JACOBIN LEGACY

JACOBIN LEGACY

*The Democratic Movement Under
the Directory*

By Isser Woloch

Princeton University Press 1970

For Nancy and David

PREFACE

SLOWLY but relentlessly Jacobinism was suppressed following Robespierre's fall. In November 1794, four months after Thermidor, the National Convention ordered the Paris Jacobin Club closed, while representatives were sent on missions to purge and subdue the provincial clubs or popular societies. In retreat and disarray, those that survived quietly complied with a decree of August 1795 that dissolved all clubs provisionally. A few weeks later, Thermidor was consummated when the Directory regime took its place under the Constitution of the Year III. Faithful to the libertarian spirit of 1789, however, the new charter offered a vague guarantee for freedom of association. Under this ostensible protection, and the general amnesty that inaugurated the transition, Jacobins began tentatively to regroup. Though their new clubs were dispersed by the Directory several times, it was not until Bonaparte swept away all the scruples of liberal constitutionalism that political clubs were definitively banned and Jacobinism interred. The August 1795 decree did not prove decisive.

Historiographically, however, it has been. The literature on the original clubs of 1789-95 is enormous, comprising over two hundred local studies and several works of synthesis. As against this impressive corpus, the only work on the later clubs is Aulard's vintage essay on the Paris Club of 1799, and studies of the Sarthe and Toulouse by M. Reinhard and J. Beyssi. As Professor Godechot has observed in his standard survey of revolutionary institutions, the clubs of the Directory years have hardly been studied at all. This striking disproportion may be explained with some justification by the state of the sources. When the government ordered the popular societies closed in 1795, it stipulated that their papers be sequestered and stored by the local authorities. Many of these records (minute books, correspondence, membership lists) therefore survive in communal archives and have since been edited or used as the basis for local case studies. During the Directory, by contrast, the sequestration of whatever papers the clubs may have kept was rarely ordered. Hence no ready-made body of detailed sources awaits the historian seeking material on the later clubs. Their history must instead be written from relatively fragmentary sources scattered among the voluminous political and administrative records of the Directory era.

The resulting imbalance of scholarship has been detrimental in two ways. In the first place it limits our perception of the phenomenon of Jacobinism itself since it serves to cut off its history arbitrarily. Secondly, it encourages our habitual underestimation of the Directory period's significance. Admittedly, the Directory years are overshadowed by two commanding peaks of French history. After the epoch-making days of revolutionary government and popular revolution they indeed loom as a depressing aftermath of social malaise, second-class leadership, and incipient militarism. Viewed from the other end, they must likewise appear as a prolonged prelude to the Napoleonic experience. But this does not mean that the conflicts and issues raised by the democratic revolution of the Year II were definitively settled or irrelevant to the Directory. On the contrary, to trace these out is to contribute part of the answer to how and why the French Revolution issued in dictatorship.

Recently some beginnings have been made towards rediscovering the history of those years. In the classic French genre of local history, two exhaustive studies have appeared after an hiatus of thirty years since Marcel Reinhard's pioneering book on the Sarthe department: P. Clémendot's volume on the Meurthe, and J. Suratteau's study of Mont-Terrible. Work on international movements of revolutionary expansion and counterrevolution by J. Godechot and R. R. Palmer has produced a substantial reevaluation of the Directory's importance in the history of Western Europe. Meanwhile, the origins of revolutionary socialism have been placed under the microscope by a veritable renaissance in the historiography of Babeuf, Buonarroti, and the Conspiracy of Equals.

Counterrevolution and Babeuvism have the virtue of being palpable and even dramatic; this book will focus on the more mundane position of the democrats or Neo-Jacobins. Its dual objective is to provide a fresh perspective on the history of Jacobinism, and on the fate of the Directorial republic. The principal advantage to the overview attempted here is that it relates a number of themes even if no single theme is examined exhaustively. To have limited the study to the clubs in one department, or to the democratic press, or to career line analysis of selected groups (to name some of the possible alternatives) would have been to rule out a perception of their interconnections. Obviously, too, there was an enormous range of local diversity in France, both circumstantial and fundamental, and it must not be assumed that this study is a blithe attempt to ignore or minimize this. Yet the existence of local diversity did not prevent a sense of common purpose from developing among the Neo-Jacobins, nor did it preclude certain similarities in their activities, which gravitated around newspapers and clubs. In short, one is confronted here with a classic forest-trees problem, and the approach offered here is one opting for a view of the forest. The focus of this study therefore fits its subject's special characteristics. Its equilibrium lies between local and national settings, between expressions of consciousness and modes of behavior, between the forms of political life and the social realities that they so imperfectly encompassed. If this must be reduced to a single concern, it is an attempt to rediscover a political culture in several of its dimensions.

Two threads of continuity in the history of Jacobinism are the role of political clubs, and the constellation of attitudes which I have labeled "the democratic persuasion." This said, it is apparent that as Jacobinism evolved after the Year II it suffered several vicissitudes. Immediately after the Directory was launched, Babeuf's program of insurrection and communism challenged, disoriented, and ultimately compromised Jacobins or, as they now appeared, traditional democrats. To put it another way, the difficulties of reorientation to the Directory regime were complicated by Babeuf's meteoric rise. After the suppression of the Babeuvists, an upsurge of royalist reaction threatened to overwhelm the Jacobins along with the republic itself. The pains of reorientation were followed by the trauma of another struggle for bare survival. Only after these obstacles were negotiated did an eventual Jacobin resurgence occur.

The Year VI (1797-98) was the year of Neo-Jacobinism. As the republic entered an unprecedented period of peace and normalcy (following the Directory's famous anti-royalist coup d'état of 18 fructidor, and the treaty of Campoformio) the Jacobins regained a significant measure of initiative. Their legacy was now embodied by several hundred clubs, or Constitutional Circles as they were called, on which this study will focus. It was an elusive movement (foreshadowing the non-communist Left of modern times), but it yields to analysis. What was the social role of these clubs? What were the patterns of political and civic activism that they practiced? What

ACKNOWLEDGMENTS

IN NURTURING this study from its genesis as a doctoral dissertation to its final form, I have enjoyed a considerable amount of human and material support. My interests in this subject were kindled in R. R. Palmer's seminar on the French Revolution. His suggestions in the early stages, combined with his sympathetic insights and healthy skepticism, were invaluable. In Paris, Professor Albert Soboul offered hospitality, interest, and encouragement for which I was and remain extremely grateful. My wife Nancy Spelman Woloch suspended her own studies for a year and assisted me in the archives to an extent that nearly doubled the amount of research that I was able to accomplish. For his critical reading of an early draft I am indebted to David Bien, and for a later draft to Eugen Weber. Reginald Zelnik, Peter Loewenberg, and Gary Nash contributed informally and perhaps unknowingly to the refinement of my ideas.

Research for the study was supported by a Procter Fellowship and a Fulbright Fellowship, for which I thank Princeton University and the United States government respectively. Generous research grants and summer fellowships from Indiana University and the University of California, Los Angeles, facilitated the later stages of writing and revision.

CONTENTS

Concordance of the Republican and Gregorian Calendars

	Year IV *1795-96*	Year V *1796-97*	Year VI *1797-98*	Year VII *1798-99*	Year VIII *1799-1800*
	1795	1796	1797	1798	1799
1 vendémiaire	23 Sept.	22 Sept.	22 Sept.	22 Sept.	23 Sept.
1 brumaire	23 Oct.	21 Nov.	22 Oct.	22 Oct.	23 Oct.
1 frimaire	22 Nov.	22 Oct.	21 Nov.	21 Nov.	22 Nov.
1 nivôse	22 Dec.	21 Dec.	21 Dec.	21 Dec.	22 Dec.
	1796	1797	1798	1799	1800
1 pluviôse	21 Jan.	20 Jan.	20 Jan.	20 Jan.	21 Jan.
1 ventôse	20 Feb.	19 Feb.	19 Feb.	19 Feb.	20 Feb.
1 germinal	21 March	21 March	21 March	21 March	22 March
1 floréal	20 April	20 April	20 April	21 March	21 April
1 prairial	20 May	20 May	20 April	20 April	21 April
1 messidor	19 June	19 June	20 May	20 May	21 May
1 thermidor	19 July	19 July	19 June	19 June	20 June
1 fructidor	18 Aug.	18 Aug.	19 July	19 July	20 July
Jours compl.	17-21 Sept.	17-21 Sept.	18 Aug.	18 Aug.	19 Aug.
			17-21 Sept.	17-22 Sept.	18-22 Sept.

Note: Since virtually all contemporary documents used the revolutionary calendar exclusively, dates will be given here in conformity with that practice. Corresponding dates from the gregorian calendar will be provided in the text but not in footnotes. In the revolutionary calendar the months are not capitalized, but such words will be capitalized here when used to designate the following notable *journées*:

Thermidor: 9 thermidor II (27 July 1794)—fall of Robespierre
Prairial: ½ prairial III (20/21 May 1795)—sans-culotte uprising
Vendémiaire: 13 vendémiaire IV (5 October 1795)—royalist uprising
Fructidor: 18 fructidor V (4 September 1797)—anti-royalist purge
Floréal: 22 floréal VI (11 May 1798)—anti-Jacobin purge
Prairial: 30 prairial VII (18 June 1799)—purge of the Directory
Brumaire: 18 brumaire VIII (9 November 1799)—Bonaparte's coup d'état

Abbreviations Used in Footnotes

A.D.S.	Archives départementales de la Seine
AHRF	*Annales historiques de la Révolution française*
A.N.	Archives Nationales
Aulard, *Paris*	A. Aulard, ed., *Paris pendant la Réaction thermidorienne et sous le Directoire: recueil de documents pour l'histoire de l'esprit public à Paris* (5 vols.; Paris, 1898-1902)
B.N.	Bibliothèque Nationale (Div. des imprimées)
B.N. Mss	Bibliothèque Nationale (Div. des manuscrits)
J. hommes libres	*Journal des hommes libres de tous les pays ou le Républicain* (Paris), November 1792=fructidor an VIII
M. of Pol.	Minister of Police
P.V.	Procès-verbal
R.F.	*La Révolution française* (periodical)

PART ONE

ORIGINS AND TESTING

CHAPTER I

Introduction: The Jacobin Clubs, 1792-95

THE FACT that Jacobinism in the French Revolution developed through the medium of political clubs is by no means incidental. This was its most generic quality and constitutes a logical starting point for analysis. By Jacobins—not simply the leadership in Paris, but the rank and file across France—I mean people who banded together in clubs in order to support and advance the Revolution. Once established, these clubs underwent significant changes in their social composition, political practices, and in the kinds of attitudes that they represented. Decisive turning points like the fall of the monarchy and the establishment of a government "revolutionary until the peace" left a permanent impact on them, though the ambiguities and local variations in these changes were enormous. In the face of such complexity it is still possible to describe the principal characteristics of Jacobinism in its classic phase after 1792, and to highlight in summary fashion the main steps in its development. The question then remains to be posed: what was likely to have abiding relevance after the climactic achievements of the Year II? Were the most striking features at that time necessarily the most enduring ones? If not, what were the other qualities of Jacobinism whose persistence marks them as equally fundamental?

‡ I ‡

The original Jacobin clubs were created by the middle-class reformers or "Patriots" of 1789. Known as Societies of the Friends of the Constitution, the clubs were organized to support the transition to a constitutional monarchy in a progressive fashion. Hoping to avoid violent upheavals, but also unnecessary concessions to the old order, the Jacobins of 1789 believed that discussion and education at the local level would facilitate the acceptance of a new constitution. Their original purpose, then, was primarily didactic; their original emphasis was on constitutional liberalism. Their libertarianism, however, was frustrated by the grip of tradition over vast segments of French society, and by the rapid development of overt counterrevolution.[1]

Even in its initial phase, when the leadership was limited to locally prominent individuals, the clubs were potentially disruptive, as far as the royal authorities and the moderate majority of the National Assembly were concerned. Almost from the beginning the clubs agitated public opinion and exerted pressure on the government, as they passed from reading newspapers and discussing issues to drawing up petitions with which they assaulted the Assembly and the new departmental authorities. The Assembly reacted harshly to this trend by declaring in April 1790 that the right of petition—a sacred right, to be sure—belonged only to individuals and could not be delegated: "Consequently, that right may not be exercised collectively . . . by clubs of citizens."[2]

This pronouncement was largely ignored. On the contrary, the clubs continued to stimulate an increasingly alert and articulate body of opinion that put great pressure on the Assembly. Moreover, in Paris and elsewhere a few clubs effectively conducted mass agitation during the crisis provoked by the king's flight to Varennes in June 1791.[3] And so as early as that year the Assembly moved to curb the clubs definitively by legislating limits on their organization and activities. The bill, reported out of committee by Le-Chapelier and passed in September, was supported by Rousseauistic arguments as well as conservative principles, for it attacked the clubs as intermediary corporations that obstructed the general will. Though the clubs had been useful early in the Revolution, Le-Chapelier maintained, their growing system of affiliation and their incessant petitions were becoming dangerous. The bill stipulated that no society or club "may assume a political existence under any form whatsoever, nor exert any pressure on the acts of the constituted powers and legal authorities. Under no pretext may they ap-

---

[1] For much of what follows the standard works are L. DeCardenal, *La Province pendant la Révolution: histoire des clubs Jacobins (1789-1795)* (Paris, 1929), and C. Brinton, *The Jacobins: An Essay in the New History* (New York, 1930). In addition see the works by R. C. Cobb cited below.

[2] A. Aulard, "La Législation des clubs pendant la Révolution," *R.F.*, xvii (1889), 255-67.

[3] See A. Mathiez, *Le Club des Cordeliers pendant la crise de Varennes et le massacre du Champ de Mars* (Paris, 1910), and I. Bourdin, *Les Sociétés populaires à Paris pendant la Révolution . . . jusqu'à la chute de la royauté* (Paris, 1937).

4

pear under a collective appellation, either to draw up petitions, or to form deputations to attend public ceremonies." In addition to petitions, deputations, and public political manifestations, the decree also prohibited deliberations, presumably meaning resolutions and votes at club meetings.[4] The legislators clearly sought to reduce the clubs to a passive, apolitical role. At most the clubs should work to educate the citizenry by reading newspapers aloud and by publicizing legislative enactments. No longer would they be permitted to act as pressure groups upon the authorities.

This decree was one of the National Assembly's last acts, for it was about to dissolve and give way to a newly elected Legislative Assembly under the Constitution of 1791. The September decree was apparently lost in the shuffle and was never enforced, so that in April 1792 the same question was raised once again. Opposition to the clubs was as strong as ever, but this time the committee's report, delivered by Français de Nantes, concluded that they were more useful than dangerous in a free society. The clubs continued to be attacked by conservatives but their survival seemed assured. Meanwhile, as the religious question became more divisive and as the original Patriot Party crumbled under the strain of new conflicts, the firm supporters of revolution became increasingly embattled in their clubs while the more conservative members tended to drop from the rolls. The formation of the conservative Feuillant Club following a mass defection of deputies from the Paris Jacobin Club in the summer of 1791 was symptomatic of this development.[5]

After the overthrow of the monarchy in the second revolution of August 1792, the clubs became an essential part of the revolutionary effort. From their ranks cadres were ready to assume local leadership and to fill the vacuum left by the fall of the monarchy. The clubs were no longer Friends of the Constitution, for there was none, but became instead Friends of Liberty and Equality—a change in name that would soon become substantive. For as Marcel Reinhard has suggested, the resort to violent, sweeping revolution in

[4] *Moniteur*, 30 September 1791 (p. 1140); J. Godechot, *Les Institutions de la France sous la Révolution et l'Empire* (Paris, 1951), pp. 67-68.

[5] Surprisingly there is no authoritative general work on the Paris Jacobin Club. We have, besides Aulard's six-volume collection of source materials, only two brief surveys: Gaston-Martin's volume in the "Que sais-je?" series: *Les Jacobins* (Paris, 1945), a recent edition of which is merely a reprinting of the 1945 version, and G. Walter's *Histoire des Jacobins* (Paris, 1946).

5

1792 could be justified and sustained only if complemented by a democratization which would cement the loyalty of politically conscious citizens from many levels of society.[6] To this end the clubs became more congenial places for the "common people" who, in many towns, had already been attending their meetings but had held a back seat before August 1792.

The atmosphere at the clubs came increasingly to reflect the presence of these men who worked with their hands, who were of low status, and who lacked much formal education. Plebeians or common people in normal times, they were the sans-culottes of the French Revolution. Though they were often referred to as *ouvriers* (a loose and misleading contemporary term), most were not day-laborers or even wage earners, and they most assuredly were not from the bottom rung of the indigent. The sans-culottes, rather, were master craftsmen, journeymen, artisans, small shopkeepers, minor clerks and functionaries, and common soldiers.[7] These types in growing numbers joined those citizens of the middle class—lawyers, bureaucrats, teachers, merchants, landed proprietors—who were already well installed in the clubs; and what is more, in the months that followed they often emerged as local leaders.

The evolution of the clubs towards both a broader social base and a more decisive political role was interrupted in the spring of 1793 by the factional conflicts revolving around the Girondin-Montagnard schism. This struggle for leadership in the capital had a paralyzing effect in the departments. In the wake of dissension and confusion the clubs lost their momentum. Only after the triumph of the Mountain and the isolation of "federalism" as a counterrevolutionary heresy did they come to life again with renewed vigor.[8] In most of those resuscitated clubs there was no trace of the earlier elitism. Amalgams of bourgeoisie and sans-culottes—of politically

[6] M. Reinhard, *La Révolution démocratique* ("Les Cours de Sorbonne," C.D.U., Paris, 1959), p. 244.

[7] Brinton, *The Jacobins*, Ch. III; DeCardenal, *La Province pendant la Révolution*, pp. 48-78; R. C. Cobb, "The Revolutionary Mentality in France, 1793-94," *History* (1957), pp. 184-85. In Brinton's statistical sample for the Year II, artisans and petty tradesmen constitute about 45 percent of the membership (p. 304); but the author himself cautions about the many ambiguities in his statistics.

[8] DeCardenal, *La Province pendant la Révolution*, pp. 154-83.

conscious citizens from many occupational and status levels—they called themselves appropriately enough *sociétés populaires*.

As sentinels of revolution—and often as isolated bastions of patriotism—the clubs won the wholehearted endorsement of the Convention after the Mountain's triumph. Now the Convention decisively reversed the tendency of the two earlier Assemblies to fault the clubs and to restrict their activities. Instead, local officials (often federalist sympathizers at this point) were forbidden to interfere with clubs or to prevent them from meeting. In the autumn of 1793 the sociétés populaires won unparalleled power when they were officially invited to denounce all disloyal citizens, and also to designate competent patriots to fill public offices. They were even directed to hold their meetings in public so that they might have greater influence in the community.[9]

The clubs, in short, were markedly transformed. Having started as educational and propagandistic associations of middle-class reformers in 1789, they had gradually evolved into socially heterogeneous political action groups. Finally in the Year II (1793-94) the sociétés populaires became the arms of a triumphant Montagnard government. Not only were they to be the Convention's "arsenals of public opinion"; by late 1793, in Crane Brinton's words, the clubs were functioning as auxiliary administrative bodies in the departments, working with the local revolutionary committees whose members were recruited from the clubs and scrutinized by them.

During the ensuing months, as the clubs increasingly came under the control of Paris, the movement became the highly centralized affair often referred to as the "Jacobin Dictatorship." This centralization had two roots: first, the system of affiliation with departmental clubs that the Paris Jacobin Club had extended by the Year II into a procedure for maintaining orthodoxy in the provinces; and second, the tightly structured institutions of the *gouvernement révolutionnaire* which were codified in the law of 14 frimaire Year II (December 1793). The revolutionary government, whose hub was the Committee of Public Safety, attempted to coordinate everything, and to repress what it could not control. The autonomous and unaffiliated clubs in the Paris sections, which were exclusively sans-culotte in composition and more militant than most clubs, were eventually suppressed by Robespierre because they resisted this centralization.

[9] Summarized in Godechot, *Les Institutions de la France*, pp. 299-300.

A few provincial "ultras," and the battalions of the terroristic *armée révolutionnaire* in the interior were eliminated for the same reasons.[10] But most local *sociétaires* fell into line, and accepted their position in what amounted to an unpaid revolutionary bureaucracy.

Once this revolutionary government was firmly in place, general political debate was taken as pointless by those in power. As Richard Cobb has pointed out, the Jacobins placed their faith in the Convention with astonishing credulity. The fall of Danton, Hébert, and Robespierre alike were accepted with relative equanimity; issues of national policy were rarely discussed, and the ground rules laid down by Paris were generally accepted.[11] This development of orthodoxy was emphasized by repeated purges of most clubs carried out under the auspices of the revolutionary government, but also influenced by local rivalries. So, while the base of the Jacobin clubs was broadened socially, it had become extremely narrow politically by the time Robespierre was overthrown.

‡ II ‡

In the course of the clubs' transition from the vanguard of revolutionary agitation to the bulwarks of an established government, certain well-known Jacobin characteristics developed. Some of these were transitory, stemming primarily from the imperatives of the crisis situation that confronted France at the time or from derivative circumstances that depended on that situation. Other attitudes and practices, it can be argued, had a more durable significance.

The political centralization was by its very nature a provisional state of affairs. The Convention, it must be remembered, ruled explicitly by temporary revolutionary fiat as opposed to fixed constitutional law. For the duration of the crisis its leaders were au-

[10] Study of the Revolution has been renewed by recent works on this popular revolution, notably Albert Soboul's thesis whose theme is given in its subtitle: *Les Sans-culottes Parisiens en l'an II: mouvement populaire et gouvernement révolutionnaire* (Paris, 1958). Other contributors include G. Rudé, *The Crowd in the French Revolution* (Oxford, 1959); W. Markov, ed., *Jakobiner und Sans-culotten: Beitrage zur Geschichte der franzosischen Revolutionsregierung 1793-4* (E. Berlin, 1956); and R. C. Cobb, *Les Armées révolutionnaires: instrument de la terreur dans les départements* (2 vols.; Paris and The Hague, 1963).

[11] Cobb, "The Revolutionary Mentality," pp. 192-94; and Cobb, "Quelques aspects de la mentalité révolutionnaire, avril 1793-thermidor an II," *Revue d'histoire moderne et contemporaine*, VI (1959), 87-93.

thorized to forge a single center of political opinion and a single source of administrative control. All the classic elements of liberty (elections, freedom of expression, checks and balances, local autonomy) were lain aside "until the peace." The rigid system of affiliation maintained by the Paris Jacobin Club—and used eventually to help destroy the popular movement in the Paris sections—was consistent with this theory of revolutionary government. It was only in this context that the popular societies were converted from private political associations attempting to mold public opinion, into quasi-official governmental organs.[12]

Jacobins of this period are familiar to posterity as terrorists, but this too was an extension of their role as instruments of revolutionary government. In the Year II terrorism was an official policy of the French republic, designed to accomplish certain specific objectives. This remains true despite the fact that the popular movement in Paris, which was instrumental in having terror placed "on the order of the day," may have conceived of it in a more sweeping and deep-seated fashion, or at any rate was more intensely committed to it than the hesitant Convention. In any case, terrorism in the form of perfunctory political trials, capital economic crimes, overflowing jails, the guillotine, and the *mitraillade*, was the most striking aspect of life in the Year II in those areas of France torn by civil war. Certainly too the victims and the imagined victims were motivated by revenge in the years that followed, and acts of revenge in turn created countercurrents, so that terrorism remained very much alive as an issue. But the actual need for and resort to terror, though a distinguishing feature of Jacobinism at the time, was a crisis phenomenon.[13]

The same may be said of the extreme exaltation or fanaticism

[12] On the development of centralization during the Terror see A. Mathiez, *La Vie chère et le mouvement social sous la Terreur* (Paris, 1927), and R. R. Palmer, *Twelve Who Ruled: The Committee of Public Safety During the Terror* (Princeton, 1941). For the popular forces working against centralization see, above all, the books by Soboul and Cobb.

[13] The *thèse de circonstance* is argued statistically in D. Greer, *The Incidence of the Terror* (Cambridge, 1935). The sociétaires' attitudes towards the Terror are discussed in Cobb's important article, "Quelques aspects de la mentalité révolutionnaire," pp. 93-104, and in *Les Armées révolutionnaires*, Vol. II, Chs. 3 and 4. See also Mathiez, "Robespierre terroriste," in *Etudes sur Robespierre* (Paris, 1958), and DeCardenal, "Robespierrisme et terrorisme après thermidor," *AHRF*, 1938 [No. 88], pp. 314-42.

9

that seems to have marked Jacobinism at the height of its power. Faced with enormous dangers—with a multifaceted and armed counterrevolution—the Jacobins were aggressive, distrustful of outsiders, and prone to believe in conspiracies. Being a tiny minority of the population (almost never more than 5 percent of any community), and surrounded by a sullen, hostile peasantry, the Jacobins of town and village shared the conviction that the Revolution depended on their action in the clubs. Their sense of being embattled understandably produced exaltation, as well as a tendency to verbal exaggeration and self-righteousness. All of this was compounded by the premium that the revolutionary leadership placed on orthodoxy and conformism.

Some historians and contemporaries have seized upon these traits in order to create a derisory stereotype of the revolutionists —reaching in Taine's exalted prose such images as "monkeys led by crocodiles." More temperately, Crane Brinton has discerned in their state of consciousness the makings of a secular, messianic religion. He describes the Jacobins in terms of their Ritual and their Faith, an undemonstrable conceptualization that has been stimulating but has been resisted by most French scholars. Recently Richard Cobb has attempted a more straightforward description of what he calls the "revolutionary mentality"—accounting for its bizarre manifestations in terms of crisis circumstances and the popular social milieu of the clubs. And it was a state of mind, he argues, that was bound to pass when the dangers as well as the novelty of political activism diminished.[14]

By germinal Year II the crisis created by inflation and scarcity of subsistence, as well as by invasion, treason, and general insecurity was mastered. The invasion was repulsed; the food supply seemed assured (though in fact it was not); internal opposition was quelled in most areas. As a result exaltation was turning into routine. Repeated purges, a narrowing political orthodoxy in which some of the Revolution's warmest supporters found themselves outside the pale, and a rigid control centered in Paris had achieved impressive results, whatever their toll: the Revolution was defended, consolidated, and broadened in its social consequences.

[14] Brinton, *The Jacobins,* Chs. vi and vii; Cobb, "Quelques aspects de la mentalité révolutionnaire," on the passing of the revolutionary mentality, pp. 116-20.

But there was a paradox in this. Success had been achieved by channeling patriotic enthusiasm into a prescribed framework. This in turn eventually sapped the spontaneity of the Revolution's support among the sans-culottes. In some places, notably the Paris sections, this situation produced open breaches between the Robespierrist government and the sans-culotte militants. More commonly it produced not conflict but a mounting apathy, which caused the clubs to contract in membership and activity even while the Montagnards seemed at the pinnacle of their influence. Several months before Thermidor, attendance at the meetings of the sociétés populaires had begun to fall off perceptibly.

After Thermidor, reaction accelerated and transformed this decline into a total rout. The clubs were denounced for their role as arms of an austere revolutionary government that had apparently lost its raison d'être. They were attacked and ridiculed particularly for those things that might have abated of themselves: the rigid centralization that had issued in "one center of opinion"; the verbal and ritualistic fanaticism that would seem ludicrous once the crisis was over; and above all the terrorism that had sentenced 16,000 to death and had sent to jail tens of thousands of suspects who were now released and eager for revenge. The point is, though, that reaction against the Jacobins was matched by confusion and disorientation within their own ranks. With the crisis abating, the postures and practices of the Year II seemed outmoded within the clubs as well as outside. But a natural evolution, as it were, was prevented by the intervention of the thermidorians. Instead, the clubs were frontally assaulted and then temporarily disbanded.

‡ III ‡

The thermidorian reaction, however, did not permanently inter the Jacobins. Therefore we must ask what there was in Jacobinism that was likely to survive the crisis situation of the Year II and to endure. The centralization, terrorism, and ritualism were fundamental but transitory. On the other hand Jacobinism was something more than the redoubtable patriotism of Frenchmen in a time of supreme crisis, for if that were the case, then the thermidorian period would have marked the demise of the movement for the revolutionary generation. What happened in the years between Thermidor

11

and Brumaire suggests instead that revolutionary France had produced in the Jacobin clubs a crucial political and social institution—an instrumentality that could affect the republic in peace as well as crisis; that could help shape the character of political life and to a certain extent the government's approach to social issues. Jacobinism is not synonymous simply with dauntless patriotism in a time of danger, nor with the strange mantle of terrorism and fanaticism that the sociétaires wore in the Year II. It had equally as much to do with what Americans call grass-roots democracy, and a commitment to equality in the sense of mitigating social distinctions.

Richard Cobb has suggested that the members of the sociétés populaires in the Year II were generally indifferent to larger political questions, or at any rate were extremely credulous in accepting the official version of events from Paris. At the same time, however, the Jacobin clubs continued to be formidable action groups in their own communities. Local issues fill the annals of each club. More than anything else the clubs rendered political life tangible and meaningful to the politically conscious, pro-revolutionary citizen. Along with the national guard, the clubs were the crucial institution through which people participated directly in the Revolution and influenced the course of events locally. Even after they were "bureaucratized" by the revolutionary government, in their towns and villages they continued to articulate local concerns.[15] In a way that should have startled Tocqueville, they invaded the insulated world of officialdom. Though the ultimate allegiance of the clubs to the Convention was never in doubt after the summer of 1793, individual clubs often fought bitterly with particular representatives-on-mission from the Convention. In one way or another the Jacobins exemplified the notion of self-help in a period when the inherited framework of monarchical authority lay in ruins. The most fundamental trait of Jacobinism was its cultivation of *civisme* and "public spirit." Citizenship (for the patriotic minority) and the corresponding notion of a responsive government remained their norm. In this important sense the Jacobins were democrats.[16]

[15] Cobb, *Les Armées révolutionnaires*, Vol. II, Ch. 2, explains the "communalist mentality" in regard to subsistence questions.

[16] The theoretical definition of democracy offered by the political scientist Pierre Duclos seems an apt description of Jacobinism's democratic thrust. Democracy, he writes, is not to be equated simply with universal suffrage and

Another aspect of Jacobinism that promised to endure beyond the emergency of the revolutionary crisis was its qualified brand of social egalitarianism. In this respect the clubs completely outgrew their origins in the constitutional monarchy period. The Jacobins of 1789 had been elitists whose outlook was indelibly middle class in character. But for the people who continued in the Jacobin movement through the Terror and into the Directory period, this outlook was diluted. This is not to say that Jacobinism became a distinctively popular or anti-bourgeois movement, as the sectional movement in Paris had become in 1793. It is a question, rather, of the effect produced when the clubs began to bring together elements of diverse social groups. As amalgams of bourgeoisie and sans-culottes, the clubs potentially, though not necessarily, weakened the hierarchies of class and status that were perpetuated in the society of the constitutional monarchy. When middle-class elitist preoccupations with liberty gave way after the monarchy's fall, it was possible for equality to become the main sustaining notion.

Jacobin egalitarianism was not essentially a matter of economic and social leveling. It was rather a moral outlook in which one's status ideally depended on civic virtue and social utility. The sanctity of work, of manual labor was affirmed, thus elevating the sans-culottes in general esteem though not necessarily in material position. At the least it offered them the opportunity for participation in civic life, and for a measure of social dignity. A constellation of other ideas and attitudes more or less followed: that extreme wealth produced evil consequences, that everyone was entitled to subsistence, that wholesome simplicity was a virtue to be cultivated rather than an estate to be overcome.[17] Similar attitudes were held

---

the like, but rather with "*civisme* or public spirit." "Democracy reposes on the dual sentiment of each individual's right and duty in relation to the community. A right to contribute maximally to the community's destiny; a duty ceaselessly to push that community towards a higher destiny, more worthy of mankind." (*L'Evolution des rapports politiques depuis 1750: liberté, intégration, unité* [Paris, 1950], p. 174.) On the role of clubs in other countries in the period of revolutionary expansion see J. Godechot, *La Grande Nation: l'expansion révolutionnaire de la France dans le monde 1789-99* (Paris, 1956), Ch. 10.

[17] Brinton, *The Jacobins*, Chs. v and vii; Cobb, "The Revolutionary Mentality," pp. 186-91; Cobb, *Les Armées révolutionnaires*, Vol. ii, Ch. 5.

much more aggressively by the Parisian popular movement. In the milieu of the Paris sections and out among the battalions of the armée révolutionnaire these notions were taken more seriously. They were emphatically programmatic, whereas in the Jacobin movement generally they were normative, and derived partly from tactical expediency. Measured by the standard of the popular movement—by the sans-culottes' demands in the *journée* of 5 September 1793, by the militancy of the armées révolutionnaires, or by the popular insurrection of prairial Year III—Jacobinism was equivocal and virtually irrelevant to the position of the popular masses. But this cannot be taken as the only standard of measurement. Above all the Jacobin outlook idealized the sans-culotte as citizen. As the moral and political orthodoxy of the Year II, this created a bridge, albeit a fragile one, between politically conscious common people and their wealthier and better educated fellow citizens who also supported the Revolution.[18]

Those who conformed to this orthodoxy without conviction dropped out of the movement at the first real opportunity, particularly when the Parisian sans-culottes were no longer capable of forcing the government to take their demands into account—as they had in 1793 by sustained agitation and the threat of insurrection. But the authenticity of these democratic and egalitarian sentiments in the Jacobin movement is suggested by their survival—in a blunted and more measured form—during the Directory period, when the clubs were no longer the standard-bearers of official orthodoxy.

[18] "Democracy" and "social equality" are provocative terms in the ideologically charged field of revolutionary historiography. It must be emphasized, therefore, that I do not have in mind the "popular democracy" of the Paris sections in the Year II or the "social democracy" of Babeuf. On the other hand, hyphenated terms such as "middle-class democrats" or "political-democrats" would not be wholly appropriate either, though they could well be used. True, typically bourgeois interests like political ambition were served in the clubs, while conversely the movement never threatened the really fundamental advantages held by the middle class. Nonetheless the sans-culottes were an integral element of the clubs and assuredly contributed to the movement's character. Secondly, even if the movement's primary concerns were political, it had an important if ill-defined social impact which the choice of a label like "political-democrat" would obscure. In addition this label might imply that the Jacobins were most interested in things like universal suffrage, which was not necessarily the case.

‡ IV ‡

Revolutionary fervor culminated and declined after germinal Year II during the height of Robespierre's ascendancy. The revolutionary government and the popular movement played out their dialectical roles, each simultaneously supporting and opposing the other, until each was weakened, subdued, and in the end destroyed by the thermidorians' intervention. As the revolutionary mentality dissipated, apathy, hostility, and fear produced mass defections from the ranks. But partisans remained, and they continued to find in the clubs a focus for their aspirations and a means of expression and organization. During the Directory, however, they were forced to operate within limitations dictated by the triumphant thermidorians. The thermidorian attempt to deal with the clubs, and the framework that they elaborated in the new constitution, must therefore form the final matter to be taken up in this introduction.

Predictably, as the thermidorians dismantled the revolutionary government and retrospectively condemned its activities, the clubs were singled out for attack. A future member of the Directory, J. M. Reubell, won loud applause in the Convention a few weeks after Thermidor when he assailed the sociétés populaires as undesirable intermediary corporations that "have established themselves as societies of inquisition all over the Republic . . . inundating the country with blood." Harking back to LeChapelier's argument of 1791, he held that the clubs had no proper role in goverment or administration. And in their "exclusive" composition (that is, selectivity of membership) Reubell managed to find an affront to the equality of all citizens. In response to this appeal the Convention forbade affiliations and correspondence between clubs as well as collective petitions, thereby demolishing the apparatus of centralization that had rendered the clubs so powerful.[19]

This measure was not lethal to Jacobinism. The prohibition on collective correspondence and affiliation did not prevent the clubs from acting on the local political scene. In fact, at the Paris Jacobin Club itself several Montagnard deputies greeted this decree as something that, while objectionable, at least served to liberate the movement from a compromised past. As the deputy Crassous put it: "This morning's decree dissipates the phantom . . . that the popular

[19] *Moniteur*, 28 vendémiaire III (pp. 126-27).

societies wished to become an intermediary power between the people and the Convention." The Montagnards did not anticipate that this was only the first blow.[20]

A few weeks later the Convention voted to close the Paris Jacobin Club itself, terming it the center of political factionalism. But even the elimination of this center of direction, and of such practices as affiliation and collective correspondence, was not sufficient to appease the thermidorians. Reactionary representatives-on-mission relentlessly purged individual clubs and reduced them to impotence and to caricatures of their former selves.[21] In the Convention the attack now shifted from the Paris Club to the provincial clubs and Reubell's argument was invoked against their very existence. Clubs were excoriated for allegedly setting themselves up as sovereign bodies (as against the sovereignty of *all* citizens), and as autonomous and oppressive public powers (as against the duly constituted authorities). In August 1795, pending the formulation of an article in the new constitution to regulate clubs, all existing clubs were ordered closed, and their papers and property sequestered. The network of clubs that had brought revolutionary government to the departments was swept away, never to reappear.

The thermidorian architects of the new constitution, however, were committed to the libertarian principles of 1789 and accordingly guaranteed freedom of association. Now in Article 361, which specifically banned the appellation of "société populaire" that most

---

[20] A. Aulard, ed., *La Société des Jacobins: recueil de documents pour l'histoire du club des Jacobins de Paris* (6 vols.; Paris, 1897), VI, 592-93. See also DeCardenal, "Les Sociétés populaires du 9 thermidor à la fermeture du Club des Jacobins," *R.F.*, n.s., X (1937), 113-43, and, on the subsequent closing of the Paris Club, *Moniteur*, 24 brumaire III (p. 233).

[21] See, e.g., A. Fray-Fournier, ed., *Le Club des Jacobins de Limoges (1790-95) d'après ses délibérations, sa correspondance et ses journaux* (Limoges, 1903); E. Chardon, ed., *Cahiers des procès-verbaux des séances de la Société populaire à Rouen* (Rouen, 1909); B. Combes de Patris, ed., *Procès-verbaux des séances de la Société Populaire de Rodez* (Rodez, 1912); M. Henriot, *Le Club des Jacobins de Semur 1790-1795* (Dijon, 1933); L. Hugueny, *Les Clubs Dijonnais sous la Révolution* (Dijon, 1905); O. Bled, *Les Sociétés populaires à Saint-Omer pendant la Révolution* (St. Omer, 1907); H. Labroue, *La Société populaire de Bergerac pendant la Révolution* (Paris, 1915); P. Leuilliot, *Les Jacobins de Colmar: procès-verbaux des séances de la société populaire 1791-1795* (Strasbourg, 1923); R. R. Tissot, *La Société populaire de Grenoble pendant la Révolution* (Grenoble, 1910); L. Bultingaire, *Le Club des Jacobins de Metz* (Paris, 1906).

clubs had adopted, they revealed the direction of their intent. Article 362 prohibited many of the features that had been characteristic of the clubs between 1792-94, but in language so ambiguous (as we shall see) it invited circumvention.

> No private society which concerns itself with political questions may correspond with another, or affiliate therewith, or hold public sessions composed of the members of the society and of associates distinguished from one another, or impose conditions of admission and eligibility, or arrogate to itself rights of exclusion, or cause its members to wear any external insignia of their association.

Article 364 held that no association may present a collective petition, and Article 360 stipulated that "corporations or associations contrary to public order" may not be formed—which in effect authorized the government to close any club it wished immediately.[22]

Clearly the framers' intention was that clubs in the future would be innocuous assemblages of citizens engaged in educational activities and barred from any direct involvement in political life. This was underscored in Article 363—a declaration of principle rather than an operative provision—which held that political rights were confined to the exercise of the franchise in the primary and electoral assemblies. The spirit behind these articles was expressed in a speech by one deputy who warned of the damage that clubs could do. P. Bordas maintained that good citizens avoided the noise, agitation, and intrigue of clubs and were content to exercise their sovereignty during election week. In his view clubs inevitably bred disorder and factionalism. "Legislators," he pleaded, "France is lost if at this decisive moment you foolishly reject the counsels of experience; if for the second time democratic ideas are allowed to prevail."[23] The notion that clubs at best were breeding grounds for "democratic" agitation continued to prevail among Directorials. But the Constitution of the Year III—for all its reservations and ambiguously restrictive clauses—still afforded the opportunity for the formation of effective clubs.

[22] J. H. Stewart, ed., *A Documentary Survey of the French Revolution* (New York, 1951), p. 611. The drafting of this constitution is discussed in G. Lefebvre, *Les Thermidoriens* (Paris, 1937), Ch. 9.

[23] P. Bordas, *Réflexions sur le nouveau projet de Constitution* (Impr. Nationale, thermidor an III), p. 12.

Under the Directory, Jacobinism as a centralized network of clubs enforcing orthodoxy and monopolizing public authority stood no chance of reviving. On this the Constitution was explicit. But Jacobinism, as a movement in which civisme, popular participation in government, and a commitment to the idea of equality were advanced, remained a viable political persuasion. True, the new regime was explicitly founded in opposition to Jacobinism, as these constitutional restrictions indicate. But in its commitment to libertarian principles the Directory was hampered philosophically and constitutionally from dealing with Jacobinism decisively. Only Napoleon's undisguised authoritarian rule succeeded in completing the reaction by extinguishing Jacobinism with finality. Willing to forego certain principles of 1789, the Napoleonic regime tolerated no independent political activity, permitted no clubs of any kind, no newspapers except those it controlled, and no truly contested elections. The Directory, as an ostensibly liberal and constitutional government, alternated fitfully between allowing such political activity and repressing it. Having conceded the principle of free association, the regime had to deal with those who took this right seriously. Clubs remained the chosen instrument of citizens who hoped to reform and democratize their newly consolidated but conservative republic.

CHAPTER II

The Problems of Reorientation

As the thermidorian reaction ground to its finish, democrats were carried far from where they had been and farther from where they had hoped to be. The convention was purged, the clubs closed, local militants disarmed, and the jails filled with the unlucky ones. Inflation again afflicted the nation's masses, unopposed except by acts of desperation. What passed for public opinion was engrossed in exorcising sans-culottism, depantheonizing Marat, and writing a new bourgeois constitution. Vendettas and betrayals formed a somber mosaic of agony across the country. Yet for all its vigor and deepening sweep, the reaction failed to annihilate the democratic movement. With the republic's survival in the Directory regime, the possibility of revival remained. The following two chapters will consider the early years of the Directory, from the Babeuf plot to the fructidor coup, a period for democrats of reorientation, false starts, and dramatic reversals of fortune, all of which formed a prologue to resurgence.

‡ I ‡

Formally, at least, the inauguration of the Directory and the general amnesty that accompanied it, offered democrats the advantages of a fresh start. They had irretrievably lost almost all their first-class leaders, the potential of mass support, and that unique configuration of opportunities that had existed in the Year II. But there were compensating advantages. The weight of a compromised past was lightened by the discontinuity. Issues of personality, concerns of the moment that had grown disproportionate might at last recede. Attitudes born under pressure could be reconsidered, just in the way that Babeuf (who had once attacked Robespierre as a tyrant) benefitted from the opportunity of viewing him in a new light.[1] Along with the idealists and truly great men who were executed or otherwise silenced, there also went a complement of demagogues, hypocrites, and false prophets—some of whom deserted to the thermidorians.

[1] K. Tonnesson, "L'an III dans la formation du babouvisme," *AHRF*, 1960, pp. 411-25.

Secondly, with the disappearance of sans-culottism as an autonomous movement threatening to turn against its would-be allies in the middle class, a fundamental ambiguity in Jacobinism was essentially resolved. Robespierrism, or to oversimplify it, middle-class leadership, could prevail unchallenged.[2] As participants and followers the sans-culottes would be welcomed, courted, and celebrated; no fear of their autonomy remained to dampen Jacobin egalitarianism. Henceforth, in other words, the distinction between Jacobin and sans-culotte—sensed by some contemporaries, lost by posterity under the general reaction against the Terror, and reestablished by recent historians—would be blurred. The democratic movement could be open-ended. Its advocates would number autodidact artisans, declassed aristocrats, petit-bourgeois functionaries, and middle-class intellectuals. Babeuf's attempt to develop and force divisions deviated notably from this development, hence the democrats' problem of reorientation was even more complicated. They faced on the one hand the Directory's entrenched conservatism and on the other Babeuf's insurrectionary radicalism. Their path lay somewhere between.

Democrats had been reluctant and powerless witnesses to the drafting of the new constitution. So complete was their rout that from the Mountain's decimated benches only the obscure voice of Julien Souhait spoke out against its major provisions.[3] Its restricted franchise, indirect elections, and elaborate separation of powers clashed with a straightforward commitment to popular government. Omission of such natural rights as free public education or the right to subsistence was a purposeful leap backward from the principle of equality.[4] This regime was not of their making. But in the event, most Jacobins proved willing to abide by it, consoled by the hope that it would cement the republic, normalize political life, and establish the rule of law. An end might then come to the arbitrary reign of

[2] See A. Soboul, *Les Sans-culottes Parisiens en l'an II* (Paris, 1958), and "Robespierre et la pratique politique jacobine" in his *Paysans, Sans-culottes et Jacobins* (Paris, 1967). On the breakdown and final manifestations of sans-culotte autonomy in the Year III, see K. Tonnesson, *La Défaite des Sans-culottes* (Paris and Oslo, 1959).

[3] *Opinion de Julien Souhait (des Vosges) sur le droit de suffrage . . .* (Impr. Nationale, an III).

[4] [Antonelle], *Observations sur le Droit de Cité et sur quelques parties du travail de la commission des onze* (Chez Vatar, an III), B.N. *E/ 5718.

the thermidorians, which had been in this sense a mirror-image of the Terror. For over a year there had been no ground rules, no recourse against proscription. Now at least the constitution would define the ostensible limits of authority and rights of citizens.

To sunder the thermidorian alliance between conservative republicans and royalists was the Jacobins' most immediate aim—the necessary prelude to any exercise of influence. Their most likely lever was the Right itself, for obligingly the royalists continued their plots against the republic. The Directory was in fact virtually inaugurated amidst an abortive uprising known as the Vendémiaire Rebellion. Protesting the two-thirds decree by which the thermidorian Convention sought to perpetuate its personnel in the new two-house legislature, the wealthier Paris sections led an armed revolt against the Convention. Their actual purpose was to block the peaceful implementation of the new constitution and thereby call into question the republic.[5] Moderates were forced to come down from the clouds and recognize that imminent dangers to their entire edifice lay on the Right. By contrast the Jacobins could appear as potential supporters of the regime rather than its subverters, not hopelessly destined to be outside the pale. With a general amnesty proclaimed, and with a period of unusually free expression inaugurated by the constitution, their reentry into political life was facilitated.

Jacobin activists had to formulate a position towards the new regime immediately, and most found it convenient to distinguish between its form and its spirit—between its vague principles and its narrow social foundations. Accepting its forms, above all its framework for political life, they continued to oppose its spirit—the parochial middle-class spirit of 1791, of Thermidor, or what later became Orléanism. As for the Directory's principles, insofar as they coincided with the universalism of 1789, they were valuable, sustaining France as La Grande Nation in Europe. But insofar as these principles were interpreted to reflect the interests and preconceptions of a narrow social elite, insofar as they promoted oligarchic tendencies, they were alien.[6]

[5] Among recent studies of Vendémiaire see H. Mitchell, "Vendémiaire, a Revaluation," *Journal of Modern History*, xxx (1958), 191-202, and G. Rudé, *The Crowd in the French Revolution* (Oxford, 1959), Ch. xi.

[6] See especially F. Lepelletier, *Réflexions sur le moment présent, ou suite de*

Accepting the forms of the new regime and opposing its spirit, the Jacobin posture precluded total opposition, especially subversive activity. Conversely it assumed that the royalists, irreconcilable to the republic, were by nature subversive and could not fail to place the Jacobins in a favorable light by comparison. Vendémiaire had not cut deeply enough to accomplish this, the Directory choosing to regard it as a kind of *fronde*. But it was still taken by democrats as an indication of how things really stood.

As they wrote to each other in these months, Jacobins were extremely conscious of this situation. (The value of such letters is unfortunately as great as their survival is rare.) Correspondence between Claude Gautherot, who had left his native Auxerre (Yonne) to study art in Paris, and his friends at home strikes a characteristic mood. His friends, active in the old Auxerre popular society and later in the Neo-Jacobin club, admired Gautherot's position as secretary to the martyred Montagnard Maure, and his participation in the government force assembled to oppose the vendémiaire insurrection. His correspondent congratulated him, expressing his relief that a wound sustained by the young artist at the time had not been fatal as originally rumored. Vendémiaire, he continued, was "a day when the patriots gave a good accounting of themselves . . . it has altered the ideas that some people hold in regard to the so-called terrorists. On that celebrated *journée* it was recognized that they were the republic's true friends." This turn of events helped relieve the writer's melancholy—a melancholy which came, he said, more from "the misfortunes of our country and the persecution of patriots" than simply from his own troubles. (These troubles, however, were not negligible; he lost his post as a grammar teacher at the normal school when the Auxerre Jacobin club was purged and was also on the list of "terrorists" to be disarmed.) Now he could write that he was becoming encouraged. "I have adopted as a principle," he concluded, "that the more blunders made by the leaders of reaction, the sooner will their reign come to an end."[7]

---

celles déjà publiées . . . en floréal de l'an III (Impr. Vatar, an IV), B.N. Lb42/ 1031; *L'Orateur plébéien ou le défenseur de la République,* Prospectus; No. 1, 21 brumaire IV, "Introduction, servant de supplément au prospectus," and No. 17, 2 nivôse; *L'Ami de la Patrie, ou journal de la liberté française,* Prospectus in A.N. ADXXª 27.

[7] Gautherot Papers, B.N. Mss (nouv. acq. fran.) No. 21700: letter from

Jacobins who had fled from Lorient (Morbihan), writing to friends and relatives at home, expressed similar attitudes towards royalist subversion in the course of their revealing correspondence. "We hope that if the royalists try something they will pay dearly for their audacity," wrote the *orfèvre* Beillet to the watchmaker Droz. At the same moment his fellow exile Ollivier (a functionary in the navy department who had been purged after Thermidor) was writing to his wife: "The patriots will triumph over all the aristocracies, but it takes patience. It is up to the patriots to be prudent, and to let the aristocrats show themselves in a way that the patriots can smash them solidly."[8] From Rochefort (Charente) the hapless watchmaker Maurice Roy maintained a correspondence with his former fellow revolutionary committeeman Daviaud, who was living in Paris with the ex-Montagnard Laignelot. Roy could scarcely believe the stories he heard about the ferment and insurrectionary movements in Paris associated with former terrorists, in view of the near "fatal" reaction that had almost brought them all "across the precipice." Groping for an explanation this ingenuous sans-culotte concluded: "I am pretty well convinced that this is yet another of Pitt's machiavellian machinations." In reply, the more sophisticated Daviaud assured him that subversion was indeed the chosen ground of the Right, and that terrorists who had mistakenly taken that road themselves had already learned or would soon learn that they were "dupes."[9]

Jacobin journalists were likewise preoccupied with anti-republican subversion, especially as it helped define their own loyalty to the government.[10] Repeatedly the newspapers called upon the Directory

Auxerre dated 14 pluviôse IV. (Gautherot's police dossier is in A.N. F⁷ 6208, dossier 3314, plaq. 2.) A similar impression is conveyed retrospectively by Louis Taffoureau, a Jacobin from St. Omer (Pas-de-Calais) who was later implicated (falsely) in the Babeuf plot. At the trial he recalled that the republicans of St. Omer buried their differences after Vendémiaire and attempted to regroup themselves, sending petitions to Paris and subscribing to newspapers. *Débats du procès instruit par la Haute-Cour de Justice . . .* (Impr. Nationale, 1797), III, 569.

[8] A.N. F⁷ 6611 [Affaires Politiques], Seine: dossier Ollivier, Beillet et Moquet: Beillet to Droz, horloguer, 7 ventôse IV; Ollivier fils à son épouse, 9 ventôse.

[9] A.N. W 564, dossier 50 [Procedure Contre Maurice Roy]: Roy to Daviaud, 3 floréal IV; Daviaud to Roy, 18 floréal.

[10] The Neo-Jacobin newspapers are enumerated in the Note on Sources

to cease regarding as suspects its "true friends" among the "pure and vigorous" patriots. Simultaneously they demanded the definitive elimination of royalist elements like émigrés, refractory priests, *chouans*, and white-terrorists. This was a capital point; it argued against the Directory's strategy of comprehensive reconciliation, of "homicidal indulgence" to émigrés and white-terrorists. Such tolerance of reaction by the "*mitoyens* . . . who extend one hand to the chouans, and the other to republicans" was producing a "mortal stagnation in public affairs," argued René Lebois, the latest Friend of the People. "It must be decided once and for all," he maintained, "one party must crush the other because it is no longer possible to reconcile the aristocrats with the patriots."[11]

Proclaiming their adherence to the new regime at every turn, the non-Babeuvist democrats assumed the role of loyal opposition. "To resist the government's abuses, is to support the government," insisted the *Orateur plébéien*—a journal whose initial subsidy the Directory quickly sought to cancel.[12] Scathing attacks on the Directory's inactivity in the face of economic crisis were penned in the Jacobin press, but without calling into question the legitimacy of that government. Abuses could be opposed within the framework of laws. Know the constitution and the laws, counseled Pierre Tissot, "in order to uphold their real meaning; in order to put an end to the usurpations of functionaries, in order to be the people's sentinels, the supporters of the poor, of the simple citizen against the aristocracy of officialdom."[13] Babeuf thrived on his conviction that the bourgeois republic was unredeemable. Democrats like Tissot continued to view it as a distasteful but reformable regime.

---

and Bibliography; the role of the press is discussed in several places including Chs. 3, 5, and 13, as well as in the present chapter, since along with the clubs it was the essential instrument of Neo-Jacobinism.

[11] *Ami du Peuple* No. 113, 17 frimaire IV; *Orateur plébéien* No. 1, 21 brumaire.

[12] A.N. F^{18} 21 [Presse]: Ministry of Interior to Directory, reporting that the Directory's decree of 18 frimaire canceling 3,000 subscriptions to the *Orateur plébéien* came too late, since the publisher had already received the money.

[13] *J. hommes libres* No. 27, 4 frimaire IV, P.F.T. "Sur l'utilité pour les patriotes de connaître la constitution et les lois." On Pierre Tissot, whose role in the Neo-Jacobin resurgence of 1798 was capital, see A.N. F^7 4775/31 [Comité de Sûreté Générale]; W. C. Holbrook, "Tissot, premier historien des derniers Montagnards: documents inédits," *AHRF*, 1937, pp. 448-59; Tonnesson, *La Défaite des Sans-culottes*, pp. 139 and 363.

In order to maintain their loyalty to the Directory regime, the Jacobins had to abandon the Constitution of 1793. This most democratic of French constitutions had been drafted by the Mountain in June 1793, approved by almost two million voters, and held in abeyance "until the peace." When the thermidorians proceeded to scrap it without ceremony they were acting illegally, as Babeuf insisted on recalling. For the non-Babeuvist democrats the loss of the 1793 constitution was regrettable, but the overwhelming fact of its stillbirth acceptable. In sympathetic disagreement with Babeuf the *Orateur plébéien* explained their position.

> As of now the Constitution of '95 is our veritable source of order and energy; every good citizen owes it, not the sacrifice of his opinion nor of his ultimate views, but a public respect, a sincere submission and the tribute of his efforts, without losing for all that the right to prepare for its reform or improvement.[14]

Such a position, however, was not incompatible with an occasional fond recollection of the lost charter, and certain Jacobins continued to eulogize its merits. In part this was a question of nostalgia, or more precisely of loyalty to one's past despite its unpopularity in the present. More important, their loyalty to the new constitution depended on the opportunity to amend or "improve" it—a consideration invariably mentioned when Jacobins discussed this question. In this respect the Constitution of 1793 remained a standard which could be invoked to encourage reform efforts through the long and cumbersome procedures that were required. Democrats certainly acknowledged that the 1793 constitution was itself impractical and imperfect, but they continued to be inspired by the level of equality and democracy that it proclaimed. They did not continue to "advocate" it, as Babeuf most decidedly did, but they defended its historical significance.

Since the Babeuvists used the Constitution of 1793 as an explicit alternative to the Directory regime, the government adopted an extreme response. In a decree dated 27 germinal (16 April 1796) it announced that anyone publicly advocating the Constitutions of 1791 or 1793 would be subject to the death penalty.[15] The line sep-

---

[14] *Orateur plébéien* No. 9, 16 frimaire IV, "Un mot à l'occasion du No. 35 du Tribun du Peuple."

[15] See M. Dommanget, "Les Egaux et la Constitution de 1793," in *Babeuf et*

arating "opinion" and "action" was blurred here, and in effect it became a proscribed subject; a favorable opinion of that charter was stigmatized as a sign of disloyalty to the existing government. On this ground the Jacobin press opposed the law. "Nothing is more inept," P. A. Antonelle had complained several weeks earlier, anticipating such a move, "than to make a show of proscribing the partisans of an opinion; and until now at least, attachment to the constitution of '93 can only be regarded as an opinion, as long as it is not accompanied by activities to overthrow the present constitution."[16]

Ironically it was under this count alone that Babeuf was ultimately convicted and executed—that is, for opinion rather than action. Needless to say, the Tribune ignored the decree. For the non-Babeuvist democrats who submitted, it was painful but not critical. When the government shortly indicated its intention of enforcing this law by making its violation one of the counts in the indictment against the Babeuvists, it undoubtedly reinforced the tendency of accommodation among Jacobins. In a sense the decree, by lifting the Constitution of 1793 beyond debate altogether, made the process of accommodation simpler and less ambiguous. On the other hand the Jacobins objected to it strenuously as an abridgment of free expression and were constrained by the inability to keep the standard of 1793 aloft for purposes of reform. But in the final analysis they continued, as they had since Vendémiaire, to come to terms with the republic's new charter.

Despite the continuing social ostracism, verbal and physical assault, and judicial persecution that they suffered, the Jacobins did not abandon or turn against the republic as Babeuf urged. While their newspapers regularly groaned under a host of grievances from persecuted Jacobins, only a few individuals were ready to follow

---

les problèmes du Babouvisme, Colloque Internationale de Stockholm, ed. A. Soboul (Paris, 1963). The decree, aimed at the Babeuvists but vague enough to cover much more, provided the death penalty "à tous ceux qui, par leurs discours ou par leurs écrits soit imprimés, soit affichés, provoquent la dissolution de la représentation nationale ou celle du Directoire exécutif . . . ou le rétablissement de la royauté, ou celui de la constitution de 1793, ou celui de la constitution de 1791. . . ." A. Debidour, ed., *Recueil des actes du Directoire exécutif* (Paris, 1911), II, 158n.

[16] *Orateur plébéien* No. 66, 2 germinal IV. The Jacobin organ in Tarbes, the *Journal des Hautes-Pyrénées* No. 22, 24 germinal IV, likewise complained about the confounding of "ces mots distincts: opinion et faction."

Babeuf into the alienation or exile that turns men into plotters. Neither did they lapse into destructive self-pity over present losses, or into immobilizing nostalgia over the fast-receding past. Though such a mood may have lurked in their writing, it did not prevail. Tenaciously, a thinned but unbroken Jacobin movement convinced itself that its rightful place could be regained. They were unresponsive to the Babeuvists' boldest contention: that "the French Revolution is merely the forerunner of another much greater revolution ... which will be the last."[17]

‡ II ‡

Another revolution. A program of insurrection and temporary dictatorship, of absolute equality and distributive communism. No wonder the non-Babeuvist democrats appear hazy and temporizing. Their differences with the Directory pale in the light of Babeuf's "Manifesto of Equals" or "Act of Insurrection." But admitting the Jacobins' penchant for compromise is not to acknowledge nebulousness. In their own right they resisted the new regime's conservatism, while offering what they deemed an alternative to the rigors of Babeuvism.

One must not be engrossed by the Jacobins' intense patriotism or by their zeal in fighting counterrevolution. This defensive aspect was simply the most obvious side of Jacobinism; its positive

[17] "Manifeste des Egaux" (written by Sylvain Maréchal) in Buonarroti, *Conspiration pour l'égalité dite de Babeuf* (Paris, 1957 edn.). The extent of Babeuf's radicalism is best measured not by Buonarroti's account (written many years after the fact), but by the documents that Buonarroti reprints as an appendix; by Babeuf's *Tribun du Peuple*, much of which is reproduced by Maurice Dommanget in his important book *Pages choisies de Babeuf* (Paris, 1935); and in the documents seized by the Police when the Babeuvists were arrested: *Copie des Pièces saisies . . . dans le local que Babeuf occupait . . .* (2 vols.; Impr. Nationale, an V).

The literature on Babeuf and Buonarroti has grown very large; its range is evident in two collections of essays in honor of Babeuf's bicentennial: one in a special issue of *AHRF*, 1960, and the other representing the Colloque Internationale de Stockholm, published under the title *Babeuf et les problèmes du Babouvisme*. The literature is reviewed in at least three other places: E. Eisenstein, *Filippo Michele Buonarroti, The First Professional Revolutionary* (Cambridge, 1959); K. Tonnesson, "The Babouvists: From Utopian to Practical Socialism," *Past and Present* (1962), pp. 60-76; and C. Mazauric, *Babeuf et la Conspiration pour l'égalité* (Paris, 1962). All of these works rely heavily on the scholarship of A. Saitta, A. Galante-Garonne, M. Dommanget, J. Godechot, and V. M. Dalin.

side was also evident at this time, though it had to be affirmed both against Babeuvism and Directorial conservatism. For Jacobins and Babeuvists alike most issues of the day were symbolized in words like "Democracy" and "Equality"—a situation, incidentally, that permitted so many Jacobins to admire Babeuf while ignoring the real implications of his argument. Babeuf's commitment to *égalité réele* reinforced his call for an insurrection against the government. The Jacobin concept of equality found adequate expression within the constitutional republic, the problem being to energize it and start it moving in the right direction. For this their main prescription was precise and pragmatic. Babeuf called for an insurrection; the Jacobins called for a revival of political clubs.

In the pages of René Vatar's *Journal des hommes libres*, a newspaper recognized by contemporaries as the authentic *porte parole* of Jacobinism, the alternative to Babeuvism unfolded. A bookseller and publisher from a venerable family of that profession, Vatar had moved from Rennes to Paris in 1791, and in the Year II he was appointed by Robespierre as printer for the Committee of Public Safety. Barely surviving the thermidor purges, he kept his newspaper alive, a beacon for persecuted Jacobins in Paris and the provinces.[18] Around his shop and offices a large circle of democrats gravitated, including Felix Lepelletier, Charles Duval, Pierre Tissot, and P. J. Antonelle. This last, an ex-noble turned democrat, was particularly prolific in the early months of the Directory, and though well known among the inner circle of Babeuvists, he provided in Vatar's newspaper and in the *Orateur plébéien* an alternative to Babeuf's position.[19]

Scandalized by the legendary corruption and public misery of the thermidorian era, Antonelle warned that the spirit of inequality

---

[18] On Vatar and his newspaper see Appendix iv.

[19] Mayor of Arles in 1790-91, member of the Legislative Assembly and the Paris Jacobin Club from 1791-92, Antonelle sat during the Terror on the Revolutionary Tribunal. There his irrepressible individualism alienated him from the Robespierrist leadership: he insisted on declaiming and publishing his lengthy opinions despite orders to the contrary and in 1794 was removed from the court to jail, to be liberated after Thermidor. (For a brief sketch of his career see the *Dictionnaire de Biographie française*. An article that promised a much-needed analysis is extremely disappointing: E. Avenard and P. Guiral, "Essai d'explication du Marquis d'Antonelle," *Provence historique*, v [1955], 263-88.) His extensive writings after Thermidor and at the beginning of the Directory were generally published by Vatar.

threatened to undermine the republic. "A distressing and excessive inequality," he wrote, "keeps the real people—the entire mass, except for a small number—under the dependence of that small number, and under a veritable oppression." His premise was that a people with France's revolutionary past could reverse this trend if it was aroused and organized, especially by joining together in clubs. "Where else can the people recover that energy and that true feeling for its rights that they are trying to extinguish, and that all conspires to destroy, if it is not in those patriotic assemblages that are their natural channel." The indispensable right, he argued, was the right of association, by which citizens could enlighten themselves and exercise surveillance over their officials. The ostensible guarantee of this right under the new constitution implied that what he called "representative democracy" would be possible even under that charter.[20] But the right was tenuous, the government having authority to close clubs that it deemed dangerous. Thus the existence of clubs became the touchstone of the democrats' position. To threaten the clubs, as conservatives repeatedly did, was to attack the mainspring of democracy. "A long-established truth is that . . . they detest the clubs because clubs are one of the formative and protective elements of representative democracy."[21]

Antonelle considered clubs not simply as a political organization but as a unique institution for promoting social integration and combatting the spirit of oligarchy that tainted other social institutions after Thermidor. "Everything promotes oligarchy," he complained.

> The boudoirs and the salons, the whore-houses and the lycees, the cafés and the schools, the balls, the festivals, the spectacles . . . good institutions and bad institutions—all are turned to profit by the oligarchs. . . . In the disastrous state of inequality in which we are sinking, everything favors and enriches the very few, while everything weighs upon the great mass of useful and

[20] *J. hommes libres* No. 134, 22 ventôse IV: Antonelle, "Mon troisième mot sur la fermeture des réunions civiques." (Cont'd in Nos. 135 and 136.)

[21] *Ibid.* No. 175, 3 floréal IV: Antonelle, "Démocratie." The Montagnard Laignelot proclaimed from the dock at Vendôme (where he was wrongly implicated with Babeuf) that a major flaw in the Constitution of the Year III was that it gave the government authority to close clubs on slight pretext. *Débats du procès*, IV, 332. See also *Orateur plébéien* No. 66, 2 germinal IV and No. 81, 17 germinal; *Ami de la Patrie* No. 15, 16 ventôse IV.

hardworking people. . . . Only one thing can hold them off and cut them down to size, that is, I repeat, attending republican clubs.[22]

Such imagery was common. Jacobins at Montcenis and Nancy complained of being unable to communicate effectively since their clubs were banned. "Meanwhile, by virtue of their wealth, the conspirators and chouans can gather . . . at balls and superb dinners where the most detestable principles are preached."[23]

Single-minded emphasis on clubs tied into a larger issue in the Jacobins' arsenal: universal public education. While this cause continued to head the list of Jacobin demands, the clubs could partially fill the existing void. Civic education, at least, could be obtained immediately, and with this advantage: that in the clubs, a man could be "simultaneously student and master." As Antonelle argued, in the clubs where public issues were discussed and criticized, "it will not be easy to impose on him for long."[24]

All republicans celebrated the function of a vigorous free press, but the Jacobins saw a complementary, indeed a superior role for the club as an instrument of civisme. An article in the *Orateur plébéien* entitled "On the necessity to complement freedom of the press with freedom for the clubs," demonstrated the relative passivity of the citizen in relation to the press. "The true organ of the people must be essentially popular, absolutely generalized, easily exercised, of common usage; this organ must be the habitual and faithful interpreter of the people's opinion." Only the clubs filled these qualifications,[25] and the very attacks of the clubs' opponents underscored this point. In support of a resolution to clamp down on clubs, the reactionary deputy Mailhe initially defended complete freedom for the press. This he would not grant to the clubs, the chief difference being "especially in the rapidity of their respective

[22] *J. hommes libres* Nos. 151 and 152, 9 and 10 germinal IV: Antonelle, "Quelques effets de la réaction—Necessité de former en tous lieux des réunions républicains." See also *Ibid.* No. 154, 12 germinal: "Réponse à un mot de Mailhe"; and articles by Charles Duval opposing limitations on the clubs' organization, No. 167, 25 germinal.

[23] *Ibid.* No. 149, 7 germinal IV: letters from Montcenis and Nancy.

[24] *Ibid.* No. 152, 10 germinal. On the role of education in democratic thought, see also Lepelletier, *Réflexions*, and Antonelle, "Un mot sur l'égalité," *J. hommes libres* No. 68, 14 nivôse IV.

[25] *Orateur plébéien* No. 92, 28 germinal IV.

effects." In clubs, he rightly observed, "a state of revolutionary electricity" can be created.[26]

Mailhe's proposed bill (which was sidetracked by the Legislature) would have plugged every loophole in the constitution through which the clubs were able to organize and act effectively, and would have drastically limited the legal size of clubs to from twenty to sixty members, depending on the size of the commune. He intended that political clubs in France should be "inapperçu dans l'Etat," and do no more than any artistic, scientific, or literary society. If they were anything more than reflective, he argued, they became coteries; far from being necessary "to revive public spirit," active political clubs undermine the republic. Essentially this remained the argument of conservatives until it was realized under Bonaparte. Meanwhile, in response to the mounting agitation of the Pantheon Club in Paris, the Directory, instead of supporting a *permanent* proscription like Mailhe's, moved on 9 ventôse (28 February 1796) to dissolve the new club temporarily.[27]

While conservatives harassed them, and Babeuf sought to manipulate them as fronts, traditional democrats viewed the clubs as their principal rallying point and hope for the future. The Lorient Jacobins who had sought exile in Paris instructed their correspondents accordingly. "In most sections (of Paris) clubs are forming like that of the Pantheon Français to which I belong," wrote the petit-bourgeois Ollivier. "These useful associations will once again save the country. It is astonishing that the patriots of Lorient still do not have one." His fellow exiles shared this conviction. "Ten or twelve clubs already formed in Paris are at work doing everything they can for the good of the country . . . we are almost 3,000 in the Pantheon club resolved to vanquish," wrote Beillet. "Be sure to take it upon yourself to advise recognized patriots to form themselves into clubs."[28]

[26] Mailhe's address and draft proposal are reprinted in *Moniteur*, 11 and 12 germinal IV.

[27] See Mathiez, *Le Directoire*, Chs. VII and VIII, on the Pantheon Club and Babeuf's penetration of it; also C. Picquenard, "La Société du Pantheon et le parti patriote à Paris du brumaire à ventôse an IV," *R.F.*, XXXIII (1897), 318-48.

[28] A.N. F⁷ 6611: Ollivier to his wife, 6 ventôse; Beillet to Lacroix, 17 ventôse; Beillet to Droz, 7 ventôse. See also *L'Observateur du Midi* (Marseilles) No. 2, 6 germinal IV, and *Journal des Hautes-Pyrénées* (Tarbes) No. 17, 6 germinal IV.

Personalities and specific issues came and went, the level of tolerance for Jacobinism varied, but the call for clubs remained constant. This initial attempt to organize such clubs foundered very shortly. Fearful of the unrest caused directly by the subsistence crisis, the Directory moved against the Pantheon Club in Paris when it seemed to become a forum for Babeuvist propaganda. With this precedent local conservatives assaulted the provincial clubs, which found themselves extremely vulnerable and with no recourse for protection.[29] Those that did manage to stave off closure eventually succumbed to the devastating anti-Jacobinism unleashed after the government exposed the Babeuf conspiracy, arrested its alleged principals, and insinuated that "foyers" of the plot existed in the provinces. The spring of 1796 was notably uncongenial to the clubs, but their day would come again.

‡ III ‡

Subsequent chapters will examine the Jacobin or democratic persuasion as it matured during the Directory years. It suffices here to indicate the survival of a limited concept of equality in the face of Babeuf's attempt to enlarge and appropriate that evocative ideal for himself. The Jacobins' disavowal of Babeuf's call for an insurrection against the Directory was paralleled by their rejection of égalité réele as an impractical utopian ideal.[30] By the time Babeuf

---

[29] Short-lived clubs were formed in the following places, among others: Angers, Arras, Avignon, Beaune, Beziers, Bordeaux, Bourges, Cambrai, Cette, Digne, Dijon, Foix, Grenoble, Marseilles, Mende, Montpellier, Nancy, Pau, Riom, St. Omer, Strasbourg, Toulon, Toulouse, Troyes, Versailles. Their significance and the circumstances surrounding their suppression are suggested in a letter about the rise and fall of a club at Fontenai-le-Peuple. (*Le Batave* [Paris] No. 1135, 9 prairial IV.) The author contrasts the intentions of the members and the constructive activities they were preparing to undertake, with the false accusations leveled against them as a pretext to close the club: namely an association with the Pantheonist and Babeuvist "conspirators." The man's answer amounts to the point that the club was purely local, having nothing to do with those remote affairs, and that maladministration by local officials in financial, economic, and political matters was the real cause of unrest.

Documents collected in the course of controversies over their composition and activities are especially informative for clubs at Beaune (Côte d'Or): A.N. F⁷ 7152, fol. 4865 and F⁷ 7418, fol. 4024; Bourges (Cher) A.N. F⁷ 4277, "Cher" and F⁷ 7158, fol. 5904; and Grenoble (Isère) A.N. F⁷ 7147, fols. 3641 and 3716 and F⁷ 7146, fol. 3622.

[30] Babeuf was one of the first men to view collectivism as an attainable objective rather than a utopian ideal. Antonelle, on the contrary, rejected

was arrested, insurrection and communism were so fused in his thought that they were indistinguishable. The Jacobins' limited notion of equality, on the contrary, reinforced their commitment to legality and compromise.

Babeuf's égalité, an economic concept, defined itself against the entire record of history. The human condition of material inequality and exploitation appeared no more tolerable in a modern republic than under the timeless oppressions of the past. "People of France," he could write, "you have been no more favored than the other nations which inhabit this unfortunate globe! Always and everywhere the poor human race . . . serves as the plaything of all ambitions."[31] Exploitation was the problem, private property the cause. Egalité réele would therefore be redemptive of the plebeians or underclass: the enormous population of indigents in town and country, the menial day-laborers, the landless agricultural classes, all those without material stake in the social order.

Since the Jacobin concept of equality was not economic, its redemptive effect was scarcely directed to the underclass. Equality was a moral and civic concept, which denoted a spirit rather than a condition. Its basic requirements were a popular, responsive government, and social institutions that minimized the consequences of

---

égalité réele as even a long-term goal for a country like France, arguing that such an ideal stood in the way of more practical commitments. "Les racines de cette fatale institution [private property] sont trop profondes et tiennent à tout; elles sont désormais inextirpables chez les grands et vieux peuples. . . . Tous ce qu'on pourrait espérer d'atteindre, ce serait un degré supportable d'inégalité dans les fortunes." Antonelle préfigured the posture of the "revisionist" opposing the "doctrinnaire" socialist: "Que ce systeme indestructible si l'on veut, soit en outre irreformable, c'est de quoi l'on me permettra de douter." (See *Orateur plébéien* No. 9, 16 frimaire: "Un mot à l'occasion du No. 35 du Tribun du Peuple"; and *J. hommes libres* No. 144, 2 germinal.) An article by A. Saitta, "Autour de la Conjuration de Babeuf: discussion sur le communisme (1796)," *AHRF*, 1960, pp. 426-35, argues that in such articles Antonelle was purposely trying to serve as a foil for Babeuf, whose views he shared. But the fact that Antonelle was an "agrégé principal" of Babeuf's inner circle does not by any means prove this. Indeed Babeuf had a skeptical attitude about Antonelle. (See Babeuf to Hesiné, *AHRF*, 1963, pp. 79-83.) On the contrary, Antonelle's case might be the foremost example of how democrats were anything but regularly consistent.

[31] This quotation is from Maréchal's "Manifeste des Egaux" (p. 94). A fuller exposition is in Babeuf's "Manifeste des plébéiens," *Tribun du Peuple* No. 35, 9 frimaire IV, reprinted in Dommanget's *Pages choisies de Babeuf*, pp. 250-64.

existing inequality and advantages.[32] The vision of equality lay not in the future but within the Revolution's history itself; the Jacobins forged their arguments not against the historic plight of humanity but against the corruption and derogations of the present. Their concern was not to eliminate inequities of wealth or talent but to prevent these advantages from producing inordinate privilege for their beneficiaries and unusual oppression for everyone else. Like Babeuf the Jacobins invoked the public welfare as against the mere sum of individual self-interest. For Babeuf, only in the *communauté des biens* could the public welfare thrive; for the Jacobins a democratic republic sufficed.

The alleviation of economic misery in the Jacobin order was supposed to come not through structural change, but through relief efforts and timely government intervention tendered in a spirit of justice. In the first respect the Jacobins were no more than self-conscious humanitarians, scarcely differing in their attitude towards the underclass than an aristocrat with noblesse oblige or a cleric of the apostolic persuasion. It might be said that the underclass remained abstract, and that as subject rather than object it continued to be invisible. For the Jacobins thought primarily of citizens. The misery that really enraged them was that suffered by the sans-culottes—men unendowed with wealth or formal education, but who had achieved a sense of their own dignity precisely by having participated in the Revolution. Implicitly the Jacobins differentiated between sans-culottes (whose prototype was "the artisan") and the real underclass of the apolitical masses. When the new clubs proclaimed as one of their objectives "bienfaisance envers les malheureux" and "correspondance avec la misère,"[33] they were talking about the sans-culottes—men who had fallen from an assumed state of self-sufficiency, both civic and material, into poverty and degrada-

[32] For a concise definition of democracy in this sense see the credo of J. N. Pache, mayor of Paris during the Terror, "Seconde Mémoire sur une affaire pendante . . . au tribunal civil" (floréal an V) in L. Pierquin, ed., *Mémoires sur Pache* (Charleville, 1900), p. 110.

[33] See e.g., A.N. F⁷ 3685/1: "Des républicains de Saint-Omer . . ."; *J. hommes libres* No. 73, 20 nivôse: "Cercle patriotique de Cette (Hérault)"; "Règlement du Cercle des Amis de la Constitution . . . de 1795" in R. R. Tissot, *La Société populaire de Grenoble pendant la Révolution* (Grenoble, 1910), pp. 188-89.

tion. It was in this spirit that the journalist René Lebois parried Babeuf while attacking the conservatives' apathy towards la misère.

> The enemies of the rich . . . do not wish, as is alleged, to equalize all fortunes . . . but they do follow the principles of popular morality. . . . The revolution was not made so that the merchants could replace the dukes and peers; so that the artisan would be deprived of necessities. . . . It was made to ameliorate the lot of the artisan and the working man graced with skills but disgraced by fortune.[34]

The minimum program of interventionist policies advocated by the Paris sections in the Year II was by now standard among Jacobin spokesmen. But just as they rejected Babeuf's *communauté des biens,* so did they ignore the sans-culottes' maximum program with its proposal to limit the size of enterprise, so that "one citizen could have only one workshop or one store."[35]

Property rights—whether "social" or "natural" in origin—were considered by the Jacobins subject to regulation, as long as "hunger is on the order of the day," as it was once again in 1796. Manifest abuses of property (rather than what Babeuvists deemed the *inherent* abuses) were what offended the Jacobins. "Property ought no longer to be regarded as the absurd right to starve and oppress, nor freedom for commerce as the power to steal with impunity," they continued to insist, against prevailing laissez-faire orthodoxy. Especially when the poor harvest and inflated currency of 1796 were aggravated by hoarding, price gouging, or speculation in paper money, the right to dispose of one's property had to be restricted. The Jacobins, at least, were not the advance agents of the Code Napoléon with its explicit sanction of the right to *abuse* property. On the contrary, Vatar's newspaper attacked "that grand and unlimited freedom of commerce, vaunted by certain men whose interests counsel it, but almost always so disastrous when it applies to necessities."[36]

[34] *Ami du Peuple* No. 116, 29 frimaire IV.

[35] Soboul, *Les Sans-culottes Parisiens,* Part II, Ch. 2: "Les aspirations sociales de la sans-culotterie parisienne." The phrase "one workshop" comes from the famous *enragé* petition 25 June 1793, reprinted in *Annales révolutionnaires,* VII (1914), 547-60.

[36] See *J. hommes libres* No. 48, 25 frimaire IV; No. 106, 24 pluviôse IV; No. 22, 29 brumaire IV; *Ami du Peuple* No. 125, 9 pluviôse IV; *Orateur*

While Babeuf used the economic crisis of 1796 to indict the entire system of private property, the Jacobins merely refurbished the regulatory measures of the Committee of Public Safety. Clubs, newspapers, and pamphlets called for severe punishment of hoarders and speculators, requisitions to force peasants to sell crop surpluses, expansion of public granaries, and prohibitions against the export of grain. Without using the provocative term *Maximum*, the *Journal des hommes libres* in addition proposed several possible methods of price control on items like bread, meat, and fuel, including Dubois-Crancé's plan for a sliding scale of prices. Full market price should be payable by "the rich," free subsidized purchases available to the indigent, with several gradations in between. The government was obliged to do this, Vatar argued, because it "must assure to everyone the means of existence."[37]

Characteristically the Jacobins emphasized the political or administrative side of such economic regulation. The key to successful intervention was a popular government whose officials were dedicated to the public welfare and unsubservient to vested interests. The kind of men in office made all the difference. In this frame of mind Pierre Tissot looked back to the hunger riots of the Year III (during whose repression his father-in-law Goujon, an author of the original *Maximum* law, had been executed) to indict the prevailing "abuse of power." "To demand bread! This crime earns the death penalty when the magistrates are rich proprietors, infamous egoists, for whom liberty is a dream, equality a monster, the people's suffering an element of the social system." The remedy lay not in the abolition of property but in the restoration of a "popular government."[38]

Understandably, the Jacobins regarded the forced loan as a key public issue. An empty treasury and run-away inflation had compelled the reluctant Legislature to decree a forced loan in 1796 as a temporary expedient for raising taxes. Initially the forced loan had

---

plébéien No. 1, 21 brumaire; *Le Batave* No. 1135, 9 prairial IV. See also petitions from clubs in Arras and St. Omer, A.N. F⁷ 3685/1 (Pas-de-Calais), and a letter from the Jacobin Germain, the Directory's commissioner to Versailles, in E. Tambour, *Etudes sur la Révolution dans le département de Seine-et-Oise* (Paris, 1913), p. 21.

[37] *J. hommes libres* No. 106, 24 pluviôse, and No. 109, 27 pluviôse IV.

[38] *Ibid.* No. 27, 4 frimaire IV.

"filled the true patriots with joy." This "violent but useful emetic" was applauded as a measure that would restore solvency and "save modest fortunes from being overwhelmed by the great ones."[39] The Jacobin press discussed the forced loan obsessively, suggesting ways to insure its effectiveness. The *Journal des hommes libres*, for instance, reprinted in its entirety a placard appearing in Paris headed *Sauvons la France*, signed by Cranfort, "ouvrier du faubourg Martin au nom de plus de 300 de ses camarades." Proclaiming that this measure exempted the unfortunate three-quarters of the French people from a tax, Cranfort emphasized that it ought to be especially effective against nouveau-riche profiteers, but only if such men were known to the authorities. Hence he urged good citizens to report the names of anyone who "made immense profits in his vile commerce and is now very rich. . . . They must at last render an accounting." To facilitate such informing Cranfort provided the address of the responsible officials in Paris, and the advice that such declarations need not be signed, lest anyone be fearful of retaliation.[40]

Unless they were vigilant, though, the law could have an opposite effect. Great local discretion was possible in the actual assessment process; maliciously motivated, the administrators could "cause the enormous burden that the rich alone should bear, to fall upon the impoverished family, which has sacrificed everything for the Revolution." Perversely, the burden could afflict "citizens who are rich in their republican virtues alone."[41] Accordingly the clubs, newspapers, and individual activists threw themselves into the effort to expose such abuses, and the issue became the center of numerous local political storms. Jacobins denounced administrators who "scourged the poor citizens by assessing the rich with sums far smaller than they could afford,"[42] while conservatives attacked ad-

---

[39] Gauthier-Bezornay, *Mémoire presenté au Directoire* (Impr. Lebois, an IV); *Orateur plébéien* No. 16, 30 frimaire IV; *J. hommes libres* No. 94, 12 pluviôse IV.

[40] *Ibid.* No. 58, 6 nivôse IV. A comprehensive plan for the collection of the forced loan and the compilation of a civic cadastre of good, bad, and indifferent citizens, is presented in *Ibid.* No. 45, 23 frimaire.

[41] *Orateur plébéien* No. 17, 2 nivôse, and No. 74, 10 germinal; *Ami du Peuple* No. 123, 7 pluviôse, and No. 127, 19 pluviôse; *J. hommes libres* No. 94, 12 pluviôse; *Ami de la Patrie* No. 10, 11 ventôse IV.

[42] A.N. F⁷ 7147B, fol. 3867: representative Villetard to M. of Pol. on unfair assessments in the Yonne, 20 floréal IV. A.N. F⁷ 7611: Ollivier à son épouse,

ministrators who in their view used the forced loan unfairly, especially when such zeal appeared related to a man's terrorist past. That was how the Directory's commissioner in Pesmes (Haute-Saône) denounced Jeannot, a Jacobin justice of the peace during the Terror. "This immoral man of blood," he reported, "was the counsel of the new departmental administration for price control and the forced loan."[43] In Fontenay a recently organized club was dissolved by the authorities who reported that among the topics discussed, with such militants as Brutus Magnier in attendance, were "the great abuses in the division of the forced loan tax."[44]

The Jacobins needed an issue like the forced loan on which to focus, for it tangibly embodied their conception of sound public policy. For Babeuf, the forced loan was yet another self-delusion by which the Jacobins avoided realities. Contemptuous of the refrain that ran through Jacobin pronouncements on the subject ("this measure will save the Republic"), the *Tribun du Peuple* attempted to expose the forced loan as a sham.[45] Even if carried out with zeal, it was merely a tax that changed nothing, Babeuf declared. The rich will find a way of getting it back from the poor by intensified exploitation. Whereas the forced loan was adjudged a failure by the Jacobins only after maladministration and vested interests perverted it so that it fell oppressively on the "little man," Babeuf held that it was intrinsically a *duperie*. If such it was, then there was little to be done within the framework of legality. Insurrection seemed incumbent.

‡ IV ‡

Babeuf's disdain for the forced loan dramatized that as far as he was concerned his aims and the Jacobins' were incompatible. But his decisiveness was not matched by the other side. In the political culture of Jacobinism, Babeuf represented a complex presence.

---

6 ventôse, describing the politics of the forced loan assessments in Vannes (Morbihan).

[43] A.N. F⁷ 7151, fols. 3630 and 4584: commissioner to Pesmes (Haute-Saône) to Directory.

[44] A.N. AF III 42, fol. 153: Ministry of Justice, report to Directory, 13 vendémiaire V. Cf. *J. hommes libres* Nos. 135 and 147.

[45] *Tribun du Peuple* No. 39 quoted in Dommanget, *Pages choisies de Babeuf*, pp. 275-76.

Though typical Jacobin spokesmen, like those grouped around the newspapers, formally repudiated his position, their kinship with the Tribune remained appreciable.

During the thermidorian period, when he was imprisoned for his crusading journalism, Babeuf had acquired a solid reputation among democrats. In the thermidorian prisons a coterie of admirers promoted his ideas among revolutionaries in and out of jail. Though the strains of confinement produced personal quarrels, a spirit of fellowship seems to have predominated in which a wide range of men were deemed potentially good democrats by Babeuf, Charles Germain, and their close friends.[46] Hence when Babeuf prepared to resume publication of his newspaper after the amnesty, he could appeal to these contacts and capitalize on the good will that existed toward him in Jacobin circles.

The one newspaper that democrats were likely to be reading—the *Journal des hommes libres*[47]—provided valuable publicity for Babeuf at the outset. On 14 brumaire IV (5 November 1795) Vatar published an announcement, submitted by one of Babeuf's circle, informing his readers that the Tribune was about to resume his course of *plébéianisme*, having "at his command the veritable lever, a strong spirit, and a great love of justice and liberty." The *Hommes libres* urged patriots to support Babeuf, who in the past had proven himself worthy of confidence; to facilitate this support it reprinted complete information on how to secure a subscription for the *Tribun*.[48] Direct evidence exists that subscribers reached Babeuf specifically through this channel. For example, the Cherbourg Jacobin Fossard, standing trial with the Babeuvists at Vendôme, testified as follows on his original contact with Babeuf: "Sometime after the 13th of vendémiaire I saw the announcement of the *Tribun*

[46] This point is best documented in V. Advielle, *Histoire de Gracchus Babeuf et du babouvisme* (2 vols.; Paris, 1884), which reprints some of the letters passed between Babeuf and Germain. See also Tonnesson, *La Défaite des Sans-culottes*, and V. M. Dalin, "Marc-Antione Jullien nach dem 9 thermidor," in his *Babeuf-Studien,* ed. W. Markov (Berlin, 1961).

[47] See Appendix IV. The testimony of Louis Taffoureau of St. Omer, standing trial at Vendôme, illustrates this in passing. As a measure of how low the fortunes of "les républicains les plus purs démocrates" had sunk during the thermidorian reaction, he noted that "*L'Ami du peuple* et *les Hommes libres* n'avaient à cette epoque tout au plus que chacun deux ou trois abonnés à St. Omer." (*Débats du procès,* III, 569.)

[48] *J. hommes libres* No. 7, 14 brumaire IV: Annonce Litéraire.

du peuple in the *Journal des hommes libres.* Our curiosity was piqued; we each sacrificed 100 sous. . . . Four or five among us resolved to write to this *Tribun du Peuple* to order his newspaper."[49] Through thick and thin Vatar's managing editor Camus continued forwarding subscriptions for Babeuf's newspaper through Vatar's office.[50]

Several days after the original announcement, however, Vatar entered a vigorous demurrer against Babeuf, having digested the first issue of the *Tribun.* "All true supporters of the republic," he claimed, will "disavow the imprudent pages which at this time can only fan the flames of discord, serve the cause of royalism, and doom the nation."[51] From then until the moment of his arrest the Jacobin press unanimously maintained that any attempt at insurrection would provoke fierce repression, not only against its authors but against all "energetic republicans." The Jacobins' first line of response to Babeuf was to warn against bringing on another Prairial, in which gullible sans-culottes would be cut down as royalists gleefully looked on.[52]

Despite numerous repetitions of this rebuke, the Jacobins did not turn completely against Babeuf. A dialogue continued in which Babeuf was treated like a misguided sibling. Vatar published several remonstrances from the Tribune himself, as well as apologetic ar-

[49] *Débats du procès,* III, 609.
[50] A.N. F7 4278: Camus to Babeuf, 1 floréal IV.
[51] *J. hommes libres* No. 10, 17 brumaire IV: "Sur le Tribun de Peuple." A similar sequence of reactions was recorded by J. Goulliart, who had been intimate with some of Babeuf's friends during his thermidorian incarceration. (See Goulliart to Babeuf, Arras, 27 thermidor III, reprinted in *AHRF,* 1934, pp. 257-58.) Babeuf wrote to Goulliart asking him to start a local subscription bureau at Bethune (Pas-de-Calais) and Goulliart agreed—testimony to some regard for Babeuf. After reading the first few issues, however, he was upset. He claimed that he had always looked on Babeuf's ideas as "Castles in Spain," not realizing that Babeuf actually hoped to provoke a "boulversement total." When Goulliart realized that "sous prétexte du Bonheur du peuple on veut de nouveau le plonger dans le chaos de l'anarchie," he dissociated himself from the Tribune. (A.N. F1c III Pas-de-Calais/ 15, fol. 82: Goulliart [Officier municipal] à Delerue [commissaire départementale], 26 brumaire IV.) Other documents indicate that Goulliart remained associated with local Jacobins. His signature is prominent among 120 others in a petition from Bethune calling for all out war against peasants who withhold food from market (*Ibid.,* fol. 134: Les Patriotes de Bethune au Directoire, 26 frimaire, IV).
[52] See e.g., *Orateur plébéien* No. 94, 30 germinal: "Coup d'oeil sur notre situation actuelle"; *Ami de la Patrie* No. 51, 22 germinal IV.

ticles by people like Felix Lepelletier.[53] It seems clear that there was a decisive consideration here: Babeuf had to be defended because of his enemies. Harassed and proscribed by the Directory, Babeuf became an object of Jacobin solicitude.

Few Jacobins realized that Babeuf seriously intended to carry out his call for insurrection by means of a secret conspiracy; rather they regarded him as a publicist with provocative, uncompromising opinions. When the government attempted to suppress these opinions, Babeuf's image as a dangerous fanatic was neutralized. He may have been misguided, but his intentions were considered pure, his record of selflessness established. The persecution of such a man, instead of the chouans and profiteers, was a matter of concern for the Jacobins. Moreover, the cause of free speech was at stake if (as they wrongly argued) a disciple of Rousseau and Mably was being muzzled.

Seen as a publicist rather than a secret conspirator, Babeuf was indisputably colorful. Already driven underground, he suffered no restraint in his thundering rhetoric. All the warnings about avoiding a new Prairial could not detract from his effect as a spellbinding critic who deftly unmasked hypocrisy. Babeuf's favorable impact accordingly seems to have been a matter of sentiment rather than intellect. His image was especially enhanced by his own courage, and by the fortitude of his wife, who stood by him in his precarious underground existence, refusing to betray him despite her own arrest and intimidation by the police.[54] The Lorient Jacobin Ollivier reflected a common concern and interest over this issue when he wrote to his own wife that "Babeuf is still in hiding and his wife is imprisoned in the Force because she has had the courage not to reveal her husband's refuge. Soon she will come up before the grand jury, and the patriots have reason to hope that she will get off."[55] From Arras (Pas-de-Calais) Babeuf's admirers gathered a substantial "patriotic collection," since they were aware of the "privations that you are suffering, as well as your family." "Continue to unmask the atrocious projects of the *patriciate*, and to merit its hatred,"

[53] See *J. hommes libres* Nos. 114, 119, 127. In No. 124 Babeuf was given over two full pages to air his views. See also *Copie des pièces saisies*, II, 9-24 and 36-40, and *Débats du procès*, I, 89.
[54] *J. hommes libres* No. 114, 2 ventôse IV.
[55] A.N. F⁷ 7611: Ollivier to his wife, 6 ventôse IV.

they concluded, "for it can only assure you of the increasing esteem and gratitude of numerous and unfortunate plebeians."[56]

The actual thrust of Babeuf's ideas, however, was blunted by the lack of doctrinal rigor or consistency that his readers were willing to summon. Remaining one voice among many, he did not drown out the others. Actually, the emphasis placed on his personal courage and seemingly utopian convictions ill served a man whose chosen role was precisely to break out of that tradition in order to lead a violent, redemptive revolution. But as a revolutionary leader Babeuf simply was not taken seriously, except by his innermost group of initiates. Babeuf's program, in short, failed to create many converts. But Jacobins generally did admire the Tribune's courage, salute his sentiments, and in many instances feed on his rhetoric.

Babeuf's ambiguous impact on the Jacobins is apparent in the case of J. B. Trotebas, whose name appeared on Buonarroti's list for an Insurrectionary Convention. A militant leader of the Metz Jacobin Club during the Terror, Trotebas had headed the list of local "Robespierrists" disarmed and imprisoned after Thermidor.[57] Following the amnesty he left prison, and as he later wrote to the Directory, found himself at sea.

> What could I do now after having lost all in serving the Revolution? . . . Unfortunately as a music teacher I no longer found pupils, and as a tailor very little work. At that time I received in the mails from Paris the prospectus of *Babeuf's* journal. I read it and showed it to a good friend of mine; we enjoyed it and decided to subscribe to it. We did more (because all must be told): upon the request of several citizens a collection was made to reprint the same prospectus.[58]

Trotebas maintained that this step was especially needed to neutralize the impact in Metz of a virulently reactionary local newspaper, the *Journal sans-titre et sans-abonnés*. Under this combination of circumstances, Trotebas decided to start a newspaper of his own,

[56] *Copie des Pièces saisies*, II, 58-59: Les égaux d'Arras à leur tribun, 25 pluviôse an 4.

[57] On Trotebas see my article "The Revival of Jacobinism in Metz During the Directory," *Journal of Modern History*, XXXVIII (1966), 13-37.

[58] A.N. F⁷ 4276 [Affaire Babeuf]: Trotebas to Directory, 8 prairial IV.

the short-lived *Observateur démocrate,* which brought Babeuf's name to the democrats of Metz.[59]

For all its militance, Trotebas' lively newspaper was not Babeuvist, but was an outspoken organ of Jacobinism resembling the *Orateur plébéien.* His principal source of ideas and information was the *Journal des hommes libres,* from which he borrowed almost verbatim extensively. While Babeuf moved toward an increasingly exclusionist position, men like Trotebas were left behind as they continued to embrace a wide range of opinions, to absorb and refract a variety of ideas that under rigorous scrutiny would appear contradictory. Trotebas' paper precisely lacked the consistency and direction that marked the inner core of Babeuvism. Sympathetic to Babeuf's posture of plebeianism, which corresponded to his own circumstances, Trotebas never even hinted at an acceptance of Babeuf's insurrectionary program on which all else really depended. Like most of Babeuf's readers, he chose what he liked from Babeuf's ideas without accepting their logical implications. Likewise Babeuf's strictures did not prevent him from relying heavily on the *Journal des hommes libres.* On the issue of communism, for example, Trotebas followed that newspaper directly in neutralizing Babeuf's thrust by according him the mantle of Rousseau, Mably, and Helvétius. Trotebas' own position on "the ticklish question of property" was rhetorically utopian and pragmatically reformist. He was most exercised by abuses of property—*dilapidation* and the like— and by callous exploitation which he considered a kind of assault on property itself.[60] When Trotebas was arrested because of his "subversive" propaganda, and in due course acquitted, Vatar justifiably celebrated it as a vindication of those who follow the *Journal des hommes libres.*[61]

Trotebas' evident unconcern with maintaining doctrinal consistency was typical. Jacobins in Paris forwarded subscriptions for the *Orateur plébéien,* the *Journal des hommes libres,* and the *Tribun du Peuple* to their "brothers" back home without distinguishing clearly between them. The Rochefort revolutionary Daviaud de-

[59] *L'Observateur démocrate ou le réveil des sans-culottes* (Metz) 5 Nos., pluviôse-ventôse an IV: B.N. Lc11/652 ter. The Directory's censorship agency described it as a "pantheonist newspaper" (A.N. F7 3448).

[60] *Observateur démocrate* especially No. 4, 1/5 ventôse and No. 5, 5/12 ventôse.

[61] *J. hommes libres* No. 155, 13 germinal IV, and No. 160, 18 germinal.

43

nounced every manifestation of insurrectionary activity in his correspondence, rejoicing, for example, that attempts to provoke the Legion of Police into rebellion had aborted. But at the same time he mailed a Babeuvist pamphlet back to his friend in Rochefort for his delectation.[62] It is not surprising that at the Vendôme trial even the most incriminating evidence and the most aggressive prosecutors failed to establish the participation of most defendants in an actual plot against the republic.[63]

Such was the case with Babeuf's correspondents in Cherbourg who were made to stand trial at Vendôme only to be acquitted. The bill of particulars assembled by the prosecution against them amounted to little more than a case of Jacobinism, flavored by a liaison with Babeuf. The Cherbourg "Babeuvists" were a group of former Jacobins who were trying to hold together and regain local influence. Their small club was regarded by its members as "an unsalaried revolutionary committee" working to enlighten public opinion, and to influence local administration.[64]

Having heard about Babeuf's newspaper, the Cherbourg democrats got together a subscription and wrote to Babeuf when the newspaper failed to arrive on time. In the course of this correspondence Babeuf exhorted them to press on with their work. The subject of Babeuf also entered into the letters they exchanged with their friend Cordebas in Paris. Damning excerpts from these letters were read into the trial record but turned out to be nothing more than the news that "Gracchus Babeuf has been indicted," and that Rayebois should "be on guard." "The Pantheon club has been closed," Cordebas informed his friends in Cherbourg. "When a new one is formed, I will let you know." Even the prosecutor admitted that the phrase "should we lose hope at a moment when everything points to a new order of things?" was simply a ritualistic exhortation to keep up hope. The most damning item with which the prosecutor challenged the defendants was Babeuf's advice to "carry out your work to the end or perish." Fossard replied that this re-

---

[62] A.N. W 564, dossier 40: Daviaud to Roy, 18 floréal IV. The pamphlet he enclosed was "Le Cri du Peuple français contre ses oppresseurs."

[63] The full import of this may be seen in the prosecution's summary statement for each defendant: *Discours des accusateurs-nationaux près la Haute-Cour de Justice, prononcé par le Citoyen Bailly* (Vendôme, an V).

[64] *Débats du procès*, III, 167-70.

ferred to their club and to what it had been doing all along. As for their subscription to the *Tribun du Peuple*, this was simply part of their effort to keep themselves informed and exposed to all viewpoints.[65] Since the police raid on Fossard's house had netted a voluminous amount of printed material including such diverse newspapers as the *Orateur plébéien*, the *Redacteur*, the *Ami des Lois*, and the *Journal des français*, in addition to the *Tribun du Peuple*, one may assume that Fossard was not trying to mislead the prosecution.[66] Moreover as late as floréal he was writing letters to newspapers like the *Patriotes de '89* to discuss the problem of chouans—a theme with which Babeuf was not notably concerned.[67]

The small group of Lorient Jacobins, almost arch-typical socially and politically, provides a further insight into this question. Their invaluable correspondence (seized precisely because of suspected subversive connections) marks them as militant but orthodox. It is suffused with a concern over rehabilitating their positions personally and politically, of bringing back "the good days" when patriots and men of virtue determined the country's destiny. Meanwhile they must struggle with aristocrats like Minister of Marine Truguet who withholds jobs from them. They work to defend each other's reputation, solicit favors for each other, and comfort each other. In Paris they are appalled by the mass misery and find in the Pantheon Club not simply a congenial political environment but a fellowship of humanitarians concerned to relieve this misery. Invariably the *Journal des hommes libres* is mentioned as their organ; they read it, submit articles to it, know its editors. They also read the *Tribun du Peuple*. Ollivier, the purged naval functionary, writes that one of his most valued friends has become Prieur de la Marne—"le père des patriotes"—who offers the hospitality of a good fire in his apartment and the company of "amiable republicans," allowing bitter winter days to be passed there in a spirit of fraternity. In this setting they play lotto and discuss politics. "I have another pleasure, which is no small thing for me," he writes. "It is to

[65] *Ibid.*, 605-11; *Discours des accusateurs-nationaux*, pp. 253-54.

[66] A.N. W 564, dossier 39 (Juri d'accusation de Cherbourg): P.V., 28 messidor IV.

[67] *Journal des Patriotes de '89* (Paris) No. 50, 5 floréal IV: "Fossard, horolger, au Cit. Réal."

read to him [Prieur] Babeuf, the *Tribun du Peuple* and other interesting works."[68]

THE DIRECTORY was not fazed by this ambiguity. Harried by administrative anarchy and a subsistence crisis, cajoled by the *honnêtes gens* to bring "order" to France, and uncertain of its own political tactics, the Directory sought to consolidate its command of the center by some decisive act. Babeuvism was an inviting target, but in reality it was the whole spectrum of democratic activism that was about to come under fire.[69] The government's response to the specter of Babeuvist sedition (actually a remote threat compared to the capacity of armed royalism) hit the rank and file of Jacobins and sectionnaires directly. Previous measures had already revealed the government's failure to discriminate between democrats willing to live with the new constitution and Babeuvists intent on overthrowing it. The decree of 27 germinal making "advocacy" of the 1793 constitution punishable by death was a restriction on the expression of sentiment rather than a curb on overt, subversive activity. The closing of the Pantheon Club, and in its wake a number of provincial clubs, struck more at the legal channels of dissent than at clandestine plotting and violence. Only when the Directory disbanded the potentially rebellious Paris Legion of Police was it acting to diminish the possibility of insurrection.[70] Its next move reverted to an indiscriminate harassment of democrats by ordering all non-resident *destitutés* (Jacobin refugees) out of Paris immediately.

Understandably, Jacobin spokesmen insisted that Babeuf would bring disaster down upon them all if he persisted, while they continued also to oppose each of the Directory's repressive acts. The end result fulfilled their predictions. Claiming that a plot was actually imminent, the Directory found its pretext for smashing the Left opposition. To a traditionally credulous public the Directory on 22 floréal IV (11 May 1796) unmasked a "monstrous conspiracy"

[68] For this paragraph see A.N. F⁷ 7611: letters from Beillet and Ollivier. The quotation is from Ollivier to his wife, 9 ventôse IV.

[69] Director Carnot was the architect of this policy. For an analysis of his complex motivation see Marcel Reinhard, *Le Grand Carnot* (Paris, 1952), II, 176-88.

[70] This important episode is treated ably by Jean Tulard, "La Legion de Police de Paris sous la Convention thermidorien et le Directoire," *AHRF*, 1964, pp. 38-64.

that allegedly reached from its organizer Babeuf out through the ranks of Parisian sectionnaires, provincial terrorists, ex-conventionnels, Jacobin publicists, and one actual member of the Legislature, J. B. Drouet. This event had two ultimate consequences. First, a spectacular political trial was eventually held in the town of Vendôme before a special High Court. More than a year after the arrests it acquitted sixty defendants, sentenced seven to deportation, and executed Darthé and Babeuf. Second, a wave of militant anti-Jacobinism was unleashed for which the Vendôme trial was only a showcase. Jacobin officeholders came under attack almost everywhere. As hundreds of citizens were investigated for possible indictment, freedom of association and opinion suffered a sharp abridgment. Close surveillance and harassment beset most cadres. All in all the Jacobins suffered a major crisis in civil liberties—doubly disturbing in view of the benefits they had expected from the new constitution. Politically the balance was tilted as far from the Left as it had ever been. The Jacobins lost virtually all influence, while the Directory attempted to share the center with willing reactionaries. Popular attitudes on social and economic questions were again muted.

This latest ordeal, however, was not without its marginal benefits. Above all it provided an occasion for Jacobin solidarity, giving impetus to the articulation of Jacobin self-consciousness and identity. The arbitrary interrogations, arrests, indictments, and purges did not silence all dissent. On the contrary, Jacobins used whatever channels they could salvage to defend themselves. Moreover, with Babeuf no longer an actual danger—with the worst over, so to speak—the Vendôme trial bridged the chasm between Jacobins and Babeuvists. In the end when the death sentence was handed down against the Tribune, he could take on the mantle of martyr, while the Vendôme trial generally assumed an honored place in Jacobin hagiography. But that was to come later. For the moment, as the arrest warrants were being executed, the charge of conspiracy threw the Jacobins entirely on the defensive, sapped their energy and morale, and called into question their survival as a public force.

CHAPTER III

The Struggle for Survival: From
Vendôme to Fructidor

PROVINCIAL officials reported the consternation of Jacobin cadres as they heard news of the "Babeuf plot" from Paris. Some officials chose to see this reaction as a sign of complicity in the alleged conspiracy.[1] More likely, one can assume that these Jacobins understood a signal for reaction when they saw it. Gloom spread rapidly in Jacobin circles. A letter from the activist Rossignol in Paris to his wife in Rochefort—intercepted by officials seeking out subversive correspondence—conveyed the prevailing sense of despair. "Scarcely had I started writing to you when I heard the news that another plot is unfolding . . . I must admit that this latest disaster will not help us and can only add to our difficulties, my poor friend."[2] The despondency of thirty Jacobin refugees from the Gard who had been forced to flee to Arles was more explicit. They had hoped for the return of normalcy and were beginning to enjoy its fruits, "but an event taking place far from us, and of which we are certainly ignorant, has given rise to a terrible reaction which will again subject us to all the horrors of proscription."[3]

Immediately the Jacobins' most determined adversaries stepped forward to urge draconian measures against the "anarchists" and to implement them where they could. Typical proposals called for a purge of all officeholders who, since the drafting of the new constitution early in the Year III, "have proven that they are loyal only to the anarchic charter." The public prosecutor of the Pas de Calais advised Paris that all *amnistiés* should be ordered back to their original communes where they would be placed under surveillance,

---

[1] See correspondence from Ariège (A.N. F⁷ 7154, fol. 5285 and F⁷ 7149, fol. 4083); Aveyron (A.N. F⁷ 7417a, fol. 3707); Vaucluse (A.N. F⁷ 7147a, fol. 3851). A particularly interesting "Note de ce qui s'est passé à Pau à l'occasion de la conspiration découverte le 22 floréal" was submitted by the departmental administration of Basses-Pyrénées: A.N. F⁷ 7154, fol. 5096.

[2] A.N. W 564, dossier 40, Paris, 22 floréal: A la Citoyenne Rossignol . . . à Rochefort-sur-Mer. His most immediate worry was whether he would be forced to leave Paris because of the law directed against terrorist *destitués*.

[3] A.N. F⁷ 7160, fol. 5267: Addresse de plusieurs républicains du Gard, refugiés à Arles, 9 prairial.

making them vulnerable to persecution as they had been after Thermidor.[4] Repressive measures in this spirit were carried out against the *amnistiés* of Angers (Maine-et-Loire), where the Directory's commissioner fulminated against them. "It is time that this clan of men proscribed by public opinion should no longer be included among the number of French citizens," he maintained, as he supervised measures to initiate this process. Equally aggressive officials in the Vienne department began to harass their own "*anarchistes féroces*" by closing the café where they used to meet, dogging their steps into the countryside, carrying out illegal domiciliary visits against them, forbidding them to leave the commune, and forbidding more than three of them at a time to assemble even in a private residence. Furthermore these officials hoped to intercept the Jacobins' correspondence. When the departmental commissioner eventually forwarded these decrees to Paris for review he anticipated possible objections to their patent illegality. His plea for indulgence was stark testimony to the erosion of civil liberties that Jacobins were facing. "Perhaps you will find these measures to be in opposition to the principles of liberty. . . . But at the same time you must decide whether it isn't appropriate to sacrifice the rigor of these principles momentarily for the sake of public tranquility."[5]

The eye of the storm was in Paris, where the government's repression was methodically unmethodical. In a sweeping but random dragnet almost two hundred arrest warrants were initially issued, producing in the end about sixty indictments.[6] For a while the threat of arrest hung over the heads of most prominent former revolutionaries, middle-class Jacobin or sans-culotte sectionnaire. The prevailing atmosphere in government circles was such that anyone was fair game provided that someone cared enough and that some shred of evidence could be unearthed linking the individual with

[4] A.N. F7 7145, fol. 3248; F7 7146, fol. 3302.

[5] A.N. F7 7154, fol. 5002 and fols. 4730, 5806, and 6172 in the same series. The last-quoted phrase from the departmental commissioner is in a letter dated 9 messidor. A.N. F7 7157a, fol. 4532 contains material on harassment of Vadier's son in Toulouse.

[6] Two groups of arrest warrants were issued on 19 floréal (30 persons) and on 24 floréal (110 persons). Others were added in the days that followed, both in Paris and in several provincial towns. See Debidour, *Recueil des actes du Directoire*, II, 330-48, 373, 383. Cf. R. C. Cobb, "Notes sur la répression contre le personnel sans-culotte de 1795 à 1801," *AHRF*, 1954 [No. 134], pp. 23-49.

Babeuf.[7] Most of these suspects had to be released since there simply was no such evidence, although the government strained to produce it. In perhaps the most blatant case, which deserves to be put on record for its own sake, Minister of Justice Merlin de Douai carried on a private campaign to implicate René Lebois in the plot. When the publisher of the *Ami du Peuple* was released after a preliminary hearing, Merlin expressed dismay and wrote to the justice of the peace in Lebois' *quartier*, requesting him to search through his records for earlier material that could be used against him. The justice of the peace—preoccupied with a raft of forced entries that was plaguing his district—replied that he could find nothing incriminating. Undaunted, Merlin turned back to the director of the grand jury requesting that *he* examine the files of Lebois' newspaper after the date of 27 germinal to find possible violations of the law prohibiting advocacy of the 1793 constitution. The official, by now an expert on the nuances of Babeuvism, replied that Lebois simply was not to be implicated in the conspiracy on the basis of available evidence, and advised that if his writings "do possibly form the basis of an accusation against him," it is a separate matter and ought to be handled by someone else. Not to be put off, Merlin followed this suggestion and had Lebois' file transferred to yet another official. In the end nothing came of this investigation and the most Merlin could do was to inconvenience Lebois by subpoenaing him to testify at the Vendôme trial months later.[8]

From the beginning, Jacobins warned that the Babeuf plot would unleash reaction and hypocrisy. Reactionaries would attempt to implicate all vigorous republicans in the conspiracy and would pose as friends of the constitution.[9] Eventually Minister of Justice Merlin and Minister of Police Cochon, themselves the chief persecutors, recognized this and called a halt to the spread of illegal measures. Errant officials in a number of places were warned to curb their

[7] See the denunciations and surveillance reports gathered in A.N. F7 4276 [Affaire Babeuf] and A.N. F7 7160, fol. 6202 [Affaire Babeuf].

[8] A.N. BB3 21: Merlin to Gerard, 9 prairial IV; J. P. section de l'Ouest to Merlin, 19 prairial; Merlin to Gerard, 27 prairial; Gerard to Merlin, 1 messidor; Merlin to Bureau Central, 7 messidor, and reply; Lebois to Merlin, 23 nivôse V.

[9] *Observateur du Midi* (Marseilles) No. 14, 6 prairial IV; No. 19, 1 messidor. The editor, Peyre-Ferry, was denounced to the police as "le Babeuf de Marseille" (A.N. F7 4276: letter dated Marseilles, 16 floréal).

ardor and keep within the limits of constitutional procedures.[10] For the fact was that loyal Directorials, too, were reporting that reaction was getting out of hand. Characteristically, representative Faure of the Meurthe wrote to Cochon agreeing that the notorious militant Phillipe of Nancy was indeed a likely coconspirator with Babeuf. But he warned in addition that local chouans were intent on profiting "from the unfortunate circumstances into which the monster Babeuf has placed us, in order to ruin the best republicans."[11] By its loyal commissioners in the departments the government was informed that "the Babeuf plot has revived the audacity of our royalists," that the "horrible conspiracy . . . is serving as a pretext for organizing a reaction . . . a general proscription of patriots." What was first considered a partisan Jacobin response thus came increasingly to be echoed by more "reliable" persons, and to be documented in royalist newspapers and broadsides.[12] Naturally the visible cadres of Jacobins were the foremost victims of this aggressively reactionary atmosphere, but when it reached a certain point the central government invoked its authority to protect its own position and constitution. Jacobin morale had been shaken, their position weakened. That was sufficient.

Jacobins defended themselves as best they could. Along with their initial response—that the government's policy would encourage reaction—they offered a more controversial argument: as presented by the government this *grande conspiration* (as they ironically referred to it with italics) was not at all convincing. They greeted the news not simply with distress and alarm, but with a pronounced incredulity. By and large they could understand the *grande conspiration* only as a transparent pretext for stifling opposition. And while most Jacobins who went on record initially disavowed Babeuf

[10] See A.N. F⁷ 7154, fols. 5285 and 7038: Merlin to Cochon, 21 thermidor; A.N. F⁷ 7154, fol. 5002: draft report by an unnamed bureau chief in the Police Ministry.

[11] A.N. F⁷ 7144, fol. 3174: representative Faure (Meurthe) to M. of Pol., 4 prairial.

[12] A.N. F⁷ 7160, fol. 6330: commissioner to the correctional tribunal of Dôle (Jura), 9 messidor, enclosing a reactionary pamphlet; A.N. F⁷ 7154, fol. 5014: commissioner to Barcellonette (Basses-Alpes), 11 prairial, enclosing a slanderous broadside entitled "Les créanciers des terroristes"; A.N. F⁷ 7147B, fol. 3889: commissioner to Lot, 6 prairial; A.N. F⁷ 7146, fol. 3634: commissioner to Aix, 1 prairial; A.N. F⁷ 3685/5: commissioner to Puy-de-Dôme, 22 prairial.

himself, they found it difficult to believe that even the Tribune was an actual conspirator.

From the outset, Vatar's *Journal des hommes libres* adopted a remarkably firm position of disbelief, admitting only that the documents seized by the government illustrated Babeuf's *desire* for some kind of insurrection. But "musings" did not add up to overt conspiracy. The evidence, it argued, revealed no actual plan for the very good reason that such a plan would have been impossible to execute. Thus, it was unlikely that even the misguided Babeuf was guilty as charged, while the culpability of most others was simply impossible. The presence of an individual's name on one of Babeuf's lists, or even actual correspondence with Babeuf, scarcely proved a man's complicity in a plot that was "imaginary" to begin with.[13]

As the actual list of indicted citizens emerged from the welter of preliminary arrests, rumors, and accusations, it seemed manifest to the Jacobins that many indictments had little to do with the central figure, Babeuf. Among the well-known individuals swept up in the net along with a group of sectionnaires were the deputy Drouet, a number of ex-conventionnels (Lindet, Ricord, Laignelolt, Amar, and Vadier), and democratic publicists Antonelle and Lepelletier. The inclusion of Drouet was striking evidence to the Jacobins of a Machiavellian design. Drouet was a veritable folk hero (the clerk who had stopped Louis XVI at Varennes), a long-suffering patriot (imprisoned by the Austrians while on mission for the Convention), and a man of vast sympathy for the common people, who upon returning to the Legislature in 1796 was scandalized by conditions in thermidorian France. The most outspoken legislative critic of the Directory, Drouet had indeed become in-

[13] *J. hommes libres, passim,* for the last *décade* of floréal. Later, in a signed article, Vatar recapitulated his view more guardedly: "Nous n'avons jamais nié l'éxistence d'un plan ou projet de conspiration; mais que nous n'avions pas cru, que nous ne croyons encore, que Babeuf n'eut jamais de moyen proportionnels aux succès de ses rêves monstrueux. . . ." On the next day he reiterated that the real plot is the "persecution dirigé contre les amis de la République." (Nos. 214 and 215, 15 and 16 prairial.) In the pamphlet he wrote to protest the temporary closing of his presses by the government, Vatar put the same point in this way: He was persecuted "pour avoir vu, sous un jour différent, les moyens de conjuration, et avoir cru à l'impossibilité de la réussite." See note 16 below. The Central Police Bureau complained on 26 floréal that Vatar "affiche l'incredulité la plus damnable dans son journal sur la conspiration." (Aulard, *Paris,* III, 186.)

volved with Darthé and other Babeuvists, but to all Jacobins it was beyond doubt that this man would never conspire. The government's problematic case against Drouet strained the limits of credulity, to say the least. But for the government this was a necessary risk, since Drouet's inclusion had a more basic purpose than the intimidation of a noisy critic. With a deputy among the accused, the trial would have to be held before a special High Court, whose procedures and verdict were not subject to appeal.[14]

To include Robert Lindet (who had helped defeat the Directory's plan to establish an "oligarchic" national bank) or Antonelle ("a man whose veritable place is in the senate, in the ranks of the courageous defenders of the people") was almost to admit that the conspiracy was a pretext for intimidating opposition.[15] But Jacobin revulsion was increased by the cynicism with which other indictments were handed down against sectionnaires and even a number of their wives. When Vatar himself was arrested on two different warrants, it became clearer still that the question was not one of conspiratorial activity.[16] In the Directory's *amalgame* the entire spectrum of democratic activism would be standing trial at Vendôme.

All of this was fair game for skepticism. The moderate, but occasionally pro-Jacobin, *Journal des Patriotes de '89* of Réal and Méhée agonized over this and gradually drifted into an open break

[14] When the record of Drouet's interrogation was published, it verified his wide-ranging opposition activity and his innocence of the actual charges. See (Haute-Cour de Justice) *Copie de l'instruction personnelle au représentant du peuple Drouet* (Impr. Nationale, frimaire an V), B.N. Lb42/233. L. Levi, "Le Retour de Drouet," *R.F.*, Vol. 69 (1916), pp. 400-26, is based primarily on this source. The Directory no doubt recognized Drouet's innocence and probably allowed him to escape once the High Court had been established on the basis of his indictment. On the arrest and police harassment of Parisian sans-culottes see R. C. Cobb, "Notes sur la répression contre le personnel sans-culotte de 1795 à 1801," pp. 23-49.

[15] See, e.g., *Journal des Hautes-Pyrénées* (Tarbes) No. 34, 9 prairial; *Resurrection du Père Duchêne* (Paris) No. 12 (n.d.).

[16] On the master list of arrest warrants in A.N. F7 4276, Vatar is listed No. 18, and again at the bottom as the imprimeur of the *Hommes libres*. The warrants were issued twice, on 26 and 30 floréal (see Debidour, *Recueil des actes*, II, 383, 424), but as in the case of Lebois the charges did not stick. Vatar's difficulties in publishing his newspaper at this time are detailed in his pamphlet "R. Vatar . . . à tous les français républicains . . . 6 prairial," reprinted in such newspapers as the *Journal des Patriotes de '89* No. 282, 7 prairial, and the *Observateur du Midi* No. 16, 16 prairial.

with the government. Even Babeuf was depicted here as a demagogic journalist rather than a conspirator, the editors' quick verdict
being that the government had simply not proven its case.[17] Before,
during, and after his own arrest Vatar's role became a newsworthy
phenomenon in itself, as reflected for example in the pages of the
Batave, a colorless and usually officious newspaper. On 25 floréal
(14 May 1796) it reported that "the *Journal des hommes libres* does
not appear to lend much credence to the conspiracy," and the following day that that newspaper "today refutes in detail the charges
of the conspiracy; it regards the plan as completely ridiculous." The
Batave grew obsessed with Vatar's persuasive polemic and on 28
floréal (17 May) itself wavered and confessed that its previous "unlimited confidence in the government" was becoming difficult to
sustain.[18] While this particular organ did regain its composure a
short time later, most Jacobins hardened their position of disbelief.

Thus did the *grande conspiration* become a clear dividing line
between Jacobins and Directorials. Open contempt for the government's case was the rule among Jacobins from the beginning.[19]
Occasionally it was expressed with provocative boldness, as in Rouen
where a group of Jacobins drew up a placard to counterattack.

> Friends & Brothers:
>
> The alleged Revolution [Babeuf conspiracy] which has recently
> manifested itself in Paris is nothing but a maneuver by the
> honnêtes gens to reach their goal of eliminating the best and
> most energetic patriots, because these patriots prevent them from
> doing as they would please. . . . Long live the Republic, one,
> individual, and immortal; down with tyrants; death to the specu-
> lators, hoarders, and egoists.[20]

But even stated more sedately skepticism served to identify a Jacobin
in his community and to cause him trouble. The record of one

[17] *Journal des Patriotes de '89* No. 276, 1 prairial IV; No. 283, 8 prairial;
No. 286, 11 prairial. Official and journalistic gossip linked Réal with Vatar
around this time (see Aulard, *Paris*, III, 202-203).

[18] *Le Batave* Nos. 1121-24, 25-28 floréal IV.

[19] Jacobin skepticism is described in correspondence from Cambrai (Nord):
A.N. F⁷ 7147a, fol. 3851 and Foix (Ariège): A.N. F⁷ 7146, fol. 3311.

[20] A.N. F⁷ 7145, fol. 3248-bis: commissioner to Rouen, enclosing a copy of
the placard, dated 3 prairial IV.

such case highlights a number of the facets of this complicated situation.

Charles Jaubert (*homme de lettres*) had returned to the Jemmappes department after working in the Paris prison bureaucracy during the Terror. A man given to wearing a red cap, a friend of Antonelle's, and a contributor to the *Orateur plébéien,* Jaubert was a conspicuous Jacobin in the town of Ath and was considered to have a potential following of some significance. The departmental commissioner, the administrative council of the department, and the local military commander all considered him a security risk and after the Babeuf plot were anxious to have him imprisoned. Jaubert finally gave them a pretext when he "permitted himself to scoff at the alleged Babeuf conspiracy, to say that the government had been misled; that the conspiracy was a fable; that patriots were being persecuted." For this he was arrested, while a search of his lodgings was carried out turning up most notably "a project for organizing popular societies throughout the republic."[21] The local authorities then dispatched him to the correctional tribunal at Mons for a preliminary hearing, whose transcript survives. When asked if he knew why he had been arrested Jaubert

> replied yes, that it was for having the newspaper entitled *Journal des hommes libres* at the town hall of Ath, in which newspaper the extent of the latest conspiracy announced in Paris was called into question. . . . That it was upon the observation of Citizen Defacqz who alleged that there existed a vast conspiracy, and who produced as proof the newspaper entitled *Le Rédacteur,* that I countered with the *Journal des hommes libres* which I produced and which contradicted Defacqz's assertions.[22]

Not surprisingly the tribunal refused to indict Jaubert on the basis of such charges, and he was freed. The authorities, however, continued to urge that the Directory include Jaubert in the measures it was taking against the conspiracy. Meanwhile they would watch him.

Viewed from the Luxembourg Palace, Jacobin skepticism was a willful attempt to undermine confidence in the government. Ac-

[21] A.N. F⁷ 7151, fols. 4588 and 4129: deptal. admin. of Jemappes, 13 prairial; deptal. commissioner, 12 and 16 prairial; Dubois (military commander), 16 messidor.

[22] A.N. BB³ 21: P.V. of interrogation, 15 prairial.

cordingly, Police Minister Cochon circularized all municipal and departmental officials to alert them against this campaign. "Blindly partisan scribblers, evil-minded persons, and even direct participants in the conspiracy, are trying to persuade you that the conspiracy is nothing but a fantasy," he warned. "Others tell you that it is going to provoke a terrible reaction against the patriots. . . . They have no other aim but to undermine the confidence that the government ought to inspire in you."[23] For once Cochon correctly estimated the Jacobin position. They had indeed lost credence in the government, or rather in the faction led by director Carnot and the controversial Police Minister himself. The long trial at Vendôme heightened this sense of alienation. But it ended by rekindling the Jacobins' commitment to their own legacy.

‡ II ‡

Unlike earlier political trials in revolutionary France, the *Procès Vendôme* was not accepted with passivity by the defendants' partisans. Dragging on for almost four months, it became a rallying point for Jacobin consciousness. In contrast to the one-sided procedures of the Terror or the thermidorian period, this was a prolonged confrontation in which defendants enjoyed the opportunity to cross-examine witnesses, justify their action, and plead their own ideals. Continued highhandedness by the government served under these circumstances to provide endless ammunition for the defendants' case. Most important, they enjoyed favorable publicity. Before the trial their desire for publicity had caused them "somber melancholy." As the concierge at the detention prison had reported, the defendants above all "seem to fear the secrecy."[24] Once the trial began, secrecy was lifted and exhaustive partisan coverage was provided in the *Journal des hommes libres* and in the extraordinary newspaper founded by a resident of Vendôme, P. N. Hesiné, for the express purpose of disseminating the defendants' point of view.[25]

[23] A.N. F⁷ 7146: Ministre de Police Générale, *Aux Administrations centrales et municipales* . . . , 7 prairial an IV. Unofficially, as pointed out earlier, Cochon did reverse himself on the second charge, by warning certain officials against carrying their anti-Jacobinism too far lest it promote uncontrollable reaction.

[24] A.N. F¹ᵃ 549: Daude to M. of Interior, 20-26 fructidor IV.

[25] The official transcripts—edited in some places to the advantage of the government—fill four volumes: *Débats du procès instruit par la Haute-Cour*

An overwhelming impression of solidarity among the defendants emerges from the trial record, and it was Babeuf who made the crucial contribution. Upon his arrest he had issued a defiant statement acknowledging even more than he was probably guilty of, and flaunting before the government the spectre of a popular insurrection to establish "égalité réele." Eventually, however, he abandoned this stand, principally for the sake of the sixty-odd defendants whose lives were also at stake. Instead of using the trial as a forum for his own particular program, he muted his defiance, masked his conspiratorial activity, and represented himself to the court as a wronged idealist, a publicist persecuted for his controversial views. He, too, denied that an actual conspiracy had been imminent and embraced the common contention that government provocateurs were the real conspirators.[26] Under these circumstances the other

---

de Justice contre Drouet, Babeuf et autres: recueillis par des sténographes (Impr. Nationale, 1797). They must be checked against two other sources. Vatar's *Journal des hommes libres* expanded its format and issued numerous supplementary pages in order to carry a running account of the testimony, the defendants' tribulations, and other news surrounding the trial. Hesiné's *Journal de la Haute-Cour de Justice, ou l'écho des hommes libres, vrais et sensibles* (Vendôme), with its behind-the-scenes revelations, intimate correspondence of the defendants, and analysis of the proceedings, is by far the most valuable source, though it has never yet been used extensively. In preparing the following brief pages I have relied on a complete reading of these sources. But since it is not my intention to cover this trial in any detail (for it deserves a separate book in itself), citations, illustrations, and references will be kept to a minimum. A word about Hesiné's *Journal*, however, is in order.

In 1866 Hatin had noted this journal in his bibliography of the press, indicating that a copy was held by M. Ponchet-Derouches. Subsequently it disappeared, and as late as 1960 specialists were unable to locate it anywhere. In fact it had disappeared from France when President Andrew White of Cornell University purchased part of that collection at an auction in 1882. It was thus transported to Cornell University, Ithaca, N.Y., where it was forgotten— so much so that my communication to the librarians there was answered initially by the devastating news that they could not locate it. (See *Catalogue of the Historical Library of Andrew Dickson White*, Part II: The French Revolution [Ithaca, 1894], pp. iii, 160, 236.) Since then a microfilm copy in the Feltrinelli Collection (Milan) and the original copy at Cornell have come to the attention of French scholars, particularly R. Bois, who first brought Hesiné to public attention in an important article written without access to most issues of the newspaper (see note 27 below). M. Bois will undoubtedly follow up his pioneering article with a fuller study, while in the interim an inexpensive facsimile edition has been published by Editions Sociales.

[26] See M. Dommanget, "Le Système de défense des babouvistes au procès de Vendôme," *AHRF*, 1967, pp. 255-58.

defendants did not have to protect themselves by turning against Babeuf. While each man justified himself individually, the defendants ended by showing the French people a popular front.

Hesiné was supremely qualified for cultivating this image. A mathematics teacher, government employee, and ardent democrat, he had not participated in Babeuvist activity before the arrests, but was a great partisan of the Tribune's objectives. At the same time he was sympathetic to more conventional democrats, and more than willing to work for them, so that he could come to Babeuf's defense without slighting the integrity of others.[27] In the pages of his *Journal de la Haute-Cour* fusion was achieved between a muted Babeuvism and an aggressive but traditional Neo-Jacobinism. Distinctions blurred before the common heritage of 1793. Communism was reduced to a speculative ideal; the talk of insurrection became the measure of an idealist's anger rather than an actual design.[28] Admittedly it was difficult for the genuine Babeuvists to abide this. In correspondence with Hesiné, Babeuf initially ridiculed such dissimulation, while Buonarroti entertained an abiding contempt for people like codefendant Vadier, and in his final address to the court was hard put not to abandon the strategy.[29] One man was adamant and simply would not go along; Darthé chose to remain defiantly silent—and for this he paid with his life. On the whole, however,

[27] See R. Bois, "P. N. Hesiné, rédacteur du 'Journal de la Haute-Cour, ou l'écho des hommes libres, vrais et sensibles,'" *AHRF*, 1960, pp. 471-87, which concentrates on his activity during the trial. My own impressions of Hesiné are supplemented by later documents, which indicate his enthusiastic, effective participation in the Neo-Jacobin resurgence of 1798. For Hesiné's broad-minded view of Antonelle see R. Bois, "A propos d'une lettre de Babeuf à Hesiné," *AHRF*, 1965, pp. 94-98. Cf. also Hesiné, *Journal de la Haute-Cour* No. 61, 2 floréal V, where he extols Lindet and Lepelletier, and *passim* for his vindication of Antonelle.

[28] Hesiné, *Journal de la Haute-Cour* Nos. 23, 25 and 26 (6, 16, and 20 pluviôse V) on the attempt to argue the utopian character of Babeuvist socialism; Nos. 63-64, 20 and 24 floréal V on Babeuf's final defense; Nos. 71-72, 5 and 6 prairial V on the "Plaidoyer de Réal," the defense attorney. Cf. the *J. hommes libres'* summary of Buonarroti's testimony, No. 169, 4 germinal V.

[29] See the revealing "Une lettre de Babeuf à Hesiné (16 decembre 1796)" published in *AHRF*, 1963, pp. 79-83. Buonarroti's attitudes are discussed and documented in A. Saitta's important *Filippo Buonarroti, contributi alla storia della sua vita et del suo pensiero* (2 vols.; Rome, 1950-51). More recently M. Dommanget has reopened this discussion with his publication of "Un inédit de Buonarroti—Réplique à la réponse de l'Accusateur National," *AHRF*, 1961, pp. 56-70.

the defendants sustained their solidarity. The government's *amalgame* did not produce the anticipated result of discrediting the mainstream of Jacobinism by linking it to Babeuf. Instead, the fervor of the Babeuvists ended by energizing a popular front position—one which might not have materialized while Babeuf was free.

Successive defendants accomplished two things in their testimony: they attacked the government's integrity, and exalted their own sentiments. The accused, their lawyers, and their partisans in the press spent a great deal of time exposing the contradictions and blatant falsities in the prosecution's presentation. The sum of distortions, false identifications, and outright lies in the government's case was enormous. Relentlessly and convincingly, the thesis was repeated that the *grande conspiration* was invented by government agents to destroy the legitimate opposition of democrats. At the end, democrats depicted the trial as "an inquisition"—a year-long persecution of "courageous defenders of the people . . . family men and workers . . . whose great crime was to have their name on a list."[30]

More important, the trial provided a forum for affirmation. To the government's charge that the democrats in the dock were a band of anarchists, plotting to overthrow the social order, the defendants offered a counterimage. While Babeuf and a few of his intimates were forced to dissimulate for the sake of a larger strategy, the others could assert their veritable principles and cultivate their memories. In a representative instance, the ex-conventionnel Laignelot closed his defense with a eulogy to the democratic revolution of 1793, and a memorial to its betrayal in the "terrible event" of Thermidor and the final devastation of Prairial.[31]

---

[30] *Père Duchêne* (Paris) No. 34 (n.d.); cf. J. N. Pache, *Sur les Factions et les partis, les conspirations et les conjurations: et sur celles à l'ordre du jour* (Impr. Vatar [floréal] an V). Mayor of Paris during the Terror, Pache was held in unusually high regard both by Jacobins and militant sectionnaires. Hence this attack on the Vendôme trial and on Carnot is especially important. Appearing shortly before the end of the trial, it is an outspoken defense of the democratic movement as personified by the collectivity of those Vendôme defendants whom Pache knew personally: Drouet, Cordas, Fiquet, Crespin, Paris, Antonelle, Lepelletier, Parein, Amar, Menessier, Bodson, Lindet, Chrétien.

[31] "Défense du Citoyen Laignelot," *Débats du procès*, IV, 328-34. For the

The verdict consummated the long process of identification. Most of the defendants were acquitted, which of course vindicated their contention of innocence. Even the state's own judges rejected all charges involving actual conspiracy. Retrospectively they seemed to be agreeing that the *grande conspiration* was fabricated, or at least so problematic as to be unprovable, despite the reams of allegedly incriminating documents that were seized.

On the other hand, this general vindication was matched by the martyrdom of nine men. The one made the other seem all the more capricious. Not only that, but for what charge were Babeuf and Darthé to be executed, and Buonarroti, Germain, and five Parisian sectionnaires to be deported? For advocacy of the 1793 constitution. For their opinions; for their writing. All of which seemed to add the charge of hypocrisy to a government that claimed to be based on law and liberty. Darthé's and Babeuf's attempt to commit suicide right in the court further dramatized the brutal character of the sentence. The *dernier supplice* of Babeuf once and for all obliterated the ambiguity about his place in the democratic movement. For most democrats he now became a martyr in the ranks of those who lost their lives in Prairial or at Grenelle. He entered the honored fraternity of sectionnaires and famous conventionnels like Goujon and Javogues. Babeuf and Darthé stabbed themselves "as the martyrs of democracy did two years ago when they were slaughtered by a military commission."[32] The "barbarous executions" capped the propaganda value that had accrued to a beleaguered democratic movement. As one democratic newspaper, which had initially disavowed the "ultra-revolutionary furies of Tribune Gracchus," now wrote: "The scaffold, exile, or the dagger—such is the lot of the benefactors of humanity, the instructors of this republic."[33]

---

general thrust of the democratic position affirmed at Vendôme see, e.g., Hesiné, *Journal de la Haute-Cour* No. 14, 6 nivôse V; No. 24, 10 pluviôse V; No. 59, 28 germinal V; Antonelle: "Sur la Prétendue conspiration" in *J. hommes libres* No. 104 (supplément), 29 nivôse V.

[32] *Ami des Principes* (Angers) No. 36, 12 prairial V. Full and dramatic accounts are presented in Hesiné, *Journal de la Haute-Cour* Nos. 72 and 73, 6 and 7 prairial V; and *J. hommes libres* Nos. 8-11, 8-11 prairial V (which sometimes relied on Hesiné).

[33] *Père Duchêne* No. 37 (n.d.)—an important source. *Journal de Toulouse* No. 128, 16 prairial V and Nos. 129 and 130 (reprinting passionate accounts

With this dramatic sequence of events Babeuvism was assimilated into the surviving democratic movement, whose center of gravity now shifted decisively into the sphere of Neo-Jacobinism. The alleged conspiracy, ensuing reaction, trial, and verdict decided several things. Genuine Babeuvism was discredited by virtue of its failure —especially in the aftermath of the Grenelle massacre, which for all its obscurity was in effect a second Prairial. True, in Babeuf's own mind the plot could have succeeded. Writing to Hesiné in frimaire Year V, he claimed that the time was ripe, but the secondary leadership timid or faulty.[34] Such assertions reveal more about Babeuf's personality than the realities of the situation, but at best it is a moot point. Secret conspiracy was now as discredited as spontaneous uprising had been after the tragedy of Prairial. Babeuf, however, could undergo an innocuous kind of rehabilitation in Jacobin eyes. While Jacobins in the future ritualistically disavowed the *communauté des biens* and "égalité réele," they did not tax Babeuf with the error of having actually plotted to bring them about.[35] The Babeuf plot remained the *prétendue conspiration*. It was a reactionary government that had committed the overt act of violence in sentencing the Tribune to death.

---

from the *J. hommes libres*); *Le Révélateur* (Paris) No. 559, 19 prairial V: "Dernier lettre de Gracchus Babeuf, assassiné par la prétendue haute-cour de justice."

[34] "Une lettre de Babeuf à Hesiné," *AHRF*, 1963, pp. 79-83. My impression is that Buonarroti was not really claiming such imminent success for the plot in his retrospective account of 1828.

[35] In Pache's book, *Sur les Factions*, disavowal of the "partage égale des terres . . . communauté des biens et toutes les autres follies qu'on a répandues sur le compte des démocrates pour les perdre" was already part of the popular front formula (p. 19). Another version—in more direct sympathy with Babeuf himself—likewise renders Babeuvism innocuous. The *Défenseur de la Vérité*, an aggressively democratic Parisian newspaper founded shortly before the Fructidor coup (see below), frequently eulogized the Vendôme defendants, as did most Jacobin journalists. They dealt with Babeuf's communism this way (No. 40, 2nd jour compl. an V):

> Que des écrivains estimables, rêvant au bonheur de l'humanité, et desirant faire partager à chaque membre du corps politique la même mesure de biens et de felicité, aient trouvé . . . que tel devait être l'état de toute aggregation primitive des citoyens—[comme] Platon. . . . Que ces publicistes se fassent illusion sur la possibilité d'appliquer leurs principes à une société toute organisée et fortement empreinte d'habitudes contraires à leur systeme, à la bonne heure; mais c'est étrangement s'abuser de croire qu'ils aient formé une secte quelconque, ennemi de la propriété, et qui ait en vue le partage des terres ou la communauté des biens.

The verdict became a bloody shirt. Invariably and often democrats referred to it as the "assassination of Vendôme." And while Babeuf's execution was their major grievance, the plight of the other defendants, and the loose ends left over from the trial also provided democrats with a reservoir of propaganda. Soon after Babeuf's fatal end, Vatar was publicizing contributions received at his office for Babeuf's widow and soliciting others. The trip from Vendôme to Cherbourg of five defendants sentenced to deportation occasioned outcries against the "crimes and wickedness" that they were made to endure. Meanwhile, two other miscarriages of justice took the spotlight. One involved two soldiers who were sentenced at Blois to twenty years' imprisonment for having expressed sympathy for the defendants. The other was the case of Hesiné himself. Embroiling him in complicated indictments based on obscure pretexts, the government was clearly trying to silence him. This it could not do, for Hesiné was irrepressible and ingenious. But he did end in prison.[36]

These matters were reopened after Fructidor, when Hesiné was released in what amounted to a one-man amnesty. He immediately took up the case of the two soldiers and simply would not let it rest. Nor were the Cherbourg prisoners forgotten. Periodically, articles appeared depicting their virtues, exposing their mistreatment, and lamenting their terrible poverty. More than one collection was taken up in their behalf.[37] At the same time, the acquitted defendants stepped up their attempt to collect compensation from the government. Several deputies headed by François Lamarque pleaded their cause and actually pushed an indemnity bill through the lower house. Its defeat in the Council of Ancients produced a

[36] *J. hommes libres* No. 14, 14 prairial V; No. 51, 21 messidor V. The statements in this and the following paragraph can be documented at length from this newspaper. On Hesiné's legal battle see the Bois article, "P. N. Hesiné."

[37] *J. hommes libres* No. 114, 24 fructidor V (on Hesiné's pardon); No. 107, 17 fructidor V; No. 141, 16 vendémiaire VI; No. 164, 9 brumaire, and Nos. 182/83, 27/28 brumaire (on the two soldiers). Occasionally such articles were signed H . . . , doubtless written by Hesiné. See also *Tribun du Peuple* [not to be confused with Babeuf's newspaper] No. 55, 26 frimaire VI, which recapitulates the case. For the Cherbourg prisoners see *J. hommes libres* No. 168, 13 brumaire VI (on Germain); No. 240, 25 nivôse VI and *Tribun du Peuple* No. 82, 26 nivôse VI (on Buonarroti). On the prisoners' mistreatment see *J. hommes libres* No. 249, 4 pluviôse VI and No. 271, 26 pluviôse; *Journal des Amis* (Metz) No. 65, 10 pluviôse VI. Collections were made by the clubs in Marseilles and the 5th arrondissement of Paris (*J. hommes libres* No. 264, 19 pluviôse and No. 303, 28 ventôse VI).

renewed wave of outrage, and further mobilized the democrats' collective self-consciousness.[38] Finally, the whole drama was replayed when the sans-culotte Mennessier, who had been found guilty *in absentia*, managed to get a new trial before the criminal tribunal of the Seine. After complicated maneuvering he was completely exonerated. Democrats followed his trial with great interest and found in this dramatic reversal further support for everything they had been saying.[39]

What we think of as the Babeuf Trial was really transformed for Jacobins into quite another thing at Vendôme. The actuality of Babeuvism receded almost to the point of vanishing, and in its place arose an image or even a myth. Reflecting the defendants' central strategy, it was the myth of a popular front. Babeuf became a democratic martyr rather than the founder of insurrectionary communism. Intending to divide "true" democrats from compromisers, Babeuf ironically contributed to the consolidation of Neo-Jacobinism. Soon his would-be militants—Trotebas in Metz, Hesiné in Vendôme, Fossard in Cherbourg, Taffoureau in St. Omer, and numerous Parisian sectionnaires—would unobtrusively resume the methods of constitutional opposition. Only a generation later would Buonarroti publicly restore to Babeuf his chosen role.

‡ III ‡

Capitalizing on the *grande conspiration*, the Directory meanwhile sought a conservative consensus. On the basis of its aggressive anti-Jacobinism, it propelled itself into a working alliance with ele-

---

[38] At least twenty defendants petitioned the Ministry of Justice between prairial and messidor year V for an indemnity. Almost all explained that they sought payment only because they were destitute; six specified that they had been forced to sell their possessions to sustain their families (A.N. BB³ 22). So convincing were these pleas that the Ministry recommended the expenditure of some funds for this cause, but it does not seem to have been implemented (A.N. AF III 42, fol. 153: rapport au Directoire, thermidor V). Lamarque's plea was made in frimaire: *Rapport . . . sur la pétition de plusieurs citoyens acquittés par la haute-cour de justice, après une longue detention* (Impr. Nationale). Coverage in *J. hommes libres* and in the *Tribun du Peuple* No. 47, 17 frimaire VI, No. 49, 19 frimaire, and No. 89, 3 pluviôse.

[39] See *Défenseur de la Vérité* No. 36, 28 fructidor V; *Le Révélateur* No. 657, 27 fructidor V; *Tribun du Peuple* No. 8, 29 fructidor V—all of which reprint a letter from Mennessier attacking the "juges-assassins de Vendôme." Coverage of the trial in *J. hommes libres* No. 193, 8 frimaire VI, No. 162, 7 brumaire VI (article by H . . .), No. 165, 10 brumaire, and No. 193, 8 frimaire VI.

ments cool to the new France in the hope of winning them over. But a durable alliance with the Right on the Directory's terms proved impossible to realize, as the elections of the Year V demonstrated. The outcome of these contests (March-April 1797) was decidedly reactionary if not royalist. All but eleven of the two hundred-odd ex-conventionnels up for reelection—most of them avowed moderates and anti-Jacobins—were defeated by virtue of their association with the revolutionary past. In the Paris electoral assembly even former Feuillants were rejected as insufficiently conservative. So greatly did these elections reinforce the Right in the Chambers that it could now assert its independence and begin to differentiate itself from the uncertain ground it had been sharing with the Directory. The day had been long in coming, and the partisans of reaction were determined to reverse the exclusion of priests and émigrés, harness the executive power, and counter the executive's aggressive conduct of foreign affairs.[40]

Now the Directory was forced to reconsider its position, which in turn created a schism within the five-man executive. Carnot and Barthélemy adopted a conservative, legalistic position which held that the electorate had spoken and that its will must be followed wherever it led. The three others, who now formed a working majority, resolved to resist the drift towards reaction regardless of its electoral sanction, and to preserve the gains of the Revolution by keeping themselves in power at all costs.[41] Understandably, the government therefore became less vehement in its harassment of Jacobins and "terrorists." With Babeuf gone, they could be counted on to support the republic against an element that seemed to be contemplating a restoration. For their part, the Jacobins appreciated the Directory's belated stand against reaction, but they remained isolated and locally vulnerable before the men who had come into office during the Year V elections. The period before the fructidor coup offered little opportunity for a Jacobin resurgence. But certain things did indicate the survival of a distinct Jacobin point of view

[40] J. Suratteau, "Les élections de l'an V aux conseils du Directoire," *AHRF*, 1958 [No. 5] pp. 21-63. The unfolding reaction is revealed through the papers of the British agent Wickham by M. W. Fryer, *Republic or Restoration?* (Manchester, 1965), and H. Mitchell, *The Underground War Against Revolutionary France* (Oxford, 1965).

[41] See M. Reinhard, *Le Grand Carnot* (Paris, 1952), ii, 189-245; A. Meynier, *Le 18 fructidor* (Paris, 1926); and Vol. ii of LaRevellière's *Mémoires*.

within the front of republicans who began rallying to defend the Revolution. The success of that effort would in turn alter the Jacobins' position.

On the most visible level—the world of high politics in Paris—two parliamentary factions crystallized after the spring elections: the Directorial "Salmistes" and the reactionary "Clichyites." Prominent reactionary deputies had begun to caucus at a house on the Rue du Clichy. In the Directory's eyes this gave the Clichyites a dangerous opportunity to organize or, as one Directorial deputy put it, to form a "permanent conspiracy against the Republic." As a counterpoise the Directory's supporters formed a club of their own, which initially met at the Hôtel du Salm. The Salmiste nucleus consisted of about fifty deputies and other republican notables, and the membership of this Constitutional Circle, as they called it, remained limited to persons "who had rendered some service to the Republic." With very few exceptions, notorious Jacobins were excluded; as one sympathetic newspaper reported, "it rejects all those whose turbulent spirit would wish to precipitate things and throw us into new revolutions." Participants like Thomas Paine were insistent on this point, stressing that the men he encountered there were "the long-standing friends of liberty. . . . I do not mean the Jacobins of recent times, but those who had formed the first clubs of free men." In the same vein Lenoir-Laroche—a friend of LaRevellière's and an editor of the *Moniteur*—declared that the Constitutional Circle of the Hôtel du Salm was composed of "names dear to liberty" from the arts, letters, philosophy, and the legislative councils. They were the "founders of liberty who have never had anything to be ashamed of in either their principles or actions; men who used to be called *moderates* . . . and who today are being stigmatized as Jacobins; men who were almost all persecuted under the reign of terror, but who cherish the republic nonetheless."[42]

Such defensiveness was prompted by the attacks of reactionary journalists and officials who were trying to smear the Salmistes as anarchists and "partisans of the Terror." One royalist newspaper unblushingly maintained that the club was "a Jacobin club, whose

[42] J. Debry, "Autobiographie," ed. L. Pignaud, *Annales révolutionnaires*, XI (1919), 386; Aulard, *Paris*, IV, 180, 188, 185; A. Mathiez, *Le Directoire* (Paris, 1934), pp. 311-13. T. Paine, *Lettre au peuple française sur la journée de 18 fructidor*, cited by Meynier, *le 18 fructidor*, p. 46; Lenoir-Laroche, "Du cercle constitutionnel et des clubs en général," *Moniteur*, 9 messidor V (pp. 1113-14).

misguided project is to renew the great work of the brothers of 1793."[43] All of this was mendacious nonsense. Moreover such polemics indicate nothing of what the Jacobins themselves thought of the Salmistes. In fact they were quite cool towards them, though they acknowledged the Salmistes' role in standing up to the Clichyites. After running excerpts from the club's principal appeal to the public (a speech by the ex-Girondin deputy Honoré Riouffe), the editors of the *Journal des hommes libres* commented on the speech with misgivings. They objected to the fact that Salmistes like Paine, Lenoir-Laroche, Benjamin Constant, and Riouffe based their positions on the claim that they spoke as victims of the Terror. They deplored Riouffe's attempt to prove his respectability by demonstrating that his own antipathy to Jacobinism was second to none, and by implication that the honnêtes gens need not embrace the dangerous Clichyites in order to defend themselves against the specter of anarchism. Moreover, the *Hommes libres* objected to the whole idea of a club like the Hôtel du Salm. While it embodied the Directory's notion of proper political leadership and activity, the principal Jacobin newspaper regarded it as an unsound enterprise with manifest oligarchic tendencies. Arguing that the Club du Salm was isolated from the people, the editors portrayed it as "a coterie with a narrow spirit" that substitutes "the petty views of a clique for the great interests of the Republic." And it advised the members to "get out into the world once in a while ... descend from the level of glittering theorizing. ... If you wish to be useful to the nation steal away from the gilded salons and banquets. Get out among the people." To Vatar and his circle, the Hôtel du Salm was far from representing a notable advance in republicanism.[44]

In the departments the situation was less clear. The Directory sanctioned the formation of clubs designed to expose the machinations of crypto-royalists, without giving head to the democrats. The Clichyites, at any rate, feared that clubs would revive in the departments under the influence of the Club du Salm; "following this

[43] Aulard, *Paris*, IV, 153, 159, 172, 177, 180, 183, 283; C. Ballot, ed., *Le Coup d'état du 18 fructidor an V: rapports de police et documents divers* (Paris, 1906), p. 6. This view is reflected in the private correspondence of one reactionary: see J. Puraye, ed., *Lettres de Gilbert Claes à son père à Fologne, 1797-99* (Desclec de Brouwer, 1957), pp. 43-44.

[44] H. Riouffe, *Discours lu au Cercle constitutionnel, 9 messidor* (Impr. Gagnard, an V); *J. hommes libres* Nos. 49-50, 19 and 20 messidor V.

example," the Central Police Bureau warned, "France will soon be one mass of associations that will finish by bringing on civil war."[45] But in the far reaches of France any effective republican club was likely to be more heterogeneous than the Club du Salm, which had Directorial deputies at its nucleus and was under the Directory's immediate scrutiny. The democratic press could therefore be more enthusiastic about the prospect of seeing clubs formed in the departments than it was about the Constitutional Circle of the Hôtel du Salm. Thus the *Hommes libres* reported buoyantly that several clubs had already been established in the Midi, and that these clubs "present a battle line on all sides."[46]

Both the spread of clubs and the consolidation of the Club du Salm in Paris were a threat to the Clichyites' legislative advance. The partisans of reaction therefore attempted to enact an organic law that went even further than Mailhe's proposal of a year before in severely curtailing the operation of clubs. Not only were they to be drastically limited in size and absolutely forbidden to undertake deliberations of any kind, but according to a proposal by the deputy Duplantier they were to be prohibited from meeting after sunset and were to convene only in rooms with open doors. These new touches brought ridicule down on their author, but in the end he achieved his objectives when, on 7 thermidor V (25 July 1797), the Legislature voted to close all clubs provisionally until a satisfactory organic law regulating clubs could be drafted. The Directory apparently acquiesced in this vote, perhaps because it was growing fearful about clubs opening over which it had no effective control. The democratic press, on the other hand, uttered a moan of despair and indignation, attacking the decree as an unconstitutional attempt "to deprive the people of the one and only *popular* means of expressing their views."[47]

The practical effect of the 7 thermidor decree is difficult to gauge. Some available data suggest that, even if symbolically crucial, it was not actually very great. Police Minister Pierre Sotin, charged with executing the new law, dispatched a circular letter to all departmental commissioners asking them to report back on any clubs

[45] Ballot, *Le Coup d'état*, p. 22 (9 messidor).
[46] *J. hommes libres* No. 60, 30 messidor.
[47] *Ibid.* No. 69, 9 thermidor V; *Ami du Peuple*, 20 thermidor; *Père Duchêne* No. 41 (n.d.); *Le Révélateur* No. 609, 9 thermidor V.

that existed in their departments, and to enforce the law accordingly. (His letter, it might be noted, scarcely veiled his opinion that the law was deplorable—an attitude that would become important after Fructidor.) Over fifty of the ninety commissioners answered promptly, and their responses constitute a useful survey of the state of political clubs before Fructidor.[48]

Twenty-eight commissioners reported that there were no clubs in their departments, while four indicated that they had no knowledge of any but that they would investigate. Twenty-one reported that there were clubs of one kind or another. In almost all cases (except those from the Midi area) these reports reveal that the existing clubs did not remotely resemble the sociétés populaires that were the nightmare of conservatives. About half were long-established, apolitical reading and recreation clubs. At Mâcon (Saône-et-Loire), typical of these, the club was supervised by the officers of the municipality and consisted "of a room in which the public met to hear the news read"; there were no deliberations and anyone could attend. The clubs at Epinal (Vosges) and Langres (Haute-Marne) were so officious that they dissolved themselves when the debate in the Legislature over clubs first began. Others followed suit immediately after the law was passed, although Sotin ruled that such reading clubs did not really come under the law's purview and could remain open.

Naturally even innocuous reading clubs could serve as screens for political activity, and it is a reasonable assumption that many Jacobins had taken temporary refuge in such clubs. The surprising thing, though, is that only two of the reporting commissioners expressed any such suspicions. The commissioner to the Aube department reported that a well-organized reading and recreation club which met in a private home was alleged to be active behind the scenes politically, especially at election time. And in Pau (Basses-Pyrénées), though it held no deliberations, the reading club was considered potentially dangerous by the authorities and was closed under the law of 7 thermidor. The point is, however, that as of thermidor Year V, whatever the potential of such clubs, the ones that existed in most towns could do little more than bide their time if they were not to run athwart of the authorities.

[48] A.N. F⁷ 7274/b, fol. 909: responses to circular letter of 13 thermidor V.

After the spring elections a few new clubs that were something more than reading societies were organized. In Perigueux, Grenoble, and Valenciennes, for example, Constitutional Circles were formed "in imitations of the Reunions that were being formed in Paris." But (excepting the Midi) only two of these new Constitutional Circles aroused the authorities, notably in Auxerre (Yonne) where a large club was formed in open opposition to the local magistrates, who in turn closed it on their own initiative several days before passage of the 7 thermidor decree in Paris.[49] In the newly formed Ourthe department the commissioner to Liege reported that three clubs of about forty members each had been organized. Two, according to him, were useful clubs which did things like reprinting Honoré Riouffe's speech; the other was composed of "anarchists." Characteristically the first two dissolved themselves forthwith upon passage of the law of 7 thermidor while the latter club expressed astonishment over the law, and apparently dragged its feet in complying.[50]

Actually the scattered cases of independent Constitutional Circles are the exceptions that underscore the rule. Despite a golden opportunity to denounce manifestations of "anarchism," the wary departmental commissioners could find little to complain about either in the older reading clubs or the new Constitutional Circles, for the Jacobins had not succeeded in gathering much momentum.

If there was a significant exception to this it was in the embattled south. The *Hommes libres* had reported the establishment of clubs in Cantal, Aveyron, Tarn, Lot, Haute-Garonne, and other southern departments. Anti-Jacobin officials also testified that Jacobins might be mobilizing in the Midi, and they hastened to frustrate any "anarchistic" activity that might occur. The departmental administrations of Aveyron, Ardèche, Tarn, and almost certainly other departments in the region, exchanged circular letters about the threat of a Jacobin resurgence. In addition the military commanders in the area (who were generally Clichyite sympathizers at this point) printed circular letters purporting that "trouble-makers are traveling through the southern departments with the intention of establishing clubs there." These officials alleged that "public order was troubled in several departments because of the meetings

---

[49] A.N. F⁷ 7271, fol. 549: report of 28 messidor V.
[50] A.N. F⁷ 7274/b, fol. 909: letter of 17 thermidor.

of certain individuals in deliberative clubs; it is to be feared that such an example will be contagious." They all stood ready to close any such club that came to their attention several days before the law of 7 thermidor was passed.[51]

In all, both before and certainly after passage of that law, the time was not propitious for any significant revival of Jacobin clubs. There was a good deal of talk on all sides about it, and some abortive activity occurred in the Midi. But both the vigilance of local reactionaries and the policies of the Clichyite deputies prevented any widespread formation of Constitutional Circles—either of a "Salmiste" or Jacobin variety. Only after the grip of the reactionaries was broken in the fructidor coup could democrats exercise their rights of free association in their preferred manner. As it stood, whatever clubs may have been formed in the spring of 1797, and whatever their composition and objectives, they were closed by decree and were likely to remain closed until the Clichyites lost power.

‡ IV ‡

At this juncture, republicans of all persuasions could find encouragement only by looking to the republican armies stationed in Italy and Germany. The generals and their men were beginning to take the initiative, making it clear that they would not sit idly by while the country drifted back into the "slavery" of a Clichyite reaction. Through his divisional newspaper, which supported the Directory, General Bonaparte was the most audible of these new voices. Petitions and proclamations pledging loyalty to the Directory flowed into Paris from the battalions, and a particularly effective propaganda technique was exploited in which the toasts drunk by officers and men at their patriotic banquets were circulated back home: toasts such as "To the reemigration of the émigrés!" or "To the unity of French republicans; may they follow the Army of Italy's example and, supported by it, regain that energy which is fitting for the leading nation on Earth!"[52] The *Père Duchêne* and

---

[51] A.N. F⁷ 7274/b, fol. 909: extrait des délibérations de l'administration centrale de l'Aveyron, 3 thermidor V; départmental commissioner (Tarn) to M. of Pol., 24 thermidor; circular letter to municipal administrations in Tarn and Ardèche, 6 thermidor V.

[52] See *La France Vue de l'Armée d'Italie* (Milan) for thermidor V; *J. hommes libres* No. 71, 11 thermidor.

the *Hommes libres* acknowledged that the republican cause seemed hopeless without these energetic defenders. "An excess of evil is often the precursor of good," wrote one of Vatar's correspondents, "but even if we are at the precipice, the armies are still there."[53]

The emergence of the armies as the vanguard of republicanism is familiar; so, too, are the Directors' efforts to enlist the support of certain generals for an impending coup against the Clichyites. What is not so commonly appreciated is that politically conscious citizens at home responded directly to the armies' exhortations. The army was obliged to shore up the republican cause, but its loyalty and determination had a perceptible effect on civilian morale.

In a petition addressed to the Army of Italy an estimated 550 citizens from Issoire (Puy-de-Dôme) declared that the Army's proclamations "have trebled our courage." Hundreds of republicans in Chambéry (Mont Blanc), Valenciennes (Nord), Rennes (Ille-et-Villaine), Dijon (Côte-d'Or), Poitiers (Vienne), and Mâcon (Saône-et-Loire) framed similar petitions proclaiming that they were inspired by the armies' activities in support of the republic, were alert to the dangers of reaction, and "know how to live freely or die."[54] A truly impressive demonstration occurred in the Haute-Vienne department, where twenty pages of signatures were gathered to accompany a printed address expressing solidarity with various army divisions and their generals. They expressed this solidarity, the signators added, even though the counterrevolutionaries might consider such "deliberations" unconstitutional.[55] Summarizing and reporting on all this a few days later, Vatar hoped that "this general explosion of patriotism would inform our brave brothers-in-arms that the nation still has in its midst numerous battalions of *enfans fidèles*."[56]

The remnants of the Jacobin press also began to show some polemical vigor in the summer of 1797, as they supported the government's efforts to halt the drift towards reaction. In thermidor

---

[53] *Père Duchêne* No. 25 (n.d.); *J. hommes libres* No. 67, 7 thermidor V; (Mathieu), *La République française réduite à zéro* No. 2 (n.d.).

[54] *J. hommes libres*, thermidor-fructidor, *passim* (especially Nos. 92, 101, 104, 105, 114, 122).

[55] A.N. AF iii 267/Haute-Vienne: *Les Citoyens du département de la Haute-Vienne soussignées, aux braves généraux, officiers et soldats composans les armées de la République française* (broadside).

[56] *J. hommes libres* No. 114, 24 fructidor V.

Year V a new democratic journal called the *Défenseur de la Vérité*
was launched by Bescher and Babeuf's former printer Lamberté.[57]
The veteran radical publicist René Lebois again took up his pen
in the *Eclaireur du peuple*, and inflammatory patriot pamphlets under
such titles as *La République française réduite à zéro* came off the
presses with increasing frequency, urging the government to strike
a decisive blow. Placards and broadsides were more likely to dent
mass apathy and by 2 fructidor (19 August 1797) the Central Bureau
reported that "partisan placards are multiplying on the walls of
Paris." Under Vatar's imprint a series of placards titled *Le Démocrate constitutionnel* blanketed sections of Paris; while rallying to the
government against the Clichyites, these placards declared that the
patriots' efforts must produce a defense of the constitution "interpreted democratically."[58]

To reactionaries the differences between Jacobins and Directorials
at this point seemed trivial in view of the common front they were
apparently forming, "rekindling revolutionary fanaticism in the
multitude." Things seemed ominous to them when these "numerous, insolent, rabble-rousing" placards were protected by the police
and not torn down as Babeuf's had been.[59] But within this republican front the democrats held special ground and were pushing
the Directory as well as supporting it. The Jacobin press recalled
the tradition of popular, direct action which was anathema to Directorials and Clichyites alike. "Men of July 14, Men of August 10,

[57] B.N. Lc2/2679. The epigram of this previously unknown newspaper reads:
"Sous les mauvais gouvernements, l'égalité n'est qu'apparente et illusoire; elle
ne sert qu'a maintenir le pauvre dans sa misère, et le riche dans son usurpation."

[58] Ballot, *Le Coup d'état,* p. 126; *Le Démocrate constitutionnel* No. 2 (n.d.).
(In folio, B.N. Lc2/2680.) J. Dautry used this newspaper in his *mis à point*:
"Les Démocrates parisiens avant et après le 18 fructidor," *AHRF* 1950, pp.
141-51.

[59] Ballot, *Le Coup d'état,* pp. 152-53 (letter of a British secret agent to Lord
Malmesbury, 17 fructidor); *Dix-huit fructidor, ses causes et ses effets* (Hambourg, 1799), I, 14. The royalist *Miroir* of 16 fructidor (Aulard, *Paris,* IV, 314)
claimed that the *Démocrate constitutionnel* was "an official" publication, while
Lord Malmesbury's informant wrote that the *Journal des hommes libres* was
"in the Directory's confidence." Vatar's relationship with the Directory was
more accurately described by Pierre Tissot, one of his contributors: "Barras
ne dirigeait pas le *Journal des hommes libres* mais il ne cessait d'y entretenir
des intelligences, au moyen desquelles il soutenait sa popularité. . . ." (P. F.
Tissot, *Histoire de la Révolution française* [Paris, 1839], IV, 92—referring to
the time of the fructidor coup.)

let us be armed and vigilant," the placards proclaimed. "French-men! Let the memory of your fundamental dignity and of your oppressor's crimes excite your noble courage . . . arm yourselves, take up your clubs, and purge France of the monsters," echoed the *Défenseur de la Vérité*. Reminding its readers of July 14 and of "the immortal insurrection of August 10," Errard's *Révélateur* urged that "the same enemies are before us."[60] Such exhortation expressed the reviving enthusiasm of a vocal minority of democrats who hoped to find new opportunities for themselves when the Clichyites were bested.

Nor was increasing fervor a monopoly of the journalists; active concern was to be found even among militant sans-culottes who had been politically dormant for more than a year. A series of reports to the Minister of Police, from an agent calling himself Antoine, reveals a good deal of agitation in that bastion of sans-culottisme, the faubourg Antoine.[61] According to this sympathetic observer, the militants [*patriots chauds*] were bristling for the kind of action that the Jacobin press was advocating, and were upset because the Directory was not calling upon them openly for support. They discussed various plans of their own, such as a maneuver in which the wounded war veterans from the Hôtel des Invalides would march en masse to the Legislature to ask for a promised bonus; "and since the [Legislature's] response would not be at all satisfactory, a commotion would ensue" (27 thermidor).

The militants even tried to win over some of the masses, Antoine reported. At one grocery store about forty of them propagandized the day-laborers who were working on the walls that ringed the city. "Each was charged with rallying as many workers as he could find to the coup that is being prepared" (6 fructidor). The patriots of the faubourg struggled to overcome the influence of conservative manufacturers who owned the large workshops situated in the faubourg. The latter apparently were making the faubourg a center of royalist agitation, with the Place des Vosges a favored

[60] *Le Révélateur* No. 647, 18 fructidor; *Défenseur de la Vérité* No. 26, 18 fructidor; *Démocrate constitutionnel* No. 6 (n.d.); *J. hommes libres* No. 107, 17 fructidor V; *Père Duchêne* No. 40 (n.d.).

[61] A.N. F7 6139 [Affaires Politiques: Bureau Particulier], dossier 17: reports dated between 23 thermidor and 8 fructidor V. Also A.N. 171 AP 1 [Barras Papers], dossier 10, on activity in the Halle au Blé section and elsewhere.

meeting place of "the chouans" who were being organized by these *gros boutiquìers.*

Royalist counteragitation only stirred the patriots into more determined action. By the 8th of fructidor (25 August 1797), according to Antoine, the militants were meeting frequently, designating leaders, and choosing men to man the exit barriers at the moment of the coup. Eighty former cannoniers from the 8th arrondissement —those stalwarts of the popular movement—were reportedly pledged to help. But the patriots despaired that the Directory was unwilling to call on them. In one of his last bulletins Antoine thought that they would abandon their projects if the government did not act.

The Directory had no intention of relying on these sans-culottes to crush the Clichyites, for this would only open a Pandora's box. According to LaRevellière's *Mémoires,* Barras and General Augereau wished to call on the faubourgs for a popular demonstration and to culminate the *journée* with the guillotining of half a dozen traitors. But even a limited and rigidly controlled insurrection was strenuously opposed by the others, with LaRevellière allegedly vowing that they would have to kill him first if they wanted to unleash the people.[62] In the end the coup was executed by the army under a carefully arranged plan and with tight discipline that left few loose ends. Still, the Directory could not prevent a show of support by interested sans-culottes and on the *journée* of 18 fructidor (4 September 1797) there was a brief flurry of armed popular activity that modestly complemented the main military thrust.

As one Parisian newspaper mentioned in passing: "the faubourgs St. Antoine and St. Marceau came in arms to offer their hands and their help. . . . That was the only popular movement that occurred; it was orderly." A British agent who observed this movement reported to London that about three hundred "Babeuvists" had marched through the faubourg Antoine with Rossignal at their head, which squared with the recollections of a royalist pamphleteer who also spoke of "three hundred bandits of the worst type armed with pikes and brandishing sabres . . . going to salute the Directory and offer it their help to finish things up."[63] These reports

[62] LaRevellière, *Mémoires,* ii, 109.

[63] *Gazette Nationale de France,* cited in Aulard, *Paris,* iv, 334; J. Godechot, "Le Directoire vu de Londres," *AHRF,* 1950, p. 5; *Dix-huit fructidor, ses causes et ses effets,* i, 33-34. Rossignol was in Barras' confidence: Barras, *Memoirs,* iii, 14.

(minus the adjectives) were not mistaken. Corroborating evidence survives, for example, in the police dossier of the sans-culotte Ducatel, where it is noted that on 18 fructidor he had come forward "bringing with him almost 600 citizens who shared his sentiments, and offered his body to the government as a rampart."[64]

The new commissioner to the Central Police Bureau of Paris was directly concerned with such activity and reported uncomfortably about it to his superior. "You are no doubt informed of the manner in which the distribution of arms was carried out the day before yesterday in the faubourg Antoine and yesterday in St. Martin: the people threw themselves onto the wagons and grabbed everything; it was really a pillage rather than a distribution. Today the trouble-makers are fanning the flames of discord...."[65]

The coup was not exclusively the concern of politicians and soldiers. In the first moments, when the outcome was perhaps uncertain, arms were broken out in the twelve municipalities. According to Baudin, in some places such as the 5th arrondissement the arms were carefully distributed by the municipal commissioners only to "well-known and brave republicans" whose names and addresses were scrupulously recorded—even if this caution resulted in some of the weapons not being utilized. "If this step had been taken in all the arrondissements," he observed, "many difficulties would have been avoided." The major "difficulty" for Baudin was the emergence of "extremely radical and truly dangerous men who dared to say right in front of me: 'the Directory and the Councils have done nothing yet, and that affairs are going to take another turn.'" These radical and dangerous citizens reportedly included "several citizens [defendants] from Vendôme" and especially former General Fion who headed an armed group in St. Martin. Of General Fion, Baudin candidly admitted he "would prefer to see him at the front."[66]

Needless to say, the Directory was not about to permit the people to arm and mobilize effectively. Besides, the activists were now few in number—militants without masses of followers—and the arms were shortly put away. But the fructidor coup did give a new impetus to other kinds of political action in Paris and the departments. The brief stirring of armed cadres of Parisian sans-culottes

[64] A.N. F⁷ 6152, dossier 875: report by Bureau Central, 27 brumaire VII.
[65] A.N. F⁷ 6139, dossier 75 (Objets diverses particulières au Ministre): Baudin to Sotin, 20 fructidor V.
[66] *Ibid.*

was only the most dramatic manifestation of the undercurrent of expectation that greeted these important events.[67] In its issue of 18 fructidor the *Révélateur* posed the issue for democrats in this way:

> If this Republic . . . is not everyone's Republic, but a Republic of dominators, of the insolent rich, of egoists, of hoarders, of speculators, of intriguers, of thieves—then, republican warriors, it still remains for you to reconquer liberty and to establish equality. . . . Should not all people profit from it equally? The feeble as well as the strong, the poor more than the rich?[68]

In summary, the months before Fructidor had not produced a resurgence of Jacobinism, but events suggested that such a development was not out of the question. Clubs had scarcely begun to revive when the decree of 7 thermidor provisionally closed them all; and the evidence suggests that even without this decree the resurrection of clubs was proceeding slowly and haltingly. On the other hand, republicans at the grass roots were not indifferent to the maneuvering that was going on in the capital. A resonance developed between the battalions of the armies abroad and the activists at home. The Jacobin press bestirred itself and emphasized that the approaching confrontation would not only save the republic from the royalists but that it could well reopen unresolved social and political questions.

THE OBVIOUS fact that the *journée* of 18 fructidor may have meant different things to different people is easy to overlook. Mathiez, Lefebvre, Dautry, and others who have dealt with the Directory period take a dim view of the fructidor coup because it was executed by a clique of politicians and generals. Implicitly they compare its narrow purpose and self-serving qualities with the élan of the great

---

[67] The literature of local history illustrates this. See, e.g., A. Bernard, "Le 18 fructidor à Marseille et dans les Bouches-du-Rhône," *R.F.*, XLI (1901), 193-215; E. Delcambre, *Le Coup d'Etat jacobin du 18 fructidor an V et ses répercussions dans la Haute-Loire* (Rodez, 1942)—not necessarily the best local studies but the most explicit on this point. The expectations and immediate reactions of provincial Jacobins to news from Paris were particularly strong in Metz (Moselle) and Auxerre (Yonne). See my article "The Revival of Jacobinism in Metz During the Directory," *Journal of Modern History* (March 1966), pp. 20-21; and the correspondence of several Auxerre Jacobins with a friend in Paris: Gautherot Papers, B.N. Mss (nouv. acq. fran.) No. 21700.

[68] *Le Révélateur* No. 647, 18 fructidor V.

revolutionary *journées*.[69] In retrospect this is a defensible perspective. But at the time, the coup stood as the Directory's most decisive achievement and signaled a perceptible shift in the balance of political forces. This in turn reopened a range of possibilities for politically conscious Frenchmen.

At the very least—and in a surprisingly effective yet bloodless way—the coup d'état overturned the disloyal majority of reactionaries and royalists that had come to power in the elections of 1797. The Legislature was immediately purged of two hundred Clichyite deputies thus producing a working majority firmly committed (so it seemed) to the maintenance of the republic. The strident, Jacobin-baiting, royalist press was muzzled by the suppression of 42 newspapers. Finally, the dismissal of local reactionaries who had been elected to departmental and municipal councils was extended to 53 departments. Their replacement was intended to produce a more efficient administration, to end the harassment of patriots, and to facilitate execution of the laws against priests and émigrés that were revived on 19 fructidor.[70]

These measures constituted a minimal republican consensus and were acclaimed in hundreds of congratulatory letters and petitions addressed to the Directory and the Legislature.[71] Predictably most of these communications were officious and rife with platitudes; indeed, to believe their language the Directors had become virtual republican saints. But nothing like this outpouring of sentiment occurred at any other point in the Directory's history. No matter how stereotyped it was it should not be discounted. It showed at least that the Directory was not hopelessly discredited and unpopular, and that firm action had won it a certain amount of good will.

Democrats shared this minimal consensus and demonstrated that they were not alienated from the republic as it then existed. But neither did they passively defer to the Directory's leadership. A re-

[69] E.g., Mathiez, *Le Directoire*, pp. 333-35: "Le 18 fructidor laissa donc indifférente la foule des démocrates. . . . La République n'était plus la chose de la Nation. Elle n'était que la chose des dirigeants." Lefebvre writes in the same spirit but does concede, without developing the point, that Fructidor "revived revolutionary ardor." (*Le Directoire*, pp. 91-93.)

[70] The best account is in Meynier, *Le 18 fructidor*. Cf. V. Pierre, *Le 18 fructidor* (Paris, 1893), an anti-revolutionary work which emphasizes the coup's harsh effectiveness.

[71] A.N. AF III 211-267 [Affaires départementales: Addresses au Directoire], *passim*.

invigorated Jacobin press balanced an enthusiastic show of support for the government with a concern over the limiting effects of the Directory's instinctive conservatism. The journalists, like the sectionnaires who so disturbed commissioner Baudin, insisted that the coup must "take another turn."

For the editors of the *Journal des hommes libres* there was a lesson to be drawn from the *journée manquée* of 13 vendémiaire Year IV. That episode had turned into a "lost victory" because it had no repercussions beyond the defeat of the armed royalist rebels. "It is easy to see," the editors declared, "that if the most active measures do not follow the *journée* of 18 fructidor . . . the moderation which characterized it will precisely favor the royalist." The broadsides that Vatar was still publishing lamented in the same vein that there was "not a breath, not a stirring of democracy" thus far in the purged Legislature.[72]

Under the suggestive rubric, "A partial revolution is a public calamity," Errard's *Révélateur* developed its earlier contention that the *journée* of 18 fructidor might open the way towards "reconquering liberty and establishing equality . . . for the feeble and the poor even more than the rich." Two adversaries to this cause existed, according to Errard, and both were now preaching moderation. The first were of course the crypto-royalists; equally dangerous were the "speculators and other public thieves who wish to conserve their ill-gotten gains and commit new acts of corruption." That they opposed a Bourbon restoration themselves was insignificant, for they feared the people more than anything else. "These various factions," he warned, "are agreed on snuffing out enthusiasm among the patriots." To the *Défenseur de la Vérité* the fructidor coup was the signal for a profound regeneration of public spirit: "Let energy and enthusiasm replace vile egoism and the cold calculations of cupidity in every heart." Calling the people to action, the editors exhorted specifically: "Let the good days of the Republic revive. . . . Let the popular clubs open everywhere at once."[73]

The same point of view was forcefully advanced by a newspaper founded immediately after Fructidor that resurrected the title of Babeuf's old organ, the *Tribun du Peuple*. In its first issue—pro-

[72] *J. hommes libres* Nos. 112 and 116, 22 and 26 fructidor V; *Démocrate constitutionnel* No. 10 (n.d.).

[73] *Le Révélateur* No. 656, 26 fructidor V; *Défenseur de la Vérité* No. 28, 20 fructidor.

claiming that "this journal is edited under democratic principles"—
it presented "an exact outline of the democratic movement." This
precis of revolutionary history culminated in an apologia for the
journées of prairial Year III and a bitter condemnation of the
government's massacre of sans-culottes on the Plain of Grenelle
shortly after Babeuf's arrest. The democratic movement had been
smashed as a result of the repression following those events, but
clearly the editors hoped that the *journée* of 18 fructidor might mark
its resuscitation. Like Bescher in the *Défenseur de la Vérité* and the
other democratic journalists, the editors identified "egoism" as the
adversary of democracy. On its masthead epigraph the *Tribun du
Peuple* threw out this challenge to France: "Vous n'avez point
de moeurs! Le luxe, l'égoisme et la corruption vous dévorent. Est-
ce ainsi que vous affermissez la République?"[74]

Parisian democratic journalists thus developed a particular angle
of vision and vocabulary; they shared the implicit values and the
special language characteristic of social movements. Invoking "democracy" as a watchword, they excoriated the "egoists" and
nouveaux riches. Avowing their opposition to "moderation," they
celebrated the "enthusiasm" of active citizenship.

But what constituency was there to respond to this message? One
looks to the Legislature in vain for a group of deputies openly seconding these sentiments. The few democratically oriented deputies
were isolated and cautious in temperament. Without a distinctive
program or organization, they were usually indistinguishable from
the majority of Directorial republicans. The journalists' independence rarely was echoed in the legislative debates, and the parliamentary history of this period therefore does not support a contention that the democratic movement was coming to life again
after Fructidor. Unfortunately, perceptions of political life are usually drawn from parliamentary history.

At the grass roots, however, a considerable number of citizens
echoed the journalists' evocative arguments. Of a mind with the
Défenseur de la Vérité they now organized political clubs to advance
their position, and in these Neo-Jacobin clubs or Constitutional
Circles the democratic movement in France survived.

[74] *Le Tribun du Peuple et l'ami des défenseurs de la patrie* [des associés
Prévost et Donnier] No. 1, 22 fructidor V *et seq.* Scattered numbers of this
extraordinary and previously unknown newspaper are in B.N. (Lc2/2678).

PART TWO

RESURGENCE

CHAPTER IV

The New Clubs: Social Consciousness
and Composition

IN THE wake of Fructidor, freedom of association was dramatically restored. The purged Legislature revoked the Clichyites' law of 7 thermidor that had temporarily banned all clubs, and on the very next day the Constitutional Circle of the Hôtel du Salm reconvened amidst public fanfare. Obviously, Neo-Jacobins did not have a monopoly on clubs, as the loftily conservative addresses of Benjamin Constant before the Hôtel du Salm demonstrated. Likewise the Directory's agents in the provinces who felt surrounded by an apathetic or hostile populace deemed Constitutional Circles useful. The administration of the Vienne department expressed a common view when it praised the club at Poitiers for its usefulness "in the days right after the fructidor coup. It rendered service to a department where there was no effective force to contain malevolence." But tactical advantages did not obscure for these officials the tendency of such clubs to produce "excesses." As the commissioner to Seine-et-Oise declared, "their exaltation must be limited if it is not to become misguided."[1]

The trouble for the Directory was that its advocates simply could not control the course of events in their communities. Once it restored the right of free assembly, the Directory lost the initiative to men who did not regard clubs merely as useful expedients for the propagation of official republican pronouncements. The members of the Constitutional Circles that began to form in most of France's ninety departments often fostered rather than feared "exaltation." They had no inclination to listen to the oratory of men like Benjamin Constant, to support official candidacies in elections, or to accept the Directory's imprecations against "anarchism." Though they did not originate as opposition groups, most of the clubs eventually clashed with the Directory. By the time the elections of 1798 were held—seven months after the fructidor coup—over 35

[1] Aulard, *Paris*, IV, 344, 348; R. Doucet, *L'Esprit public dans le département de la Vienne* (Paris, 1910), p. 322; E. Tambour, *Etudes sur la Révolution dans le département de Seine et Oise* (Paris, 1913), p. 54.

of these clubs had been ordered closed in separate actions, while others were investigated, threatened, and harassed into dissolution.

Through the new clubs a politically conscious minority, unbeholden to the Directory, attempted to revitalize public life locally. In different ways and to different degrees most of the Constitutional Circles echoed and amplified the sentiments expressed in the democratic press after Fructidor. Their aims took them considerably beyond the Directory's studied purpose of returning the republic to normalcy. Instead, many of the new clubs in 1798 attempted to infuse into the framework established by the Directorial constitution the spirit of equality and the practice of civisme.

This chapter will discuss the composition of these clubs, the social consciousness that they fostered, and controversies that developed over their membership and leadership. The following chapter will survey the clubs' educational, civic, and political activities. In both these chapters the local or (to use an Americanism) grass-roots character of the clubs will be emphasized, and case studies will be introduced to explore in detail some of the arguments. Chapter VI, on the other hand, will consider cohesive or common elements that tended to bind these local efforts into a national movement.

‡ I ‡

Even in the most radical phase of the Revolution, Jacobinism was not the movement of what French historians call the "popular masses." When masses of the people did participate directly in the Revolution they had their characteristic means of expression and distinctive concerns. Their great impact on the course of events came through unstructured pressure and rioting, particularly in response to economic privations and overt or imagined threats of counterrevolution and betrayal. In addition, and perhaps more important, the popular masses existed in the Year II as a residual clientele for the militants (mainly artisans and shopkeepers) who staffed the revolutionary committees, attended the clubs, and in Paris dominated the section meetings. It was these few thousand militants—as Albert Soboul has shown in impressive detail—who actually constituted the Parisian popular "movement."[2]

[2] See the chapter entitled "Masses populaires et militants sans-culottes" in A. Soboul, *Les Sans-culottes Parisiens en l'an II* (Paris, 1958), pp. 433-55.

What happened to them is a subject for speculation, and something will be said about this later. But with the thermidorian reaction and the repression of the Parisian hunger riots of the Year III, the popular masses disappeared almost completely from the active political scene, reverting to more traditional and isolated forms of social protest. The absence of severe economic crisis after 1797 in a sense sealed this fate, and though some conservatives may still have feared it, open mass agitation was unlikely to recur. Consequently, what survived of an even vaguely organized or self-conscious democratic movement no longer had to take cognizance of such potential mass pressure. Nor was it remotely probable that the surviving democrats would, under any circumstances, make much of an impact on the knowing apathy of the masses. In turning to the Neo-Jacobinism of 1798, then, one anticipates that the "popular masses" would be unmoved by the efforts of the democrats. But this does not exhaust the only significant alternative. It does not necessarily imply, as we have tended to assume, that the new clubs were "limited to the bourgeoisie."[3]

Actually the new clubs drew their members from a sprawling and ill-defined expanse of urban and semi-urban French society. Membership lists that might reveal in statistical detail the social composition of the Constitutional Circles are fragmentary because their records almost never survived. Three extant lists indicate that artisans and shopkeepers formed the largest identifiable group, but this material is too inconclusive to support any statistical argument.[4]

---

[3] Obliged to discuss this question in 1951, Professor Godechot came to the understandable but premature conclusion that "during the entire period of the Directory the clubs remained institutions limited to the bourgeoisie." (*Les Institutions de la France sous la Révolution et l'Empire* [Paris, 1951], p. 425.)

[4] From three lists the following breakdown emerges:

	A	B	C
Officials	7	—	5
Professionals	5	12	6
Merchants and Manufacturers	4	5	12
Cultivators	2	—	11
Artisans and Shopkeepers	11	25	19
Soldiers and Veterans	2	3	6
Miscellaneous	2	4	9

A. Carcassonne (Aude), A.N. F7 7404, fol. 4114: petition to the Directory, signed by 80 of which 33 add their occupations. B. Lunéville (Meurthe): *Profession de foi politique des républicains de la commune de Lunéville, soussignés réunis en Cercle Constitutionnel*, placard in F7 7399, fol. 3663. C. Limoux (Aude): F7 7417, fol. 5390 (see discussion below).

Jean Beyssi has attempted to reconstruct from lists of electors and officeholders the likely composition of the Jacobin "party" in Toulouse—the one major city where the Jacobins remained in power almost throughout the Directory. His valuable analysis shows in detail that the officeholding or leadership group came primarily from the professional and merchant group of the middle class, while two hundred-odd "militants" came from the ranks of artisans, shopkeepers, and clerks.[5] Despite the absence of similar studies and of direct evidence that could yield statistical data, there is still a large amount of material available from which a good deal can be seen or inferred.

Almost every surviving document—whether hostile, friendly, or disinterested, whether coming from the clubs or written about them—affirms that they were socially heterogeneous. Under a constitution that was designed to revive the *régime censitaire* of 1791, the clubs that were founded (with a few exceptions like the Hôtel du Salm) differed from the original clubs of 1789-91 that were top-heavy with the classic elements of the bourgeoisie.

The leaders, the permanently politicized members of the new clubs, were the same Jacobins of the Year II that Crane Brinton has portrayed: "middling" citizens, often with solid standing in the community, and economically secure. But with the break in political life afforded by the fructidor coup these men attempted to reach beyond their immediate peers and to fraternize with citizens from other social groups. By way of introduction the case of Bordeaux illustrates this social context of Neo-Jacobin activity in the Year VI.

Before Fructidor, Bordeaux Jacobins found refuge in a club called "The Literary Circle of the Grande-Quille." In inquiring whether or not this club came under the law provisionally closing political clubs in thermidor Year V, the commissioner to the municipality recorded several details about its composition. He explained that it had as many as two thousand members and that it rented a vast apartment whose rent was paid by annual dues "that were more or

---

[5] Jean Beyssi, "Le parti Jacobin à Toulouse sous le Directoire," *AHRF*, 1950, pp. 28-54 and 109-33. Arguing that Neo-Jacobinism was essentially middle class, Beyssi stresses that in its stronghold of Toulouse there were no attempts to revive the programs of 1793, particularly the directed economy, and that the bourgeoisie "imposed reserve" on the sans-culottes (see, e.g., p. 47).

less high." It contained a reading room where silence was obliga-
tory, as well as billiard and card rooms, and was open at all
times of the day. In short, it was an exclusively middle-class social
club, and as such did not come under the law.[6]

Immediately after Fructidor the Jacobins transformed it into a
political club. Preempting the title (whether legitimately or not),
about two hundred members petitioned the Directory to congratu-
late it for the coup and, in typically vague Jacobin rhetoric, to urge
the government to "develop social institutions, reestablish morale,
and revive public spirit." They asked for and were granted by the
municipal authorities permission to occupy a technical college
(formerly part of a monastery) for meetings of this reconstituted
club. A similar club, the Circle of the Niveau, was established in
another part of the city.[7]

Where the club stood in relation to the Directory is suggested in
a dispassionate report by the commissioner to the Central Police
Bureau of Bordeaux. The trouble with the Circle of the Grande-
Quille, he observed, was that it "developed too great an elan when it
was trying to second the salutary efforts of the Executive Directory."[8] In plain language this meant that the club operated inde-
pendently of the Directory. One Bordeaux newspaper supported
the clubs: the *Courrier de la Gironde*, edited by a defrocked priest
and former "terrorist" named Latapy. Against the dominant conservative public opinion expounded in the city's other newspapers,
Latapy defended the political rights of the "workers and laboring
citizens," and campaigned in the spring for electors who were
"ardent friends of liberty, equality, and democracy"—an appeal that
was used as evidence to support the charge of local conservatives
that Latapy was an "anarchist."[9] The point is that Latapy's stance

[6] A.N. F⁷ 7274/b, fol. 909: to M. of Pol., 15 thermidor V.

[7] A.N. AF iii 232/Gironde: Adresse des républicains composant le Cercle
Littéraire de la Grande-Quille . . . ; Ville de Bordeaux: *Inventaire sommaire
des Archives Municipales: période révolutionnaire* (4 vols.; Bordeaux, 1929),
iv, 516, on the Grande-Quille's application; Archives Municipales de Bordeaux,
i/79: petition headed "Au Bureau Central de Bordeaux" from the Cercle du
Niveau.

[8] A.N. F⁷ 3677/10 (Gironde): Rapport sur les cercles du canton de Bordeaux,
pluviôse an VII.

[9] *Courrier de la Gironde* (Bordeaux) Nos. 182 and 185, 2 and 5 germinal
VI. Latapy was violently denounced by the departmental commissioner for his
activities in behalf of the clubs: A.N. AF iii 232/Gironde [Elections]: letters

reflected the presence of these "workers and laboring citizens" in the clubs, and the dependence of middle-class Jacobins on them for support. According to the Commissioner's report, the Grande-Quille was composed in the main of "men without much education who have no treasure other than their moral and political virtue." They were to be compared, he noted, with the "wealthy and educated men" (and former federalists) who frequented a club of their own, the Société de l'Académie. For the commissioner both groups had their place and each could serve the republic in its own way. But he reiterated that the members of the Grande-Quille and of the Niveau clubs were mostly "from the working class."[10]

Simply to dismiss the Constitutional Circles as "bourgeois" is therefore inadequate and misleading, for their existence precisely served to create a framework that went beyond the Directory's middle-class republicanism. This was true in small towns as well—for example in Limoux, a town in the Aude department with a population of between four and five thousand. A Constitutional Circle was founded there by 68 citizens whose composite portrait exemplifies the Jacobin social milieu.[11]

5 officials (1 commissioner, 1 judge, 3 justices of the peace)
6 soldiers or veterans
6 professionals (3 teachers, 2 lawyers, 1 surgeon)
12 fabricants
11 farmers [agriculteurs]
6 shopkeepers
13 artisans (3 bakers, 2 tanners, 1 each: launderer, gunsmith, cooper, carpenter, gardener, shoemaker, weaver, metalsmith)
9 miscellaneous (2 greffiers, 4 clerks, 1 rentier)

Under the leadership of Brousset, the commissioner to the municipality, "a large proprietor" and holder of national lands, the club

to M. of Pol., 5, 9, and 21 germinal VI, and to Minister of Interior, 25 germinal. For a brief note on Latapy's career, see E. Labadie, *La Presse Bordelaise pendant la Révolution* (Bordeaux, 1910), pp. 211ff.

[10] A.N. F7 3677/10: Rapport sur les cercles. . . . In this report the Niveau Club is described as "du même genre" as the Grande-Quille, though its members are slightly more "turbulent."

[11] A.N. F7 7417, fol. 5390: Renseignemens confidentiels donnés au commissaire provisoire près l'administration central del'Aude, floréal VI.

appealed to the town's sans-culottes with some success, and its meetings reportedly attracted as many as three hundred citizens. To accommodate the throng the club rented a meeting hall in a local hospital and covered its expenses with dues "from which the poor were exempt." The club's activities eventually gave rise to the charge that it "gave false hopes" to these poorer members. At the very least it initiated a drive to incorporate them into the national guard. In addition Brousset, certainly in accord with the club, was charged with granting exemptions to over one hundred draftees primarily "from the working class," while seeing to it that the remaining twenty *requisitionnaires* in the canton—who belonged "to families that were well off"—were inducted.[12]

To conservatives the Grande-Quille of Bordeaux and the Constitutional Circle of small-town Limoux presented a common social specter. They were disturbed that educated, respectable, and even prosperous citizens should be courting and flattering "workingmen"; that middle-class demagogues or *meneurs* (as they were stigmatized) were giving "false hopes" to uneducated, discontented, and credulous sans-culottes. No matter how clearly they professed loyalty to the new constitution, these clubs appeared dangerous and disruptive by virtue of this suspicious social amalgam.

If the word "intelligentsia" had been handy, it probably would have been invoked as yet another epithet. Especially in the larger towns where democrats advanced their views through the press, these spokesmen must have seemed a distasteful kind of visionary intelligentsia. Though this concept cannot be borrowed from nineteenth-century Russian history with any rigor, there are crucial similarities. Like the Russian intelligentsia the Neo-Jacobin *meneurs* were of diverse social origins, ranging from displaced aristocrats like P. A. Antonelle and G. Chaumont-Quitry to autodidact plebeians like the tailor and music teacher J. B. Trotebas of Metz. In between were a variety of writers, publishers, teachers, and an occasional government employee, physician, or lawyer.[13] Their com-

---

[12] A.N. AF III 216/Aude: several reports, especially Copie d'une lettre au M. de Pol., 15 germinal VI. Cf. a letter from the Constitutional Circle of Quesnoy complaining that "des jeunes gens riches trouvent moyen de faire plier la loi, qui veut que tout requisitionnaire rejoigne; ils se substituent des remplacans." (*J. hommes libres* No. 181, 26 brumaire VI.)

[13] The following, among others, could be characterized as constituting a Neo-Jacobin intelligentsia: Chantreau in Auch, Parent l'aîné in Nevers, De-

mon bond lay in the realm of values and consciousness, where a tension existed between ideals and reality. Here, though, the similarity ends, for the Russian intelligentsia were alienated "intellectuals of the opposition" who had a distinctive "sense of apartness."[14] Directorial France, in contrast, offered opportunity unavailable in Tsarist Russia to bridge that gap—or at least what some might consider the illusion of opportunity. Neo-Jacobins could and did organize clubs, circulate petitions, denounce officials, campaign for candidates in local elections, and in general insist that their country live up to the best within its own heritage. One ought not insist too strongly on this concept, however. Even if it rings true for democratic elements in Paris and certain larger towns, it is not particularly relevant to the smaller towns where the local *meneurs* were not likely to have stood out as social types but still appeared to conservatives as abrasive and troublesome.

The tenor of complaints and warnings received by the Directory was typified by a letter from the commissioner to the tribunals at Beaucaire (Gard) denouncing the local club for its "incendiary motions." Twenty "intriguers" have made three or four hundred proselytes, he claimed, including "many sans-culottes without property" who are being armed and integrated into the national guard. The commissioners to the Puy-de-Dôme and Gard departments filed similar, and on the whole fair-minded, reports acknowledging that the members of the clubs at Clermont and Nîmes were patriotic and loyal to the constitution. But both were worried because the members were mostly "ouvriers et cultivateurs faciles à égarer" and "ouvriers peu éclairés."[15] From the Côte-d'Or department the

---

lattre in Metz (journalists and professors at the école centrale); Latapy in Bordeaux, Peyre-Ferry in Marseilles, Touquet in Evreux, Bazin in Le Mans, Ballois in Perigueux (provincial editors); Hesiné in Vendôme (mathematics teacher, journalist, sometime government employee); Faulcon in Grenoble (bookseller and publisher); LePelletier in Versailles (wealthy pamphleteer). In Paris there were men like Publicola Chaussard, Caignard, Leclerc des Vosges, Marc-Antoine Jullien, Tissot, Xavier Audouin (sometime government employees and journalists); the *instituteur* Valentin Huay, the physician Victor Bach, the jurist Gaultier-Biauzat, journalists like Bescher, Gabriel, Valcour, and publishers like Vatar.

[14] See Martin Malia, "What is the Intelligentsia?" in *The Russian Intelligentsia*, ed. R. Pipes (New York, 1961), pp. 1-18.

[15] A.N. AF iii 228/Gard: letter of 15 germinal (Beaucaire); A.N. F⁷ 7405, fol. 4176 (Clermont); F⁷ 7391, fol. 2787 (Nîmes). Cf. Head Judge of the

Directory was warned that the club at Beaune was composed "for the most part of the useful and industrious class," and of a few "incorrigible anarchists" who mislead them, while a signed denunciation of the club at Arnay in the same department maintained that the three leaders of the club were former terrorists (now a doctor, a local commissioner, and a tax collector), and that "the great majority of the Circle is composed of shoemakers, cobblers, weavers, bricklayers, and other workers under their dependence." Similar language was used by the conservative deputies of the Moselle department; their most serious charge against the Jacobin club leaders and editors in Metz was that they "deceive and mislead unsuspecting workingmen who wrongfully give themselves over to the hope that they are given of a better lot."[16] For all their bias these officials and deputies accurately estimated the social thrust of Neo-Jacobinism.

This orchestration of complaints and denunciations of course had local variations. Charging that "incendiary motions" were made in his town's Constitutional Circle, a notary in Mèze (Hérault) reported also that "several of the members made a collection of six livres each which went toward supplying the poor with grain and money"—further proof, it seemed to him, of an attempt to seduce and stir up the working classes. Reports on the clubs at Amboise (Indre-et-Loire), Valence (Drôme), and Joinville (Haute-Marne) maintained (in the last case approvingly) that the leaders agitated "the less fortunate citizens" over their tax burdens and preached to the "feeble men" who composed the bulk of the membership that they pay the kinds of taxes they do because they have allowed the

---

Criminal Court of Dinan (Sambre-et-Meuse), to M. of Pol., 13 nivôse: "ces sociétés sont . . . composés pour la plupart, dans les petites villes surtout, des simples artisans à qui on ne peut accorder des principes; il n'est point étonnant qu'il n'y regne que des passions." (F⁷ 7369, fol. 846.) Or, departmental commissioner (Lys) to M. of Pol., 12 nivôse on the club at Bruges (F⁷ 7369, fol. 885).

[16] A.N. F⁷ 7432, fol. 7007: municipal commissioner (Beaune) to M. of Pol., 19 germinal; F⁷ 7415, fol. 5235 (Arnay); A.N. AF III 515, plaq. 3281: four deputies from Moselle to Directory, 11 germinal. Naturally, ex-revolutionary personnel—"men who made themselves despicable in the Year II"—were singled out for attack. See e.g., A.N. AF III 258/Saône-et-Loire: Des Vrais Républicains d'Autun au Directoire, floréal (with two pages of signatures); AF III 523, plaq. 3377: municipal commissioner to Villefranche (Aveyron), to M. of Pol. and Interior; F⁷ 7414, fol. 5079: public prosecutor of Vannes (Morbihan).

rich to monopolize local offices. The plausibility of such charges is borne out in the town of Dôle (Jura) where the Constitutional Circle addressed a pamphlet to its "brothers" in the department "who cultivate the land and work in the ateliers." The club openly declared that the tax burden was excessive because of its "unfair distribution" and because of the "infidelity" of the officials who apportion it. According to the members of the club, this was one of the major obstacles to be vanquished "in order to accomplish our revolution and to affirm the reign of equality."[17]

The clubs of the Year VI directed their appeal both to the dwindling revolutionary elements of the bourgeoisie and to politically conscious sans-culottes. The more energetic and successful clubs would scarcely have flourished but for the participation of citizens from the ranks of what was called the "workingmen" (*ouvriers*). As then used, this term was not equivalent to the wage-earning proletariat but rather was an extremely vague designation that could signify master craftsman, small shopkeeper, or journeyman, as well as day-laborer. The sociétaires and their critics undoubtedly stretched this rubric excessively, using it more to connote a subjective quality than to describe a specific relationship to production or the ownership of capital. A "workingman" in revolutionary parlance could also own an atelier or shop and could employ journeymen and apprentices himself. But since he worked with his hands alongside his employees, both could be considered and could call themselves *ouvriers*.[18] When in the documents the term is used in conjunction with the word *pauvre* we might suspect, however, that we are not dealing exclusively with the workingman who is owner-employer, but also with some of the wage earners themselves, as well as the citizen who may once have had a workshop but who has now fallen on hard times.

[17] A.N. F⁷ 7390, fol. 2714: Tableau des événements facheux qui se sont passés à Meze . . . par Bosc, notaire public; A.N. F⁷ 7437, fol. 7519: signed denunciation from Amboise, to M. of Pol., floréal VI; F⁷ 7423, fol. 6060: Renault, cultivateur, to Directory 30 germinal; F⁷ 7428, fol. 6550: ten citizens of Joinville to Directory (the ten were not members of the club but defended it for its stand in this matter); *Les Républicains membres du Cercle Constitutionnel de Dôle, à leurs frères les habitans des autres communes du Jura* (A Besançon, Impr. de Briot, an VI), pp. 1 and 4 (in A.N. F⁷ 7417, fol. 5361).

[18] See Albert Soboul's important articles: "Problèmes de travail en l'an II," *AHRF*, 1956, pp. 236-54, and "Classes et luttes de classes sous la Révolution française," *La Pensée*, No. 53 (1954).

In any case the bulk of the members and the most characteristic types seem to have been a conglomerate of intellectuals, white-collar employees, and "workingmen" or artisans of all varieties with fairly low status and poor education. In Cherbourg (Manche) they included—as the random notations on a sequestered membership list indicate—a vitrier, captain, douanier, facteur, tailleur, laidier, orfèvre, garde magasin, epicier, gendarme, and two marchands. These, in turn, might have represented themselves as the members of the club at Blois (Loir-et-Cher) did in a petition to the Directory: "We are all workingmen, good fathers, from the same canton."[19]

The use of the term "workingman" in this fashion suggests that the clubs were distinguished not so much by their social composition as by their social consciousness. In generalizing about the composition of the new clubs we can scarcely go beyond saying that they did not represent any one group; they were neither distinctively "popular" or "bourgeois," as the sectional clubs in Paris and the Paris Jacobin Club were respectively in the Year II. But the atmosphere, the rhetoric, and the actions of the clubs reflect a common social consciousness cultivated by the citizens who united in them. The sociétaires' view of themselves, as well as the misgivings that their activity created among the Directory's conservative supporters and officials, tells us much about the clubs' significance in Directorial France.

To bridge the gap between social classes in some form or manner seems to have been one of the Neo-Jacobins' enduring aspirations. Clubs achieving some success in this on occasion congratulated themselves. The Constitutional Circle of Auxerre, chef-lieu of the Yonne, was organized by members of the old société populaire who were eminently petit-bourgeois. Fragments of a correspondence they maintained with one of their friends who had migrated to Paris (where he was an art student and a Jacobin) have survived and offer a rare glimpse into the private thoughts of these meneurs.

[19] A.N. F⁷ 7408, fol. 4503: sequestered MS membership list (Cherbourg) on which only a few occupations are listed alongside the 85 names; A.N. F⁷ 7390, fol. 2706: Les membres réunis en cercle constitutionnel au Directoire (Blois) 20 ventôse VI. (A member of this club who corresponded with Jacobins in the Police Ministry explained that he could not afford the postage involved, being "poor like almost all republicans." A.N. F⁷ 3681/13: Dubreuil to Tissot, 13 nivôse.)

Labrune, a minor functionary in Auxerre, wrote to Gautherot as follows:

> The Constitutional Circle is coming along. We are all reunited. This refreshing air is necessary to me since for so long I lived under a regime that promoted despair—not hope. For the friends of the common good . . . this is the way to be revived. We all live in the principles of our former fraternity; it is even more intimate now because of the difficulties in which we have seen each other involved.[20]

But the fresh air, the revival, the "principles of our former fraternity" were not the exclusive affair of a small clique. In a petition to the Legislature the club boasted of the fraternity and mutual respect enjoyed by persons from various social groups: "the administrators, the farmers, the majority of workingmen are burning with patriotism. On the *décadi* seven to eight hundred patriots habitually assemble in the constitutional circle." And the reason that this petition is signed only by about one hundred members, it stated, was because "the majority of the patriotic peasants and artisans do not know how to write."[21]

In the environment of the small town it is not surprising to encounter extreme cases of social solidarity in the local club. The town of Cadours (Haute-Garonne) seems to have been singularly fertile soil for the Jacobin ideal, according to this communication in the local Jacobin newspaper from a member of that club. We do not have long-winded speeches to tire the members, punned the writer (who could well have been thinking of Benjamin Constant), but we do have "indefatigable laborers, precious workers. . . . In the club the man who lives by his work and the proprietor who lives off his rent—*often augmented by his own labor*—mingle, united by

---

[20] B.N. Mss (nouv. acq. fran.), Gautherot Papers: Labrune to Gautherot, 14 frimaire VI. See also Chardon to Gautherot, 25 fructidor V, reporting that the Constitutional Circle of Auxerre is being revived immediately. Gautherot, secretary to the Montagnard Maure, was under surveillance throughout the Directory period (A.N. F^7 6208, dossier 3314).

[21] A.N. C 431 [Conseil des Cinq Cents: pièces annexes], fol. 167: Adresse au Conseil des 500, 11 ventôse VI. A description of this club appears in the *Observateur de l'Yonne* (Sens) No. 60, 15 pluviôse VI.

the pleasant bonds of fraternity and civisme. Both the one and the other enjoy an *honnête aisance*."[22]

The achievement of such egalitarian harmony was rare, however. In the Year VI the establishment of a club more commonly forced an awareness of the imperfect condition of local society, and of the Revolution's mixed legacy of fraternity and animosity. Most of the clubs did not see themselves as the end product or fulfillment of a social transformation, but as vehicles for promoting a certain point of view that might contribute to such a transformation. If the aim was a wistful and undoubtedly visionary harmony, the business at hand included the identification or definition of enemies.

Insofar as the perception of social conflict was articulated by the Neo-Jacobins it did not involve capital *vs.* labor, or (as Babeuf would have it) the poor *vs.* the rich. The polar terms, the ideal types were words like "democrat" and "egoist," heavy with moral connotations. Immensely vague polarities, they were rarely drawn with enough precision to be very convincing in retrospect, but to contemporaries they stated the case at hand plainly enough.

An elemental social consciousness was implicit, for example, in this item in a provincial Jacobin newspaper: "A constitutional circle was formed at LaFlèche (Sarthe); it is composed not of the rich and the aristocrats, as we had been led to believe [like the Academy Club in Bordeaux], but of artisans, veterans, and citizens strongly attached to the Republic." More explicit was an editorial in the *Journal des Amis* of Metz, one of the most vigorous and polemical Jacobin newspapers. Summing up many of its previous articles, and expressing the sentiment of the town's clubs for which it acted as spokesman, the *Journal* observed that there were two parties in Metz: "the party of the people and the party of aristocrats." And for the Jacobins the aristocratic party was "the party of the grandees, the nobles, the priests, and the rich egoists who detest the people."[23]

These "egoists" were not people of wealth, education, or status

---

[22] *Journal de Toulouse* No. 87, 24 ventôse VI: "Aux rédacteurs, Cadours." On *honnête aisance* as a sans-culotte norm, see R. C. Cobb, "The Revolutionary Mentality in France 1793-94," *History*, XLII (1957), 187.

[23] *Ami des Principes* (Angers) No. 16, 2 pluviôse VI. *Journal des Amis* (Metz) No. 87, 24 ventôse VI. This was one of the most vigorous and articulate provincial democratic newspapers. For a detailed discussion see my article, "The Revival of Jacobinism in Metz During the Directory," *Journal of Modern History*, XXXVIII (1966), 21-33.

per se, but those fortunate citizens who in addition bore "aristocratic" attitudes towards their fellow citizens, and concomitantly a callousness towards the well-being of those citizens. (At their worst they might indeed have "detested" the pretensions of the common people.) The formation of clubs sometimes served to bring out this latent antagonism between democrats and "egoists." Thus, a correspondent from St. Affrique (Aveyron) wrote that his club was being harassed, and he laid the blame on certain citizens who had once been Jacobins, but who had since "gained honors and wealth" and have now dissociated themselves from political clubs and instead are arousing the authorities against them. More bitterly a correspondent for the Constitutional Circle of Montauban (Lot) complained that "the egoism of the wealthy has reached such a high point that it is unbelievable. . . . The Mercantile interests are maneuvering imperiously: instead of facilitating the establishment of the Constitutional Circle, they have done everything possible to place obstacles in its path." In Montauban, he continued, public spirit was a virtual monopoly of the *patriotes pauvres*: "only the poor know how to commiserate with the woes of humanity and with misfortune." The members of the Versailles (Seine-et-Oise) Club implied the same thing when they claimed in one of their pamphlets that "an honorable poverty is the lot of most of us."[24]

In the prickly atmosphere created by the Directory's persistent surveillance, hostility to the "egoists" could be most openly expressed in terms related to patriotism. A favored contention of the democrats was that the "egoists" or "honnêtes gens" made poor citizens, and conversely that the average "workingman" was the exemplar of civic virtue. This implied what the *Révélateur* had stated on 18 fructidor: that the Revolution—if it were not to be a mockery—"must benefit the weak as well as the strong, the poor even more than the rich" (or at least as much). The alleged callousness and selfishness of the rich "egoists" accordingly served as a foil against which some of the clubs nurtured their social consciousness.

---

[24] *J. hommes libres* No. 284, 9 ventôse VI (St. Affrique); *Journal des campagnes et des armées* (Paris) No. 701, 3 ventôse VI (Montauban); *Discours lu le 20 nivôse an VI au cercle constitutionnel établi à Versailles* (Impr. Jacob) in A.N. F⁷ 7415, fol. 5227.

An apposite occasion for displaying this amalgam of patriotism and social consciousness was afforded by an appeal from the government to all official agencies, religious cults, literary clubs, and political clubs to contribute to a fund being raised by the government to help finance an invasion of England—the *summa* of patriotic aspirations.[25] Jacobins generally advocated relatively progressive forms of financing and were usually prepared to call for forced loans in emergencies. But it would be to misunderstand their mentality completely if it were assumed that they were not equally prepared for self-sacrifice in patriotic causes. They responded to the Legislature's appeals for contributions to the invasion funds, and for a variety of reasons.

Naturally there were ulterior motives for making public displays of patriotism along prescribed lines, notably to reassure a suspicious government that the clubs were both useful and loyal. Such tactics are apparent in the case of a contribution from the Constitutional Circle of the faubourg Antoine, for example. An agent of the Police Ministry named Bacon who was assigned to observe the club had suggested that the club respond with alacrity to the appeal. Such a gesture, he wrote secretly to the Minister, would defend the honor of the faubourg, and in addition "would produce a great effect, and would bring millions into the treasury"—presumably meaning that the artisans of the faubourg would be setting a dramatic example for the whole country.[26] Bacon, though, could not have prevailed on the members to do something against their own inclinations, and it is reasonable to assume that the members who contributed were manifesting authentic patriotic feelings in laying down their sous. At any rate, the act of contributing was accompanied by an opportunity to express their sentiments in a petition, and this they did not fail to do. "That which others take from their superfluity,

[25] *Moniteur*, 17 nivôse VI (p. 430).

[26] A.N. F⁷ 7319, fol. 5656: Copie de l'adresse des membres du cercle constitutionnel séant au faubourg Antoine (12 nivôse), and covering letter. Also among the first to respond to the Legislature's appeal were the *chasseurs* Barbier and Meunier who were languishing in prison because of their support for Drouet. Their *don patriotique* (made "despite the persecution" they were suffering) was accompanied by a plea that the Legislature intervene in their case. (*Moniteur*, 24 nivôse V, p. 459.)

we take from our necessities," they wrote.[27] This self-conscious sentiment is the key to the significance of these contributions.

The call for contributions gave rise to several episodes even more
newsworthy than the response of the faubourg Antoine. In the
Marseilles Club an incident so notable occurred that the local
Jacobin newspaper verified it and published it twice: "the deed of a
worker who sold the blanket on his bed in order to donate its price."
This was soon matched by a second spectacular act of self-sacrifice
in the same club: the donation by a destitute citizen of one day's
relief rations. Such incidents were picked up and recounted in
other newspapers with approving sentimentality, and the moral
was obvious: the most humble citizens were the most ardent
patriots.[28]

In this spirit the clubs sent communications to friendly newspapers
describing their collections, and thereby fixed their own self-image
in the press. The money raised by the Constitutional Circle of Pau
(Basses-Pyrénées), the *Journal des hommes libres* related, "came
out of the subsistence of the wounded war veteran, the worker, the
father ruined by the revolution who nonetheless make the most painful sacrifices to the Republic."[29] At Versailles the members of the club
explained that the contributors to their collection did *not* include
those "energetic" citizens who had become enriched by the Revolution, and who perhaps scoff at the small amount raised by the club.
But the *sociétaires* were consoled since even "if the republicans do
not enrich the altar of the fatherland with their offerings, at least
they embellish it by the sentiments that accompany them." The collection made in the Dijon Constitutional Circle was represented as
"the homage of a club composed almost entirely of artisans on

[27] The Legislature was impressed, and this was the only petition from a
Constitutional Circle in the Year VI that was given the honors of the session
and printed at its expense: A.N. ADxvi[71] Seine/an VI: *Corps législatif,
C 500: Les soussignés, membres de la Réunion républicaine, séante au faubourg Antoine, au Corps Législatif* (Impr. Nationale, nivôse an VI).

[28] *L'Antiroyaliste ou le républicain du Midi* (Marseilles) Nos. 15 and 16,
20 and 26 nivôse VI. Reprinted in the following newspapers: *J. hommes libres*
No. 251, 6 pluviôse; *L'Indépendant* (Paris) No. 127, 7 pluviôse; *Républicain
du Nord* (Brussels) No. 808, 10 pluviôse; *Journal de Toulouse* No. 61, 2 pluviôse; *Journal des Amis* (Metz) No. 65, 10 pluviôse.

[29] *J. hommes libres* No. 256, 11 pluviôse VI; *L'Indépendant* No. 132, 12
pluviôse; *Ami des Principes* (Angers) No. 23, 16 pluviôse. Cf. *Journal des
Hautes-Pyrénées* (Tarbes) No. 14/15, 16 germinal VI.

whom the misfortune of circumstance presses heavily." Further, the club predicted that "this offering will seem slight to our *parvenus,* who . . . know only how to sacrifice for their own pleasure, and to laugh from their gilded mansions at the efforts of patriotism. . . ."[30]

These and other letters offer an insistent polarity in which the nexus of artisans' and workers' virtue is exalted while the wealthy "egoists" are attacked as both selfish and unpatriotic.[31] Good democrats could make demands on others, but they also gloried in their own sacrifices, which were the greater for their relative lack of wealth. The laying down of a few sous by an artisan or worker who could ill afford them served to underscore the social consciousness of the club members. If they contributed, while the egocentric, unpatriotic rich allegedly failed to, then their determination to fight against the social and political pretensions of those "egoists" would presumably be stronger. The simple, even banal, act of raising a *don patriotique* could accordingly heighten social consciousness by affording a safe opportunity to attack the "egoists."

In sum, the members of these clubs were citizens to whom equality and fraternity were congenial ideals; their clubs stood as symbolic challenges in the community to those whose political conservatism entailed a distasteful class consciousness. In the clubs these citizens were trying to assert or symbolize their commitment to equality as an ideal value, and to demand from the community the recognition of this value. The clubs—to use a phrase that appears on occasion—were considered by their members "temples of equality." The Jacobins cultivated a sentimentalized democratic vision of the veritable goal of a revolution: "in which the nation will be composed only of simple citizens, in which everyone will achieve well-being

---

[30] *Ami des Principes* No. 10, 20 nivôse; *L'Echo des Alpes* (Chambéry) No. 56, 27 nivôse. *Journal de la Côte-d'Or* (Dijon) No. 31, 5 ventôse.

[31] E.g., in Bordeaux, where the wealthy citizens reportedly evaded their responsibility and "did not part with a fraction of their superfluity," while the poor contributed in number to the club's collection (*J. hommes libres* No. 298, 23 ventôse); or Toulouse, where the club members, "mostly workers of this commune," made contributions but expect that "the royalists will sneer at the sight of this generous sacrifice by the poor and the artisan." (*Journal de Toulouse* No. 116, 22 floréal VI.) The *Moniteur* reported on collections submitted by other Constitutional Circles, but not on the statements accompanying them. (E.g., the clubs at Perigueux, Laon, Tarbes, Rochefort, Verneuil, Beaune, Auxerre, Moulins.)

through work, in which misery will no longer afflict the soul."[32]
If this vision was completely unrealized in society at large, it could
at least be celebrated and possibly even approximated at the clubs
for brief moments. There may have been an element of self-
delusion in the process; some citizens might simply be receiving a
clear conscience, and others, "false hopes." Sociologically, after all,
the clubs were but one of many reference groups for the individual
members, far more vulnerable and temporary than the occupational and social groups to which the members unalterably belonged. For most of the members politics was not an all-consum-
ing preoccupation. But by the same token the clubs' importance
lies precisely in this sociological quality of being collectivities that
cut across groups and categories to integrate citizens on the basis
of ostensibly shared values.[33]

‡ II ‡

As symbols of an unfulfilled egalitarian sentiment, and as forums
for the articulation of such sentiment, many of the clubs quickly
won themselves a variety of enemies among local conservatives.
The critics (frequently including the constituted authorities) were
particularly uneasy over the way a few "factious meneurs" (generally former revolutionary personnel or terrorists) were able to win
popularity among certain sans-culottes whose passivity in the previous two years had evidently been grudging. But it was difficult
for anti-Jacobins to attack the clubs immediately since the government officially sanctioned the clubs after Fructidor as useful
rallying points for republicans of all persuasions. Having sundered
its alliance with the ultra-conservatives, the Directory was temporarily anxious to placate its other flank and had to concede the Jac-

---

[32] *J. hommes libres* No. 61, 1 thermidor V.

[33] The categories of reference group theory include voluntary associations
that do not follow other patterns of differentiation (social, religious, economic),
but create a new pattern of association or interaction. The clubs, accordingly,
were groupings of people who achieved a sense of solidarity by virtue of
sharing common values, and who acquired a sense of obligation to fulfill role-
expectations. But reference group theory cannot indicate the relative importance of such a group to the particular members, since "multiple groups
or statuses, with their possibly divergent or even contradictory norms and
standards, are taken as a frame of reference by the individual." See R. K.
Merton, *Social Theory and Social Structure* (Glencoe, Ill., 1957 and 1962).

39986

obins' permanent demand for the right to free association. A city like Rouen where the town fathers persistently blocked the establishment of a Constitutional Circle as "disguised Jacobinism," was therefore an exception.[34] Elsewhere, rather than working to bar the clubs altogether, conservatives scrutinized them closely; denounced them for real or imagined abuses and violations of the law; or attempted in some way to control or neutralize them.

The restrictive clauses of the constitution offered ample pretext for scrutinizing the clubs, and the interpretation of Article 362 became a crucial matter for their survival. A cardinal point in the thermidorian attack on the original clubs, and in persisting conservative opinion, was that the clubs had been tyrannically "exclusivist" in arbitrarily selecting their membership and claiming a monopoly on patriotism.[35] In a moment of rich irony, the director Reubell had actually argued in the Convention that the clubs were thereby an affront to the equality of all citizens. The framers of the new constitution did not follow this reasoning to the extent of categorically prohibiting clubs from screening their members. Shrinking from such a dogmatic position, they left the wording ambiguous. Referring to clubs as "private societies which concern themselves with political questions," the constitution at the same time stipulated that clubs could not establish prerequisites for membership "or arrogate to themselves rights of exclusion." Altogether this would appear to mean that clubs could select their members as long as they did not exclude *categories* of citizens. Yet one could also plausibly argue from the wording that the clubs simply had to accept anyone who came along and asked to join.

Resolution of the inevitably conflicting interpretations in this matter ultimately lay with the Executive Directory, but in practice it was the Directory's Police Minister who was required to rule on

---

[34] *J. hommes libres* Nos. 261 and 301, 16 pluviôse and 26 ventôse VI, on Rouen. Jacobins also reported on their inability to establish a club in Angers (Maine-et-Loire) and L'Orient (Morbihan). (*Ami des Principes* [Angers] No. 17, 4 pluviôse and No. 36, 12 ventôse; and *J. hommes libres* No. 262, 17 pluviôse.) For an official government statement sanctioning clubs see *Lettre du Ministre de la Police générale aux administrations centrales et municipales de la République* (Impr. Nationale, 17 pluviôse an VI), B.N. Lb42/1773.

[35] For this reason the Neo-Jacobins continued to be called "exclusifs" as well as "exagérés" and "anarchists" by their opponents. See e.g., the conservative *Journal du département de Seine-et-Oise* (Versailles), 10 germinal VI.

101

such disputes. In addition, local authorities (such as departmental administrations, municipal administrations, or justices of the peace) might initially interpret the laws, as might the Directory's commissioners, subject to review in Paris by the Police Minister. Such imperfectly ordered layers of authority gave many individuals the opportunity to challenge and harass the clubs.

The Police Minister in the first five months after Fructidor was Pierre Sotin who was eager to assure the clubs' relatively unimpeded revival—a policy that eventually lost the favor of the Directory and led to his dismissal.[36] Earlier Sotin had reluctantly carried out the law of 7 thermidor Year V provisionally closing all clubs. After Fructidor, with the law now on his side, he received the numerous denunciations of allegedly illegal activities by the new clubs with marked coolness; the complaints of the sociétaires that they were being harassed and persecuted, on the other hand, he treated sympathetically. In general he tried almost always to interpret Article 362 liberally, thus preventing the clubs from being thwarted piecemeal by the interference of local officials who would have tied the clubs' hands completely.

The following letter, written by Sotin to two men in the town of Langres (Haute-Marne) about a month after Fructidor, indicates the kind of harassment the clubs were up against, and Sotin's intervention in their behalf:

You inform me, citizens, that a municipal clerk has gone from door to door to persuade persons who are known to be unpatriotic to present themselves in your Constitutional Circle—arguing that its sessions are supposed to be public.

You ask me if such a claim is legitimate; if everyone, even the enemy of the public interest, has the right to attend a constitutional circle without anyone being permitted to bar him? Here is my answer to your questions. The clubs authorized by Article 362 of the constitution are designated there under the name of *sociétés particulières*. From that name alone it follows that there is no necessity for the sessions to be public. . . . Article 362 certainly does not oblige them to hold public sessions. . . . Thus, I believe that your constitutional circle, not wishing to be a public

[36] For a discussion of Sotin's ministry see below, Ch. VIII.

assembly, and remaining a private club, has the right to close its doors to those who do not belong to it.[37]

The more such complaints Sotin received the more resolute he became in extending the protection of his office to the clubs. When the Constitutional Circle at Nice (Alpes-Maritimes) protested that local officials were using Article 362 to claim that the club did not have the right to screen its members or to collect dues, Sotin replied that the clubs "have the right to choose their members as they please," and that they could certainly collect money to pay their expenses. (Dues, incidentally, were almost always voluntary or according to ability to pay.) Moreover, he went on to praise the Nice Club and to assure it of his protection "against the attacks of its enemies." Eventually the club used this letter to defend itself against these enemies by publishing it in a friendly newspaper.[38]

By nivôse (December), having received many complaints and queries about the organization and activities of the clubs, Sotin had formulated his views on a wide range of disputed points. He ruled that admission to club meetings could be limited to members, and on the crucial matter of screening new members had this to say:

> There is nothing unconstitutional about screening committees [*commissions de reception*] as long as they do not concern themselves with the status [*état*], occupation, wealth, or birth of the individuals who apply, or require from them a certificate, a declaration or an oath; as long as they limit themselves to giving their recommendation for the admission or rejection of the candidates on the basis of the information they have on the candidate's *moralité et civisme*.[39]

In effect this was granting the Jacobins exactly what they wanted. It allowed them to judge prospective members according to the individual's moral and civic demeanor—his probity and patriotism.

---

[37] A.N. F⁷ 7298, fol. 3001: draft letter of 23 vendémiaire VI. Sotin followed this up with a letter to the departmental authorities requesting that the individual accused of harassing the club be investigated.

[38] A.N. F⁷ 7365, fol. 543: 16 frimaire VI; later reprinted in *Antiroyaliste* (Marseilles), 6 ventôse VI.

[39] A.D.S.: VD*, dossier 180 (pièce 2148): Sotin to the Municipal Administration of the 1st Arrond. (Paris), 8 nivôse VI. A similar letter was sent to the justice of the peace at Avallon (Yonne) on 12 nivôse (A.N. F⁷ 7364, fol. 424).

This remained the official view until Sotin was dismissed, and it constituted the declaration of rights for the Constitutional Circles. Sotin's view accordingly rankled conservatives; the central administration of the Seine-et-Marne carped to Sotin that the club at Melun "organized itself in an exclusive manner, basing its position on an alleged letter from you." But despite such grumbling, Sotin's ruling had its desired effect. As a report on the Cherbourg Club (which had been denounced for violating Article 362) observed, "this infraction was general in all the constitutional circles."[40]

There was no uniformity in the way the founders of the clubs selected new members—the procedures ranged from the informal to the intricate. The *règlement* (bylaws) of the Vendôme Club (Loir-et-Cher) echoed Sotin's ruling by stating simply that "candidates will have their moralité et civisme discussed." Sotin's language is also reflected in a declaration by the important Club of the Rue du Bacq in Paris: "We accept [members] indiscriminately from among all the citizens of our arrondissement—whatever may have been the nuances of their political opinions during the various periods of the Revolution—as long as we are assured of their probity, their morality, and their attachment to the Republic." The club insisted on freedom to choose its members, but went on to affirm the necessity of exercising this freedom responsibly, and of avoiding the factiousness and exclusivism of a bygone era. The editors of the *Journal des Amis* similarly advised abandoning a past exclusivism and "political intolerance," and appealed to their fellow Jacobins to welcome those "virtuous artisans" who had once been beguiled by the royalists. At the outset the clubs by and large were anxious to avoid opening old wounds, but were equally unwilling to risk being swamped by hostile persons.[41]

The screening procedures of some clubs were designed to avoid public discussions of prospective members which might cause needless ill-will. The Constitutional Circle of Versailles (Seine-et-Oise)

[40] A.N. F^7 7353, fol. 9486: letter from Seine-et-Marne dated 4 ventôse—by which time Sotin had been dismissed; F^7 7408, fol. 4503: report by the public prosecutor at Cherbourg, 9 floréal VI.

[41] A.N. F^7 7366, fol. 551: MS règlement of Vendôme Club, forwarded to M. of Pol. on 28 frimaire VI. F^7 7402/b, fol. 3960: Les républicains soussignés, membres du cercle constitutionnel du 10e arrondissement, séant rue du Bacq [Paris], 6 ventôse. *Journal des Amis* (Metz) No. 87, 24 ventôse and No. 65, 10 pluviôse VI.

required that a candidate be nominated by six members, that there be a ten-day waiting period, and that a vote would then be taken without discussion. The Chateauroux (Indre) Club had a similar procedure: nomination by ten members, a ten-day wait, and then a secret ballot. At Cherbourg (Manche) secret ballots were also used, and the club in the 7th arrondissement of Paris required only two members to nominate a new candidate. The Toulouse Club probably had the most elaborate rules: daily lists of nominees were posted for ten days, and a committee existed to receive information "against the probity and republicanism of the candidates." If no derogatory information was received, the committee would then present the candidate without further delay. If there was derogatory information the committee would make no report at all, though it would present the candidate after twenty days if he still desired to try his luck. All of these clubs tried to avoid some of the abrasiveness that open discussion of an individual's character could produce, but they still insisted on the right to screen members.[42]

Needless to say the moralité et civisme of a number of prominent citizens was found wanting by one club or another, and such occurrences invariably revived the charge of "exclusivism" against the clubs. The Cherbourg Club—to take a striking example—accepted the horloger Fossard, one of the defendants at the Vendôme trial of the Babeuvists, and designated a second Vendôme defendant named Rayebois as an "honorary member." But it rejected the local justice of the peace Ingoult because, according to his partisans, he did not share the club's "anarchic furies." When this incident provoked an investigation of the club, the members admitted that they screened candidates carefully, and one member even boasted that he had once proposed the admission of Ingoult "par dérision."[43]

In Poitiers (Vienne) the rejection of Faye, who held the prestigious post of *commissaire des guerres*, was a cause célebre, but the club stood fast and used the *Journal des hommes libres* to attack

---

[42] A.N. F⁷ 7351, fol. 9345: MS règlement of Versailles Club; F⁷ 7362, fol. 238: MS règlement of Chateauroux Club; F⁷ 7408, fol. 4503: report on Cherbourg Club; *Règlement de Police Intérieur adopté par la Réunion du 7ème arrondissement* [Paris] (Impr. Institut des Aveugles-travailleurs, an VI) in B.N. Lb40/2364. *Réunion d'hommes libres, établie en Cercle à Toulouse conformément à la loi* [Toulouse, an VI] in A.N. F⁷ 7362, fol. 270.
[43] A.N. F⁷ 7408, fol. 4503: reports and MS membership list.

Faye as a "polygame et nouveau riche" who fully deserved the scorn of his fellow citizens. Public controversies over the screening and exclusion of individuals also flared in Louhans (Saône-et-Loire), Villefranche (Ayeyron), and Vesoul (Haute-Saône). In the latter a hostile informant claimed that many "good republicans" turned out to join the club but that "several factious people repulsed them, declaring themselves a purifying core; they drew up bylaws, opened a register, and admitted only citizens who they could manipulate." From Douai (Nord) one of Vatar's correspondents promised a similar use of the right to review the membership of a club, when he wrote that the "mass of true republicans" in the club would purge it of undesirable elements "by the means provided in its bylaws."[44]

As this last case suggests, some of the clubs were initially organized on a broad base and experienced a brief period of harmony. Only after a while did differences emerge among the members and factions form—factions that underscored the heterogeneous social composition of the clubs. In still other towns antagonistic groups went their own way from the beginning and formed separate clubs which coexisted uneasily. Both kinds of cases (the establishment of rival clubs and the conflicts for control within single clubs) reflected the conservatives' resistance to Neo-Jacobinism, at a time when free association was officially sanctioned by the government.

The departmental capitals of Lyon, Orléans, Pau, Caen, and Evreux were the most important cities in which two rival clubs were founded. Fragmentary reports on France's second city suggest that Lyon's two Constitutional Circles differed from each other considerably. One was top-heavy with most of the city's important officials. The Club of the Rue Dominique, on the other hand, was a Neo-Jacobin club composed largely of "artisans and workingmen," and only a very few public officials. During the elections the independence of this club became intolerable to the Directory's supporters and they had it closed.[45]

[44] *J. hommes libres* No. 212, 17 frimaire VI; reprinted in *Tribun du Peuple* (Paris) No. 48, 18 frimaire. A.N. AF III 508, plaq. 3212: Bondot, pharmacien à Vesoul, to Directory, 13 ventôse VI; and A.N. F⁷ 7414, fol. 5058: municipal commissioner (Vesoul) to Directory, 23 floréal VI. AF III 258/Saône-et-Loire: municipal commissioner (Louhans), 3 germinal. AF III 523, plaq. 3317: Copie de la lettre du Croissac, commissaire à Villefranche. *J. hommes libres* No. 290, 15 ventôse VI (Douai).

[45] A.N. F⁷ 7341, fol. 8263: report dated frimaire VI. Cf. General Rey to the

In Orléans (Loiret) and Pau (Basses-Pyrénées) rivalry between two clubs was overt and acrimonious. A special investigator sent by the Police Ministry to Orléans reported that "the mercantile spirit and the egoism of the merchants" constituted a scourge against patriotism, and that public spirit had been virtually destroyed by the influence of "the opulent party and the religious zealots." Two rival clubs had been formed which reacted quite differently to this situation. As in Lyon, one was established under the auspices of the town's constituted authorities and represented a commitment to the status quo. According to the *Journal des hommes libres* (which surely received its information from the other club), its membership included several crypto-royalists and a good number of reactionaries and "honnêtes gens"—a synonym for "egoists" in the Jacobin lexicon. Conservatives maintained that the second club was dominated by men in "general little educated . . . and ultra-revolutionary," and they kept up a surveillance on this club that amounted to harassment. The club responded in kind and was persistently badgering the authorities.[46]

A similar but even more rancorous conflict developed in Pau. After Fructidor a Constitutional Circle was organized by "several educated and principled men" with the blessings of the moderate departmental administration. Apparently uncongenial for the local Jacobins, it was soon challenged by a second club that was founded "in the quarters of Citizen Garra at the Theater. . . . Its nucleus consists of several men who were the scourge of their fellow citizens during a certain period of the Revolution," as well as "a certain number of good patriots who were brought in by them." Garra must have been popular because his club reportedly attracted a great number of "workers and artisans from the commune"— "feeble and credulous" men who were easily "misled" by Garra and the other meneurs. Capitalizing on its success, Garra's club tried to infiltrate the other club and proposed to merge the two, but

---

deputy Vitet, 9 frimaire (from Lyon): "J'oubliais de vous dire que deux cercles sont formés, le 1er par les soins des authorités séant à St. Pierre, le deuxième au ci d. Dominicans." R. Harmand, "Poullain-Grand-prey et ses correspondants: lettres inédites," *Annales révolutionnaires*, XIII (1921), 130.

[46] A.N. F⁷ 6150 [Affaires politiques], dossier 742: Beadeduit to Tissot (the bureau chief), 18 pluviôse VI (from Orléans); *J. hommes libres* No. 232, 17 nivôse VI and *L'Indépendant* (Paris) No. 131, 11 pluviôse; A.N. F⁷ 7364, fol. 374: municipal commissioner (Orléans) to M. of Pol., 6 nivôse.

at the last moment these overtures were rejected, and on its own initiative the municipal administration closed Garra's club. A similar sequence of events took place in Evreux, chef-lieu of the Eure department.[47]

Towns in which groups or factions struggled within a single club saw the same division as towns where there were rivalries between two clubs: a conservative and quasi-official group against a more popular, ex-revolutionary group. Schism of this kind occurred in the clubs of at least three departmental capitals: Poitiers (Vienne), Auch (Gers), and Marseilles (Bouches-du-Rhône).

At the outset the Poitiers Club exemplified and implemented the republican consensus of Fructidor. Following the Directory's lead it pressed for the implementation of the law of 19 fructidor, which was designed to bring the effects of the fructidor coup to the departments by proscribing priests and émigrés once again, and by purging royalists from local offices. All elements of the club agreed that the vigorous execution of such existing laws would strengthen the republic.[48] But a significant element or faction within the Constitutional Circle gradually pushed beyond this consensus and attempted to create a more egalitarian atmosphere in which the sans-culottes were again thrust into center stage. The Directorial moderates resisted this drift and eventually a fatal schism occurred. In a report by the municipal administration the crux of this conflict is revealed, and it suggests once again how misleading it is to dismiss Neo-Jacobinism as a "bourgeois" movement.

Having received reports that the sessions of Poitier's large club were becoming disorderly, the municipal administration dispatched an observer to its meeting of 24 pluviôse (12 February 1798). He reported in detail that there was sharp debate concerning a former terrorist named Bernarais and his role in the club. Some of the mem-

---

[47] A.N. F[7] 7413, fol. 5012: especially departmental administration (Basses-Pyrénées) to M. of Pol., 28 ventôse VI. The *Journal des Hautes-Pyrénées* (Tarbes) No. 14/15, 16 germinal VI, referred to the "pauvres ouvriers faisant partie du cercle." Evreux will be treated in a separate case study below. The merging of two clubs in Caen (in the chouanized Calvados department) was applauded in the *Journal des campagnes et des armées* (No. 703, 5 ventôse VI) and *J. hommes libres* (No. 279, 4 ventôse VI). The unified club put up a front against the royalists in which there was no mention of the "anarchist threat." See *Aux Habitans de Calvados* (par le cercle constitutionnel de Caen, ventôse VI) in F[7] 7411, fol. 4759.

[48] Doucet, *L'Esprit public dans . . . la Vienne*, pp. 345-48.

bers reportedly considered Bernarais a demagogue, and rather than listen to his denunciations of "dangerous enemies to the popular cause," they left the club. Bernarais was accused of "having formed in the Circle a substantial party of workers whose good faith he won over, and of using this party to direct the operations of the Circle to his liking." Allegedly he was seeking political power "and attempting to monopolize the suffrages of the workers whom he misled." When reproached for this behavior, Bernarais reportedly ignored his critics and "appeared continuously to dissociate himself from the educated and patriotic men in order to attach himself exclusively to the mercenary class of workers whom he has subjugated." The issue was resolved in the end when the municipality ordered the club closed just as its counterpart in Pau had done with Garra's club.[49]

A schism also rent the club at Auch after some of the members began to launch public attacks against what they called "post-thermidorian Girondins"—a tactic that was not common, for most clubs avoided such open polemics over past differences. Other members, espousing directorial moderation, tried to counteract this by speaking in praise of the *journée* of 9 thermidor or by claiming that the royalists invoked the notion of "democracy" in order to mislead the people. Predictably this aroused the democrats who made things so uncomfortable for the conservatives that they left the club. Henceforth they took to denouncing the club to the authorities in Paris, and sought particularly to expose a "clique" of nine leaders, six of whom had "no known property," and most of whom were active in the revolutionary movement of the Year II. Led by Chantreau, a veteran revolutionary journalist who was currently a professor at the école centrale, the club ended up in open conflict with the Directory's representatives in the town.[50]

[49] A.N. F⁷ 7394, fol. 3069: P.V. de l'administration municipal de Poitiers, 24 pluviôse VI.

[50] A.N. F⁷ 7413, fol. 4960: Duville (sous chef au bureau des contributions) to M. of Pol., 27 ventôse VI, explaining that he had been a member of the club; municipal administration (Auch) to departmental commissioner, 6 floréal. (The clique of leaders allegedly included two professors at the école centrale, an aubergiste, an apothecary, a printer, and a journeyman printer.) On Chantreau see G. Brégail, "Chantreau, journaliste et professeur sous le Directoire," *Annales révolutionnaires*, XIII (1921), 23-36. From the town of Gand it was also reported that "good citizens" abandoned the club when it became "an arena of denunciations" (F⁷ 7408, fol. 4477: departmental commissioner [Escaut] to M. of Pol., 13 ventôse).

Finally, a most revealing battle for control occurred in Marseilles' large Constitutional Circle, although all supporters of the republic in Marseilles had good reason to unite after Fructidor. This metropolis had been plagued by militant reaction ever since Thermidor and the first white terror. The Directory's attempt to pacify the area by conciliation with Fréron's mission in 1796 had failed dismally, and the triumph of the reactionaries was sealed in the elections of the Year V. After that the city was racked by violent extremism that ranged from the harassment of republicans, their cafés, and their newspapers, to outright assassination. General Willot, a royalist sympathizer who was military commander of the region, permitted the returning émigrés and other anti-republicans to commit their outrages with impunity, and stifled every attempt of the republicans to defend themselves effectively. The fructidor coup was therefore of vast importance for Marseilles, since Willot (elected a deputy in 1797) was deported along with the editor of the most reactionary newspaper in Marseilles. So marked was the change in atmosphere that, according to one historian's estimate, thousands of émigrés, royalists, and thermidorians left Marseilles in anticipation of the consequences.[51]

The Directorial program of implementing the laws of exception revived on 19 fructidor, and of purging the constituted authorities of royalists, had a particular urgency in Marseilles. Quite logically, the Directory at first encouraged the formation of a large political club to help rally the republicans. But, as in so many other towns, the Jacobins in the club emerged as a distinctive, and in this case, dominant element not about to be controlled or manipulated by the Directory's supporters.

As described by the local Jacobin newspaper the Constitutional Circle was composed in the main of men active in the Revolution at its height—"those unfortunate patriots whom three virtually uninterrupted years of proscription . . . have reduced to the most frightful misery." The bulk of the members were sans-culottes, according

---

[51] P. Gaffarel, "Le gouvernement du Général Willot à Marseille (mars 1796-mars 1797)," *R.F.*, LXV (1913), 133-66; A. Bernard, "Le 18 fructidor à Marseille et dans les Bouches-du-Rhône," *R.F.*, XLI (1901), 200-201, 210. See also R. Gérard, *Un Journal de province pendant la Révolution: Le "Journal de Marseille" de Ferréol Beaugeard* (Paris, 1964), Part II.

to the same source, which admired "the generosity of its workers, who constitute the majority of the Circle, of those poor artisans who come each day to devote part of their daily wages to help relieve the indigent." A hostile official was in effect testifying to the same impression when he stigmatized the mass of members as "the least educated class which attaches itself to certain men because it believes them to be better republicans than the others."[52] Here was one conservative, it seems, who grudgingly admitted that the sans-culottes could distinguish their allies in the ranks of the middle class.

In Marseilles, according to the Directory's agents, the meneurs included some of the men "who dominated the popular society in 1793, with this difference: that the present spirits are infinitely more exasperated now than they were then." The Central Police Bureau of Marseilles identified from among these meneurs two particularly prominent individuals: Granet, Montagnard deputy to the Convention, and Massy, a printer and bookseller who was a wealthy family man but too "ardent" in his politics. The alleged leaders also included Peyre-Ferry, editor of the *Antiroyaliste*.[53]

Initially the Constitutional Circle was not the exclusive domain of these former Jacobins and "terrorists," for the civil and military authorities in the area maintained a close rapport with the club. "The commissioners to the department and the generals here occupy the tribune and make their voices heard in order to urge citizens to obey the laws," reported the *Antiroyaliste*; Generals LeBon and Chabert both paid their respects to the club and had speeches read at various times.[54] But these officials failed to impose their moderation on the club. In Marseilles as in Auch past grievances were so strong that attacks were openly made against the "thermidorians," and the Directory was criticized for its attempt to curb democratic ardor. The "Directorials" (as the loyal supporters of the Directory came to be called) tried to stop this, but to no avail. In a personal letter to

[52] *L'Antiroyaliste ou le républicain du Midi* (Marseilles) No. 15, 20 nivôse and No. 35, 10 germinal VI. A.N. AF III 217/Bouches-du-Rhône: departmental commissioner to Directory, 24 germinal VI.

[53] A.N. AF III 46 [Ministre de Police: Rapports au Directoire], dossier 168: report of 22 frimaire VI, based on information supplied by the Marseilles Central Police Bureau.

[54] *Antiroyaliste* No. 10, 26 frimaire; Nos. 24 and 27, 9 and 16 ventôse; *Journal de Toulouse* No. 83, 16 ventôse.

the Directory, the newly appointed commissioner to the Central Police Bureau admitted this in unguarded language:

> I mounted the tribune of the club on the 25th of ventôse [15 March 1798]. I unmasked all [the Jacobins'] maneuvers . . . but it was fruitless; from his side Chabert administered a death blow, but nothing helped; the leaders have convinced the imbeciles that the government no longer has any use for the pure republicans, and that it is attempting to smear them under perfidious labels.[55]

The writer added that the Directory's supporters were able to deal with the club only by closing it down a few days later.

THE CONSTITUTIONAL Circles of 1798 were short-lived because the only way the Directory could effectively control them was to close them or harass them out of existence. In many towns the Directory's supporters—either inside or outside the clubs—tried first to intimidate or outmaneuver the "anarchist" leaders, before resorting to the final expedient of having the clubs closed. Usually they failed to gain this control or influence because they represented the narrow middle-class point of view in whose spirit the constitution had been drafted, and which emphatically distrusted the political participation of the sans-culottes.

That individuals or groups of revolutionary bourgeoisie were more popular with politically conscious "workingmen" and petits-bourgeois can be explained by assuming that their behavior and attitudes corresponded more closely to the sans-culottes' attitudes and inclinations. Certainly their preferences were not identical and presumably they differed over many issues. But they did share a minimal preference for a republic where political oligarchy and social pretension would be attacked, and where the "workingman" had a rightful place in civic and political life. The clubs continued to be led by the middle class, but these leaders tried often with some success to draw in men who worked with their hands, who had relatively poor education, who were suffering from hard times or at least realized that others were suffering. To such men the Directory's warning about "anarchism" had little meaning—except to

---

[55] A.N. F⁷ 3659/4 (Bouches-du-Rhône): letter headed "Marseille, le 8 Germinal VI," and clearly from the commissioner to the Central Bureau.

reveal the Directory's hostility to them. The existence of such clubs was the last hope that politically conscious sans-culottes would not be effectively banished from political life. In Directorial France the best such sans-culottes could do was to distinguish their allies in the middle class and make common cause.

CHAPTER V

Jacobin Civisme: The Clubs in Action

‡ I ‡

WHAT FUNCTIONS did the new clubs ascribe to themselves? What patterns of activity can be reconstructed from their fragmentary records?

To begin with, the clubs had for proponents and antagonists alike a symbolic significance. Appreciating that their history was virtually synonymous with the progress of the revolutionary cause, conservatives restricted the clubs extensively in the constitution and exercised a continuing surveillance over them thereafter. Reactionaries and royalists went even further by trying periodically (as in germinal Year IV and thermidor Year V) to ban them altogether. Conversely, Jacobin publicists defended the sanctity of the clubs even when they were in a state of dissolution; Antonelle's articles in the Year IV provided almost a body of theory positing clubs as the essential institutions in a "representative democracy." The existence of clubs emerged from this history and on-going controversy as a standard by which the Jacobins could estimate their position in the commonwealth. They clung to the clubs as symbols that legitimized an imperfect republic and held out hope for its reform. It bears repeating here that the closing of clubs always foretold reaction. In the end, this was one of Bonaparte's earliest blows against the republic.

Regaining the right to associate freely after Fructidor, the Jacobins could begin to enjoy political life in their preferred and familiar way. "Deprived for so long of the opportunity to meet together that the Constitution assures us," wrote a neighborhood club in the capital, "we were reduced to suffering in silence the evils that afflicted the Republic." Thanks to the fructidor coup, explained another club, they could "begin to breathe freely . . . and peacefully enjoy the rights that the Constitution accords to all French citizens." Undaunted by the ambiguities that potentially could circumscribe or even jeopardize this right, the Neo-Jacobins maintained that their clubs "exist in keeping with the formal text of the constitution . . . knowing no permission except that sanctioned by the law."[1] In

[1] A.N. AF III 260/Seine: Les Citoyens soussignés réunis en cercle constitu-

turn they pledged to uphold that law. Renouncing the "audacity" once necessary to begin the Revolution, they promised now to promote the "wisdom and meditation" needed to maintain it. Even militant former revolutionaries admitted that "it is no longer a question of revolutionizing but simply of republicanizing." While they did not disown their heritage—deploring the "calumnies" that had engulfed the original popular societies—they asserted that the new Constitutional Circles would be "schools of republicanism."[2]

To bolster an insecure republican regime, then, was the clubs' explicit purpose. Considering themselves the most committed opponents of counterrevolution and apathy, the members called themselves *patriotes prononcés*. There was a contrast to be noted, as one of the Directory's commissioners explained, between the mass of apathetic citizens in his district who "do not even bother to discuss the affairs of government," and "a certain number of citizens who take a greater interest in those affairs and who have formed themselves into a constitutional circle."[3] The Directory could not but appreciate such efforts.

At the same time, however, most of the clubs pursued a second objective. If one purpose was to bolster the existing republican regime, the other was gradually to refashion that regime in their own image. While rallying to the constitution, the clubs interpreted it distinctively and liberally. Though claiming to support the government, they meant that only in an ultimate sense, for they did not hesitate to exert pressure on it concerning questions of personnel and policy. They sought to democratize the operations of government, and when necessary challenged the authority of local officials. Republicans first but democrats second, the Neo-Jacobins

---

tionnel, Rue Avoye 7ème arrondissement de Paris. A.N. F⁷ 7402/b, fol. 3960: petition from the Club of the Rue du Bacq, 10th arrondissement; *L'Indépendant* (Paris) No. 172, 22 ventôse VI: Profession de foi des républicains du cinquième arrondissement de Paris.

[2] A.N. F⁷ 7406, fol. 4264: Des Républicains, nouvellement formés en société politique sur le 4ème arrond. de Paris, ventôse. A.N. C428, fol. 131: Des Républicains de Paris amants passionés de la liberté et du gouvernement actuel . . . , 4 ventôse (signed by such Parisian militants as Cardinaux and Vafflard). F⁷ 7353, fol. 9486: Les Membres composant le cercle constitutionnel du 7ème arrond., ventôse. A.N. C429, fol. 151: Des Républicains du 2ème arrond. de Paris réunis en cercle constitutionnel, 26 pluviôse.

[3] A.N. F⁷ 7388, fol. 2561: Lanthenas to M. of Pol., 17 pluviôse, *compte décadaire* for the 2nd arrondissement.

115

could pursue both objectives in the relative security and normalcy of 1798. Locally the clubs became a kind of loyal opposition. Though they remained, as they claimed, the most forceful supporters of certain policies initiated by the Directory itself, their activism carried them considerably further. They would not become mere appendages of the official political establishment. From the government's side, the value of such supporters soon became dubious. With a precision unaffected by his bias, the Directory's devoted commissioner in the Seine department later summarized the government's attitude. "Experience has proven that these clubs—even the best intentioned ones—cannot limit themselves simply to educational discussions of political interest. All, more or less, wanted to involve themselves in government."[4] Here was the crucial point. The "schools of republicanism" were also the potential nuclei of independent local parties.

ANOTHER way of putting this is to distinguish between the clubs' educational and political activities. Chief among the former—and certainly the least controversial—was the dissemination of republican newspapers. Certain clubs were, in fact, so cautious as to style themselves reading clubs at the outset, like the Niveau Club in Bordeaux, which petitioned the authorities for a meeting hall as "A Society of subscribers to periodical papers." The Versailles Club —which like the Niveau later became aggressive politically—was ostensibly founded "to read newspapers and discuss political questions."[5] Likewise the Toulouse Club proposed to offer "a very large number of poor citizens" the means of learning the news. Months later, when the middle-class leaders had temporarily allowed that club to decline for tactical reasons, the *Journal de Toulouse* reported that the meeting hall was still being frequented by "workers who come peacefully to hear the news read." This was an effective defense against the attacks of conservatives and was used also in Montauban (Lot), where the club was portrayed primarily as "a means of making known to the hard working but poor class events which concern the republic's welfare."[6] Most of the extant règlements or

[4] Dupin's *compte rendu* for prairial VI in Aulard, *Paris*, IV, 730.
[5] Archives Municipales de Bordeaux, 1/79, pièce 35: Au Bureau Central de Bordeaux, n.d.; A.N. F⁷ 7351, fol. 9345: letter from 14 of the members to municipal administration of Versailles, 6 frimaire.
[6] *Discours prononcé par un membre du Cercle Constitutionnel de Toulouse,*

bylaws provided for the public reading of newspapers, some setting aside a particular hour for it, and others stipulating in addition that "the newspapers will always be on the bureau."[7]

Reading newspapers was not usually an end in itself but was meant to stimulate the discussion of issues by which the citizens would really become educated in republicanism. Newspapers would help in the more general enterprise of "assembling our views and our wisdom upon objects of concern to public well-being." For according to their bylaws, one purpose of the clubs was to discuss and define "social and republican virtues," "liberty, equality, and the amelioration of customs." At their meetings the clubs would "marshal public and private virtues to oppose the disastrous advance of immorality and corruption." They might, with the Toulouse Club, debate the principles of proposed laws until the laws were passed; then, naturally, they would "execute them." In a speech to the Vesoul (Haute-Saône) Club a leader enumerated the kinds of issues they would consider: the restoration of the country's finances; the uprooting of superstition from the countryside; measures of public safety required by circumstances; "the means of destroying the devouring scourge of poverty, and of utilizing all branches of the social order."[8] According to their public statements, then, the clubs were not committed to a passive acceptance of the status quo. If revolutionizing was abjured in favor of civic education and "republicanizing," this did not amount to a renunciation of change or reform.

Ever since 1789, moderates had been attempting to limit the clubs simply to an educational role, while the democrats attributed a

---

le 22 frimaire an VI (in A.N. F⁷ 7362, fol. 270); *Journal de Toulouse* No. 86, 22 ventôse; F⁷ 7415, fol. 5178, 4 floréal (Montauban).

[7] See the following règlements: Versailles (Seine-et-Oise) in A.N. F⁷ 7351, fol. 9345; Arras (Pas-de-Calais) reprinted in E. Lecesne, *Arras sous la Révolution* (Arras, 1883), III, 338; Chateauroux (Indre) in F⁷ 7362, fol. 238; Arnay (Côte-d'Or) in F⁷ 7415, fol. 5235.

[8] *Discours prononcé le 2 brumaire de l'an VI . . . au Cercle constitutionnel de Vesoul par le Citoyen Poirson fils* (in A.N. F⁷ 7404, fol. 4114); *Discours prononcé . . . Toulouse*; "Déclaration des principes des membres du cercle constitutionnel séant à Douai (Nord)," reprinted in G. Aubert, "La Révolution à Douai," *AHRF*, xv [1938], 546; règlement of Arras and Arnay clubs, *op.cit.*; F⁷ 7353, fol. 9486: Les Républicains, membres du cercle constitutionnel du 10ème arrond, séant rue du Bacq, 6 ventôse; *Courrier de l'Armée d'Italie* (Milan) No. 53, 12 brumaire VI: Plan d'organisation du cercle constitutionnel.

political purpose to them from the start.[9] Robespierre's early argument that the clubs must serve as sentinels of the people remained axiomatic for the Jacobins, and in the Year VI the issue was fought once again in words and practice. The critic of Neo-Jacobinism who best restated the traditional conservative argument in the Year VI was A. M. Roederer, a future Napoleonic counselor of state. Attacking the tendency of the clubs to scrutinize, censure, and denounce officials, he held such activity to be both illegal and unjustifiable. To Roederer all political functions claimed by the clubs were either "a public function and the act of a magistrate, or the exercise of individual rights." Between duly constituted magistrates and individual citizens, he was unwilling to have any secondary groups or "corporations" imposed. He deemed it an affront to a free government to suppose that clubs were necessary to protect and represent individuals. Only educational clubs—"societies of friendship and instruction"—should be tolerated, he argued. Such clubs, moreover, ought to be limited to fifty members who could then discuss things calmly, and should be expressly forbidden to form any collective opinion or consensus. Deliberations, votes, and resolutions would be prohibited, as well as "collective correspondence" and affiliation. Such orderly, educational clubs, according to Roederer, "cannot help but produce moral and intellectual benefits since they unite only spirits and hearts; they have—if we may put it this way—neither arms nor legs."[10]

The Jacobins opposed this view emphatically. They insisted on giving their clubs "arms and legs" in order to exercise some influence in their communities. The pro-Jacobin *Indépendant* countered Roederer's quasi-Rousseaustic attack on the Constitutional Circles by finding its own text in Rousseau: "as soon as someone says about the affairs of state: 'What does it matter to me?'—then the state is doomed." From this the *Indépendant* argued that "the continual vigilance of every citizen in a republic is necessary," and that this was a legitimate function of the clubs.[11] Many Constitutional Circles

[9] Cf. A. Soboul, *Les Sans-culottes Parisiens en l'an II* (Paris, 1958), p. 614.

[10] A. M. Roederer, *Des Sociétés particulières, telles que clubs, réunions* (Impr. Demonville, an septième), B.N. Lb42/751. This pamphlet summarizes views that appeared in the *Journal de Paris* the previous year.

[11] *L'Indépendant* No. 174, 24 ventôse VI. (The principal editor was Aristide Valcour, a revolutionary pamphleteer in the Year II.)

wrote this notion into their bylaws and manifestos, thereby staking a place in the political arena.

Surveillance was aimed first of all at exposing counterrevolutionary "conspirators." Even if the leaders had been effectively proscribed in Fructidor, there remained, as one club put it, "the secondary agents of corruption." Secondly, the clubs would scrutinize "the morality, the capacity, and the republicanism" of local officials. Such vigilance by the clubs was deemed essential to the well-being of the republic; as the Nîmes Club stated in a petition to the Legislature, it is only through the clubs "that a multitude of truths will reach you."[12]

Certainly the members were wary of unfounded accusations, but they felt this could be avoided without sacrificing the clubs' right to make legitimate denunciations. As a spokesman for the Vesoul Club maintained, though they would not allow their club to become a "foyer de dénonciations," they would continue to expose "liberticide activities." In their declarations of principle certain clubs proclaimed this as their major purpose: the St. Benoist (Indre) Club intended "to unmask the enemies of republican government, to scrutinize, and to disconcert their counterrevolutionary maneuvers," while the tiny club at Chauderaigues (Cantal) would "inform the supreme authorities of the poor spirit which prevails in the canton . . . and call for the dismissal of the officials"—which it did in the same petition.[13]

Surveillance and denunciation by clubs resulted in a continuous flow of petitions into the Police Ministry and the Directory. Individuals or groups of officials were accused of royalism, malfeasance, ineffectiveness, or "anti-republicanism." Occasionally sev-

---

[12] A.N. F⁷ 7406, fol. 4264: Des républicains . . . en société politique sur le 4ᵉᵐᵉ arrond., ventôse; *Discours d'un grenadier . . . à ses camarades prononcé au cercle constitutionnel le 27 brumaire VI* (Paris, n.d.), p. 5 (B.N. Lb 40/2362); A.N. C431, fol. 431: Les Républicains de Nîmes composant le cercle constitutionnel, pluviôse; règlement of Arnay Club, *op.cit*. Cf. M. Reinhard, *Le Département de la Sarthe sous le Régime directorial* (St. Brieuc, 1935), pp. 305-306.

[13] *Discours prononcé . . . au Cercle constitutionnel de Vesoul*; A.N. F⁷ 7373, fol. 1150: petition from club at St. Benoist, n.d.; F⁷ 7390, fol. 2710: petition from club at Chauderaigues, 10 pluviôse. Cf. Les Patriotes d'Ornans réunis en cercle constitutionnel to M. of Pol., n.d., in which 22 members of this club in the Doubs department submitted a detailed list of persons whom they charged with *incivisme* or with being émigrés. The list contained no less than 160 names! (F⁷ 7410, fol. 4636.)

eral clubs in a department concerted informally to denounce some-one. For example, the Circles at Laval and at Mayenne (both in the Mayenne department) submitted virtually identical petitions, one day apart, to protest against the appointment of a certain individ-ual to the post of *captain de gendarmerie*, on the grounds that he was an aged, illiterate drunkard. The principal clubs in the Haute-Saône department (at Vesoul, Luxeuil, and L'Ure), all evidently in close touch, each petitioned to warn against Goisset, who had been dismissed as president of the department council following the fructidor coup, and who was now accused of intriguing to be reinstated.[14]

On occasion the clubs printed these petitions or submitted them to friendly newspapers, in the hope of embarrassing the culprit. Such publicity was one way of striking at men who would otherwise be safe behind their parliamentary immunity, local political influence, or social prominence. The petition on Goisset, for example, was circulated in both of these ways, as was an attack by the Nîmes Club on Rabaud, a reactionary deputy from the department who had escaped the fructidor purge. The petition portraying Rabaud as a protector of émigrés and persecutor of republicans was printed in at least two Jacobin newspapers.[15]

Adverse publicity generated by the clubs against local officials in the press frequently had its desired effect, as the targets reacted angrily. Denunciations of alleged ineffective or "anti-republican" be-havior must have mattered since these officials took the trouble to prepare elaborate counterclaims and to demand redress against libels. Beyond simply defending themselves, a few of the accused warned the government of what was at stake. Officials of the Rhône depart-ment wrote to the Police Ministry that "several of us have been rep-resented in the *Journal des hommes libres* under the most hideous characteristics and as perpetrators or protectors of crimes." In a separate letter the departmental commissioner voiced the same com-plaint, and with some insight connected the formation of political

[14] A.N. F⁷ 7376, fol. 1531: petitions from the Laval and the Mayenne clubs, 20 and 21 nivôse; F⁷ 7400, fol. 3723: petitions from the Vesoul, Luxeuil, and L'Ure clubs, pluviôse. In both cases the Police Ministry followed the matter up.

[15] *J. hommes libres* No. 301, 26 ventôse VI (on Vesoul); A.N. F⁷ 7391, fol. 2787: departmental commissioner (Gard) to M. of Pol., 6 floréal; *J. hommes libres* No. 258, 13 pluviôse; *Antiroyaliste* (Marseilles) No. 26, 6 ventôse (on Nîmes).

clubs with the efforts of the "exclusifs" to regain power by means of such denunciations.[16] The municipal administration of Pont-à-Mousson (Meurthe) likewise wrote to protest a squib in Vatar's paper which claimed that public spirit was dead in that commune, that brigands went unmolested, and that the king's health was toasted. After attempting to refute these charges, the officials went on to accuse the *Journal des hommes libres* of "accepting indiscriminately all the calumnies that are addressed to it from points all across France," making it appear that the constituted authorities are incompetent and thereby undermining confidence in them.[17] Similar complaints came to the Police Ministry from indignant officials in Versailles, Jemappes, LeHavre, St. Omer, Orléans, Dunquerke, and Toulon, among others. And the charge was largely correct. Without taking much trouble to verify their informants' claims, newspapers like the *Journal des hommes libres* or the *Ami de la Patrie* published these accusations to assist the local Jacobins in their efforts to embarrass hostile and "anti-republican" officials.[18]

In addition to denouncing individuals, some clubs sought "to seek out and inform the magistrates of abuses which exist, in order to instigate reforms." They remonstrated with the authorities to speed reorganization of the national guard, arrest refractory priests, celebrate the décadi, and reorganize the local bureaucracy. Beyond this the range of issues raised in the clubs' petitions was extensive, as a few examples will suggest. From Beaune (Côte d'Or) came a protest against a proposal that "is causing despair amidst the class of our poorer fellow citizens"—the suppression of the *hospices civils* in communes of under 12,000 population. Less portentously, but of equal consequence to their sensibilities, the members of the Rheims (Marne) Club denounced a local center of subversion, "a house of ill-fame—fanatic and royalist" where country folk were duped into spreading "the most poisoned principles." Two petitions from the

---

[16] A.N. F[7] 7341, fol. 8263: letters of 1 frimaire VI.

[17] A.N. F[7] 7393, fol. 2969, 22 pluviôse VI.

[18] Examples may be culled from entries in the Police Ministry registers for "Affaires Diverses": F[7]* 465-89. Coesnon-Pellerin's *Ami de la Patrie* was attacked for publishing the same type of alleged slanders: e.g., F[7] 7323, fol. 6160 (Glos/Orne); F[7] 7388, fol. 2596 (Chateauthierry/Aisne); F[7] 7412/b, fol. 4895 (Cergy/Seine-et-Oise); F[7] 7353, fol. 9527 (Siguy/Ardennes). Likewise Errard's *Révélateur* ("ce journaliste jacobin") was denounced by the municipal administration of Pointoise (Seine-et-Oise) for its attack on them: F[7] 7323, fol. 6196.

Orléans (Loiret) Club urged the municipal authorities to reorganize the national guard and to provide better provisions for a detachment of the Army of Italy that was stopping there. The municipality rejected the petitions, warning the club not to meddle in administrative affairs, since the aim of political clubs should be limited "to spreading education and maintaining the flame of patriotism."[19]

Petitions were used both to express local grievances and to register opinions on issues of national rather than local character. (This latter type will be discussed in Chapter VI.) In both cases the petitions were functional, bringing pressure to bear for specific objectives; they were the most important of the "arms and legs" against which Roederer inveighed. In addition, framing petitions possibly contributed to the clubs' morale, for it rendered the individual's participation tangible and concrete. Putting himself on record, the signer committed himself to a cause and publicly identified himself with his fellow members.

When retrieved from the scattered repositories where they were ultimately buried, these petitions reflect how the clubs busied themselves. The small club at Nîmes (Gard), which averaged about forty members at its meetings, sent off at least five petitions to the legislative or executive branches of the government during the months of pluviôse and ventôse: it denounced the deputy Rabaud; it denounced a local notable named Chabaud-Latour, and deplored the fact that the fructidor coup had thus far brought little change to their commune; it petitioned the Directory to request that the town be placed under martial law; it petitioned for that a second time, and added that royalists dominated the national guard; and it petitioned to inform the Legislature (for some unknown reason) that it had amalgamated with a small club in the faubourg of Porte d'Alais.[20] In the month of nivôse the Constitutional Circle at Vendôme (Loir-et-Cher) sent in at least three petitions: one called for the reorganization of the national guard; a second requested the Legislature to decree that liberty trees be planted in all communes "as in the great days of the Revolution"; and a third petition

---

[19] A.N. C434: petition from Beaune, 2 ventôse; *L'Abeille des gazettes et journaux* (Metz) No. 140, 8 pluviôse, reprinting the Rheims petition; F⁷ 7397, fol. 3423: two petitions headed "Cercle constitutionnel d'Orléans, aux administrateurs de la commune . . . ," 30 pluviôse, and draft reply.

[20] A.N. C431, fol. 167, pluviôse; C432, fol. 180, 25 ventôse; A.N. F⁷ 7391, fol. 2787: to the Directory, 25 pluviôse; *ibid.*: to M. of Pol., 26 pluviôse.

asked the Legislature to empower municipal governments to conduct domiciliary visits in search of priests, émigrés, and draft-evaders.[21] The functional and the morale-boosting character of these exercises appear to be in equal evidence.

No ONE had questioned the clubs' right to submit petitions when they were officiously congratulating the Directory for the fructidor coup, or affirming their loyalty to the constitution. But the right of petition did come under attack once the petitions began to express grievances, demands, and denunciations. Directorials on all levels resented this outside pressure and wished to stop the unfavorable publicity the clubs were generating. Increasingly, one of the favorite grounds on which officials attacked the clubs was for violating the vague constitutional provision against "collective" petitions.

Article 364 read: "All citizens shall be free to address petitions to the public authorities, but they must be individual ones; no association may present them collectively. . . ." Like most of the articles on clubs, this one was just ambiguous enough to invite circumvention; it did *not* say categorically associations or clubs may not submit petitions. During his tenure as Police Minister, Sotin deflected all criticism by an extremely liberal interpretation of this article. The clubs' petitions were customary and legal, he ruled, as long as the members also signed their names individually at the bottom—which is precisely what they had been enthusiastically doing all along.[22]

Sotin's interpretation of the law could easily be overturned if the government decided that it would no longer tolerate such pressure. About two weeks after his dismissal, the issue came to a head in the Council of 500. Interrupting the announcement by the presiding officer of a petition from one of the clubs, the deputy Riou observed that the constitution forbade the clubs not only correspondence among themselves "but also correspondence with the constituted authorities, other than as individuals [autrement qu'en non individuel]. If the petition being announced is collective, I request the

---

[21] A.N. F^{1c} III [Ministre de l'Intérieure: ésprit public et élections] Loir-et-Cher/8: petition to C500; A.N. F^7 3681/3 (Loir-et-Cher): petition to C500; A.N. F^7 7386, fol. 2366: to M. of Pol.—all dated nivôse.

[22] E.g., A.N. F^7 7382/a, fol. 1959: draft letter from Sotin to the central administration of the Ourthe department, 5 pluviôse, in answer to their complaint that the Liège Club submitted "collective" petitions.

order of the day." His objection was sustained and the petition was put aside. On 24 ventôse (14 March 1798) the Directory followed this up with a sweeping executive decree. "Each day there appear addresses or petitions headed 'The citizens of ——, united in a constitutional circle,'" read the preamble, thereby acknowledging the volume of the clubs' petitions. And it proceeded to cut them off forthwith.

> I. Every address or petition presented . . . under any collective denomination whatsoever will, by dint of that alone, be lain aside and go unanswered. . . .
>
> II. Every club called a constitutional circle, or meeting under any other collective denomination, will be closed if it undertakes any collective act whatsoever, or if its members, in petitioning individually, refer to their alleged quality as members, or mention their meeting in a club or circle.[23]

A curious mixture of technicality and political principle, the 24 ventôse decree clearly revealed the Directory's opposition to the Jacobin brand of civisme. In cutting off the flow of embarrassing petitions, it would shut down the clubs' most significant outlet and would probably undermine the morale of the members who took great pains in fashioning these thunderbolts. Authorities on all levels were given license to ignore the petitions that had already been drawn up. In one sense the whole matter turned on a technicality and represented simply a reversal of Sotin's liberal interpretation of "collective" petitions. Ostensibly the Directory was not disputing the right of an individual to petition his government. In reality the Directory would simply not abide effective remonstrance.

This decree embodied more than the resolution of a technical conundrum about petitions. In general it gave writ to the kind of argument that Roederer and others had been advancing and drastically limited the effectiveness of the clubs. In truth, as the decree stated, the clubs were behaving like "corporations within the state," not only in drawing up petitions, but in a wide variety of manifestations and "collective acts" more appropriate to pressure groups than to "schools of republicanism." It is debatable whether the existence of pressure groups was desirable for a healthy civic life. But for the Directory there was a certain logic in now taking a narrow stand

---

[23] *Moniteur*, 20 ventôse VI (p. 683), and 27 ventôse (p. 709).

on the constitution's language. Since Fructidor the Constitutional Circles (to use Roederer's simile) had indeed sprouted a variety of arms and legs.

‡ II ‡

Effective internal organization contributed to the clubs' corporate identity in their communities. Like the right to screen their members, this prerogative was challenged from the beginning, but Police Minister Sotin affirmed it as long as he was in office. A memo dated 8 nivôse (28 December 1797) summarized Sotin's rulings on several disputed points: clubs could hold deliberative meetings and pass resolutions; choose rotating officers such as moderators, presidents, and secretaries; form committees to examine the speeches of members and arrange for their publication; and appoint people to collect dues or contributions.[24] Many of the clubs proceeded to frame bylaws (règlements) providing for responsible officers, planned agendas, facilities for publishing documents, and modest treasuries (which were sometimes in the red). In their new-found moderation, they were careful to erect barriers against illegal motions, unsubstantiated denunciations, and the general disorder that had prevailed in the Year II.[25] Most, however, stopped short of the Vendôme Club, which established an aura of puritanism at its meetings: drunkenness and smoking would not be tolerated; the wives of members would be the only women allowed on the premises.[26]

[24] A.D.S.: VD*, dossier 180 (pièce 2148): MS *instruction* of 8 nivôse VI.

[25] A.N. F⁷ 7415, fol. 5235 (Arnay); F⁷ 7351, fol. 9345 (Versailles); F⁷ 7362, fol. 238 (Chateauroux); *Déclaration des Principes du Cercle Constitutionnel établi à Vesoul* (Impr. J. B. Poirson) in F⁷ 7404, fol. 4114; *Reunion d'hommes libres, établie en cercle à Toulouse, conformément à la loi* [an VI] in F⁷ 7362, fol. 270; F⁷ 7393, fol. 2919: MS règlement of the Constitutional Circle of the 2nd arrondissement in Paris; *Règlement de police intérieur, adopté par la Réunion du 7ème arrondissement* (Impr. Institut des Aveugles-travailleurs, an VI) in B.N. Lb40/2364; *Règlement des Amis de la Constitution séant au faubourg Antoine* (Impr. Lamberté, an VI) in F⁷ 7292, fol. 2585. On the prevailing disorder in the original sociétés populaires see L. deCardenal, *La Province pendant la Révolution* (Paris, 1929), pp. 91-95. A *compte* (budget) for the club in the 4th arrondissement (A.N. F⁷ 7406, fol. 4264) shows income from 39 payments of 12 sous each as voluntary contributions, and from the sale of 94 copies of the règlement at 6 sous each. Payments were made for supplies like candles, ink, paper (32 l.); the concierge (12 l.); printing the règlement (12 l.). This left a deficit of 25 l. for one month's arrears in the rent.

[26] A.N. F⁷ 7366, fol. 551: MS règlement of the Vendôme Club.

Basically the clubs' bylaws provided the stability and organization necessary if they were to act effectively as groups. Thus organized and permitted to pass resolutions, the clubs could go beyond discussion and education.

Certain undertakings were unexceptionable and could be condoned by the clubs' sternest critics, but even these contributed to defining the clubs' corporate presence in the community. For example, the bylaws of several clubs mentioned that they would volunteer "acts of charity for unfortunate republicans," and the record occasionally reports collections taken up for "the indigent" or some act of relief for a particularly "unfortunate" republican. The plan for a Constitutional Circle drawn up by French and Italian democrats at Milan called for an ambitious program of periodic collections for "poor but virtuous" young couples about to be married. The gift would be presented to them at a "simple rustic fete" with song and dance, which was meant to be the counterpart of "the theaters and concerts that embellish the existence of the rich."[27] More controversial, no doubt, was a collection taken up by the Marseilles Club "to be sent to the unfortunates jailed in Cherbourg as a result of the Vendôme proscription," that is, the Babeuf trial.[28]

Charity and relief may be classed with other activities under the heading of self-help. In these projects the Jacobins not only gave tangible expression to their vaunted civic-mindedness, but also cultivated their sense of fraternity. Thus, when no one else seemed to be taking the responsibility, several clubs decided to repair the local roads. "The members of the constitutional circle of Marseille," reported the *Antiroyaliste*, "indignant at seeing the rich obstinately refuse the least sacrifice for the motherland, decided to work at repairing the roads for three days [every tenth day]." The operation was approvingly publicized in the press, where it was explained how "over four thousand persons assembled" singing republican

[27] E. Lecesne, *Arras sous la Rèvolution*, III, 338; *Journal de Toulouse* No. 86, 22 ventôse; *Antiroyaliste* (Marseilles) No. 35, 10 germinal; *Récit de ce qui s'est passé à la fete civique du Cercle constitutionnel de Versailles . . . le 2 pluviôse an 6* (Impr. Locard fils) in B.N. Lb42/497; "Notice exacte des séances du cercle constitutionnel de la Rue du Bacq, 10ème arrond." (MS) in F7 7402/b, fol. 3960 (entries for 22 pluviôse and 2 ventôse); *Courrier de l'Armée d'Italie* (Milan) No. 53, 12 brumaire VI.

[28] *Antiroyaliste* No. 28, 13 ventôse; *J. hommes libres* No. 303, 28 ventôse, referring to the prisoners as the "first victims" of the royalist reaction before Fructidor.

songs, and eventually repaired over a league of impassable road.[29] When the club in the 11th arrondissement of Paris agreed to participate in a similar project, the members turned it into a fraternal outing, combining it with a *repas frugal* at which they also discussed the coming elections.[30] In the same spirit of self-help the club at Caraman (Haute-Garonne) concerted to hunt out a band of brigands that had been ravaging the local woods, and the club at Chambéry (Mont Blanc) raised a subscription and a volunteer force to assist the patriots of Vaud, across the Swiss border, who were being menaced by the "oligarchs of Berne."[31]

The members of the clubs could generally be counted on to turn out in force for routine republican festivals and ceremonies. But, in incidents that appear uniformly minor, they managed to irritate the local authorities by their cliquish aggressiveness. The real issue in such disputes was clearly the corporate image that the clubs projected. The Club of the Rue Dominique in Lyon, for example, was issued a stern rebuke by the town fathers for its disrespectful contentiousness over the placement of the club's posters and decorations in a public festival that was being prepared. The administration of the Jemappes department complained testily that the club in one commune was violating the laws by parading at public festivals with a flag bearing the inscription "Cercle Constitutionnel de Libre-sur-Sambre."[32] Friction could even arise over that most innocuous of republican symbols, the liberty tree. Why, suspicious officials in several places grumbled, did the clubs plant trees of their own in public ceremonies, instead of simply assisting the officials in planting their trees?[33] Still other complaints testify to this official edginess over

---

[29] *Antiroyaliste* No. 21, 19 pluviôse; *Journal de la Côte-d'Or* (Dijon) No. 30, 30 pluviôse; *L'Indépendant* No. 149, 29 pluviôse; *Journal de Toulouse* No. 68, 16 pluviôse; *Abeille des gazettes* (Metz) No. 153, 4 ventôse.

[30] A.N. F⁷ 3688/13, "dossier secrète": report on a meeting of the club in the 11th arrondissement, 22 ventôse. Cf. *Bulletin de l'Eure* (Evreux) No. 114, 15 pluviôse, and *Abeille des gazettes* (Metz) No. 147, 22 pluviôse on the club at Verneuil (Eure).

[31] *Tableau politique* (Paris) No. 143, 18 pluviôse; *L'Echo des Alpes* (Chambéry) No. 67, 19 pluviôse (edited by the Savoyard physician, soldier, and revolutionary propagandist, Amadée Doppet).

[32] A.N. F⁷ 7383/a, fol. 2010: administration du section Midi (Lyon), to M. of Pol., 1 pluviôse; F⁷ 7410, fol. 5603: administration of Jemappes to M. of Pol., 18 germinal.

[33] A.N. F⁷ 7387, fol. 2486: president of the municipality of Puget-Theniers (Alpes-Maritimes) to M. of Pol., 3 pluviôse; *Journal de Toulouse* No. 66, 12 pluviôse, on the club at Caraman (Haute-Garonne).

public signs of the clubs' corporate existence. In Rennes (Ille-et-Villaine), St. Hipolite (Gard), and Puget-Theniers (Alpes-Maritimes), municipal officers reprimanded and attempted to close the clubs for announcing their meetings in the streets by means of placards or criers.[34]

"It is truly by means of civic gatherings that public spirit is maintained," wrote the Versailles Club. But patriotism was sometimes overshadowed by corporate identity at the clubs' banquets and celebrations. For one thing, the speeches delivered at these civic gatherings usually had significant emphases and omissions. Offering the usual imprecations against kings and aristocrats, as well as that vague idealism that any republican could applaud, the speakers nonetheless departed from the Directory's standard formula for such occasions, which was to attack the "tyranny" of both royalism *and* anarchy.[35] Instead, speakers like citizen Wallier of the club in the 7th arrondissement talked exclusively about the excesses of reactionaries. On the anniverary of Louis XVI's execution Wallier rehearsed the perfidies of that monarch, and took occasion to note how his escape in June 1791 was stopped by an obscure citizen named Drouet, who thus became a national hero, only to end up being "persecuted" as a defendant at the Vendôme trial. The speaker then passed to August 10 and to the "just punishment" of the king, but observed that the fight was not over, for there came "a long and cruel reaction against the *ardent and pure* sectaries of liberty." Throughout his speech, which paid tribute to Drouet and to all "pure republicans," no reference was made to the "crimes of anarchy" or the Terror.[36]

More than the speeches, the toasts drunk at these festivals seem

[34] A.N. F⁷ 7406, fol. 4265: municipal administration of Rennes, 17 ventôse; F⁷ 7411, fol. 4815: municipal administration of St. Hipolite; F⁷ 7387, fol. 2486: Puget-Theniers, 3 pluviôse (Sotin did not agree that this was cause for rebuking the club).

[35] *Récit . . . Cercle constitutionnel de Versailles*; A.N. F⁷ 7414, fol. 5072: MS Discours prononcé par le cit. F. N. Moureau, ébeniste, régulateur du cercle constitutionnel du faubourg Antoine; *Discours prononcé par J. M. Lequinio, le 2 pluviôse an VI . . . sur la place publique de Valenciennes, et imprimé par ordre du Cercle constitutionnel* (n.l.) in F⁷ 7386, fol. 2358; F⁷ 7383/a, fol. 2055: Rapport succinct de la célebration de la fête du 21 janvier par le cercle constitutionnel du sixième arrond.

[36] A.N. F⁷ 3688/13 (Seine: fol. pluviôse): Réunion patriotique du 7ème arrond. de Paris, séance du 2 pluviôse.

to have provided evocative slogans for the initiated. Innocent enough on the surface, they were a safe way of nurturing sentiments that were not part of the Directorial orthodoxy. Invariably there was a toast drunk "to the martyrs of liberty and the victims of reaction." Any reading of the Jacobin press suggests that this referred not simply to the victims of the white terror after Thermidor but also to the sans-culottes who were cut down following the *journées* of prairial Year III, and to the defendants of the Vendôme trial. Toasts "to the republicans who have remained inviolably committed to the principles of liberty and equality," or "to the regenerators of the Constitutional Circles" further served to identify the celebrants as a group apart from the generality of republicans. When the Jacobins became suitably enthused at these banquets, they might even pass beyond circumspect, recordable toasts into more spontaneous outbursts. At a banquet held by the Brive (Corrèze) Club, according to the municipal commissioner, toasts of *Vive les pierrons* were heard, "which in vulgar usage means partisans of Robespierre."[37]

Thirty ventôse (20 March 1798)—the day before the primary elections began—was a patriotic holiday known as the Festival of the Sovereignty of the People. A club planning to celebrate with a banquet apart from the municipality's public ceremony was the Versailles Club, which was strongly given to the corporate separatism that conservatives deplored in the Jacobins. Wishing to be scrupulously legal, the club submitted a detailed proposal for its banquet to the municipal authorities, and the document has survived. In its conception and detail the plan evokes the atmosphere that the club hoped to generate. It incorporates a familiar Jacobin sentimentality, but avoids the more pronounced ritualistic overtones of similar events in the Year II.[38]

The celebration was to take place around a platform on which products of the various crafts would be displayed; over the platform a banner would be placed reading: "Les Besoins de tous forment leur réunion; l'amélioration du sort de tous est le but de la Société"

---

[37] *Ibid.* Cf. *Récit . . . Cercle constitutionnel de Versailles*; *Journal des France* [a sequel to *J. hommes libres*] No. 38, 25 thermidor VI. A.N. F⁷ 7413, fol. 4944: municipal commissioner (Brive) to M. of Pol., 1 germinal (referring to a banquet held on 30 pluviôse).

[38] A.N. AF III 262/ Seine-et-Oise: MS Projet de fête le trente ventôse à la souveraineté du Peuple, pour faire suite à celle de la Municipalité. (Another copy in A.N. AF III 512, plaq. 3250.)

—a succinct summary of Jacobin social consciousness. After the official ceremonies the club members and their guests would adjourn to this stand. Entertainments would be held around it, including foot races, the prize being a flag with the inscription "Vigor and activity are necessary for a free people; slackness for despotism." Next the banquet would be served and the inevitable toasts drunk. Some were carefully prepared in advance, balancing enthusiasm and moderation and expressing a synthesis of enlightenment ideals and revolutionary fervor.[39] Finally, prepared speeches would develop these sentiments, particularly in regard to the exercise of sovereignty in the upcoming elections.

The club wanted "republicans from the environs" to attend as guests, and planned to publicize the banquet and to distribute copies of the program in the vicinity. But all non-members were to be screened by a committee which reserved the right to reject them under a factitious formula: "our locale does not permit us to admit anyone else." The Jacobins publicly insisted on their right to bar anyone from their fraternity whom they deemed undesirable. But clearly they were anxious to bring in as many guests as possible and had no desire to conduct themselves as a cabal.

The proposal for the festival noted in conclusion that a committee of ten would plan and execute it and report back to the club on their progress. On 27 ventôse (17 March 1798) two members of this committee submitted the proposal to the municipal administration of Versailles, which found a variety of reasons for rejecting it and prohibiting the affair. Some of the objections were mere technicalities: that the proposal was not properly stamped and not in correct form, whatever that was. But the officials also deemed the proposal contrary to Article 362 of the constitution, arguing that two members had attempted to speak for a number of citizens claiming corporate existence in a club. The departmental administration of Seine-et-Oise made this even more explicit when it reviewed the case the next day. Supporting the municipality of Versailles wholeheartedly, it attacked the club's proposal because it claimed

---

[39] E.g., "*A la République*: Puisse-t-elle, fondée sur la morale, être aussi terrible au-dehors pour les tyrans qui voudront la combattre avec les armes, que redoutable dans l'intérieur par la *vertu*, à la corruption qui voudrait l'avilir par son or impur! Puisse-t-elle avec le tems et sans sécousses remplir le voeu des philosophes et des hommes libres."

the right to exclude people, and above all because it undertook "external correspondence" as a collective association.[40] Relying on several technicalities, these officials in effect were blocking the constitutional right of free association. But they must be credited with substantial insight. The Versailles Jacobins were planning a banquet designed to create an atmosphere and to propagate sentiments that departed from the official brand of republicanism.

WHEN THE clubs thrust themselves directly into local administrative or political affairs, their corporate presence was most acutely resented. In attempting to dominate, embarrass, or simply pressure the existing power structure, the Jacobins were exercising what they took to be their freedom. In relatively few places were the local officials in complete harmony with the clubs. An informant from Lunéville (whose anonymity was most unusual since almost all such denunciations were signed) did complain bitterly that "the clubbists spoke as if they had in their hands the authority that the Constitution accords solely to the magistrates." What was worse, these very magistrates "who should guard against all types of association are part of this one." Similar dismay was expressed over some of the clubs discussed earlier such as Limoux (Aude) and Vesoul (Haute-Saône).[41] Rarely, however, was the accord between clubs and officials as complete as was purported in these cases. The relationships ranged from friendly to indifferent to hostile; and the clubs used whatever means was appropriate to bring pressure to bear. At Villefranche (Aveyron), where officials and clubs were implacably hostile, the club made a point of boycotting the officials, and allegedly threatened to expel members who had misguidedly joined them in a public celebration.[42]

Whether the officials suffered domination or obloquy from the clubs, they were, in the Directorial view, losing the independence and dignity due their office. Once elected or appointed, they were not supposed to be subjected to intimidation or pressure; tech-

[40] A.N. AF III 262/ Seine-et-Oise: extrait des registres des délibérations de l'administration central du Seine-et-Oise, 28 ventôse VI.

[41] A.N. F7 7399, fol. 3663: letter received on 18 germinal from Lunéville; F7 7404, fol. 4114: Memoire justificatif des citoyens de Vesoul, floréal (35 signatures); F7 7414, fol. 5058: municipal commissioner (Vesoul) to Directory, 23 floréal; A.N. AF III 216/Aude.

[42] A.N. AF III 523, plaq. 3377: copie de la lettre du Croissac, commissaire à Villefranche, to M. of Pol. and Interior, n.d.

nically they were responsible only to the Directory. Obviously the clubs did not accept this narrow version of representative government. They chose to ignore the constitution's non-operative Article 363, which held that political rights were exercised only during election week. In the Jacobin view elected or appointed officials ought to be responsive to the opinions of the sovereign citizenry. Consequently the clubs attempted to remonstrate with these officials and to influence their behavior. The record rarely offers any two instances that were identical, but in each case this conflicting view of representative government was a fundamental source of disagreement.

Most scandalous in the eyes of conservatives were clubs that demonstrated before the authorities, as when the Constitutional Circle at Dôle (Jura) sent deputations to the city government "to intimate their wishes to it," or when the Brive (Corrèze) Club marched en masse to the town hall to present its views to the municipal administration. No doubt the members believed that they were enjoying the fruits of freedom and the responsibilities of citizenship, as a spokesman for the club exhorted the officials against timidity in exercising their functions "when it is a question of the people's welfare," and assured them that the club "will always be ready to support you with all their forces."[43]

The clubs were most prone to exert pressure on the authorities before the elections over matters like voter eligibility and registration procedures, and this will be discussed in detail elsewhere. But these were not the only issues that elicited intervention from the clubs. The question of taxation was a common target for agitation. At Joinville (Haute-Marne), according to ten citizens who claimed that they were not members of the club but who endorsed its actions, the club antagonized the municipal officers by complaining about the unfair distribution of direct taxes, and about the indirect taxes "extorted from all those who bring comestibles to Joinville." When the authorities refused to correct these abuses the club was forced to denounce them to higher authorities, "which accounts for the rancour between the officials and the circle." Other clubs

[43] A.N. F⁷ 7417, fol. 5361: letter to the Directory, floréal; F⁷ 7413, fol. 4944: municipal commissioner (Brive) to M. of Pol., 1 germinal.

agitating the question of local taxes included Dôle, Amboise, and Valence.[44]

Taxation proved an issue capable of driving certain Jacobins into direct and violent action. After the spring elections, which brought in their wake the suppression of many clubs, the government moved to reestablish municipal toll barriers for the purpose of collecting a new road tax. This provoked an outburst of resistance in southern France in which the Jacobins were plausibly singled out as the instigators. Former members of the suppressed club at Pau (Basses-Pyrénées) were accused of banding together once again in order forcibly to prevent the establishment of these toll barriers. The barriers were torn down, the town's carpenters refused to rebuild them, and the tax collectors were intimidated into resigning. At Beziers and elsewhere in the Hérault the clubs (which had managed to survive the repression) were now closed by the government, "considering that the agitation, the delay in the establishment of the barriers, the resignation of the greater number of toll collectors . . . are the fruits of the criminal maneuvers of the leaders of the constitutional circles."[45]

The clubs also took an interest in court cases dating back to the thermidorian reaction. Before Fructidor the Jacobin press had attempted to shed the light of publicity on some of the dubious proceedings against former revolutionaries. Four Jacobin activists in Metz (Moselle) went further and formed a legal aid bureau, pledging to assist their fellow citizens "who find themselves unjustly persecuted and brought before the courts" and subjected to "arbitrary measures and odious slanders." They hoped "to spare them, as much as possible, the expensive and even ruinous costs of complicated legal proceedings."[46]

Petitions denouncing the judiciary as a stronghold of reaction were common after the fructidor coup. In several places clubs tried

---

[44] A.N. F⁷ 7428, fol. 6550: letter to the Directory, 1 prairial. On the agitation of other clubs see above, Ch. IV, note 17.

[45] A.N. F⁷ 7482, fol. 573: M. of War to M. of Pol., 29 thermidor VI; A.N. AF III* 155 [Registre de délibérations: police générale] No. 496, 26 frimaire VII.

[46] Pamphlet entitled *Conseil public et correspondance générale, ou direction centrale d'affaires dépendantes des administrations quelconques . . . établi à Metz* (Impr. Verronnais [an V]) in AF III 250/Moselle. *J. hommes libres* No. 190, 25 germinal V, and No. 167, 12 brumaire VI.

to intervene in court cases as advocates of the defendants. The president of the tribunal at Dinan (Sambre-et-Meuse) taxed the local club with interference over a case before his court, and in Autun (Saône-et-Loire) a group of outraged citizens charged that the club had formed a "committee of surveillance and investigation," which intervened to secure the reopening of a case that had been closed the previous year.[47] When the militant revolutionary from Avignon, Agricole Moreau, was acquitted after a prolonged trial, the Constitutional Circle of Grenoble (Isère) hailed the verdict and presented a banner to the defendants with the inscription: "Les hommes libres de Grenoble aux Avignonais martyrs de la liberté." Presumably they had followed the case closely.[48]

While most of the clubs' remonstrances and demonstrations concerned civic matters like elections, taxes, court cases, celebrations of festivals, and reorganization of the national guard, the record indicates several other departures. The Autun Club, whose "committee of surveillance and investigation" has been mentioned, also established a "committee of conciliation" designed, according to its detractors, "to adjudicate all differences which might arise among the so-called patriots." Likewise pushing its activities into the sphere of private relations, the energetic club at Brive was accused of arrogating to itself "an inspection over domestic affairs" because it sent out commissioners to the head of a factory to protest his dismissal of three workers who were members of the Circle. The Constitutional Circle of the faubourg Antoine undertook a more sweeping campaign to secure the employment of patriotic factory workers, and it is possible that the same issue was raised by other clubs.[49]

Factory workers were not the usual constituency for the Neo-Jacobin clubs, but the republic's soldiers were. For the Jacobins the *défenseurs de la patrie* were presumptive allies whose interests had to be supported and who in turn might bolster the position of the patriotic civilian minority. Before Fructidor, groups of patriots had expressed their solidarity with the legions of the republic by means

[47] A.N. F⁷ 7369, fol. 846; président du tribunal de la police correctionel (Dinan) to M. of Pol., 13 nivôse; A.N. AF ɪɪɪ 258/Saône-et-Loire: Des vrais républicains d'Autun au Directoire, 17 floréal.

[48] *Journal des campagnes et des armées* No. 729, 1 germinal VI.

[49] A.N. AF ɪɪɪ 258/Saône-et-Loire on Autun; A.N. F⁷ 7413, fol. 4944 on Brive. On the club of the faubourg Antoine see Ch. vɪɪɪ below.

of petitions. After the coup some of the clubs seized occasions to demonstrate their enthusiasm for the soldiers, and if possible to involve them in the local struggle for freedom. To fraternize with a passing column of the triumphant Army of Italy or with a battalion of the Army of the Interior was for the clubs a political as well as a patriotic pursuit.

No club was more systematic than the Constitutional Circle of Clermont (Puy-de-Dôme) in regaling the armed force that was stationed nearby. Each of the members took charge of "one, two, or three soldiers, according to his ability"—the wealthier members being responsible for the officers, while the humbler members entertained the rank and file.[50] The clubs at Nice (Alpes-Maritimes) and Orléans (Loiret) passed beyond fraternization and sought to enlist detachments of soldiers in their running quarrels with the local municipalities. Taking up the soldiers' perennial grievances over poor quartering and provisioning, the clubs aroused them by laying this alleged mistreatment at the doorstep of those officials. In Nice the club's agitation and support goaded the commanding officer into threatening violence against the municipal officers. The town council at Orléans was no less irritated over what it took to be the club's unwarranted meddling.[51]

Running quarrels erupted into violence when the town of Laval (Mayenne) honored a passing column of the Army of Italy with an official civic banquet. The Constitutional Circle allegedly seized the moment to denounce the municipal officers and the local gendarmerie as enemies of the republic and successfully "aroused the brave soldiers of the Army of Italy to commit excesses against [these officials]." (One suspects that the club's grievances must have been impressive, or the wine terribly strong.) An analogous melee occurred in Perpignan (Pyrénées-Orientales), where the Constitutional Circle had recently been closed by order of the Directory. Trying to enlist the support of the regulars in a nearby garrison, the

---

[50] A.N. F⁷ 7405, fol. 4176: departmental commissioner (Puy-de-Dôme) to M. of Pol., 15 ventôse.

[51] Pamphlet printed by the Orléans Club: *Réunion Patriotique: A la brave Armée d'Italie* (in A.N. F⁷ 7393, fol. 2996); petitions from the club to the municipal administration, 30 pluviôse, and draft reply in F⁷ 7397, fol. 3423. On the controversy at Nice see A.N. AF III 516, plaq. 3304 and F⁷ 7318, fol. 5577: municipal administration to M. of Pol., 16 vendémiaire VI.

members of the defunct club baited certain municipal officers and provoked a brawl in which they were supported by the troops.[52]

THE VARIETY of civic activity, petitioning, and agitation described in this chapter suggests that political clubs remained the chosen instrument of democratic activists in France. Admittedly the Constitutional Circles appear as pale imitations beside the epoch-making sociétés populaires of the Year II. But in its aftermath, certain gains of the Revolution were still in question and remained to be consolidated or lost. The crisis of the Year II—and its immediate problems and consequences—had passed. The thermidorian reaction had undone many achievements as well as excesses of the democratic revolution and had decimated its staunchest advocates. Restrictions were placed on the elections and clubs through which the movement had advanced. But the constitution's strictures were ambiguous enough to allow evasion and circumvention. Accordingly, when the clubs did revive after Fructidor, they soon proved in a most significant way to be lineal descendants of the old Jacobin clubs. True to their origins they invaded the insulated world of officialdom—the very bastion of Directorial republicanism. With their committees of conciliation, deputations to the town hall, banquets and conclaves, vocal complaints about taxation, scrutiny of court cases, fraternization with the army, denunciations of "antirepublican" officials, and their endless flow of petitions to all branches of the government, the clubs continued to promote the direct participation of citizens in politics. Embodying the ideal and the practice of civisme, they were keeping alive the promise of democracy in the French Revolution.

‡ III ‡

Thus far discussion has centered on affairs in the clubs' own communities—on local issues and situations. This emphasis was consistent with the history of the original clubs, for although the sociétés populaires had been affiliated with the Paris Jacobin Club, their field of action generally stopped at the town barriers and

[52] A.N. AF III 274/Mayenne: Les Représentans du peuple (Mayenne) to Directory; A.N. F⁷ 7417, fol. 5407: M. of Interior, to M. of Pol., 15 germinal. F⁷ 7449, fol. 8661: municipal commissioner (Perpignan) to departmental commissioner, I messidor VI.

the outlying agricultural hinterland. Still, when due weight has been given to the local or "grass-roots" character of the clubs, it must be added that this orientation was never exclusive. Inevitably the sociétés populaires had become involved in regional and national affairs, and the same was true of the Constitutional Circles.

True, affiliation between clubs headed the list of proscribed practices in the new constitution, in theory leaving each club to an isolated existence. To the extent that this precluded the reemergence of a centralized apparatus controlled from Paris, it was of no consequence; the new clubs arose autonomously out of local circumstances, without looking for signals to a "mother club" in Paris. But the ban on affiliation and correspondence between clubs also seemed to foreclose cooperation among clubs within departments, and this posed a serious problem for the Neo-Jacobins. In the normalized constitutional republic, the locus of electoral politics, for one thing, simply did not stop at the town barriers. Moreover, if a prime goal of the clubs was to revive public spirit, what would be the good of "regenerating" one or two towns in a department if the rest remained hopelessly unresponsive?

In yet another respect, then, the Neo-Jacobins could not abide a rigid interpretation of the constitution. Just as they circumvented restrictions on screening members, on "collective" acts, and on petitions, so too did they elude the ban on affiliation. The problem was to establish contacts with other clubs and build an identity of interests without overtly breaking the law.

Several clubs accomplished this by means of "ambulatory visits" to distant towns and villages in their departments—a practice banned as unconstitutional by the Directory only in ventôse at about the time it prohibited the clubs' petitions. *Ambulance* has been described in detail by Marcel Reinhard as it was practiced in the Sarthe, the department where it seems to have originated and where it had an unparalleled success.[53] But the use of ambulatory visits was widely discussed in other Jacobin circles and was being adopted elsewhere before it was suppressed.

The Sarthe had at least two advantages as a springboard for clubs: its administration composed of former Jacobins, and the presence of an outspoken pro-Jacobin, General Cambray, in charge

[53] M. Reinhard, *Le Département de la Sarthe sous le régime directorial* (St. Brieuc, 1935), pp. 298-308.

of the Army of the Interior in that region. An almost legendary nemesis of counterrevolutionaries, the General had "regenerated" the Manche department before Fructidor through the use of martial law and civilian militias.[54] He was then transferred to the Sarthe, though his popularity among Jacobins in the Manche persisted to the point where the club at Valognes petitioned to have him re-assigned there.[55] Since free association was once again permitted after Fructidor, Cambray no longer had to rely exclusively on military force, but instead supported a campaign to revive political clubs.

The members of the Constitutional Circle in the chef-lieu of LeMans were the spearhead of a drive to organize throughout the department. Each décadi a cortege headed by General Cambray or another local leader would set out from LeMans and travel to a predetermined town or village, there to celebrate the décadi and to impress upon local patriots the virtues of forming their own clubs. The assembled citizens (up to three hundred strong) would enjoy a banquet, visit the town hall and the local school, plant liberty trees, and conclude the day's festivities with a mass recital of the patriotic oath. For undertaking such expeditions the LeMans Club became known as an "ambulatory circle"; eventually two or three other clubs in the Sarthe emulated LeMans.

A crucial step in this process of fraternization came several days after the visit, when the whole affair would be written up in the *Chronique de la Sarthe*, a local newspaper edited by Bazin, a leader of the LeMans société populaire in the Year II. The publicity and exhortation offered by the *Chronique* was an effective cement for holding the scattered groups together; in addition, circulation of information through the newspaper facilitated gatherings of delegates from around the department in LeMans. By ventôse these efforts had produced clubs of some sort in as many as 25 of the department's 53 cantons. Feeding on the democratic rhetoric of the *Chronique*, the clubs nonetheless tried to present a broad front publicly, and indeed were warned by the leading Jacobins to avoid "a rigorously exclusive spirit that will enervate public spirit." By all accounts the movement was enormously successful, and the Direc-

---

[54] G. Dubois, "Le Général Cambray et les administrations municipales de la Manche en l'an V," *R.F.*, XLVIII (1905), 512-33, and XLIX, 24-36.

[55] *J. hommes libres* No. 224, 9 nivôse VI. Hardly a week went by that this newspaper did not lavish praise on General Cambray.

tory found itself confronted with what amounted to an independent political party.[56]

The impact of this aggressive fraternization was not limited to the Sarthe. Word of the ambulatory activities of the LeMans Jacobins gradually spread. For their visits to the far corners of their department they were celebrated by the *Journal des hommes libres* as "troubadours of liberty"—a phrase that appeared subsequently in other Jacobin newspapers. The Jacobin press advocated the use of ambulatory visits, recognizing how they "multiplied the bonds of fraternity," brought to far-off communes a sense of unity with other patriots, and laid the groundwork for the coming elections. Jacobins in Angers, Toulouse, Marseilles, and elsewhere were told in their own newspapers how the clubs had "singularly revived public spirit" in the Sarthe. As far away as Chambéry in the Alps the "troubadours of liberty" in LeMans were held up as an example to local Jacobins.[57]

Admiration for the "civic crusades" in the Sarthe was commonplace; but launching an effective ambulatory club proved difficult in practice. It was no coincidence that the adjacent Loir-et-Cher department—to which General Cambray was also assigned—became the second place where *ambulance* developed. While this department did not enjoy the Sarthe's advantage in having a central administration or local newspaper under the control of *patriotes prononcés*, it did boast its own natural resource in the person of Pierre Nicholas Hesiné, one of France's most ardent democrats. Hesiné had thrust himself into the very center of the democratic movement during the Vendôme trial. Under the most difficult circumstances he became the defendants' advocate, publishing a newspaper to present the Babeuvist case during the trial. For his pains he was eventually imprisoned, but as a symbolic gesture of good will towards the democrats after Fructidor the Legislature

---

[56] Reinhard, *Le Département de la Sarthe*, pp. 303-304 and n. The author explains how these clubs were usually led by the local officials, who in this case were mostly Jacobins or *exclusifs*.

[57] *J. hommes libres* No. 245, 30 nivôse VI; *Tribun du Peuple* (Paris) No. 87, 1 pluviôse; *L'Indépendant* (Paris) No. 121, 1 pluviôse. *Ami des Principes* (Angers) No. 3, 6 nivôse; *Journal de Toulouse* No. 76, 2 ventôse; *Antiroyaliste* (Marseilles) No. 21, 19 pluviôse; *L'Echo des Alpes* (Chambéry) No. 62, 9 pluviôse. The suppression of *ambulance* on 17 ventôse was sharply criticized by the *Journal des hommes libres* as "disgusting" (No. 293, 18 ventôse), and by the *Journal de Toulouse* No. 87, 24 ventôse.

ordered his immediate release. Hesiné returned to Vendôme, where
he had a devoted personal following, and resumed his post as secretary to the municipality. The energy that he brought to his work
and to his political activity testified to the democrats' optimism that
Fructidor might really mark a resurrection for them.[58] With
the impetus of Hesiné's return, clubs were soon founded in the department's leading towns, Blois and Vendôme. Visiting both during
the winter, General Cambray encouraged them and established a
close rapport with Hesiné—one critic later denouncing him as
"General Cambray's secretary."[59] These two men, in turn, were in
personal contact with Police Minister Sotin whose solicitude was
undoubtedly reassuring. Writing from Blois in pluviôse, Cambray (who was actually under orders from the War Ministry)
informed Sotin unofficially of what was happening: "We are now
forming constitutional circles everywhere; there will also be ambulatory clubs a little later . . . though that is not yet what it should
be."[60]

A short time later the Blois and Vendôme clubs did begin to make
ambulatory visits to other towns. At a banquet at Vendôme on
20 pluviôse (8 February 1798)—attended, the press claimed, by eight
hundred persons—Jacobins from several communes assembled and
planned for the future. Next an ambulatory cortege visited Oucques,
where two hundred citizens assembled for a fraternal banquet after
the fashion of the Sarthe Club, and visits were subsequently arranged to some of the other clubs that dotted the department.[61]

[58] See Hesiné's account of his activities: Mémoire sur la situation politique
du département de Loir-et-Cher . . . (MS), fructidor VI in A.N. F⁷ 7436, fol.
7451. Hesiné's name appears on several petitions from the department's Constitutional Circles, and in virtually all the other documents concerning them.

[59] On the clubs at Blois and Vendôme see *Ami du Peuple* (Paris) No. 99,
8 vendémiaire VI; *J. hommes libres* No. 124, 4ème jour compl. an V; No. 143,
18 vendémiaire VI; No. 172, 17 brumaire VI; No. 182, 27 brumaire. A.N. F⁷
7366, fol. 551: Rimbault, employé à l'administration du Marehenoir to departmental commissioner (Loir-et-Cher), 5 ventôse VI, explaining how he had attended the club at Vendôme and describing its demeanor. On General Cambray's early visits to the Blois and Vendôme clubs see *J. hommes libres* Nos.
137 and 141, 12 and 16 vendémiaire VI.

[60] A.N. F⁷ 3681/3 (Loir-et-Cher), fol. "pièces examinés": Cambray to Sotin,
11 pluviôse. This dossier also contains correspondence from Hesiné and his
lieutenants to the Police Ministry.

[61] *J. hommes libres* No. 261, 16 pluviôse VI; No. 273, 28 pluviôse; No. 285,
10 ventôse; *Ami des Principes* (Angers) No. 23, 16 pluviôse.

No local newspaper existed to stimulate and chronicle these activities, but in the pages of the *Journal des hommes libres* their success was broadcast to Jacobin circles. Word spread to Orléans (Loiret), where a member of that club proposed on 18 ventôse (8 March 1798) that they ought to form ambulatory circles in the Loiret "in imitation of the constitutional circle of Blois." Reacting to this proposal enthusiastically, the club instructed the speaker to write (as an individual) to Blois for advice on how to organize ambulatory visits.[62] Ironically it was on the previous day that the clubs at LeMans, Blois, and Vendôme had been ordered closed by the Directory, which suddenly decided that *ambulance* was unconstitutional.

Before the Directory closed out this option, at least two other departments had begun to spawn ambulatory networks. From Aurillac in the Cantal the municipal commissioner exposed that club's success at *ambulance*. In pluviôse the members "had gathered on several consecutive sundays [sic?] with one circle after another in different cantons of the department, where even members from circles in neighboring departments betook themselves." The example that he gave (a visit to the town of Pleaux) resembled the expeditions of the Sarthe ambulatory club, featuring a march through the town out to a faubourg where a banquet and a meeting were held. The Constitutional Circle of Mauriac, the other principal town in the Cantal, also undertook ambulatory visits until the decree of 17 ventôse (7 March 1798) prohibited these sorties.[63]

Operating out of Brive, another ambulatory club visited at least four communes in the month of pluviôse, and in addition arranged a successful conclave on the 30th of that month (18 February 1798) for delegates from Corrèze and proximate parts of Lot and Dordogne. These activities prompted varying reactions. To the pro-Jacobin deputy Marbot (who was evidently in close touch with the club) their exertions warranted special praise, and this he lavished on them in a speech to the Council of Elders. "Distances are nothing for patriots," he intoned; "ambulatory constitutional circles have recently been formed in the departments of Corrèze, Lot and Dordogne; the patriots travel 10, 20, 30 leagues without calculating

---

[62] A.N. F⁷ 7364, fol. 374: report headed "Cercle constitutionnel d'Orléans, séance du 18 ventôse," and other letters.

[63] A.N. F⁷ 7418, fol. 5436: municipal commissioner (Aurillac) to M. of Pol., 4 prairial; Constitutional Circle of Mauriac to M. of Pol., 10 germinal; municipal commissioner (Mauriac) to M. of Pol., 5 germinal.

the remoteness, and people from all around come to see and hear them." For the Directory's commissioners, on the other hand, the club's success gradually produced qualms and began to take on "exclusivist" coloration.[64] One man's patriotism was another's factionalism. Had the Directors seen the imposing petition that the assembled delegates addressed to the Legislature they might have been further discomfited. For while it contained no subversive propositions, its tone and rhetoric recalled bygone festivals-of-federation and offered an independent brand of enthusiasm that the Directory had ceased to tolerate.[65] In any case the Brive organization was the final network of ambulatory clubs to wither under the Directory's blows at the end of ventôse.[66]

In at least four departments, then (Sarthe, Loir-et-Cher, Cantal, Corrèze) did the larger clubs systematically make ambulatory visits to smaller towns and villages. But these were by no means the only clubs attempting to "regenerate" more benighted areas and to fraternize with brothers who lived outside the cities. The clubs at Dijon, Poitiers, Metz, Versailles, Caen, and Dôle all tried in various ways to stimulate patriotic activity and political consciousness in other corners of their departments.[67] Local Jacobin newspapers in

[64] Marbot's remarks in *Moniteur*, 22 pluviôse (p. 572) and correction, 27 pluviôse (p. 590); A.N. F⁷ 7413, fol. 4944: municipal commissioner (Brive) to M. of Pol., 1 germinal; F⁷ 7406, fol. 4282: departmental commissioner (Corrèze) to M. of Pol., 15 germinal.

[65] A.N. C431, fol. 167: Des Républicains du cantons de Brive, Turenne, L'Arche, Meusac, Beyrac, Curemont, Beaulieu, Conzenai, Massac, Agen, St. Robert, Tulle, Ségur-et-Serviers (département de la Corrèze); Terrasson, Lacassagne, Solignac (département de la Dordogne); Martet-et-Souillac (département du Lot) to Council of 500, 1 ventôse VI. The petition concerned the disfranchising of counterrevolutionaries.

[66] No doubt other clubs made occasional forays into the countryside, without the organization of the ambulatory circles: E.g., the club at Chateau-Gontier (Mayenne): *J. hommes libres* No. 264, 19 pluviôse VI.

[67] See L. Hugueny, *Les Clubs Dijonnais sous la Révolution* (Dijon, 1905), p. 232; R. Doucet, *L'Esprit public dans le département de la Vienne pendant la Révolution* (Paris, 1910), p. 349; *Journal des Amis* (Metz) Nos. 78 and 85, 6 and 20 ventôse VI; A.N. AF iii 262/ Seine-et-Oise: report headed "éspirit public—Challan" and A.N. F⁷ 7410, fol. 4689: copy of a broadside entitled *Echo du Cercle Constitutionnel de Versailles* (Impr. Locard fils); F⁷ 7415, fol. 5227: *Aux Habitans de Calvados, par le cercle constitutionnel de Caen* (Caen, an VI); F⁷ 7417, fol. 5361: *Les Républicains membres du cercle constitutionnel*

Moulins, Evreux, Toulouse, Marseilles, Perigueux, and Metz contributed to such efforts by allowing a frequent exchange of information. In Puy-de-Dôme, where there was no Jacobin journal, a central committee was formed, composed of delegates from the department's clubs as well as other citizens from communes without clubs. This central committee allegedly set up an executive bureau to process information and denunciations received from all over the department.[68] Here was one case, though, in which the laws against affiliation were being flagrantly violated; most other clubs managed their fraternization and coordination more delicately.

The usual culmination of a successful fraternization and propagandizing campaign within a department was some sort of conclave in which delegates (or citizens) would assemble at the cheflieu. In the flush of enthusiasm, however, some of the clubs opened themselves to charges of illegal operations. This was the case in Dordogne, where the Jacobins held important departmental offices as they did in the Sarthe and were evidently tempted into overreaching themselves. In planning an elaborate gathering, the Perigueux Club was indiscreet enough to use printed broadsides inviting delegates from other clubs "to fraternize as free men." The Constitutional Circles in various parts of the department further disseminated the information "to a recognized republican in each canton" who was to solicit participants; these in turn would be cleared by the Constitutional Circles before they set out for Perigueux.[69] Similarly, as the elections approached, a number of clubs prepared to use the official gathering of electors in the department's chef-lieu for a kind of party caucus that would precede or parallel the electoral assembly's sessions.[70] In sum, while few Constitutional Circles matched the LeMans ambulatory club in forging a department-wide party machine, some of the larger ones rec-

---

de Dôle, à leurs frères les habitans des autres communes du Jura (Besançon, an VI).

[68] A.N. F⁷ 7405, fol. 4176: departmental commissioner (Puy-de-Dôme) to M. of Pol., 15 ventôse VI.

[69] A.N. C531, fol. Dordogne: broadside headed "Perigueux, 25 pluviôse," and letters exchanged with members of the Ciprien-sur-Dordogne Club, 7 ventôse. On the Jacobin cadres in Dordogne, see H. Labroue, *L'Esprit public en Dordogne pendant la Révolution* (Paris, 1911), pp. 152-56.

[70] See Ch. ix, below.

ognized this as a primary goal and pursued it with varying degrees of vigor and ingenuity.

‡ IV ‡

Direct contacts among the clubs in general (as distinct from the liaisons of clubs *within* departments) were relatively rare and unimportant. Thus, when the Dôle (Jura) Club needed a printer it used the presses of P. J. Briot, who was also president of the Besançon Club in neighboring Doubs. Or, when the Valenciennes Club had printed Lequinio's speech on the anniversary of the king's death, it mailed out copies to other clubs—accompanied by a sheet bearing Rousseau's epigraph: "Soyons hommes et citoyens jusqu'au dernier soupir!" (At Perpignan, where the Constitutional Circle had been banned in the interim, the parcel was seized by the authorities.)[71] Besides this type of casual contact, a flow of mail undoubtedly passed between individual club members and friends in Paris. A few cases on record document what was surely a widespread practice of reading such letters at club meetings; pro-Jacobin deputies, like Marbot, Lamarque, and Gay-Vernon, clearly maintained such liaisons with some of the clubs.[72] This exchange of information and opinion, while certainly important in neutralizing the sense of isolation that the clubbists must have suffered, was still a long way from representing a system of affiliation uniting the clubs.

But if direct contacts among the clubs were incidental and occasional, there existed a kind of affiliation that linked them indirectly.

[71] The Dôle pamphlet (*op.cit.*) bears the imprimateur: A Besançon, de l'imprimérie de Briot. Briot's career is discussed in M. Dayet, *Un Révolutionnaire Franc-Comptois, Pierre-Joseph Briot* (Paris, 1960), p. 63 *et passim*. The documents on the correspondence between Valenciennes and Perpignan are in A.N. F⁷ 7398, fol. 3494.

[72] See F. Lamarque, *Lettre . . . à son collègue P.G. sur la cloture du cercle constitutionnel de Perigueux . . .* (Impr. Baudouin, germinal VI) in which this deputy defends the club's activities and protests against the censorship of his mail to and from Perigueux. A.N. F⁷ 6174, dossier 458 (plaq. 2): letter to Reubell from a correspondent in Nantes, 10 brumaire VI, reporting that "antigovernment" opinions were expressed in letters from two deputies that were read to the club by members who had received them. B.N. Mss (nouv. acq. fran.) No. 21700, Gautherot Papers, for correspondence between Gautherot in Paris and his friends in the Auxerre (Yonne) Club.

Through the Jacobin press, autonomous, locally oriented clubs were able to exchange information and cultivate a sense of solidarity. In their favored newspapers they became aware of each other's existence and of the identity of interest that they shared no matter what their local circumstances.[73]

The Jacobin press had barely survived the pre-Fructidor reaction and was one of the coup's most direct beneficiaries. Existing Jacobin papers were temporarily freed of the endless abuse directed against them by other newspapers, since the coup banned the most reactionary ones. In addition a score of Jacobin publicists was able to establish new journals, a number of which survived the financial pitfalls of publishing, though not the Directory's ultimate distaste for independent journalism. Several papers remained on the brink of insolvency throughout their existence and were forced to solicit subsidies from the government, thereby losing a measure of their independence. But the editors of such papers (the *Indépendant*, the *Ami de la Patrie*, the *Journal des campagnes et des armées*), while generally supporting the government, still managed to encourage new departures and to oppose the government's anti-Jacobinism.

Each constituent of the Jacobin press—including about fifteen provincial and fifteen Parisian journals—was of course autonomous. Nonetheless a far greater spirit of cooperation than of competition seems to have prevailed among them. In effect they formed a

[73] The following remarks are based upon research in the Parisian and provincial Jacobin press (for titles and other information see the Note on Sources and Bibliography); documents concerning the *Journal des hommes libres* and its editors (see Appendix IV); and material on the Directory's surveillance of the press (especially A.N. F⁷ 3449-53 and A.N. AF III 45). The secondary literature on the revolutionary press (e.g., Deschiens, Gallois, Hatin, Goncourt, LePoittevin, and Tourneux) has almost nothing to say about the Jacobin press after 1795. However, a good general introduction is provided by A. Soderhjelm, *Le Régime de la Presse pendant la Révolution française* (Helsingfors, 1901), Vol. II. Albert Mathiez made a reconnaissance of the Directory's manipulations of the press in "Le Bureau politique du Directoire," *Le Directoire*, pp. 356-74. This essay is based primarily on carton AF III 45, and concerns those journals subsidized by the Directory; it has little to say about the Jacobin press, and in some particulars (i.e., its comments on the *Indépendant*) tends to be hasty and misleading. The study of the press has recently been revitalized by Jacques Godechot and some of his students. His methods of assessing a newspaper's readership by analyzing the sources of letters to the editor and news items are summarized in "The Origin of Mass Communications Media," *Gazette*, VIII (1962), 81-87.

guild among themselves, known to each other, sympathetic to each other's difficulties, and united in a common orientation. Moreover, it is clear that there was a preeminent leader, a kind of *pater familias* of Jacobin publishers and editors, in René Vatar and his *Journal des hommes libres.*

Vatar's significance as a focal point for dispersed democrats during the early months of the Directory and the period of the Babeuf trial has already been discussed; it has been explained how his publishing background, connections with prominent democrats, and ideological commitment combined to make him a figure of unparalleled importance, even if his role was played behind the scenes. To knowledgeable friends and enemies alike, however, Vatar's position was well understood and he remained "The advocate-and-chief of the anarchists" (as his antagonist Poultier put it) until Bonaparte deported him. In 1798 Vatar's involvement with the Jacobin resurgence was direct in his own 10th arrondissement club, and all-encompassing in his newspaper. The experience and financial leverage provided by his publishing and bookselling operation enabled him to endure frequent persecutions, and to enjoy a relatively wide circulation. From this position he cultivated his connections with the other Jacobin journalists, both Parisian and provincial.

Systematically exchanging publications and maintaining personal contacts with them, he openly came to their defense when they ran into difficulties with the authorities. (The journalists that he defended at one time or another included Bazin of the *Chronique de la Sarthe*, Ballois of the *Observateur de la Dordogne*, Touquet of the *Bulletin de l'Eure*, Latapy of the *Courrier de la Gironde*, Trotebas of the *Observateur démocrate* and the *Journal des Amis* [Metz], and in Paris, Errard of the *Révélatuer*, Coesnon-Pellerin of the *Ami de la Patrie*, Leclerc of the *Tableau politique*; Bescher of the *Défenseur de la Vérité*.)

Scrutiny of the *Journal des hommes libres* reveals how the other Jacobin newspapers fed its columns with local news. Conversely, and more important, the *Journal des hommes libres* was probably the most basic source of information and opinion for the provincial editors. Excerpts from it—sometimes acknowledged and sometimes verbatim but unacknowledged—appeared in virtually every Jacobin newspaper in the Year VI, from the militant *Tribun du Peuple* in Paris (which borrowed shamelessly) to Marc-Antoine Jullien's

Courier de l'Armée d'Italie in distant Milan. At one time or another most of the Jacobin papers found themselves stigmatized as the "acolytes" or the "faithful echos" of Vatar's newspaper. The stark testimony of at least one Jacobin editor underscores how dependent they were on this lifeline from Paris. Defending before the authorities in Metz a controversial article that he had published, an editor of the outspoken *Journal des Amis* explained that in any case "he was only copying the *Journal des hommes libres* which had announced the existence of the plot . . . and whose editors were *patriotes prononcés*."[74]

This nationally circulating newspaper was a clearinghouse for information about the Neo-Jacobin movement. By way of the provincial Jacobin newspapers a certain amount of information about the clubs came to Paris and was in turn disseminated throughout the country. But this was only a secondary source of such news. Far more important for Vatar was direct communication from individuals in the provinces writing to inform his editors about local conditions, especially the progress or frustrations of their clubs, and to publicize the denunciations discussed earlier. During the Directory years there is scarcely an important town in France that did not have some correspondent who wrote to the editors and who presumably subscribed to the newspaper. Communications from provincial correspondents were either printed in full as letters to the editor, or summarized (usually in combination with other items) as news stories, sometimes accompanied by editorial commentary. The overall effect was to establish a reciprocal relation between newspaper and clubs; in effect the *Journal des hommes libres* was the organ of the clubs, open and accessible to their views and to their use.[75] But more than simply serving as a forum for the exchange of informa-

---

[74] Archives Municipales de Metz, 21¹/20: Extrait des registres des délibérations de l'administration central du département de la Moselle, 18 pluviôse VI. See, e.g., A.N. AF III 45: rapport sur *L'Indépendant*; A.N. F¹ᶜ III, Seine/19: report by Bureau Central on the press, 12 prairial; Aulard, *Paris*, IV, 716; F⁷ 3452: report on the *Eveil des Républicains* (Gers).

[75] Examples of clubs openly identifying with the *Journal des hommes libres* may be found in F⁷ 7417, fol. 5361 (Dôle); F⁷ 7430/b, fol. 6771 (Villefranche); F⁷ 3688/13, "dossier secrète" (club of the 11th arrondissement in Paris); F⁷ 7413, fol. 4960—in which it was reported that the club at Auch (Gers) "proposed that they read only the *Journal des hommes libres* and that they burn the *Ami des Lois*," which had attacked the former.

CHAPTER VI

The Democratic Persuasion:
Attitudes and Issues

B Y MANY standards Neo-Jacobinism was not cohesive. A collection of local groups in urban or quasi-urban settings, it represented no single economic, regional, ethnic, or class interest. Affiliated only through the informal ties of the democratic press, the new clubs boasted neither a centralized party apparatus nor any recognized national leaders. Moreover, there was available to the Neo-Jacobins no distinctive body of inherited doctrine or single document that could unite them in an explicit public position. But Neo-Jacobins did share a persuasion: "a broad judgment of public affairs informed by common sentiments and beliefs."[1] And in articulating this persuasion they were attempting to reopen significant questions about the republic's future.

Obviously the attitudes of sans-culottes, former Montagnard functionaries, and bourgeois journalists varied in certain particulars and implications. In 1793 such differences had been of capital importance, setting the Paris sections against the Paris Jacobin Club. At some future date (especially with the rise of an industrial proletariat) differences would again loom large, causing democrats to fragment into more clearly defined and conflicting groups. But in the aftermath of revolution and reaction, Neo-Jacobinism stood as a minimal synthesis of democratic aspirations, which tentatively drew together middle-class Jacobins and politically conscious sans-culottes. No matter how much their interests and motivations varied, they shared a commitment to certain values, and a disposition to view certain issues in similar ways.

In its most developed form the democratic persuasion may be found in several all but forgotten books written between 1797 and 1799. In a full and even systematic fashion these essays attempted to examine the state of the commonwealth from the democratic perspective. Together they provide a substantial insight into the surviving elements of democratic thought during the Directory. By

---

[1] This formulation I owe to Marvin Meyers, *The Jacksonian Persuasion: Politics and Belief* (Vintage edn., N. Y., 1960), pp. 10 and vii.

ignoring them one is erroneously led to believe that the democratic-revolutionary tradition jumps directly from Robespierre to Babeuf and Buonarroti. Actually, between these familiar landmarks, the writings of such men as M. J. Satur, Guy Chaumont-Quitry, Marc-Antoine Jullien, and E. G. Lenglet resynthesized and perpetuated the assumptions of Robespierrist or Jacobin democracy, without making Babeuf's leap to communism.

A review of the democrats' assumptions (especially as measured against representative conservative spokesmen) provides a background for examining the kinds of issues that democrats raised in one way or another during the Directory years. This consideration of issues will constitute the second, and lengthier, section of the present chapter. Altogether, this survey will assess the legacy of the democratic revolution after the periods of crisis and extreme reaction had passed. It will focus on the Year VI, when the democratic persuasion was transformed into a movement for reform within a conservative republic.

‡ I ‡

Discontented with the tone and direction that the revolutionary experiment had assumed under the Directory, the Neo-Jacobins constituted an embryonic party of movement, anxious to revive the momentum of revolution without its violence. Their more speculative writing tended therefore to be alternately bitter and optimistic about the state of the republic, but it was surprisingly free of abstraction. Their inspiration was the telescoped epoch of the previous decade. For its more educated advocates the democratic persuasion may have had roots in the Enlightenment, but these were secondary compared to its roots in yesterday's history.

While all republicans—conservative or democratic—were heirs of 1789, they disagreed emphatically about the "second revolution" of 1792-94. Conservative Frenchmen judged the results a disastrous interlude of demagoguery, social upheaval, and pillage—all of which they summarized as "anarchy." To the Jacobin minority this period presented a positive image that was part of their heritage. By a selective, somewhat sentimentalized, reading of recent history the Neo-Jacobins had a standard by which they found the present regime wanting on a variety of counts. They looked back to the days of the egalitarian revolution and sought to disinter its achievements, spirit, and promises from the excesses that had marred it. Keeping references to the Year II vague, they tried to free the substance from the factional politics and personalities whose memory had yet to be exorcised.[2]

In one of the most searching and original critiques of the Directory regime, M. J. Satur penned a remarkable tribute to the efforts of the democratic revolution. One by one he recalled the federations, the Paris Commune, the popular societies, the *levée en masse,* the committees of surveillance, the Revolutionary Tribunal, and the *Maximum.* Aware of their mixed blessings, of their ambiguities and ultimate failures, he nonetheless concluded: "all those circumstances together or successively identified the national spirit to the nation—and did so by a bond other than vanity. The people were proud to govern, they believed themselves on the same level as their officials; they believed they could march forward."[3]

Much in the same vein were the observations of Guy Chaumont-Quitry, a former aristocrat turned democrat. In a bitter indictment of the Directory, published after the *journée* of 30 prairial when optimism for the last time infused the Jacobin ranks, Chaumont-Quitry tried to summarize the essence of the egalitarian revolution; he sought to define "the constant index of republican vigor" that

---

[2] Despite their differences in 1793, representative democrats now generally agreed that (a) the revolutionary government had had its shortcomings; (b) its intentions had been pure. The *Journal des hommes libres,* whose publisher had been the official printer for the Committee of Public Safety, put it this way: "Le Comité de salut public blessait sans cesse la liberté; mais ne la gangrenait pas." Not only did it save France militarily, but "il força les hommes d'être probes. La corruption était presque inconnue . . . il ne prodiguait les richesses que pour créer des moyens de destruction contre nos ennemis." (No. 5, 5 messidor VII.) By contrast, the writers grouped around the *Démocrate* in the Year VII (see Ch. xiii below) were mainly of "hébertist" background. They recalled that the Cordeliers Club had opposed the law of 14 frimaire, which gave such great powers to the Committee of Public Safety, and the abridgment of popular freedom and initiative that followed. Yet they now labeled those policies as "error" rather than "crime." The men who ran the revolutionary government at least "pensaient de bonne foi atteindre à leur fin par de pareils moyens, et cette fin était le bonheur de l'humanité." (*Le Démocrate* Nos. 27 and 29, 12 and 14 fructidor VII; *Ennemi des Tyrans* [new title] No. 56, 10 vendémiaire VIII.)

[3] M. J. Satur, *Les Préjugés constitutionnels de l'an VI, digression sérieuse et nécessaire sur la liberté politique* (Impr. Logerot, an VII), B.N. Lb42/1998, pp. 22-23. I have been unable to find any biographical information about this author.

had marked the triumphs of the Year II. And he found it in the civic-mindedness (civisme) of the people, and in "that general modesty of fortune" that obtained at the time, which was the best way "to assure the effectiveness of political equality"—a theme that is to be encountered in Satur's work also. Chaumont-Quitry went on to recall the austere days when the nation-in-arms stripped itself of frills and luxury, and concluded on virtually the same note as Satur, anxious not to turn the clock back to that trying period, but simply to impart a just appreciation of its triumphs. "Whatever the bloody images may have been that flowed out of that epoch, let us admit that it was splendid and that it will cause French honor to be forever memorable. At that time—hardly any selfish motives, hardly any great fortunes."[4]

In Neo-Jacobin rhetoric the ideal of civisme—"national spirit" and "republican vigor"—was exalted; its antithesis was described in terms like "vanity" and "selfish motives." The achievement of the Year II was seen as the triumph of civic-mindedness over individual self-interest. This in turn was related to two specific changes: first, the development of political equality and the consequent popular participation in the governing process; second, the attempt to curb the extremes of wealth and poverty. The public spirit of a nation, its political institutions, and its economic life were integrally linked; if the state failed to mediate or neutralize the thrust of individual interest, then democracy would be impossible.

At least one astute conservative recognized this central thread of the democratic critique. Unlike most men of his persuasion, Edouard Lefebvre did not rely on invective to portray the opposition; in a book published in 1798 this apologist for the bourgeois republic took the Left's measure with a combination of insight and graciousness. Indeed, Lefebvre even granted them the honorable label of "democrats," and refrained from belaboring them as exagérés or anarchists.

With more than a passing nod in his *Political and Moral Considerations on the French Republic* the author acknowledged the

---

[4] Guy Chaumont-Quitry, *Essai sur les causes qui, depuis le 18 fructidor, devaient consolider la République en France: et sur celles qui ont failli la faire périr* (Impr. Vatar-Jouannet, an VII), B.N. Lb42/2393, pp. 36, 38. Cf. *L'Indépendant* (Paris) No. 334, 14 fructidor VI, "Démocrate et Demagogue sont deux."

democrats' idealism and the outward attractiveness of their views which stemmed, he conceded, from their love of mankind. Far from being an isolated group of demagogues or criminals, they had many partisans in France and in Europe. Their ranks, he correctly observed, were filled principally with artisans who came out of their workshops to enter public life. Consequently he argued that there was no warrant or need to persecute these citizens; for just as a river settles back into its bed after a tempest, so will these artisans gradually return to their workshops.[5]

But if the proponents of democracy ought not to be persecuted, the writer continued, their ideas must be decisively rejected, and France must undergo no further democratization. Though it may be attractive in theory, democratization is simply unsuitable to the customs and habits of the French people. Shifting now to the conservative argument, Lefebvre maintained that France cannot be expected to pass immediately from the "slavery" of the *ancien régime* to democracy, since the necessary spirit of patriotism is insufficiently developed. Specifically, the French are "un peuple libre marchand" whose attachment to government and state necessarily derives from *self-interest*. France is a commercial country where liberty must contribute to the advancement of commerce if it is to have a secure foundation. From this perspective the democrats' point of view is a brand of wishful thinking. They cherish freedom too passionately without understanding its foundation; in effect they have things backwards, believing that everything, "including the arts, commerce, and manufacturing" must be subordinate to liberty. Thus they envisage a "purer" social bond than mere self-interest— but they are mistaken. For if self-interest is not the "purest" of social bonds, it is nonetheless the most realistic and appropriate to France's condition. And when this principle is grasped, other controversial issues will be resolved—notably, the place of luxury and opulence in society will be granted, and indeed it will be recognized that luxury and opulence are *necessary*, however much this may conflict with democratic idealism.[6]

[5] Edouard Lefebvre, *Considérations politiques et morales sur la France constituée en république* (Chez Bertrand, an VI), B.N. Lb42/1897, pp. 206-209. This book was listed at A. M. Cécile's *Tableau historique littéraire, et politique de l'an VI de la République* (Impr. de Valade), p. 292; Lefebvre is identified as a member of the Société libre des sciences, belles lettres.

[6] Lefebvre, *Considérations politiques*, pp. 16-19.

No book on either side of the question better pinpointed the essence of the democratic persuasion and its practical implications than Edouard Lefebvre's critique. But his work is far from unique in revealing the conservatives' concern over commercial freedom and private property, and in emphasizing that the crux of the argument involved the principle of self-interest. Several texts illustrate Edouard Lefebvre's brief that the democrats rejected "self-interest" as the binding social tie in their quest for a "purer" bond, and secondly, that they did not rate the advancement of commerce or the defense of private property as the paramount imperative of the state.

M. J. Satur took his stand precisely on this point as he expounded principles that would have been anathema to Lefebvre. To begin with, however, Satur thought it necessary to dissociate himself from the stigma of Babeuvism, and to this end he rejected the "errors" of extremism which conservatives were always imputing to the Jacobins. But Satur's disavowal of communism, the agrarian law, and direct democracy was in the form of stating that such concepts had always been recognized as chimerical and had never constituted a real threat to anything. What France genuinely had to fear was "an error that grips society much more tightly, an error that corrodes society through its *mores*." What was this stark threat to the well-being of the commonwealth? Simply "self-interest considered as the deliberate motive of all our actions." In Satur's view this self-interest was the favored "principle and sentiment" of the educated segment of the population before Fructidor; unfortunately it continued to prevail, along with the corruption that came in its wake. Translated into political terms this implied that "egoism" was not only the great sin of royalists and reactionaries who had been driven underground by the Directory in Fructidor, but was the attribute of the educated conservatives who constituted the Directorial establishment itself. As a consequence the French people generally found themselves squeezed "between the power of riches which dispenses money and work, and the authority of the government [which dispenses] sophisms."[7]

[7] M.J.S., *Correspondance trouvé dans le porte-feuille d'un jeune patriote assassiné sur la route de Paris* (Chez Leroux, an VI), B.N. Lb42/524, pp. 10-11, 42. (Attributed to Satur in G. Walter's *Catalogue*.)

Men like Satur taxed the conservatives with a nexus of attitudes and policies that the conservatives willingly defended. Former moderates, federalists, or turnabout Montagnards who had suffered under the popular revolution, the conservatives retained an uncompromising attitude about the role of the educated propertied elite in running a country. With this came a conviction that reform and innovation tended to get out of hand and to menace property rights, which they regarded as the cornerstone of individual liberty. Hence they preferred a government of elaborate checks and balances in which direct intervention and participation by the people would be minimal. In effect wealth would be protected by political institutions and prerogatives. All of this was seen by conservatives as the necessary foundation for a truly open society, with liberty and opportunity for all citizens. In the democrats' view, however, they were fostering oligarchy.

Democrats detected a relationship between an overemphatic insistence on the sanctity of property rights and a tendency towards oligarchy in the public utterances of Benjamin Constant. One of the bourgeois republic's most articulate spokesmen, Constant was, like Mme. de Staël, an advocate of individual liberty, but in other respects a conservative. Since he enjoyed the patronage of prominent citizens like Barras, and of France's eminent conservative organ, the *Moniteur*, a speech that he gave in ventôse was widely publicized and has become for historians a classic exposition of the Directory's anti-Jacobinism.

The better part of Constant's speech was a bitter attack against an unspecified "anarchist" opposition. Not only did he lay the horrors of the Year II at their doorstep, but he argued that the anarchists had changed for the worse since then: "With all your crimes you are not terrorists, you are merely criminals." To these "maladroit clamourers of distorted declamations" he would not grant sincere motives let alone acceptable aims. "Ils reclament la haine des aristocrates pour calomnier l'indignation des hommes de bien," he added, ironically underscoring the Jacobins' contention that the "homme de bien" was often a new kind of aristocrat. But this invective was only the introduction to Constant's message. "All interests," he warned his audience, "are grouped around property. The slightest blow against it will resound in all parts of the empire;

whoever dispossesses the rich menaces the poor; whoever pro-scribes opulence, conspires against modest fortune."[8]

In coupling an attack on democrats with an extreme apotheosis of property rights, Constant provoked an open polemical clash that revealed the Neo-Jacobin's predilections. The *Journal des hommes libres* took the lead in rebutting "the young Swiss orator of the salons and professor of oligarchy." Equally outraged, the *Journal des campagnes et des armées* ran two items in response. The first was in the form of a poem whose theme was that in attacking so-called factions of anarchists, Constant was merely masking his own reactionary intentions—the standard Jacobin response to what might be called Jacobin-baiting. A few days later an article "On Benja-min Constant's Discourse" examined the implications of his speech, whose danger was seen less in what it stated than "in what it insinu-ated." As the article explained, Constant attacked "terrorists and exagérés," scoffed at the threat of royalism and then introduced his formula for what distinguished a "true republican": namely, "his zeal in defending property." This, according to the writer, was "a mutilated and perfidious" formula. Defending property rights in a republic is necessary, but scarcely sufficient; it is certainly not the characteristic quality of a republican, for such zeal is frequently found among the declared enemies of liberty who nonetheless stoutly defend property. The real criticism of Constant is that he "clearly designates the wealthy class as the eminently republican class that is particularly destined to fill public functions—a marvelous principle for giving our republic a violent impulsion towards aristocracy." With the *Journal des hommes libres*, this article concluded that Constant was in effect a "fauteur d'une olygarchie française."[9]

Fear of a new aristocracy was central in the democratic persua-sion. The volatile revolutionary mentality of the Year II had sub-sided, but its legacy in a less perilous day was an abiding hatred of the "egoists." Consequently the ritualistic denunciations of aris-

---

[8] Benjamin Constant, "Discours prononcé au cercle constitutionnel [de la Rue de Lille] le 9 ventôse an 6," *Moniteur*, 21 and 22 ventôse (pp. 686, 690). The club in question was the conservative club of the Hôtel de Salm. This speech is cited by A. Meynier, *Le 22 floréal an VI et le 30 prairial an VII* (Paris, 1928), pp. 32-35, and G. Lefebvre, *Le Directoire*, p. 124.

[9] *J. hommes libres* No. 300, 25 ventôse VI; also No. 166, 11 brumaire VI. *Journal des campagnes et des armées* (Paris) Nos. 708 and 723, 20 and 25 ventôse VI; *Ibid*. No. 732, 4 germinal VI.

tocracy made by the Directory itself were inadequate—such strictures being aimed merely against the émigrés and the old hereditary nobility. Sieyès' proposal to strip the latter of its citizenship was endorsed with ferocious relish by some of the clubs, but this hardly appeased their qualms about aristocracy.[10] For as the *Journal des Amis* of Metz declared: "the party of the aristocracy . . . is that of the grandees, the nobles, the priests, and the rich egoists who detest the people." And the "aristocracy of great wealth," in Satur's words, "was the hardest, the most real, and the most difficult to displace of all aristocracies."[11]

The Jacobin critique of the incipient middle-class aristocracy was all encompassing: It was seen as a threat to the economic well-being of the population, the political freedom of the citizenry, and the moral fiber of the republic. Not only did the "egoists" perpetuate the extremes of wealth and poverty, but in defense of their depredations they bred class hatred and suspicion. According to the *Indépendant*, the aristocrats "erect a barrier between the rich and the poor by painting the second as partisans of the agrarian law, as the born enemy of the rich—seeing as he has no gold. For him, the rich are everything, the poor nothing." At bottom the Jacobin critique held that the "egoists'" interests and attitudes promoted social disintegration.[12]

[10] Sieyès, the consummate middle-class elitist, pursued his vendetta against the old Second Estate by urging that former nobles be proscribed once and for all. (Lefebvre, *Le Directoire*, pp. 99-100 and Meynier, *Le 22 floréal*, pp. 6-7, comment with appropriate cynicism on this demarche.) The Directory was unenthusiastic (Barras, *Memoirs*, III, 70-71), but agreed to this compromise in frimaire VI: former nobles would be reduced to the status of foreigners and consequently deprived of political rights unless they went through naturalization procedures. Exceptions were granted in principle to anyone who had proven his loyalty to the republic by holding civil or military office. Since the method of applying these exemptions was never worked out, the law remained a dead letter. Numerous club petitions supported such action against "those maniacal oppressors," "conspirators," "those spoiled people . . . that insolent and proud caste." (A.N. C426, fols. 96-98.)

[11] *Journal des Amis* (Metz) No. 87, 24 ventôse VI; Satur, *Les Prejugées constitutionnels*, summary of Ch. IV; Chaumont-Quitry, *Essai sur les causes*, pp. 74-75.

[12] *L'Indépendant* No. 214, 4 floréal VI. The *Journal des campagnes et des armées* No. 703, 5 ventôse VI, made the same complaint in reference to education and manners; that is, it complained about the tendency of the *bien élèves* to distinguish "two classes of republicans"—themselves, and the uneducated populace.

The palpable symbol of this social disintegration was the extravagant opulence allegedly flaunted by rich "egoists." Armed with arguments from the eighteenth-century debate over luxury, Neo-Jacobin intellectuals could marshal their arguments around this central image. Unfettered, arrogant luxury exemplified for them the nexus of "egoism" in which public spirit was eroded in the name of self-interest. "Political liberty and the wise economics of public welfare suffer equally the luxury and the aristocracy of great wealth," wrote Satur. "How can one justify luxury in a system of justice that wishes to maintain the enjoyment of private life, without enfeebling the ties of public life and its virtues?"[13]

The term "egoist" was the Jacobin's counterpart to the label of "anarchist" that had been tied to them. Stripped of polemical excess, and interpreted in relation to questions of public policy, "egoists" and "anarchists" become conservatives and democrats. For the democrats, true political liberty was affronted by the extremes of wealth and poverty which constituted both a menace and a challenge to the republic. But underlying both the economic and political institutions of the nation was the nature of its social bonds and public spirit. Self-interest as the democrats saw it was too easily translated into "insolent luxury" and political oligarchy.

The antidote to these interconnected evils lay in "democratic institutions." Summarizing a decade of history in which the Jacobins had sought to translate this ideal into policy, the Parisian journalist Publicola Chaussard succinctly explained the two things meant by democracy. In the first place, democratic institutions were "those which, without violating the principles of our constitution, tend to restore to the people the rights that they are able to exercise themselves, without danger to the public interest."[14] It goes without saying that the chief instrumentality for this was the political club. More generally, this represented an optimistic view about the participation of citizens in government and about "enthusiasm." As

[13] Satur, *Les Prejugées constitutionnels*, Ch. IV, *passim* and esp. p. 68. Cf. *Défenseur de la Vérité* (Paris) No. 54, 12 vendémiaire VI.

[14] Publicola Chaussard, *Coup d'Oeil sur l'intérieur de la République française, ou esquisse des principes d'une Révolution morale* (Impr. Moutardier, an VII), B.N. Lb42/2475, pp. 19-21. Chaussard had worked at the War Ministry during the Terror. As a journalist he wrote for several newspapers including the *Décade philosophique*. In 1799 he was prominent in the Club du Manège in Paris.

another pro-Jacobin intellectual put it in a book that was virtually an electoral platform for the Year VI: "One might say that representative government is the natural domain of petitions, discussions, clubs, newspapers, civic banquets, political parties, and polemical disputes. Out of this turbulence wisdom emerges; from all these elements liberty is nurtured."[15]

Secondly, according to Chaussard's quintessential summary, democratic institutions are "those whose effect will be to diminish the inequality of wealth [*jouissances*, lit. use or possession] and to give a politic direction to riches and luxury." The effect of such measures would be, in the author's opinion, "to maintain the spirit of equality and of simplicity, which in turn maintain the love of virtue and fatherland."[16]

‡ II ‡

Democratic institutions, as Publicola Chaussard envisaged them, would not violate the constitution. Jacobins might regret the abandonment of unicameralism and universal suffrage, which had been promised in their constitutional draft of 1793. But in practice they could carry on within the less congenial pattern of checks and balances, indirect elections, and restrictive suffrage forced upon them by the Directorial constitution. As the crisis mentality of the Terror abated, the Jacobins became constitutionalists; when conservatives accused them of being secretly committed to imposing the untried charter of 1793, they were ignoring the Jacobins' pragmatism.[17] Per-

[15] Français de Nantes, *Coup d'Oeil rapide sur les Moeurs, les lois, les contributions, les secours publics, les sociétés politiques . . . dans leur rapports avec le Gouvernement représentatif . . .* (Grenoble, pluviôse an VI), p. 3. A member of Legislative Assembly and a disciple of the *philosophes,* he was described by a friend as "un homme lettré, instruit, et d'une société aussi douce qu'aimable." With such a background Français became what might be described as a reluctant democrat. It was his report that stopped the conservative effort to circumscribe the clubs during the Legislative Assembly. During the Convention he overcame an initial sympathy for the Girondins to become an administrator in his department and an active member of the Grenoble société populaire. (See A. Piquemal, "La Conversion d'un Jacobin," *La Nouvelle Revue,* n.s., xvii [1902], 372-82.) In the Year VI he stood for election and this pamphlet was in effect his platform; he won handily, and in Paris took an active part in the "coup d'état" of prairial Year VII. (See A.N. AF iii 237/Isère, and A.N. AF iii 47.)

[16] Chaussard, *Coup d'Oeil,* p. 21.

[17] Early in ventôse copies of the Constitution of 1793 were found circulating

haps the Jacobins continued to nurse a nostalgia for that symbol of unfulfilled hopes, but in practical political life the document grew increasingly irrelevant. For all its unpalatable features the Directory's constitution did demarcate and ostensibly guarantee a broad range of elective and participatory institutions. The Jacobins therefore accepted it, not as the ultimate formula dictated by wisdom and experience, but as a set of rules under which substantive political controversy could be carried on. As they presciently anticipated, the same could not be said of other possible arrangements such as the Bonapartist charters.

Three considerations buttressed the Jacobins' new posture of constitutionalism. First, in light of the document's built-in provision for legal amendment, they could argue that its worst features had to be endured only temporarily. Second, they could in good conscience sing the constitution's praises in the interim since they were fearful of assaults from the Right which would produce far worse results than the Directory regime. Third, and most important, they could at the same time hope to effect reforms even without amending the charter itself, by securing passage of "organic laws" to amplify the constitution's general provisions, and also by interpreting its provisions liberally. They assumed that as the climate of opinion changed, "representative democracy" could develop even under the disabilities of the Constitution of 1795.

No doubt when a Jacobin qualified his declaration of fidelity to the constitution by mentioning the ultimate need for amendments he was guilty of self-delusion. The actual process of amendment was extremely cumbersome, requiring up to nine years and favorable majorities in three successive legislatures. Still it remained necessary for morale in democratic circles vaguely to recall the original objections to the new charter. Democrats continued to refer to

---

in Avignon. Investigation revealed two possible explanations: that the person distributing them (a concierge in charge of a warehouse where they had been stored for several years) was an individual "d'un incivisme reconnu," who was acting out of royalist sympathies as a provocateur; or that the concierge allowed the leaflets to get out of his hands merely by a chance occurrence. In the end no one considered the incident a willfull act of political opposition by the Jacobins. See A.N. F^7 7408, fol. 4472: "Proclamation de l'Administration Municipale . . . d'Avignon, à ces Concitoyens"; and *J. hommes libres* No. 302, 27 ventôse VI, for the first version; F^7 7408, fol. 4472: "Mémoire" in behalf of the concierge by his chef de bureau, and other documents in his favor.

themselves as citizens who "have felt obliged to express frankly their opinions or their doubts over certain articles"; as citizens who saw certain "vices" in the compact which "gave wealth an advantage over spirit, talent, and virtue." By their account democrats were citizens who "find several articles in the constitution that violate the rigor of their principles."[18] But if it had imperfections it also had mechanisms for peacefully and legally correcting them. As the Arnay (Côte d'Or) Club pompously declared, the constitution itself offers "legal means for arriving at that state of perfection which it is possible for men to give to the art of government."[19]

Above all, each and every one of these statements warned, there must be no "attacks," "assaults," or "shocks" against the charter. It must be accepted as the foundation of political life; those addicted to faith in "chimerical solutions" or utopias must recognize that the present constitution is their only defense against forces that would destroy them and the republic altogether. Impelling the Jacobins' constitutionalism was their conviction that the Right was truly the great opponent of the Directory, eager to subvert it in order to establish a more reactionary, anti-democratic government. Except when traitors openly threatened the state—as in the pre-Fructidor crisis— the democrats now claimed non-violence as their credo, while violence was seen as the characteristic of aristocrats and chouans. A deep fear about subversion from the Right—not only by royalists but by conservative politicians—was implicit in their defense of the constitution.

Periodically the Jacobin press made this explicit by publicizing alleged plots to alter the constitution. Immediately after Fructidor, for example, rumors circulated about proroguing the Legislature illegally in order to cool things off and to correct imbalances between legislature and executive. In a well-known article, Albert

---

[18] *J. hommes libres* No. 319, 14 germinal VI; A. Didot, *Réflexions sur les ennemis de la République française* (Impr. Institut des Aveugles-travailleurs, an VI) in A.N. F⁷ 7408, fol. 4506 (Didot was a founder of the Constitutional Circle in the 7th arrondissement of Paris); *Le Démocrate* No. 1, 24 fructidor V (a short-lived sheet edited in Paris by Méhée).

[19] A.N. F⁷ 7415, fol. 5235: MS règlement. Also *Discours prononcé par un membre du Cercle constitutionnel de Toulouse* (frimaire an VI) in F⁷ 7362, fol. 270; *Profession de foi politique des républicains de la commune de Lunéville . . . réunis en cercle constitutionnel* (Impr. de Messuy) in A.N. F⁷ 7399, fol. 3663. This document is based on the manifesto of the Club of the Rue de l'Université in Paris, which was led by Jacobin deputies Marbot and Lamarque.

Mathiez adduced indirect evidence to suggest that conservative republicans or "Salmistes" (Benjamin Constant, Mme. de Staël, Talleyrand, Sieyès, and Lauraguais) hoped to go even further in "reforming" the constitution along conservative lines. Already, in short, certain conservatives were contemplating the kind of constitutional coup that Bonaparte engineered.[20]

When the rumors started again in pluviôse one of the most insistent warnings came from the *Journal des Amis* of Metz, which drew upon Vatar's paper as its source. The *Journal* reported the rumor that a faction was planning to convert the Legislature into one house of one hundred members, and to install a one-man executive (possibly a president for life) to replace the unwieldy Directory. Conservative deputies rose to denounce these rumors, claiming that royalists were spreading them in order to promote unrest. But the *Journal des Amis* was not satisfied; it commented that such a faction might indeed exist and need not be the chimera of royalist subversives. How often "have intriguers shown themselves to be in accord with the royalists, in order to give the revolution twists profitable to their ambitions and cupidity?" In other words, certain politicians might well be interested in securing a firmer grip over the government by strengthening the power of the executive and making the Legislature more oligarchic. Against this threat of oligarchy, the *Journal des Amis* declared that strict adherence to the constitution must be maintained, and no "organic alterations" allowed. To the letter the editors anticipated the disaster for democracy that would result from Bonaparte's coup. But at the same time they were careful to qualify their support for the Directorial constitution in a most revealing way. Obliquely they reminded their readers that the constitution was actually the work of thermidorians and anti-Jacobins whom they detested, like the notorious Merlin de Thionville of their own Moselle department. Their own support of the constitution came despite its tainted origins; Jacobins were loyal to the constitution even without having "enriched them-

---

[20] A. Mathiez, "La réforme de la Constitution de l'an III après le coup d'état de 18 fructidor," *Le Directoire*, pp. 336-55. It must be remembered that Brumaire began as the consummation of "oligarchic" tendency that had long been evident in the thinking of certain conservative republicans. For additional insights into this tendency see R. Guyot's seminal article on French constitution-making in the sister republics: "Du Directoire au Consulate: les transitions," *Révue historique*, cxi (1912), 1-31.

selves" and without "flaunting an opulence as scandalous in its formation as it is revolting in its uses." But even if the constitution's thermidorian architects were oligarchs, profiteers, and social climbers who reemerged after Robespierre's fall, their charter could be made to serve all citizens.[21]

By the Year VI, then, the Jacobins were constitutionalists, prophetically fearful that erosion of the compact would open the way to unmitigated oligarchy. Meanwhile they could salve their consciences over the constitution's unpalatable features by recalling the possibility of amendments. More practically, they could work from within the constitutional framework to build legislative and administrative majorities that would introduce reforms; that would see to it that "the organic laws interpreting the constitution are made to favor democracy."[22]

A veritable master plan incorporating this stance was circulated in democratic circles during the resurgence of the Year VI. The anonymous pamphlet entitled *Quelques Conseils aux Patriotes Cisalpins* was almost certainly written by Marc-Antoine Jullien, a youthful protégé of Robespierre. After the anti-Jacobin repression of 1796, this mercurial democratic activist had followed Bonaparte's army to Italy, where he edited the *Courrier de l'Armée d'Italie* from Milan. His pamphlet was addressed to Cisalpine patriots in 1797, but its circulation in Paris the following year (where a copy was seized by the police) indicates its relevance to the Jacobin minority in La Grande Nation itself.[23]

[21] *Journal des Amis* (Metz) No. 68, 16 pluviôse VI. A few days later the editors reiterated their opinion even more prophetically: "Les vrais anarchistes sont ceux qui chercent a rompre la démarcation et la balance des pouvoirs constitués, sous prétexte de les centraliser." (*Ibid.* No. 70, 20 pluviôse.)

[22] A.N. F⁷ 7368, fol. 823: Les hommes libres et laboreurs, réugnis en société patriotique à Evans (Jura) to Directory, 19 frimaire VI. Cf. the petition from 150 republicans of Lot and Corrèze, asking for the purging of aristocrats and "the strengthening of democratic government." A.N. C426, fol. 96: 30 vendémiaire VI.

[23] *Quelques Conseils aux Patriotes Cisalpins* (n.l., n.d.) in A.N. F⁷ 3054 (Elections, an VI). A handwritten notation on the cover reads: "L'auteur de cet écrit est Julien de la Drôme fils." An important article based on Jullien's papers and notebooks (which came to be deposited in the Marx-Lenin Institute) ignores this pamphlet: V. M. Dalin, "Marc-Antoine Jullien nach dem 9 thermidor," in his *Babeuf-Studien*, ed. W. Markov (Berlin, 1961). Dalin does portray in depth the attempt of a former "Robespierrist" to find his way back to a political persuasion with which he could confront the world. Dalin's

Jullien prescribed the organization of a political party—a kind of legal conspiracy, by the standards of that period. This party was to be based on the philosophy of non-violent, gradual reform by means of concerted political action. With republics already established (in Italy and in France), the destiny of nations lay in their legislatures; democracy could be promoted and consolidated by legally gaining control of the legislature from the grass roots up. Only then, wrote Jullien, can laws be passed "that will satisfy you; then, you can improve the social system to your liking." Meanwhile violence as well as adherence to exaggerated aims ("une perfection imaginaire") must be avoided. "Those who might have the secret design of modifying or changing the constitution must nonetheless support the constitution until the moment when legal and peaceful means are available to correct it. . . . If you fail to observe the constitution inviolably you will end up being proscribed." Jullien went on to urge that instead of fretting over the constitution, patriots concentrate on more immediate reforms: "Popular laws must be passed . . . in favor of the poor, the tillers of the soil, the workers, the soldiers." But here too caution was necessary. "To begin with," he continued, "the interests of the rich and the large proprietors must not be directly attacked."[24] Torn between what the Soviet historian V. M. Dalin has called his petit bourgeois predispositions and his commitment to social revolution, Jullien clearly did not believe that "popular laws" could be achieved by mere palliatives. Implicitly he recognized that the progress of democracy involved redistribution of wealth; but he rejected expropriation as a suitable means, since it would provoke open warfare. Instead of "a system of persecution that would alienate the rich," Jullien proposed to promote equality through more gradual means. If the thrust of social revolution was dulled in the process, this was the necessary price of realism. One thing that the Neo-Jacobins had in common with Babeuf was their determination to pass beyond exalted but abstract sentiments and to descend into the arena of political action —one way or the other.

---

thesis is that Jullien's "petit bourgeois" class bias determined his compromises. The only quarrel one can have with this generally unsympathetic interpretation is that it implicitly makes Babeuvism the yardstick of integrity.

[24] *Quelques Conseils* Nos. 1, 6, 8, 23, 60; Nos. 48 and 49.

Jullien prescribed that patriots must articulate issues and popularize the revolution with the mass of citizens, while avoiding imprudence, illegality, or violence. Since the Jacobins were reduced to virtual passivity before Fructidor, their subsequent attempts to develop such issues were embryonic at this stage. Understandably, most of their efforts centered on the upcoming elections of 1798—a subject to which a separate part of this study will be devoted, including a chapter on the issues of franchise reform. Putting first things first, the Jacobins were in effect implementing Jullien's strategy of seeking political power legally. But it is possible to glean the other kinds of issues that were going to be debated and that some people already were raising. Some tentative answers can be proposed to an all-important question: with the evolution of Jacobinism into a constitutional movement for reform, what were the issues that might distinguish their party? Into what substantive issues was the democratic persuasion being translated?

‡ III ‡

The national issue (apart from the coming elections) that commanded the Jacobins' greatest attention was the veterans' bonus. In the Year II the Convention had pledged such a recompense to the *défenseurs de la patrie*, without fixing the amount, method of finance, or time and conditions of payment. Like the Constitution of 1793 or the Ventôse laws, the bonus was one of the Convention's grander gestures that remained on paper. Presumably the government would have preferred to forget all three, but since it was dependent on the good will of the army, it continued to discuss this promise. The Legislature affirmed that the bonus should total the round figure of a *milliard*, and that it would be proffered through long-term annuities underwritten by émigré property. But taking back with one hand what it seemed to be giving with the other, it added that nothing would actually be done "until the peace." Since the government was committed to an aggressive foreign policy this boded ill for the bonus.[25]

The clubs did not accept this indefinite postponement and pressed the matter vigorously. The bonus was the perfect issue around which Jacobins and soldiers—the two strongest revolutionary elements in French society—could coalesce. It was understood that most

[25] A. Meynier, *Le 18 fructidor* (Paris, 1927), p. 179.

of the soldiers came from families of "modest fortune"; by means of the bonus the nation's resources could be utilized for the benefit of these citizens who (in one of the Jacobins' favorite phrases) had profited least from the Revolution while doing the most to defend it.

The clubs therefore kept up a continuous flow of petitions on the subject of the bonus. For the republic's invincible armies—which they had just honored at a fraternal gathering—the members of the club at Magnac (Haute-Vienne) demanded "the prompt distribution of the milliard promised by the nation." Similarly the Constitutional Circle of Verneuil (Eure) explained that it had done what it could to honor the soldiers by providing a banquet for a division that was passing through their town. But it was much more important for the Legislature to implement "that beneficent law which will assure them their due recompense." "Acquit this long-suspended debt," wrote the club at Florac (Lozère), "and fulfill a sacred engagement—one contracted with the illustrious defenders of liberty in order to assure them an old age free from indigence."[26] The petitioners were in no mood to wait "until the peace"; some raised a more immediate argument than the need to assure veterans a retirement free from want: they called attention to the soldiers' parents—old people who would normally depend on their children for assistance or sustenance. As one club put it, "we say frankly, citizen legislators, we sadly witness that most of the fathers and mothers of our brave brothers-in-arms are devoid of all assistance and relief." Prompt action was therefore incumbent; it was necessary "at least to begin with the soldiers' parents to apply the national recompense that their children have merited." Petitions like these came in such numbers that the sympathetic deputy Marbot proclaimed from the Tribune: "it may truly be said that today the voice of the Nation has made itself heard."[27]

[26] A.N. C 426, fol. 98: Les républicains de Magnac réunis en banquet civique, 11 brumaire VI; C 428, fol. 133: Les citoyens soussignés composant le cercle constitutionnel de Verneuil, 26 nivôse; C 431, fol. 166: Les républicains de Florac soussignés, 20 pluviôse VI. See also a pre-Fructidor pamphlet bristling with egalitarian sentiment: Treich-Desfarges, *Projet de distribution du milliard promis aux défenseurs de la patrie, par un Général de Brigade réformé* (Impr. du Révélateur) in A.N. AF III 144b, and covering letter dated 23 messidor V.

[27] A.N. C 428, fol. 133: Les républicains de La Rochefocault (Charente) réunis en cercle constitutionnel, 27 nivôse; petition from Fougères Constitutional Circle, reprinted in *J. hommes libres* No. 240, 25 nivôse; see also *Ibid.* No. 196, 11 frimaire. *Moniteur*, 4 ventôse VI (p. 620) for Marbot's comment.

The bonus issue offered a particularly appropriate chance for Jacobins to expand on two of their favorite themes: first, the need to exact retribution from citizens who had amassed illicit fortunes through war profiteering and speculation; second, the desirability (if at all possible) of creating small, independent proprietors out of the nation's patrimony.

That corrupt, counterrevolutionary elements survived and indeed flourished in the midst of revolutionary France was a common, heartfelt grievance in Jacobin circles. The press was always lamenting "the striking contrast between the insolent luxury of the *nouveau riche* and the profound misery of the masses ruined by stock-jobbing and fraudulent financial speculation." Jacobin spokesmen typically traced "public deprivation" to the speculation of corrupt counterrevolutionary elements, and it was their conviction that "the colossal fortunes which are born from such origins must undergo expiation and must support amends for the body politic."[28] In the name of the bonus many Jacobins revived these demands that the malefactors be brought to justice and be made to underwrite support of the Revolution's defenders.

Most could agree that the émigrés should be the first target for this expiation, but as the Constitutional Circle of Pau (Basses-Pyrénées) declared: "If the property of the émigrés' relatives is insufficient, then the colossal fortunes of the ex-nobles and of the blood-suckers who have pillaged the republic must not be spared." A petition from Foix (Ariège) echoed the demand that the bonus be financed from "les tresors des dilapidateurs et des royalistes," and from Valenciennes (Nord) a club proposed that the milliard should come from "les biens des parens d'émigrés, les fortunes scandaleuses des nouveaux riches, et les rapines sans nombre des commissaires des guerres."[29]

No one, however, troubled to list the names of these "blood-suckers" or to suggest the exact nature of their crimes. On the other hand we need not conclude that because their rhetoric is dismayingly vague the Jacobins were not serious about this "expiation." The Jacobins were at one with almost all chroniclers of the Direc-

[28] *Défenseur de la Vérité* (Paris) No. 54, 12 vendémiaire VI; Chaumont-Quitry, *Essai sur les causes*, p. 72.

[29] A.N. C 428, fol. 131: petition from Pau Constitutional Circle, 11 nivôse VI; *J. hommes libres* Nos. 193 and 197, 8 and 12 frimaire VI, reprinting petitions from Foix and Valenciennes.

tory epoch to whom it was obvious that fortunes had been made by profiteering, and the Directory, if not guilty of such acts itself, seemed altogether unwilling to pursue the culprits. Even if they rarely passed beyond epithets to present a convincing case about the "blood-suckers," we can infer that the Jacobins wanted an investigation of corruption that would bring to justice the worst offenders whose plunder could then be seized with impunity. One organ of Parisian sans-culottism, however, approached the issue in a more sweeping fashion. With the other clubs the *Défenseur de la Vérité* agreed that the bonus should be underwritten not only from the émigrés' property but by "all the rich who have constantly worked for the counterrevolution." But why not go even further; why not let the milliard be supported by "all the rich, without distinction, in proportion to their wealth"? No one could legitimately object to this, maintained the editors. The *nouveau riche* and the corrupt—"those vampires who quietly helped themselves to the republic's treasures, while execrating the republic"—must certainly pay, "since their rapines are the people's patrimony." As for patriotic rich citizens, they will not complain, "for they will only be acquitting a legitimate debt." The Legislature's proposal to utilize only émigré property "tends to destroy one class of rich citizens, only to create another no less dangerous, and to substitute a different caste of privileged men."[30] This was an advanced position on the bonus, though it was consistent with Jacobin attitudes on taxation, as we shall see shortly. In any event the editors no doubt would have settled for that investigation of corruption, speculation, and profiteering that in the end eluded the Jacobins and the French nation.[31]

The pro-Jacobin deputy from the Corrèze, General Marbot, saw the bonus as a means for reviving another receding hope: the distribution of land to create a nation of small independent proprietors. Marbot rose to propose that the Legislature reconsider its decision to distribute the milliard eventually in the form of long-term annuities. He proposed instead that the Legislature offer the veterans a choice between an annuity and an actual parcel of

[30] *Défenseur de la Vérité* No. 11, 28 brumaire VI.

[31] In his study of the army commissioners Jacques Godechot largely exculpates this group from the contemporary charge that they were corrupt profiteers: *Les Commissaires aux armées sous le Directoire* (2 vols.; Paris, 1937).

national lands. Such a choice, he explained, would foster "the incalculable advantages which would result from any measure tending to turn the soldier into a proprietor."[32]

It was characteristic of Neo-Jacobins to seize on a tactically promising issue like the bonus as means of pressing for a new distribution of national property. Had the Jacobins gained a majority in the Legislature—one composed even of moderates like Marbot or Français de Nantes—might they not have reopened the question of the milliard? They might have attempted to underwrite it through special taxes, similar in conception to the forced loans of the Year IV. They might have essayed the distribution of land in small parcels to veterans by liquidating the property of émigrés held by their relatives. Or they might simply have expedited payment of the annuities that had already been voted in principle, before the elusive peace with England was achieved. Any and all of these moves—any real attempt to do something concrete about the veterans' bonus—would have effected a significant redistribution of wealth in the country. Manifestly the clubs and editorialists sensed this. Like the call for a single tax or greenbacks, the milliard was a supreme, all-encompassing issue. In a slightly more advanced stage of development, the democratic movement would surely have used it as a rallying issue and party slogan. In 1798 there was no party to seize it; on the contrary, party-like sentiment was crystallizing from below around such potential issues.

LIKE THE bonus, other issues raised by a club, newspaper, politician, or writer reflected a view of how the Revolution should progress. Frequently these issues involved ways by which the state could allocate its resources for the benefit of the average or disadvantaged citizen.

One question seen in this context was education. Throughout the Revolution almost everyone paid lip service to the idea of public education, but there was great variation in the urgency that individuals attached to it, and also in the purposes they felt an educational system should serve. The collective wisdom of France's statesmen had been virtually exhausted during the Convention in

[32] *Moniteur*, 4 ventôse VI (p. 620). Cf. Français, *Coup d'Oeil*, p. 6, praising the men of 1793 for taking "wise measures" to divide the national lands into small parcels "thus multiplying the number of proprietors."

endless debates over compulsion *vs.* free choice; priority to higher *vs.* priority to lower education; technical *vs.* humanistic disciplines; academic *instruction vs.* civic and moral *éducation*. As one plan superseded another, determination evidently waned to bridge the gap between intention and realization. The thermidorians put their chief commitment into a system of secondary schools or écoles centrales (one per department) and essentially left primary education to seek its own level on a local basis. On paper the bourgeois republic remained committed to education for its citizens, but the lack of urgency attached to this task was reflected in the language of the constitution. Where the Declaration of Rights in the Constitution of 1793 had said that the state "must place education within reach of all citizens," the right to education was entirely omitted from the 1795 Declaration of Rights. Instead the section on education provided only the vague promise that "there shall be primary schools in the Republic."[33] Though the leading thermidorian intellectuals like Daunou were committed to public education, they no longer lent to this issue the charged ideological or political significance with which many citizens still viewed it. From the Neo-Jacobin milieu, however, the demand persisted to commit the state explicitly and forthwith to free, public, universal education.

Shortly after Fructidor the former Montagnard Léonard Bourdon—who in the Year II had presented one of the most comprehensive, democratic, and practical proposals for mass education—came out of his political retirement to signal a campaign over this issue. In a petition that he delivered in person to the bar of the Legislature he reiterated the people's need for "une education commune et nationale."[34] In the following months a steady trickle of petitions from the clubs—usually stigmatized by conservatives as comprising the "uneducated" or "little educated"—kept this demand before France's legislators, trying to convey the anxiety of citizens who

[33] The conflicting proposals submitted to the Convention by various deputies between 1792-94 are reviewed in Robert Vignery, *The French Revolution and the Schools: Educational Policies of the Mountain 1792-94* (Madison, 1965). For the constitutions see J. H. Stewart, *A Documentary Survey of the French Revolution* (New York, 1951), pp. 457, 604.

[34] *J. hommes libres* No. 161, 6 brumaire VI. On Bourdon's educational ideas and experiments in the Year II see Vignery, *The French Revolution and the Schools,* pp. 85-86.

recognized that their ultimate progress depended on free, public education.[35]

Several of the statements made by pro-Jacobin intellectuals reflect their continuing view of education as a social issue. In his platform for the Year VI elections Français de Nantes put the matter plainly. "The working classes are so overloaded with work and so pressed in their needs, that they are unable to pay for their children's education. Therefore it is necessary to provide for it." The state must fill this need, but in the process "the establishment of public primary schools should indeed produce these *two* advantages: a free education for the poor and a republican education for the rich." The cautious *Indépendant*, edited by a group of Jacobin intellectuals in Paris, declared even more vigorously that "Bread and Education" was the persistent cry of the French people, and that the Revolution could be completed only when the rich were made to support the education of poor children. To carry its argument further, this newspaper called for the establishment of a Ministry of Education in an article pointedly entitled "Ideas on education and on the means of making men of letters useful."[36] Again, then, there were spokesmen and a constituency for whom public education remained an issue of paramount importance, potentially central to the emergence of a political party.

On economic questions there was also a distinctive though equivocal Jacobin point of view. While remaining staunch advocates of property rights, the Jacobins insisted that they be qualified by other basic human rights, such as the right to subsistence. They believed in private property and the free market economy, but also that the state could and should regulate possible abuses. In 1795-96, during the most extreme of all seasonal crises in the revolutionary period, the *Journal des hommes libres* had maintained that "the misfortunes of the poor [are caused] by faulty management of the social order" that can be corrected. Without referring explicitly to the Constitution of 1793, Vatar went on to reaffirm one of the "natural rights" proclaimed in that charter—the right to subsist-

---

[35] E.g., A.N. C 427, fols. 122 and 115; C 426, fol. 98; C 429, fol. 148: petitions from clubs in Valognes, Cambray, Uzes, Richelieu.

[36] Français, *Coup d'Oeil*, pp. 61-62; *L'Indépendant* No. 215, 5 floréal VI and No. 255, 15 prairial VI.

ence."[37] After 1796 when relative economic improvement took the edge of urgency off this question, the *Journal des hommes libres* was not inclined to press the point. However, the organs of Jacobinism did continue to raise questions about economic dislocations and to imply that the state could assist in freeing citizens from a helpless dependence on the marketplace. To this end they advocated neither economic equality nor any form of systematic planning and control. They did, however, propose intervention that falls into two categories: (1) public works programs to relieve unemployment and stimulate the economy; (2) intervention to remedy *abuses* of the free market, especially if allegedly counterrevolutionary groups might be behind such abuses.

In the *Journal des Amis* of Metz we find the most fully developed plan for public works conceived by any local Jacobin group. The editors presented a sweeping plan for reform on the eve of the elections, first suggesting the need to elect deputies who would be devoted to the interests of their constituents, "notably to the amelioration of the condition of the unfortunate classes." Once elected these deputies must attempt to secure for Metz "the benevolent and paternal consideration of the government." Though the particular problems afflicting their city were special, the editors' prescription had a general relevance.[38]

Part of Metz's problem was that the frontiers had been pushed eastward during the Revolution, thereby destroying the strategic importance of this key citadel and garrison town. Since economic stagnation was particularly acute, the deputies of Moselle must work to foster recovery. The military schools and colleges already established by the government were of no use "to the unfortunate class . . . which has long been asking to enjoy the benefits that it has a right to expect from a popular government, for whose establishment it has ceaselessly made the greatest possible sacrifices." At present the city offers nothing to the young, the aged, or the unemployed workers. Its deputies must therefore press for a program of public works, which would stimulate commerce, "fertilize the resources of the needy classes, and offer great advantages to the small shopkeepers." These Jacobin spokesmen saw in a kind of modernization an answer to their problems. Their demands were

[37] *J. hommes libres* No. 106, 24 pluviôse IV.
[38] *Journal des Amis* (Metz) No. 89, 28 ventôse VI.

pre-socialistic, conceived in terms of class harmony fostered by a popular government. They do not precisely look backward, nor do they anticipate the consequences of modernization. Their approach was remarkably free of dogma, unencumbered by the strictures of agrarian physiocracy or communism. It cannot be reduced to any one "interest" but assumes (not without naïveté) a harmony of interests growing out of a just social order and nurtured by a popularly elected government, responsive to the needs of all citizens.

It was not the Jacobins' concern to lift the wage earner to a position of economic equality with the man of means. But it was their hope to protect all citizens (particularly the "unfortunate") from some of the remediable depredations that could be inflicted on them in the name of freedom for commerce and property. Complaints and admonitions expressed by the clubs and newspapers constitute a decidedly populistic kind of protest against the abuse of economic power. And three such complaints turn up often enough to be taken as more than isolated cases; given the sparseness of explicit documents and the unorganized quality of political protest, we may assume that a substantial number of citizens were worried about these problems. We might further infer that as a party standing for a reformed and "popular" republic, the Jacobins could likely have been responsive to these residual grievances had they won power.

In any case the political freedom of the Directorial republic at least allowed these complaints to be voiced. And so it was that the age-old specter of free trade in grain, including its export, still came under attack. Since so many of the republic's ill-wishers belonged to the wealthy and propertied classes, fear continued to exist over a later-day version of the "famine pact."[39] An extraordinary petition from Bordeaux—scrawled in a laborious and barely literate hand, and claiming to speak for "a horde of patriots" who were presumably illiterate—voiced in rapid succession a catalogue of popular fears and hopes. It warned the Directory that

the aristocrats will never pardon you. Therefore do not spare them, especially those émigré tigers. See to it that political clubs are well and quickly organized . . . so that they can act as guardians to uncover the plots of these evildoers, and so that they can terrify the aristocrats. *See to it that no kind of grains, vegetables,*

[39] *J. hommes libres* No. 88, 28 thermidor V; *Journal des Amis* No. 89, 28 ventôse VI.

and other edibles leave the Republic, because the aristocracy seeks to starve us, in order to make the Legislature and the Executive hateful to us.[40]

In the same populistic vein petitions from Falaise (Calvados) and Maringue (Puy-de-Dôme) attacked another abuse of economic freedom that resulted in misery for working people. Regretfully observing that "until public morals were regenerated, money was the great mover of men," they claimed that most wealth was in the hands of aristocrats and counterrevolutionaries. One of their worst crimes was to hoard this money—except when they loaned it out at usurious rates. "Under a free government commerce should thrive by virtue of the country's wealth," they complained; "however, this wealth is nourishing crime" and weakening the fabric of the republic. This evil "must be attacked at its source," for only then would republicans gain "the true measure of their liberty."[41]

A third alleged crime against the republic perpetrated in the name of economic freedom was the creation of unemployment by means of factory closings or lockouts. More palpable than the effects of hoarding but also more justifiable in the name of private property than exporting grains, the freedom of employers to put hundreds of workers out of jobs at one blow was denounced by the *Journal des hommes libres* and others. Lacking any power to remedy such abuses, however, they could merely report and deplore factory closings at Rouen, Orléans, and Chalons.[42] We can infer that at

[40] A.N. AF III 232/Gironde: Adresse au Direct. Exécutif par une foulle des patriotes, 24 fructidor V.

[41] A.N. C 428, fol. 133: petition from Falaise dated 11 nivôse VI and signed by 150 citizens. A petition signed by 100 citizens of Maringue likewise accused the aristocracy of "generally not spending their money and hoarding the republic's precious metals." (C 428, fol. 132; 19 nivôse VI.) A related complaint came from the Constitutional Circle of La Ciotat (Bouches-du-Rhône). Counterrevolutionaries, they warned, observe both the décadi and all religious days of rest, thus raising "to an insupportable number" the days without pay. Their prescription was to limit days off to 36 (the number of décadis) and enforce this by a law which says: "que tout individu qui en prendra d'autres sera reputé riche et payera comme tel une double imposition dont le produit sera appliqué aux besoins des pauvres." (C 432, fol. 180: 30 pluviôse VI.)

[42] *J. hommes libres* No. 232, 17 nivôse VI (on Orléans), and No. 187, 2 frimaire VI (on Rouen). From Chalons the *Journal de la Marne* reported that counterrevolutionary manufacturers "menace la classe ouvrière de ne plus l'employer et veut la punir de son attachement au nouvel order de choses en

most the thrust of the Jacobins' position would have been for an investigatory apparatus to examine such cases, and for the assumption by the state of temporary responsibility for the plight of the effected workers.

‡ IV ‡

Denunciations of economic abuses in petitions or newspaper articles could be ignored indefinitely by the government—that is, until a legislative majority could compel action. But the question of taxation was a more immediate issue that to a certain extent had to be confronted directly. While foreign plunder kept La Grande Nation from complete insolvency, debate droned on intermittently over the kinds of taxes that ought to be levied.

Theoretically all Frenchmen now believed in equality of taxation, but in fact there was little agreement over what this meant. Conservatives routinely invoked the principle of equality to justify regressive taxes. Speaking on the question of billeting soldiers— which he correctly considered a form of taxation—"B. L.," a correspondent to the *Journal des campagnes et des armées*, attacked the hypocrisy of this stance.

> Is it reasonable, is it in keeping with the principles of distributive justice, that the person who occupies only one room—who lives pitifully off the product of his daily toil—should billet the same number of soldiers, and as often, as the man who owns a large house?

> In this case, the rich—as is his wont when this sophism will serve his interest—is going to invoke the principle of equality. He will not fail to state that since his cobbler and he are equal in the eyes of the law, therefore they must billet equally . . . without regard to the difference in their wealth.[43]

---

lui refusant tout travail." R. Nicolas, *L'Esprit public et les élections dans le département de la Marne de 1790 à l'an VIII* (Chalons, 1909), p. 153. (For the campaign of some Parisian militants against such a situation, see Ch. VIII below.) By the same token, Jacobin newspapers tended to oppose strikes by workers.

[43] *Journal des campagnes et des armées* No. 725, 27 ventôse VI: Au Rédacteur, by "B. L." (It is likely that this writer was Benoist-Lamothe, a pro-Jacobin intellectual who edited the *Observateur de l'Yonne*.)

The logic that "B. L." attacked was carried by the *Moniteur* so far as to argue that a consumer salt tax was both more just and more beneficent than an inheritance tax. While the government never quite adopted this position officially, it did gradually revive the execrated and regressive indirect taxes of the old regime. A levy on tobacco at the manufacturer's level was passed in the Year VI after lengthy debate, and in that year too the municipal *octroi* (taxes on goods, including food, coming through town barriers) were revived to pay for road maintenance. Finally in the Year VII the Council of 500 proposed a modified *gabelle* or salt tax. In the opinion of the Legislature's majority these taxes were fair, since everyone paid equally and no one paid very much. And as the old regime officials had known, they were effective sources of revenue since they were relatively easy to collect.[44]

Various Jacobin spokesmen protested against these measures and in the process espoused a consistent philosophy of taxation. Once again their position was summarized by Marc-Antoine Jullien's pamphlet: tax policy should "lighten the burdens of the poor . . . and curb the rapid augmentation of fortunes." In this light even a mild tax on a popular item like tobacco was denounced as "a new weight with which the unfortunate are burdened. Have you not reflected that all these [indirect] taxes weigh only on the poor and pass lightly over the fortune of the rich?" For the *Défenseur de la Vérité* such taxes "maintain the opulent man in his monstrous usurpation and the unfortunate in his shocking indigence."[45] Nor was the opposition to indirect taxes limited to popular democrats like this journal's editors; it was shared by distinctly bourgeois but pro-Jacobin intellectuals as well. In substance moderates like "B. L." or Français de Nantes took the same line as militants like Bescher and Lamberté whose sole constituency was the Paris sans-culottes.

---

[44] *Moniteur*, 11 ventôse VI (p. 646), reviewing favorably a pamphlet by J.B.M. Jollivet, *De l'impôt sur les successions, de celui sur le sel, et comparaison de ces deux impôts.* . . . For the arguments used to justify indirect taxes on basic consumer goods see Marcel Marion, *Histoire financière de la France depuis 1715* (6 vols.; Paris, 1927), IV, 95, 98-99, 126-28. A convenient summary of the Directory's financial policies is provided in Lefebvre, *Le Directoire*, pp. 133-43.

[45] [Jullien], *Quelques Conseils*, No. 50; *Défenseur de la Vérité* No. 54, 12 vendémiaire VI; *Ami de la Patrie* (Paris) No. 582, 11 vendémiaire VI. The *J. hommes libres* and the *Journal des Amis* (Metz) were among the other newspapers opposing the proposed tobacco and salt taxes.

In his platform for the Year VI Français proposed "to eliminate the idea of any indirect tax on the commodities which the working and poor segment of the people consume." And as a logical corollary to this approach, he repeated the characteristic Jacobin demand for an extensive program of luxury taxes.[46]

In the legislative debates, meanwhile, a spokesman for the democratic philosophy of taxation emerged in the person of Julien Souhait, the backbench Montagnard who almost alone had defended universal suffrage and the egalitarian revolution in 1795. His opposition to the tobacco tax was persistent and so well prepared that he helped delay its passage for several months. As far as the growers were concerned Souhait portrayed the tax as violating genuine freedom of commerce, for it was both discriminatory and obstructive. Looking at it from the consumers' point of view, he invoked the principle that "all taxes must reach the taxpayer according to his capacities. But in this tax the rich will be paying no more than the poor."[47] Souhait used the same mixture of arguments to oppose the octroi; such a tax, he cried, was "contrary to the will of the people, to liberty, to justice, and to the constitution." Again he complained that on the one hand such taxes placed an impediment on free commerce, and on the other hand violated the proper principle of taxation, for they tended "to place support for the rich man's consumption on the shoulders of the poor." Moreover, according to the version of his speech reported in the *Journal des hommes libres*, Souhait warned that the people simply would not tolerate such taxes: "The revolution began with the tearing down of town barriers," he accurately recalled; "do not place the people in a position where they will use iron and fire to throw them down again." These remarks infuriated some of the other deputies who greeted the speech with familiar "murmurs"; one deputy called it "the most anarchic speech" he had ever heard. But the fact was that when the barriers were revived a few months later, cadres of former club-

---

[46] Français, *Coup d'Oeil*, p. 90; Satur, *Les Préjuges constitutionnels*, p. 70. Cf. *Ami de la Patrie* No. 571, 4th jour compl. an V: "Aperçu d'un impôt républicain, ou cri du peuple pour une taxe sur les cabriolets, les chevaux de selle, les voitures de luxe." Deputies continued to introduce proposals to tax such things as "glaces des appartements . . . chiens de chasse et de luxe . . . voitures de luxe"; opponents replied that such taxes would depress the luxury trades and thus hurt the artisans. (See Marion, *Histoire financière*, iv, 127-28.)

[47] Reported in *Moniteur*, 2 nivôse VI (p. 369) and 21 ventôse (p. 687).

bists did take direct action to prevent their installation in several areas of southern France.[48] Evidently there was a significant constituency opposing regressive taxes.

AN EVEN more fundamental tax question than the pros and cons of indirect or consumer taxes was the nature of direct taxation. In his letter on the injustices of current billeting practices, "B. L." had gone on to assert a general principle: "it is fundamentally just that all taxes be graduated and proportional to the value of individual property." For billeting, some people argued against a proportional approach; in direct taxes conservatives most assuredly argued against graduated or progressive taxation. And here in fact lay the ultimate clash between the conservative and democratic positions.

Conservatives justified their tax policies by a literal interpretation of fiscal equality, and also by an assumption to which Benjamin Constant gave the classic formulation. Since property rights were the foundation of the state, they had to be protected by "surrounding them with a sacred barrier . . . the slightest blow against property would have fatal ramifications." Progressive taxation was regarded by conservatives as precisely such a blow against property. When the former Montagnard Garnier de Saintes proposed in the Year IV to introduce progressive taxation in order to meet a desperate financial crisis, the conservatives reacted emphatically. Speaking in the name of the Council's Finance Committee, Dauchy portrayed the proposal as "a law of exception against prosperity," which penalized wealthy citizens and especially "the great capitalists" who are so useful to the republic. Furthermore, "its effect will be inevitably to subdivide (*morceler*) properties to an extreme degree. This system of subdividing property has already been far too prevalent in the disposition of the national lands." Indeed, according to Dauchy, progressive taxation "is the veritable germ of the agrarian law [communism], which must be stamped out at its

[48] *J. hommes libres* No. 169, 14 brumaire VI. The *Moniteur*'s account (16 brumaire, p. 186) differs slightly, but essentially conveys the argument that the "classe du malheureux et de l'indigent" consumes the most and therefore will suffer most from the toll barriers; his statement about tearing down the barriers is not reported. On destruction of the barriers see above, p. 133.

inception."[49] These arguments prevailed and the idea of progressive taxation was dropped, stigmatized as a subversive proposition.

The dormant question was revived in the Year VI, not in France but by democrats in the newly founded Cisalpine Republic of Italy. According to Jacques Godechot some lively debates ensued in which Italian conservatives took up Dauchy's cry that progressive taxation was in effect a war on wealth and property: "There is nothing more ominous than the idea of a progressive tax; in principle, it will be recognized as impossible; in fact, its effect would be disastrous for the state, despite its democratic enticements."[50]

These debates in the Cisalpine Legislature seemed extremely important to France's conservative *Moniteur*, which entered the controversy as an unreserved partisan. The vehicle for the *Moniteur's* argument was a pamphlet originally published in 1793 by a former member of the Legislative Assembly named Jollivet, *De l'impôt progressif et du morcellement des patrimonies*. This attack against progressive taxation (which the Convention had voted in principle) was lauded as "a fine work, ever useful to reread." The familiar argument was spelled out thoroughly: progressive taxation was unjust as well as ruinous of commerce since it discouraged and even penalized the accumulation of wealth. Though this sound view had prevailed in France, the "fatal" measure was being proposed in Italy, "where enthusiasm and inexperience can lead them to the precipice before they know it." Accordingly, the *Moniteur* warned those who might be taken in by its "specious air of humanitarianism"; progressive taxation must be seen as a form of expropriation, "a veritable agrarian law" that would bring about "the ruin of society."[51]

In the face of its "democratic allure" and "specious humanitarianism," progressive taxation was denounced by conservative republicans. But for democrats it remained the ultimate issue, the ultimate

---

[49] Constant, "Discours," *Moniteur* (p. 690). Dauchy's speech is described as "a classic résumé of all the objections ever raised against the system of progressive taxation" by Marcel Marion, who shared Dauchy's indignation against it. Indeed Marion's standard history is actually a vast polemic against the Revolution's "demagogic" financial policies, notably proposals for progressive taxation and the elimination of indirect taxes. (*Histoire financière*, III, 408-409.) Dauchy's speech is quoted by Mathiez, *Le Directoire*, p. 99 and Soboul, *Précis d'histoire de la Révolution française* (Paris, 1962), p. 403.

[50] Quoted in J. Godechot, *La Grande Nation* (Paris, 1956), II, 498.

[51] *Moniteur*, 18 ventôse VI (p. 674).

instrument of public policy for peacefully consummating the Revolution. This could be inferred from the various statements on taxation already cited from press, pamphlets, and legislative debates—an admittedly random collection. Fortunately a more compelling case for this proposition can be offered.

Even while the *Moniteur* was roundly attacking progressive taxation, the most elaborate contemporary statement of the democratic point of view was being prepared for the presses—a book in which progressive taxation became the very core of a political philosophy. The book, announced in the *Journal des hommes libres* on 13 germinal (2 April 1798), was E. G. Lenglet's *On Property and its Relations to the Rights and the Obligations of Citizens*. Possibly when it becomes better known this book will be recognized as a landmark between the revolutionary thought of Robespierre and the tradition of revolutionary socialism launched by Buonarroti in his famous work of 1828. Though Lenglet's book never had much direct influence and was surely forgotten after Brumaire, it reflects how the thrust of the democratic revolution was sustained during the Directory years. It further suggests that the basic course of the non-socialist Left had been firmly charted by 1798 and grew directly out of the French Revolution.

E. G. Lenglet was an outstanding example of the pro-Jacobin intellectual type. A distinguished lawyer, Lenglet had been a colleague of Robespierre's in the bar at Arras. Like Sotin or Français de Nantes he was probably disaffected by the purge of the Girondins, but continued nonetheless to support the revolutionary cause. By the Year VI he had assumed his natural place, as it were, as a judge on the principal tribunal of the Pas-de-Calais department.[52] Though he was a member of the republican elite by virtue of his background and education, in his political thinking he retained an abiding sympathy for the democratic cause.

In the Year VI he proposed to stand for election in his depart-

[52] There is no reliable biographical sketch of Lenglet. The entry in Robert, Bourleton, and Cougny's standard *Dictionnaire des parlementaires français* is extremely brief, superficial, and in one instance erroneous (i.e., its reference to his "royalist tendencies" after he was elected—wholly inconsistent with his hostility to the Brumaire coup, authorship of the book we are about to consider, and political support in Pas-de-Calais). Lenglet's friendship with Robespierre is mentioned in J. M. Thompson, *Robespierre* (New York, 1936), I, 27.

ment, and like Français de Nantes he assisted his candidacy with a book which set forth his views. But where Français' *Coup d'Oeil* was a wide-ranging survey of numerous specific questions—almost a complete political platform—Lenglet's was a weightier and more analytic effort. Moreover, while its tone was in certain respects similar to Français' effort at seeking consensus, the thrust of Lenglet's argument was designed to cheer the substantial democratic constituency in his Pas-de-Calais department. Here the movement was dominated (as the Directory's agent reported) by "the wisest friends" of the late Montagnard pro-consul Joseph Lebon, who inspired fierce partisanship among his admirers and detractors.[53] The Neo-Jacobins had firm control of the department's electoral assembly in 1798, and endorsed Lenglet's candidacy by a vote of 378 out of 449 votes cast.[54] For all its unique qualities, then, Lenglet's book grew out of a distinct Neo-Jacobin milieu.

Lenglet's three-part treatise first established the validity of property rights, then justified universal political rights or suffrage, and finally considered what system of taxation was just in light of the two prior principles. By the time the author was finished he had produced a fully developed theory of democracy.[55]

Part I was designed to have a double effect. To conservatives who believed with Benjamin Constant that democracy was really disguised Babeuvism or "anarchism," Lenglet demonstrated that the sanctity of property could hardly be questioned by any right-thinking person. At the same time, he was appealing to those who may have believed with Babeuf that property rights were a usurpation of natural rights; his argument was meant to persuade them to abandon this conviction. Lenglet hoped to show that any notion of abolishing private property had to be renounced as a requisite for advancing the democratic cause.

Having legitimized property rights, Lenglet proceeded in Part II

[53] A.N. AF III 254/ Pas-de-Calais: transcribed report, germinal. Lebon's reputation (which for a long time was about equal to Carrier's) has been rehabilitated in a study by Louis Jacob.

[54] A.N. AF III 254/ Pas-de-Calais: P.V. de l'Assemblée électorale; renseignements diverses. See also A.N. AF III 522, plaq. 3365, on the Jacobins' control of this department's elections.

[55] E. G. Lenglet, *De la Propriété et de ses rapports avec les droits et avec la dette du citoyen* (Chez Moutardier, an VI), B.N. *E/1844. Publication of the book was announced in *J. hommes libres* No. 318, 13 germinal VI.

to defend universal suffrage. Here he was making greater demands on conservatives; yet in one sense he was still trying to reassure them, for he maintained that property rights were actually best protected by granting political rights to all citizens. This contention he supported by reexamining the thermidorian position on the franchise question and indeed on the whole experience of the Year II.

The thermidorians had argued from that experience that the poor (i.e., the sans-culottes) abused political power. To this Lenglet first made the standard reply that outright denial of their political rights was the most blatant abuse of all. But beyond that, what if it was admitted that men without property (i.e., sans-culottes) took over virtually exclusive power and even abused it in the Year II? The question remains, why did this happen? And the answer is that it did not happen because the laws *permitted* them to share political power, but rather because the laws previously had excluded them altogether. They became *exclusifs* not because of political equality but because before 1793 such equality was contested and denied.

Lenglet then delved further into the history of the popular revolution. There were times during the Year II, he admitted, when popular leaders threatened the propertied classes; when they inveighed against "the aristocracy of wealth" for its readiness to ally with the hereditary aristocracy or else to rise in its place. Such charges by the sans-culottes (and the policies based on this view) were sometimes exaggerated; but all too often they were well justified because of "the insensate clamours of arrogance"—by the pretensions of the bourgeoisie. Lenglet implicitly went on to justify not only the political equality of 1793 but also the social democracy of that period. His theoretical defense of equality was coupled with a defense of the actual thrust of popular revolution. From the whole experience, far from being soured on democracy, he concluded that "there is nothing as good as equality."

The author's sympathy for the democracy of the Year II was further bolstered by his invocation of the Rousseauistic argument that it is wrong to reinforce a privilege such as wealth with further political privileges. In addition he refuted traditional arguments in favor of a restricted franchise, such as the notion that the poor are too easily corrupted at election time. To this he answered plausibly: "if we exclude from the elections those who might sell themselves, should we not almost for the same reason exclude those who might purchase votes?"[56]

With the validity of property rights and of universal political rights now established, Lenglet posed a fundamental question. Given property rights which are by nature unequal in extent, and given equal political rights, what are the relative obligations of each citizen? Should the decisive factor be the equality of political rights, therefore requiring uniformity in obligations such as taxation? Or should the decisive factor be the (unequal) amounts of property with consequent variations in a citizen's obligations according to his wealth? Lenglet flatly opted for the latter: "each individual must render to society in accordance with the advantage which he receives from it."

To illustrate this dictum Lenglet offered the following example. Suppose that there was a large landholder whose property equaled that of 100 small holders. The first man would receive, in effect, 100 times as much protection from the state and society as each of the others. The 100 small holders could each plow their own fields, whereas the large proprietor required a social order that provided labor with which to plow his fields. The 100 could defend themselves and their possessions in many instances, but the large holder would be more vulnerable and more directly dependent on the state for protection. The large proprietor would benefit most from the maritime commerce and foreign trade, which are protected at great cost to society by the state. Likewise public facilities such as courts of law would be of most direct benefit to large property holders.

To assure that the wealthy citizen repaid society for the benefits and advantages inherent in his position, Lenglet proposed simply that "*taxes must not be proportional but progressive.*" The detailed plan that he presented for levying a graduated income tax is of antiquarian interest only, but his own summary of the scheme is of striking importance as a conception of social policy:

[56] *De la Propriété*, Parts I and II, especially pp. 70, 100, 105. L'aristocratie, quelle qu'elle soit, républicaine ou royale, dorée et sansculottes, est donc partout également malfaisante ou dangereuse; enfin, et ceci s'adresse aux hommes qui veulent faire, comme à ceux qui veulent consolider une révolution, en politique il n'est rien de bon que l'*Egalité*. C'est a dire, la justice (p. 111).

183

> Secours aux individus qui manquent du nécessaire
> Exemption d'impôts pour ceux qui n'ont rien au délà
> Réduction d'impôts pour les petites fortunes
> Augmentation pour les grandes.[57]

Taxation was for Lenglet the great engine of progressive social reform, balancing the interests of the indigent, the man barely scraping by, the average property holder, and the very wealthy. Most fundamentally, progressive taxation was intended directly to diminish the extremes of wealth and poverty. For according to Lenglet's plan the high taxes to be drawn from the wealthy must be immediately used "to relieve misfortune." Repeatedly Lenglet emphasized that the alleviation of poverty was a fundamental obligation of the state in general and the wealthy citizen in particular; in his plan, the form of this relief anticipates the "negative income tax" that is being proposed in the 1960's.

Indigence and poverty, however, are not the only conditions to be taken into consideration. For the average citizen who is self-supporting but of limited means Lenglet also proposed relief in the form of exemptions. And like Français de Nantes and others, Lenglet asserted that "necessities must not be taxed." Further, the basic subsistence income that was the lot of many citizens would be strained by any kind of direct taxation. As Lenglet explained, the citizen of modest income acquitted his debt to society simply by the sum of wealth put into circulation by his labor. Finally, as regards the wealthy, Lenglet was forthright in explaining that by his plan the progressive augmentation of taxes in relation to wealth would in effect place a maximum on income.[58]

In summary, Lenglet proposed that property rights and political rights be guaranteed to all citizens. Out of the animosities generated by the Revolution between rich and poor, he was seeking an area of agreement: it was to the poor and to their utopian advocates that he urged the recognition of property rights; it was to the wealthy bourgeoisie that he recommended acceptance of universal suffrage. The consequent imbalance of debts or obligations to society—deriving

[57] *Ibid.*, pp. 123-34. In passing, Lenglet advocated public education "payés à frais communes," p. 118.

[58] *Ibid.*, pp. 130-31, 121, 143, 147. Lenglet pointed out, however, that his plan would not limit the amount of capital (*fonds*) that a person could hold or pass on to his children (pp. 140-41).

from the fact that the social order was of more direct benefit to the wealthy—must be righted by rigorously progressive taxation. This in turn would be used to relieve the needy and would gradually work to reduce the extremes of wealth and poverty. From the way in which Lenglet wove his arguments together he demonstrated that progressive taxation was the hallmark of non-socialist democracy.

His book, then, draws together many of the assumptions and pre-occupations of Jacobin activists, but in addition focuses on a long-term program for reform. In effect Lenglet detailed what Publicola Chaussard later referred to as "democratic institutions." Lenglet's thought demonstrates how the Jacobins rejected not only Babeuvism but any idea of class war and expropriation, positing instead the possibility of a durable harmony between various social classes —provided that the basic political and economic institutions were sound. At the same time, Lenglet, like Satur, Chaumont-Quitry and others, explicitly defended the popular revolution from the criticism of those who saw only its excesses and not its causes or accomplishments. Lenglet presented what is essentially a fully real-ized theory of democracy, consistent with the attitudes expressed less systematically by other Jacobins. Politics here is intimately re-lated to social and economic questions. Classic middle-class inter-ests like private property or law and order are made consonant with some of the popular revolution's substantive goals.

Admittedly the Neo-Jacobins did not pursue such goals insistently. Certainly they did not share Babeuf's complete alienation from pre-vailing middle-class values. Gradualists and constitutionalists, they were content with keeping alive certain ideals of the democratic revolution of 1793, while accepting the framework of 1795. Yet Marc-Antoine Jullien was not merely paying lip service to these ideals when he wrote: "It is necessary to pass popular laws in favor of the poor, the tillers of the soil, the workers, and the veterans." This chapter has suggested the areas in which "popular laws" might have been passed, without the *bouleversement* of state and society that Babeuf advocated. The Jacobins did not invoke the Constitu-tion of 1793 as their standard, but implicitly they wished to revive certain of its features that had been dropped from the program of the bourgeois republic, among these the right to subsistence and the right to free public education. The problem of extremes in

185

wealth and poverty was at the heart of the Jacobin persuasion, though as often as not it was treated in moral or political terms. The importance of the veterans' bonus as a tactical way of keeping this issue alive can hardly be overrated. Beyond that, taxation would have remained an important arena for confronting this problem, and in Jacobin circles the idea of progressive taxation was clearly in the air.

In sum, the Neo-Jacobins were hopeful of reviving basic components of Robespierrist democracy. This is not to suggest that they identified with the person of Robespierre; far from it, since as political leader the Incorruptible was hopelessly stigmatized as a tyrant. But Robespierre's vision for society informed Neo-Jacobinism just as it had informed the Jacobin movement of 1793. After the dust had settled, after the passage of time allowed an admirer of Robespierre's like Buonarroti to separate the enduring from the ephemeral in his hero's career, it was this social vision that stood out, rather than the unhappy role of chief executioner. In an unpublished fragment entitled "Benefactors of Humanity," Buonarroti entered Robespierre into that pantheon with these lines:

> He proposed progressive taxation and public education. He wished to limit property rights, to assure the people the real exercise of their sovereignty, and to banish opulence, luxury, hypocrisy and oppression from society.[59]

If this was the essence of Robespierre's greatness (and Buonarroti's opinion is as valid as any), then Robespierre clearly left a legacy independent of a loyalty to his own person—a legacy that survived in Neo-Jacobinism.

[59] Buonarroti Papers, B.N. Mss (nouv. acq. fran.) No. 20804, undated MS.

CHAPTER VII

Ideology and Patronage: A Case
Study of Evreux

Purges carried out from above punctuated political life in Directorial France much the way insurrectionary *journées* had in 1789 or 1793. Devoid of the *journées'* drama and social depth, these mutations in political personnel offer the spectacle of a dreary spoils system. But if personal ambition and careerism animated these struggles for place, so too did ideological conflict. This case study of one department will suggest that while the point of politics may have been the competition for official positions, its counterpoint was the clash of political persuasions. In this interplay, the position of the Neo-Jacobins was defined.

To begin with it must be understood that the Directory was an immensely powerful patron to local officeseekers, commanding much of the discretionary authority that one usually associates with Louis XIV, the Committee of Public Safety, or Napoleon. True, the Directorial constitution provided for autonomy and decentralization, with local elections on all levels of government in the normal course of events. But the power of the central Executive Directory intruded nonetheless in two ways. First, through a system of commissioners who represented the Directory in each department and municipality, sharing authority in an ill-defined fashion with locally elected councils. Secondly, through emergency powers that the constitution granted the Directory to dismiss members of these local councils and to appoint their successors until the next elections. Citizens seeking political office would have to secure themselves on two flanks: the patronage of the Directory, and the suffrage of their politically conscious constituents.

In the absence of an organized party machine the Directors depended on informal recommendations for making these appointments and were therefore often ill informed about local circumstances and personalities. Hence their appointments lacked consistency, leaving a good deal of room for subsequent recrimination and maneuvering. Ideally the Directory tried to fill the vast number of positions with experienced, loyal moderates whose views harmon-

ized with official conservative republicanism. But as Marcel Reinhard has suggested, the upheaval of the Revolution had soured many
well-to-do citizens on the attractions of officeholding, and consequently many positions were hard to fill effectively.[1] The Directory
was then forced to turn to citizens whose views were either more
reactionary or more progressive. Indeed the more factional or ideological a man's politics, the more likely he was to seek office for himself or like-minded citizens. The paucity of disinterested moderates
probably accounts for the fact that at least twice the Directory found
it necessary to conduct wholesale purges that encompassed its own
appointees. Thus, following the Babeuf plot it dismissed former
Jacobins, despite their valuable experience and relative moderation. In their place were appointed extreme conservatives recommended by deputies newly elected to the Legislature and thoroughly
hostile to the work of the remaining two-thirds carried over from
the Convention. Eventually this group openly broke with the
Directory, and in Fructidor it was therefore purged in turn. Both
purges were extensive but not thorough. Certain departments and
towns were passed over altogether; in others individuals were dismissed while equally "anti-republican" officials were allowed to stay
on.

For the Jacobins Fructidor presented a significant opportunity
to regain lost footholds in local political office. The new Constitutional Circles and the reinvigorated Jacobin press uniformly demanded a broadening of the purge. "Proven and energetic patriots,"
as they put it, must now be appointed everywhere. The factional
character of this demand could hardly be missed since the Jacobins
were usually a visible group in any given place. But the tedious
wrangling that followed in most departments and towns was
more than a pursuit of the rather meager spoils of local office. The
careerism of individual Jacobins and the aspirations of the movement as a whole were both served; the struggle for office cannot be
understood exclusively in terms of one or the other.

‡ I ‡

Local histories abound in details of the competition for this or that
position. The political attitudes that the officeseekers may have

---

[1] M. Reinhard, *Le Département de la Sarthe sous le Régime directorial* (St.
Brieuc, 1935); A. Mathiez, *Le Directoire*, Chs. II-IV.

shared with a broader constituency are more difficult to uncover. In the almost total absence of their personal papers, one possible source is the local press—a source admittedly superficial and unsatisfactory for many kinds of research. Approximately fifteen provincial newspapers of the Directory years were factional or "party" organs run by the local Neo-Jacobin intelligentsia. For three reasons most are actually defective as sources: some were too ephemeral; others remained cautiously unpolemical and thus are short on manifest ideological content; still others apparently have not survived intact and are known only by a few miscellaneous numbers or by secondhand traces. The newspaper published in Evreux, chef-lieu of the Eure department, is therefore outstanding: it published continuously for almost a year and a half, including the entire period of the Jacobin resurgence in 1798; it became unusually explicit in its political and social commentary; and it is well preserved in the Bibliothèque Nationale, where it has enjoyed an undeserved neglect.

The *Bulletin de l'Eure* first appeared on 15 frimaire Year V (5 December 1796) and after thermidor Year V was published regularly every other day until it was suppressed by the Directory on 21 germinal VI (10 April 1798) in the midst of that year's elections. Not only was it the organ for the department's Jacobins, but it was virtually a chronicle of their activities. The editor (who thereby became an important personage in the Eure's public life) was J.B.P. Touquet—a man who was not especially prominent in the early years of the Revolution. Various accounts of the pro-Girondin "federalist" movement in the Eure mention him nowhere among the partisans of either side; nor is Touquet's name among the 24 chief "Robespierrists" of Evreux satirized in a local ballad.[2] Yet we know that he was a resident of Evreux and not wholly inactive since he remarks once that he was arrested in the Year II by the revolutionary committee of Evreux, and that the department's famous deputy to the Convention and member of the Committee

[2] Articles on the federalist revolt are listed in G. Walter's *Répertoire de l'histoire de la Révolution française*, Vol. ɪɪ: Lieux (Paris, 1951), under the headings of Evreux and Eure. The standard history of the Eure department (an antiquarian work that is superficial and undocumented) mentions Touquet only once in passing, noting that he edited "a very violent newspaper." Boivin-Champeaux, *Notices historiques sur la Révolution dans le département de l'Eure* (2nd edn., Evreux, 1894), ɪɪ, 378. "Partisans de Robespierre"—a ballad to the tune of the Carmagnole—is reprinted in *Souvenirs et Journal d'un bourgeois d'Evreux 1740-1830* (Evreux, 1850), B.N. Lk7/2707, pp. 93-94.

of Public Safety, Robert Lindet, helped secure his release. Whether the revolutionary committee regarded him as an *ultra* or a *citra* is unknown.[3] Touquet's principal collaborator on the *Bulletin* was Guy Chaumont-Quitry, an ex-noble who had been mistakenly inscribed on the list of émigrés but who secured his removal at a time when the government was denying most such requests. He and his brother François were lawyers in the department as well as partners in publishing the *Bulletin*.[4]

By the time of the Vendôme trial, both Touquet and Chaumont were visible spokesmen for the Left. At a public session of the Criminal Tribunal of the Eure where he practiced, Chaumont openly attacked the government for its persecution of the Vendôme defendants, and declared that the verdict sending Babeuf and Darthé to the gallows was a murder.[5] Touquet's opposition was based on his realization that Jacobinism as well as Babeuvism was on trial, especially in the person of Robert Lindet who was being tried *in absentia*. For Touquet the indictment against Lindet was an affront to the republic and to the patriots of the Eure who had sent him to the Convention in 1792. Publicizing and endorsing the memorials written by Thomas Lindet to defend his brother, Touquet further registered his disbelief in the whole alleged conspiracy. One of the government's most embarrassing moments had come when the key witness had discredited himself in trying to associate Lindet with the plot; after testifying about the ex-conventionnel's alleged part in a meeting of the conspirators, the witness "identified" Lindet among the prisoners in the dock when in fact Lindet was not in the dock at all. But in commenting on this Touquet seized on the incident's broadest implications: "They accuse Lindet of extravagant speeches in meetings which he did not attend and whose existence occurred only in the reports of those fabricators of conspiracies."[6]

[3] *Bulletin de l'Eure* [B.N. Lc10/127 (4)] No. 22, 14 prairial V.

[4] A.N. AF iii* 154 (Délibérations et arrêtés du Directoire concernant la Police), entry for 22 nivôse VI.

[5] Guy Chaumont-Quitry, *Essai sur les causes qui, depuis le 18 fructidor, devaient consolider la République* . . . (Impr. Vatar-Jouannet, an VII), B.N. Lb42/2393, p. 29n.

[6] *Bulletin* No. 22, 14 prairial V; Thomas Lindet, *Second Mémoire pour R. Lindet accusé devant la Haute-Cour de Justice* (Evreux, Impr. Touquet). For a detailed account of this testimony, see Hesiné's *Journal de la Haute-Cour de Justice* No. 61, 2 floréal V.

While Touquet by no means endorsed Babeuvism—labeling it later as "a theoretical and perhaps chimerical ideal"[7]—he did explicitly and vigorously oppose the Directory's anti-Jacobinism.

Apart from his attacks on the Vendôme trial, Touquet's journalism was far from incendiary in 1797—a time when the reactionary press all but deluged the republic and when few departments had any pro-revolutionary newspapers at all. Long speculative articles on education, religion, the émigrés, and public spirit filled the journal's pages in the early months of the Year V. At the same time the *Bulletin* provided a highly partisan coverage of that year's elections, supporting the pro-revolutionary elements in the department—the so-called "terrorists"—against the reactionary ground swell.[8] Achieving no success at the polls, the Jacobins were then exposed to the confident onslaught of their opponents, and in the process the *Bulletin*, too, became more combative, carrying on a running polemic with reactionary leaders like the deputy Pavie. Its pages increasingly reflected the revival of fighting spirit among republicans who felt threatened by a massive effort to undo the Revolution. The Directory's anti-Jacobinism was temporarily forgotten, as republicans of all persuasions made common cause. Touquet joined the chorus of publicists urging the Directory to take decisive action against the royalists and their cyphers and was jubilant when the Directory did in fact execute the fructidor coup. The Jacobins in the Eure could particularly rejoice in the fact that their nemesis Pavie was among the deported deputies.

Soon, however, the differences among republicans reappeared. Patriotism and solidarity among Evreux's republicans were celebrated in a banquet attended by 250 people—"the flower of republicans and sans-culottes"[9]—but in its afterglow the substantial questions of personnel and policy had to be faced. As a man who had put his career on the line before Fructidor by leading the crusade against reaction, Touquet felt entitled to serve as spokesman for the *patriots prononcés*. As early as 29 fructidor (15 September 1797) he wrote privately to the Directory to denounce remaining royalist sympathizers and laggards in the Eure administration, and to propose

---

[7] *Bulletin* No. 61, 29 fructidor V; Cf. *Ami de la Patrie* (Paris) No. 564, 27 fructidor—from which Touquet seems to have copied his article.

[8] *Bulletin* No. 11, 19 germinal V; *Souvenirs et Journal d'un bourgeois d'Evreux*, p. 118.

[9] *Ibid.*, p. 125.

candidates for these posts, including Chaumont-Quitry.[10] When his correspondence failed to secure results, he began using his newspaper to attack the departmental administrators and the departmental commissioner Crochon (an initiator of the federalist movement in 1793). With increasing harshness he criticized them for being too moderate, for not acting effectively against counterrevolutionary elements. His attack culminated in a "Solemn Denunciation" in the *Bulletin* of 15 brumaire VI (5 November 1797).[11]

In response to this mounting abuse the departmental administration decided upon the drastic measure of suppressing the *Bulletin,* and despite Touquet's angry protests his presses were sealed on 17 brumaire (7 November). Like most provincial Jacobins Touquet had contacts in Paris to whom he now turned for help. On the presses of Coesnon-Pellerin (publisher of a pro-Jacobin newspaper in Paris called the *Ami de la Patrie*) Touquet brought out a special issue of the *Bulletin* so that his subscribers could be apprised of the "tyrannical" actions designed to deprive them of their newspaper. In addition, the *Journal des hommes libres* took up Touquet's case, attacking the administration of the Eure for attempting to silence legitimate criticism in this fashion. Vatar noted that without such criticism the Directory would never be able to learn when disorder or neglect prevailed in a department. If there had ever been any doubt about the administration's culpability, Vatar concluded, it has certainly proven by this act of suppression that it merits dismissal.[12]

The department's decrees and Touquet's protests were all appealed to the authorities in Paris, and there the case issued in a stalemate. Characteristically, Police Minister Sotin sided with the aggrieved Jacobin and ordered the seals on Touquet's presses lifted immediately; the Directory sanctioned this, but decided not to suspend the

[10] A.N. AF III 518, plaq. 3322 (pièces 10-11); also A.N. F⁷ 7299, fol. 3167.

[11] *Bulletin* Nos. 79-82, 1-7 brumaire VI, and No. 86, 15 brumaire. Crochon, the relative of an émigré, had been *procurator-syndic* of a district in the Eure and had played an important part in the abortive federalist movement. See A. Montier, "Le Département de l'Eure et ses districts en Juin 1793, épisode du mouvement fédéraliste dans l'Ouest," *R.F.,* xxx (1896), 138-41.

[12] *Bulletin de l'Eure* [De l'impr. Coesnon-Pellerin, rue Nicaise, Paris] No. 87, 19 brumaire VI; *J. hommes libres* No. 176, 21 brumaire VI, and No. 194, 9 frimaire VI; Thomas Lindet to Sotin, 19 brumaire VI in A.N. F⁷ 7299, fol. 3167.

administration. In a letter to Touquet and to the administration the Directory conceded to Touquet's credit that there were disorders in the department's administration. But wishing to retain the services of these moderate and respectable citizens, the Directory observed that surely they would hasten to overcome their shortcomings with impeccable republican behavior. For the moment Touquet could only publish this inconclusive letter, and comment that he indeed hoped the administration would reform. Implicitly he reserved the right to continue his criticism since the government had at least acknowledged its usefulness.[13]

Hostility between Touquet and the spokesman for the administration, commissioner Crochon, of course increased after this indecisive confrontation. The attempted suppression of the *Bulletin* made them irreconcilable enemies, while the struggle continued over who should fill local offices, and what policies should be pursued in the department. An increasingly important forum for opposition to the present administration developed in the new Constitutional Circles.

‡ II ‡

Less than two weeks after Fructidor the *Bulletin* was promoting Constitutional Circles, where republicans could unite and where "public spirit will thrive." As the weeks passed, Touquet was able to report on the establishment of clubs in at least eleven cantons and to describe their activities as examples for other citizens. He noted too with scorn the unsuccessful opposition to clubs mounted by the local "honnêtes gens" in several places.[14]

Undoubtedly these Constitutional Circles were small. The signatures that they could muster on their petitions probably represent minimal membership figures since illiterate members did not generally sign the petitions; since some members might have been absent at the time; and since the clubs might have grown as the elections approached. In any case the club at Verneuil (population 4,000) could muster 45 signators, while clubs in 3 hamlets managed 35 (Lacroix-Leufroid), 25 (Pacy), and 15 (Tillières).[15]

[13] *Bulletin* No. 88, 23 frimaire VI.

[14] *Ibid.* No. 68, 9 vendémiaire VI, and Nos. 88-118 *passim*. There were clubs in Bernay, Beuzeville, Bourgachard, Breteuil, Gaillon, Lacroix-St. Leufroy, Pacy-sur-Eure, Ruglès, Tillières, Verneuil, and later in Evreux.

[15] For these petitions, see notes 16, 17, and 19 below.

These small groups were nonetheless energetic, effectively seconding the *Bulletin* in its campaign to regenerate public spirit in the department and to oust the departmental administration. A scathing indictment of these officials was drawn up by the Verneuil Club. In general it accused them of unpatriotic and virtually antirepublican behavior. In particular it charged that the department failed to enforce the décadi; permitted counterrevolutionary plays to be performed; allowed irregularities in conscription; failed to reorganize the national guard properly; allowed unpatriotic employees to remain unmolested; and did nothing positive to revive public spirit.[16] Following the lead of Verneuil, several other clubs submitted similar petitions which added to the bill of particulars. They claimed that the administration allowed biased jurors to be chosen who then acquitted the known murderers of republicans; that it allowed émigrés to return; that it harassed republicans in their clubs; and that it appointed tax commissioners who assessed "reductions for the rich and overcharges for the poor."[17] The general thrust of this criticism was summarized by the Verneuil Club. It demanded an administration which is "more animated, more energetic, more FRIENDLY towards republicans; one which has the courage to destroy all the abuses that cover the area of the department; one which will itself set an example in the practice of republican institutions." In conclusion, the club urged the Directory to recognize "that all the courageous men who have for so long been represented to it as *anarchists, jacobins,* and *terrorists* are its true friends."

The Constitutional Circles in the Eure operated on three levels. Primarily they constituted a department-wide network, linked together by the *Bulletin,* which publicized their activities and encouraged them. In this respect their major campaign concerned the replacement of the departmental administration. Locally each club worked to bolster republican institutions in its own canton by goading the cantonal authorities into action. When they were not

[16] A.N. F^{1c} iii [Ministre de l'Intérieure: esprit public et élections], Eure 12: Les Citoyens soussignées composant le cercle constitutionnel de Verneuil, Au Gouvernement, n.d.

[17] A.N. F^7 7388, fol. 2558: Des républicains du canton de Pacy-sur-Eure réunis en cercle constitutionnel au M. de Pol. The petition concludes: "nous savons que les républicains de Verneuil vous ont dénoncé cette administration royale." For discussions of this and other petitions, see *Bulletin* No. 105, 27 nivôse VI; No. 117, 21 pluviôse; No. 123, 3 ventôse.

thwarted by local conservatives, the clubs reported success in cele-brating the décadi in their communes or helping to reorganize the national guard. The Verneuil Club undertook to repair the local roads after the fashion of the Marseilles Club and fraternized with a detachment from the Army of the Rhine and Moselle that was pass-ing through the town.[18] Finally, the clubs were concerned with national issues and sent in petitions on such matters as franchise reform and the distribution of the veterans' bonus.[19]

The most obvious emphasis of this coordinated push by the clubs and newspaper was towards vigorous application of already exist-ing revolutionary legislation, and the cultivation of a republican "spirit" in the affairs of local government. In this sense the Jacobins were the most effective supporters of the Directory's professed policies, and it would be difficult to understand why the Directory did not support the *Bulletin's* party against the allegedly lethargic officials whom it condemned. The explanation is that the Jacobins stood for more than the application of venerable revolutionary laws about émigrés, national guards, and the décadi.

Through the media of clubs and newspapers the Jacobins were cultivating a persuasion that was democratic as well as republican —a spirit or point of view suspect to the Directory. While disavow-ing the "theoretical and perhaps chimerical ideal" of the Babeuvists, Touquet nonetheless placed himself among the "passionate cham-pions of democracy." The message he preached to his readers often centered on the question of democracy. In a sense "democracy has been established in France," he felt; the problem lay in continued attempts to undermine it. The aristocracy of hereditary nobility had already been destroyed and posed no threat. But according to Tou-quet a new aristocracy—"celle des riches"—was in a menacing posi-tion, though he felt that "it can be easily defeated." Most of the new aristocrats of wealth, he observed, are not even royalists, because they fear that a restored monarchy might despoil their ill-gotten gains; they too are republicans, and there lies the snare. The differ-ence between them and the democratic republicans is that the new

[18] *Bulletin* Nos. 96, 98, 99, 103, 114; *L'Indépendant* (Paris) No. 127, 7 pluviôse VI.

[19] A.N. C 431, fol. 167: Des républicains du canton de Tillières réunis en cercle constitutionnel; Des républicains du canton de Lacroix-Leufroid réunis en cercle constitutionnel; A.N. C 428, fol. 133: Les Citoyens soussignées com-posant le Cercle Constitutionnel de Verneuil, au Corps Législatif.

aristocratic republicans support the republic so that they can maintain their wealth, while democrats support the republic because they wish to be free.[20]

From such rhetoric Touquet passed to issues, declaring open warfare against this new "aristocracy" and its alleged stalwarts in the departmental administration. While Touquet demanded enforcement of Directory-sponsored laws against émigrés and ex-nobles, he advocated in addition other kinds of laws whose thrust was altogether different. "At the moment when the aristocrats are being attacked," he wrote, referring to current laws against émigrés, "how can things be arranged so that the rich do not have to pay anything; so that luxury taxes and progressive taxes are labeled unjust ... in our democratic republic?"[21]

Moreover, according to Touquet and his correspondents in the clubs, the honnêtes gens had the present departmental administration at their beck and call; large landowners were favored in tax assessments by the officials whom they regaled and patronized. Citing numerous and seemingly well-documented instances of such corruption and favoritism, Touquet concluded that the administration practiced "the protection of the rich and the oppression of the poor." "Such marked and scandalous injustices," he concluded, "destroy equality, throw the *petit contribuable* into despair, and sap the republic at its foundations."[22] It was this type of criticism that estranged these *patriotes prononcés* from the Directory—particularly as they attempted to implement their persuasion by organizing independent clubs. In the face of such a threat the Directory was obliged to support the status quo in the person of officials who may have lacked sufficient energy in carrying out official policy but who at least did not question the established order and reopen the issue of "equality."

The struggle over the personnel of the departmental administration thus reflected differences in political and social attitudes. Soon it crystallized around the formation of two rival clubs in Evreux, one behind Touquet, the other behind Crochon. The clash of the two clubs in turn served to articulate the issues that were at stake.

According to Touquet, Crochon was preparing a double move to wrest the initiative from his Jacobin critics: he planned first to start

[20] *Bulletin* No. 61, 29 fructidor V; No. 72, 17 vendémiaire VI.
[21] *Ibid*. No. 21, 29 pluviôse VI.   [22] *Ibid*. No. 134, 27 ventôse VI.

an official departmental newspaper to which all local functionaries would be required to subscribe; and second, to establish a Constitutional Circle in Evreux under the aegis of the departmental administration. Touquet denounced both possibilities. An official newspaper that controlled the sources of most local news he deemed an intolerable abridgment of the free press—besides which he had no desire to compete with a second paper in this relatively small department. As for a club under official auspices, he held that it would be a disaster for the Jacobins: "they would be amalgamated with the enemies of the public interest: the honnêtes gens would be in a majority. The Jacobins have no desire to be involved with that horde assembled by an administration."[23]

Meanwhile the Jacobins consummated their own efforts to form a club in Evreux, where "abuses and threats" had previously thwarted them. In placards addressed to the citizens of Evreux they explained that their objectives were "to demonstrate the advantages of a free and popular government . . . to develop the wise and immutable principles of the Constitution . . . to confer public office only upon upright, virtuous, modest, patriotic, and enlightened men."[24] Starting with a nucleus of thirty to forty men, the club held its opening meeting on the first of ventôse (19 February 1798) in a former church, the Ursulines.

Almost immediately this club was denounced to the Police Ministry by a local official who claimed that he had been invited to join but had refused. His letter described the manner in which the club "illegally" screened its applicants, with nomination by five members, an investigation by a committee that reported back to the club, and a final vote by secret ballot. Moreover, he charged, "I recognize among them good republicans, but also persons whom I have heard declare in front of over a hundred people that Babeuf was murdered at Vendôme"—a reference to Chaumont-Quitry. Crochon

---

[23] *Ibid.* Nos. 106-107, 29 nivôse and 1 pluviôse VI. The issue of an official newspaper came up also in the Maine-et-Loire department, where there seemed to be a connection between the suppression of the Jacobin *Ami des Principes* and the creation of an official organ controlled by commissioner Moreau, the *Journal du département de Maine-et-Loire*. See B. Bois, *La Vie scolaire et les créations intellectuelles en Anjou pendant la Révolution* (Paris, 1928), pp. 463-66.

[24] *Aux Républicains de la Commune d'Evreux par le Cercle Constitutionnel séant aux ci-devant Ursulines* (Impr. Touquet) placard in A.N. F⁷ 7401, fol. 3769.

also wrote to Paris in order to denounce "fifteen or twenty" prime movers in the club "who wish to be the only republicans," and who blackballed several local officials in the process.[25] To these charges, which were more or less legitimate, the club provided an answer in its placards, by defending its principles of selection. "Have we refused to admit any friend of the revolution? Is there among us a single member who has not given proof of a pronounced patriotism?" Unity was desirable, the club declared, "but we want it only with the republicans who have shared our principles, our oppression, our triumphs, and who still share our sentiments."[26]

Unable to breach this group or render it innocuous, the local establishment led by Crochon finally did organize a club of its own. Accepting as members anyone who came to its meetings, the second club (which met at a local Collège) was larger than the first and did form a successful counterpoise to it. The Collège Club met twice per décade and devoted its sessions primarily to hortatory readings of government communications and the speeches of men like Benjamin Constant.[27]

There were some citizens in Evreux who were disturbed by this division, this spectacle of two Constitutional Circles "devouring each other." In a relatively small city like Evreux a rivalry of this kind was deemed particularly dangerous because the principals were in such close proximity; there was nothing impersonal about it. In fact an attempt was made to effect an amalgamation of the two clubs in the name of republican unity. But when the Collège Club proposed a "réunion en masse," the Ursulines Club "unanimously" rejected the idea, suggesting instead that each club appoint twenty commissioners who would form the nucleus of a new, united club, and who would then proceed to screen and admit other members. In the end no agreement was reached. Meanwhile the Ursulines Club eased its entrance procedures in order to counteract the adverse charges about its exclusiveness; henceforth a candidate need only be recommended by one member and would then be voted upon in secret. This it was hoped would make it clear that no

[25] A.N. F⁷ 7401, fol. 3769: substitute commissioner to the Criminal Tribunal to M. of Pol., 11 and 13 ventôse VI; Crochon to M. of Pol., 17 and 27 ventôse.
[26] *Aux Républicains de la Commune d'Evreux.*
[27] F⁷ 7401, fol. 3769: Crochon to Directory, 12 germinal VI; *Bulletin* No. 129, 13 ventôse VI.

patriot would be turned away while no "political chameleon" would be admitted, as they were to the Collège Club.[28] The differing complexions of the two clubs did not change, however. As one chronicler put it, the Collège Club was composed "of almost all the officials and of the federalists," while the Ursulines Club contained "all of the terrorists." Besides Touquet and Chaumont, the most prominent figure in the Neo-Jacobin club was the ex-conventionnel Francastel, an unrepentant Montagnard who was back in his department as a national forestry agent, and who personified for conservatives the Jacobin as terrorist or exagéré.[29]

‡ III ‡

Local struggles of this kind frequently spilled over to Paris where the principals sought favorable publicity and influence. Touquet's friend Coesnon-Pellerin accordingly editorialized for him in the *Ami de la Patrie*, explaining how "royalists, oligarchs, and scoundrels" are terrified of the Constitutional Circles, and how in some places they have formed rival clubs when they were unable to muzzle the original ones by intrigue and slander. Citing Evreux as a case in point, he reported that the second club of the Collège had failed in its ruse to effect a réunion en masse with the Ursulines Club, but had sown needless discord in the process. Touquet evidently had another champion at the Police Ministry, for an undated, unsigned report in its files praised the Ursulines Club for reviving public spirit and deplored the formation of a second club "which troubled public tranquility, dividing the republicans. The necessity to close the second club has become urgent," it concluded. Presumably on the basis of this report the Ministry ordered the departmental administration of the Eure to close the Club of the Collège.[30]

This setback caused Crochon to redouble his attacks on the exagérés of the Ursulines. He pointed to the participation of Francastel, "whom public opinion accuses of having rivaled Carrier in ferocity," and for the first time the word "anarchist" appeared in Crochon's letters. Eventually he threw aside all restraint and

---

[28] A.N. F⁷ 7401, fol. 3769: Delamar to M. of Pol., 29 ventôse VI; *Bulletin* No. 129 (supplément), 13/15 ventôse, and No. 130, 17 ventôse.

[29] *Souvenirs et Journal d'un bourgeois d'Evreux*, p. 131. On Francastel, see A. Kuscinski's *Dictionnaire des Conventionnels*.

[30] *Ami de la Patrie* No. 723, 24 ventôse VI; F⁷ 7401, fol. 3769.

charged that "the most execrated agents of the Terror can be counted in its midst; ex-nobles who—to make themselves appear as the best republicans—reprinted and placarded the infamous libels of Babeuf; men who regard the Constitution of the Year 3 as insufficiently republican." Crochon enlisted the support of another leader of the Eure federalists of 1793, the abbé LeCerf who was now a deputy to the Legislature. LeCerf intervened at the highest level and persuaded director Merlin de Douai that Touquet's club and newspaper must be suppressed; a draft memorandum to this effect was drawn up on 10 germinal (30 March 1798), and after a brief delay it was executed.[31]

The struggle that was now coming to a head in the elections was more than a conflict between the "ins" and "outs" for political place, in which old epithets like "terrorist" or "federalist" were used as grist for the mill of political maneuvering. The Jacobins were trying to free themselves from unpopular, and allegedly lethargic officials; the Directorials were trying to curb the activism of self-proclaimed patriots who irresponsibly attacked public officials in order to replace them with their own men. Below this tangible conflict two political persuasions, two concepts of republican citizenship, were clashing. In Touquet's exaggerated rhetoric it was nothing less than a struggle between good citizens ("people interested in the practice of virtue") and "egoists" or honnêtes gens ("rich people, people with pretensions and privileges, people given to idleness and accustomed to luxury and pleasure seeking, people who scorn common folk").[32]

The small Jacobin party in Evreux engaged the Directorials in a fierce conflict which they might easily have avoided by seeking their advancement through accommodation. Touquet himself surely stood to lose rather than gain in a prolonged fight with the administration, since he was initially a journalist acceptable to the whole spectrum of republicans. But instead Touquet and his supporters identified themselves as the party of the *petit contribuable*—the little man whose primary goal remained the fulfillment of "equality." And clearly this vague social issue had to be formulated and fought in political terms. Identification with the revolutionary past had to

[31] A.N. F⁷ 7401, fol. 3769: Crochon to M. of Pol., 12 and 19 germinal VI; A.N. F⁷ 3688/13 (Eure): LeCerf to M. of Pol., 10 germinal.
[32] *Bulletin* No. 124, 5 ventôse VI.

be sustained rather than obscured. Thus the Ursulines Club proclaimed that in the elections it would support only "proven republicans" and not, as others were advocating, those "who have been inconspicuous in the revolution." Moreover the peoples' electors must be men of probity, good family men who regard their fellow men as equals. "We will seek these modest, true republicans, and we will find them in the most certain retreat of virtue, *l'heureuse médiocrité.*" These electors will in turn choose deputies "capable and worthy of defending the sacred cause of liberty."[33] While these deputies would not necessarily come from the same "modest" circumstances as the voters, they should be men who stand for the same principles and who are capable of defending them in Paris—men like the Montagnards of 1793, perhaps.

The heat of this preelection controversy served no doubt to exaggerate the specific charges being hurled back and forth—as when Crochon, feeling increasingly beleaguered, started labeling individuals as Babeuvists. At the same time the intensity led people to speak their minds more openly than usual. So it was that François Chaumont-Quitry published an article on the eve of the electoral assembly designed to expose decisively the department's social malaise, and to demonstrate its connection with the political power structure.

Directorials frequently described the Jacobins as exclusifs—meaning that they supposedly considered themselves the only true republicans, to the exclusion of less ardent citizens. The author took this label and turned it around on his enemies. The anti-Jacobins were the real exclusifs, he declared; they who, like the aristocrats of the old regime, "despise or at least disdain the agricultural and mechanical professions."[34]

Like the "gentlemen" they wish to monopolize all positions. They have retained the haughtiness of the bourgeoisie and have acquired the pride of the nobility; they always stand aloof from the laborer, the artisan, the worker, the people whom in their feudal vocabulary they call "the *canaille of the faubourgs.*" Such is that

[33] *Ibid.* No. 129 (supplément), 15 ventôse. This article begins: "L'adresse suivant circule dans ce département. . . ." Presumably it was being circulated in the clubs.
[34] *Bulletin* No. 143, 19 germinal VI: "Des Exclusifs"; continued in No. 144, 21 germinal, which was the last issue.

company of ambitious oligarchs who consider the rest of the patriots *gross* people who use *improper* language, who lack precision in their *ideas*, and whose republicanism is *uninformed*. They exclude that mass of citizens if not from the constitution then at least from all positions. . . . The insolent designation of *"petits gens"* is being renewed; they are ashamed to shake the hand of a man of the people . . . while they effusively embrace known aristocrats.

Thus, society is being reinfested with *gens comme il faut*. Two orders are being established. One grafted upon the nobility, forming cliques, and requiring at least the title of bourgeois to be admitted to them; new patrons with a gilded clientele of ex-nobles, the hypocritical motto of priests, the phalanx of men with nice manners, nice style, fine dinners. . . . The other order is composed of those unfortunate republicans who have no estate other than their own morals, no ambition other than to be free, no wealth other than their work, no pleasures other than those of a good household—*"gross"* men who are accosted on one day for their vote, and ignored the next day; a sovereign in tatters who is granted one hour of independence in order that he may be subdued and humiliated for the rest of the year; a squalid mass of 27 million men whose fate it is to be eternally degraded and despised by the million oligarchs.

In Chaumont's indictment, the offenses of the new "gentlemen" lie not only in the barriers to social equality that they erect, but in their political practices. They do not participate in the political clubs (those "temples of equality"); instead they speculate in national lands, traffic in certificates of disability for draftees, and close their eyes to the corruption that surrounds them. The local officials serve the oligarchs, he added, "[they] protect the manufacturers against their own workers . . . allow decrees, contracts, procès-verbaux, and judgments to be placed on auction at their offices." They are obsequious to a pretty "lady" whom they call *Madame,* while adopting a brusk, disdainful tone with the widow of a war veteran whom they call *Citizen*.

This same combination of social climbing, corruption, and political favoritism was the target of Jacobin journalists elsewhere—in Metz, for example, where the "grandees and rich egoists," the frivolities of high society, and the self-seeking corruption of the men who served it were repeatedly attacked in the *Journal des Amis*.[35] Rarely was the confrontation as explicit or as skilfully conducted as it was in Evreux. But most Neo-Jacobin spokesmen maintained that a political system which sought to limit the people's active participation in civic life fostered these social pretensions and this divisive class consciousness. The ideal of social equality and dignity for all citizens (integration, we might call it today) could be upheld only by means of broad political participation and constant vigilance. Meanwhile one could raise the banner of virtuous simplicity while exposing the alleged hypocrisy and invidiousness of the upperclass. With transparent sentimentality, Chaumont-Quitry concluded his article with a passionate sans-culotte peroration:

> I prefer the shopkeepers of the market, the workers, the spinners who get together to buy a newspaper . . . I prefer the conversations and common sense of the artisan who is concerned with his country's politics, to the puerile tales of a perfumed old man surrounded in a salon . . . I prefer the patriotic simplicity of a worker . . . a popular circus where a chapter of the constitution is recited with enthusiasm, to those little academies where they read licentious pamphlets . . . I prefer a simple civic banquet at which, amidst a fraternal disorder, toasts are proclaimed to wellbeing on earth and the expulsion of tyrants.[36]

On the following day the *Bulletin* was suppressed, never to reappear.

RHETORIC can be a distracting smoke screen that obscures the doings of political activists. In Directorial France this was not necessarily the case. On the contrary, what often obscures is the surface battle of personalities and patronage that is usually taken to characterize the period's political life. The attitudes and issues articulated by the *Bulletin de l'Eure*—and especially the remarkable article by Chaumont-Quitry—offer an unusually clear insight into the Neo-Jacobin persuasion. Though the Eure Jacobins stopped short of formulating a party program, they did manage to express a wide-ranging consciousness in regard to social, moral, and political questions. Their

---

[35] See my article "The Revival of Jacobinism in Metz During the Directory," *Journal of Modern History*, xxxviii (1966), especially 25-28.

[36] *Bulletin* No. 144, 21 germinal VI.

persuasion—their view of how politics should be conducted and how politics might influence social issues—was no secret in Evreux.

Though this case study provides little hard information about the social composition of the clubs in the Eure, it is clear that the members came neither from the department's wealthy and prominent citizens, nor from its uneducated, indigent masses. How many of the petit contribuables for whom they claimed to speak might have eventually developed a political consciousness and supported these activists, we have no way of knowing. And whether the movement would eventually have addressed itself to the workers for whom Chaumont-Quitry expressed a passing concern is even more problematic. The relatively ill-defined status of the three primary leaders (Touquet, Chaumont-Quitry, and Francastel) seems to mirror the supposition that Jacobinism did not represent any well-defined social group, like the commercial bourgeoisie or the workers in the Norman textile industry. As social types Touquet and Chaumont belong to that unalienated intelligentsia clustered around the Neo-Jacobin newspapers. They were by no means outsiders; each could have secured his livelihood and status by a policy of cooperation with the prevalent brand of conservative republicanism. Instead they opted for opposition, risking their present positions and standing for the uncertain rewards of factional politics. And they attracted followers whose ranks may not have been very large numerically but who were strong enough to support a newspaper with pronounced dissenting views, and to put up a good though ultimately losing fight in the departmental elections of 1798.[37]

This case study further illustrates that the representative institutions and constitutional guarantees of Directorial France were in principle adequate as a framework for Jacobinism. Under such conditions politics still had an expressive function that could reflect the attitudes of politically conscious citizens; it was not simply a vehicle for advancing individual careers or special interests. The Jacobins in the Eure—as in other departments—promoted their own candidates for office, justifying their attacks on the incumbents by pointing to the alleged lethargy and inadequate republican "spirit" of these officials. More difficult to express was their desire to use a purge of local officeholders as a wedge for putting equality back in

[37] See A.N. AF iii 266/Eure: renseignemens diverses and P.V. de l'Assemblée électorale, which will be discussed below, Ch. x.

the Revolution's program. Here their formulation remained essentially negative; they knew what they opposed. Wherever Neo-Jacobinism found its voice, social pretension came under attack. The Directorial establishment was denounced as an incipient oligarchy that was reducing the average person—the petit contribuable —to the status of a second-class citizen, and betraying the Revolution's egalitarian promise.

CHAPTER VIII

Neo-Jacobinism and the Parisian
Sans-Culottes

Paris led a dual life at the height of revolution. The hub of a nationally organized Jacobin government, it was also a collection of 48 quasi-autonomous sections. The newly organized cadres of sans-culottes or sectionnaires did not fuse harmoniously with the Jacobin leadership. Robespierrist or government-oriented in its politics, the mighty Paris Jacobin Club remained essentially middle class in composition. Outside its orbit the sans-culottes had their own clubs and sectional assemblies, which formed the institutional basis for a kind of popular democracy at the local level that was incompatible with Jacobin centralization. In addition, the Mountain's pragmatic egalitarianism appeared insufficiently defined or aggressive to suit the sectionnaires. Jacobins and sans-culottes in Paris were necessary but uneasy allies, their relationship aptly described by Albert Soboul as dialectical. Depending on popular support for such causes as the expulsion of the Girondins and war mobilization, the Mountain occasionally had to move beyond its own goals. For example, on the *journée* of 5 September 1793 it bowed before a determined mobilization of sans-culotte pressure, to decree several distasteful terroristic measures like the creation of the armée révolutionnaire. But in the end, in Soboul's phrase, schism was ineluctable. As the tactician of a consolidated revolutionary government, Robespierre personally took the lead in curbing the strident democracy of the sans-culottes. Under the guise of his assault on the rival hébertist faction in germinal Year II, he brought about the disbanding of the independent sectional clubs and menaced recalcitrant militants with arrest. Henceforth the popular movement that had carried the Revolution forward by successive *journées* and continuous pressure lost its power of intimidation and initiative.[1]

Robespierre's curtailment of sans-culotte autonomy proved to be a mere prologue to what followed after his fall. During the thermi-

[1] See the essential works of Albert Soboul and Richard Cobb, cited in Ch. 1 and elsewhere, and A. Mathiez's *La Vie chère* for the Robespierrist perspective.

dorian reaction the sans-culottes were completely driven out of political life in the sections. Their views were ignored, their past actions censured, their persons attacked. A winter of severe shortages and disastrous inflation, surpassing even the years 1789 and 1793, culminated the ordeal of 1795. By the spring, masses of sans-culottes (especially in the faubourgs and the crowded central market districts) were driven by privation and despair to rise in protest. For several days they massed, with what arms they could raise, before the Convention to demand economic relief and the restoration of political democracy. Demonstration turned into insurrection on the first of prairial (20 May 1795)—the final episode in the popular movement. Military force crushed the uprising, and its supposed leaders were executed (including half a dozen sympathetic but innocent Montagnards), to become for democrats "the martyrs of prairial." More important, over two thousand militants who had participated in sectional life during the previous year were disarmed or imprisoned for several months, whether or not they had taken part in the Year III *journées.*[2]

What became of the militant sectionnaires who had constituted the popular movement in the Year II? Or, more pertinently, what options were available to those who remained politicized? What options were open, that is, short of the tenuous autonomy that had been possible in the unique situation of the Year II? For an undetermined number, Babeuf's program filled the void with its bold new vision. The spontaneous rising of an armed sovereign people had proven futile in the Year III; Babeuf proposed in its place that the people's vanguard organize a secret conspiracy to overthrow the middle-class republic and establish a reign of egalité réelle. This program doubtless inspired more sympathy in the Paris sections than

[2] See the excellent studies of K. Tonnesson, *La Défaite des Sans-culottes: mouvement populaire et réaction bourgeoise en l'an III* (Paris and Oslo, 1959), and R. C. Cobb and G. Rudé, "Le Dernier mouvement populaire de la Révolution à Paris: les journées de germinal et de prairial an III," *Revue historique* (1955), pp. 250-81. For the Montagnard perspective see *Mémoires de R. Levasseur (de la Sarthe), ex-conventionnel,* Vol. IV (Paris, 1831); J. Claretie, *Les Derniers montagnards: histoire de l'insurrection de prairial an III* (Paris, 1867); and P. Tissot's *Souvenirs de la journée du 1er prairial an III* (Paris, an IV), which was important as democratic propaganda. J. Dautry's essay on the attempted suicides of the "martyrs of prairial" is extremely suggestive: "Réflexions sur les martyrs de Prairial: sacrifice héroïque et mentalité révolutionnaire," in *Gilbert Romme et son temps* (Paris, 1966).

can ever be documented. But there is scant evidence that many sans-culottes actually endorsed Babeuf's call to action. Babeuvist logic and passion roused few sectionnaires to move from sympathy to commitment.[3] In the event, the Conspiracy of Equals and its lugubrious sequel on the plain of Grenelle proved a complete failure. The middle-class republic was not likely to be taken by storm. Uncompromising opposition and conspiratorial subversion in turn became something to be pondered skeptically by the much-abused militants.

Repeated setbacks reduced the greater number of sectionnaires to a disillusioned indifference. But from an imponderable mixture of conviction and opportunism, others accepted the prevailing facts of middle-class ascendancy, and instead of succumbing passively or trying to overthrow it, these politicized militants hoped to dilute it. To accomplish this they had in some measure to join ranks or at least cooperate again with middle-class revolutionary groups.[4] To put it simply, the Neo-Jacobin resurgence of the Year VI became a suitable umbrella for their own activity. What ensued was remote from the aggressive autonomy of the Year II, but it was likewise a far cry from the enforced passivity that came with Neo-Jacobinism's final defeats.

‡ I ‡

During the thermidorian reaction Paris had been redivided into twelve arrondissements, each absorbing four of the old sections. Predictably, the revival of political life after Fructidor spread unevenly among them, being strongest where the surviving cadres were relatively cohesive. Nonetheless, by the beginning of pluviôse a new club had been organized in each arrondissement (see Figure 1). Symbolically, several offered a physical link with the

[3] A. Soboul's important analysis of Babeuf's lists does not really answer this question, but it does show that the potential cadres of Babeuvism were not identical to the cadres of the popular movement: "Personnel sectionnaire et personnel babouviste," *AHRF*, 1960, pp. 436-57. See also M. Shibata's footnote to this article "Sur le personnel ci-devant sectionnaire sous le Directoire," *AHRF*, 1967, pp. 381-84.

[4] Cobb and Rudé have emphasized the breakdown of communication between Montagnards and sans-culottes in the Prairial debacle: "Le Dernier mouvement populaire," pp. 180-81.

past, meeting in buildings that had once housed local popular societies.[5]

Four of these neighborhood clubs seem to have been hopelessly ineffective in overcoming apathy or generating excitement. "Their means are almost nil, their sessions languid; public spirit cannot be warmed by them," concluded the local commissioner about the club in the 3rd arrondissement. Clubs in the 2nd, 9th, and 12th arrondissements trod the same lonely road and left few traces. More than the others they fell victim to the persecutions and calumnies directed against the original clubs. Stigmas from the past produced apathy in the present, according to the Constitutional Circle of the 2nd arrondissement. "Today the family man, the peaceable artisan fears to compromise himself by coming to our meetings."[6] Clubs in the 8th and 10th, on the other hand, enjoyed a marked success, probably as great as any neighborhood club of the Year II, attracting a substantial attendance and making a perceptible impact on their communities. The other six (in the 1st, 4th, 5th, 6th, 7th, and 11th arrondissements) ranged somewhere in between. The documents suggest a measure of success but without demonstrating it conclusively.

In the absence of minutes (except for the 10th arrondissement club) or membership lists, the basic source for studying these clubs remains their petitions. From a variety of repositories one or more such petitions have been retrieved for nine of the twelve clubs. Altogether they offer an indication of the clubs' concerns and activities, as well as a basis for inferences about their size and composition.

On the surface, at least, local political life in Paris was no longer unique; the objectives of the Parisian clubs were virtually indis-

---

[5] By nivôse, nine of these clubs were noted in a list prepared by the Paris Central Police Bureau: "Liste des lieux où sont situés les divers cercles constitutionnels existant dans la commune de Paris." A.N. F⁷ 7353, fol. 9486. Founded shortly thereafter were clubs in the 5th arrondissement (A.N. AF III 516, plaq. 3304, pièces 10-11), 3rd arrondissement (*J. hommes libres* No. 264, 19 pluviôse VI), and Rue du Bacq, 10th arrondissement. See Figure 1. Clubs meeting where popular societies had met in the Year II were those in the 3rd, 5th, 7th, 8th, and 9th. (Cf. Soboul, *Les Sans-Culottes*, pp. 1079, 691, 1084, 1086; Tonnesson, *La Défaite des Sans-culottes*, p. 139.)

[6] A.N. F⁷ 7388, fol. 2560: Rapport . . . première décade de ventôse, 3rd arrondissement; A.N. C 429, fol. 151: Des républicains du 2ème arrond. de Paris, réunis en cercle constitutionnel, 26 pluviôse. Cf. reports by the reliable police observer Gros de Luzenne on the "alarming apathy" encountered by some of the clubs: A.N. F⁷ 3688/13, reports dated 19 and 24 ventôse.

FIGURE I

The Parisian Constitutional Circles

Arrondissement	Locale	Number of Signatures on Petitions
1	Couvent de la Conception Rue Honoré, Div. Place Vendôme (?)	70
2	Rue de Bellefond No. 225, faub. Montmartre	65
3	Maison dite des Petits-Pères, Div. Guillaume Tell	—
4	Place de la Liberté No. 116, Div. Gardes françaises	67
5	Couvent St. Laurent, Div. du Nord	35
6	Institut des Aveugles-travailleurs, Div. des Lombards	60
7	Rue de l'Avoie No. 155, Div. Réunion	75
8	Enfants de la Patrie, faub. Antoine	225
9	Rue de Glatigny No. 10, Div. de la Cité	—
10	Rue du Bacq, Div. Fontaine de Grenelle	140
11	Collège ci-dev D'Harecourt, Rue de la Harpe, Div. Thermes	90
12	Rue de la Vieille Estrapade No. 10, Div. Observatoire	—

SOURCE: see note 5. Signators represent a minimum number of members. The names gathered from the petitions of five of these clubs are reproduced in Appendix I.

tinguishable from the new provincial Constitutional Circles. They wished to bolster republican institutions like the national guard and the décadi, and to cultivate an egalitarian spirit. A report on the 10th arrondissement club speaks of its members' efforts to "democratize the working class."[7] They demanded an end to the persecution of

[7] A.N. F⁷ 3688/13: report dated 19 ventôse on the Rue du Bacq Club: "Les membres ne portaient plus le nom de *patriotes,* de *républicains,* de *jacobins*; ils s'appelaient les *démocrates.* Des officiers et des soldats faisaient partie de cette société. Les membres se repandaient dans toutes les sections pour democratiser la classe ouvrière, et s'y repandent encore. Les bureaux de la police sont remplis de leurs affidés."

former revolutionaries under such labels as "terrorists" or "anarchists," conversely calling for purges of anti-republicans and reactionaries. Such causes as public education and the war veterans' bonus received their support, and they were particularly active in advocating the franchise reforms that will be discussed in the next chapter. Finally, like the provincial clubs, they were the nuclei of local parties at election time.

The founding cadres of these clubs numbered from thirty to sixty men, acting sometimes upon the initiative of smaller groups or particular individuals like the legal clerk and former revolutionary commissioner Aristarque Didot in the 7th arrondissement,[8] or the *instituteur* at the Maison des Aveugles-travailleurs, Valentin Huay in the 6th.[9] A minimal indication of how the clubs grew is offered by the number of signatures on their petitions (Figure 1), but the total memberships were invariably greater. The club in the 11th arrondissement, for example, had to request the use of a medical-school amphitheater to replace the original quarters that it had outgrown. The smaller 4th arrondissement club, which could muster only 67 signatures on its petitions, sold 95 copies of its printed by-laws at a nominal charge. A club meeting in the St. Laurent Convent (5th arrondissement), which once housed a sectional club, reportedly attracted hundreds of participants, though it was founded by 35 men, while the Rue du Bacq Club in the 10th stated that it had almost 400 members, though its meeting place could not accommodate so many people at one time.[10] The less successful clubs attracted be-

[8] Didot's role in founding the 7th arrondissement club is documented in A.N. F⁷ 7353, fol. 9486; and in F⁷ 7408, fol. 4506, enclosing his pamphlet *Réflexions sur les ennemis de la République française* (Impr. Institut des Aveugles-travailleurs), and a covering letter dated 25 ventôse VI. His turbulent career may be glimpsed in Soboul, *Les Sans-culottes*, pp. 119, 428, 594, 698, and Tonnesson, *La Défaite des Sans-culottes*, p. 108n.

[9] Valentin Huay's hand was apparent in every document concerning the 6th arrondissement club, which met at his Institut des Aveugles-travailleurs. Earlier he was described by Babeuf's agent in the arrondissement as a "patriote, bon pour administrer et révolutionner," *Copie des Pièces saisies . . . dans le local que Babeuf occupait lors de son arrestation* (2 vols.; Impr. Nationale, nivôse an V), II, 89. Other activists in this club were Cordas and A. Fiquet who both stood trial at Vendôme; Martin, justice of the peace in the Gravilliers section in the Year II, and sectionnaires LeCreps, Crêté (limonadier), and Lefebvre (menuisier).

[10] A.N. AF III 260: Des républicains du 11ème arrondissement réunis en cercle constitutionnel to M. of Interior, 8 ventôse VI. (A police observer

tween forty to ninety, which compares favorably with the admittedly more numerous local clubs of the Year II.

Contrary to the accepted periodization, sans-culottes had not disappeared as a group from Parisian political life. The twelve neighborhood clubs in the capital were composed primarily of sectionnaires, including a significant number who had suffered persecution for their activities in the Year III. In the main they came from the *monde boutiquier et artisanal* that had provided the elite of the popular movement. Leaders with a larger, more plebeian following in the Year II, these militants in 1798 were simply the remaining activists with a negligible following. Furthermore (a point to be examined shortly) some by this time had abandoned their earlier trades to seek government employment of some kind.[11]

A smaller but influential group in the clubs came from within the orbit of the middle class (professionals, men of letters, and high-status white-collar employees), but with this additional quality: their milieu, too, was the neighborhood. Though belonging to the bourgeoisie themselves, they did not fraternize exclusively with their social peers. Their political world was at least in part spatial, rooted in the *quartier* and in connections with the artisans and shopkeepers who were willing to associate with them. All of these neighborhood clubs contrasted to another Parisian Neo-Jacobin club, the Constitutional Circle of the Rue de l'Université. Like the original Paris Jacobin Club, this one had a nucleus of deputies

---

reported 70 to 80 persons in attendance at a meeting in ventôse: A.N. F⁷ 3688/13: rapport du 22 ventôse—dossier secret.) The budget of the 4th arrondissement club, listing sales of the règlement, is in A.N. F⁷ 7406, fol. 4264. On the 4th and 10th arrondissements see below.

[11] Identification of the petitions' signators in terms of their participation in the popular movement was made through the following sources: Police Records—notably the *fichier* of the Committee of General Security (C.S.G.) in the Archives Nationales; references in Soboul and Tonnesson; the MS electoral lists for Paris in the Year VI (A.N. AF III 260/Seine); documents published by Markov and Soboul on the popular movement; and lists in the *Copie des Pièces saisies* of Babeuf. Of these, only the electoral lists give information on occupation as a matter of course; however, the other sources contain occasional references which cumulatively become fairly uniform. For use in future research, the signators on petitions of several clubs are included in Appendix 1.

(including Marbot and Lamarque) and concerned itself with general questions, domestic and foreign, rather than local problems.[12]

Typical of the cadres that formed the neighborhood clubs were the 35 founders of the 5th arrondissement Constitutional Circle, of whom a number can be identified from police and section records of the Years II and III. A group of its militants came from section faubourg du Nord, where the new club met, including four members of the old revolutionary committee: the lawyer Guibert, the sculptor LeRoux, the sectionnaire Mauvage, who had been disarmed in the Year III, and the amidonnier Dupont, stigmatized as "the second most dangerous man" in the section after the justice of the peace Isambert, for whom Dupont had served as greffier. Other founders of the new club included the sectionnaires Nogaret and Dupré, who had organized petitions on hoarding and price-fixing in the Year II; the musician Leblanc, the porcelain-designer Constant, and the journalist Destival, who in the Year VI was an editor of Valcour's *Indépendant*. Police reports indicate that such sectionnaires at Hébert (painter) and deLormelle (carpenter) were also active in this club.[13]

Members of the successful Rue du Bacq Club came from three sources. The nearby Hôtel des Invalides contributed what was

[12] Colliot's *Journal des campagnes et des armées* acted as printer and publicist for this club. Its "Profession de Foi" and its address on the eve of the elections were reprinted here (see Nos. 681 and 706, 13 pluviôse and 8 ventôse) as well as in other papers and in pamphlet form. But see also its "Adresse . . . à l'assemblée constituante de la Nation Batave," and its "Adresse . . . au corps législatif de la République Ligurienne," in No. 714, 16 ventôse; follow-up articles in *Ibid*. Nos 723 and 726, 25 and 28 ventôse; *J. hommes libres* No. 298, 23 ventôse; and *Le Persevérant* No. 3, 29 germinal. The wide circulation of its addresses, even in the *Moniteur*, would suggest the prominence of its leadership; this is verified in an unprocessed police report (A.N. F^7 3688/13: rapport du 26 au 27 ventôse by Agent No. 43): ". . . le cercle constitutionnel séant rue de l'Université dont les représentans Marbot et Lamarque sont régulateurs."

[13] The petition from 35 founders to the Police Ministry, 3 pluviôse, is in A.N. F^7 7381, fol. 1863. The growth of the club is described in a report to the Directory dated 24 germinal in A.N. AF iii 516, plaq. 3304 (pièces 10-11), in which other names are mentioned. Soboul, *Les Sans-culottes*, pp. 297 and 691, refers to the popular society that met in the Eglise St. Laurent in the Year II. Identification of the signators was facilitated by documents reprinted in Markov and Soboul, *Die Sansculotten von Paris: Dokumente zur Geschichte der Volksbewegung 1793-94* (Berlin, 1957), pp. 240, 242, 186, 162, 498. Another bourgeois founder of the club was the municipal administrator Vigier on whom see A.N. F 1b Seine/24, dossier 5ème arrond.

probably an important group, including Caillot, Gomegéon, Groslaire, and LeMonnier. Secondly came former employees of the revolutionary government (such as Jacquemin, Laugier, Marcellin, Raisson, Sijas) and intellectuals like the physician Victor Bach, jurist Gauthier-Biauzat, journalist Caignard, and artist Gautherot. The *Journal des hommes libres* was represented here by no less than four men: publisher Vatar, and editors Camus, Eon, and Girard. Finally there were the militants of the Year II from sections Fontaine de Grenelle and Unité (including Blondiot, Copie, Dorlé, Magendie, Paulin, Pierron, Pilon, Pons, Rondel, Rouval).[14]

The percentage of identifiable signatures on the clubs' petitions rises for the 4th and 7th arrondissements thanks to the information in the lists compiled previously by Babeuf's agents. Together with material from police files and the references in Soboul and Tonnesson, this allows one-third of the signators to be identified as participants in the sectional life of the Year II. With great zeal Babeuf's agent in the 7th arrondissement assembled lists of *patriotes démocrates*, basing this designation on reputations from previous years rather than commitments to the as yet unborn Conspiracy of Equals. Among the 75 signatures on petitions from the Rue de l'Avoie Club, 23 appeared on these lists, including 3 with the special designation *propre au commandement* (the house painter Garnier, the glazer Roche, and the fruit-seller Laquier). Two of the more militant individuals were the glazer Bernard and the foundry worker Duval, who were both arrested during the prairial *journées*.[15]

Eleven names from Babeuf's list of democrats in the 4th arrondissement turn up on that club's petitions, bringing to 22 out of 67 the total identifiable as sectionnaires in the Year II. In all there were at least four revolutionary committeemen (Blussaud, Chassein, Fillion, and LeMaitre), several cannoniers, and at least nine people disarmed or arrested during the Year III *journées* (including Bot,

[14] Two petitions yielded 140 signatures: A.N. F7 7402/b, fol. 3906, and A.N. C 431, fol. 167. Besides identifications made from C.S.G. files and electoral lists of the Year VI, material in Markov and Soboul, *Die Sansculotten*, pp. 460-64, helped identify activists from the Fontaine-de-Grenelle section.

[15] Two petitions yielded 70 signatures: A.N. AF III 260/Seine, and A.N. F7 7353, fol. 9486. The lists of Babeuf's agents are in *Copie des Pièces saisies*, II, 181, 197, 215. (Bergeret, Chevalier, Houdaille, Mercier, Valet—section Droits de l'homme; Noury, Foresse, Servent, Duval, Baudequin, Petielle, Chapuis, Lefort, Garnier, Bernard, Roche—section Homme armée; Jahyer, Hardy, Dimay—section Réunion; Laquier, Boucotte, Hanique, Servant.)

Ceré, Boutaud, Deladreux, and Cousin, president of section Museum).[16]

Information in the police dossiers and section papers on the occupations of these men is unfortunately spotty, but Babeuf's lists frequently contained some reference to this. In these two clubs the identifiable members were from one strata or another of sansculotterie, with few exceptions like certain *employées* who may have been from the bourgeoisie. Parenthetically, three names on the 7th arrondissement list bore the added notation *instruit*: the saddlemaker Petielle, the employée Chapuis and the wig-maker Foresse. Only two or three were identified as ouvriers or held manifestly menial jobs like courriers. Far more numerous were the artisans and shopkeepers including four cobblers, two glazers, two hatters, and two wig-makers.[17]

‡ II ‡

The first and the most remarkable of these Parisian clubs was located in the faubourg Antoine. Founded on 24 fructidor Year V (10 September 1797), the Réunion Politique du Faubourg Antoine assembled in the Enfants de la Patrie, a neighborhood orphanage that had formerly been a church.[18] To those who now gathered together a continuity with the revolutionary past was surely manifest, since this building had housed the last of the Parisian popular societies, the Société des Quinze-Vingts, spearhead of the germinal *journées* in the Year III.

[16] Two petitions yielded 67 signatures: A.N. F⁷ 7406, fol. 4264, and A.N. F⁷ 3688/13 (denouncing the commissioner to the 4th arrondissement). Babeuf's lists in *Copie des Pièces saisies*, II, 111, 116, 118, 122. (Auvray, Bot, Boquet, Burguburu, Dumoy, Fabre, Kelar, Jacquinet, Jouvre, Langlois, LeMaitre, Ravet.)

[17] Occupations (mainly from Babeuf's lists) are as follows. 4th arrondissement: 2 cordonniers, 2 chapeliers; one each: limonadier, gendarme, rentier, concierge, courrier, loueur de carrosses, mercier, bottier. 7th arrondissement: 3 employés, 2 cordonniers, 2 vitriers, 2 perruquiers; one each: tailleur, ceinturonnier, chirurgien, sellier, peintre en batimens, peintre en miniatures, doreur, tireur au banc(?), fruitier, ouvrier fondeur, serrurier.

[18] This historic building is discussed in L. Lambeau, *L'Hôpital des Enfants-Trouvés du faubourg Saint-Antoine* (Paris, 1903). In September 1792 section Quinze-Vingts petitioned the Legislature to expel the nuns who lived there. On the Société des Quinze-Vingts see Tonnesson, *La Défaite des Sans-culottes*, pp. 72, 139, 147.

Six men, all artisans and neighbors, organized the Réunion Politique:[19]

F.J.B. Caron, carpenter, rue Charonne
L.J.P. Letailleur, gazier, rue Charonne
Louis Moreau, carpenter, rue Traversière
L. E. Hardevillé, gazier, rue Montreuil
Philippe Herré, cobbler, rue faub. Antoine
P. Z. Dertus, gazier, rue faub. Antoine

They were typical of the more than two hundred men who took part in the club's deliberations and activities. (A list of some 220 signators of its petitions and letters may be found in Appendix I.) Though it was less "popular" or populous than the crowded working-class districts of the central market area, its concentration of artisans had made the faubourg a bastion of sans-culottisme. Reflecting the social character of its neighborhood, the Réunion was composed almost exclusively of artisans, shopkeepers, journeymen, and petty functionaries. Virtually no identifiable middle-class elements can be found in its ranks. Rather, it was a club of carpenters, stonemasons, locksmiths, harness-makers, textile craftsmen, and wine-sellers, to name some of the more common occupations (see Appendix II). While elusive occupational nomenclature, and the usual absence of detailed membership lists, make it impossible to determine how many were self-employed and how many were wage earners in the faubourg's larger *ateliers*, it is clear that most members were skilled or semi-skilled artisans by training and that few were wealthy or solidly independent.[20]

In any event, to perceive the Reunion's milieu it is not sufficient to catalogue the ostensible occupations of its members. Yesterday's gazier or menuisier might still list himself as such even though he was today's unemployed or underemployed artisan. The contraction of the luxury trades, the persecution of sectionnaires after Thermidor, and the recession of 1797 all intensified the dislocations

[19] A.N. F⁷ 6140, dossier 165: Declaration faite au Bureau Central par divers citoyens d'ouvrir une assemblée. . . .

[20] The names of the members (Appendix 1) have been gathered from all the petitions and documents that will be cited in the notes to this chapter. Information about some of these individuals comes primarily from the C.S.G. card file, from references in Soboul and Tonnesson, and from the documents of the Babeuf plot (see Appendix II).

of economic life that France's sans-culottes suffered.[21] The various strata of sans-culotterie found themselves in a tenuous condition whose problems were mirrored in the case of one Diochet. This member of the Réunion—whose story illustrates common themes by way of exception—had been a wig-maker in 1789. By 1793 he was employed in the post office, government work being an occupational refuge for many sans-culottes, and title to it a part of their revolutionary ethos. But for Diochet this was a temporary expedient, for by 1798 he had become a café-keeper. Perhaps his café brought him chronic debt rather than profit, but in following a path that Frenchmen still find irresistible, he was trying to raise himself once again to an independent status. While Diochet's capacity to marshal the necessary capital was unusual, the pressures upon him were the common lot of his fellow sectionnaires.

Members of the Réunion likewise shared a common political background. At its meetings militants from the faubourg's sections in the Year II now reassembled. With the exception of General Rossignol (a famous if unvictorious "sans-culotte" general in the Vendée), the Réunion's members had been active mainly in their own sections and were almost certainly unknown outside of the faubourg. Over 35 can be identified from police records, which also document their difficulties during the thermidorian reaction (see Appendix II). At least twelve (Boyer, Brisvin, Demony, Gillé, Henriet, Hivert, Humblet, Laurent, Leban, Mercier, Thiboust, and Vacret) had been members of civil or revolutionary committees in sections Montreuil, Popincourt, Indivisibilité, and Quinze-Vingts. Five militants who had gone off with the armée révolutionnaire in the Year II reappeared in the Réunion in the Year VI.[22] More important, among the Réunion's members were men who were denounced, disarmed, or imprisoned for their alleged connection with the Year III *journées*. Several had been branded as instigators even before the uprisings. Hardevillé, Gillé, and Humblet, for example, were ordered arrested by the Committee of General Security in pluviôse III as leaders of the Société des Quinze-Vingts, which had been denounced by the thermidorian committee of surveillance

---

[21] See R. Schnerb, "La Dépression économique sous le Directoire après la disparition du papier-monnaie: an V-an VIII," *AHRF*, 1934, pp. 27-49.

[22] Brabant, Laurent, Placet, Potemont, and Vingternier. Cf. R. C. Cobb, *Les Armées révolutionnaires: instrument de la terreur dans les départements* (2 vols.; Paris and The Hague, 1963).

in the 8th arrondissement. Boyer, Cochery, Fournerot, and Thiboust were denounced for their part in secret meetings that preceded the germinal days, the so-called "conspiration Lagrelet," while
others participated in the section meetings that helped place the
faubourg on an insurrectionary footing. After the germinal days,
the arrested included Brisvin, Laudet, Leban, and Potemont—all of
whom reappeared in the Réunion Politique in the Year VI. A second wave of arrests following the *journée* of 2 prairial swept up
Laurent, Henriet, Letailleur, and others who had never held even
local office.[23] This element of rank-and-file sectionnaires was the
backbone of the faubourg's new Constitutional Circle.

Here, then, was a remarkably cohesive cadre of surviving sectionnaires. More substantial and better organized than similar ones in
other arrondissements, their club was nonetheless far from unique.
The absence of members from the revolutionary bourgeoisie did set
it apart from other clubs, provincial and Parisian, for elsewhere
such cadres generally worked with or under Jacobin tutelage. But
this very circumstance makes it all the more significant that the Réunion Politique established direct liaisons with middle-class Neo-
Jacobin elements in the capital. Indeed their whole effort was possible largely by virtue of a sympathetic Police Minister's intervention.
The history of the Réunion indicates therefore not only the survival
of political activism among typical sans-culottes, but a renewal of
cooperation with the revolutionary bourgeoisie.

‡ III ‡

Ever since the Directory's inauguration the Police Ministry had
been the democrats' nemesis. Reaction had been incarnated by Minister Cochon, known familiarly as the "assassin of Vendôme." His
power to overrule or instruct local officials in the handling of dissi-
dents gave the ministry considerable leverage over political life
everywhere, but in Paris its role was emphatic. With its network of
agents and informers it systematically harassed democrats and kept
them on the defensive. Such was Cochon's zeal that his loyalty to
the republic itself was eventually questioned. In preparation for the
fructidor coup the Directory therefore dismissed him, and sought to

---

[23] See Tonnesson, *La Défaite des Sans-culottes,* pp. 147, 366-67 and *passim.*

replace him with a reliable republican of proven experience and integrity.

Pierre Sotin seemed eminently qualified. The son of a Breton *parlementaire*, Sotin possessed the elitist qualities that the Directory sought in its appointees. His commitment to revolution and republicanism was early and constant in his department. But moderation seemed implicit in his involvement with the federalist movement and his subsequent arrest by Carrier at Nantes in November 1793. At the ensuing trial, however, Carrier himself testified that Sotin had been an excellent citizen who never deviated from revolutionary principles except for that indiscretion. The jury of the Revolutionary Tribunal accordingly found him innocent of counterrevolutionary intentions, and along with most of the Nantais in that group he was acquitted. Remaining in Paris, he held a variety of positions in the Parisian administration under the Directory and was serving as its commissioner to the Seine department when he was nominated by LaRevellière for the Police Ministry.[24]

LaRevellière soon rued that day. While Sotin fully justified the Directors' confidence that he would act vigorously in his key post, he passed far beyond their intentions. Conversely, the *Journal des hommes libres*, which greeted the appointment of this "excellent republican" with an enthusiasm usually reserved for Jacobin stalwarts, had reason to grow increasingly pleased. To the Directory's surprise and the democrats' delight, Sotin turned out to be a Neo-Jacobin.[25]

Significant changes ensued. Under his tenure the ministry metamorphosed from persecutor to paladin of democrats. A purge brought the dismissal of the most notorious reactionaries in the ministry and their replacement with former Jacobins in top posts

---

[24] Biographical information from V. Pierre, *La Terreur sous le Directoire* (Paris, 1887), pp. 38-39, and S. Lacroix, *Le Département de Paris et de la Seine pendant la Révolution* (Paris, 1904), pp. 331-32, 341-44, 353-54; LaRevellière, *Mémoires*, II, 117-19.

[25] *J. hommes libres* No. 70, 10 thermidor V; *Démocrate constitutionnel* No. 10 (20/21 fructidor V); *Défenseur de la Vérité* No. 54, 12 vendémiaire VI and No. 100, 28 brumaire VI; *Tribun du Peuple* No. 64, 6 nivôse VI; *J. hommes libres* No. 272, 27 pluviôse: "Situation rapprochée et comparée de la République avant et après fructidor." LaRevellière uncomprehendingly blamed Sotin's "betrayal" on the influence of Barras (*Mémoires*, II, 119).

and sectional militants in lesser ones. The secret political bureau, which supervised investigations of Parisian political activity, was conferred upon the brother-in-law of the martyred Montagnard Goujon, Pierre Tissot. One of the most principled and admired democrats in Paris, Tissot's liaisons had extended both into the world of the old Paris Jacobin Club and the sections. As secretary of the ministry, Sotin appointed LaChevardière, a member of the Paris Jacobin Club and the Paris municipality during the Terror, whose standing among Jacobins survived his association with Danton. The Jacobin journalist Caignart was named head of the émigré bureau, while Veyrat and Niquille—men known in the sections— were appointed inspectors in charge of surveillance. Subordinate positions went to sectionnaires like Cavagnac, Chefdeville, Pepin, Pierron, and Warin.[26]

Once a stronghold of reaction and royalism, the ministry now showed unbending rigor against royalism. Sotin personally advised the Directory against making exceptions in the deportation of priests and émigrés. Playing down the threat of renewed terrorism, he circularized the departmental authorities to warn that even after Fructidor royalism remained the nation's paramount threat.[27] To help the constituted authorities purge undesirable officials his ministry gathered information under these revealing categories: individuals who had opposed the *journée* of 18 fructidor in any way, who had opposed the forced loan, and who had "smeared excellent patriots as terrorists and blood drinkers." A pragmatic Jacobin could hardly have asked for more.[28]

Aggressive prosecution of alleged royalists was only part of the change. Unforeseen by the Directory, its appointee was also a determined protector of democrats and their clubs. As indicated earlier, Sotin consistently handled the denunciations against the

[26] A.N. AF III 509, plaq. 3224 (pièces 43, 58, 60, 62, 69); A.N. F⁷ 3006, dossier 4 (Bureau particulier); A.N. F⁷ 3007, dossier 7 (Bureau de l'émigration); A.N. AF III 45: No. 155-56 (Personnel: brumaire VI). On Tissot, see Ch. II, note 13; on LaChevardière see Lacroix, *Le Département de Paris*, pp. 411, 417, 461.

[27] A.N. F⁷ 7298, fol. 3097: rapport au Directoire, 4ème jour compl. an V; *J. hommes libres* No. 171, 16 brumaire VI. Sotin's pursuit of "royalists" was so implacable that on 9 pluviôse he apologized to the Directory, which had apparently criticized him for excessive zeal (A.N. AF III 47, fol. 169, pièce 46).

[28] A.N. F⁷ 3007, dossier 3: M. of Pol., to deptal. admin. (Seine), vendémiaire VI.

clubs that crossed his desk by interpreting Constitutional Article 362 as liberally as possible. Essentially this prevented the clubs from being impeded piecemeal by the interference of unsympathetic local officials. In Paris this protection was especially sustained. With secret funds Sotin subsidized the publishers of four precarious pro-Jacobin newspapers and advanced small sums to Constitutional Circles in eight of the arrondissements, presumably to cover the cost of things like fuel, printing, or furnishings.[29] The Réunion of the faubourg Antoine received three such sums, but that was the least of what Sotin did for this club and its members.

THE *faubouriens* had encountered obstacles from the outset. Considering the Enfants de la Patrie their natural meeting place, they found the orphanage's director, Castille, unwilling to turn over a key. On the scene, one of Sotin's agents assisted them, but this failed to resolve the problem of access. Castille still questioned the group's right to use the public facilities under his charge, this being a difficulty encountered by a number of Constitutional Circles. Moreover his misgivings were encouraged by his superior, the Minister of Interior, who answered Castille's inquiry by stating that a public building may not be furnished gratis to a group of private citizens. He therefore instructed his subordinate to retrieve the keys forthwith, if necessary with the aid of officials in the 8th arrondissement. If the club wished to rent the building, he concluded, they would have to arrange it with the Ministry of Finance. Though the minister later claimed that it had not been his intention to frustrate the club but merely to keep it within legal procedures, his ruling actually resulted in the club's temporary dissolution.[30]

After receiving these instructions, Castille reclaimed the keys. The club remonstrated vigorously and three sans-culottes (Brisvin, Potemont, and Moreau) threatened the officials he had summoned

---

[29] A.N. AF III 509, plaq. 3224 (pièces 125 and 127): M. of Pol., Dépenses secrètes: vendémiaire-pluviôse an VI. The publishers were Colliot, *Journal des campagnes et des armées*; Bescher, *Défenseur de la Vérité*; Coesnon-Pellerin, *Ami de la Patrie*; Leclerc des Vosges, *Tableau politique, littéraire et moral*. Girardin, the owner of a popular reading-room, also received a subsidy. Constitutional Circles in the 1st, 2nd, 3rd, 9th, 10th, 11th, and 12th arrondissements each received one or two small sums; the one in the 8th received three.

[30] The affair can be reconstructed from these sources: A.N. F⁷ 3688/13, dossier "Orphelins"; A.N. F⁷ 7292, fol. 2585; and A.N. F⁷ 7293, fol. 2743, which all contain reports and letters from the principals.

for assistance. But Castille stood fast, insisting that he was under "the most imperative orders" to close the club. When the commissioner to the 8th arrondissement supported him, the sans-culottes were forced to leave.

Only Sotin's prompt and direct intervention saved the day. A letter from Castille to Sotin written two days later reviewed the sequence of events.

> Last night at six o'clock I received your letter which relieved me of the orders contained in the Minister of Interior's letter. I immediately made use of it: I returned the keys . . . and the constitutional circle immediately convened; the threats I had received on the occasion of the club's dissolution ceased when it reopened.[31]

What arrangement Sotin made with the two other ministers is unclear, but the correspondence between them indicates that his decisive personal intervention removed all obstacles to the club's use of the Enfants de la Patrie. Sotin had no basis for objecting to the payment of some kind of rent, but he opposed the abrupt attempt to dislodge the club without working out some sort of arrangement. Considering the hostility that existed between the sans-culottes and the 8th arrondissement officials, his protection was all the more necessary.[32]

When the Réunion convened on the evening of 9 vendémiaire (30 September 1797), a letter from Sotin was read aloud recapitulating what had happened and closing with the phrase "I take the responsibility and will answer for everything." The members were gratified by this official protection, according to the agent Antoine who was at the meeting. No illusions existed about the possibility of real autonomy; in its stead there was an open working relationship between Sotin and the sectionnaires. At the next meeting the former revolutionary commissioner Boyer praised the minister for protecting patriots "openly and loyally." Sotin, he said, "has declared open war on the royalists." When right-wing innuendo was directed against the club to discredit it, Sotin in turn issued a

---

[31] A.N. F⁷ 7292, fol. 2585: Castille to Sotin, 10 vendémiaire VI.

[32] *Ibid.*, M. of Finance to Sotin, 9 vendémiaire, acknowledging Sotin's visit to his home the previous night for the purpose of inquiring about his role in closing the club; M. of Interior to Sotin, 13 vendémiaire.

statement to the press flatly denying all rumors that the police intended to close it.[33] On the following day the members voted an address to thank him for his protection. In addition they praised his devotion to the people as manifested in the way he treated sans-culottes at his bureau, and in the exemplary republican atmosphere maintained in his ministry. As a token of their esteem the clubbists made him an honorary member.[34]

‡ IV ‡

Under such circumstances it is hardly surprising that the Réunion's prevailing tone, as expressed in its petitions and bylaws, was circumspect. For one thing, the club publicly affirmed that all had not been perfect in the Year II. Expressing their belief in the absolute right of free expression in political clubs, the members nonetheless retained "painful memory of the political clubs that preceded these new ones; the memory of the bad faith of certain men who at that time [the Terror] wished to control public opinion in order to gain their own ends. . . . Far from us are those men who under the guise of patriotic exclusion wished to place their own power above the laws." But with such disclaimers, the Réunion remained committed to "that sacred equality on which our political constitution is based."[35]

As in most other Constitutional Circles, the Réunion's bylaws were designed to assure orderly meetings and a reasonably efficient formal organization. Meetings were held on the first, fifth, and

[33] *Ibid.*, Antoine to Sotin, 9 and 12 vendémiaire; *J. hommes libres* No. 143, 18 vendémiaire; *Moniteur*, 18 vendémiaire (p. 72).

[34] A.N. F⁷ 7292, fol. 2585: Au Citoyen Sotin, 19 vendémiaire (90 signatures); reprinted in *Ami du Peuple* No. 111, 24 vendémiaire. Many similar expressions of appreciation reached the minister from other clubs in the following weeks: e.g., A.N. F⁷ 7400, fol. 3705, from Versailles; A.N. F⁷ 7400, fol. 3705, from Nice; A.N. F⁷ 3688/13; fol. "Seine, pluviôse" from the club of the 7th arrondissement, Paris; and "Les Militaires républicains de la garnison de Paris, réunis en cercle constitutionnel," including the *révolutionnaire* Vafflard: A.N. F⁷ 7351, fol. 9293. The spirit of fraternity in Sotin's department is conveyed in an account of a civic banquet that it held, including the toasts that were drunk. *Rédacteur*, 7 nivôse VI, reprinted in Aulard, *Paris*, IV, 504-505.

[35] A.N. AF III 260/Seine: Les Citoyens composans le Cercle Constitutionnel, séant aux Enfans de la Patrie, Au Directoire, n.d.; A.N. F⁷ 7414, fol. 5072; MS Discours prononcé par le Cit. F. A. Moreau, ébeniste, régulateur du Cercle Constitutionnel du faubourg Antoine le jour de la fête de la souveraineté du peuple.

ninth days each décade, beginning at seven o'clock, a late hour suitable to working men. New members were admitted when proposed by two current members; officers were rotated once a month. Instead of dues, each member could place whatever he wished into a special box for expenses. A standard item of business was the reading of newspapers, five members being charged with this duty at each meeting. Otherwise the agenda was fixed in advance and a member allowed to speak only when recognized by the regulator or president. "Indecent and unconstitutional motions" would be ruled out of order; if repeated, the offender would be denounced to the authorities.[36]

Within such an orderly framework what was accomplished? The Réunion's activity ranged over the common fare of other Constitutional Circles but also struck a characteristic note of its own. Several petitions echoed the Jacobin press in its call for a broadening of the fructidor coup and the punishment of anti-republicans with "inflexible justice." In particular the Réunion attacked the municipality of the 8th arrondissement, which was alleged to be a typical refuge for lower-echelon reactionaries. The members' concerns were explicit in the bill of particulars assembled against these officials. They had opposed the fructidor coup, "the arming of citizens in favor of the government," and the formation of political clubs. They protected "fanatics," while disdaining republican institutions and even the word "citizen." They refused the civic inscription to qualified citizens, while allowing domestics and other royalist types to vote in the Year V. In fact, declared the club, the municipal officials were nothing less than opposed "to the progress of reason and republicanism."[37]

In petitions to the Ministers of Police and Interior the club also demanded vigorous support of republican institutions. Symbolically they made an issue of the décadi, insisting that its observance be assured by force. Presumably they felt that this was necessary to promote an atmosphere in the city conducive to republicanism.

[36] *Règlement des Amis de la Constitution séant au faubourg Antoine* (Impr. Lamberté, vendémiaire VI) in A.N. F⁷ 7292, fol. 2585. Lamberté was a Vendôme defendant and the *Défenseur de la Vérité*'s printer.

[37] A.N. F⁷ 7293, fol. 2743: Réunion Républicain séant aux Enfans de la Patrie to M. of Pol., 23 vendémiaire and 13 brumaire VI. A.N. AF III 260/Seine: Les Républicains réunis en société politique aux Enfans de la Patrie, Au Directoire, n.d.

Eight of the members further proposed to organize public celebrations of the décadi at the Enfants de la Patrie.[38] The kind of class
consciousness alluded to in previous chapters apparently surfaced
during the discussions of this issue. As reported by a hostile observer, the members lapsed into inflammatory rhetoric that attacked
affluent merchants, "a class [according to this observer] as useful
as the working class, which in fact depends on that class for its
livelihood."[39]

Implicit in its petitions on the décadi or the ouster of reactionary
officials, social consciousness was explicit in the club's stand on unemployment. Especially in the faubourg's large workshops, unemployment before Fructidor had been chronic and had resulted in
non-political unrest, including scattered strike movements against
the related fall of wages and long hours. The events of Fructidor
gave a new edge to the problem, bringing it into the political arena.
Unemployment rose perceptibly following the coup, with the owners
claiming that Fructidor itself was responsible for a breakdown of
confidence in the business community and a resulting "stagnation
of commerce."[40] The sans-culottes countered that reactionary owners
were using lockouts for political reasons. But this serviceable conspiracy thesis, invoked as an explanation for hard times, led into
a more fundamental argument over the right to subsistence.

At the Réunion's meeting of 12 vendémiaire (3 October 1797)
president Boyer rose to denounce "the industrialists and manufacturers for holding secret meetings in their respective trades, for the
purpose of putting the workers out of work. . . . The aim of these
conclaves is to confound the government with an unemployed
working class." A committee of eight was named to investigate this
charge and to report back with a draft petition.[41]

[38] A.N. F⁷ 7292, fol. 2585: petition to Ministers of Interior and Police 29
fructidor V; reprinted in *Le Révélateur* No. 659, 29 fructidor V. A short time
later Boyer, Cochery, Potemont, Mithou, Ducatel, Letailleur, Moreau, and
Kerchov indicated that they hoped to organize public celebrations (*Ibid.*).
Cf. A. Mathiez, *La Theophilanthropie et le culte décadaire* (Paris, 1904), pp.
241-42.
[39] A.N. F⁷ 7293, fol. 2743: Malepeyre to M. of Interior, 26 fructidor V.
[40] C. Ballot, ed., *Le Coup d'état de 18 fructidor an V: rapports de police et
documents divers* (Paris, 1906), pp. 38, 48 (reports for messidor V); pp. 185,
188, 192 (reports for 28 and 30 fructidor and 2nd jour compl. an V). Cf.
Lefebvre, *Le Directoire*, p. 141: "La conjoncture politique multipliait les crises.
Le 18 fructidor alarma les riches et restreignit le commerce parisien."
[41] A.N. F⁷ 7292, fol. 2585: Antoine to Tissot, 12 vendémiaire VI.

Completed on 22 vendémiaire (13 October) and signed by about one hundred members, this petition is a singularly important document in the history of sans-culottisme. In its solemn text, attitudes and programs from the Year II were refurbished and perpetuated. Its laborious execution reflected the faint but surviving hope that "popular" policies might still be exacted from the republic. The faubouriens accordingly began their petition with two axiomatic propositions that they shared with all Neo-Jacobins: "Governments find their force only in the welfare of the people," and "Political clubs are temples of equality."[42] Under this formula they proceeded to their special grievances and proposals. The body of the petition vehemently attacked the employers as enemies of the public welfare who are attempting

> to turn the working class against the government by plunging it into despair. With cold-blooded calculation they have locked out their workers, at a time when the hardships of winter are about to set in. When the workers ask for jobs they are told: "The brigands have armed the jacobins on the 18th fructidor, and have thereby conspired against the honnêtes-gens and the state. Commerce cannot tolerate such oscillations in the government; go to those whom you have defended and ask them for bread."[43]

But the issue of political lockouts was a wedge for winning sympathy over the more general problem of unemployment and depressed wages. "Thousands of workers are without jobs and are tormented by hunger. . . . More than half the workshops and factories are closed, and the entrepreneurs who have retained their workers have lowered the rate of pay by a third or a half," the petition continued. "And if a worker is caught defending the government for the *journée* of the 18th he is fired from his shop.—In a

[42] A.N. F⁷ 7319, fol. 5656: Les Membres de la Réunion politique séant au faubourg Antoine to M. of Pol., 22 vendémiaire VI.

[43] The police observer Bacon supported this contention. In brumaire he reported that workers were being refused employment and were told "vous en aurez lors que vous vous reunirez à nous pour terrasser les scelérats qui sont la cause de nos maux et de votres." A.N. F⁷ 7319, fol. 5656: Bacon to M. of Pol., 4 brumaire VI. Evidently others also considered this a police problem, one anonymous letter warning the ministry about its magnitude ("I was told about one carpentry workshop where fifty lost their jobs."), A.N. F⁷ 7361, fol. 185, 29 frimaire VI.

word never has the worker been as humiliated and abused as he is today."

Could the worker obtain redress with the assistance of local officials? No. "The justice of the peace is almost nil for him; he is stifled in every way." Therefore they must ask the central government "to extend a helping hand to its friends . . . [to] put an end to public misery." In order to stop this plot against the people's welfare, the government must recognize its true friends and change its policy of political "balancing." It must realize that "the republic cannot strengthen itself if republicans have nothing to eat."

Without using the phrase, the faubouriens were defending the right to subsistence guaranteed by the Jacobin Constitution of 1793 and omitted from the Constitution of the Year III. Two months later a petition submitted by another group of Parisian sectionnaires (who probably met at Cardinaux's café) supported the claim that the workers were being degraded, and explicitly demanded that their right to subsistence be assured. "The word citizen alone," they complained, "is enough to exclude anyone from the workshops that dares utter it. . . . There will be no strongly pronounced republicans among the workers as long as the Nation fails to render them independent of tyranny's zealots by assuring the laboring classes all the work necessary for their subsistence."[44]

To solve the problem exposed in both these petitions, the faubouriens proposed three specific alternatives.

[1] Force the manufacturers and entrepreneurs who have closed their shops to reopen them immediately. . . .
[2] Establish a welfare fund (*caisse de bienfaisance*) to assist indigents and unemployed workers, and to this end levy a tax on all rich capitalists.
[3] Establish public works, and make the capitalists support the costs. Of these three methods we invite the government to adopt that which it feels conforms most to justice. . . .

The anonymous functionary who first dealt with the Réunion's petition when it arrived at the Police Ministry went to the heart of the matter by recognizing that it advocated the right to subsistence.

---

[44] A.N. C 428, fol. 131: Des Républicains de Paris amants passionnés de la liberté et du gouvernement actuel . . . , au Conseil des 500, 4 nivôse VI (*ca.* 50 signatures including Cardinaux and the *révolutionnaire* Vafflard).

Endorsing this demand, he prepared a long report, incorporating large sections of the petition itself and adding his own views. The fundamental requirement of a great republic, he maintained, was to provide opportunity for the worker "to exchange his labor for the bread on which he must nourish himself." To this end he proposed that the Directory solicit from the Legislature the establishment of public workshops. In an elaborate draft report complete with oratorical flourishes, the official suggested that while the Directory should leave the exact methods of paying for the workshops to the Legislature's discretion, its message should lash out against the capitalist malefactors in unequivocal terms: "those who wish to starve the people to punish it for its patriotism, those whose superfluous wealth serves only to flaunt a scandalous luxury and a revolting immorality, must pay for the expenses of the public workshops."[45]

Though Sotin's nameless subordinate endorsed the petition in full and proposed that the Directory sponsor public workshops, the minister himself was unprepared to press such a controversial demand. Arguing in effect that it was not his province, he merely ordered an investigation of the particular charge about political lockouts in the large workshops. Sympathetic to the victims, he stigmatized such lockouts as "a maneuvre that royalism has always used at times when the government strikes at its partisans." Beyond this he doubtless realized that the Directory would never countenance the sweeping attack on the integrity of the business class that was proposed in the petition and draft report. Short of proving an actual conspiracy, there was little he felt in a position to do. When the conservative Central Police Bureau completed its inquiry, it presented the arguments that would inevitably have been used against the petitioners. On the whole, reported the Bureau, manufacturers maintain full employment though some have been forced by circumstances to lay off workers. "But from what we can tell, no spirit of party or of counterrevolution appears to enter into these measures—measures difficult for the government to regulate."[46]

Ultimately the Réunion received no satisfaction in its attempt to reclaim the right of subsistence. While there is no evidence that Sotin personally rejected the petitioners' claim, he was manifestly un-

[45] A.N. F⁷ 7319, fol. 5656: rapport au Directoire (rough draft), unsigned.
[46] *Ibid.*, Sotin to Bureau Central, 5 frimaire VI; Bureau Central to M. of Pol., 6 nivôse VI.

prepared to offer them real support. As in the Year II, Jacobins and sans-culottes at the very least divided over the question of urgency, over the implementation of appealing theoretical principles like the right to subsistence, which of course clashed with other principles. Still, the emphasis of this episode ought not to be exclusively negative in retrospect. The survival among the sectionnaires of this program is extremely significant in itself, as is the favorable draft report from within the Police Ministry. Moreover, the limits of Sotin's support for the Réunion do not mean that beneficial cooperation was entirely lacking. On the contrary this club, along with others, enjoyed a fruitful collaboration with this Jacobin Police Minister in a number of ways. If Sotin did nothing for the "working class" as a whole, he at least offered the sans-culotte militants a significant measure of support and patronage.

‡ V ‡

Was the government friend or antagonist of the people? Central in the Réunion's petition on unemployment, this question pervaded democratic rhetoric. "Friends of the people" must control the government. Its policies and also its patronage must advance the people's welfare.

"Bureaucratization" of the sectionnaires in the Year II was part of the process in which each triumph of the popular movement brought its spontaneity and autonomy closer to extinction. As Albert Soboul put it, "many militant sectionnaires, even if they were not prompted solely by ambition, considered the gaining of a position as the legitimate recompense for their militant activity." But the eventual effect, in Richard Cobb's parallel analysis, "was to put a brake on the political independence of the sans-culotte by accentuating the employees' incentive to orthodoxy." Behind this development lay the economic dislocations of the *monde boutiquier et artisanal*. With the decline of the luxury, food, and clothing trades among others, many sans-culottes were forced to change occupations. In large numbers they sought positions as salaried revolutionary commissioners, cannoniers in the armée révolutionnaire, and employment as watchmen, drivers, clerks, and concierges in the agencies of the revolutionary government.[47]

---

[47] Soboul, *Les Sans-culottes*, pp. 1033-34; Cobb, *Les Armées révolutionnaires*, I, 211-12. In the long run the corporate or professional structure of the central

Long after the popular movement had expired, the militants remained bureaucratized in this sense. Collectively and individually they continued to regard government employment as a rightful prerogative and as a necessary means of subsistence for their social group. The archives of Sotin's ministry reveal a flow of requests from sans-culotte militants for patronage. To return to an earlier example, if the wig-maker Diochet relied on employment in the post office as a temporary expedient until he was able to open a café, others with narrower options continued to regard such employment as a necessary resort. And if such work did not fulfill the sans-culotte's aspiration for independent status, at least it satisfied his political ethos. Until Fructidor, however, they were totally frustrated. Ministers like Cochon considered the sectionnaires dangerous criminals rather than unfortunate patriots in need of assistance. The change in personnel at the Police Ministry was therefore of capital importance.

Besides bringing certain sectionnaires into his own ministry, Sotin helped place beleaguered sans-culottes in other kinds of positions. To the War Minister he recommended among others ex-brigadier Vingternier, a militant who had served with the armée révolutionnaire. Through his offices the *fabricant de bas* Brément was employed at the archives, the gazier Ducatel became a concierge at the Force prison, the porcelain-engraver Boyer a customs official, and the cabinet-maker Leban a local police constable. Shortly after Fructidor, Sotin circularized various officials of the Seine department in behalf of 28 sans-culottes, at least 23 of whom were members of the Réunion. This "List of citizens recommended for the Municipal Administration of the 8th arrondissement, and for other positions" (see Appendix III) almost compels the conclusion that the club served as a means of channeling patronage into the faubourg. Most of the 28 (as comparison with Appendix II will show) had backgrounds as sectional militants in Years II and III. Under Sotin this became title to consideration rather than suspicion.[48]

government bureaucracy which began to take shape under the Directory was affected only marginally by the demands of the sans-culottes. See Clive Church, "The Social Basis of the French Central Bureaucracy under the Directory," *Past and Present* (April 1967), pp. 59-72.

[48] A.N. F7 6140, dossier 134, plaq. 2: "Liste des citoyens . . ." reproduced in Appendix III; also Sotin to M. of War, 2nd jour compl. an V. Cf. A.N. F7

Sotin and his subordinates unfortunately received far more requests for positions than they could hope to fill. The post of prison concierge, for example, was solicited by a variety of people including LeRoy, a Jacobin *homme de lettres*; Pathiot, "a wine-seller reduced to indigence"; and the bonnetier Vacret, a militant faubourien who wrote to Sotin, "persuaded that you are the friend of the patriots," to explain how he had been ruined by his imprisonment during the Year III.[49] The continuing scourge of unemployment and the "growing misery" in the arrondissement, according to the police observer Bacon, were exasperating the sectionnaires. "The confidence that the government began to inspire amongst those unfortunate patriots is being extinguished," he reported. "Several had been led to believe that they would obtain positions to which they had the most legitimate claims; they presented petitions to several ministers; promises were made, and they obtained nothing. . . ."[50] It is untrue that nothing was obtained. Dozens of sans-culottes did gain the government employment that they desperately sought. But where dozens succeeded, hundreds still bore the weight of economic dislocation.

Though he failed to place the bulk of sectionnaires who sought positions, Sotin resorted to other expedients for coming to their aid. Diverting some of the so-called secret funds at his disposal—most of which went into routine channels like the Paris Central Police Bureau—Sotin dispersed several hundred small sums to needy ex-Jacobins and sans-culottes.[51]

The money was used in several ways. For one, Sotin commissioned sans-culottes for specific, temporary jobs of police work. Sectionnaires like Vachard, Cardinaux, and Taillandier received sums marked in the records as "for the 18th fructidor" or "for captures on the 18th fructidor." Others were paid for occasional work such as following a suspect, transporting a prisoner for the ministry, or for some unspecified task for which he was reimbursed under the heading "*frais de mémoire*." A few individuals were granted com-

---

6152, dossier 859, plaq. 1: Talleyrand to Merlin, 7 germinal VI, about Rossignol and Jorry, for whom Sotin had personally solicited jobs.

[49] A.N. F⁷ 3688/13.

[50] A.N. F⁷ 7319, fol. 5656: Bacon to Sotin, 4 brumaire VI.

[51] A.N. AF III 509, plaq. 3224 (pièces 125 and 127): Ministre de Police, Dépenses secrètes: vendémiaire-pluviôse an VI. These documents are indispensable for appreciating Sotin's role in Paris.

missions for plying their trade. Thus on 3 nivôse (23 December 1797) Potement (a locksmith) and Tounette (a carpenter) were paid 55 and 112 livres for "furnishings," while the glazer Huin received 215 livres.

Far more numerous were the small sums distributed as outright relief and marked in the records simply as "assistance" (*secours*). A few went to relatively well-known democrats like Fournier l'Americain, the Vendôme defendants Morel and Bouin, and the café-keeper Cardinaux. A far larger percentage of these disbursements went to rank-and-file sans-culottes, particularly in the faubourg Antoine, which seems to have been Sotin's special concern. At least 29 men identifiable as members of the Réunion Politique (see Appendix I) received one or more such secours:[52]

Bal (or Bas)	Ducatel	Laurent
Bernard	Duclos	Letailleur (2)
Bouché	Duchesne	Marcellin (3)
Boyer (3)	Gregoire de Lyon	Moreau
Brabant	Hardivillé	Moreau l'ainé
Chappuis	Herré	Potement
Chefdeville (2)	Humblet (2)	Segretin
Cochery (2)	Joly	Vacret
Cuvillier	Landron	Vigner
Dormoi	Lanoy	

In addition, sums went on several occasions to unspecified "inhabitants of the faubourg," while 43 secours were given to persons identified only as *divers*. This secret list of disbursements reveals a veritable underground of liaisons between the Police Ministry under Sotin and the sectionnaires. As one member of the Réunion later put it, Sotin inaugurated "a good turn . . . [to help] citizens who have sacrificed for the Revolution and who are out of work."[53] In this capacity Sotin doubled as a minister of relief.

‡ VI ‡

Sotin's solicitude for the democrats and their clubs eventually lost him favor with the Directory. His enforced resignation on 27

[52] *Ibid.*

[53] A.N. F[7] 7319, fol. 5656: Bellanger (c.d. capitaine) to M. of Pol., 13 ventôse VI.

pluviôse (15 February 1798)—scarcely seven months after his appointment—revealed the Directory's hardening stand against a Neo-Jacobin resurgence that the minister had encouraged. While democrats everywhere had reason to lament this turn of events, his dismissal bore directly upon the faubourg Antoine.

A tentative but promising interlude of cooperation came abruptly to an end. Sotin had demonstrated the material and moral concern that sans-culottes expected from a true republican government. His fall brought a return of hostility. Once again sectionnaires would become "prairialistes" and "anarchists" in the government's eyes. Once again political activism would be suspect. Reports from the police spies who were increasingly set upon the faubourg reveal that after his dismissal substantial unrest developed among a group led by the popular faubourien Leban. A widower with several children, cabinet-maker by trade, and one of the prime movers in the Réunion, Leban was currently a police constable thanks to Sotin's patronage. To the faubourg's sans-culottes Leban explained that Sotin's loss was theirs. "You have the proof," he alleged, "because Sotin provided money to relieve you, while [Dondeau, his successor] gives you very little." Besides this falling-off and mismanagement of relief, the political consequences disturbed him equally.[54]

In the preceding months there had been no evidence of open opposition to the ministry's intrusion into the Réunion's affairs. Certainly some former militants had had nothing to do with the club and in private doubtless scorned its liaisons with officialdom. But such sentiment was never voiced strongly enough to have come to anyone's attention. The sectionnaires seem to have trusted the minister and his men; accepting his help, they proceeded to revive the old Société des Quinze-Vingts. With the dismissal of Sotin, and soon afterwards his lieutenants, the relationship lost its justification in the eyes of Leban and his followers. Only now did they proclaim that the Réunion was being undermined because its leaders were "sold to the government." Protection under Sotin became intolerable domination under his successor.[55]

[54] A.N. F⁷ 3668/13: reports by "Agent A," 24 and 27 ventôse VI. Cf. eleven members of the Réunion to M. of Pol., 22 ventôse VI, complaining of favoritism and graft in the way assistance was being distributed: A.N. F⁷ 7319, fol. 5656. On Leban see A.N. F⁷ 4770, dossier 3 and F⁷ 4746, dossier 2.

[55] A.N. F⁷ 3688/13: report dated 21 ventôse.

Particular conflict arose over the role of veteran police agents who had once served under Cochon. Men like Linage (who had helped the founders secure keys to the Enfants de la Patrie), or Bacon *père* and *fils* (who monitored the meetings, and who had supported the sans-culottes' claims for patronage and as well as their protests against unemployment) had been acceptable while working under Sotin's congenial stewardship.[56] Their continued prying in the faubourg under Dondeau now aroused resentment. Towards the end of ventôse, Leban and his friends were overheard denouncing Linage's presence at the Réunion. Niquille, one of Sotin's subordinates who had not yet been fired, agreed, cursing Linage as a "f**** g*****," accusing him of being "attached to the government," and of spying for Dondeau. When Niquille and Tissot were themselves dismissed, relations with the Police Ministry and "the government" deteriorated further.

> Since the dismissal of Veyrat, Niquille, Cavagnac and others [summarized a police spy], Leban, Humblet, Vacret, and Brisevin are doing everything they can to denigrate the government's operations. Leban, a *commissaire de police*, makes the most infamous remarks against Minister [Dondeau's] performance; he says that one has to be as big a moderate and scoundrel as Dondeau to have dismissed pronounced democrats like Niquille and others.

Vacret's brother-in-law, whose remarks in a faubourg café were overheard by the same agent, likewise argued that the government no longer deserved confidence. "It has dismissed our best friend. Sotin was kicked out only because of his staunch republicanism. . . . Don't listen to Boyer, Diochet and other *baconnistes*: they are government men. . . . Leban will warn us about how we should conduct ourselves."[57]

[56] Linage was cited for his work in the faubourgs Antoine and Marceau in a memorandum from Cochon to the Directory dated 28 brumaire V. Bacon's tenure extended further back to the Year III. He or his son was paid 10,000 livres as recompense for special services rendered in germinal and prairial III, vendémiaire IV, floréal IV (the time of the Babeuf arrests), and fructidor IV. See Debidour, *Recueil des actes du Directoire exécutif*, III, 604, and IV, 311-12, 379.

[57] A.N. F7 3688/13: report dated 24 ventôse. See also report marked "Paris le 21 germinal VI."

This last comment indicates that Leban and his friends did not enjoy unanimous support among the sectionnaires. Ex-revolutionary commissioner Boyer headed a second faction that continued to maintain relations with Bacon and Dondeau. As late as germinal, Boyer was writing to the minister about "gratification for citizens Ducatel and Moreau . . . who have merited it," as well as other letters "relative to the secours." Dondeau evidently destroyed most of this correspondence upon Boyer's advice, "so as not to compromise yourself," but it is still clear that Sotin's dismissal had caused a break over tactics in the Réunion.[58]

Lamenting this "disunion that reigns among all the faubourg's patriots," one observer attributed it to "petty personal quarrels." "So-and-so says, you cannot be a republican because you associate with such-and-such."[59] But this was not entirely correct. Such cliques did thrive on obscure personal conflicts and petty ambitions, but at the same time genuine differences over tactics hardened the lines of antagonism. With sometimes rancourous intensity, the quarrel persisted into the following year, and when a comprehensive history of the faubourg is written these factions will have to be traced out in detail.[60] Presently it suffices to say that certain sectionnaires like Leban and Humblet drew clear limits to the possibility of collaboration, while others like Boyer and Potemont were more opportunistic. One must hesitate, however, to make a decisive judgment. In most apparent respects—occupational status, wealth, and revolutionary background—they did not differ appreciably. Chosen as electors in

[58] *Ibid.*, Boyer to Dondeau, 6 germinal VI. (Boyer had been regarded by his section as a "government man" in the Year II as well, according to Tonnesson, *La Défaite des Sans Culottes*, pp. 360-61.)

[59] A.N. F⁷ 7404, fol. 4148: 18 ventôse VI.

[60] Almost a year later Boyer and ten other sans-culottes (Ducatel, Brément, Vaquier, LeCuis, Moreau, Potemont, Herré, Moreau l'ainé, Ducatel, Terrasson) complained that seven others (Leban, Humblet, Kerchov, Derré, Gonchon, Yo . . s, Dejon) were constantly harassing and vilifying them in the faubourg. "Selon toutes apparances," the eleven wrote "(ils) ne s'acharnent contre nous que parce que nous vous defendons . . . ils vous abhorent et déclarent hautement qu'ils conjurent contre vous. S'ils parlent de nous, ils disent ce sont des coquins vendus au gouvernement." A.N. F⁷ 6191, dossier 2476 (pièce 105) to M. of Interior, 22 floréal VII. This letter is only one of over two hundred documents that include charges, countercharges, and surveillance reports on the groupings, alignments, and purported activities of the faubouriens. To untangle this web fairly may prove impossible. Other pertinent documents may be found in A.N. F⁷ 6197, dossier 2774; F⁷ 6168, dossier 1702; F⁷ 6196, dossier 2730; and A.N. AF III 47.

the spring elections, Boyer and Leban each occupied a dwelling assessed at 150 livres.[61] The accommodating Potemont had been as militant in the Year II as any faubourien, which is presumably why Babeuf had hoped to make him commander of the Montreuil section during his insurrection. Furthermore, the commissioner to the 8th arrondissment continued to describe Boyer as "the most notorious anarchist and greatest enemy of the present government," and as a leading spirit behind constant meetings of "anarchists" in his bailiwick before the elections.[62] During those elections, finally, it seems probable that differences were temporarily patched over for the sake of a common effort against common antagonists. Be that as it may, Boyer, Potemont, and others did avoid breaking openly with Dondeau, thereby pushing opportunism to the limit and antagonizing others.

What might be most significant in all of this is that Leban's aggressive group had earlier associated itself with the Réunion. The split between the Boyer/Potemont faction and the Leban/Humblet faction underscores by contrast the lack of such discord during Sotin's tenure. Those who went into opposition after his dismissal signed the club's petitions before it, as did the Boyer/Potemont group. Along with Boyer, Leban was a chief dispenser of Sotin's relief funds. Under Sotin's sympathetic protection these militants collaborated in a club that effectively reflected their community's concerns, and which in this sense was a revival of the Société des Quinze-Vingts. In most respects, however, its style and activities resembled the other Constitutional Circles of the Year VI.

The brief history of the Réunion Politique—until now unwritten and unknown—suggests two possible conclusions among others. (1) Under the Constitution of the Year III sans-culottes were not necessarily doomed to exclusion from political activity. (2) The breach or lack of community between middle-class Jacobins and sectionnaires was appreciable but not wholly unbridgeable. Politically conscious sans-culottes were encouraged after Fructidor to bestir themselves. The cautious Neo-Jacobinism of journalists, functionaries,

[61] A.N. AF III 260: MS list of electors for the Year VI with the assessed value of their residences.

[62] A.N. F⁷ 3688/13: Hamburger to departmental commissioner (Seine), 17 germinal VI; A.N. F⁷ 6152, dossier 869: Hamburger to Reubell.

and bourgeois revolutionaries was not totally irrelevant to the sectionnaires in the Year VI.

There can be little doubt that the majority of sectionnaires were *"hommes politiques de passage,"* in Richard Cobb's phrase.[63] Once the forward elan of Revolution had been broken early in 1794, they lapsed into apathy. But these archetypical sans-culottes of the faubourg Antoine force a qualification of this view, if only by posing a striking exception. At least some of the militants, who had stood between the anonymous masses and the well-known radicals like Marat or Hébert, remained active. Exceptional in their sustained political consciousness, they were otherwise typically plebeian in their occupational, educational, and social status. They had been hommes du quartier and so they remained. In the Year II they had been aggressively independent, self-consciously radical, and defiantly anti-liberal. The intervening years had cooled their ardor considerably, whereas the element of "bureaucratization" grew more pronounced and further sapped their autonomy. Their quest for popular democracy was abandoned. By the Year VI they acquired a grudging capacity to engage in political action within a constitutional framework prescribed by others. They could live politically and struggle mundanely without the boundless ferment and opportunities of crisis. Subdued, and opportunistic up to a point, they distinguished their possible allies in the middle class. Out of this grew a tactical working alliance, a tenuous popular front (to use a distinctly anachronistic term), whose benefits included some desperately needed patronage and relief funds. It also permitted a modest revival of activism in which politics could play its expressive role in the continuum of community life. Who can measure the importance of this? And who can reckon the toll of enforced quiescence under Bonaparte?

[63] R. C. Cobb, "Quelques aspects de la mentalité révolutionnaire: Avril 1793—thermidor an II," *Revue d'histoire moderne et contemporaine*, vi (1959), 119.

PART THREE

CONFRONTATION:

THE ELECTIONS OF 1798

CHAPTER IX

Franchise Reform and Electoral Organization

LECTIONS under the Constitution of the Year III were held
in two stages. On the first of germinal, primary assemblies
in the cantons and municipalities chose electors. Beginning on the twentieth, these electors convened in departmental electoral assemblies to choose deputies to the Legislature, departmental
administrators, and judges. French males over twenty-one were
eligible to vote in the primary assemblies if they were domiciled in
the canton for a year, paid a direct personal property tax, were inscribed on the civic register, and were members of the national guard
reserves. Citizens who were not on the tax rolls could still vote if
they paid (anytime during the month of messidor preceding the
elections) a voluntary contribution or poll tax equivalent to three
"journées de travail"—the wages of an unskilled laborer for one
day, the value of which was to be set by the local authorities. In
order to qualify as an elector, a citizen had to own or rent property
worth (depending on where he lived) between one hundred and
two hundred times the value of a journée de travail.

These provisions amounted to a marked departure in principle
from the direct elections and universal male suffrage promised in
the Jacobins' draft constitution of 1793. E. G. Lenglet and a few
others kept alive the theoretical arguments in support of that universal suffrage, just as a handful of individuals had tried to defend
it in 1795 when the Directorial constitution was being drafted.[1] Most
democratic activists, however, became less concerned with this vanquished principle than with the actual electoral contests about to
be conducted. In 1798 it was not the abandonment of universal
suffrage that they fought, but rather the rigid interpretation of
existing laws, obstructive administrative procedures, and massive

[1] *Opinion de Julien Souhait (des Vosges) sur le droit de suffrage* . . . (Impr.
Nationale, an III); Lanthenas, *Division organique des citoyens . . . avec les
moyens de faire les meilleures élections possibles* . . . (Impr. Nationale, an
III); [Antonelle], *Observations sur le Droit de Cité et sur quelques parties du
travail de la commission des onze* (Chez Vatar, an III). Thomas Paine was
also in this group.

voter apathy—all of which were the palpable obstacles to electoral democracy in the French Republic.

‡ I ‡

Like the charter for the constitutional monarchy of 1791, the Constitution of the Year III disfranchised some adult males. Judging from the figures for Paris, however, the limitation on the primary suffrage was not extensive. Out of a total population of 550,000, approximately 120,000 men were eligible to vote under the Directory regime.[2] All the more reason that the practice rather than principle commanded the Jacobins' attention. Within the existing laws and constitutional stipulations there were enough ambiguities and possible interpretations to provide the substance of electoral reform. No masses of disfranchised citizens were clamoring for the right to vote. But there were small groups of politically conscious citizens who were not regular taxpayers and property owners, who might have been made to qualify by paying the poll tax and getting themselves registered. Most citizens showed little interest in negotiating these obstacles; the problem was that even those who did might be blocked by the persons administering the law.

In the Year V, when the first regular elections under the new charter were held, the thermidorians had used the cumbersome procedures and ambiguities in the laws to discourage voting. According to the democratic journal *La Résurrection du véritable Père Duchêne,* they purposefully disfranchised citizens by keeping the civic registers closed during the year. If the registers had been kept open, this newspaper argued, "imperceptibly, drop by drop, the worker, the artisan . . . free men by temperament . . . would have enrolled." The *Père Duchêne* further charged the "royalists" with spreading rumors that workingmen would be required to pay three or four years back taxes if they attempted to register. The Jacobins maintained, in exactly the opposite spirit, that a citizen was

[2] A.N. F[20] 381: Département de la Seine, denombrement de la population . . . terminé au commencement de l'an IX (MS); *Département de la Seine: Assemblées primaires an VII: tableau de distribution* (Impr. Ballard). See R. R. Palmer's remarks on the Constitution of 1791 in *Age of the Democratic Revolution* (Princeton, 1959), I, 522-28, and J. Suratteau's recent methodological discussion "Heurs et malheurs de la 'sociologie électorale' pour l'époque de la Révolution française." *Annales E.S.C.* (1968), pp. 556-80.

required only to produce an old tax receipt or *avertissement* to show that he had once been on the rolls, and that he need not necessarily pay a tax for that year. Evidently there was considerable uncertainty about the meaning of the laws.[3]

Furthermore, unsympathetic officials at the bureau were able to exercise arbitrary discretion. When the officials finally opened the registers, the *Père Duchêne* later charged, "fat bankers whose sons evade the draft . . . and lackeys of aristocrats" were registered while the virtuous if impoverished *père de famille* and workingman was repulsed.[4] It was no wonder, then, that the elections of the Year V produced a clean sweep for the reactionary forces.

With renewed determination born of the fructidor coup, the Jacobins prepared to assault some of the obstacles that continued to inhibit unregistered citizens who wished to vote or who might be convinced to vote if they could be made to qualify. Most of their exertions before the elections concerned ambiguities in the laws about tax rolls and civic registers, with the aim of facilitating registration by interpreting the laws as permissively as possible. This strategy was pursued with singular vigor by the Constitutional Circle of the Rue du Bacq in the 10th arrondissement of Paris. To survey its activity is to demonstrate concretely the issues of electoral reform in the Year VI.

Meeting every other day for about a month—until the Directory abruptly ordered it closed on 15 ventôse (5 March 1798)—the Rue du Bacq Club considered numerous proposals designed to liberalize the election laws and increase the number of voters.[5] Sug-

---

[3] *La Résurrection du véritable Père Duchêne* (edited by Labisol and published by Coesnon-Pellerin), B.N. Lc2/937. See the undated issues for pluviôse-fructidor an V, especially Nos. 4, 15, 17, and 22. Also *Ami de la Patrie* (Paris) No. 330, 1 pluviôse V; J. L. Vachard, *Reveillez-vous gens qui dormez, priezdieu pour les trespasses* (Paris, Impr. Vatar [an V]), B.N. Lb42/1341.

[4] *Père Duchêne* Nos. 20 and 22, n.d. (articles signed by Caignart). In a mémoire dated fructidor Year VI the militant democrat P. N. Hesiné recalled that at Vendôme (Loir-et-Cher) hundreds of citizens were denied their right to vote by the royalists in the Year V. "Figurez vous," he added, "l'élan de cette population nombreuse rentrant dans l'exercice de ses droits en l'an VI." (A.N. F7 7436, fol. 7451.)

[5] This was one of the few clubs to have kept minutes which survived. The original MS entitled "Notice exacte des séances du Cercle constitutionnel de la Rue du Bacq" may be found, with covering letters from the club, in A.N. F7 7402/b, fol. 3960. An abbreviated version was published by Vatar, who was a member, under the title *Résumé des travaux du cercle constitutionnel de la*

gestions about how to bring out the vote and how to prepare for the elections were discussed and then submitted to the club's executive committee (*comité d'instruction*) for study and implementation. Lesser proposals included framing "an address to the people on the exercise of their rights in the coming assemblies"; drawing up "a triple or quadruple list of citizens to elect in the arrondissement's primary assemblies"—that is, slates of candidates; and publishing a manual of rules for use by citizens in registering and voting.[6] The committee had not yet acted on these proposals when the Directory closed the club. It did complete a petition in support of the effort "to bring about the admission of the soldiers' fathers to the primary assemblies," thus joining clubs in the 1st and 11th arrondissements in backing this popular cause.[7] In addition it launched an effective appeal over the tax requirement for eligibility in Paris, and an unsuccessful protest over the technicalities of registration and eligibility.

Several months earlier the departmental administration of the Seine had fixed the value of the journée de travail at the rate of sixty sous or three livres, three times higher than what was considered normal. Its rationale was plausible enough: discipline within the national guard was enforced through a system of fines, the most common of which happened to be fixed at three journées de travail. Thus, as the department put it, "to give these fines more effect" the value of the journée de travail had to be fixed at a maximum level. The journée de travail, however, was also used as the standard in determining eligibility both for the primary and electoral assemblies. According to this ruling a person not on the tax rolls who wished to vote in the primary assemblies would have to pay the poll tax of nine livres instead of three. And to be named as an elector in Paris a citizen would have to own property or rent a dwelling assessed at 450 livres instead of 150 livres.

The clubs of the 10th and 11th arrondissements petitioned against this decree, claiming that it made the right to vote "illusory." They warned that it would have a particularly devastating effect on the composition of the electoral assembly. "Where is the virtuous pa-

---

Rue du Bacq (Impr. Vatar, an VI); it is discussed briefly in A. Meynier, *Le 22 floréal an VI et le 30 prairial an VII* (Paris, 1928), pp. 30-31.

[6] "Notice exacte des séances," sessions of 16, 20, 26 pluviôse and 2 ventôse.

[7] See below, pp. 251-52.

triot who—after the incalculable sacrifices that he has made for the establishment of the republic—can still have the means that would enable him to occupy a dwelling assessed at 450 livres?" The decree, argued the petitioners, would give the primary assemblies over exclusively to "nouveau riche scoundrels, public thieves, and bankers of the counterrevolution."[8]

This local administrative decision setting the journée de travail at such a high level had dangerous implications which were spelled out by the Constitutional Circle of Besançon (Doubs)—a club that certainly read Vatar's *Journal des hommes libres.* In a petition to the Legislature the members deplored the ruling under which, they alleged,

> a multitude of good citizens who have sacrificed all to reconquer their precious rights to vote in the people's assemblies will be excluded from those assemblies; in particular a large number of those intrepid men of the faubourgs Antoine and Macreau who have protected the cradle of liberty. . . . The outcome of future elections will be compromised, because it is principally in that class of estimable artisans that the Republic's most sincere supporters are to be found.[9]

Such outside encouragement must have been gratifying to the Parisian democrats; more gratifying was the department's decision to reverse itself after reviewing the matter. On 2 ventôse (20 February 1798) the Seine administration decreed that the journée de travail was fixed at one livre. It noted that the infractions of discipline in the national guard, subject to fines equivalent to three journées de travail, were no longer common. But in addition it granted the Jacobins' main premise: "our less fortunate citizens—who are in this state by virtue of the numerous sacrifices that they have made—must have the exercise of their rights in the primary and electoral assemblies facilitated."[10]

---

[8] *J. hommes libres* Nos. 261 and 266, 16 and 21 pluviôse; "Notice exacte des séances," 14 pluviôse.

[9] A.N. C 431, fol. 167: Les Citoyens composant le Cercle constitutionnel de Bescançon, n.d. (80 signatures). Briot, the president of this club, became one of Vatar's contributing editors the following year.

[10] Broadside headed *Département de la Seine*, 2 ventôse VI, in B.N. Mss (nouv. acq. fran.) No. 2717; résumé in *J. hommes libres* No. 284, 9 ventôse; *Journal des campagnes et des armées* No. 708, 10 ventôse.

According to at least one police observer, the import of this decision to lower the journée de travail was not lost on some reactionaries; when it was announced, they attacked the administrators as "terrorists," and declared that "the class of artisans will cause a good deal of trouble in the elections."[11] Whether the actual turnout in the primary assemblies was affected we have no way of knowing; undoubtedly some citizens paid three livres for the right to vote who would not or could not have laid down nine livres. But we can say for certain that the complexion of the electoral assembly would have been substantially altered had the electors been required to own or rent property assessed at 450 livres instead of 150 livres; over two-thirds of the electors subsequently chosen did not meet the 450-livre standard.[12] In any event, by agitating over the journée de travail the Neo-Jacobins of the Rue du Bacq Club were not directly challenging the Directorial position which made the suffrage contingent on property-holding; rather they sought to minimize its application and practical effect. Acting from contrary motives, Bonaparte would eventually reaffirm and strengthen conservative principles in the state by increasing the amount of property electors were required to hold.

THE WHOLE process of registration was another area for possible reform. Pons de Verdun, one of the few former Montagnards in the Legislature, addressed himself to this by proposing what could be called an open registration bill. His premise was that reactionaries had purged republicans from the voting rolls and national guard rosters, had kept the civic registers closed, and had made it impossible for citizens to utilize the special constitutional provision for payment of a poll tax in lieu of a personal property tax assessment. Primarily it was a question of following up the fructidor coup by undoing the damage perpetrated when the reactionaries had been in power. But the final item—the poll tax issue—brought the deputies into the social dimension of electoral politics and the question of enfranchising sans-culottes who might otherwise be excluded

[11] A.N. F 3688/13: report by "Agent No. 3," 14 ventôse.
[12] A.N. AF III 261/Seine: Commune de Paris: La Commission des contributions directs, au Citoyen Mathieu, 8 floréal VI. Enclosed is a complete list of the assessed valuation of each elector's residence.

from voting. Pons thus explained the poll tax situation in the most reactionary departments:

> The counterrevolutionary authorities employed every bit of force and finesse at their disposal to snatch away the advantages of the poll tax for the poor but hardworking and truly republican class—to thus prevent that class from acquiring its right to vote . . . to reduce these men of redoubtable civisme to inaction.[13]

Impressed by such considerations, some of the clubs tried to support this effort. When the bill, passed by the Council of 500, seemed headed for defeat in the upper house after an adverse report by its committee, the Club of the Rue du Bacq voted to petition the elders in support of the bill. A detailed brief was assembled by a member named Gaultier-Biauzat, one of the judges who had voted to acquit Babeuf at the Vendôme trial. To lend added weight to the appeal, Vatar printed it in pamphlet form; as such it is a capital document illustrating the issues and tactics of Jacobin franchise reform efforts.[14]

Three major arguments were given to support the three main sections of Pons' bill. (1) The constitution required that a citizen be inscribed on the civic register for one year in order to vote, but these registers had not been kept up to date. Many citizens had been inscribed in the Year II but had subsequently been excluded from political life during the reaction. By the Year V the registers were generally inaccessible to these citizens. Moreover there was no legislation prescribing the procedures for establishing and maintaining the rolls; therefore, standards set up in each locality were open to challenge. In the light of all these circumstances, the petition urged that all citizens be recognized as duly registered if they had been inscribed at any time in the past, even before the promulgation of the Constitution of the Year III.

(2) Another requirement for eligibility was payment of a direct property tax, or of a special contribution for those who did not own

---

[13] *Conseil des 500: Rapport fait par Pons (de Verdun) au nom d'une commission spéciale, sur les inscriptions civiques, celles au rôle de la garde nationale, et celles de contribution personnelle, séance du 13 nivôse an 6* (Impr. Nationale), p. 6. This pamphlet, as well as speeches by other deputies on this issue, may be found in the B.N. and in the Maclure Collection, University of Pennsylvania Library.

[14] *Adresse au Conseil des Anciens, sur les inscriptions réquises pour être admis à voter dans les assemblées primaires, presentée le 27 pluviôse an VI* (Impr. Vatar), B.N. Lb42/508.

or rent enough property to be on tax rolls. The constitution also specified that this special payment be made at a designated time: in the month of messidor, eight months before the elections. But the petition argued that the tax rolls had not been drawn up in many departments by messidor V. Citizens who subsequently learned that they were not on the rolls, but who still desired to vote and were willing to pay the poll tax, should therefore be allowed to do so even now. In other words, since the provision about messidor nullified the more basic provision about an alternative to paying a property tax, the messidor deadline should be overlooked for the current year.

(3) Yet another requirement for eligibility was that a citizen be enrolled in the national guard reserves. Here the petition noted that the national guard had been manipulated politically; under royalist influence a "repulsive purge" had been carried out in which "proletarians" were excluded and "only wealthy citizens were admitted." Therefore this requirement too should be waived temporarily.

The Jacobins of the Rue du Bacq Club, and the bill's supporters in the Legislature, were not assaulting the idea that a citizen must be truly "active" to merit the franchise—that he be in some fashion a taxpayer, a national guardsman, and a duly registered citizen. But they held that it should be made as easy as possible for citizens to be deemed active; that their taxpaying should be minimal and in some cases virtual. That in essence a sectionnaire of the Year II was an active citizen. In the aftermath of reaction the Jacobins asked that most of the formal requirements and red tape be waived altogether, so that the citizens who were forced out of political life during the reaction be allowed to reenter with a minimum of difficulty. As the deputy Ysabeau stated during the debate: "The primary task that the constitution itself imposes upon us is to render to the totality of citizens the incontestable right that they have to exercise their sovereignty in the primary assemblies; and if some unforeseen obstacle prevents this, it is up to us to remove it." Thomas Lindet put it more simply. "No, he who was prevented from fulfilling the formalities of registration during the prescribed period will not be turned away by republicans."[15]

[15] *Opinion d'Ysabeau sur la résolution concernant les inscriptions civiques* (Impr. Nationale), p. 3; *Opinion de Lindet . . . (séance du 9 ventôse)* (Impr. Nationale), p. 2.

Such logic—or rather, such sentiment—was resisted by the Council of Elders. Not even allowing the text of Biauzat's petition to be read publicly, it reasoned that the bill's adoption would allow the triumph of certain "coteries" in the elections.[16] Open registration, in other words, was opposed as a partisan Jacobin measure. While the arguments against the bill ranged from a scrupulous insistence on the letter of the constitution (inconsistent, of course, with the fructidor coup) to the contention that the exclusion of republicans from the voting roles during the reaction was an unproven claim, opponents also lost no opportunity to bait the Jacobins who allegedly wished to manipulate the electoral laws for partisan advantage. The bill's handful of proponents tried in vain to counteract this innuendo; Thomas Lindet and Lacombe Saint-Michel defended the "idolâtre de la liberté," and the "patriotes chauds" from attempts to impugn their motives. What better friends of the republic existed than those zealous republicans who suffered proscription and oppression during the reaction? The majority had its doubts, however, and insisted on regarding the bill as an unconstitutional, factional maneuver. As representative Regnier maintained, the whole issue of the closed civic registers was only recently being raised, having not previously been included among the crimes charged to the royalists. "It is easy enough to understand this belated allegation."[17]

In Regnier's eyes the bill had further objectionable implications. Responding to an earlier plea for the bill, Regnier commented: "In hearing the previous speaker, one would be tempted to believe that the only republicans are those who pay no taxes at all, and that the Republic's safety depends on them alone."[18] Such ponderous sarcasm had the raw edge of class consciousness that was latent in most debate on franchise reform. And it was a sense of class consciousness that dovetailed nicely with the Directorials' concern over factions. As representative Laussat observed, the reason poll taxes were to be paid months in advance of the election was to assure "the purity of motives" among those taking advantage of it in order

---

[16] *J. hommes libres* No. 275, 30 pluviôse VI.

[17] See the speeches by Baudin, Cornudet, Creuzet-Latouche, Laussat, Porcher, and Regnier against the bill, and speeches by Lindet and Lacombe St. Michel in its favor (Maclure Collection).

[18] *Opinion de Regnier sur la résolution relative aux inscriptions civiques, séance du 13 ventôse* (Impr. Nationale), pp. 1-2.

to qualify. By imposing an eight-month waiting period before registration, he felt, it would be possible to prevent any bribery of workingmen that might be contemplated—a roadblock to the "calculations and tactics of factions and parties."[19]

Under the weight of such arguments the bill was buried by the elders, but not without provoking audible discontent. In section Unité (10th arrondissement) the police constable reported that "republicans seem disturbed. The rejection of the resolution on civic inscriptions has alarmed them and seems to have plunged them into apathy."[20] The more determined Jacobins continued their efforts. In the 6th arrondissement, for example, the Constitutional Circle petitioned the lower chamber to deplore the elders' action and to urge the Council of 500 to resubmit the bill "in order to secure for republicans the rights of which royalists deprived them."[21]

The issue was dead as far as the Legislature was concerned, and it was clear that royalists were not the only ones depriving certain citizens of their opportunity to vote. Still, the issue could be dealt with on the local level. Thomas Lindet had argued that one aim of the bill was "to prevent a host of particular disputes by means of a general measure." When this general measure failed to pass, the issue was contested locally. Sympathetic administrators in the Seine department, for example, tried on their own authority to satisfy the demand for open registration. They decreed that all citizens who had been inscribed on the civic registers *before* promulgation of the Year III Constitution, who were not inscribed on last year's rolls (and who were otherwise entitled to vote), should present themselves to their arrondissements where they would be registered.[22]

But even on a local level uniformity was difficult to enforce. In the 6th arrondissement a citizen complained that reactionary officials were simply ignoring the decree and insisting that a citizen be

---

[19] *Opinion de P. C. Laussat* . . . (Impr. Nationale), pp. 4-5, and *Opinion de J. Cornudet* . . . (Impr. Nationale), pp. 2-3. In the course of this debate conservative legislators raised cogent theoretical queries about the nature of "free" elections, but there was also a great deal of hypocrisy. The arguments in Lenglet's book provide a notable contrast.

[20] A.D.S., 4 AZ 105: rapport du comm. de police de la division de l'Unité, deuxième décade de ventôse VI. (Few of these valuable weekly reports by the police constables in each section survived the 1871 fire in the Paris Municipal Archives.)

[21] Cited in *Moniteur*, p. 670 (session of 13 ventôse).

[22] *J. hommes libres* No. 302, 26 ventôse VI.

inscribed as of last year; in refusing to accept registration dating from before brumaire IV, he concluded, the municipality was continuing to interpret the law "in favor of the honnêtes gens." Similarly a member of the Constitutional Circle of the 11th arrondissement denounced the officials of his municipality for refusing a registration permit to a certain citizen; another member replied that the man would succeed if he tried a second time after the magistrates received official notification of the new ruling.[23] At the very least, though, the unwillingness of the Legislature to satisfy this demand in a uniform fashion continued to leave registration of excluded citizens a problematic affair.

ALONG WITH the rate of the journée de travail and the open registration bill, a major question of franchise reform was the potential effect of the veterans' bonus. As noted earlier, the milliard had been advocated not simply as a debt of honor to the soldiers but also as a relief measure for the soldiers' parents. The Constitutional Circle of Versailles seized on this point to make the following argument. Many parents, deprived of their son's help while he was serving in the army, were reduced to impoverishment. Unable to pay any taxes, they were then disfranchised. But the promised benefits of the bonus were legally due them, and at the current moment they were supposed to be deriving support from it in the absence of their children. They should therefore have the vote as virtual taxpayers, so to speak. The Versailles Club accordingly launched the proposal that the fathers of soldiers be given the vote regardless of how poor they were, even though the bonus was not yet actually being paid. Felix Lepelletier, who was active in the club and a close friend of the publisher Vatar, saw to it that the club's petition was publicized and endorsed on 27 nivôse (16 January 1798) by the *Journal des hommes libres*. In reprinting it the paper invited "all patriots, particularly the constitutional circles, to support this measure, which will avenge the national honor against the insolent sarcasms of the rich counterrevolutionaries, and which will give to thousands of republicans a right precious to all good Frenchmen."[24]

[23] *L'Indépendant* (Paris) No. 181, 1 germinal VI; A.N. F⁷ 3688/13, dossier secret: police report on the club of the 11th arrondissement.
[24] *J. hommes libres* No. 242, 27 nivôse VI; *Tribun du Peuple* (Paris) No. 84, 28 nivôse.

Other papers printed the proposal, and a campaign of petitions gained momentum rapidly. The club at Mayenne, for example, specifically affirmed its support of the Versailles Club and submitted its own petition, which capitalized on the obvious emotional appeal of the proposal: "The men that [the parents] gave to the republic are surely well worth three days' [wages]." To this plea for sympathy Vatar added a purely legalistic argument for allowing the impoverished fathers to vote. If France's finances had permitted the immediate payment of the promised bonus, there would have been a significant addition to the parents' income and they could pay the tax.[25] The petition of the club at Uzès (Gard) combined the emotional and legalistic arguments. Speaking in the name of the destitute parents, the club wrote: "If the vigorous arms of our children were available to assist our feeble hands, we would be in a condition to pay the tax required by the constitution . . . the indemnity is due us, the public treasury is overburdened and we ask nothing. But . . . we do ask to participate in the most precious of rights." Scores of clubs submitted petitions to endorse this proposal.[26]

‡ II ‡

These attempts to increase the electorate by interpreting the eligibility laws as loosely as possible and by enfranchising the indigent fathers of soldiers formed one side of the Jacobins' electoral reform campaign. The other side consisted of demands for disfranchising several types of citizens.

The fructidor coup had not eliminated the potential ability of the local "aristocrats" and "honnêtes gens" to dominate future elections through their personal influence. Moreover, the Jacobins remained a small minority of the electorate (not to mention the population) and had little to hope for at present in genuinely free elections, should that unlikely occasion ever have arisen. Distrust of the honnêtes gens was by now endemic in the Jacobin political out-

[25] *J. hommes libres* No. 255, 10 pluviôse VI.

[26] A.N. C 431, fol. 167: Les membres composant le cercle constitutionnel d'Uzès (Gard), 1 ventôse VI. The club of the 11th arrondissement in Paris advanced the argument a step further by suggesting that wounded soldiers would be entitled to a greater share of the bonus and should therefore qualify both as electors and voters (A.N. C 431-434, and *J. hommes libres*, pluviôse-ventôse, *passim*).

252

look. Above all, then, many Jacobins feared that the Revolution's antagonists might once again regain power through the very republican institutions that they disdained. Consequently they urged on the government a policy of exclusions and disfranchisements.

Immediately after Fructidor the Directory on its own initiative had reinstituted the laws against priests and émigrés. The Jacobins hoped to expand this repression with measures against other alleged opponents of the Revolution. They sought from the government, in the words of a petition from Vannes (Morbihan), "means by which the patriots can be given the influence that they ought to enjoy in the coming primary and communal elections." Here was no commitment to the right of all citizens to vote; the franchise was seen as a prerogative to be denied to the disloyal and unpatriotic—above and beyond priests and émigrés about whom there was no longer any question. For their part the citizens of Vannes suggested the establishment of a *juri de sûreté nationale* in each town, whose function would be "to repress the leaders of the party that opposes the revolution."[27]

The demand that the Revolution's enemies must somehow be barred from defeating the Revolution through its own electoral procedures was expressed in more excited language by fifteen "Hommes libres et laboreurs en société particulière à Evans," a hamlet in the Jura: "The only citizens in a Republic are the Democrats; consequently the right of citizenship for men or women has never belonged and can never belong to aristocrats, nobles, royalists, papists, or any of their sectaries." And of the many measures that this tiny club deemed necessary to affirm "the reign of democracy," the most pressing was to exclude from the primary assemblies "the aristocrats or conspirators against democracy, the monarchiens, the fanatical papists, and the vacillators."[28]

Throughout the period between the fructidor coup and the spring elections, the Constitutional Circles importuned the Legislature to disfranchise "anti-republicans." Too sweeping to be meaningful, many of these pleas bespoke anguish rather than calculation, as when the patriots in Alet (Aude) declared (without explaining

[27] A.N. C 426, fol. 97: Les citoyens soussignés de Vannes, 29 vendémiaire VI (120 signatures).

[28] A.N. F⁷ 7368, fol. 823: Des hommes libres et laboreurs en société particulière à Evans (Jura) to Directory, 19 frimaire VI.

how to accomplish this) "that every man who had publicly shown his aversion for the republic" should be disfranchised.[29] Eventually, though, a few concrete proposals about how to diminish the influence of the reaction in the coming elections crystallized and were taken up by the Constitutional Circles.

The foremost category singled out in these petitions were persons whom the Directory itself had removed from office after the fructidor coup; according to the Jacobins' logic they should now be banned from the elections. These *destitués de Fructidor* included the administrators of over fifty departments, a few judges, hundreds of municipal officials, and many of the Directory's former commissioners to the departments and cantons. In most cases they were prominent citizens of a reactionary temperament whom the Directory had embraced after the Babeuf conspiracy. Events before Fructidor had shown that these honnêtes gens above all were vehement anti-Jacobins intent upon snuffing out the least sign of democratic agitation. Their exclusion from the political arena was deemed necessary by many clubs if the Fructidor coup was to have any lasting significance. In the words of the Constitutional Circle of Amiens (Somme): "we demand a *décret sauveur* which will exclude from the electorate and from all public offices . . . all those who were ousted by the law of 19 fructidor: all of those judges and perfidious administrators whom the Directory has dismissed."[30]

Dozens of Constitutional Circles echoed this proposal, including the small and closely linked clubs in the Eure and in the Loir-et-Cher departments, as well as the ambulatory club of the Corrèze.[31] Some of the petitions demanding the disfranchisement of the *destitués* at the same time urged that the indigent fathers of soldiers be allowed to vote. This coupling of propositions was so common that, according to the *Journal des hommes libres*, in pluviôse the government was receiving a mass of petitions in support of these two causes.[32]

---

[29] A.N. C 431, fol. 167: Les Patriotes d'Aleth (Aude), 6 ventôse.

[30] A.N. F⁷ 7386, fol. 2378: Des Républicains composant le cercle constitutionnel d'Amiens to the Council of 500, 7 pluviôse VI.

[31] A.N. C 431, fol. 167: petitions from the Constitutional Circles of Ouquès (30 signatures); Morée (23 signatures); Villedieu (19 signatures); and Blois (120 signatures)—all in Loir-et-Cher. *Ibid.*, petition from Brive (Corrèze), 1 ventôse (120 signatures).

[32] *J. hommes libres*, No. 246, 1 pluviôse VI and *passim*; A.N. C 431-34,

Other Constitutional Circles went further than advocating the disfranchisement of the *destitués de Fructidor*. Like the club in Paris' 6th arrondissement, they urged the Legislature to exclude from the primary assemblies in addition "all those electors whose choices were struck down (*frappés de nullité*) by the salutary law of 19 fructidor."[33] This referred to those thousands of electors who had participated in the fifty-odd electoral assemblies of the Year V whose choices were subsequently annulled by the Directory because of their reactionary character. This extreme measure was endorsed by large clubs in Tours (Indre) and Nevers (Nièvre) among others. In Metz (Moselle) over 350 persons signed the club's petition asking that the *destitués de Fructidor* be excluded along with "those who have notoriously shown themselves as their accomplices by intriguing for them openly in those assemblies whose operations you have annulled." The club further pledged to support "any measure of public safety" that might be necessary to assure the republic's security.[34]

Still other petitions coupled these demands with proposals concerning changes in electoral procedures, or relocation of the seat of electoral assemblies to avoid reactionary strongholds. Several omnibus petitions were received by the Legislature summarizing the several planks in this program of exclusionary electoral legislation. The Constitutional Circle of St. Omer (Pas-de-Calais) for example, suggested that six categories of citizens be deprived of the vote: Roman Catholic priests, relatives of émigrés, electors of the Year V, *destitués de Fructidor*, individuals who have harbored refractory priests or held clandestine religious services, and individuals who have provoked desertion or who have given refuge to deserters.[35]

The Directory resisted almost entirely this pressure to disfranchise

---

including vigorous petitions from clubs in Tournus (Saône-et-Loire), Sarlat (Dordogne), Angoulème (Charente); A.N. AF III 252/Nord: petition from Cambray.

[33] A.N. C 429, fol. 151; 20 pluviôse (40 signatures).

[34] A.N. C 431, fol. 167: Des Républicains composant le cercle constitutionnel de Metz to the Council of 500, ventôse; *Ibid.*: petition from club at Tours (110 signatures); A.N. F⁷ 7396, fol. 3315: petition from Nevers (150 signatures).

[35] A.N. C 431, fol. 167: Des Républicains réunis en cercle constitutionnel à St. Omer, 10 ventôse (45 signatures). Also *Ibid.*: petition from club at Tinchebray (Orne); *J. hommes libres* No. 280, 5 ventôse. Prominent among the St. Omer signators was Vendôme defendant Louis Tafourreau.

various categories of reactionaries; it was not about to expose its flank. To be sure, the *destitués de Fructidor* were no friends of the regicide republic, no matter how conservative of property and order it was supposed to be. They remained opposed to the foundations of the Directorial settlement and to the Directory's policy of expansion in Europe. But to keep the *destitués de Fructidor* under control was not the same as eliminating their presence on the local political scene. By virtue of their social positions they were part of the natural political nation in a conservative, libertarian republic. Should their influence be completely eliminated the door would be open to the uncertainties of uncontrolled democracy and "enthusiasm." Once the counterweight of conservative influence was removed, the Jacobins might consolidate their influence, however small a minority they were. It is therefore not difficult to imagine, as Barras claims in his *Memoirs*, that several of the Directors were rumbling about disfranchising not the *destitués de Fructidor* but the "terrorists."[36]

Consequently, the Directory allowed only minor changes in the electoral laws for the Year VI. The *scrutin de réduction et de rejet* was eliminated (lists of candidates drawn up before the convocation of the assemblies, from which the electors could vote against individuals). The exact procedures for balloting were further detailed, and the hours of the primary assemblies were fixed from between 9 A.M. to 7 P.M. This would ostensibly keep the leisured voters from prolonging the proceedings excessively in order to tire those citizens who happened to work for a living. But as far as the major demands for changes in eligibility were concerned, the Legislature made only one concession. On 5 ventôse (23 February 1798) it passed a law disfranchising citizens who held civil or military positions among the "rebels"—a measure designed to exclude leaders of the chouan and Vendée rebellions.[37] But this decree was ambiguous enough to serve as a pretext in Paris for barring certain "vendémiarists"—conservatives and royalists who had participated in the primary assemblies of the Year IV in Paris that had proclaimed a state of insurrection aimed at preventing the smooth transition from the Convention to the Constitution of the Year III. Beyond this, how-

[36] Barras, *Memoirs*, III, 216.
[37] *Bulletin des Lois* Nos. 183-86, 24 and 28 pluviôse VI; 5 and 9 ventôse VI.

ever, the Jacobins failed to limit the influence of the honnêtes gens by disfranchisement.

‡ III ‡

The campaign to modify the franchise laws in order to register new voters and disfranchise others secured slim results. On the contrary, the Directory's primary response to the demand for electoral reform was to limit the right of petition itself in the decree of 24 ventôse (14 March 1798). While minor points were gained on a local level (as over the value of the journée de travail in Paris), no comprehensive legislation was passed to open registration, enfranchise the fathers of soldiers, or exclude proven reactionaries like the *destitués de Fructidor*. But these issues were preliminaries to the actual electoral contests of the Year VI; a great deal remained to be done even within the unyielding framework of existing laws. From petitioning to modify these laws in advance by legislation, the clubs turned to the task of organizing their forces, recruiting voters, and generating enthusiasm for the pending confrontation.

Defeat of the Jacobins' open registration bill did not imply that the voting lists were definitively closed; it meant that no important changes in the registration rolls could be effected simply or straightforwardly. The rolls could still be altered under several circumstances: names could be challenged as ineligible under existing laws; names could be added with the connivance of friendly officials. Nor did the lists themselves necessarily constitute the *sine qua non* of admission to the primary assemblies, for these meetings of citizens were in a sense self-regulating and reserved the final word about who could and could not vote. The electors chosen by such an assembly might be challenged in turn at the department's electoral assembly, but that eventuality could be faced in due course.

At the very least, then, the clubs constituted organized pressure groups that could comb the rolls for alleged errors and demand redress from the authorities. For this purpose the club at Dôle (Jura) sent a public deputation to the town hall, where it requested that the official list of eligible voters be immediately drawn up and a copy sent to the club "which would render its observations."[38] At Langres (Haute-Marne) the club wrote to the municipal com-

[38] A.N. F⁷ 7417, fol. 5361: letter to Directory, floréal.

missioner asking him to help remove the names of three citizens from the list of eligible voters by virtue of several laws that were cited. The letter concluded with these words: "sent to citizen Brugnon [the commissioner] by the Circle of which he is a member, with an invitation to make use of these notes." Unfortunately for the club, Brugnon, whose membership was evidently nominal, deemed the letter a violation of the 24 ventôse decree against "collective correspondence." He therefore sent the letter to Paris as evidence against the club—a good illustration of that decree's intent as well as its effect in hampering the clubs.[39]

Where a club was fortunate enough to have support somewhere in the local administration it could sometimes achieve impressive results in pruning or enlarging the voter rolls according to its lights. Unfortunately, we can document such cases only by the reactions they provoked, since the clubs did not keep records of such maneuvers. The built-in irregularity of the primary assemblies where a majority could set its own ground rules with a certain degree of impunity presumably determined many clubs to proceed with efforts to recruit and bring in citizens whose eligibility might be questionable. Where their own partisans were concerned, the letter of the law proved to be flexible in the extreme for the Jacobins. As a result, a host of outraged citizens denounced the clubs to the Directory for illegally recruiting voters. Following a pattern that seems to have been repeated in dozens of towns, the Jacobins of Luxeuil (Haute-Saône) and Besançon (Doubs) evoked bitter denunciations by their tactics. From Luxeuil the municipal commissioner wrote to the Directory that he was powerless to stop the irregularities perpetrated by Fady, the official agent or clerk of the commune, who was active in the town's Constitutional Circle. He charged in particular that the clerk had drawn up "supplementary lists" of voters, generally registering these citizens without anyone witnessing the process of certification. At the primary assembly the club saw to it that these names were accepted despite their putative ineligibility.[40] From

[39] A.N. F⁷ 7416, fol. 5334: Brugnon to M. of Pol., 10 germinal, enclosing a copy of the letter from the club. Fragmentary minutes from the clubs at Orléans and the 11th arrondissement in Paris indicate similar kinds of pre-election activity; it is virtually certain that if the minutes of other clubs had survived they would likewise document this point.

[40] A.N. F⁷ 7414, fol. 5058: municipal commissioner (Luxeuil) to M. of Pol., 3 germinal.

Besançon came a petition with ten pages of signatures attacking the Constitutional Circle for sharp practices in electioneering, with a special denunciation of the municipal administration—"a satellite of the club"—for striking off voters it claimed to be ineligible and adding "a horde" of people who were allegedly ineligible to vote either because they did not meet the residence requirement or because they had paid no taxes.[41] Such disputes erupted in the assemblies themselves, and the success in recruiting new voters therefore depended on the effectiveness of organization that the clubs brought to these assemblies, of which more will be said shortly.

People outside of the Constitutional Circles viewed the clubs' recruiting efforts with dismay, and not simply because of their alleged illegalities or sharp practices. A distinct aspect of the denunciations that accumulated against the clubs was social in nature—a reflection of the prevalent sense of class consciousness among conservatives. Their indictment essentially held that the Jacobins recruited support outside the bounds of the political nation; in thus organizing their efforts the Jacobins were therefore upsetting the precarious social equilibrium that the constitution was supposed to protect. In Basses-Alpes, for example, the conservative leaders maintained that the club's electioneering "stirs up discord within that class of citizens whose neediness and lack of education makes it susceptible to every impression." As a result the assemblies were allegedly disorderly and full of ineligible people. Seventy-five citizens of Torigny (Manche) conveyed the same impression when they signed a petition complaining of the Constitutional Circle's role in the elections, especially that people were admitted to vote, "who haven't payed the required tax"; the clubs, they concluded, "finding in those kinds of persons a surer docility."[42]

Perhaps the outstanding monument to the class prejudice that the Jacobins' electoral activities seemed to arouse came from the town of St. Bonnet (Loire). Here the aggrieved anti-Jacobins took the

[41] A.N. AF III 224/Doubs: Des Citoyens de la commune de Besançon to the Council of 500, 15 germinal. Cf. A.N. AF III 251/Nièvre: Les Citoyens soussignés de Clamecy . . . , 5 germinal; A.N. F1c III Pas-de-Calais/2: Robert (de Neuville) to the Legislature, 4 germinal; and petition from citizens of Wismer (arrondissement of St. Omer).

[42] A.N. AF III 212/Basses-Alpes: Mémoire par les deputés . . . ; A.N. F7 7446, fol. 8376: Les citoyens soussignés de Torigny . . . (75 signatures). Also A.N. C 530/Bouches-du-Rhône: municipal administration of Aix to M. of Pol., 6 germinal.

trouble to print a detailed account of the scandalous events that enveloped their primary assembly. The pamphlet rehearsed the usual complaints about credulous and unruly sans-culottes recruited by the local Jacobins—citizens "having no property, and assuredly not inscribed on the tax rolls." To document this charge, however, the pamphlet did not list the names of the allegedly ineligible recruits or any precise fiscal data about them. Instead it conveyed its argument simply by noting in detail the group's social composition, as if this were self-explanatory: seventeen compagnon serruriers, two journaliers, one tisserant, one ci-devant voiturier et actuellement sans état, one cordonnier, one charpentier, one garçon serrurier, one deserteur (!), and six others, all led by Arnaud, adjoint municipal.[43] Testimony to this kind of class tension comes from the other side as well, for example in a complaint by former members of the club at Montmarsan (Landes) that the commissioner to the department showed open disdain towards "savetiers, cordonniers, boureliers and perruquiers."[44] This aura of class consciousness surrounding the primary assemblies had been prefigured during the legislative debates on the Jacobins' open registration bill, and it was not without cause. To be sure, the great bulk of Neo-Jacobin voting strength came from duly registered and taxpaying citizens. But clearly the Jacobins were attempting, despite the bill's defeat, to recruit new voters from that suspect body of sans-culottes who had not been heard from since the Year II.

DIRECTORIAL conservatism and (what is really the same thing) bourgeois class prejudice did not pose the only obstacles for the clubs trying to recruit new voters among the sans-culottes. The chief barrier to widespread electoral participation was mass apathy, a condition sans-culottes shared with many honnêtes gens. Voting may have been the cornerstone of political life in Directorial France, but it was a tedious and time-consuming affair that could easily disenchant the less-than-committed. Jacobins and Directorials alike deplored the resultant apathy among their fellow citizens. But where the

[43] *Procès-verbaux de l'Assemblée primaire du canton de St. Bonnet-le-Chateau, département de la Loire . . . 1 et 2 germinal an 6* (Impr. de Boyer à St. Etienne) in A.N. AF III 240/Loire.

[44] A.N. AF III 239/Landes: Les citoyens de Mont-de-Marsan individuellement soussignés, 10 thermidor 6. Many of the same signatures appear in a petition from the Constitutional Circle dated ventôse.

Directory's numerous electoral proclamations denounced non-participation in general terms,[45] the clubs were particularly concerned with the uncivic attitudes of workingmen. The stark justification for non-voting among that class was capsulated in an exchange overheard and reported by a reliable and sympathetic police observer in Paris. A workingman complained to his friend that he was not registered, to which the latter replied: "You're really a dupe if you worry about that. The time that you spend in the assembly won't bring you one sou for bread."[46]

Some of the clubs worried. At Pont St. Esprit (Gard) the Constitutional Circle petitioned to express its regret over "the large number of people, principally among the cultivators and artisans who, though generally good citizens, are guilty of an indifference to public affairs. . . . They worry more about the loss of a day's wages than about the election of a good magistrate." The best this club could propose was the suggestion that the government declare election day a compulsory national holiday.[47] Others took the more direct, but equally ineffective tack, of exhortation by means of pamphlets. In Paris an electoral pamphlet that bristled with egalitarian sentiment ended with a plea to the "respectable class of WORKERS," asking that they open their eyes and "sacrifice a day's work in order to vote." Similarly the Constitutional Circle of Dôle (Jura) addressed a pamphlet to "the cultivators and workers in the ateliers" of the Jura urging them to join the struggle "to complete our revolution and to affirm the reign of equality." Vote, it pleaded, and do not listen to those who tell you to "stay in your workshops or at the head of your plows—the time that you would spend at your assemblies will be lost time for you."[48]

Pointed as they were, such spirited pamphlets or mournful petitions were unlikely to overcome apathy; only a more direct and

[45] E.g., "Proclamation relative aux assemblées primaires de l'an 6, du 9 ventôse," in *Moniteur*, 14 ventôse (p. 658).

[46] A.N. F⁷ 3688/13: report for 13 ventôse by Gros de Luzenne; also report by Morand, 28 ventôse.

[47] A.N. C 429, fol. 151: Les Citoyens soussignés composant le Cercle constitutionnel du Pont St. Esprit to the Council of 500, 4 pluviôse VI (45 signatures).

[48] A. Thiébaut, *Le Tocsin de l'Opinion publique* (Impr. Guilhemat, an VI) in B.N. Lb42/535. *Les Républicains membres du Cercle Constitutionnel de Dôle, à leurs frères les habitans . . . du Jura* (Impr. Briot à Besançon, an VI) in A.N. F⁷ 7417, fol. 5361.

intensive effort could have any effect. Recruiting "workingmen" was related to the larger task of mobilization and organization. The Jacobins were not interested in enrolling new voters for the sake of good citizenship as a principle; they were seeking allies in their effort to shape the outcome of elections. Several Clubs evidently attempted to follow the most direct method possible of recruiting support among workingmen, who may or may not have been legally eligible to vote, but who in any case were understandably reluctant to take the time off. To allay such reluctance, these clubs moved to indemnify the men for the wages that they would lose while attending the assemblies—thus producing (in the eyes of the denouncers) the most contemptible kind of electioneering in the republic's annals.

In the most detailed account of this tactic a signed letter from Limoux (Aude) claimed that the local club raised a fund "to engage the day-laborers and the poor" in the elections—the money being distributed in the form of "*bienfaisance* and indemnity accorded to the day-laborers (*journaliers*) for the loss of time that they spend at the elections." The informants stated that as a result of these efforts the number of registered voters rose to one thousand, two hundred more than the previous year's total. A parallel measure to encourage participation by workingmen in the assemblies involved changing the locale of one meeting hall to a faubourg far from the homes of many voters in the district but near to those of the "workingmen."[49]

"A fund to indemnify indigent workers for the days that they would spend in attendance at the primary assemblies" was also distributed by the Constitutional Circle of Louhans (Saône-et-Loire), according to several outraged citizens in that town. Likewise in Mauriac (Cantal) the municipal commissioner reported that the Constitutional Circle had swelled the roll of voters with unqualified persons: "The worker, the peaceable artisan," he charged, "were pulled from their workshops for a price."[50] The commissioner to the tribunals at Laval (Mayenne) denounced the

---

[49] A.N. AF iii 216/Aude: copie d'une lettre au M. de Pol., 15 germinal.

[50] A.N. AF iii 258/Saône-et-Loire: municipal commissioner (Louhans) to M. of Pol., 3 germinal; also A.N. F⁷ 7414, fol. 5052: municipal administration (Louhans) to departmental commissioner, 26 floréal VI. A.N. F⁷ 7418, fol. 5436: municipal commissioner (Mauriac) to M. of Pol., 5 germinal.

club in his town for its strenuous efforts to bring unqualified "work-men" to vote in the primary assemblies, some of whom were paid for their troubles. A similar claim was leveled at the club in Paniers (Ariège) by the justice of the peace, who reported "that it was even agreed to pay daily wages for the attendance of some ringleaders" —though he did not indicate whether this proposal was actually implemented.[51]

Of the host of accusations leveled against the clubs for their at-tempts to recruit voters from among "workingmen" and "non-taxpayers" these were the most damaging, and struck the most responsive chord among conservatives. A long-standing assumption in conservative ranks held that workingmen or sans-culottes with little property were likely to be venal. This became the principal rationale for limiting the franchise and reviving the dichotomy of 1791 between active and passive citizens in the Constitution of 1795. By admitting to the franchise only regular taxpayers, the archi-tects of the Directorial republic intended that the electorate would consist of persons who would be able to afford the financial sacri-fices of active citizenship and thereby be above corruption. Indem-nities for income lost during attendance at the primary assemblies therefore completely contravened a major premise of the constitution.

The Jacobins rejected these assumptions about active and passive citizenship. Arguments against a limited suffrage had been recapitu-lated by Julien Souhait and Antonelle in their pamphlets of 1795, while Lenglet's book of 1798 further advanced the democratic theory of political participation. All the while democrats insisted that re-gardless of the letter of the law, citizens who were civic-minded enough to desire a vote and who were properly domiciled members of the community ought to participate. Such was the premise of their campaign for new registration legislation, knowingly rejected by the conservative majority in the Council of Elders. But the issue, as suggested at the outset of this chapter, was not being joined principally on the level of theory. And the fact remained that exer-cise of the franchise did take at least a whole day or more, and hence could be costly in wages or business lost. Fully aware of this, certain clubs attempted in some fashion to cushion the losses that their

[51] A.N. AF III 247/Mayenne: "Rapport sur divers évenemens arrivés à Laval . . . depuis le 21 ventôse jusqu'au ce jour 6 germinal." A.N. AF III 215/Ariège: justice of the peace (Paniers) to M. of Pol., 11 germinal.

more vulnerable members might sustain. For most of the clubs this doubtless went no further than trying to build morale and inculcate voters with a sense of strength and purpose—to create the feeling that they were regaining control over their political destiny for the first time since 1793. A few Constitutional Circles, however, went beyond this (or at least intended to) by actually offering "indemnities." Possibly some of these clubs did nothing more than raise a fund to provide food and drink on the days of the primary assemblies—a customary practice in George Washington's Virginia at this time.[52] But even if the charges about indemnities were literally accurate, they must be judged in the full context of electoral organization undertaken by the clubs. They were but a small part of the larger effort to loosen restrictive franchise laws, overcome the inertia of apathy, and recruit new voters. Conservatives might just have been confusing corruption with effective electioneering.

‡ IV ‡

Altogether the clubs produced a burst of political vitality in France. Though the number of voters did not increase in 1798, changes occurred in the kinds of men turning out to vote, and above all in the prevailing atmosphere.[53] A small measure of the populistic style that had developed during the Year II again infused political life. But even this mild hint of sans-culottisme clashed with the sense of propriety prized by middle-class Directorials. While sans-culottes delighted in acting through the mass amidst noise and excitement, such group duress was antithetical to middle-class

[52] See William N. Chambers, *Political Parties in a New Nation: the American Experience 1776-1809* (New York, 1963), pp. 21-27.

[53] This section and much of the following chapter are based largely on materials collected by the Directory, especially in series A.N. AF III 211-67: Affaires départementales (élections). Included here are the manuscript procès-verbaux of each departmental electoral assembly; reports by the Directory's commissioners and other agents, accompanied by supporting documents; unsolicited denunciations, petitions, unprocessed notes, and rejoinders. Other sources include series A.N. C 530-35: Conseil des Anciens, an VI, some of which duplicates the above, but which also contains original documents; A.N. F1c III: Ministry of Interior: Esprit public et élections; A.N. AF III 501-23: Directory: minutes des arrêtés et pièces annexes. To support each generalization or detail here by a particular reference would multiply the size and number of footnotes excessively. But enough citations will be made to indicate the kinds of sources and the nuances involved.

individualism. Indeed election week exposed a tension in the Directorial prescription for republicanism. It saw them celebrating the virtues of civic participation on the one hand and insisting, on the other, that the prescribed place of the elite—with its property, education, and instinct for the *juste milieu*—be honored. Only under the more restricted electoral system of the Restoration and July Monarchy could these ideals be harmonized in actual practice. Meanwhile, the Directorials labored under their own constitution, which turned out to be more of a compromise between egalitarianism and elitism than they had intended. Popular participation had a price in this politicized country that the moderates were reluctant to pay. For the Jacobins this price of "enthusiasm" was a positive virtue.

As the primary assemblies convened on the first of germinal (21 March), the clubs presented a formidable front. With slogans still ringing from previous rallies—"Aux bons sans-culottes, pour chasser de leur sein les ennemis du peuple"[54]—they willfully disregarded the fine points of procedure and precipitated confrontations with the forces of order. Tumult may have served the designs of ambitious bourgeois Jacobins, but it was also the style of sans-culottes. Extreme partisanship—that tangible expression of political consciousness—is what truly marked the entry of the new clubs into the electoral process. The assemblies in 1798 provided a catharsis for accumulated ill will and enmity. As one observer commented, former revolutionaries "wish to revive class distinctions between 'plebeian' and 'patrician' citizens . . . to reestablish sans-culottisme under other forms."[55]

Solidarity fostered by the clubs produced a partisanship conducive to the psychology of mass action, albeit through the ballot. But the line between partisanship and overt intimidation was sometimes crossed. Jacobins in Vaucluse and Bouches-du-Rhône declared a rhetorical "war on the thermidorians," but in Besançon (Doubs) this was carried out literally when a fraternal banquet on election eve ended with an assault on the *Café Au 9 thermidor.* Directorials who walked out of hostile primary assemblies were hectored through

[54] A.N. AF III 258/Saône-et-Loire: reports on General Parrein, former president of the Lyons Temporary Commission, addressing clubs at Chalons and Louhans.
[55] A.N. AF III 211/Ain: Girod to Merlin, 16 germinal.

the streets—in Brive (Corrèze) to the alleged cry of "Vive Robespierre"; in Vendôme (Loir-et-Cher) to shouts of "à bas les grands maisons, à bas les grands chateaux." Pushing, catcalls, and other forms of harassment fell upon "the veritable bees of the nation, those who pay taxes," as the outraged commissioner to Montmarsan (Landes) put it. One of the most raucous incidents occurred in Chambéry (Mont Blanc) where "a number of workers permitted themselves to menace citizens" on their way to vote, attaching "papers bearing the words *I am a CHOUAN* to those whom opinion purports to designate as not being ardent friends of liberty."[56]

Two décadis latter at the departmental electoral assemblies, beleaguered conservatives continued to complain of partisan crowd activity—"a multitude seduced by the factious" surrounding the meeting hall, harassing unpopular electors, and yelling "ferocious cries." In Allier, Basses-Alpes, Gard, Nièvre, Basses-Pyrénées, Saône-et-Loire, Seine, and Vienne, Jacobin electors received significant moral support from these milling, slogan-shouting, and in some cases, armed crowds numbering in the hundreds, who spurred them on with shouts like "Vive les sans-culottes, haine implacable aux thermidoriens."[57]

The notion of popular sovereignty was fundamental in sans-culottisme or populism. Under the Directory this principle was severely limited; the primary assemblies were allowed only to choose electors, and were strictly enjoined from becoming deliberative bodies. Nonetheless they provided forums in which citizens could cultivate the sense of their ultimate power. Their prevailing spirit in 1798 was anti-paternalistic. Citizens tore down the Directory's proclamations (Paniers/Ariège), or refused to hear the Directory's instructions read, "stating that when the sovereign has risen, it receives no orders or advice from anyone whatsoever" (Emile/Seine-et-Oise);

[56] A.N. F⁷ 7441, fol. 7935: Observations . . . concernant le dept. du Doubs. A.N. AF iii 515, plaq. 3285 (pièce 13): Lefranc to Merlin, 5 germinal, on Montmarsan. A.N. F⁷ 7336, fol. 551 on Vendôme. A.N. AF iii 516, plaq. 3304 (pièces 12-13): departmental commissioner (Mont Blanc) to M. of Pol., 6 germinal.

[57] E.g., A.N. AF iii 212/Basses-Alpes: Mémoire presenté par les deputés du Basses-Alpes . . . ; AF iii 228/Gard: departmental commissioner to Directory; [Butaud, administrateur de la Vienne], *Sur les doubles élections de Poitiers (Vienne)* (Paris, Impr. Tutot, n.d.) B.N. Lb42/554; AF iii 258/Saône-et-Loire: Observations sur les assemblées primaires et électorales.

"that while the primary assemblies are in operation there are no longer any laws" (St. Reverein/Nièvre). These rhetorical blasts at incipient paternalism reflected the conviction that primary assemblies could become effective instruments of representative democracy. The members came to the assemblies with the attitude, expressed in Clamecy (Nièvre), that "the government has made its 18 fructidor, let us also make our own."[58]

But all the demonstrations, slogans, and provocative challenges hurled at conservatives were the icing on the cake of sound organization that preceded the elections. Verbal intimidation was effective only when buttressed by preparations for controlling the actual voting. The cornerstone of the Jacobins' approach was to prepare a slate of nominees and organize enough support to put it over one way or another. From numerous, well-documented accounts of the club's electoral preparations, a composite portrait can be drawn.

In advance of the elections, a special meeting of the club would be well publicized by letters, public placards, or word of mouth; usually it would be held in conjunction with a fraternal banquet. Speeches would be made emphasizing the need for tenacity and solidarity. The members would then deliberate on slates of officers for the assemblies and for electors to be chosen by the assemblies. Once the slates had been hammered out the members would usually take a mass oath to support those and only those names. (In a few places these names would be written on cards and distributed to make sure that there were no misunderstandings; such artifacts of Jacobin party organization actually survive in the Directory's files.)[59]

On the morning of 1 germinal (the day the primary assemblies opened) the clubbists would converge on the hall, often en masse. They would invariably arrive early—before the official opening hour of 9 A.M. Frequently, it was charged, they would start the proceedings before that hour, that is, before all the other voters had arrived.

---

[58] A.N. AF III 215/Ariège: justice of the peace of Paniers to Directory, 11 germinal. AF III 262/Seine-et-Oise: departmental commissioner to M. of Pol., 7 germinal. AF III 251/Nièvre: Observations sur plusieurs assemblées primaires . . . ; and Les Citoyens soussignées . . . de Clamecy, 5 germinal. Cf. AF III 255/Hautes-Pyrénées: departmental commissioner, *compte décadaire* for germinal, reporting that voters were "egarée . . . par l'espérance qui lui a été donnée de voire reduire les contributions et d'avoir le pain à un sol la livre."

[59] E.g., A.N. AF III 258/Saône-et-Loire; A.N. F7 7417, fol. 5361 on Dôle (Jura).

(The assemblies began by designating the oldest member present as acting president, who would then supervise the balloting for permanent officers. Once elected, these men would then conduct the business of the assembly.) Their predesignated men would be chosen as presidents, vice-presidents, and secretaries of the assembly. Then certain citizens would be expelled from the assembly on the grounds that they were émigré relatives, chouans, and the like. Attempts to challenge the eligibility of club members on the grounds that they were not properly registered or not on the tax rolls would be repulsed. At this point conservatives in some assemblies would walk out and form a rump of their own; in others where the Jacobins found themselves on the losing end of these decisions, they would undertake a walk-out. Now the voting for electors would begin, and if all had gone well the Jacobins would be in a position to name their slates of electors, if not by a clear majority on the first ballot, then after some lobbying and maneuvering on the second or the final third ballot.

This kind of organization—limited to voters within a single town or city—was common. But in a few departments Jacobins were even more advanced in the art of party organization, with plans to coordinate activities in several towns, and to concert for final preparations before the departmental electoral assembly. A glance at the Allier department will recapitulate the major points in this discussion, add a few concrete illustrations, and suggest how far certain cadres were able to go in forming effective local parties.

When they had a foothold on some level of local administration, the Jacobins certainly found the tasks of party organization facilitated, even if other local officials (like the Directory's commissioners) remained hostile. This was the case in the Dordogne, Landes, Sarthe, and Pas-de-Calais departments, as well as the Allier, where several Jacobins had been brought into local administration by the Directory in its quest for effective republican officials after Fructidor. In addition, the Moulins Jacobins published a local newspaper, like their counterparts in LeMans and Perigueux. Accordingly the Moulins Club was able to convene a large fraternal banquet one month before the primary assemblies with a minimum of harassment. Here middle-class Jacobin leaders cultivated their liaisons with politically conscious sans-culottes and began organizing for the coming elections. At this point they already were arranging for a second banquet to be held on 19 germinal (8 April) —the day before the departmental electoral assembly was to convene. Participants took an oath to join together at that time, "with the greatest possible number of their friends," to mount a show of support for their fellow electors. Meanwhile those attending this preliminary meeting would return to their own communes to prepare for the primary assemblies.[60]

In Moulins the Constitutional Circle issued a public manifesto proclaiming their imminent triumph "by uniting all their choices on the same patriots." In a broadside that was freely distributed, the Jacobin strategy was stated with complete candor, and with the implied sense that certain conventions had to be discarded:

> Yes, on the same names! Because if they divide their votes they will lose the majority. . . . We recognize the citizens worthy of our confidence; but to respond to the desire of our fellow citizens . . . we will indicate here those whom we are planning to name to the bureaux, as electors, as municipal administrators, as justices of the peace, as assessors.

There followed three sets of slates : for officers in the several primary assemblies of Moulins, for electors, and for local officials in each section of the commune.[61] According to a hostile petition signed by forty opponents of the club, this list included "the most influential members of that club," some of whom had been revolutionary commissioners in Moulins or outlying communes in the Year II, or members of the Lyon Temporary Commission, such as the procurator Verd. The denouncers also contended that the Jacobins' most vociferous partisans included several couteliers and manoeuvriers—continuing the practice of stigmatizing such support by the mere indication of a citizen's plebeian status. Other testimony about the primary assemblies indicates that many of the club's choices won majorities on the first ballot.[62]

[60] A.N. C 530/Allier: printed P.V. of the civic banquet held on 1 ventôse. See also two anti-Jacobin pamphlets: *Faits relatifs à la scission des élections du dept. de l'Allier* (Moulins, an VI), B.N. Lb42/547; and Beauchamp et Chabot, *Sur la scission de l'Assemblée de l'Allier* (Impr. Ami des Lois), A.N. AF III 212/Allier.

[61] *Avis au Républicains* (Impr. Burelle à Moulins), placard by the Constitutional Circle, signed F. G. [Givois] in A.N. F7 7415, fol. 5161.

[62] A.N. F7 7415, fol. 5161: Les Citoyens soussignées des sections Liberté et Egalité de Moulins au Directoire, 1 germinal.

Jacobins in other cantons of the Allier, no doubt encouraged by their ventôse conclave, were equally effective, though not without provoking cries of "foul." One incident, not unique here, underscores the urban character of Jacobinism that is, after all, rather obvious from the start. According to twenty protesting citizens from the canton of Izeure, the Jacobins prolonged the sessions of the primary assemblies until most farmers had to return home, primarily to care for their livestock. "Then there remained at the session all the citizens from the bourg of Izeure, the majority of whom were day-laborers not entitled by law to vote." (The municipal authorities later submitted documents purporting to show that 50 of the 215 voters in that assembly were not on the tax rolls.) In the commune of Gannat, according to a complaint signed by a dozen citizens, the Constitutional Circle "insinuated to the illiterate and credulous class of men that . . . whoever did not belong to it could only be considered as a chouan or royalist." With this and other techniques of intimidation—like marching en masse to the primary assembly —the club dominated the voting completely. A club at Cusset likewise won support among local sans-culottes by such tactics as allegedly allowing to vote the sons of parents who did not even pay taxes themselves. And at Varennes, when someone challenged the eligibility of one elector-designate on the question of his property, the protester was silenced by force. Several towns of the department, in short, were as well organized and dominated by the Jacobins as the chef-lieu of Moulins.[63]

Success brings its own rewards. Now the local newspaper could report the resounding triumphs of *patriotes prononcés* in many corners of the department. It could remind its readers of the 19 germinal conclave with buoyant optimism. Meanwhile preparations proceeded apace. New electors and their friends were urged to travel to Moulins early. "The patriots will hasten to show you to suitable lodgings or will offer you their own homes; during the sessions of the electoral assembly you will join us at the permanent banquets to be provided by citoyenne Grobon." Tammany Hall could hardly have done better.

Once housed and fed, the electors would concert for the final step: the choice of a slate for deputies and departmental office.

[63] All of these anti-Jacobin petitions are in A.N. C 530/Allier.

"Once the choices have been determined, let our votes be unwavering on the first ballot, that is to say that all republican votes must be cast for the same candidates."[64] So well prepared were the Allier Jacobins that they could weather the retaliatory blows that were about to be administered by the Directory. Conservatives would prevail on the government to close the Moulins Club and to prohibit the 19 germinal banquet at the last moment. But here, at least, the club was able to adjust by simply going underground. Its preparations were so well advanced that the Jacobin electors (who, incidentally, constituted only a hairline majority of all electors) were still greeted and cared for when they arrived. They were still able to concert and to move efficiently in the electoral assembly. Their ultimate failure came not for want of party organization but precisely because the Directory decided to prevent the emergence of parties.

[64] *Département de l'Allier: Journal* [Moulins, Impr. Burelle] No. 36, 10 germinal VI, in A.N. C 530. For a similar sequence of events see A.N. AF III 251/Nièvre: Réclamation des citoyens de Nevers, against the *Journal de la Nièvre* and the Nevers Constitutional Circle. In Landes, where there was no regular Jacobin newspaper, a printed newsletter was gotten up specially for the period of the elections: *Bulletin de l'Assemblée électorale du dept. des Landes* (Impr. Delaroy) Nos. 1-5, 20-24 germinal, in A.N. AF III 239/Landes.

CHAPTER X

Party Conflict: Jacobins and Directorials

T HE FAILURE of parties to evolve out of the Revolution indisputably darkened France's prospects and eased the way
to dictatorship. By contrast, across the ocean in America
parties were crucial for the survival and viability of the young fed-
eral republic. So divergent a development, however, was not as stark
as it appears in retrospect. Within the framework of the Directorial
constitution, France nearly did achieve the formation of rival parties
during the 1798 election campaign as a consequence of the Neo-
Jacobin resurgence. Precisely because the process of party formation
came so close to fruition and yet aborted so totally, these elections
merit particular scrutiny.

Without questioning the uniqueness of the French experience,
one can call upon the American case as a comparative yardstick.
The vaunted stability of the United States was neither inevitable
nor painless, its public life free from serious political conflict only
for a short time. Perhaps when George Washington was inaugurated it did seem as if the electoral system would guarantee a non-
partisan exercise of power by the nation's elite. An unstated but
virtually universal assumption of this system condemned organized
opposition parties. But Americans began increasingly to differ over
questions of political ideology, regional loyalty, and foreign relations. As they clashed and impugned each other's motives, men
like Hamilton and Jefferson shattered the framework projected in
1787 at Philadelphia.

Consensus was salvaged in the face of this discord through the
creation of rival political parties that channeled the conflicts into
manageable forms. Ultimately these parties served to consolidate
rather than undermine the republic. And as David H. Fischer has
recently shown, conservative federalists as well as Jeffersonian democrats adapted to the methods of party rivalry, while continuing to
hurl epithets of "Jacobin" and "aristocrat" at each other. After a
period of stress which saw more than one ill-conceived effort at repression—including President Washington's strictures against "self-

created" democratic-republican clubs—Americans agreed to disagree. By 1800 conflict was formalized, opposition accepted as part of the legitimate political process. The generation of statesmen that had drafted a constitution predicated on a distrust of parties ended by presiding over America's first party system.[1]

Reference to America in the 1790's is intended simply to raise the question of party—the forms and functions of opposition.[2] Conditions in France were obviously more complex, but a similar political problem existed there: how could conflicts (whatever their roots and intensity) be normalized or expressed in a fashion that would not demolish the republican framework. In France and America the assumption that organized opposition was itself destructive posed a major obstacle to political stability, but in both countries it appeared as if the logic of events would surmount this attitude.

‡ I ‡

Conspiratorial or insurrectionary forms of opposition appeared early in France and America, and no doubt confirmed the prejudice against organized opposition. A more delicate question was raised by movements that proceeded through legal political channels. In France it was the other side of the spectrum that presented the first organized political movement. The year 1797 saw reactionary-royalist elements moving in several ways towards party formation. Through front groups called "philanthropic institutes" grass-roots support was organized, and in the wake of a sweeping electoral triumph their leading deputies began caucusing at the Clichy Club

[1] A growing literature on American party development has been synthesized by William N. Chambers, *Political Parties in a New Nation: the American Experience 1776-1809* (New York, 1963), and R. R. Palmer, *Age of the Democratic Revolution* (Princeton, 1965), II, Ch. 16. On the short-lived clubs in America see E. P. Link, *The Democratic-Republican Societies* (New York, 1942). David H. Fischer, *The Revolution of American Conservatism* (New York, 1966), traces the adaptation of the younger generation of Federalists to party rivalry.

[2] Despite his critique of parties, M. Ostrogorski provides a classic statement of their role in the process of representative government: *Democracy and the Organization of Political Parties* (2 vols.; New York, 1902). For a variety of insights on politics and parties I have drawn on Seymour M. Lipset, *Political Man: the Social Basis of Politics* (Garden City, N. Y., 1960), without necessarily sharing his assumptions.

to prepare parliamentary strategy. Here was the visible nucleus of a party. At first it appeared to be law-abiding. Though the Clichyites were opposed to the Directory's most basic policies in areas like religion, finance, and foreign policy, they proceeded cautiously in their attack. But despite its scruples, the group was hopelessly entangled with émigrés and British agents. Soon prominent Clichyites were involved in plots linked to the Bourbons and subsidized by Pitt's gold. In the end, then, this uneasy coalition of constitutional and ultra-royalists became like the Babeuvists a subversive group. Far from standing as a possible stabilizing influence in the republic's political life, it evolved into a temporary alliance for toppling the government. Though there is dispute over whether or not the Clichyites were actually on the verge of a coup d'état, their every action portended the republic's gradual demise.[3] The Directory, applauded by republicans of all persuasions, acted to prevent this. Whatever its self-serving qualities, the resulting fructidor coup solidified the republican cause.

Once the decision had been taken to disperse this anti-republican party of royalists and extreme conservatives, could the Directory afford to fragment the political fabric of the republic further by dealing similarly with the Jacobins? This was precisely the question confronting the Directory when, after several months between fructidor Year V and pluviôse Year VI, an incipient Jacobin party became visible. Here was a party substantially different from the Clichyites. Lacking a tangible center, and assuredly without a parliamentary nucleus of any significance, the Jacobin party consisted of autonomous local political clubs linked by the democratic press and by indirect ties of common outlook and background. Now it was predictable that the Directory would react unsympathetically to this presence and attempt to resist its challenge. Open combat, however, might have been immensely healthy for France, leading to the consolidation of rival parties each committed in its own way to the republic. And for a while it seemed as if the Directory would engage in such salutary combat. Only when the adverse results of the 1798 primary assemblies began coming in did the Directory lose its equilibrium and panic. In a change of policy that can be

[3] Harvey Mitchell, *The Underground War Against Revolutionary France* (Oxford, 1965), Chs. 8-11; Jacques Godechot, *La Contrerévolution: doctrine et action* (Paris, 1962), Ch. 14.

dated from 9 germinal (29 March 1798), it turned from competition to repression. It was a turn that pointed towards Brumaire.

Of course this whole question could be dismissed if it were assumed that Jacobins and Directorials were simply two competing factions—"ins" and "outs"—of the same socio-political group. And indeed both the older anti-revolutionary historiography and today's scholarship, with its emphasis on the imperatives of class structure, tend to converge around this assumption. Clerico-royalist historians portray the Jacobins and Directorials as cut from the same unwholesome moral cloth. Arguing that in its policies towards priests and émigrés the Directory perpetuated the revolutionary tradition of arbitrary measures and reprehensible brutality, Victor Pierre writes of a Directorial "terror" following Fructidor. For Ludovic Sciout, who lavished four pioneering volumes on a subject he seems to have detested, the Directorials were unprincipled revolutionaries who occasionally raised the Jacobin menace in order to keep themselves in power. The two groups, he wrote (referring to the elections of 1798), "were not divided by any principles"; one wished to gain, the other to retain power. The Directorials "pose as moderates, . . . adopt a conservative mask" simply as a tactic.[4] Likewise in current views of the Directory period, the distinctiveness of the Jacobins is implicitly contested because their social origins and interests appear essentially bourgeois—a point that is true as far as it goes, but one which does not go far enough.[5]

The preceding chapters have argued for the distinctiveness of the Jacobins as compared to the Directorials. The Jacobin or democratic persuasion was based on attitudes uncongenial to conservatives; it translated into controversial stands on potentially divisive issues. This persuasion was principally articulated not in the Legislature but in clubrooms, printing shops, and town halls. In demanding an intensification of the republicanizing process, the Jacobins were at the same time perpetuating the Revolution's democratic promise. By contrast the Directorials were conservatives. True, they may have seemed radical and Jacobinical to the English or the Federalists, who deplored their aggressive foreign policy. And for the deported priests and émigrés there may indeed have seemed little to choose

---

[4] See Victor Pierre, *Le 18 fructidor* (Paris, 1893), and Ludovic Sciout, *Le Directoire* (4 vols.; Paris, 1895-97), especially III, 446, 458.

[5] Cf. discussion of the work of Beyssi, Dautry, and Godechot in Ch. IV.

from between them. But among citizens who accepted the republic —and if it was to thrive, these, after all, were the Frenchmen that mattered—the Directorials were conservatives on most unsettled issues. While they joined the Jacobins in opposing émigré intruders and royalist agents, the question was, how would these Frenchmen—conservatives and democrats—deal with each other?

THE DIRECTORY's first unambiguous move against Neo-Jacobinism in the Year VI was legitimate by any standard. Police Minister Sotin, who had cleared away the legal obstacles to a revival of Neo-Jacobin clubs, was dismissed. True, his departure was veiled in the fiction of resignation and reassignment to a diplomatic post, allowing the Jacobin press to save face publicly by denying claims made by the reactionary press that Sotin was "in disgrace."[6] But the government's political motivation was an open secret, the Prussian ambassador reporting home, for example, that the Directory would no longer suffer the Jacobins or the Police Minister who "favored and supported them from his position."[7]

An intriguing sidelight involving General Bonaparte adorns this episode. Several weeks earlier Sotin had come under attack because of his alleged role in the Garchy affair. A favorite haunt of royalists, the Café Garchy had been visited by a rowdy group of soldiers from General Augereau's staunchly patriotic division. A predictable melee had ensued in which the café was wrecked and several people mortally injured. Who had actually provoked the brawl remained a matter of conjecture, but it was clear that the police had not intervened promptly enough to minimize the damage.[8] Conservatives used the incident to stigmatize the troops as brigands and to insinuate that a minister who permitted such scandals to occur with impunity in the heart of Paris was incompetent. After the Garchy affair, according to the *Journal des hommes libres*, innuendo against Sotin mounted with the aim of forcing him out of office

[6] *J. hommes libres* No. 272, 27 pluviôse VI: "Situation rapprochée et comparée de la République avant et après fructidor"; *Journal des campagnes et des armées* No. 719, 21 ventôse VI.

[7] P. Bailleu, ed., *Preussen und Frankreich von 1795 bis 1807: Diplomatische Correspondenzen* (Leipzig, 1881), I, 183. Cf. Lefebvre, *Le Directoire*, p. 125.

[8] For a relatively objective account of this celebrated incident see A. M. Cécile, *Tableau historique, littéraire et politique de l'an VI* (Impr. Valade, 1798), pp. 340-41.

before the elections.[9] Behind the scenes one of his critics was Bonaparte.

"The general did not conceal his indignation at that killing," a companion of Bonaparte's later recalled. "He had it out openly with Sotin, the Police Minister, in Barras' own salon."[10] Nor did he let the matter rest with this tongue-lashing. In the *Diary* of Wolfe Tone (an Irish revolutionary residing in Paris), the matter comes up in a reference to one of Tone's friends. "Lewines was the other night with Bonaparte, when a conversation took place . . . worth recording." A person of Jacobin persuasion from the Police Ministry called on the general and had a private interview, which according to Lewines presumably concerned "some overtures from the chiefs of that party." Bonaparte eventually reacted "with great heat" and launched into a diatribe against the ambitions "of those gentlemen who call themselves chiefs and leaders of the people. . . . They shall soon be made sensible of their absolute nullity," he warned. "From two or three words Bonaparte dropped," added Tone, "Lewines concluded that Sotin, the present minister of police, will probably not continue long in office."[11] Lewines, of course, was right. On 27 pluviôse VI (15 February 1798) Sotin "resigned" and was immediately dispatched on a mission to Genoa.

Shortly thereafter Merlin de Douai assumed the rotating presidency of the five-man executive. An official proclamation followed which struck a new note. Instead of its earlier and rather bland warnings against royalism and extremism, the government now dwelled on the danger of factions and parties in the coming elections. Repeatedly denouncing "the spirit of coterie" and the agitators who bred factionalism, the message of 9 ventôse (27 February) left no doubt about the identity of the factions. A lexicon of terms traditionally used to traduce the Jacobins was invoked to the full. Moreover a new metaphor was introduced: the specter of *royalisme à bonnet rouge*. Royalists could be expected to disguise themselves

[9] *J. hommes libres* Nos. 243 and 244, 28 and 29 nivôse VI, and No. 248, 3 pluviôse. For an account slanted against Sotin see, e.g., *Courrier de l'Escaut* (Malines) No. 11, 3 pluviôse VI.

[10] Arnault, *Souvenirs*, IV, 52-53. On Bonaparte's Parisian sojourn see A. Espitalier, *Vers Brumaire: Bonaparte à Paris: Décembre 1797-Mai 1798* (Paris, 1914); Barras, *Memoirs*, III, for that period; and Bailleu, *Preussen und Frankreich*, pp. 162, 167.

[11] *Life of Theobold Wolfe Tone*, Vol. II: *Journals of General Tone During his Mission in France* (Washington, 1826), pp. 462-63.

as ultra-revolutionaries: "spreaders of intrigue . . . unbalanced spirits . . . wild exaggerators, who by the abuse of their principles and their previous excesses will spread alarm among citizens, and sow discord within the legislative body."[12]

A rare piece of explicit political commentary in the lofty *Moniteur* echoed this warning against Neo-Jacobinism. Descending to expostulate on the threat of royalisme à bonnet rouge, it closed the circle by implicating the Constitutional Circles in that design. Noting that notorious royalist exiles were boasting of their imminent return to power, the *Moniteur* reasoned that since they could not possibly manage this under their true colors the royalists would disguise themselves in the very mantle of republicanism. They will invoke "generous sentiments" in order to mislead the people; they will push "ardent patriotism" to excess. Presently "they work to corrupt that salutary institution of constitutional circles. They wish to transform them into those clubs which—in principle such useful supports of liberty—became the most active and baleful instruments of anarchy. Who directs those missionaries whose ambulatory civisme spreads error from canton to canton?"[13]

Identifying the Jacobins as their enemies in the coming elections, to the neglect of actual royalists, the Directory mobilized its power and patronage against them. For form's sake, appeal was made to those Jacobins who were nonetheless "de bonne fois dans leur exageration"! They were urged to forego choosing their own kind as electors, but at the same time not to boycott the elections. Rather, they must vote for the moderate and wise men who are "far removed from intrigues and parties," and who will therefore send to the Legislature "only conservative spirits."[14] Such ingenuous invitations were quickly followed by more serious measures. At the very moment that it was attacking coteries and factions the Directory moved to construct its own party. But because of its opposition to the principle of party, it wielded its levers in the shadows.

A loosely coordinated network of supporters was invited to promote safe candidacies, circulate lists of nominees, and bolster in all

[12] Contrast the two proclamations dated 28 pluviôse and 9 ventôse, reprinted in several newspapers including the *Moniteur*, 4 ventôse (pp. 618-19) and 14 ventôse (pp. 657-58).

[13] *Moniteur*, 15 ventôse (p. 662): "Sur le renouvellement du Corps Législatif."

[14] *Ibid.*, 14 ventôse.

278

ways the forces of moderation. Government funds were provided to facilitate the effort. While they relied primarily on their own commissioners and other friendly local officials, the Directors also sent out a group of secret agents. More dramatic but less important than the normal channels of communication, these agents posed as road inspectors purportedly checking on the condition of the national highways. Their dispatches back to Paris were accordingly couched in a crude code in which the metaphor of engineering and road repair cloaked political intelligence. They, too, were enlisted to identify and organize the most reliable citizens in the provinces and also to warn the Directory about the strength of other factions.[15] As information was received in Paris certain local Jacobins were reprimanded or dismissed from office, and some of the more aggressive Constitutional Circles were closed. But it is important to note that they were closed individually and by separate decrees. No general ban on the clubs was undertaken, except insofar as *ambulance* and "collective petitions" were prohibited at the end of ventôse. The same was true in regard to the press. Selectively the government harassed local Jacobin editors and during the elections suppressed several papers. But no all-out censorship was imposed despite the broad powers held under the law of 19 fructidor V. Finally, with but two unimportant exceptions, not a single arrest was ordered from Paris during this controlled campaign of pressure.[16] A certain amount of highhandedness was manifest on both sides, but until the primary assemblies were over this was indicative precisely of genuine, one might almost say healthy, party competition. In effect the Directory was building its party from the top down by means of official propaganda, patronage, electoral funding, and a relatively restrained use of intimidation. On balance it was contributing to the crystallization of parties by its response to the Jacobin challenge,

[15] These documents are in A.N. AF III 99, and have been used by Sciout, *Le Directoire*, and by A. Meynier, *Le 22 floréal an VI et le 30 prairial an VII* (Paris, 1928). Barras (*Memoirs*, III, 226-31) discusses the disbursement of subsidies.

[16] The decrees against individual clubs or newspapers may be followed most conveniently in A.N. AF III* 154 (Délibérations et arrêtés du Directoire concernant la police), nivôse-messidor VI. The arrests of Jorry and Vauversin in Paris were special cases, but since Jorry was an active candidate his was interpreted as an act of intimidation against the Jacobins. Though it may in fact have been, the pretext involved a large sum of money that he was accountable for and that had temporarily disappeared.

regardless of its theoretical opposition to parties. Democrats and conservatives both seemed to be following the logic of their positions rather than the conventional wisdom of political theory.

Until the primary assemblies the Jacobin resurgence continued to build momentum. Confident that political normalcy had arrived at last, the Jacobins believed that the Directory would abide by its own constitution. As the *Antiroyaliste* of Marseilles noted prematurely on the eve of the elections: "for the first time since the constitution was inaugurated, republicans are cheerful at the prospect of coming freely to the primary assemblies, without having to fear the arbitrary blows of magistrates who have sold out to the royalist faction."[17] Local organization and preparation (described in the previous chapter) proceeded apace. Campaign literature—admittedly aimed at those already committed, but still circulating publicly—diverged sharply from official pleas for a "conservative spirit." In their notions about the kinds of men to choose as electors, and the directions that their legislators might chart for the nation, the Jacobins launched a party appeal to democratic sentiment.

While the Directory warned against choosing exagérés and former terrorists, the Jacobins argued that such terms were designed to smear the "proven patriots" who actually made the best electors. They urged support for men who "took their place in the popular ranks," "the ardent men whose pure and sincere zeal has since found reasonable limits." At the same time the voters must repudiate those who try to set apart so-called anarchists from republicans. Citizens who choose to see in their more enthusiastic fellows nothing but ex-terrorists must be defeated at the polls.[18] The Versailles Club carried this further by openly challenging the Directory's elitist assumptions. "Political chameleons" and men who have been "inconspicuous in the Revolution" must be rejected, regardless of their standing in the community. "Education [les lumières] is not *de rigueur*," the club declared; all an elector needed was "a pure heart . . . and a love of the Republic." Likewise in Evreux the Jacobin newspaper promoted the choice of those "modest but true

[17] *Antiroyaliste* (Marseilles) No. 31, 23 ventôse VI.

[18] *J. hommes libres* No. 284, 9 ventôse; *Chronique de l'Eure et Loire* (Chartres) No. 2, 6 ventôse; *Observateur du département de la Dordogne* (Perigueux) No. 26, 20 germinal.

280

republicans . . . to be found in the most certain retreat of virtue: l'heureuse mediocrité."[19]

Election pamphlets in Paris called for a vindication of "pure patriots" and a repudiation of self-styled moderates. Voters in the primary assemblies were urged to defeat "the friends of LaFayette, the butchers of the Reaction, the vendémiairists, the assassins of Vendôme, the executioners of Grenelle," and instead to call upon the very victims of these persecutions. Such elections would carry forward the Revolution's promise. "Let there be a trend towards the establishment of equality; let fraternity not become an empty word; let the influence of corrupting wealth be weakened and even destroyed; and let the poor be counted as a MAN."[20] Another Jacobin pamphleteer defended the men noted "for their attachment to democratic government" from the charge that they sought to undermine property. At the same time he warned against letting a concern over property rights obscure the truly overriding social issues. The worst enemy remained those who wish "to muzzle the true defenders of the people's rights in order to put those whom they call the *populace* back into irons." The pamphlet disavowing an assault on property ended by attacking that "self-styled privileged class that insolently gorges itself on the subsistence of the poor."[21]

The Directory's exhortations to prudence, moderation, and "a conservative spirit" were countered by the Jacobins' reference to the democratic promise of the Revolution. At Dôle the club members expressed a hope that the coming elections might achieve nothing less than "A Republic of brothers, where distinctions are abolished, where the pride of wealth will be trampled, where the workingman is everything, the useless man nothing."[22] In this spirit the *Journal des Amis* of Metz saw the chance to elect deputies devoted not only to the republic but to the particular interests of their constituents, "notably to the amelioration of the condition of the unfortunate classes," while in Bordeaux Latapy's *Courrier de la Gironde* cele-

[19] *L'Echo du Cercle Constitutionnel de Versailles* No. 1, n.d. (in A.N. F7 7415, fol. 5227); *Bulletin de l'Eure* (Evreux) No. 129 (supplément), 15 ventôse.

[20] *Au Peuple française* (Impr. Leguay, an VI) in A.N. F7 3054.

[21] *Un Mot aux électeurs patriotes* (Paris, n.d.) in B.N. Lb42/1335.

[22] *Les Républicains membres du cercle constitutionnel de Dôle, à leurs frères les habitans . . . du Jura* (Besançon, an VI) in A.N. F7 7417, fol. 5361.

brated an impending victory by "those integral patriots, ardent friends of liberty, equality, democracy . . . devoted to the cause of the people." Electors chosen by such assemblies, Latapy concluded, would have the flattering mandate from their fellow citizens to choose "a democratic legislature."[23]

‡ II ‡

Over fifty French cities experienced the impact of an organized Jacobin party primed with slates and prearranged maneuvers.[24] In several important towns they were a minority voice, though a loud one nonetheless. Fierce conflicts in Paniers (Ariège), Chalons (Marne), Vesoul (Haute-Saône), and St. Omer (Pas-de-Calais) led the Jacobins to walk out of the regular assemblies.[25] Forming *assemblées scissionnaires* they chose nominees who would later demand admission to the departmental electoral assemblies on various pretexts. The same was true in Poitiers (Vienne), where Bernarais led a schism, allegedly followed by "workingmen, ignorant men easy to mislead."[26] And in Lyon, that stronghold of reaction where they were a decided minority, the Neo-Jacobin Club of the Rue Dominique battled the municipal authorities and carried out schisms so that their voice could be heard. So remarkable did their action seem that the sympathetic deputy from the Rhône Vitet was led to wonder "how the republicans [of Lyon] had enough drive to make a schism and brave the steel of assassins."[27]

Lyon was not typical, however. In most cities where effective clubs had previously been organized, they prevailed with some-

[23] *Journal des Amis* (Metz) No. 89, 28 ventôse; *Courrier de la Gironde* (Bordeaux) No. 185, 5 germinal.

[24] See Ch. IX, and the discussion of sources in note 53 of that chapter.

[25] On Paniers, where the Jacobins were opposed by a conservative municipality recently installed by the Directory, see A.N. AF III 507, plaq. 3210 and A.N. AF III 215/Ariège: report and letters from justice of the peace and municipal administration. The tactics of the Vesoul Club are described by the municipal commissioner in A.N. F⁷ 7414, fol. 5058. The bitter divisions in St. Omer are described in A.N. AF III 522, plaq. 3365. On Jacobin successes in other towns in that department see A.N. F¹ᶜ III Pas-de-Calais/2; and *Aux deux conseils . . . protestation des électeurs des cantons du Pas de Calais* (Impr. Ami des Lois) in AF III 254/Pas-de-Calais.

[26] A.N. C 535/Vienne: municipal commissioner to M. of Pol.; commissioner to the tribunals to M. of Pol.

[27] A.N. F⁷ 7413, fol. 5009: Vitet to M. of Pol., and to Poulain-Grandprey.

what less strain, though in few places did the conservatives disappear as a substantial force. Neo-Jacobin success in Paris—where almost half the seats in that department's huge electoral assembly were captured—was so striking as to warrant separate consideration later. Other strongholds included:

Moulins (Allier)	Dax (Landes)
Limoux (Aude)	Montmarsan (Landes)
St. Affrique (Aveyron)	Laval (Mayenne)
Marseilles (Bouches-du-Rhône)	Mayenne (Mayenne)
Aix (Bouches-du-Rhône)	Chambéry (Mont Blanc)
Mauriac (Cantal)	Metz (Moselle)
Brive (Corrèze)	Clamecy (Nièvre)
Tulle (Corrèze)	Nevers (Nièvre)
Dijon (Côte d'Or)	Pau (Basses-Pyrénées)
Perigueux (Dordogne)	Tarbes (Hautes-Pyrénées)
Besançon (Doubs)	Clermont (Puy-de-Dôme)
Evreux (Eure)	Issoire (Puy-de-Dôme)
Auch (Gers)	Autun (Saône-et-Loire)
Bordeaux (Gironde)	Louhans (Saône-et-Loire)
Chateauroux (Indre)	LeMans (Sarthe)
Blois (Loir-et-Cher)	Versailles (Seine-et-Oise)
Vendôme (Loir-et-Cher)	Avignon (Vaucluse)

Here were concentrated the "proven patriots" extolled in Jacobin campaign oratory; here former terrorists, *amnistiés*, and their anonymous supporters were vindicated. Though extensive local research might be inadequate to quantify these results meaningfully, the testimony of contemporaries and the profusion of familiar names leave little doubt about the issue: members of revolutionary committees, officers of popular societies, agents of the Convention, and members of special revolutionary commissions now found their past activities title to political influence rather than persecution. Less divided than they were in the Year II by immediate problems and clashing personalities, France's most committed revolutionaries were no longer outside the pale of their own republic. What is more, they owed their reviving position not to government patronage but to citizens who ignored that government's instructions.

Heading the list of Jacobin electors were a number of former Montagnards who had been driven out of the Convention by the thermidorians, and whose nomination was certainly deliberate: Dartigoyète (Landes); Lanot (Corrèze); J. B. Lacoste (Cantal); Maignet (Puy-de-Dôme); Freciné (Loir-et-Cher); Peyssard, Roux Fazillac, and Pinet (Dordogne). Even the shades of executed Montagnard proconsuls returned to haunt the Directorials: local collaborators of Joseph Lebon in Pas-de-Calais, and of Claude Javogues in Loire and Saône-et-Loire were carried back to power by the voters in those departments.[28] Veterans of the notorious Lyon Temporary Commission, too, were in the vanguard of Neo-Jacobinism—for example, Grimaud and Marbut in Puy-de-Dôme; Verd, Delan, and Perrotin in Allier.[29] An Agricole Moreau in Avignon, a Bernarais in Poitiers, a Tenaille in Nevers were the kinds of local militants who personified the Jacobin movement in their cities and who were chosen as electors in 1798. For the self-styled experts on Babeuvism there was a good deal to ponder also. Numerous individuals on Babeuf's subscription list or on his factitious rosters of insurrectionary patriots turned up among the electors, including prominent men like D'herbez Latour (Basses-Alpes) and Gregoire Chana (Loire) who had been honored as appointees to Babeuf's "Insurrectionary Convention."[30]

[28] One measured comment about Lebon's legacy in Pas-de-Calais is particularly suggestive: "L'opinion publique serait dominée par les plus sages des amis de Lebon qui se signalerent par une exaltation de principe mais en s'isolant de ses meurtres si nombreuses dont ce département porte encore le deuil." A.N. AF III 254/Pas-de-Calais: Observations . . . sur l'assemblée électorale. The *Javoguistes* in the Loire allegedly included St. Didier, Chana, Phalipon, Renard, Rochal, Monate, and Dubessay. A.N. AF III 240/Loire: Extrait du compte rendu au M. de l'Intérieur par le commissaire central, 13 germinal; *Sur les élections du département de la Loire, an 6* (Impr. Baudoin) by three deputies (Forest, Duguet, and Meudre) who were conservative incumbents. Cf. St. Didier, *Réponse au libelle diffamatoire des représentans . . .* (Paris, Impr. veuve Galetti, an VI) B.N. Lb42/573. In Saône-et-Loire the *Javoguistes* allegedly included Bozon, of the Maçon temporary commission, and Duriau and Maugin, local administrators in the Year II. A.N. AF III 258/Saône-et-Loire.

[29] See *Faits relatifs à la scission des électeurs du département de l'Allier* (Impr. Moulins, an VI) in B.N. Lb42/547—a wild attack on the Jacobins which, however, gives specific information on the revolutionary background of several electors. On Puy-de-Dôme see A.N. F⁷ 3685/5 (Puy-de-Dôme): "Notes sur le département . . ." and A.N. F⁷ 7405, fol. 4176: departmental commissioner to M. of Pol. Other ex-revolutionaries active here included Dumont, Bret, and Laporte.

[30] Jean Suratteau has written on this point in "Les Babouvistes, le péril rouge, et le Directoire (1796-1798)," *Babeuf et les problèmes du Babouvisme*, ed. A. Soboul (Paris, 1963). He does not resolve the problem of what a "Babeuvist"

Anxiety in the Directorial camp was matched by a wave of enthusiasm in democratic circles over these results. Jacobin newspapers in Metz, Moulins, Marseilles, LeMans, Tarbes, Nevers, Bordeaux, Toulouse, Perigueux, and Paris applauded the choices of their own local assemblies and of other "patriotic" departments—a common reaction that illustrates the liaisons of the Jacobin journalists.[31] Editors of several papers—the public spokesmen for the party, as it were—were themselves chosen as electors: Pirolle and Delattre of the *Journal des Amis* (Metz), Latapy of the *Courrier de la Gironde* (Bordeaux), Peyre-Ferry and Reybaud of the *Antiroyaliste* (Marseilles), Parent l'ainé of the *Bulletin de la Nièvre*, and in Grenoble the former publisher and proprietor of the Jacobins' favored reading room, Faulcon.[32] The Parisian elections won universal praise in these papers, but equal enthusiasm was lavished over the results in Dordogne. A Jacobin contingent led by the three Montagnards who had been purged after Thermidor was named here, despite the fact that the Directory had dismissed them from departmental posts during the preceding month.[33] The vindication of these Jacobins, and the transparent affront to the Directory, was lost on neither side.

For all the éclat of these Jacobin victories, however, the Directory was scarcely facing a complete rout. Success in forty or fifty cities and the sweep of perhaps two dozen departments still left a majority of departments virtually untouched by their resurgence. Moreover, in

---

was, but simply indicates the names of certain electors or nominees who had been on Babeuf's various lists or in some other way supposedly implicated in the conspiracy.

[31] See *Journal des Hautes-Pyrénées* (Tarbes) Nos. 14/15, 16 germinal VI.

[32] On cadres in these cities see my article "The Revival of Jacobinism in Metz," *Journal of Modern History* (1966), p. 31. *Courrier de la Gironde* (Bordeaux) No. 185, 5 germinal; A.N. AF III 232/Gironde: letters from departmental commissioner. A.N. F1c III Bouches-du-Rhône/1: commissioner to section Nord (Marseilles), 4 germinal, and A.N. F7 3659/4 (Bouches-du-Rhône): commissioner to the Central Police Bureau of Marseilles, 8 germinal. A.N. AF III 251/Nièvre: P. V., assemblée électorale, and other documents. A.N. C 532/Isère: *Tableau alphabétique des électeurs nommés en l'an VI. . . .* Comparison of these names with names found in a history of the Grenoble Jacobin Club in 1793-94 indicates that over half the electors were active in that club. Cf. R. R. Tissot, *La Société populaire de Grenoble pendant la Révolution* (Grenoble, 1910).

[33] H. Labroue, *L'Esprit public en Dordogne pendant la Révolution* (Paris, 1911), pp. 157-61.

several key places the Directory's commissioners predicted that the electoral weight of the countryside would counterbalance the city when the departmental assemblies convened. The commissioner to Gironde, for example, expected the rural cantons to compensate for the "exaltation" of the Bordeaux electors, while his counterpart in Bouches-du-Rhône hoped that rural electors would neutralize the admitted "exaggeration" of electors from Marseilles and Aix.[34] Here in fact a schism later occurred in the electoral assembly which completely justified this view of a division between town and country: the assemblée scissionnaire of Directorials had only six electors from the metropolis. In the Rhône the reverse would happen, as the Jacobins withdrew from the regular electoral assembly and formed an assemblée scissionnaire composed almost exclusively of electors from Lyon.[35] Yet another example of a town-country split was Côte d'Or where the "patriotes invariables et éclairés" of the countryside would neutralize the Dijon Jacobins and give the Directory's commissioner a working majority.[36]

Another point in the Directory's favor was the large percentage of electors in many departments who were government employees likely to be responsive to pressure in the final contest. In Seine-et-Oise, for example (where a complete list of electors was published, giving the occupation of each man), at least half were connected in some way with government or administration.[37] In summary, results of the primary assemblies need not have caused panic among the Directorials. Only a minority of departments were hopelessly lost to the Jacobins at this point; most were divided, some entirely safe. Rather than either side holding a preponderant advantage, it seemed as if an equilibrium had been struck between the two incipient parties.

Psychologically, however, the Jacobins had scored startling gains and thus held a kind of advantage. The first round was resound-

---

[34] A.N. AF III 232/Gironde: Lahary to M. of Pol., 5 germinal; A.N. AF III 217/Bouches-du-Rhône: Constant to M. of Pol., 3 germinal.

[35] A.N. AF III 217/Bouches-du-Rhône: P. V., and Chabert to M. of Interior, 28 germinal; A.N. AF III 257/Rhône: P. V.

[36] J. Brélot, *La Vie politique en Côte d'Or sous le Directoire* (Dijon, 1932), pp. 133-40.

[37] *Liste des Electeurs du département de Seine-et-Oise, 20 germinal an 6* (Versailles, Impr. Jacob) in B.N. Le40/78. This included 56 assessors, 28 commissioners, 27 municipal administrators, and 21 justices of the peace.

ingly theirs in the major cities, which were certainly more visible than the numerically superior countryside. Even if dispatches from the provinces held out comforting information of the sort suggested, the impact of the Paris assemblies (see next chapter), and the pattern in places like Allier, Dordogne, Landes, Loire, Loir-et-Cher, Nièvre, Pas-de-Calais, Basses-Pyrénées, Saône-et-Loire, and Sarthe broke the aura of invincibility that French governments relied on to keep face. Explicit warnings by the Directory "to thwart the deadly ambitions of those authors of the execrable '93 regime"[38] had been ignored. Constitutional Circles had been victorious, and no "partisan of '93" seemed too sullied for rehabilitation—be he a Montagnard, a member of the Lyon Commission, or a defendant at the Vendôme trial.

‡ III ‡

Taken together and regarded coolly, the results of the primary assemblies added up to competition and probable equilibrium. Taken selectively and nervously, they augured defeat for the government. Insecure and uncertain in its posture of constitutional liberalism— which had thrived in the preceding six months—the Directory lapsed into authoritarianism. Since its reading of the Neo-Jacobin resurgence was exaggerated, its response was accordingly severe. That response was made in a singularly important proclamation dated 9 germinal (29 March). It stated in effect that a Jacobin party would not be tolerated. Since it thereby blocked the rise of parties, the new policy undermined the viability of constitutional republicanism.

Merlin de Douai, who drafted this crucial policy in his own hand, was clearly preoccupied with the scene in Paris. "In view of the results of the primary assemblies of Paris and several other cantons," he began, "a general uneasiness has gripped the public spirit."[39] Direct allusion to the capital was dropped from the final version, but the message was unaltered. Failing to master the primary assemblies by means of propaganda, selective intimidation, monetary disbursements, and secret commissioners, the Directory now resorted to open threats. The Jacobins' effective electoral organiza-

---

[38] See *Adresse du Directoire exécutif aux électeurs de l'an VI* (Paris, 2 germinal VI).

[39] A.N. AF iii 514, plaq. 3276 (pièce 53).

tion was denounced as a new conspiracy whose "aim is to introduce into the Legislature and all other positions men who are universally execrated and whose names alone are frightening to peaceful citizens and vigorous patriots alike. Already, on the list of electors, persons ignominiously famous in revolutionary annals can be found, who do not even hide their threats and projects. . . ." In Fructidor the Legislature had "chased from its midst traitors who had already been seated for four months; it will surely know how to exclude those whom some are trying to bring in." If the democrats persist in choosing their stalwarts as deputies, they will have their choices annulled. There was even an implication that they could be deported, as some royalists had been in Fructidor.[40]

The obvious import of this proclamation is underscored by several specific developments. First, the extraordinary effectiveness with which it was disseminated; second, the unusual care with which press reaction was monitored; and third, the pronounced reactions among Jacobins.

With great efficiency the Directory blanketed the country with the proclamation. The elections were only ten days away but, as the *Journal des hommes libres* reported with dismay, "from all over we are informed of the successive arrival of extraordinary couriers sent from Paris . . . with orders to give them the greatest publicity by posting them and by other means." Placards and broadsides reprinting the proclamation and a favorable commentary from the *Patriote française* were broadcast in the cities where electoral assemblies were due to convene. In several places copies were distributed to every elector.[41]

Special arrangements were made for the distant southern departments, with the commissioner to the Rhône acting as chief agent. Packets of the proclamation and the offprint from the *Patriote française* were dispatched to Lyon by express couriers. There, the commissioner redistributed them to five special couriers who set off for Aurillac, Mende, Grenoble, Montpellier, and Valènce. Others would be sent from Grenoble to Gap and from Valènce to Privas. The couriers "will turn the packets over to the commissioners situated along their routes, and these commissioners, with the aid of the

[40] *Proclamation du Directoire exécutif sur les élections, du 9 germinal an VI*, placard in A.N. AD xx^c 67 (No. 47); reprinted in most newspapers.
[41] *J. hommes libres* No. 327, 22 germinal VI.

postmasters, will dispatch them to neighboring departments." "Without this measure," the commissioner to the Rhône later claimed, "the proclamations would not have been received by most of my colleagues until the 25th of this month [germinal]." In order to pay these special couriers, the alert official advanced the postmaster in that region the sum of 2400 francs, acquired through the comptroller of the Rhône department acting on authorization of the departmental administration. With its careful attention to such details, this proved to be one of the Directory's most efficient propaganda efforts.[42]

While the couriers were on their way, the Directory was apparently apprehensive over its strategy. The proclamation was such a bald threat to control free elections that it might possibly backfire. A forceful approach, it was also unconstitutional. Even moderate republicans might therefore resent it as a remedy posing greater dangers than the evil it purported to cure. It was just possible that Merlin had miscalculated. This risk—disaffection of moderate constitutionalists—was assuredly the reason why the Directory monitored public reaction to its proclamation with unusual care. For this task it called on V. R. Barbet, its press secretary whose normal job was to disseminate press releases, plant articles in friendly newspapers, and disburse subsidies to certain journalists.[43] Barbet now prepared a report on newspaper reaction to the proclamation. His detailed résumé is the only document of its kind that appears in the Directory's papers at this time, contrasting notably with the perfunctory daily reports on the press compiled by the Central Police Bureau. Barbet's survey was designed to assess press opinion on a particular issue, as if what the press thought really mattered. One can infer that the Directory was fearful of criticism from the moderate press —which might or might not have caused it to modify its strategy. In the event, the report allayed such qualms.[44]

Disregarding a few small-circulation democratic newspapers like the *Révélateur*, Barbet noted the predictable opposition of the *Journal des hommes libres*. In addition he registered the fact that

[42] A.N. F⁷ 7413, fol. 5009: departmental commissioner (Rhône) to M. of Pol., 15 germinal VI.

[43] On Barbet's career see A. Mathiez, "Le Bureau politique du Directoire," *Le Directoire*, pp. 356-74.

[44] For the following two paragraphs see A.N. AF III 514, plaq. 3276 (pièce 51): Résumé des réflexions faites par les journaux sur la proclamation du 9 germinal an 6.

two newspapers, which had been receiving small subsidies in exchange for modulating their pro-Jacobin position, finally balked. Of Coesnon-Pellerin, himself one of the Parisian electors, more will be said shortly. A second Jacobin journalist who was finally driven into opposition against a Directory which had been floating his newspaper was Leclerc des Vosges. Since his *Tableau politique, littéraire et moral* had earlier reacted enthusiastically to the results of the primary assemblies, describing well-known Jacobin electors as "pure patriots," he understood what was involved. Following conviction and consistency, he protested "with anguish" against the proclamation, against the government's reaction which "can cause principles to be forgotten to the point of menacing an entire electorate and the citizens that it will send to the Legislature."[45]

If this kind of opinion had been widely held in middle-class circles, the Directory's policy of coercion might have been undermined. But when Barbet turned to eleven major organs of respectable opinion, he could report that two approved the proclamation with hesitation and that nine were unreservedly enthusiastic. Of these, four were probably somewhat to the right of the Directory (*Annales de la République, Nouvelles du jour, Fanal, Ami de l'Ordre*), and five represented the republican center in which the Directory was firmly planted (*Ami des Lois, Publiciste, Nécessaire, Patriote française, Pacificateur*). The *Patriote française* spoke for all nine when it described the proclamation as the voice of necessary authority and virtue; the *Pacificateur* termed it indispensable. A tenth paper (*Echo de la République*) regarded the threat to annul the elections unfortunate, for it preferred the more mildly unconstitutional action of postponing them. Finally came the most prestigious newspaper of all, the *Clef du Cabinet des souverains*. This eminent organ of moderate republicanism (which boasted distinguished intellectuals like Daunou on its editorial board) questioned the proclamation on the grounds that it might encourage the royalists. Yet it minimized this possibility and in the end affirmed its support for the Directors who surely would not "throw themselves into the arms of the [royalist] rebels that they have vanquished." Without condemning the Directory's intervention, the *Clef du Cabinet* simply cautioned the government not to swing too far right in the process. In Barbet's

[45] *Tableau politique, littéraire et moral* Nos. 186, 189, 192; 5, 8, 12 germinal VI.

survey, then, the moderate journals of opinion endorsed the Directory's threats almost to a man.

Since moderates did not openly balk at unconstitutionality, the self-validating quality of resolute action again prevailed as it had during the Convention. Uncommitted republicans, who might otherwise have been "seduced" by the Jacobins, were doubtless impressed by the astute psychology of the proclamation. The Jacobins were stigmatized not simply as dangerous fanatics, but as inevitable losers.

On the Jacobin side this had its effect also, but it was a mixed effect. Barbet's survey reveals that even the most accommodating pro-Jacobin journalists were finally driven into open dissent. Consciousness of party, of division among republicans, was at its height. In this sense 9 germinal marks the culmination of party crystallization at the very moment when toleration for rivalry was coming to an end. This in turn produced discouragement on the one hand, and anger on the other. The threat of a purge—stigmatizing the Jacobins as inevitable losers—was bound to be discouraging and cause a downward revision of Jacobin hopes. If the Directory intended to annul elections, then it would be self-defeating (perhaps) to invite this by electing "ignominious" revolutionary personalities. Yet such calculation did not necessarily produce surrender; on the contrary, dismay easily turned into anger. Realizing the proclamation's devastating significance, thrown on the defensive despite their successes, the Jacobins responded with surprising resolution.

Coesnon-Pellerin, publisher of the *Ami de la Patrie*, exemplified their predicament. This Jacobin's tortuous attempt to accommodate his militant past with a more subdued present was not uncommon. His revolutionary career began in L'Aigle (Orne) after 1789, when he left domestic employment (probably as a clerk of some kind) to become a printer and journalist. Elevated to the presidency of his local revolutionary committee, he exercised authority with a militance that marked him for a jail sentence after Thermidor.[46] When

---

[46] See "Notes sur le rédacteur du journal de l'*Ami de la Patrie* extraites d'un mémoire imprimé contre lui par la ville de l'Aigle, après le 9 thermidor," *Le Renommée ou Journal de Mortagne* No. xciv, 11 ventôse VI (in A.N. F⁷ 3450). According to the *Père Duchêne* No. 19 (n.d.), Pellerin had previously won a libel suit against the editor of the *Renommée de Mortagne*. This highly detailed biographical sketch must obviously be used with caution.

he was released after the general amnesty he was forced to flee to Paris where, despite the loss of his capital in the inflation, he started a newspaper. Perpetually hovering on the brink of destitution, he was compelled to entreat the government repeatedly for assistance in any and all forms: subscriptions, loans, subsidies. In the end he received a few meager subsidies, and that only after his presses had been closed by the government once. His circumstances determined his style; the price of survival was the modulating of his Jacobinism.[47] Modulation, but not repudiation. In the Year V he still managed to publish Paris' one distinctively popular newspaper, Labisol's "resurrection" of the *Père Duchêne*, along with the mildly pro-Jacobin *Ami de la Patrie*, which he and Caignart edited. Obsessed with the hope of subsidies, he placated the Directory yet insistently rejected that government's anti-Jacobinism. For a while he presumably satisfied no one. But on balance he remained closer to the Jacobins than the others.[48]

The elections of the Year VI were crucial. Like Leclerc, Valcour, and Colliot—three other pro-Jacobin moderates who sought subsidies for their newspapers—Pellerin saw these elections as the decisive opportunity for legally shifting the balance of political power in the direction of Jacobinism without any dramatic breaks. Police reports accurately placed him in the ranks of Jacobin activists preparing for the elections, and he was himself named an elector in the 1st arrondissement. The proclamation of 9 germinal, and the threat that lay behind it, therefore came as a stunning blow to that hope.

[47] His plight is spelled out in pathetic letters to various government agencies: A.N. F[18] 21: Pellerin to M. of Interior, 2 messidor IV; A.N. F[7] 7155[a], fol. 5378: Pellerin to M. of Pol., 18 prairial IV; A.N. AF III 45: Pellerin to Directory, 3 thermidor IV; and *ibid.*: Pellerin to the secretary-general of the Directory, 30 ventôse VI. In addition, see letters from Caignart and others in his behalf, asking that his presses be restored after the government had shut them down in frimaire VI because of an article it found offensive (A.N. F[7] 3450). According to one police report, Pellerin had also attempted to find a job in the Ministry of Police during the Year IV, but this "intime ami de tous les plus scélérats d'anarchistes" had no success (A.N. F[7] 4276: "Sûreté politique extraordinaire," 22 prairial IV).

[48] On his solidarity with other Jacobin journalists see, e.g., *J. hommes libres* No. 178, 13 germinal V (announcing publication of the new *Père Duchêne*); *Ibid.* No. 178, 23 brumaire VI (announcing a fund being raised by Pellerin for the widow of the martyred Montagnard Huguet); *Tribun du Peuple* No. 63, 5 nivôse VI; *Ami de la Patrie* Nos. 563 and 570, 26 fructidor V and 3rd jour compl. V.

What is worse, it forced the kind of open choice for or against the government that such men had tried to avoid. With some courage Pellerin at last made that choice. Indeed, he moved to the forefront of the Jacobin opposition. In characteristically measured but unmistakable terms he gave his answer to the Directory:

> This proclamation of the Executive Directory grieves me as an elector, but without frightening me; because I never act except by following my spirit and conscience. I shall read the Directory's proclamation with respect, but I shall betray neither my duties nor my fellow citizens. . . . It is the duty of the Executive Directory to enlighten the citizenry . . . but it must not in any fashion menace the mass of electors just because a few intriguers have slipped into their ranks.[49]

The *Journal des hommes libres* had already registered its dismay with the Directory, urging it "not to transform that imposing mass of republicans who have risen this year into conspirators against the Republic." On the following day it published the complete text of Pellerin's declaration, thereby indicating that this would be the Jacobins' position. As such, it was reprinted in a four-page handbill to be distributed in Paris and the provinces.[50]

The journalists were not overreacting. Alert citizens recognized the proclamation as a crucial policy statement. A police observer described feelings on both sides:

> The Directory's proclamation on the choice of electors made by the primary assemblies has been reassuring to good citizens, but has been a thunderbolt for the anarchists. No, never have men been so furious and at the same time so frightened. The more timid already seem themselves [deported] in Guiana. The most brazen swear that they will revenge themselves.

[49] *Réflexions du Citoyen Coesnon-Pellerin, Redacteur de l'Ami de la Patrie, et électeur, sur la proclamation d'hier* (n.l., n.d.), handbill in the Melvin Collection, University of Kansas Library.

[50] *J. hommes libres* Nos. 316 and 317, 11 and 12 germinal VI. The collaboration of Jacobin journalists is suggested in several police reports. "La veuve Tremblay, propriétaire du Journal intitulé *le Révélateur* a dit hier au soir chez l'anarchiste Chateauneuf, en parlant du ministre de la police et des destitutions qui ont eu lieu dans ces bureaux, qu'elle attend, ainsi que Vatar et Caignart redacteur des *Hommes libres* et de l'*Ami de la Patrie* des notes de Niquille et Veyrat contre le citoyen ministre [Dondeau] pour le faire connaitre aux patriotes. . . ." (A.N. F⁷ 3688/13: report dated 19 germinal VI.)

Unhappy, and perhaps frightened, they were assuredly angry and resolved to fight back. On 12 germinal (1 April) the Police Ministry learned that "the greater number of the Directory's proclamations have been torn down this evening in Paris and in the faubourg Antoine"; that men were in the streets distributing the *Ami de la Patrie* handbill and generally stirring up "workingmen, women and soldiers" to win popular support. "In their gross harangues," reported a police agent, "they do not cease to repeat that the people will never be happy as long as their true friends are persecuted."[51]

In the provinces, too, hostility was vented upon the proclamation. When the placards were posted in Moulins (Allier) they were "ripped down almost everywhere the next morning." Citizen Marcon, subsequently elected public prosecutor in the Ardèche department, reportedly tore down the proclamation and declared: "soon we will be in force in the Legislature, and we will set everyone straight."[52] The same pattern described in Paris was enacted in the provinces. "The anarchists—momentarily stunned by the proclamation of 9 germinal, which was torn down as soon as it was posted —have redoubled their audacity since Chana received some secret packets," reported the commissioner to the Loire department. Presumably the packets contained copies of Pellerin's statement and other material from Paris.[53] The handbill definitely reached the Saône-et-Loire, where Jacobins distributed it at the electoral assembly.[54] In the Loire, at any rate, Jacobin resistance was manifest in the sentiment reportedly expressed that "the Directory is more afraid of them than they are of the Directory." To repeat: the meas-

[51] Numerous police reports in A.N. F⁷ 3688/13.

[52] A.N. C 530/Allier: commissioner to tribunal of Moulins to Directory, 24 germinal; Rouchon, Boisset, Garilhe, *Sur les opérations de l'Assemblée électorale du département de l'Ardèche* (n.l., an VI), p. 5 in A.N. AF III 100. Cf. *L'Indicateur du département de la Sarthe* (LeMans) No. 15, 14 germinal (A.N. AF III 516, plaq. 3297, pièces 21-24), and *Observateur du département de la Dordogne* (Perigueux) No. 26, 20 germinal (AF III 517, plaq. 3310, pièces 8-9).

[53] A.N. AF III 240/Loire: Extrait du compte rendu au M. de l'Interieure par le commissaire central, 13 germinal. He reported in addition that St. Didier, the leading Jacobin meneur was in correspondence with Parisian democrats like Tissot.

[54] A.N. AF III 258/Saône-et-Loire: Observations sur les assemblées primaires et électorales—noting that the *Ami de la Patrie*'s "bloody critique" of the Directory's proclamation was widely distributed here, and enclosing a copy.

ure designed to undermine a nascent Jacobin party served to draw the lines of party more distinctly than ever.

THE POSSIBLE effects of the 9 germinal proclamation, however, cast an ambiguous shadow over the electoral assemblies. Rumors plausibly circulated that the Jacobins would disguise their ambitions in response; that certain candidates were being dropped as too controversial while others would settle for less visible local offices like judge or administrator instead of deputy. A complementary supposition held that Jacobins would elect a number of impeccable moderates in order to further the disguise. Obviously this cannot be disentangled. We will never know the real potential of the Jacobin resurgence to elect its stalwarts, or what might have happened if Jacobins and Directorials had played out their rivalry without this arbitrary intervention. But one thing seems clear. Even if the Jacobins altered their strategy or choices, their opposition to the Directorials was intensified by this attempt to establish a one-party system. In the approximately forty departments where the Jacobins were organized, whether controlling a majority of electors or not, there was some kind of resistance.

The final choices themselves were not always as controversial as the way they were effected. A plaintive report by the Directory's commissioner to Nièvre, who had been mauled in the election, conveys that essential point.

> How dare [the "exclusifs"] present as acts of despotism the wise and enlightened invitations of a paternal government, which in its place at the summit of affairs knows better than anyone the direction that must be provided for safety and public well-being; which in any case is simply fulfilling the spirit and the letter of the constitution when it recommends *prudent choices* to those who are called upon to participate. Well! Instead of that prudence, the elections were prepared by clandestine meetings, tumultuous and incendiary speeches, scandalous orgies where people were not ashamed to drink toasts to *la queue de Robespierre*.[55]

The Directory's party "managers" and commissioners themselves were the logical targets of this rebelliousness. While the Directory's success in over thirty departments was marked precisely by the vic-

[55] A.N. C 533/Nièvre: Dupin to Directory, 9 floréal VI.

tory of such men, opposition to them in others generally signaled a Jacobin presence. In Lot, where the Jacobins did not carry the day, they nonetheless destroyed the candidacy of the Directory's local manager. "The exclusifs have unleashed themselves against me with so much fury," lamented Merlin's confidant, "that in order to put an end to their declamations it was necessary that peaceful republicans cease thinking of me [as a candidate]." The commissioner to Gironde, a long-standing antagonist of the Constitutional Circles named Lahary, garnered a paltry sixty votes on one ballot and then withdrew his candidacy, while in Dordogne, where a slightly outnumbered group of conservatives resisted a well-organized Jacobin majority, commissioner Beaupui was the embarrassed loser in several successive contests.[56]

But Jacobin presence is not to be measured solely by victory. Rarely did they control a department without the need to win over uncommitted electors, and frequently the voting was close. In fact the Jacobin party can occasionally be perceived in an *unsuccessful* attempt to block a Directorial candidate. One well-documented instance of this situation was in the Eure. The running feud between commissioner Crochon and the Jacobin newspaper and clubs has been discussed elsewhere. Naturally it culminated in the elections, with Crochon the Directory's obvious candidate and the Jacobins' obvious target. An initial skirmish saw Crochon chosen as president of the electoral assembly by 191 out of 365 votes cast. The *Bulletin de l'Eure*—in what was to be its last issue before its suppression—reported that the oligarchs and nouveaux riches had won but that their victory was not yet conclusive.[57] That night the Jacobin electors met at the Constitutional Circle of Evreux and attempted to rally their forces. According to depositions by three citizens who overheard the noisy proceedings, members deplored the election of that "monster" Crochon, but agreed that the trend might be halted if they could agree on a slate for other officers of the assembly's *bureau* instead of "groping." A slate was then designated for these positions, but comparison of the names with the assem-

[56] A.N. AF III 242/Lot: commissioner to the tribunals to Merlin, 24 germinal; A.N. AF III 232/Gironde: Lahary to M. of Interior, 25 germinal; A.N. C 531/Dordogne: P. V.

[57] A.N. AF III 226/Eure: P. V.; *Bulletin de l'Eure* (Evreux) No. 144, 21 germinal.

bly's procès-verbal for the following day shows that none were elected. The Jacobins could not muster a majority to impose their choices. They continued to oppose Crochon, but he was subsequently elected as a deputy 200/352. In the balloting for other candidates, however, the hard core of about 150 pro-Jacobin electors could win support for some of their candidates. Robert Lindet for example, was chosen 180/343, along with his less controversial but pro-Jacobin brother, the incumbent Thomas Lindet. Public prosecutor Dupont was chosen by the substantial margin of 306/350 as a consensus candidate. On the other hand, local positions were contested with great vigor, and most of the votes went the legal maximum of three ballots. Party commitment was more open and determined on this level.[58] Within the grayness of the Moselle elections a similar unsuccessful attack to block a key Directorial candidate can be seen. Commissioner Husson played the same role in Moselle as Crochon did in the Eure. And whereas 5 of the 7 nominees for the Legislature received over 200 votes here, Husson won by the lowest margin of all, squeaking out victory by only 150/282.[59]

‡ IV ‡

Before attempting an overview of the election results—notwithstanding the built-in ambiguities—some attention must be given to the Directory's final tactic for intimidating the Jacobins, the schism, for it was a tactic that illuminated the outlines of party conflict in a number of departments. Orders went out to the Directory's local managers that if the opposition dominated the initial proceedings—such as balloting for officers of the assembly, or the validation of disputed credentials—they were to organize a walk-out. The scissionnaires were to withdraw from the "tumult and intrigue" of the regular assembly (*assemblée mère*), convene at another locale, and form a purified assemblée scissionnaire—one composed (as they variously described themselves) of the "sane" or "honest" electors. They would then proceed as if they were the duly authorized electoral college. Pretexts for such walk-outs would never be wanting since the extremely complicated regulations were difficult to observe faithfully wherever there was serious dispute over creden-

[58] A.N. F⁷ 7401, fol. 3769; AF III 226/Eure: P. V. and renseignemens diverses.
[59] Woloch, "The Revival of Jacobinism in Metz," pp. 32-33.

tials. Charges of foul could easily be raised on technicalities, not to mention objections to an "unruly atmosphere" in the regular assembly that allegedly prevented proper deliberation. Contested delegations unseated by the assemblée mère offered a ready-made nucleus for schism.

Possible effects of this act were twofold. First, it would serve as an emphatic warning to the opposition that it had better avoid patently offensive candidacies; it would graphically reinforce the threat of 9 germinal. Second, the impeccable slate that would presumably be chosen by the scissionnaires would be available to fill the department's seats should the deliberations of the assemblée mère still prove "dangerous." An aura of legality would be preserved, and the department would not lose its representation.

Schisms did abound in these elections, occurring in at least 23 out of 98 departments.[60] But actually the Directory's plan did not succeed uniformly here, for only nine of these schisms followed the textbook scenario. Only in nine did the assemblée scissionnaire successfully fulfill its task and prove worthy of subsequent validation, stealing success from a Jacobin majority. Elsewhere the schisms (a) were so paltry, irregular, or tainted by royalism as to be useless for their prescribed role (Allier, Basses-Alpes, Aube, Jura, Landes, Loire, Seine-et-Oise, Vaucluse); (b) were directed by or against royalists and did not involve the question of Jacobinism (Forêts, Gard, Jemappes, Lys); (c) were executed by a minority of Jacobins who vainly separated from the conservatives of the regular assembly (Rhône, Seine-et-Marne).[61]

---

[60] The basic source for studying the outcome of the elections is the manuscript procès-verbal of each assembly (usually in series AF III 211-67: Affaires départmentales), as well as the renseignemens diverses for each department in the same series. Work on this subject is facilitated by the lists in A. Kuscinski, *Les Deputés au Corps Législatif: Conseil des 500, Conseil des Anciens* (Paris, 1905)—a standard *instrument de travail*, and A. Aulard, ed., "Reimpressions: Texte de la loi du 22 floréal an VI," *R.F.*, xxxviii (1900), 428-60, which lists by department the final validations and purges. The standard secondary work on this subject, heretofore basic but still superficial, is Meynier's *Le 22 floréal*. Jean Suratteau will shortly be publishing a comprehensive study of these election results as his *thèse complementaire*. Some of his preliminary observations are contained in his article "Les Babouvistes, le péril rouge, et le Directoire."

[61] Meynier, *Le 22 floréal* (p. 89) and Suratteau "Les Babouvistes" (p. 170) have implied that Rhône and Seine-et-Marne were Jacobin victories snatched away by the Directory. Actually the Jacobin scissionnaires were in a distinct minority. In the Rhône they numbered no more than 80 (almost all from

In an indeterminate number of other departments schism was contemplated, but the Directory's managers proved unable to deliver for want of initiative or support. It was, after all, a dubious procedure in most cases, and uncommitted republicans electors were reluctant to participate unless forcefully led. There were doubtless other departments where the managers assumed they could prevail without schism, only to be outmaneuvered in the end. In Hérault, for example, commissioner Devals reported on 22 germinal (11 April): "I am determined to bring about a schism at the first nomination that is made outside of the list, and you may believe that they will be numerous." But by 25 germinal he was writing that all is well; three of the Directory's choices have been secured by good majorities, including his own. Only on 29 germinal did the Jacobin force emerge to push through several former militants for local posts, including Julian de Sette and Escudier. By then it was too late for schism.[62]

The nine departments that played out the Directory's scenario for schism command a detailed review. They illustrate the range of variations and ambiguities, but also point to the underlying element of party conflict not always obvious in the final results. Here, briefly and in alphabetical order, are the highlights of the contests in eight departments, with the Seine to be treated separately in the following chapter. They are reconstructed from the manuscript procès-verbaux, reports by observers, and ensuing polemics.

ARDÈCHE. The assemblée mère chose a slate with several well-known Jacobins, including former Montagnards Gleizal (176/216) and Thoulouze (135/224), and a former secretary of Couthon's, Dumont (119/230). This was as "ignominious" a list as one was likely to find in the Year VI, but it was broadened by the addition of a moderate incumbent, St. Prix (179/212). An assemblée scissionnaire

---

Lyon). The ex-Police Minister and celebrated protector of the Jacobins, Sotin, was elected here amidst hearty applause 63/67 (A.N. AF III 257/Rhône: P. V. assy. scissionnaire). In Seine-et-Marne the conservatives in the regular assembly numbered over 250, while the scissionnaires who elected a slate including ex-Montagnards like Mauduyt and Giot numbered less than 50. (A.N. AF III 263/Seine-et-Marne: P. V. of both assemblies.) These are interesting departments, showing an organized Jacobin group, but they can scarcely be counted among the Jacobin departments or the victories stolen by the floréal purge.

[62] A.N. AF III 233/Hérault: Devals to M. of Interior. For an obscure reason Devals himself was later purged on 22 floréal.

numbering around fifty electors also chose St. Prix, and returned two other conservative incumbents (Boisset and Garilhe) who were not exactly disinterested in the final outcome. Their subsequent polemic to discredit the assemblée mère and its nominees was successful and is a classic of its type.[63]

BOUCHES-DU-RHÔNE. When Massy, a wealthy bookseller and presumed Jacobin, was chosen president of the assembly by a slight majority (159/310), the Directorials set in motion a schism. Eventually they numbered 130, while 190 remained at the regular assembly, including a reported 120 Marseillais. The Directory's commissioner, Constant, observed that the schism contained the "best republicans" who could not make themselves heard among the exagérés who proposed "infamous" candidates and who allowed ineligible electors to be seated. However, he continued, the schism had a sobering effect on the majority and most of its choices for deputy were not terribly objectionable. Men like Peyre-Ferry, the "Babeuf of Marseilles" and local Jacobin editor, were passed over. Instead more respectable pro-Jacobins Escallon, Venture, and Massy were chosen almost unanimously, along with Directorials Barras, Chenier, and Constant himself. In short, a well-disguised slate was produced, which bowed to the imperatives of the situation while remaining pro-Jacobin on balance.[64] In much closer balloting for departmental offices, however, Jacobins elected a clearly partisan slate whose principals were described by Constant with either of two labels: "sans talents" and "trop exalté"—mild but unmistakable variations in the anti-Jacobin lexicon. The scissionnaires, of course, chose an entirely different slate of administrators who were subsequently installed.[65]

CORRÈZE. A schism of fifty electors chose the Directory's official candidates Brival (incumbent) and Berthelmy (departmental commissioner). Back in the regular assembly, 180 electors, including

[63] A.N. AF III 213/Ardèche: P. V.; Rouchon, Boisset, and Garilhe: *Sur les operations de l'Assemblée électorale du département de l'Ardèche* (n.l.) in A.N. AF III 100; *Réponse du Citoyen Gleizal, à une partie de l'écrit signé Rouchon, Garilhe* . . . (Paris, Impr. Bailleul) in B.N. Lb42/1871.

[64] A.N. AF III 217/ Bouches-du-Rhône: P. V. of both assemblies; Chabert to M. of Interior, 28 germinal; Constant to Directory, 26 germinal.

[65] *Ibid.* Constant to Directory, 28 germinal.

Jacobin contingents from Brive and Tulle, chose two local officials who were pro-Jacobin but not particularly notorious: Sauty and Plazanet. The local historian V. de Seilhac correctly observes that their background and social standing did not differ much from the official candidates; he concludes, therefore, that it was a "rivalry of personalities and not of opinions." But are these the only alternatives? Perhaps the rivalry was in the base of support; the real question was not necessarily the militance of those chosen (especially in view of the 9 germinal proclamation) but the independent power of the Jacobins and other republicans willing to support them.[66]

MARNE. The assemblée mère was not really controlled by the Jacobins but they were influential. Disputed Jacobin electors from Pogny and Chalons were seated, which proved to be the pretext for a schism. Over 100 conservatives left the assembly, leaving about 220 electors. The former Montagnard Thuriot—one of the better known Jacobins purged after Thermidor—was returned to the Legislature 137/219, but his former colleague Battelier was defeated by a moderate after three ballots (Vallin, 132/213). Pierret, a Jacobin, was chosen on second ballot by the slimmest of majorities (113/213), while the fourth seat was given to the popular Charles Delacroix, who was also chosen by the assemblée scissionnaire. The schism was validated though it was only half the size of the assemblée mère.[67]

NIÈVRE. The Jacobins were well-organized, aggressive, and strongly opposed by conservatives. During the primary assemblies the urban Constitutional Circles had made a scathing impact on the Directory,[68] but the occurrence of a schism, when 85 conservatives walked out of the regular assembly, clearly had a dampening effect. Party lines here crystallized around personalities in a rather involved struggle. The Directory's commissioner Etignard was dismissed on

[66] Comte V. de Seilhac, *Histoire politique de la Corrèze* (Tulle, 1888), pp. 23-42.

[67] A.N. C 533/Marne: P. V. For local background see R. Nicolas, *L'Esprit public et les élections dans le département de la Marne de 1790 à l'an VIII* (Chalôns, 1909), pp. 147-51.

[68] A.N. AF III 251/Nièvre: Les Citoyens soussignés de Clamecy . . . , 5 germinal; Reclamation des Citoyens de Nevers—two anti-Jacobin petitions. Also reports on Chatillon and St. Reverien.

the eve of the elections as pro-Jacobin. Naturally he became a rallying point for the Jacobins, while his successor Dupin stood as their nemesis. The latter was a relative of Duviquet, an official in the Ministry of Justice who apparently had great influence among local conservatives of pre-Fructidor days. Faced with a disagreeable choice, the Directory opted for the scissionnaires. In few places was its choice so manifestly beholden to extreme conservatives, but it was the necessary price for neutralizing the Jacobins. As described by a relatively dispassionate pro-Jacobin pamphlet, the schism was composed of ambitious men, a small number of royalists, electors not admitted to the regular assembly, and "several feeble men."[69] Duviquet was duly elected there, 75/83. The choices of the regular assembly that were annulled included Etignard (92/155) and the incumbent Sautereau (140/150). More important, it reelected the departmental administration that had recently been dismissed by the Directory as pro-Jacobin. And at the bottom of the roster, a militant from the Nevers Constitutional Circle was chosen *greffier* of the courts (Gillois, 70/132).[70]

Puy-de-Dôme. This was another department where the clubbists seem to have been forced into moderation by the events starting with the 9 germinal proclamation and ending with a schism of thirty electors. Instead of standing for the Legislature—as they were expected to—the most notable "exagérés" settled for slipping into lesser departmental offices: former Montagnard Maignet was chosen *haut juré* (309/334) and the notorious Dumont, public prosecutor. Likewise the departmental administration was elected from persons who were part of the Jacobin movement. The eight deputies, however, were top-heavy with moderates clearly meant to act as protective coloration for the lesser candidates and one or two Jacobins. One of the local meneurs, the *officier de santé* Bret, was chosen on the third ballot, defeating an incumbent elected by the scissionnaires, Girot-Pouzol. Though the figures suggest that the Jacobins were strong enough to indulge their preferences, their own slate in-

---

[69] *Précis historique des causes et des effets de la scission dans le département de la Nièvre* (Paris, Impr. des républicains, an VI) in A.N. F⁷ 7414, fol. 5054.
[70] A.N. AF III 251/Nièvre: P. V. of both assemblies; "Faits-Notes-Observations."

cluded three incumbents who were also chosen by the conservative scissionaires (Artaud-Blanval, Dulaure, and Enjelvin). The ruse did not work, however, and the entire slate of the assemblée mère was annulled, while the Directory had the audacity to seat the choices of a mere thirty scissionnaires.[71]

HAUTES-PYRÉNÉES. Here the contest was less lopsided. A Jacobin party was centered in the Constitutional Circle in Tarbes, supported by the *Journal des Hautes-Pyrénées,* and led by the brother of Bertrand Barère. The assemblée mère, originally numbering 156 electors, was reduced to 107, while an assemblée scissionnaire of 67 (including contested electors) proceeded to do the Directory's bidding by reelecting 2 conservative incumbents (Dauphole and Lacrampe).[72] The Jacobins did not flinch from naming their two obvious candidates: an incumbent long associated with their cause, Guchan (73/106), and Jean Barère, presently *haut juré* (82/107). Predictably they were annulled.[73]

VIENNE. Jacobin candidates for the two legislative seats were supposed to be Dardillac, a "Robespierrist" administrator and supporter of the Poitiers Constitutional Circle, and Ingrand, a former Montagnard.[74] But a schism by about 100 of the 240 electors led by the Directory's manager, Butaud, made the Jacobin party vulnerable. In the end they chose Dardillac (96/132) and the Directorial incumbent Creuzé-Latouche (129/132), who was also chosen by the scissionnaires. Again, significant differences were more apparent in the conflicting slates for departmental administration. Thanks to the schism, the Jacobin slate could be annulled. It was a most skillful running of the scenario.[75]

[71] A.N. AF III 254/Puy-de-Dôme: P. V. On the background see "Faits-Notes-Observations," and A.N. F7 7405, fol. 4176.

[72] A.N. AF III 255/Hautes-Pyrénées: P. V. assy. scissionnaire. It is interesting to note the commissioner's prior estimate that the government can count on about 75 of the 166 electors (*compte décadaire,* 2nd decade of germinal). To ensure success he called for the closing of the Tarbes Constitutional Circle.

[73] *Ibid.*: P. V. assy. mère. Cf. *Journal des Hautes-Pyrénées* (Tarbes) No. 98/9, 8 pluviôse VI on Guchan. (AF III 517, plaq. 3307.)

[74] A.N. C 535/Vienne: Butaud to Directory, 21 germinal. Other letters warned of the influence of Bernarais, an elector who was a leader of the "ouvriers" in the Poitiers Club.

[75] *Ibid.*: P. V.; [Butaud, administrateur de la Vienne], *Sur les doubles élections de Poitiers* (Vienne) (Paris, Impr. Tutot, n.d.) in B.N. Lb42/ 554;

IN THE overall results these eight departments plus the Seine form a first group (see Table 1). Here a *minority* of Directorials carried out a schism whose choices were subsequently validated, while the slates chosen by the *majority* of Jacobins in the regular assemblies were annulled. In a second group of departments the Directory felt itself so bested or considered its influence so minimal that it annulled all the results outright. This included three schisms (Landes, Loire, Allier) that were unsatisfactory for its purpose. Seven departments suffered this serious insult to their sovereignty. For it meant that they would lose all the representation due them that year, as well as all control over their judges and administrators.

This drastic reaction was suited to at least five of the seven cases. The slate turned in by Loir-et-Cher, for example, was as defiant as any. Headed by two former Montagnards (Venaille, 132/211 and Fréciné, 137/212), it ended with Ballayer among the departmental administrators (107/207), he being P. N. Hesiné's faithful comrade during the Vendôme trial and after.[76] The results in Loir-et-Cher came in the face of stiff opposition from conservatives. Not so in Landes. Here Jacobin organization was peerless and was carried out under the cloak of patriotism and republicanism in a department that had suffered a severe resurgence of royalism. The results were virtually unanimous, with two of the four deputies being recognized Jacobins: ex-Montagnard Dyzez (165/167) and administrator Batbedat (174/176). But opposition from conservatives somehow breached this formidable achievement, and although the Directory was forced to ignore an almost fabricated schism of two dozen electors, it did annul the entire election.[77] The vigorous Jac-

---

and an answer: *Dardillac, ex-administrateur: au Corps législatif, au Directoire éxecutif, à tous les Républicains* (Poitiers, an VI), A.N. F⁷ 7414, fol. 5083—a piece of humble pleading that is as misleading as Butaud's wild charges. A local newspaper, the *Journal de Poitiers et du département de la Vienne* No. 6, 30 germinal VI, did not admit to understanding the cause of the schism, which it regretted.

[76] A.N. AF III 241/Loir-et-Cher: P. V.; "Faits-Notes-Observations."

[77] A.N. AF III 239/Landes: P. V.; *Bulletin de l'Assemblée électorale du département des Landes* Nos. 1-5, 20-24 germinal VI (Impr. Delaroy); on royalist agitation that produced a factitious schism of 21 alleged electors see A.N. F⁷ 3680/Landes: Batbedat to Dondeau, 12 germinal VI, and L. S. Batbedat, *Exposé de ce qui s'est passé dans le dept. des Landes, relativement aux élections de l'an 6* (Impr. Lemaire), A.N. F⁷ 7421, fol. 5898. The Jacobins' archadversary was representative Darracq. See A.N. F⁷ 7411, fol. 4750: Darracq to Directory, 24 ventôse.

TABLE 1

Principal Jacobin Victories Invalidated by the Floréal Purge[1]

I. Jacobin majority assembly annulled, minority scissionnaires validated[2]

Ardèche (5)
Bouches-du-Rhône (7)
Corrèze (2)
Marne (4)
Nièvre (2)
Puy-de-Dôme (8)
Hautes-Pyrénées (2)
Seine (16)
Vienne (2)

II. Department's elections completely annulled

*Allier (2)
Dordogne (7)
*Landes (3)
Loir-et-Cher (2)
*Loire (5)
Basses-Pyrénées (2)
Haute-Vienne (2)

III. Selected Jacobins purged, other results validated[3]

A. *Deputies*

Pas-de-Calais (4/9)
Sarthe (3/6)
Saône-et-Loire (3/7)
Ariège (2/3)
Eure (2/6)
Nord (2/13)
Ain (1)
*Aube (1)
Aude (1)
Mayenne (1)
Mont Blanc (1)
Ourthe (1)
*Seine-et-Oise (1)

B. *Departmental offices only*

*Basses-Alpes
Alpes-Maritimes
Gers
**Hérault
Moselle
Var
*Vaucluse

Numbers in parentheses refer to the number of deputies in question.
* Schisms by conservatives not validated.
[1] A fourth group of Jacobin-oriented departments, whose results were not purged at all, includes Doubs (3), Haute-Garonne (3), and Gironde (11).
[2] Out of 48 deputies purged from this Group I, 8 were still seated since they were moderates also elected by the validated scissionnaires: 3 in Puy-de-Dôme, and one each in Ardèche, Bouches-du-Rhône, Marne, Seine, and Vienne. Hence the Jacobin loss from this group totaled 40.
[3] In addition to the purged deputies from Group A, local officials were purged as follows: Sarthe 3, Saône-et-Loire 2, Ariège 4, Ain 1, Ourthe 5. Most were judges or public prosecutors. In Group B, Hérault and Moselle lost 2 each, Vaucluse all, and the others 1 each.
** Hérault is an anomaly; two judicial officials were purged as Jacobins, but so was commissioner Devals—a Directorial elected deputy as part of the official list.

obin offensive in Allier during the primary assemblies has been described in the previous chapter, but it was blunted by a vicious and royalist-tainted schism which the Directory in the end had to ignore. The regular assembly nonetheless proceeded to include in its slate the ex-conventionnel Martel (119/120) and to recall the pro-Jacobin departmental administration, including activists from the club like Bohat, Huet, and Perrotin. Again the entire painstaking effort of party-building was for nought.[78]

Loire was another department where Jacobins had regrouped and reorganized for the elections. The schism that occurred here of fewer than forty electors had little effect. Notorious meneurs like the "Babeuvist" Chana (136/159) and St. Didier (139/157) won easy victories, along with a few moderates like commissioner Ferrand (also chosen by the scissionnaires) to make the slate more palatable to the Directory. Such consideration was of no avail, and for good reason, all things considered![79] Perhaps the outstanding bastion of Neo-Jacobinism was Dordogne, with its wealth of former terrorist personnel and ex-Montagnards to fill the many positions up for election. Directorials led by commissioner Beaupui waged a good battle, forcing most contests to go two or three ballots, but they were bested in every case. Here the Jacobins were particularly resolute in ignoring the 9 germinal proclamation; an article in their local newspaper, the *Observateur de la Dardogne*, had pretended that the proclamation could not possibly have any relevance to their department. Their slate was headed by former Montagnards who had recently been dismissed by the Directory from local positions: Peyssard (196/386) and Roux-Fazillac (206/386); in lesser positions exiled Montagnards like Elie Lacoste and Noel Pointe

---

[78] A.N. AF III 212/Allier: P. V.; Beauchamp et Chabot, *Sur la Scission de l'Assemblée de l'Allier* (Impr. Ami des Lois). This pamphlet contained the arguments that would lead to the annulling of the regular assembly. But the assemblée scissionnaire contained too many *destitués de Fructidor* to be a useful alternative.

[79] A.N. AF III 240/Loire: P. V. A voluminous dossier established the presence of well-known Jacobins among the leading electors, but the most damaging charge was contained in a memo, later printed as a pamphlet, by three conservative incumbents, Forest, Duguet, Meudre, *Sur les Elections du département de la Loire, an 6* (Impr. Baudouin, floréal 6). The departmental commissioner Ferrand, elected by both assemblies, on the whole supported the majority in this case.

were chosen *haute juré* (240/334) and *gréffier* (212/373).[80] To accept these results the Directory would have had to abandon its policy of coercion completely. The two other departments to suffer a blanket annulment in the purge of 22 floréal—Basses-Pyrénées and Haute-Vienne—were not nearly as formidable in their Jacobin resurgence, though the candidates elected were not particularly to the Directory's liking.[81] The ferocity in these two cases must appear as somewhat anomalous.

A third group of departments saw the Jacobins deprived of their victories only selectively (see Table 1). Instead of annulling the elections altogether, or validating the choices of a rival assemblée scissionnaire, the government validated the regular results but purged particular individuals. In four departments the purge was considerable, reflecting Jacobin strength comparable to the two previous groups of departments. Pas-de-Calais lost four out of seven deputies,[82] Sarthe and Saône-et-Loire lost three each, while Ariège lost two. Judicial personnel in the latter three were also included in the purge.[83] In addition Eure and Nord each lost two deputies who

[80] A.N. C 531/Dordogne: P. V., whose nuances are revealing. Much of the material concerning this department is included in H. Labroue's study, *L'Esprit public en Dordogne.* Charges of the conservatives are summarized in *Sur les élections de la Dordogne: Organisation et plan . . . a dirigé les choix comme il a voulu* (n.l.) in A.N. AF III 100.

[81] G. Cassagnau, *L'Esprit public et les élections dans le département des Basses-Pyrénées de 1789 à 1804* (Paris, 1906), pp. 96-99, detected no irregularities here, but noted that Lafont and Lanabère (each members of the departmental administration before their election to the Legislature) supported the "anarchists." Just before the purge, four deputies wrote to Merlin asking that both men be included instead of Lafont alone, as originally proposed (see A.N. AF III 99 and Cassagnau, 98-99). The case of Haute-Vienne is more puzzling.

[82] Pas-de-Calais was like Dordogne a Jacobin stronghold facing determined conservative opposition. Many contests went to three ballots; the margins of two leading "anarchists" were Thery 257/455, and Crachet 226/435. Among the Directorials who were beaten were Poultier and Parent-Réal. Four of the eight candidates for the Legislature, however, received much larger majorities: Lenglet (378/449); the Jacobin commissioner Coffin (374/433); and moderate incumbents Daunou and Lefebvre-Cayet (virtual unanimity). On the balloting for departmental administration Parent-Réal did win election (216 votes) but so did the terrorist Goulliard (180 votes). (A.N. AF III 254/ Pas-de-Calais: P. V.)

[83] On the Sarthe see Reinhard's definitive study. On Ariège see A.N. AF III 215, and on Saône-et-Loire see AF III 258.

were well known in Jacobin circles, while Ain, Aude, Mayenne, Mont Blanc, Ourthe, and Seine-et-Oise each lost one deputy who was identifiable as a Jacobin stalwart.[84] Another subgroup of seven departments had all deputies seated but had selected departmental officials and judges purged. Vaucluse was the most severely hit of these, having all its nominations below the level of deputy invalidated. At least three departments, possibly more, form an anomalous fourth group whose fate was entirely different. For in Doubs, Haute-Garonne, and Gironde conspicuous Jacobin success was validated without reservation.[85]

Thus far we have considered departments dominated or influenced by an organized Jacobin party. A fifth and open-ended group forms a borderline case of departments whose results were validated and generally favored the Directorials, but which nonetheless sent individual Jacobins to the Legislature. These were Jacobins of two kinds. One, the less numerous, were incumbents noted for their support of local Jacobin cadres or causes. The purged Lamarque and Gay-Vernon would be prototypes of this group; those not purged included Oudot (Côte d'Or), Talot (Maine-et-Loire), and Pons-de-Verdun (Meuse). One could add men like Merlino (Ain) and Lesage-Senault (Nord) who were seated despite other purges in their departments. A second group is composed of men from moderate departments, entering the Legislature of the Directory period for the first time, who proved in subsequent months to be deeply involved in the Jacobin opposition, along with the deputies from Doubs, Gironde, and Haute-Garonne: Bertrand (Calvados), Bel-

---

[84] The case of General Fion in the Ourthe was one instance where the Directory's notion of *royalisme à bonnet rouge* may have been relevant. A defendant at Vendôme, Fion was considered by the Directory's commissioner a patriotic but unreliable exagéré. To the former's embarrassment Fion received the highest vote of all candidates in this department, 197/268. To explain this result, the commissioner maintained that royalists were supporting this radical out of some nefarious design, and it is possible that he was accurate. Needless to say Fion was purged in floréal. (A.N. AF III 253/Ourthe: P. V. and departmental commissioner to Directory, 26 germinal.)

[85] On the Doubs see J. Sauzay's encyclopedic but unorganized *Histoire de la persecution révolutionnaire dans le département du Doubs de 1789 à 1801* (10 vols.; Besançon, 1867-73), IX, *passim* and especially 523-26. On Haute-Garonne see J. Beyssi, "Le Parti Jacobin à Toulouse sous le Directoire," *AHRF*, 1950, pp. 124-33. On Gironde see A.N. AF III 232/Gironde: P. V. and renseignemens diverses. The margin of the Jacobin candidates here ranged from clear (Garrau, 253/435) to very close in the balloting for departmental office.

legarde (Charente), Blin (Ille-et-Villaine), Texier-Olivier (Indre-et-Loire), Français de Nantes (Isère), Guesdon (Manche), Stevenotte (Sambre-et-Meuse), Marquezy (Var).[86] Individual deputies from departments that were partially purged like Lenglet (Pas-de-Calais), Dessaix (Mont Blanc), and Dethier (Ourthe) fit into the same category. Again, this list is open-ended and could doubtless be tripled with further information on the careers of individual deputies.[87]

Finally we come to the departments that fulfilled all the Directory's hopes. And this accounts for over half the total. These results reflected the spirit of '95, of republican oligarchy, paternalism, and moderation, as recapitulated in the Directory's numerous electoral proclamations. They included a number of the larger and even relatively urbanized departments, though by and large Jacobinism carried the cities. Of the eighteen largest departments, in the sense of seats to be filled, five were unambiguously in the Directory's camp, and seven in the Jacobins'. Six produced a few Jacobin candidates but a majority of moderates wholly acceptable to the government.[88] Of necessity, it must be noted, the Directory could not cut itself off entirely from the experienced, capable *patriotes prononcés*, even if they were potential partisans of Jacobinism. It is not surprising that a number of past, present, or future Jacobins escaped the purge.

THAT PURGE of 22 floréal (11 May 1798) was the culmination of a chain of events set in motion by the 9 germinal proclamation. The Legislature's right to review and certify election results had been reaffirmed in pluviôse of the Year VI. It was made clear then that the lame-duck Legislature would carry out this review before the new deputies took their seats on the first of prairial. However, it was the Executive Directory that seized the initiative in this process all

[86] See A.N. AF III 42 (Police): surveillance reports for the month of prairial VII, and *J. hommes libres*, messidor-fructidor VII, *passim*.

[87] Suratteau, "Les Babouvistes," p. 173, estimates that up to 80 Jacobins slipped through the purge.

[88] *Directorial*: Seine-Inférieure (14), Somme (9), Loire-Inférieure (8), Côtes du Nord (8), Bas Rhin (7). *Jacobin*: Seine (16), Gironde (11), Pas-de-Calais (9), Puy-de-Dôme (8), Bouches-du-Rhône (7), Dordogne (7), Saône-et-Loire (7). *Mixed but predominantly moderate results:* Nord (13), Ille-et-Vilaine (10), Manche (8), Calvados (8), Seine-et-Oise (8), Moselle (7). Number of seats due to be filled are listed in parentheses.

along. When the election results were in, the executive branch supervised the piecing together of a purge list. To prepare the way a series of agitated messages was sent over to the Legislature, warning about irregularities and conspiracies in the elections. The Legislature in turn abandoned its customary procedures, and instead of forming separate committees for each departmental election that was in question, established one *ad hoc* committee to take the Directory's list in hand and deliberate upon it. With only a few minor additions the list was recommended in an omnibus, all-or-nothing bill that was completely contrary to normal methods of deliberation. After short debates in each house the bill was overwhelmingly adopted in unrecorded voice votes.[89]

With due allowance for an element of capriciousness and inconsistency, the Directory made good on its threat of 9 germinal. Eighty-six Jacobins or candidates sponsored by the Jacobins, duly elected by a majority of their departmental electors, were barred from the Legislature (see Table 1).[90] More important is the fact that the Jacobins of at least twenty departments (Groups I and II plus Pas-de-Calais, Sarthe, Saône-et-Loire and Ariège) saw the fruits of their efforts wiped out almost completely. The painstaking work of building up a constitutional party of opposition was arbitrarily canceled out and stigmatized as subversive. It was not simply the individual candidates who were the objects of this arbitrary purge, but the nascent party formations themselves.

[89] The Directory's original list is in A.N. AF III 99; the final list approved by the Legislature as the law of 22 floréal VI has been reprinted by Aulard, (See note 60). The Directory's messages, the legislative committee reports, and the speeches are available in the Maclure Collection, University of Pennsylvania Library. See especially *Conseil des Cinq-Cents: MESSAGE . . . Le Directoire exécutif au Conseil des cinq cents* (Impr. Nationale, 13 floréal).

[90] Previous estimates such as Suratteau's 106 have been too high, possibly because they include the 8 deputies also elected by scissionnaires who were ultimately seated; the 9 Jacobins elected by the minority assemblies of Rhône and Seine-et-Marne and legitimately excluded; and individuals who were purged as royalists or for obscure reasons.

CHAPTER XI

Electors and Elections in Paris

EVEN WHEN its political life was relatively subdued, Paris commanded attention. As the seat of national government and the center of political journalism its affairs were subjected to intense public scrutiny. Control of Paris in the elections of 1798 by the opposition would entail a particularly serious loss of prestige for the government, not to mention the prize of a sixteen-man deputation due to be elected. With increasing apprehension the government monitored the primary assemblies as they completed their balloting. The results seemed so dangerous that the Directory adopted a policy of repression, which it announced by the proclamation of 9 germinal (29 March). Paris therefore offers a graphic case study of the nature and tactics of the democratic opposition, the results of the assemblies, and their implications.

‡ I ‡

Considerable effort by the clubs to secure franchise reform and to overcome mass apathy had achieved little. Therefore there was no reason to expect an unusually large turnout for the assemblies. With the same ground rules in force throughout the Directory period, figures on the number of eligible voters in Paris for the Years V and VI reveal virtually no change: the potential electorate remained at about 120,000. Changes in registration within the city's twelve arrondissements—which probably reflect variations in the administration of the laws as well as internal population movements —were negligible.[1]

As against the large number of eligible citizens, the number that actually voted seems to have been small. For such information there are no compilations like those recording the number of eligibles. Actual participation, as well as the votes in each contest, would have to be reconstructed from the procès-verbaux of the nearly 170 primary assemblies in Paris—an impossible task since these local records were almost entirely destroyed in the 1871 fire at the Paris

[1] A.N. F²⁰ 381: Département de la Seine: tableau de distribution des Assemblées primaires an V (MS); *Département de la Seine: Assemblées primaires an VII: tableau de distribution* (Impr. Ballard).

311

Municipal Archives. At least six of these procès-verbaux, however, came to rest elsewhere, and in addition figures are available for two other assemblies. This sampling of eight districts can at least suggest something about voter turnout.

In section Bon Conseil, part of the 5th arrondissement, the three primary assemblies had approximately 830, 870, and 750 eligible voters. But the largest number of citizens actually voting in 1798 was 101, 139, and 103. Participation was not much above 15 percent.[2] Three assemblies in the 4th arrondissement had between 650 and 750 eligible voters (population shifts and redrawn district lines created variations here). The maximum number of voters on any ballot in these assemblies was 104, 137, and 146.[3] Two other samples show only a slightly higher percentage of participation, and these came from sections where the clubs were unusually active. Thus, 194 citizens cast their ballots in a Fontaine de Grenelle district (10th arrondissement) where between 600 and 800 were eligible. And a district of section Quinze-Vingts in the faubourg Antoine (8th arrondissement), where the number of eligibles lay between 800 and the constitutional maximum of 900, saw 204 faubouriens vote in 1798.[4]

These statistics reinforce impressionistic testimony about elections under the Directory, suggesting that only 15 to 30 percent of the eligible voters cast their ballots. And if the eligibility figures are inflated by inclusion of people who had moved or died, this is offset by the fact that the figures of participation cited represent the maximum number voting in each assembly. Actually some assemblies took several ballots over a period of days without all voters participating throughout. For example, in a 4th arrondissement district where the voting for electors went the legal maximum of three ballots, 146 citizens voted in the inconclusive second *scrutin*, but only 126 were present for the decisive third ballot.

Besides illustrating a state of apathy, the figures suggest that a small group of voters could prevail if it was well organized and able to sway some uncommitted votes. Notwithstanding its meager-

[2] A.N. F^{1c} III, Seine 1: P. V. of the 1st, 2nd, and 3rd districts.

[3] A.D.S., VD* Nos. 5414, 5416, and 5463: P. V. of the 2nd, 4th, and 12th districts.

[4] A.N. F^7 3054, fol. "Elections, an VI": Rapport du 9 germinal by Agent No. 46 on 10th district of 10th arrondissement; A.N. F^7 3688/13: Boyer to M. of Pol. Dondeau, 6 germinal.

ness, our sample of procès-verbaux shows that in some districts slates were well prepared and carried on first ballots; in others a more fluid situation existed where several candidates vied for two or even three ballots. Two of the districts in the 4th arrondissement were open in this fashion, going the maximum of three ballots. (In one district a first elector was chosen on the first ballot, a second on the second round, and two others on a third ballot.) But in the third district of this group the local club was probably in control and brought in a majority for its slate on the first ballot with an almost uniform vote:

Duboscq, md. papetier	79/137
Delchamp, rentier	76/137
Nourry, corroyeur	77/137
Corbie, orfèvre	74/137

The Directory's commissioner passed a predictable comment, calling the proceedings of this assembly "precipitous," and its choices "peu avantageux."[5]

"Agent No. 46," a police observer who participated in and reported on the assembly of a Fontaine de Grenelle district (10th arrondissement), and who was sympathetic to the Jacobins there, illuminates the workings of these assemblies. The district was a bastion of the Rue du Bacq Club with its amalgam of former Jacobins, sectionnaires, and wounded veterans of the Hôtel des Invalides. A slate drawn from members of the club included names well known in the democratic movement: Gaultier-Biauzat (the judge who had voted to acquit Babeuf, and who drew up the petition in support of open registration); Raisson (a Jacobin stalwart and administrator in Paris during the Terror); Magendie (a surgeon and sectional militant in the Year II); and Vatar's collaborator Antonelle (a member of the Revolutionary Tribunal, and a defendant at Vendôme). In a suggestive pattern of voting three were elected on the first ballot:

Biauzat	115/194
Raisson	119/194
Magendie	120/194

[5] A.D.S., VD* No. 5416: P. V. of 12th district; A.N. F⁷ 7412, fol. 4856: report by commissioner to the 4th arrondissement.

But Antonelle polled only 83 votes, 16 short of a majority and almost one-third fewer than the others. Something about the balance of power in that assembly can be inferred from this: evidently there were about eighty democrats, probably members of the Rue du Bacq Club, acting in concert; they garnered support for the first three names on their slate from about forty voters who were, however, put off by Antonelle's notorious reputation. After this first ballot Antonelle's friends lobbied for him, introducing him to some of these citizens so that Antonelle could convince them that he was not a mad anarchist. The effort succeeded, for Antonelle was chosen on the second ballot, 103/167.[6]

Generalizing about some of the other districts in Paris, this observer concluded that a rapprochement was taking place between the generality of "inconspicuous republicans" and those who "have led the way in Revolution."

> Republicans in general have recognized the necessity . . . of choosing men whom they have come to realize have been given false reputations as partisans of the constitution of '93. . . . [Their election] is a sacred debt, feebly redeemed, which renders to these same men the esteem and recognition of republicans and which eases somewhat the suffering that they have endured from persecutions. . . . It is said, if we wish to remain republicans, we must rely on those men whose republicanism is beyond doubt.[7]

Naturally this movement back to men "who have led the way in Revolution" was not uniform in the city's 170 electoral districts. Conservative and reactionary forces were far from subdued, and the democrats had to fight bitterly, even to the point of making electoral schisms in a few places. Indeed according to the reports of the twelve commissioners to the arrondissements (who were the Directory's principal observers) the choices were especially "mixed" in the 2nd, 3rd, 4th, 5th, 7th, and 12th arrondissements. By this it was meant that Jacobins, Directorials, and reactionaries had all made their presence felt.[8]

---

[6] F[7] 3054: report by Agent No. 46.

[7] *Ibid.*: "De l'Esprit des Assemblées primaires," by Agent No. 46. The agent's obvious sympathies for the Jacobins were denounced by some of his fellow agents, whose allegations are on file in this same dossier.

[8] Most of the commissioners' reports and supporting documents are scattered in two places: A.N. AF III 260 (Seine)—especially "Résumé . . . Assemblées

The Right on the Parisian political spectrum was held by the so-called vendémiairists—named after that coalition of reactionaries and royalists who had attempted an abortive rebellion against the Convention as it was about to inaugurate the Directory regime. This same coalition had produced the Clichyite party in the Year V, and despite its setback in Fructidor, had not expired. In an unrelated decree dated 5 ventôse (23 February) the Legislature had decided to bar "rebels" from the coming elections, having in mind chouans and vendéeans. But the Jacobins in Paris attempted to expel some of the vendémiairists on the basis of this law, arguing that the leaders of the primary assemblies of the Year IV that had organized the vendémiaire demarche were themselves rebels. Serious commotions and isolated acts of near violence resulted from this confrontation, but the vendémiairists and their sympathizers were not easily intimidated.[9] In the 3rd arrondissement, for example, thirteen of the electors chosen were described by the Directory's commissioner as vendémiairists or *réacteurs*; in the 5th, the commissioner reported that vendémiairists had carried two assemblies, naming seven electors. Fierce battles had to be waged even in the 10th arrondissement, where in one assembly the forces were so closely matched that the vendémiairists succeeded in nominating the presiding officers, but the Jacobins were able to rally and put across their choices for electors. More revealing were contests in which Jacobins opposed Directorials who received support from the far Right. Staunch Directorials like Camus (a conservative ex-conventionnel), Sibuet (publisher of the *Ami des Lois*), Lenoir-Laroche (one-time editor of the *Moniteur* and a personal friend of director LaRevellière), and Limodin (a crusading anti-Jacobin on the Central Police Bureau) were all opposed in bitter contests and found themselves allied in electoral schisms with the vendémiairists.[10]

But when due attention has been given to the "mixed" outcome in certain districts—the scattering of vendémiairists chosen, and the

---

primaires an VI"; and A.N. F⁷ 7412, fol. 4856—especially "Tableau analytique des differentes pièces . . . relatives à la tenue des assemblées primaires de la commune de Paris." Other pertinent material is in F⁷ 3054 in a catch-all dossier marked "Elections, an VI"; A.N. F⁷ 3688/13 and 14; and A.N. C 534, fol. "Seine."

[9] *L'Indépendant* (Paris) No. 188, 8 germinal VI; A.N. F⁷ 3054, Agent No. 46; A.N. F¹ᶜ III, Seine 1: P. V. for 5th arrondissement.

[10] A.N. AF III 260 and A.N. F⁷ 7412, fol. 4856.

far larger number of substantial conservatives, including members of the Institut, high officials, and the Directory's own commissioners—it must be stated that the democrats prevailed. All of the Directory's observers (who would have done better to report good news) shared the view that the elections were dominated by former Jacobins, sectionnaires, and terrorists. While they reported few acts of overt violence or corruption, they complained endlessly about "intrigue," high-pressure tactics, and a disregard for the fine points of the laws. Their most common contention was that "partisans of '93"—notorious revolutionaries and their "little known friends"—trampled over peaceful, disinterested voters in order to put across their slates. In most arrondissements the clubs were identified as the centers of this effort, and in the 1st, 6th, 8th, and 10th arrondissements it was beyond doubt that the Constitutional Circles dominated the proceedings.[11]

Prior to the elections the clubs of the Rue du Bacq and of the faubourg Antoine were the best organized and most effective. It seems no coincidence that the Directory's commissioners found the greatest number of "dangerous" electors in the 10th and 8th arrondissements: 24 and 23 respectively. At least eighteen electors in the 10th arrondissement were active club members who had signed petitions.[12] In the faubourg Antoine only eight electors were signators, but others were almost surely members, including several who were on Sotin's patronage list for the faubourg Antoine.[13] Another piece of evidence reveals the role of club members and former sectionnaires in the 8th. Of the ten primary assemblies held there, three chose as presidents militants who went on to be designated electors

[11] *Ibid.*, especially "Résumé . . . Assemblées primaires."

[12] Bach (médecin), Caignard (journaliste), Caillot (invalide), Gauthier-Biauzat (juge), Giraud (employé), Groslaire (invalide), Jacquemin (employé), Lebrun (rentier), Magendie (surgeon), Marcellin (employé), Martin (imprimeur), Paragon (employé), Pierron (employé), Pons (rentier), Raisson (administrateur), Rouillard (employé), Rouval, Senéchal (fonctionnaire), Sijas (employé). See AF III 260: liste générale des électeurs du 10ème arrond. (with comments), and Appendix, below, for members of the Rue du Bacq Club.

[13] Signators on petitions of the Réunion include Boyer (ouvrier en porcelain), Delvigne (ouvrier ébéniste), Duchesne (md. de bierre), Guidet (cizeleur), Moreau (ouvrier ébéniste), Leban (menuisier), Lejeune (bourrelier), Vacquier (md. de vin). Likely members include Damois (propriétaire) and Rollet (tapissier). See A.N. AF III 260: rapport du commissaire au 8ème arrond.; A.N. F7 3688/13: letter to departmental commissioner (Seine), 17 germinal; and Appendix, below.

(Rollet, Duchesne, Cochois); two others chose sans-culotte militants as presidents without subsequently naming them as electors—perhaps because they were wholly deficient in their property qualifications: Vacret and Brisvin, both of whom were active in the Réunion.[14]

We have information about a more typical area in a report on the 6th arrondissement. Here the commissioner observed that "former members of the revolutionary committees and popular societies . . . working through the medium of the constitutional circle," controlled four of the assemblies, and chose nine electors whose reputations were notorious. These included three members of the revolutionary committee of the Gravilliers section (Berthaud, Daux, Michel); a leader of the insurrectionary *journées* of the Year III (Vanheck), and two "Babeuvists" who were tried at Vendôme (Crespin and Fiquet). In addition, Vanheck and Michel were elected to the municipal administration of the 6th arrondissement, from which position they were eventually ousted by the Directory.[15] Clubbists of the 1st arrondissement who captured their municipal administration among their prizes were likewise pursued by the government.[16]

In the seven arrondissements where the democrats made the strongest impression on the Directory's observers, these commissioners singled out 18, 9, 8, 23, 16, 24, and 7 electors as undesirable because of their revolutionary backgrounds. In all, about 130 of the approximately 650 Paris electors were stigmatized as "partisans of '93" and thus as "poor" or "dangerous" choices, and these lists represented only about half the total of such electors. While some of these individuals may have changed their outlook substantially since

[14] A.N. F⁷ 3054: Etat nominatif des présidents des Assemblées primaires des douze arrondissements. In the 8th arrondissement there were ten districts which chose Vacret, Benard, Rollet, Brisvin, Fleuriselle, Duchesne, Cochois, Jaladon, L'Aîné, and Massiaux-Chevallier as presidents. Vacret and Brisvin are mentioned in Ch. viii.

[15] A.N. AF iii 260. On Vanheck and Michel see A.N. F¹ᵇ II, Seine 24. Petitions from the Constitutional Circle of the 6th arrondissement may be found in A.N. F⁷ 7361, fol. 143 and A.N. C 429, fol. 151. Electors who were signators include Fiquet, Creté (limonadier), Huay (instituteur), Leclerc (ex-employé), Lefebvre (menuisier).

[16] See A.N. F¹ᵇ ii, Seine 24, dossier, "1ᵉʳ arrond.": M. of Interior to Directory, thermidor VI, and letters from three of the newly elected municipal officers protesting against their impending ouster. Five members who signed a club petition (A.N. C 431, fol. 166) were elected: Brulard, Follope, Perdrix, Bazelot, and Marquet.

the Year II, it is likely that they were chosen in such numbers precisely because they represented certain associations for the voters.[17]

Within this "popular front" of democrats were two groups: middle-class Jacobins and sans-culotte sectionnaires. The first consisted of men who had held positions in the revolutionary government, some of whom were active in the Paris Jacobin Club. Heading this roster in prominence were ex-Montagnards (Jullein de Toulouse, Panis, Prieur de la Marne), followed by men who had worked for the executive commissions or the Paris department (Xavier Audouin, Clémence, Daubigny, Raisson, Réal, Santerre, Sijas, Tissot); personnel of the Paris Revolutionary Tribunal (Antonelle, Brochet, Chrétien, Naulin); and military officers with radical reputations (Brutus Maignier, Jorry, Rossignol). With a few exceptions (notably Chrétien and Rossignol) these men were essentially bourgeois; they moved in fairly high political circles, and if they had reputations these were city-wide or even national in scope. Also among this group were recent arrivals in Paris (as well as some long-time Parisians) who are notable not so much as terrorists of the Year II but as Neo-Jacobins of the Year VI. Police Minister Sotin (who was not an elector) would have been a prototype for this group. In Paris it included journalists like Destival of the *Indépendant*, Caignart and Coesnon-Pellerin of the *Ami de la Patrie*; Gaultier-Biauzat and Victor Bach of the Rue du Bacq Club; and Valentin Huay, director of the Institut des Aveugles-travailleurs, theophilanthropist, and a founder of the club in the 6th arrondissement.

With a man like Valentin Huay—an educated professional whose ties to the Directory are indicated by his theophilanthropy—we merge into the second group, for Huay was a *personalité du quartier,* a recruitment target for Babeuf's agents, with deep roots among the common people of his neighborhood. Quite possibly Huay's *maison de secours* was a focal point of community life. In any case, the second group was sans-culotte socially and entirely local politically. These were the sectional militants of the Year II—justices of the peace, members of revolutionary committees, and club leaders—whose constituency was the quartier or section: men like Baudrais, Bodson, Briffaut, Crespin, Damois, Daux, Duchesne,

---

[17] When Albert Soboul publishes his lists of sectionnaires who were members of revolutionary committees, etc., it will be possible to deal more rigorously with such questions.

Durant, Fiquet, Hu, Lacombe, Leban, Lebrun, Magendie, Mennessier, Moreau, Pierron, Toutain, Vanheck. Along with these names—familiar enough to the local thermidorians who had ousted them from political life in the Year III—were also chosen rank and filers, day-to-day activists who had participated unspectacularly in the *beaux jours* of the Year II and the grim days of the Year III. Such second-line militants would not have stood out on any list of electors, but they were known to those who were paid to keep watch on each section. To these informants the list of electors bristled with exagérés. For every Rossignol or Tissot there were more obscure sectionnaires who did not escape notice: a Jacquemin, "furious in his exaggeration"; a Rollet, "without character, allowing himself to be led towards the constitution of '93." When all these identifications were passed on to the Directory, they understandably led to the conclusion that the Paris elections had been held "under the yoke of terrorism and anarchy." Allowing for the tendentious rhetoric used by Directorials to describe their opposition, this conclusion was largely correct. Jacobins and sectionnaires, cooperating as they rarely had in the Year II, won almost half of the seats in the Paris electoral assembly for 1798.

This resurgence of former revolutionaries or exagérés (as the Directory called them) reflected a shift in the social foundation of political power in Paris. The Seine department had virtually no countryside to offset the urban constituencies of Parisian democrats. Hence comparative analysis of the Parisian electoral assemblies during the Directory period reveals what are probably unique correlations between political trends and social composition (see Table 2). Triumphant political reaction in the Year V[18] brought to the electoral assembly of that year strong contingents from the classic commercial and professional strata of the bourgeoisie: merchants, lawyers, and notaries. In addition a fairly large number of electors indicated no profession and were presumably wealthy men living off their property.[19] The social configuration of the electoral assembly of the Year VI contrasts markedly. Here were substantially fewer merchants and lawyers; an average number of government

[18] See J. Suratteau, "Les Elections de l'an V aux conseils du Directoire," *AHRF*, 1958 [No. 5], pp. 43, 47 and *passim*.
[19] *Liste des électeurs du département de la Seine, imprimée par ordre de l'Assemblée Electorale de l'an V* (Impr. DuPont), B.N. Le40/21.

TABLE 2

Social Composition of the Paris Electoral Assemblies: Years IV-VII[a]

Occupations	Year IV	Year V	Year VI	Year VII
Elected Officials	41	23	32	39
Employees	135	80	125	136
Commissioners of the Directory	—	1	11	11
Judges	7	10	8	8
Old Regime Notables	—	12	—	—
Négociants	55	41	15	16
Manufacturers and Entrepreneurs	16	11	10	6
Bankers	2	4	1	—
Proprietors	19	22	13	25
Cultivators	10	9	—	9
Rentiers and pensioners	21	19	27	25
Professionals	(180)	(138)	(101)	(109)
Lawyers	91	83	54	56
Doctors	6	3	7	1
Architects and Engineers	14	9	12	8
Notaries	44	31	13	22
Teachers, etc.	25	12	15	12
Artists	9	7	12	3
Men of Letters	14	4	8	13
Soldiers	7	2	12	6
Sans-culottes	(114)	(146)	(219)	(143)
Artisans and Shopkeepers	63	121	174	105
Marchands[b]	51	25	45	38

Sources: *Liste des Electeurs du dépt. de la Seine de l'an IV* (Impr. Ballard), B.N. Le40/77; *Liste des Electeurs du dépt. de la Seine . . . an V* (Impr. DuPont), B.N. Le40/21; *Assemblée Electorale: Liste générale . . . des électeurs du dépt. de la Seine* (Impr. Jacquin, an VII), B.N. Le40/33; *Liste Générale des électeurs du dépt. de la Seine pour l'an VI* (Impr. Ballard), A.D.S. 2AZ 156.

[a] Does not include electors who list no occupation.

[b] Listed here are marchands who do not specify what they sell; others were classified with artisans and shopkeepers.

functionaries; and above all a significantly greater number of artisans and shopkeepers: the principal strata of sans-culotterie.[20]

As Paris moved politically away from royalist reaction and Directorial conservatism, the preponderant bourgeois influence over the elections diminished. Elections that were dominated politically in 1798 by former Jacobins and sectional militants produced a broader spectrum of social participation in political affairs where the sans-culottes had a numerically strategic place. At least seventy more sans-culottes sat in the electoral assembly of the Year VI than in those of the three other years, while fewer lawyers, notaries, and merchants were chosen. Occupational groups characteristic of sectional life in the Year II and of participation in the revolutionary *journées*, but almost totally absent in the Year V elections, were again in the ranks (see Table 3): carpenters (12), jewelers, (8), pharmacists (8), café-keepers (7), house painters (6), shoemakers (5), tailors (5), saddlers (4), locksmiths (4). Moreover, in the light of what we know about the placement of former sectionnaires in lower-echelon government jobs after Fructidor, we can assume that a substantial number of *employés* in the Year VI (some of whom were already losing these newly acquired jobs) were sans-culottes unable to support their families in their accustomed trades.

No comparative statistics on the property assessments of the electors are available, but we do have the data for the Year VI. The very reason for its existence in accessible form is significant: the government was seeking to establish the ineligibility of certain electors. An equally ambitious search for such data was carried out by the Directory's agents in Marseilles where over thirty electors—including prominent local revolutionaries—were declared ineligible. On a smaller scale, such charges were raised in at least six departments,[21]

---

[20] *Liste Générale des électeurs du département de la Seine pour l'an VI* (Impr. Ballard), A.D.S., 2 AZ 156.

[21] The Directory's most zealous agent in Marseilles, the commissioner to the Central Police Bureau, wrote on 8 germinal (after denouncing the election of exagérés by the primary assemblies): "Je m'occupe de prouver que la majorité des électeurs ne remplissent pas les conditions exigées par la constitution pour pouvoir l'être." At that point he could name 12 specifically, and estimated that 20 others were unqualified. Of the electors chosen in the 6th district he observed: "entre les quatre il ne font pas 150 l. de location"; those in the 11th district were only slightly better off: "les 4 ne font pas 200 l. de location." A.N. F⁷ 3659/4 (Bouches-du-Rhône): letter headed Marseille, le 8 germinal 6. This charge eventually became commonplace in the correspondence of the

TABLE 3

Artisans and Shopkeepers in the Electoral Assemblies, Years V and VI

Occupations	Year VI	Year V
Grocer	16	17
Carpenter	12	3
Bookseller	8	6
Jeweller	8	1
Pharmacist	8	3
Café-keeper	7	1
Gold/Silversmith	7	10
Mercier (haberdasher)	6	11
House painter	6	1
Shoemaker	5	0
Tailor	5	0
Upholsterer	5	3
Locksmith	4	0
Perfumer	4	1
Saddler	4	1
Watchmaker	4	4
Hatter	3	2
Doreur (gilder)	3	1
Baker	3	1
Engraver	3	3
Mechanic	3	0
Stationer	3	7
Cabinetmaker	2	1
Designer	2	0
Embosser	2	0
Enameller	2	0
Bonnetier (hosiery)	2	4
Marble cutter	2	1
Smelter	2	1
Fumiste (stove repair)	2	0
Brewer	1	4
Hardware	1	4
Glazer	1	3
Currier and Tanner	1	5
Fur/Skin dealer	0	4
Seed dealer	0	2
Other trades and crafts— on each:	27	16

SOURCE: Same as Table 2.

but it was evidently in the two metropolises that the trend was especially perceptible.

Most electors in Paris were actually perfectly eligible, living in dwellings assessed at between 150 and 300 livres. (If the journée de travail had been set at three livres instead of one, as the Paris department had originally proposed, over two-thirds of the electors would have been ineligible.) Still, 73 electors did fail to meet the property requirements for eligibility—either because they were not on the tax rolls, or more commonly, because they lived in residences assessed at under the minimum requirement of 150 livres.[22] In and of itself this is inconclusive: a few of these electors (like Victor Bach) turned out to be men whose principal property was located outside of Paris. In other cases the voters may have been unaware of the ineligibility. But there can be no doubt that in many of these instances the voters were conscious of what they were doing. When they chose Besanemot, mercier, 70 livres, or Guillot, ouvrier rubanist, 50 livres—as they did in the faubourg Antoine—they signified that one thing they were *not* concerned with was choosing substantially propertied men to represent them.

‡ II ‡

Though the Directory had repeatedly cautioned voters to keep "those execrable men of '93" at arm's length, in Paris and other cities such "proven patriots" now swelled the electoral lists. The government's counsel had been flaunted, and in the proclamation of 9 germinal the government gave its response. This in turn further crystallized the breach between Jacobins and Directorials. Jacobin journalists—including those who had been receiving subsidies from the Directory—balked at the threats contained in this proclamation. Vatar's unsubsidized *Journal des hommes libres* and Coesnon-Pel-

---

Directory's other agents. See A.N. C 530/Bouches-du-Rhône. Other departments where the charge was made that some electors were "sans qualité et sans propriété" include Allier, Ardèche, Aude, Basses-Alpes, Hautes-Pyrénées, and Vaucluse, but only in Vaucluse was it alleged that a substantial number of electors were ineligible.

[22] A.N. AF iii 261 (Seine): Commune de Paris: La Commission des contributions directs, au Citoyen Mathieu, commissaire près l'administration central, 8 floréal VI. Enclosed is a list of the assessed valuation of each elector's residence. Also, A.N. C 534/Seine: Liste des Citoyens . . . qui n'avaient pas le droit de voter.

lerin's *Ami de la Patrie* led the resistance. In Paris and the provinces the Directory's posters were torn down, its motives impugned, its persecution of "the people's true friends" attacked. But the Jacobins' chagrin was diluted with disappointment and fear. New moves by the Directory, including the dismissal of Pierre Tissot and other men who had been brought into the Police Ministry by Sotin, were seen for precisely the warnings they were meant to be. Democratic circles were rife with rumors that others, such as the municipal officials of the 10th arrondissement, were about to be dismissed. There was even talk of the impending arrest of people like Victor Bach, and on 16 germinal (5 April) the Central Police Bureau reported a rumor circulating in the Tuilleries that certain "anarchist" electors had already been arrested.[23]

Under these circumstances the men who were trying to organize for the electoral assembly had to reconsider their strategy, especially their choice of candidates for the Legislature. We will never know who might have been elected in Paris had the Directory not intervened on 9 germinal. But it was likely that bold candidacies would have been put forward in the free elections that Jacobins had anticipated. Now such plans were being scuttled. Here, for instance, is the convincing report of one police observer who monitored the Café Chrétien.

> It was being asked whether, after the Directory's proclamation, they should elect those citizens who had previously been proposed, such as *Bouchotte* [War Minister in the Year II], *Pache* [Mayor of Paris in the Year II and now retired to the countryside], *Antonelle, LePelletier* [like Antonelle, an outspoken democratic publicist, defendant at the Vendôme trial, and activist in the Versailles Constitutional Circle], *Xavier Audouin* [Pache's son-in-law and Bouchotte's assistant], *Duhem* [an unbending Montagnard expelled from the Convention after Thermidor], etc. A citizen replied that if the Electoral Assembly names those men, the Legislature will annul the election.[24]

The need to pass over such admired figures seemed clear, though

[23] A.N. F⁷ 3688/13: report dated 12 germinal, and report marked "du 11 au 12 germinal"; report by Agent No. 46, 13 germinal, and by Agent No. 33, 14 germinal. The Central Bureau's report is in Aulard, *Paris*, IV, 597.
[24] A.N. F⁷ 3054.

the observer reported the bitterness of the café's habitués over the tyranny that deprived them of a really free choice.[25]

When the electoral assembly convened at the Oratoire on 20 germinal (9 April), certain electors busily promoted individual candidacies while others were trying to draw up whole slates.[26] The inner workings of the assembly were chronicled in detail by the Directory's principal observer: assistant commissioner to the Seine department, Dupin, who submitted three or four reports daily. On the second day he told of a list of nominees that was winning approval even among such militants as Daux, formerly on the revolutionary committee in Gravilliers section. Safe moderates who could scarcely offend the Directory dominated the slate, along with a sprinkling of democrats who would presumably ride in on the others' respectability if the Directory was serious about annulling elections. Now a balanced slate would have been necessary under any circumstances since the democrats did not have a clear majority. But as a response to the Directory's threats, the balance of this slate was tilted far to the center and represented a fatalistic compromise. It included ex-conventionnels Cambacérès, Genissieu, and Berlier (men of the Plain who had on occasion supported the Mountain); the Minister of Justice in the Year II, Gohier; Monge and Berthollet, respected savants who symbolized the role of the Institut's intellectuals in Directorial France; and three lesser known republican officials who were probably directorials: Duviquet, Bexon, and Faure. The democrats were represented by Tissot, Biauzat, Raisson, and from the *Invalides*, Groslaire.[27] The latter

[25] In the weeks before the elections, the young protégé of Robespierre's, Marc-Antoine Jullien, jotted in his notebook the names of 60 possible candidates for the coming elections. This list is a likely indication of the men that might have been chosen had the Directory not intervened with its threat. The names include Sotin, Prieur de la Marne, Lindet, Réal, Biauzat, Xavier Audouin, Raisson, Tissot, Antonelle, Hesiné. See V. M. Dalin, "Marc-Antoine Jullien nach dem 9 thermidor," *Babeuf-Studien*, ed. W. Markov (Berlin, 1961), pp. 196-97.

[26] See A.N. F⁷ 3688/14 and F⁷ 3054. Some of the names mentioned in rumors were the "Babeuvist" Claude Fiquet; adjutant-general Jorry; former justice of the peace Hu; the journalist and defense lawyer at Vendôme, Réal; Antonelle; Daubigny; Lémery, and Baudrais.

[27] A.N. C 534 (Seine): Dupin to Directory, 21 germinal, evening. A slate that was even closer to the center was proposed in Baslieux, *Aux Electeurs* (n.l., n.d.), B.N. Lb42/1819: Gohier, Cambacérès, Bexon, Berlier, Oudard,

three had belonged to the Rue du Bacq Club, whose members (including Vatar, not an elector) were extremely active behind the scenes and in the assembly.[28] The inclusion of Tissot was no accident; by all accounts he was the symbolic standard-bearer of the democratic cause—a man admired almost universally among politically conscious democrats, Jacobin and sans-culotte alike. As one police report put it: "Tissot's partisans are stirring in every direction to see to it that he is borne to the Legislature. It is already agreed among them that Tissot will immediately propose the [distribution of the] milliard to the troops."[29]

UNCERTAINTY prevailed in the initial act of the electoral assembly—the designation of presiding officers. When the first ballot for president of the assembly was taken, according to the *Journal des hommes libres*, Genissieu was the Jacobins' candidate, while Cambacérès "was considered by public opinion . . . as likely to bring about a division in the Electoral Assembly," that is, to do the Directory's bidding. A third candidate, Delavigne, was described as a "pure royalist."[30] With a majority of 341 votes needed for victory, the first ballot failed to produce a winner: Genissieu: 335; Cambacérès: 194; Delavigne: 46; scattered votes: 105. Genissieu carried the second ballot 371/606, but Cambacérès edged out the democrats' candidate Tissot for the post of secretary, 325/607 on the second ballot. Division further crystallized, without yielding a decisive victory, in the voting for three assistant secretaries (*scrutateurs*). After two ballots failed to produce a clear majority for either side, the final ballot yielded mixed results, with two conservatives and one Jacobin

---

Faure, Gaultier-Biauzat, Goupillau de Fontenay, Genissieu, Duviquet, Paganelle, and Réal.

[28] In one of his illuminating reports, Agent No. 46 wrote: "I later found myself with several republican electors against whom I myself had certain misgivings. . . . I found myself with Vatar (who was not an elector) and with Réal, Brutus Maignet, Marcellin, Bach, Raisson, Bonhommet, Biauzat, Magendie, Lacombe, Coesnon-Pellerin, Antonelle, etc., etc." These "men whom circumstances have kept at a distance until now," convinced the observer that they did not wish to provoke a return of the Terror—a message that they would presumably try to impart to other uncommitted electors. (A.N. F7 3054, 9 germinal.) Note that most of those mentioned belonged to the Rue du Bacq Club.

[29] A.N. F7 3688/13: report of 22 germinal.

[30] *J. hommes libres* No. 326, 21 germinal VI.

elected by close votes. Thus, with the balloting for presiding officers completed, it was still uncertain where the balance of power lay.[31]

A break came in the next order of business, the verification of credentials. Contested delegates were required to go before committees chosen by a standard and impartial method. A committee reporting on the first disputed case recommended that an elector named LaMaignière be expelled by virtue of the law of 5 ventôse Year VI which barred "rebels" from the assemblies, since he had been the presiding officer of a seditious primary assembly during the vendémiaire revolt of the Year IV. The full assembly then debated this recommendation, with conservatives arguing that old conflicts should be forgotten, and that only persons specifically indicted after Vendémiaire came under the law of 5 ventôse. Jullien de Toulouse, a former Montagnard, replied that the committee's report should be adopted "since there was a conspiracy in vendémiaire," and presidents of the primary assemblies at that time had supported it. When Limodin, whom the Jacobins execrated, tried to speak in support of the accused vendémiairist, commotion erupted; Biauzat demanded that Limodin be arrested as a *provocateur*, which he later revealed himself to be. After order was finally restored, and the question further debated at length, president Genissieu took the floor and proceeded to justify the Jacobins' confidence in him. He maintained that the law of 5 ventôse *was* applicable to the presidents of sectional assemblies in the Year IV. A vote was taken— twice—and each time it was decided that LaMaignière should be expelled. This set the pattern, for in all other disputed cases the rulings supported the Jacobin position. In all, thirty-two other vendémiairists, ex-nobles, and scissionnaires were expelled. The fight over credentials proved to be decisive.[32]

Agent Dupin reported to the Directory with increasing consternation that some of its most loyal supporters—including its commissioner to the Seine department, Mathieu—were being ruled against in cases where schisms had occurred in the primary assemblies. Conversely, notorious "anarchists" like Victor Bach were being

<hr/>

[31] B.N. Mss (nouv. acq. fran.) No. 2718: P. V. de l'Assemblée Electorale, Département de la Seine, an VI (original copy). The third ballot for three scrutateurs produced the following results, with 659 voting: Minier 333, Biauzat 320, Belard 318 (elected); Vollée 310, Tissot 298, Cretté 298 (defeated).

[32] A.N. C 534: Dupin to Directory, 24 germinal; A.N. F⁷ 3054: rapport du 24 germinal, Agent No. 46; *L'Indépendant* No. 206, 26 germinal.

seated. In the case of Bach it was alleged that he was unqualified because he was neither a resident nor a taxpayer. (Bach later proved that he was a property holder in his native Allier department.) Meanwhile, Bach's success cheered his partisans who were heard to murmur, "il se f**** de nous avec leurs contributions; n'avons nous pas assez contribué de nos personnes?" And on the next day La-Revellière's friend Lenoir-Laroche and his fellow delegates were excluded, while a group of former terrorists headed by Leymerie was admitted in their place.

Even a well-planned attempt to challenge Antonelle's eligibility failed. While Dupin himself submitted accusatory documentation to the committee, Antonelle's friends were busy. "Several detached themselves," Dupin related, "and roamed around the committee, apparently to prepare their batteries in advance." The documents designed to impugn Antonelle's eligibility happen to have survived among the assembly's working papers and are a revealing blend of technicality and political bias. The first charged that he had recently requested and received a civic inscription from the 10th arrondissement municipality, claiming that he had lost his original, but that there was no record of his having received one previously. The second charged that his opinions were anti-governmental, particularly in his *"Lettres de l'hermite* which were reproduced in their entirety in the *Journal des hommes libres*." (They were written while he stood trial with Babeuf at Vendôme.) A third document accused him of intriguing to be elected. The committee rejected the challenge on all three grounds and voted to seat him.[33]

When the impartially chosen committees had completed their work, all electoral schisms were decided in favor of the democrats, with Directorials and vendémiairists coming out on the losing side. Lenoir-Laroche, Mathieu, and other conservatives were excluded, while Bach, Leymerie, and Antonelle were seated. The democrats were picking up momentum, and perhaps for this reason the Directory tried another countermeasure. On 23 germinal (12 April) it suppressed the *Journal des hommes libres* and Coesnon-Pellerin's *Ami de la Patrie* as "the habitual echoes of the anarchist faction." But even this blow did not produce the desired sur-

[33] B.N. Mss (nouv. acq. fran.) No. 2718: report by the 12th committee of the electoral assembly; A.N. C 534: Dupin to Directory, 25 germinal, 4:30 and 10 P.M., and 28 germinal, 9 P.M.

render. As one pro-Jacobin police observer wrote, the suppression "has caused an outcry among republicans who, however, are not in the least frightened." Dupin's running commentary on the assembly indicates that although this decree was a harsh blow, each victory over credentials made the democrats more energetic. Dupin even commented on how they deployed themselves physically: "The exagérés have changed tactics. Instead of gathering on one side of the hall, they are developing a broad front, spreading across the whole hall; by thus taking up so much space they appear to be in even greater number." Their deportment as a group seemed manifest to him: "The friends of the government are not in force," he lamented; "they leave for dinner, while the exagérés bring a piece of bread with them." Success appeared to be cumulative and self-generating. "The only energy is to be found in the party of the exagérés. The others are discouraged and disheartened. They are relying on the Directory to annul the whole proceeding."[34]

Besides the ultimate threat of complete annulment two other dangers loomed more imminently for the electors. First, a lack of time to complete their work. Second, a schism or walk-out by Directorials. Protracted balloting for officers and the arguments over credentials had used up six of the ten days allowed by law for the convocation of the electoral assemblies. Disorder and controversy had caused exorbitant delays that irritated everyone, and which each side blamed on the other. On the 25th the pro-Jacobin *Indépendant* suggested that since many more deputies had to be elected than was usual, in order to fill the seats emptied by the Fructidor purge as well as the regular number of vacancies, the rule allowing only ten days ought to be suspended by the Legislature. On the same day one of the electors—Brutus Magnier, a well-known democratic activist—personally petitioned the Legislature for such a suspension of the rules. In addition to its need of electing additional deputies, he explained that implementation of the law of 5 ventôse "requires a staggering amount of work in order to expel the

[34] A.N. F⁷ 3054: rapport du 24 germinal, Agent No. 46. Dupin observed in his report for 23 germinal, evening (A.N. C 534) that the decree suppressing the Jacobin newspapers was "un signal heureux que donne le gouvernment aux électeurs qui lui sont fidèles. D'autres sont étourdi du coup." But his three reports for 25 germinal (1, 4:30, 10 P.M.) described the democrats' continuing aggressiveness. See also *Journal des campagnes et des armées* No. 753, 25 germinal VI.

émigrés' relatives, the rebels, the nobles, and the vendémiairists."
And if the Legislature could not grant an extension, he asked that
the assembly at least be allowed to prolong its daily sessions beyond the hours set by law. The petition was rebuffed out of hand,
the Council passing to the order of the day.[35]

At the midway point a second danger was the possibility of schism.
Rumors about such an impending maneuvre by the Directorials had
started during the controversy over Victor Bach's admission. But
Dupin's opinion at the time was that it was unlikely because "I
do not see a man of courage to lead it."[36] Unbeknownst to him,
however, a plan was afoot. Those who were anxious to break away
from the Jacobins at the Oratoire were doubtless encouraged by a
massive output of inflammatory propaganda designed to sully the
assembly. Pamphlets and placards appeared in great volume, smear-
ing some of the ex-terrorists who had been chosen as electors—a
useful preliminary if the Directorials were to pose as a pure rem-
nant that must separate from such a rabble in order to discharge its
duty in orderly fashion. Placards began to announce that a schism
was inevitable and necessary "so that the fanatics can be identified
and excluded from the Legislature." With audacious mendacity,
Directorial publicists ground out their allegations linking people as
varied as Réal and Antonelle in an anarchist plot, and reaching
down into the ranks of more obscure electors to point out who had
belonged to a revolutionary committee, who had been a *septembriseur*, or who had been on Babeuf's famous lists. This attack culminated later in one placard naming no less than 26 electors as
part of a "Babeuvist conspiracy" entitled inconsistently enough
*Tentatives de réaliser le système de Babeuf par la voie des
élections.*[37]

With the way prepared by such libels, the expulsion of the
vendémiairists and contested delegates created a ready-made nucleus
for a schism. The alleged irregularities in their expulsion, as well as
additional charges of fraud or illegality, provided a suitable pretext.
By 26 germinal (15 April) about sixty men were ready to form an

[35] *L'Indépendant* No. 205, 25 germinal. A.N. C 432, fol. 181: Un électeur de
l'an VI au Conseil des 500, 25 germinal (signed Magnier).

[36] A.N. C 534: Dupin to Directory, 25 germinal, 10 P.M.

[37] The pamphlets and placards may be found in A.N. AF III 100. Reports
on their circulation are reprinted in Aulard, *Paris*, IV, 600-601, 603, 606, 634.

assemblée scissionnaire. Retiring to the Institut de France in the Louvre, where they held their sessions under protection of the authorities, their number eventually totaled about two hundred. Two of the Oratoire's duly elected scrutateurs deserted to the Louvre. Other prominent scissionnaires included Limodin, Mathieu, Lenoir-Laroche, and a reactionary lawyer named Guyot-Desherbiers who became a *porte-parole* for the group. The scissionnaires were a mixed lot of crypto-royalists, Directorial conservatives, and a few employees whose prime motive might have been fear for their jobs. (Dupin, for his part, had ordered all electors who were employees of the Seine department to join the schism.) Some scissionnaires may have been genuinely affronted by the alleged frauds and the palpable disorder of the "exagérés," not the least being the presence of a partisan crowd outside the Oratoire. But politics was the controlling motive, and the *Indépendant* was on firm ground when it charged that the schism had been planned so well in advance that special credentials "were ready from the first moment." Moreover, scrupulous honesty was scarcely a virtue that could be claimed by scissionnaires since some of their number attempted to sabotage the majority at the Oratoire by absconding with the procès-verbal, and by having the porters abruptly dismissed.[38]

The assemblée scissionnaire of the Institut or Louvre almost immediately published its formal protest against the assemblée mère of the Oratoire. This *Acte de Scission* declared that the verification of credentials at the Oratoire was decided without regard to law, and that the assembly had seated people who had no right to be there. (The full details on the 73 ineligible electors only came to light later.) Therefore the signators separated from it and from "the choices that violence, intrigue, cabal, and the influence of conspirators had dictated." They did so "in order to offer the Legislature pure choices that the entire Republic could recognize as worthy of its constitution." A typical comment in the Directorial press provided the necessary gloss. The schism "will at least have the effect of preventing the larger assembly [Oratoire] from assigning its votes to violent and fearsome men; because in that case

[38] *L'Indépendant* No. 209, 29 germinal; A.N. C 534: Dupin to Directory, 27 germinal.

the majority will expose itself to seeing its choices annulled, in favor of those chosen by the minority scissionnaire."[39]

For the democrats, then, the worst had happened. The Directory's threats to annul their choices were likely to be fulfilled since the great department of the Seine could still be represented by a slate of deputies chosen at the Louvre. It had been hard enough to draw up an acceptable slate before; now their hands were further tied, and the need for compromise even greater. According to Dupin, some electors still insisted on voting their consciences instead of bowing to expediency. Leymerie, Jullien de Toulouse, Michel, and Daubigny, among others, purportedly continued to press for the election of Bach and Antonelle. But others like Réal opposed this, arguing "we must not spoil our chance too much." Dupin now had the satisfaction of reporting that the spirited words which had been shouted during the victorious verification battles were no longer to be heard.[40] Some evidently became despondent: in a printed broadside that revealed timidity and despair, Raisson placed himself out of the running. Antonelle, too, bowed out, though in a more affirmative spirit of pragmatism. A police observer reported: "Antonelle is canvassing various groups and saying: 'I have just learned, my friends, that you wish to name me to the Legislature; don't do any such thing. You will ruin me. I will be more useful to you without any public role.' "[41]

‡ III ‡

By the time the assembly began balloting for deputies on the 27th of germinal (16 April) it was operating under extraordinary strains. Only three days remained for choosing no less than sixteen deputies, plus departmental officials. The problem of agreeing upon slates in the face of numerous possible combinations had not been definitively solved; no unified group had a clear working majority, so that bargains still had to be struck. Successive threats by the Directory—each more specific than the next—had culminated in the ultimate act of schism. With the tensions exacerbated, and the

[39] *Acte de Scission,* reprinted in *Moniteur,* 30 germinal (p. 841); *Publiciste,* 28 germinal, quoted in Aulard, *Paris,* iv, 607.

[40] A.N. C 534: Dupin to Directory, 28 germinal, 9 p.m.

[41] A.N. F⁷ 3688/14: Coup d'oeil sur ce qui s'est passé à l'assemblée électorale séant à l'Oratoire; *Moniteur,* 28 germinal (p. 834), on Raisson.

problem of strategy complicated, it is understandable that the balloting did not produce an harmonious pattern. Some winning candidates garnered over 325 votes but others won less than 200; 6 choices polled over 80 percent of the votes cast—with Gohier winning 91 percent—but others won fewer than 60 percent (see Table 4).

TABLE 4

The Votes for Deputies in the Paris Electoral
Assembly (Oratoire)

Deputy	Votes for/ Total Vote	Percentage of Votes cast
1. Gaultier-Biauzat	304/445	68
2. Monge	360/452	80
3. Cambacérès	336/396	85
4. R. Lindet	320/429	74
5. Oudard	240/425 [2nd ballot]	56
6. Gohier	325/355	91
7. Leblanc	317/363	87
8. *General Moulin	326/406	80
9. Tissot	254/431	59
10. Castel (de Vincennes)	207/326	63
11. Berlier	286/403	71
12. *Lamarque	282/406 [2nd ballot]	70
13. Roger Ducos	277/327	84
14. Sijas	171/265	64
15. Dupuch	243/337	72
16. Gomegeon	190/373	51
17. Prieur de la Marne	155/395	38

SOURCE B.N. Mss (n.a.f.), No. 2178: procès-verbal [original copy].
* Declined.

The difficulty of explaining these variations is compounded by the fact that the number of voters on each ballot varied, in most cases between 450 and 350, but falling below 350 four times, with a low of 265 voters in one case. Still, when all this is noted, a sense of direction or an underlying consensus can be discerned within the divided and disorderly proceedings.

In choosing Gaultier-Biauzat as its first candidate, the assembly struck a perfect balance between respectability and pro-Jacobin orientation that its majority was seeking. An experienced judge who was a member of the political elite, Biauzat's close association with the Neo-Jacobins was no secret, and he could even be identified with the image of Babeuf as democratic martyr. The three next choices were heavily weighted to the side of moderation with Cambacérès and Monge representing the center, and Robert Lindet, the past glories of the Committee of Public Safety from which he was purged by the thermidorians. All were highly experienced and impeccably middle class; all won over 300 votes, and more than two-thirds of the votes cast (see Table 4).

Indecisiveness, however, reigned in the voting for the fifth seat, with two ballots required before someone obtained a majority. According to the *Indépendant*, one of whose editors sat as an elector, the competition was principally between Oudard (chief of the criminal division in the Ministry of Justice) and Antonelle.[42] It was presumably at this point that Antonelle urged his supporters to pass over him; in any case Oudard carried the second ballot, 240/425. Following this, consensus was restored and the next three seats were allotted without any significant contest: Gohier (Minister of Justice in the Year II), Leblanc (a pro-Jacobin who served on the departmental administration at various times), and Moulin (a pro-Jacobin general). Again, each won over 300 votes and over 80 percent of the votes cast. Moulin, however, declined to accept the nomination.

For the ninth seat the democrats made their decisive bid. Mustering 59 percent of the vote, they elected Pierre Tissot, 254/431. The reports are unequivocal on the impact that this had. "The moment that the ballot was counted the cry of long live the nation and the Republic arose; inside and outside [Tissot's] partisans declared: *this one is worth more than all the others put together*."[43] One more vote was taken on this next-to-last day and Castel, identified only as commander of the national guard in the outlying canton of Vincennes, was chosen. While there is a paucity of information about this candidate, the Directory's agents reacted negatively and one suspects that he was a Jacobin candidate produced to replace some more controversial or hesitant figure.[44]

[42] *L'Indépendant* No. 210, 30 germinal.
[43] A.N. F⁷ 3688/13, dossier "Bureau de Direction": rapport du 29 germinal.
[44] Comments on the men elected may be found in the Directory's papers,

There remained but one day in which to fill seven more legislative seats and to choose all departmental administrators and judges. Under such tremendous pressure tempers flared and disorder was inevitable; "incredible . . . hideous," Dupin declared. General Jorry, whose candidacy had been rebuffed, fell out publicly with his fellow electors, cursing them as "intrigans, agioteurs de scrutins, des f***** coquins."[45] Réal, who had served as an attorney for the Vendôme defendants, was working feverishly to be elected, but was passed over in favor of the ex-conventionnel Berlier who was also elected at the Louvre. For the next choice (seat No. 12) uncertainty again prevailed. Réal made another bid and picked up a number of votes; the "Babeuvist" Claude Fiquet had somewhat less support, and a third candidate—from the moderate side—was Champagne, a member of the Institut and respectable enough to have been named by the assemblée scissionnaire. Other votes were scattered for as many as thirty different candidates. Three worksheets of the bureaux or sections into which the assembly divided for the casting and counting of votes have survived for this ballot, and one can see precisely what happened.[46] Finding themselves badly split in so many directions, a large group of electors concerted to find a way out by shifting their votes on the second ballot to an entirely new or outside candidate: the popular deputy from the Dordogne, François Lamarque (see Table 5). Lamarque won handily, 282/406 on this second ballot. Unfortunately it was to no avail, since having also been chosen in his own department he was later forced to decline.

One more moderate was chosen for the Oratoire's slate—ex-conventionnel Roger Ducos who later became an accomplice of Bonaparte's in the brumaire coup. But his candidacy represented the last effort to compromise, or the last time the moderates would prevail. On the next vote, when attendance was at its lowest point ever (one recalls Dupin's earlier complaint about the exagérés and their piece of bread), the militants put across Sijas—a veteran of Bou-

A.N. AF III 261; other excerpts have been reproduced uncritically in A. Kuscinski, *Les Deputés au Corps Législatif: Conseil des 500, Conseil des Anciens* (Paris, 1905), Appendix. (This book is an *instrument de travail* providing lists of deputies by departments and years.)

[45] A.N. C 534: Dupin to Directory, 29 germinal, first letter.

[46] B.N. Mss (nouv. acq. fran.) No. 2718: P. V. and worksheets of the bureaux.

TABLE 5

Balloting for the Twelfth Seat in the Electoral
Assembly (Oratoire)

First Ballot: Bureau 2		*First Ballot: Bureau 1*	
Claude Fiquet	16	Fiquet	12
Champagne (de l'Institut)	15	Champagne (de l'Institut)	23
Réal	35	Grandin	8
Grandin	4	Réal	7
Fillassier	4	Prieur	4
Scattered Votes	27	Scattered Votes	30

Second Ballot: Bureau 2	
Lamarque	71
Champagne (de l'Institut)	13
Réal	10
Scattered Votes	13

chotte's War Department in the Year II—who by reputation was a Jacobin stalwart and to the Directory's informants, a *maratiste outré*. After Sijas, an obscure ex-Montagnard from the Colonies, Dupuch, was named; a second look reveals that in the Year III Dupuch had been among the few conventionnels to support the sans-culottes who rose against the thermidorian Convention.[47]

The assembly was drawing to a frenzied close with the prospect of not even electing all the deputies, let alone local officials. But before time expired a gesture was made to a major group within the democrats' ranks—the *invalides*. Though the militant *invalide* Groslaire had been frequently mentioned in earlier speculation about candidates, the electors chose instead Gomegeon, who like Groslaire was active in the Rue du Bacq Constitutional Circle. Possibly the fact that Gomegeon's wounds were extensive, including the loss of a hand at Jemappes, was an asset in the prevailing circumstances. But for all the confusion (including yet another attempt by Réal to take the seat for himself) and the possible mixed motives, it is significant that electoral politics still involved such a fundamental kind of group representation. As a reflection of this, the naming of Gomegeon, like Tissot's election, had some direct meaning to

[47] On Dupuch see Kuscinski's standard *Dictionnaire des Conventionnels*.

those who thronged outside the assembly. The choice "was received with great satisfaction among all the soldiers."[48]

The final ballot was an equally ringing affirmation. But for a technicality (which will be examined directly) Prieur de la Marne would have been the final deputy chosen at the Oratoire. As a member of the Committee of Public Safety in the Year II, Prieur had represented not simply the patriotism of that body, but also its commitment to the egalitarian revolution, as Prieur's fellow member Lindet really had not. Like Lindet, Prieur had been unreconcilable to the Directory and had endured a kind of self-enforced exile. Uncompromised, he remained a popular figure among democrats through 1798. The choice of Prieur, along with the Jacobin *invalide* Gomegeon, was thrown at the Directory as the sun set on the last day of the electoral assemblies.

Officially, however, the tabulations of the last ballot indicate that Prieur, though the leading candidate, received only 155 out of 395 votes cast—43 short of the necessary majority. The assembly was then forced to dissolve under the governing statutes, and the seat was left unfilled. Because the worksheets of all four bureaux of the assembly were preserved for this particular ballot, one can see that this appearance of a losing try is misleading. Whatever ways the voters in each of the four sections had of communicating with each other to concert on candidates evidently broke down under the tumult that marked the assembly's inadequate final hours. The worksheets show that Prieur received all 155 votes in three of the four sections. Signals had apparently been crossed; in the first bureau— not notably different from the others in its random composition —he failed to receive a single vote, with over seventy votes going to the person of one Bernier.[49] It would seem likely that the necessary 43 votes could have been won in the first bureau had the candidacy been signaled. In that case the frustrations of that last day would have been at least slightly diminished.

[48] A.N. F⁷ 3688/14: rapport du 4 floréal.
[49] B.N. Mss (nouv. acq. fran.) No. 2718:

Bureau 1		Bureau 2		Bureau 3		Bureau 4	
Bernier	72	Prieur	39	Prieur	59	Prieur	57
Misc.	19	Réal	34	Sotin	7	Chazal	22
		Chazal	12	Réal	7	Sotin	5
		Misc.	22	Champagne	6	Misc.	20
				Misc.	14		

‡ IV ‡

The delegation chosen at the Oratoire was composed of three types of men. First, respectable moderates whose politics were essentially Directorial, though generally lacking the pronounced anti-Jacobinism of the latter: Berlier, Cambacérès, Ducos, Monge, Oudard. Second, experienced and respected republicans who were associated in some degree with the Jacobin cause, past or present: Biauzat, Dupuch, Gohier, Lamarque, Leblanc, Lindet, General Moulin, Prieur de la Marne. Finally, three men were chosen directly from the ranks of local Parisian democrats: Gomegeon, Sijas, and Tissot. Castel is difficult to place with any accuracy, but might belong in the last group.

Other frequently mentioned candidates had not been elected: Antonelle, perhaps because he withdrew; the Vendôme defendant Claude Fiquet, because he had only a small group of backers. Disappointments and recriminations mounted, especially on the last day, when Dupin reported that little agreement prevailed among the electors: "This one pushed himself forward, that one was insulting." Jorry exploded at being passed over and so did the former sectionnaire and justice of the peace Hu. Furious at not having been elected, Hu publicly declared that he had been betrayed and that he was finished with politics; "that the others are a bunch of hotheads; that he realizes how they are being manipulated by some powerful person, behind the scenes, who is misleading them and will end up having them all shot or deported." Réal, who seems to have been a perennial loser on each ballot, "was in a very bad humor and clamored against ingratitude." He, too, claimed to have been betrayed, especially by those whom he had defended as a lawyer at Vendôme; according to Réal, they had previously agreed to back him but evidently "ils aiment mieux leurs complices que leurs défenseurs." Réal maintained to the end that if they had elected him he would have defended them from the Legislature's tribune and would have used every means at his disposal "to humble the Directory's arrogance."[50]

In addition to such ambitious and disappointed individuals, an-

[50] A.N. F⁷ 3688/14: rapport du 4 floréal, Agent No. 33 (on Hu); *Ibid.*: suite du rapport sur l'assemblée électorale, 2 floréal (on Réal). Réal's career is sketched in L. Bigard, *Le Comte Réal, ancien Jacobin* (Versailles, 1937).

other group in the assembly that made agreement difficult was the moderates who remained at the Oratoire instead of deserting to the Louvre. As one such individual later tried to explain to his patron Merlin, he had remained at the Oratoire, despite the presence of the anarchists, in order to fight them along with other good republicans. And if Tissot ("chaud"), Castel, Gomegeon ("nul") and Sijas ("dangereux") had been elected there, so had many acceptable candidates.[51] But despite all the pressures of time, threats, personal ambition and a hostile minority, the results were impressive and the agreement considerable. Only twice did the voting go more than one ballot. And only on the first ballot for the twelfth seat was there a wide-open contest. Even then, on the second ballot a compromise candidate was found on whom a substantial majority of electors could unite.

Meanwhile the two hundred electors who had seceded to the Louvre completed their work with dispatch, winning extravagant praise in the Directorial press. The assemblée scissionnaire also chose moderate ex-conventionnels like Berlier and Chenier, and savants Cabanis and Champagne. But its slate was top-heavy with second-line conservatives like Lenoir-Laroche (personally beholden to the Directory), and outright reactionaries like Guyot-Desherbiers, who were attempting to forge a conservative coalition. Seven deputies-elect were chosen from the ranks of the scissionnaires themselves. Working so efficiently that they had enough time to choose a new departmental administration as well, the scissionnaires unblushingly rewarded three more of their own adherents.[52]

From almost any point of view (except the fact that most candidates of any political persuasion were bound to be bourgeois with previous experience in government) there was a marked contrast between the slates of the Oratoire and the Louvre. The first was dominated by former revolutionaries and men for the most part sympathetic to Jacobinism; the latter was a purposefully conservative slate of *gouvernistes* ready to do the Directory's bidding.

A corresponding difference is apparent in the social composition of the rival assemblies (see Table 6). The scissionnaires represented

[51] A.N. AF iii 261: Fournier to Merlin, 3 floréal.
[52] For the deputies, see Kuscinski, *Les Deputés au Corps Législatif;* for the departmental administrators see S. Lacroix, *Le Département de Paris et de la Seine pendant la Révolution* (Paris, 1904), pp. 369, 382-84.

TABLE 6

Social Composition of the Two Paris Electoral
Assemblies, Year VI

Occupation	Total No. of Electors[1]	Scissionnaires[2]	Percentage of Scissionnaires[3]
Elected Officials	32	13	41
Employees	125	40	32
Commissioners of the Directory	11	11	100
Judges	8	2	25
Négociants	15	5 ⎫	
Fabricants, etc.	10	7 ⎪	50
Bankers	1	1 ⎬	
Proprietors	13	5 ⎭	
Rentiers and Pensioners	27	7	30
Professionals	(101)	(45)	
Lawyers	54	26 ⎫	
Doctors	7	1 ⎪	
Architects	12	3 ⎬	45
Notaries	13	5 ⎪	
Teachers	15	10 ⎭	
Artists	12	—	
Men of Letters	8	3	38
Soldiers	12	1	08
Sans-culottes	(219)	(33)	
Marchands	45	8 ⎫	
Artisans and Shopkeepers	174	25 ⎬	15

[1] *Liste Générale des électeurs du département de la Seine pour l'an VI* (Impr. Ballard) in A.D.S., 2 AZ, 156.

[2] *Liste des Electeurs de la Seine en l'an VI qui se sont réunis au Louvre . . . le 26 germinal* (Impr. Ballard) in A.N. AF III 261.

[3] The definitive number of electors was 668; the final number of scissionnaires 207. The approximate percentage of scissionnaires was therefore 31 percent, but in a sense was higher since the maximum number of electors who actually voted at the Oratoire after the schism was 452.

31 percent of the total number of electors. Middle-class businessmen (négociants, etc.) who joined the schism constituted 50 percent of all electors from that group, while the professionals who went over to the Louvre represented 45 percent of all electors from that category. Conversely, only 15 percent of the sans-culotte electors (artisans, shopkeepers, and "ouvriers") left the Oratoire for the Louvre.[53] While they formed by far the largest single category of electors in the original assembly, the sans-culottes were only the third largest group at the Louvre, even in absolute numbers: there were 51 employees (including all 11 government commissioners), 45 professionals (including 26 lawyers), but only 33 artisans and shopkeepers voting at the Louvre.[54] As many as 186 (representing 85 percent of the total number of sans-culotte electors) stayed on at the Oratoire for at least some of the laborious balloting.

Differences in the property assessments of the electors in each assembly are not nearly as marked as the contrast in their social rank. For instance, ninety Parisian electors lived in dwellings assessed at over 1,000 livres. Of these 61 percent remained at the Oratoire, while 39 percent went over to the Louvre—a higher percentage for the Institut relatively (since it had only 31 percent of all electors), but of inconclusive significance. (Fourteen electors, incidentally, were in the over-2,000 bracket, and of these half left the "disorders" of the Oratoire to sit in the assemblée scissionnaire.) At the other end of the spectrum there is an indication of cleavage along economic lines. Of the 73 electors who were ruled ineligible because they lived in dwellings below the required 150 valuation or because they were not on the tax rolls, 63 (86 percent) remained at the Oratoire. Only 10 (14 percent), including vulnerable government employees, joined the schism.[55]

The social composition of the rival assemblies underscored the democratic aspect of the elections of the Year VI. The group of sans-culottes at the Oratoire—the largest group to begin with—emerged

---

[53] *Liste des Electeurs de la Seine en l'an VI qui se sont réunis au Louvre . . . le 26 germinal* (Impr. Ballard) in A.N. AF III 261.

[54] Imprimeur-libraire (4), épicier (4), papetier (3), mercier (2), bijoutier (2), orfèvre (2), parfumeur (2), one each: apothicaire, chapellier, dessinateur, fourbisseur, éventailliste, horloger, and 8 marchands (*Ibid.*). The more mechanical and manual crafts are notably underrepresented in this group.

[55] See A.N. AF III 261: La Commission des contributions directes . . . ; and A.N. C 534: Liste des Citoyens . . . qui n'avaient pas le droit de voter (cited in note 22, above).

as an even more prominent group after most Directorial conservatives withdrew, taking with them a disproportionately large number of high-status electors. At the Louvre the assemblée scissionnaire fulfilled the kind of middle-class domination that the architects of the Directorial constitution had anticipated. The composition of the Oratoire assembly indicated, on the contrary, what the complexion of political life could become even under that charter when democrats campaigned aggressively and effectively. Moreover, it suggests that politically conscious sectionnaires from the Years II and III could form a front with middle-class Jacobins to challenge the monopoly of authority held by the Directorials. The elections, in short, could have worked against the consolidation of a purely middle-class republic by broadening the range of constituents and attitudes represented in the Legislature, even if almost all the deputies were themselves from the middle class.

WITH NATIONAL attention fixed on Paris for the past month, the validation of its disputed elections became the touchstone of the campaign. A cascade of anonymous and libelous pamphlets had stigmatized the Oratoire assembly as a nest of subversion and impugned its proceedings with exaggerated charges of fraud and illegality. In its aftermath the lawyer Guyot-Desherbiers—a leader and nominee of the scissionnaires—produced a pamphlet summarizing these alleged charges against the majority assembly. To dispute his version a number of Jacobins in turn took up pen in friendly newspapers and set the record straight on damaging falsehoods like the supposed ineligibility of Victor Bach and Antonelle.[56] The fullest and more or less "official" Jacobin response to Desherbiers came in a pamphlet by Gaultier-Biauzat.[57]

Even Biauzat was pessimistic. The best to be hoped for was that at least the scissionnaires would also be excluded by the Legislature.[58] But even this hope was shattered. A special five-man legislative

---

[56] *Le Républicain* [formerly *J. hommes libres*] No. 11, 11 floréal VI: letter from Antonelle; *L'Indépendant* No. 223, 13 floréal: letter from Jullien de Toulouse; *Ibid.* No. 224, 14 floréal: letter from Valant.

[57] Gaultier-Biauzat, *Réfutation de toutes les imputations faites par le citoyen Desherbiers à l'Assemblée électorale du département de la Seine* (n.l., an VI) B.N. Lb42/ 549; *Le Républicain* Nos. 19-21, 19-21 floréal VI.

[58] See F. Mege, *Gaultier de Biauzat* (Paris, 1890), 1, 314: Biauzat to the municipal administration of Clermont, 8 floréal VI.

committee was appointed to scrutinize the Seine elections, and its laboriously detailed majority report did recommend that the choices of both assemblies be annulled. However, a minority report delivered by Guillemardet, at the undoubted behest of the Directory, urged that the Oratoire slate be annulled and that the Louvre scissionnaires be seated.[59] To the professed surprise and outrage of the entire spectrum of Jacobinism, this motion was approved: not only was the delegation from the Oratoire barred, but the minority deputation of Directorials was validated.[60] Thus was the signal given for enactment of the Directory's entire purge list, known to posterity as the law of 22 floréal Year VI.

[59] *Conseil des 500: Rapport fait par Savary au nom d'une commission spéciale . . . 16 floréal an 6* (Impr. Nationale), and *Discours de Guillemardet . . . 16 floréal an 6* (Impr. Nationale).

[60] See, e.g., *L'Indépendant* No. 229, 19 floréal VI.

PART FOUR

TOWARDS BRUMAIRE

CHAPTER XII

The Vicissitudes of Opposition: From Floréal
to the *Journée* of 30 prairial VII

L OOKING back on the Year VI, Buonarroti briefly described
its major event. In 1798, he recalled, "the struggle between
the immoral ones and the democrats was renewed; the latter prevailed and succeeded in choosing popular republicans as
deputies; [but] the people's will was ignored by the Directory
which exercised dictatorship. The democratic elections were annulled."[1] What must be added is that this was the most gratuitous
of setbacks. The era of upheaval was supposed to be over, constitutional normalcy to have arrived at last. Clubs, newspapers, and
elections had replaced conspiracies and armed demonstrations. Nonetheless the Directory resorted to arbitrary measures, and with this
crucial decision brusquely closed a promising chapter in the republic's history.

To account for this decision one need not emphasize personal
factors like the hypersensitive temperaments of directors Reubell,
Merlin, or LaRevellière. Their policy was representative of conservative republican opinion. A crucial step in this decision to purge the
elections was the Directory's careful monitoring of respectable newspaper opinion after it issued its threatening proclamation of 9 germinal. Only when satisfied that such opinion endorsed this policy did
the Directory act overtly. In so doing it affirmed its unwillingness to tolerate organized opposition or to legitimize public division
among republicans over certain issues. Jacobin opposition was
neither murderous (as opposition had once been), nor Babeuvist,
nor anything of the kind, but this was not necessarily the point.
Differences of opinion and conviction did exist, and no one was sure
where such differences might lead. From this point of view the
emergence of local Jacobin formations, built around clubs and newspapers and seemingly unsusceptible to manipulation by the Directorials, foretold new trials and tribulations for the forces of order.

Sitting in Paris, the Directory received hundreds of reports from

---

[1] Buonarroti Papers, B.N. Mss (nouv. acq. fran.) 20804, 6ème liasse: undated
fragment for an historical sketch of the Revolution.

the provinces recounting the development of these parties, the ensuing "disorders" in the primary assemblies, and the election of local meneurs. The exaggerated and tendentious language of these reports doubtless affected the Directory's perceptions, but even so it was responding to a real situation. The Parisian assemblies, directly observable by the government, served to confirm its worst fears. Hence, with the consent of respectable opinion, a policy of repression was announced. The momentum of the Jacobin resurgence was broken, as local cadres were thrown into tactical confusion by the 9 germinal proclamation. In addition it is likely that uncommitted electors were persuaded to abandon the *patriotes prononcés* whom they might otherwise have supported. The threat of schism and the resort to it in over twenty departments was further proof of the government's determination, though even so it was unable to control the thirty-odd electoral assemblies whose deliberations we have analyzed. The final step—the drafting and passage of the actual purge list of 22 floréal VI (11 May 1798)—was something of an anticlimax. The names ultimately included reflected anomalies of image and reputation as well as the influence of special-interest lobbying behind the scenes by conservative incumbents. In general the Directory was striking more at local parties than at particular individuals, who in a few cases were later provided with compensatory employment. The local basis of independent support rather than their own qualities is what barred such deputies-elect from the Legislature. The individuals could recover easily, the movement could not.

Paradoxically, then, the year VI showed the Jacobins embracing the constitution (liberally interpreted), and the Directorials suffering its mutilation in order, they would have said, to save it. In fact their own constitution was suited neither to their political objectives nor their elitist style. Their conservatism (relative to the advanced state of French public life) proved increasingly irreconcilable with their constitutional liberalism, though they did not admit this problem to be insoluble until Brumaire. Until then the governing elite presumed that with adjustments like Floréal, opposition would be contained and the republic would find its veritable direction. But this was not to be. The Jacobins were not stilled. On the contrary, being wrenched from their gradual adjustment to constitutionalism, they proved more contentious than before. In response the Directory was obliged to further tighten its grip and erode the liberties of 1789. Freedom of association and freedom of the press were indefinitely suspended in the wake of Floréal, though Vatar's incredible resourcefulness kept the *Journal des hommes libres* alive under several successive names until frimaire Year VII (December 1798). As its high-handed but indecisive methods became more common, the Directory's own reputation gradually declined, so that even conservatives grew disenchanted with it.

‡ I ‡

First impressions were misleading, however. A weak response by incumbent Jacobin deputies suggested that the Directorials would prevail without serious repercussions. Few in number and habitually committed to prudence, these deputies were unmoved to cause any dramatic scenes in an effort to prevent the purge. They might have felt in addition that outspoken criticism would be used by the Directory as evidence that an anarchist faction really did threaten the republic. Occasionally an appropriate hint of outrage was uttered in the legislative debates, only to be stifled as soon as spoken. Quirot, for instance, declared that the proposed purge was designed "to carry out a 9 thermidor to the journée of 18 fructidor," but this cogent insight was not taken up. The avalanche of propaganda about disorders, illegality, and intrigue in the elections, as well as several threatening messages from the executive, proved too much for the deputies to resist. Instead of outrage, a tone of resignation characterized the arguments against the purge bill.[2]

Distress was admittedly expressed over constitutional questions. It was argued that Fructidor was no precedent for the proposed purge since Fructidor had come months after the elections as a response to overt acts of subversion. Even notorious royalists had not been excluded *in advance* after being duly elected, whereas the government now wished to bar certain deputies only because of their reputations and surmises about their future activities. Secondly, a few speakers warned that by allowing the bill to be pushed through

---

[2] The debate is summarized in A. Meynier, *Le 22 floréal an VI et le 30 prairial an VII* (Paris, 1928), pp. 72-85, and Buchez and Roux, *Histoire parlementaire de la Révolution française*, xxxvii (Paris, 1838), 473-507. The repetitious speeches of individual deputies are available in the Maclure Collection (University of Pennsylvania Library) as well as the B.N.

without such normal procedures as a committee investigation of each disputed election, the legislature would be surrendering to dictation by the executive, thus disrupting the constitution's balance of power. As to the more basic question of sovereignty and the government's prior interference with the electoral process, only a muted concern was expressed in the legislative debates. Only from the outside was this issue given suitable emphasis, notably by the Parisian elector and deputy-designate Gaultier-Biauzat. In a pamphlet circulated among the deputies, he attacked the "system of schisms" illegally promoted by the Directory in order to manipulate the elections. But this damaging argument was scarcely taken up with the vigor that would have been justified.[3]

Most of the opposition speeches were in fact concerned not with principles but merely with anomalies in the proposed legislation. The inclusion of comparatively tranquil departments, and of respected incumbents like Gay-Vernon and Lamarque, was supposed to make one question the wisdom of the entire, hastily assembled bill. But even this cautious tactic failed to accomplish anything. As the debate proceeded, the opposition became increasingly demoralized, stoical, and acquiescent. Representative Guchan, returned by the Jacobins in Hautes-Pyrénées whom he had supported, meekly accepted his own purging with a dispiriting accommodation. Though General Jourdan spoke vigorously against the purge, he ended on a note of republican solidarity, adding the important proviso that he would completely support the law once it passed. François Lamarque, finally, was a central personage in this drama. The most influential incumbent destined for purging, he had been returned simultaneously by two of the assemblies most under attack: Seine and Dordogne. In the embarrassing position, along with seven others,[4] of having to deliberate on his own purge, this former spokesman for the Vendôme defendants and the Constitutional Circles ended his opposition by urging republicans to bend with the wind and support the government's decisions. What is more, rather than continue his opposition, he resigned. A police

---

[3] Gaultier-Biauzat, *Appel aux principes contre le système des scissions* (Impr. Guilhemat), B.N. Lb42/1855; *Le Républicain* No. 13, 13 floréal VI.

[4] Martel (Allier), T. Lindet (Eure), Ducos (Landes, Seine), Sautereau (Nièvre), Guchan (Hautes-Pyrénées), Dupuch (Seine), Gay-Vernon (Haute-Vienne).

report claims that this resignation—taken by most as a supreme gesture of compliance—was intended to serve as a trigger for "thirty or forty" other resignations, and thus to produce a dramatic gesture of opposition. If so, it aborted. Furthermore Lamarque was among the floréalized deputies who later accepted an ambassadorship offered by the Directory both as compensation and as a way of spiriting embarrassing individuals out of the country.[5]

Outside of the Legislature other floréalized nominees seemed to promise as little trouble. A number took up pen to defend their reputations and their departments' integrity, but like the legislative opposition, these pamphlets were marked by a spirit of grumbling acquiescence rather than outrage. Pamphlets defending the assemblies of Ardèche, Landes, Mont Blanc, Nièvre, and Vienne concentrated on refuting charges of irregularity and on describing the forces of local counterrevolution that had required firm resistance on the part of patriots. The authors took particular pains to justify their own conduct, past and present, and in so doing created an image of moderation that was decidedly overdrawn. To take them literally one could not conceive of such persons as Gleizal, Dardillac, Doppet, or Batbedat suffering the fate of purged oppositionists. These apologias were no more than self-righteous protestations rather than documents of principled opposition. Generally avoiding the ominous issues raised by the floréal purge, they concentrated on the alleged misrepresentation of local situations and reputations.[6]

---

[5] Lamarque's speeches are excerpted in Vatar's *Le Républicain* and in Buchez and Roux, *Histoire parlementaire*. For information on his career see Ch. Chevreux, "Les Papiers du Conventionnel François Lamarque," *R.F.*, LXXII (1919), 289-313. It is interesting to compare two comments on Lamarque in reference to this episode: the malevolent sarcasm of LaRevellière (*Mémoires*, II, 359-60), and the grudging respect of the royalist-leaning deputy Felix Faulcon (*Mélanges législatifs, historiques et politiques* [Paris, 1801], II, 178). The police report mentioned is in A.N. F7 3688/13, dossier "Direction," marked du 17 au 18 floréal VI.

[6] *Réponse du Citoyen Gleizal, à une partie de l'écrit signé Rouchon, Garilhe, Boisset* (Paris, Impr. Bailleul), B.N. Lb42/1871; *Précis historique des causes et des effets de la scission dans le départment de la Nièvre* (Paris, Imp. des républicains), A.N. F7 7414, fol. 5054; *Dardillac, ex-administrateur: au Corps législatif, au Directoire exécutif, à tous les Républicains* (Poitiers, an VI), A.N. F7 7414, fol. 5083; L. S. Batbedat, *Exposé de ce qui s'est passé dans le départment des Landes, relativement aux élections de l'an 6* (Impr. Lemaire), A.N. F7 7421, fol. 5898; Amadé Doppet, *Essai sur les calomnies et les persecutions dont on peut-être accablé en révolution, et sur la manière avec laquelle doit y repondre un bon citoyen* (A Carouge, an VI), B.N. Ln27/6193.

Restrained speeches like Jourdan's or stoical pamphlets like Doppet's were not likely to disrupt the republic's unwholesome equilibrium seriously. Unfortunately for the Directory, other Jacobin activists were unwilling to accept and abide by the floréal coup. While their numbers were now significantly reduced by the inevitable apathy that ensued, the committed rekindled their combative spirit and attacked the purge as intolerable and unacceptable. Indeed, the Directorys' repressive policies of the Year VI operated like a veritable self-fulfilling prophecy. The conspiratorial faction whose existence it had fabricated and denounced gradually came into being. Forced into disaffection, excluded from effective channels of legal protest, the Jacobin opposition adopted a posture of contemptuousness towards the Directory. The pamphlet became its major weapon —generally signed and defiant, occasionally unsigned and vituperative. From a period of healthy and open party competition the republic entered a kind of *fronde* in which both sides stood to lose.

‡ II ‡

The nature and significance of this opposition can only be grasped by appreciating the Jacobins' sense of frustration at the purge and the dissolution of their incipient parties. Villain d'Aubigny—a veteran of Bouchotte's War Department in the Year II, and a Parisian elector with wide-ranging contacts among democrats—perhaps expressed this as emphatically as anyone when he wrote over a year later:

> The sole recompense that I ask from the friends of liberty . . . is that when I have ceased to live they will engrave on my tomb just these words: *Named by the people elector in the Year VI, he never betrayed their confidence; he was faithful to his obligations and remained at the Oratoire.*[7]

The desire for such an extraordinary epitaph suggests the emotional investment of democrats in the electoral campaign of 1798, and their

---

[7] Villain d'Aubigny, *Le Pot aux roses decouvert et réponse au manifeste de Bailleul, deputé, propriétaire et seigneur suzerain des chateaux* . . . (Impr. Vatar, messidor VII), B.N. Lb42/729, p. 24. General Herlaut's otherwise solid article on D'Aubigny is sketchy and misleading for the Directory period. ("La Vie politique de Villain D'Aubigny, adjoint de Bouchotte," *AHRF*, 1934 [No. 61], pp. 50-75).

abysmal disappointment at its abortion. What to their mind was the best that France could accomplish under its new constitution was reduced by the Directory to another dreary conspiracy. Playing by the Directory's own rules and still forfeiting their gains, democrats were bound to suffer an acute sense of alienation. And if the government was misled by the legislative debates into assuming that opposition would subside once the purge became law, it was soon disabused.

In a pamphlet published less than two weeks after 22 floréal, the controversial elector Victor Bach publicly aired the feelings that democrats were sharing in private. The tone and content of his words were anything but accommodating. He wished, he stated, to expose the *real* conspiracy and lay it at the door of its true authors. "It lies in the usurpations of your sovereignty, in profiteering off the public as well as private wealth, in the army of *mouchards* [police spies] . . . in the exactions of every kind that afflict you . . . in the proscription of honest and virtuous men who alone can improve your condition." While Bach included a detailed accounting of his own eligibility—thus putting to rest a prominent charge leveled against the Oratoire assembly—he was more interested in attacking the government rather than defending his own reputation: attacking censorship, electoral corruption, abuse of power, and the neglect of real issues like the veterans' bonus, tax reform, payment of rentiers, and relief of indigence.[8]

Bach expected his words to result in a jail sentence or even deportation. "What does it matter!" he exclaimed in exasperation. In fact, his defiance did bring about his arrest, though the grand jury subsequently refused to indict him on a charge of conspiracy against the public safety, and he was released a short time later. His case was followed intently by Jacobins, for Bach's pamphlet, like Coesnon-Pellerin's response to the 9 germinal proclamation, was a kind of "official" party response to Floréal.[9] Just after Bach's release (which he applauded) a volatile lawyer named Metge served up a second unguarded attack on the tyranny of the Directory and the supineness of the Legislature, coupled like Bach's with an indictment of

[8] Victor Bach, *La Grande conspiration anarchique de l'Oratoire renvoyée à ses Auteurs* (n.l., n.d.), B.N. Lb42/550.

[9] Aulard, *Paris*, iv, 684-85, 695, 704; A.N. F⁷ 3688/14: report for 8 prairial, Agent I.; *Le Républicain*, No. 49, 19 prairial VI.

their neglect of public welfare. Metge may have assumed that Bach's release cleared the way for such polemics, though his career (which ended with an assassination attempt on Bonaparte) suggests that he was beyond caring about the consequences. In any case, Metge found himself under indictment for the same charge. Only after eight months was he finally acquitted, to the "great astonishment" of the public prosecutor.[10]

Such pamphlets were widely disseminated. In Bach's case the government suspected plans to distribute up to 10,000 copies in Paris and the departments. Though the Central Police Bureau was charged with preventing this, evidence exists to show that copies were mailed out to such addresses as "the municipality of ——."[11] Evidence also exists to show that Jacobins in the provinces generated their own polemics against Floréal. Dordogne and Pas-de-Calais gave the government particular concern, while petitions circulating in a number of other places were publicized in Vatar's new newspaper, *Le Républicain*.[12] The most systematic manifestation of opposition occurred in the Ariège. Printed model petitions were circulated there, attacking "this extraordinary act which undermines the greatest of all rights." Cautiously limiting its argument to the Ariège itself, the petition demanded only the repeal of Article 10 of the law of 22 floréal, which concerned that department. Still, the petition appeared extremely dangerous, and when the government learned of "its almost menacing language," it ordered the petition's circulation stopped.[13]

[10] *Des Représentans du peuple, aux gouvernans, à nos très grands, très sublimes et très puissans membres du Directoire*, par Metge, Section Gravilliers (à l'insigne de la liberté violée), A.N. F⁷ 6175, dossier 2021, plaq. 11 (pièce 616)—this particular copy was found in the apartment of Vatar's managing editor, Camus. See also A.N. F⁷ 6172, dossier 1899, plaq. 8, on Metge's case and his release on 5 ventôse VII.

[11] A.N. F⁷ 7436, fol. 7389: departmental administration (Seine) to Bureau Central, 8 prairial VI. A.N. F⁷ 7450, fol. 8804: municipal administration of Falaise (Calvados) to Directory, 3 messidor VI, reporting on the receipt of three copies of Bach's pamphlet via post from Paris.

[12] A.N. F¹ᶜ III (Pas-de-Calais): compte analytique de la situation du département, messidor VI; A.N. F⁷ 6153, dossier 1047, plaq. 15: departmental commissioner (Dordogne) to M. of Pol., 21 messidor VI. See also *Le Républicain* for prairial *passim*.

[13] *Projet d'Adresse: Des Citoyens du département de l'Ariège, au Corps législatif* and relevant correspondence in A.N. F⁷ 7419, fol. 5570. Vatar's *Journal des Francs* No. 13, 30 messidor VI, defended the petition's legality.

More difficult to stop was the street-corner agitation and café meetings that were the milieu of opposition, especially in Paris. In the first two months after Floréal militants not only attempted to shore up their own sagging spirits but tried as they always did to take their case to soldiers and workingmen. Workers were scarcely interested in the purely political ramifications, but it was possible to connect these with issues that did concern them. As the police constable in division Réunion (7th arrondissement) reported: "towards the end of the day the anarchists await the gathering of workingmen in public places. . . . They openly attack the government, accuse it of persecuting patriots . . . of not doing anything for the workingmen, for the people who, they say, are crushed by taxes and have great difficulty in finding work."[14] Such contact at least helped overcome the sense of isolation that militants were bound to feel, even if they received no tangible support from this would-be constituency. And it served to focus their attention on issues that were implicit in the Jacobin position. Chronic complaints in popular quarters that "the toll barriers have been reestablished, the poor people are being crushed with taxes," and that the government should "establish [public] works, and pay the pensioners and rentiers," coincided with the Jacobins' attacks on the government's neglect of public welfare.[15]

WHILE POPULAR grievances in Paris provided a context for continued political opposition to the Directory, the cadres of war veterans living in and around the Hôtel des Invalides (10th arrondissement) constituted an immediate target for agitation. Among the most cohesive and politicized groups of Parisians, *invalides* had participated in the Rue du Bacq Club, and had been represented in the Oratoire by the election of their comrade Gomegeon. Not only was he floréalized, but the election of a popular sectionnaire named Marcellin as justice of the peace in the 10th arrondissement was also

[14] A.N. F⁷ 7429, fol. 6689: commissaire de police, div. Réunion to Bureau Central, 4 prairial VI; departmental administration (Seine) to Bureau Central, 3-4 prairial.

[15] Numerous reports by police spies reiterate the concern of "meneurs" with issues like the veterans' bonus, oppressive taxes, and unemployment, as well as the persecution of democrats. See the important collection of such reports in A.N. F⁷ 3688/14, floréal-messidor VI.

being challenged and blocked by the government.[16] Echoes of the *invalides'* intense disaffection moved the government to repressive action which only provoked them further. To still the more dissi-dent voices, the Directory chose the moment to institute drastic re-forms in the housing of wounded veterans. Claiming that the Hôtel was overcrowded and that those living outside its precincts created disciplinary problems, the government announced that it was establishing other retreats for *invalides* in the countryside. In private the government's correspondence reveals the political mo-tives that were obvious anyway, since among those destined for transfer out of Paris were militants like Groslaire and Gomegeon.[17]

The multifaceted discontent of Jacobin *invalides* found its voice in lieutenant-*invalide* Louis Gilbert, who published a pamphlet on 18 messidor (6 July 1798). Its ostensible object was to protest the transfer policy and other "vexations and injustices" against the *invalides*. But in frenetically abusive language Gilbert linked the *invalide* reform with the law of 22 floréal as two aspects of a tyran-nical plot. Focusing on Gomegeon's exclusion, Gilbert examined current political questions, and attacked the government for manip-ulating the elections. If Gomegeon had been allowed to take his seat, he contended, he would have denounced the abuses suffered alike by soldiers in the ranks and veterans.[18]

Gilbert was attempting to register his disaffection in all its ampli-tude and to flail the government as severely as possible. Yet at the same time he held to the notion of legality and indeed used it as the crux of his argument. Renouncing insurrection or the Constitution of '93 as Bach also did, he demanded scrupulous adherence to the Constitution of the Year III, in contrast to the Directory's cavalier violation of its principles. But there was tension built into his pos-ture and this inexperienced polemicist strayed several times into dangerous territory. For one thing, he chose to turn Fructidor against the Directory, to condemn it not simply for its limited effects (which all Jacobins now deplored), but as a dangerous precedent

---

[16] See the long, detailed reports on the *invalides* dated 18 floréal VI, "Notes pour le min. de police" in *Ibid.*, and "Notes pour le président du Directoire exécutif," in A.N. AF III 47, dossier 169, pièce 134.

[17] A.N. AF III 521, plaq. 3359 (pièces 66-67) and plaq. 3361 (pièce 9).

[18] *Des Invalides mutilés en combattant pour la République, au Corps législa-tif, sur les vexations et les injustices qu'on exerce envers eux et leurs camarades* (18 messidor VI) signed Gilbert, lieutenant-invalide. B.N. Lf221/13.

now being used against virtuous republicans. Secondly he made the heated assertion that the soldiers "will no longer march except at the orders of the true representatives of the people"—a legalistic corollary, perhaps, to his view of Floréal. Yet what exactly did such a challenging statement really imply—that the current Legislature was not to be obeyed? Finally, Gilbert made an imprudent appeal to "those among the royalists who are honest and virtuous" to renounce their opposition and rally to the republic. Such forays would return to haunt this angry pamphleteer and his would-be enthusiasts.

Initially, however, awkward statements about royalists and the like were overlooked, and Gilbert's pamphlet caused a sensation among democrats. Distributed abundantly in such quarters as the Invalides, Ecole militaire, Rue dominique, Gros Caillou and faubourg Antoine, it had all the earmarks of a great polemical coup. Rumors at once linked the author to Gomegeon, Marcellin, and Bach, and implied that Vatar was behind it. But very quickly the effect was dissipated by the growing concern over the pamphlet's wilder propositions. On second look democrats detected the possibility that it could be attacked as a brand of royalisme à bonnet rouge. Simultaneously, they were concerned over the pending expiration of the press censorship law (law of 19 fructidor V), being anxious to avoid a pretext for its renewal. Hence they ended by disowning what was in reality an authentic and typical statement of their attitudes. Within a week after it was issued, police observers were reporting on heated discussion of the pamphlet's flaws and merits in "anarchist" circles, and noting a disavowal that had appeared in Vatar's newspaper. The tide turned against Gilbert. According to one report, Bach himself was allegedly overheard in an exchange with the lieutenant, explaining that he disapproved of it because of certain imprudent passages. By 5 thermidor VI (23 July) it was reported that "The individuals who initially had most applauded the *invalides'* pamphlet are now the first to blame that infamous writing on the leading police agents."[19]

The "Affaire Gilbert" reflected the acid mood of Jacobin sentiment at this time, the tactical and operational difficulties of expressing it, and finally the incredible suspicion of agents provocateurs. Later investigation reveals that Gilbert was far from being a provocateur

[19] All of these reports are in A.N. F⁷ 3688/14.

or royalist. Simply a volatile Jacobin *invalide*, his career as pamphleteer ended abruptly, drowned in this chorus of admiration, disavowal, and confusion. A few months later the police discovered him running a modest wine shop in the *invalides* quartier under the sign "A la buvette des hommes libres."[20]

The pamphlet war against Floréal subsided after the Gilbert uproar, but was renewed a few weeks later in a lower key by the Jacobins clustered about Vatar's publishing house. Robert Crachet (floréalized deputy from Pas-de-Calais) and P. A. Antonelle (Vendôme defendant, publicist, and Oratoire elector) together produced a series of pamphlets—designed to keep the issue alive—reiterating what had been said before and adding a few new touches.

Robert Crachet was one floréalized deputy who did not accept his fate. He wrote as a mandated deputy illegally prevented from taking his seat, defended the Pas-de-Calais elections, and exposed the Directory's futile attempts to control them. Six weeks later, on the first day of Year VII (22 September 1798), his second pamphlet passed to the offensive. Like Bach, Crachet turned the charge of conspiracy around against the Directory and enumerated all of the Directory's acts that violated the constitution and fit together in an ominous pattern. Floréal, for example, was related to the muzzling of the press, and most recently to the government's policies in Italy. The purges of the Cisalpine government conducted by the French commissioner Trouvé were assailed as acts that reflected the same erosion of constitutionalism that was occurring in France. In conclusion Crachet demanded the repeal of the 22 floréal law and the seating of duly elected deputies.[21]

Antonelle made his characteristic contribution by enlarging the

---

[20] A.N. F⁷ 6168, dossier 1684: Etat-Major Generale, 17th division, rapports de 1-4 frimaire VII; also "Rapport sur un nommé Camus"—noting that Vatar's collaborator was observed at Gilbert's shop. The Jacobin newspaper *La Révélateur* came to Gilbert's defense when the government tried to indict him (Aulard, *Paris*, v, 83-84: 29 fructidor VI).

[21] Robert Crachet, *Appel aux principes, ou première lettre . . . aux républicains* (Impr., Rue de l'Université [Vatar], 15 thermidor VI), B.N. Lb42/1952; notices in *Journal des Francs* No. 45, 2 fructidor VI, Nos. 52 and 54, 9 and 11 fructidor; and in the *Révélateur* for 3 fructidor (cited in Aulard, *Paris*, v, 49). *Appel aux principes, ou deuxième lettre de Robert Crachet* (Impr. Rue de l'Université [Vatar], 1 vendémiaire VII), B.N. Lb42/1997; notice in Vatar's *Correspondance des représentans* No. 18, 18 vendémiaire VII. The pamphlets are discussed by Meynier, *Le 22 floréal*, pp. 96-101.

issue into the defense of "representative democracy" against oligarchy. With Crachet he underlined recent events in the Cisalpine republic as a confirmation of designs that the floréal coup had earlier revealed. Under such assaults, he warned, representative democracy was about to be obliterated once and for all.[22] Coincidentally Antonelle set out on a trip to the south of France at this time, ostensibly to put his affairs in order at his native Arles. Cutting an arc through cities like Nîmes, Marseilles, and Toulon, he was feted by local Jacobins and distributed these pamphlets attacking Floréal and the specter of oligarchy. Sensitive to the slightest manifestation of such opposition, the government ordered a surveillance of his movements which was undoubtedly the object of derision among Antonelle's provincial friends.[23]

BY NOW such pamphlets were the Jacobins' sole artifacts of opposition, except for the *chansons* that circulated privately.[24] Though

[22] P. A. Antonelle, *Quelques observations qui peuvent servir d'appendice à la seconde lettre de Robert Crachet sur le 22 floréal* (n.l., n.d.), B.N. Lb42/1894. Antonelle, *La Constitution et les principes opposés aux floréalists* (n.l., n.d.), B.N. Lb42/1953.

[23] A.N. F7 6174, dossier 2007, plaq. 11: "Rapport sommaire" of the surveillance ordered by the Police Ministry, dated 6 nivôse VII. Other anti-Floréal pamphlets include an essay by M. J. Satur, *Le Cri de la Constitution, contre l'immoralité des patriotes et la conspiration des flatteurs* (Impr. J. Baillis), B.N. Lb42/1896, esp. pp. 17-19; and the polemic by J. Lambert (des Hautes-Alpes), *La Conspiration anarchique mise à la portée de tout le monde* (Paris, n.d.) in A.N. AF III 45, fol. 164, pièce 56.

[24] Police spies sometimes managed to obtain what seem like authentic transcriptions of the *chansons* that circulated in allegedly subversive *rassemblements*, for example (A.N. F7 3688/14: dossier messidor VI, pièce 29):

> Voyez donc cette constitution
> faite pour enrichir les fripons:
> ils la trouvent bonne avec raison
> tout ça est une nouvelle methode.
> Pauvre peuple, que tu es trompé!
> que tu es mal gouverné!
> Te voilà cette fois bien empietre
> c'est le régime à la mode.
>
> Propager les abus;
> avilir la vertu;
> placer l'intriguant;
> prodiguer l'argent;
> pauvre peuple languissant;
> tout le monde mécontent,
> c'est la nouvelle méthode:
> usurper les droits plébeiens.

The following month a copy of the "Complainte pour le neuf Thermidor par le Republicain Mamin. Air du cantique de Monsieur St. Roch" was obtained, whose first two stanzas are as follows (*Ibid.*, dossier thermidor, pièce 28):

> Peuple français, on offre à ta mémoire
> Ce jour affreux qui ouvrit le tombeau
> aux citoyens qui au champ de la gloire

they undoubtedly made few converts, they were essential to the morale of the already committed. Moreover, from what we know about their circulation, we may infer that they represented merely the visible portion of a larger but perforce mute opposition. Even though they scarcely posed a direct challenge to the status quo, the Directory judged them dangerous enough to either prosecute the authors or place them under surveillance. Even at the low ebb of Jacobin fortunes, one forceful pamphlet was apparently enough to revitalize Jacobin spirits and throw the government into a minor frenzy of repressive activity.

This was particularly true of François Dubreuil's *Hommage à la Vérité*, published in nivôse VII (January 1799). As Fournier l'Americain was overheard remarking in a café, this was the best pamphlet of them all for the government's "act of accusation is perfectly composed there."[25] The Directory's zeal in attempting to prosecute its author, stop its circulation, and discover its printer testified to the same judgment.[26] In Dubreuil's pamphlet this genre of opposition reached its natural limits and achieved its maximum success.

> à tes cotes detruirait ton bourreau.
> Non je ne puis y songer sans fremir;
> Ah! mes amis, jusqu'au dernier soupir,
>   Malgré les armes
>   donnons des larmes
>   à nos saveurs
>   victimes des voleurs.
>
> Neuf thermidor, journée abominable,
> tu vas encore rejouir les tyrans;
> tu n'es pour moy qu'un fardeau qui m'accable
> tu n'appartiens qu'aux fripons, aux chouans;
> Si tu es beau, c'est pour les affameurs,
> pour les catins et pour tous les chauffeurs.
>   Mais l'homme sage
>   dans son menage
>   verse des pleurs
>   sur toutes tes horreurs.

[25] A.N. F⁷ 6175, dossier 2021, plaq. 10 (pièce 59): report for 16 nivôse VII. See also A.N. F⁷ 6173, dossier 1955, plaq. 6; *J. hommes libres* No. 6, 6 messidor VII; A.N. 171 AP 1 [Barras Papers], dossier 10.

[26] The government initially suspected Vatar and his circle as the authors and printers of the pamphlet. Giraud, Eon, and Vatar were all placed under close surveillance, and their premises subjected to searches; Vatar's employee Camus was arrested for distributing it. See A.N. F⁷ 6194, dossier 2627, plaq. 5 [dossier Vatar] 21 nivôse-14 pluviôse VII. Dubreuil himself was arrested on 23 nivôse

For twenty-five years before he returned to France in May 1792, Dubreuil had served as surgeon-dentist to the Tsarist Court in St. Petersburg. The fortune of 80,000 livres that he amassed he invested in a French state paper, only to see it depreciated and repudiated by successive regimes until it was all but gone. However, it was not this dire personal situation, this destitution, if we are to take him literally, that drove Dubreuil to despair. Money was not the sum total of his loss, he claimed, since his hope for *égalité* and *bonheur de tous* were near to being lost as well.[27] Adding a personal *cri de coeur* to the usual party appeals, Dubreuil infused his polemic with a unique passion. But despite his singular background, he may be viewed as yet another member of the distinguishable social type that was supplying almost all of these opposition pamphlets: the Jacobin intelligentsia. Dubreuil's *Hommage à la Vérité* capped the earlier efforts of jurist Biauzat, physician Bach, lawyer Metge, lieutenant Gilbert, journalist Antonelle, and functionary Crachet.

Dubreuil insisted on viewing his own unhappy fate in its largest context. He identified his plight with that of other purportedly oppressed groups in French society: soldiers and *invalides*, rentiers, functionaries who had been harassed by political purges, and artisans and workers who had lost their livelihoods. If one disentangles the meandering arguments and rhetorical digressions, Dubreuil's indictment of Directorial tyranny is found to rest on two grounds: its destruction of political sovereignty, and its erosion of the Revolution's social promise.

VII, along with his landlord and a bookseller who had sold the pamphlet. When charges were dismissed by the court, the Directory placed him on the list of émigrés (8 prairial) and arrested him for that. He was temporarily released on 15 messidor VII when Metge petitioned in his behalf to the Council of 500, which referred the case back to the Directory. It was still pending under the consulate, and seems to have been resolved when Dubreuil was included on Bonaparte's list of anarchists to be deported. See Dubreuil, *Au Citoyen Directeur du Jury d'accusation du département de la Seine* (Paris, 28 prairial VII), B.N. Lb42/704, and *Dubreuil à Bonaparte* (Paris, 1 frimaire VIII) in A.N. F⁷ 6175, dossier 2021, plaq. 8.

[27] *Hommage à la Vérité contre l'oppression, l'injustice, l'inhumanité, et les rapines du DIRECTOIRE et de ses représentans au Corps législatif; ou second et dernier appel à leur cruauté, pour en obtenir la mort. Par une famille de Rentiers et Créanciers de l'Etat réduits à l'agonie du désespoir par l'extrème besoin* [Paris, nivôse VII], signed Dubreuil. B.N. Lb42/582 (another edition B.N. Lb42/704), pp. 24-25.

Dubreuil's view of the Revolution's history seemed to contain a "hébertist" animus against the rigid policies of the revolutionary government and the way it applied the law of suspects. But his central concern from beginning to end was the thermidorians. Not to Robespierre but to revolutionaries like Merlin, Barras and Reubell were attributed both the excesses of the revolutionary government itself and the catastrophe that followed 9 thermidor.[28] Couched in abusive terms like "barbarians," Dubreuil's indictment of the thermidorians built towards the conclusion that the worst was yet to come. "Emboldened by their previous successes and infatuated by the *journées populicides* of Fructidor and Floréal, they will attempt to give us a new constitution in order to perpetuate themselves in office." Against this commonly feared threat Dubreuil rather unconvincingly invoked the familiar Neo-Jacobin position: strict adherence to the Constitution of the Year III and cultivation of an aroused sovereign people whose vigor and vigilance will overcome apathy. But the author could not help despairing and wondering whether this would avail. At one point he was constrained to write that "extreme means of insurrection" might be required if the tyranny worsened.[29] Thus, by the time the Neo-Jacobin position had been perfected it was being outmoded by the contrary movement of the thermidorians.

As in most of the other opposition pamphlets, Dubreuil's political stance took as its context the vexing social issues in France. Arguing that the present government favored the rich at the expense of the poor, when it was the poor who needed protection against the rich, Dubreuil did not advocate a Babeuvist-type regime of *plebeianisme*. Rather he invoked the venerable Jacobin formula of cooperation among productive social groups (ranging from ouvriers to négociants), bound by a sense of social justice and interdependence. Public welfare (*bonheur commun*) would be achieved only after the inequities of the social structure were corrected, only after excessive imbalances were regulated. Dubreuil's lyrical images of social justice and harmony were offered along with concrete proposals to make them feasible, notably the subsistence clause of the 1793 constitution which he reverently endorsed. The right to subsistence must be guaranteed, he maintained, "either by providing work or

[28] *Hommage à la Vérité*, pp. 10-15.   [29] *Ibid.*, pp. 3-4, 21-22, 32-35.

by assuring the means of existence to those who are unable to work."[30]

For all its peculiar tangents and idiosyncrasies, Dubreuil's *Hommage à la Vérité* is another landmark in the history of Jacobinism. It forcefully avowed the democrats' alienation from the "tyranny" of the second Directory, which had betrayed its own constitution. It rooted the act of political opposition within the larger public issues of the day and justified it by the vision of a better society. At the moment, however, it was the intensity of the opposition itself that commanded attention, both from admiring democrats and a hostile Directory. The pamphlet was acrimonious and inflammatory, virtually proclaiming the impossibility of any accommodation with the present ruling group.

In turn the prolonged prosecution of Dubreuil and the attempts to suppress the pamphlet's circulation reveal the growth of a police-state atmosphere and the narrowing outlets for the expression of opposition. Printing shops were searched repeatedly on the suspicion that they were publishing subversive pamphlets; former activitists were subjected to police surveillance in cafés, wine shops, and public places, as well as in their homes. Guilt by reputation or association became the commonplace standard of this police work, whose net ranged from prominent deputies to obscure, unemployed artisans.

‡ III ‡

Where this would end was difficult to say. Men like director LaRevellière professed a sincere commitment to republicanism and abhorrence of tyranny, yet their policies seemed to be leading towards an improvised dictatorship. Gradually, however, their manipulations and purges, as well as their contemptuous neglect of the legislators' prerogatives, earned them enemies where they had once had support. An angry open letter from the deputy Texier-Olivier to LaRevellière, summarizing such complaints, solicited in reply a self-righteous and rigid defense, which publicly signaled an untenable deadlock within the government itself.[31]

It is true that in this period between Floréal and the elections of 1799 durable reforms were consummated in such areas as the future

---

[30] *Ibid.*, pp. 10-11, 36-39.

[31] See LaRevellière, *Mémoires*, III, 64-92. Most local monographs, whatever their other shortcomings, illustrate the extent of these purges.

funding of the national debt and the restructuring of tax collection. Yet the immediate fiscal situation remained precarious, and the economy suffered from deflation and depression that compounded the difficulties of raising revenue. Since the government's principal solution to this problem lay in the exploitation of sister republics and conquered territory, the Directory's diplomatic failures in those areas were particularly serious. Moreover, to the charges of tyranny and ineffectiveness the issue of corruption was added. From across the political spectrum the executive was accused of either willfully or inadvertently turning the state's wealth over to a horde of profiteers or *dilapidateurs*. Finally it was widely believed that the Directory was muzzling patriotic French generals, while allowing military supplies to become depleted.[32] Conservative republicans who were supposed to be represented by this Directory therefore chafed under its stewardship. By the time the spring elections were due to be held, the incumbent executive found itself isolated.

Preparations by the Directory for the annual elections were coordinated by Interior Minister François de Neufchateau and bore the familiar stamp of the previous year's techniques. With most Jacobin party organs already suppressed, the task remained simply to issue the usual proclamations denouncing the extremes, to promote official candidacies, and to recommend schism as a last resort. But in the face of massive apathy and widespread disaffection among the Directorials themselves, these efforts proved unsuccessful. According to the accepted calculations of Albert Meynier, 187 candidates were supported by one or more members of the Directory, but only 66 were elected.[33] More important, the Legislature this time refused to play politics with the 27 schisms that occurred, and in all but two unusual cases followed the straightforward procedure of validating the results of the majority assemblée mère. The Jacobins were by no means the exclusive beneficiaries in these depart-

[32] The Directory's accomplishments and difficulties are assessed by A. Goodwin, "The French Executive Directory—a Revaluation," *History*, xxii (1937), 201-18; Meynier, *Le 22 floréal*, Ch. "Dilapidations, déficit, réformes financières"; and J. Godechot, *Les Commissaires aux armées sous le Directoire* (Paris, 1937), Vol. ii. For a balance sheet see Lefebvre, *Le Directoire*, pp. 133-43, and more recently A. Soboul, *Le Directoire et le Consulat* (Paris, 1967), pp. 57-68.

[33] Meynier, *Le 22 floréal*, pp. 186-201; Kuscinski, *Les Deputés au Corps Législatif*.

ments. In at least five cases (Corrèze, Hérault, Landes, Loire, Basses-Pyrénées) *they* were the scissionnaires, and accordingly such men
as Generals Marbot and Bernadotte and ex-conventionnels Lacombe
St. Michel and Saurine were excluded. But in the schisms in Dordogne, Doubs, Haute-Garonne, Saône-et-Loire, Sarthe, Var, Vaucluse, and Haute-Vienne, validation of the assemblée mère sealed
Jacobin victories and brought to the Legislature about fifty pro-
Jacobins, including at least five who had been floréalized in the
Year VI.[34] Offsetting these gains, however, were departments like
Allier, Ariège, Gironde, Nièvre, Pas-de-Calais, Seine, and Vienne,
which had been strongholds of Jacobinism in the Year VI but where
one or another group of conservatives prevailed in the Year VII.
Thus, the Directory's defeat in these elections was due in part to
the Jacobins, and in part to a series of localized rebellions within
the ranks of the thermidorians.[35]

When the new deputies took their seats on the first of prairial,
the executive found itself faced with two influential groups of
enemies who together dominated the councils. Disaffected Directorials constituted the first group, which in turn can be broken down
into two categories. Some wished to be rid of the present executive
in order simply to restore confidence in the regime, eliminate the
most blatant corruption, and place the constitution back into reasonable working order. Others, including key legislators like Boulay
de la Meurthe and Daunou, may be called revisionists. They had lost
confidence not simply in the personnel of the Directory, but in the
whole unwieldy regime, with its ambiguous libertarian principles,
its ineffectual separation of powers, and its annual ordeal of new
elections. Though each group may have considered itself republican in some fashion, the revisionists hoped to redesign the republic
on what the Jacobins kept calling oligarchic lines.[36]

[34] For Jacobin successes see Reinhard on the Sarthe, Beyssi on Toulouse
(Haute-Garonne), and Labroue on Dordogne, all previously cited; A. Fray-
Fournier, *Le Département de la Haute-Vienne . . . pendant la Révolution*
(Limoges, 1909), I, 169-79; and E. Poupé, "Les Dessous des élections de l'an
VII dans le Var," *Annales de la Société d'études provençales*, III (1906), 171-
96.
[35] For a good case study of such intra-Directorial factionalism see H. Poulet,
"Le Département de la Meuse à la fin du Directoire et au debut du Consulat,"
R.F., XLVIII (1905), 5-39.
[36] On the revisionists see R. Guyot, "Du Directoire au Consulat: les transitions," *Révue historique*, CXI (1912), 1-31; and J. Bourdon, "Le Mécontente-

The second major opposition group was of course the Jacobins, greater in number than ever, bent on revenge for Floréal and emboldened by dissension among the Directorials. A series of special police surveillance reports for the month of prairial informed the government of the "exagérés'" increasing activity.[37] Twenty to thirty deputies were among the main movers, particularly men like Guesdon, Marquezy, Briot, Dessaix, and Stevenotte who had collaborated with Vatar in various resurrections of his newspaper before it finally succumbed. Not surprisingly, Vatar and his associates Eon and Camus were at the very center of this group.[38] Through such intermediaries, contacts were established between the deputies from the provinces and a variety of Parisian democrats : certain sectional leaders from the Year II, former employees of the revolutionary government, defendants at the Vendôme trial, and Oratoire electors. Over two hundred names can be extracted from these reports, and typical of them are Villain d'Aubigny, Felix Lepelletier, General Jorry, Fournier l'Américain, Chrétien, Leban, Lacombe, and Niquille. The impression emerges that each side provided necessary encouragement for the other. The deputies were made to feel that they were supported by an active constituency of *patriotes à tetes chaudes*, as the reports call them. Conversely, the Parisian democrats were heartened to see men in high places responsive to their own complaints. Though these reports doubtless contained exaggerations and erroneous identifications, they were generally correct in their revelation about the composition and liaisons of Parisian Jacobin opposition. For it was precisely such an amalgam that emerged openly in the famous Neo-Jacobin club of the Manège that was founded the following month. Meanwhile, however, there were neither clubs nor newspapers. Opposition was forwarded by personal contacts, private meetings, speeches in the Legislature, and pamphlets. Old pamphlets like Dubreuil's were circulated, while new anonymous ones were produced, like *La Situation de la République sous le regne des tyrans*. Such items, one report suggested,

---

ment public et les craintes des dirigeants sous le Directoire," *AHRF*, 1946 [No. 103], pp. 218-30.

[37] A.N. AF III 47, dossier 171: pièces particulières, prairial et messidor VII (surveillances secrètes ordonnés par le ministre).

[38] *Ibid.*: reports for 2, 10, 22, 24 prairial and especially "pièce no. 19," for 25 prairial.

were meant to disseminate sentiments that were "too strong" to be stated openly in the Tribune.[39] The most common targets of these attacks were political tyranny, *dilapidation*, and the muzzling of the press; the most immediate demand was to replace the present executive.

New impetus for the anti-Directorial coalition was provided by military reversals. In the month of prairial (May-June 1799) poorly supplied and unreinforced French armies were compelled to evacuate most of Italy and were yielding in Switzerland before an Austro-Russian invasion. The Jacobins now found their special animus against the executive merging into a generalized chorus of discontent. Gradually their own posture became more aggressive and self-confident, reverting at least in its rhetoric to the war-crisis mentality of the Year II. Joined now by the disaffected conservatives and revisionists, the Neo-Jacobins pushed their assault to a successful conclusion. First, the lawful replacement of two directors was engineered: Reubell, who drew the lot for annual replacement, and Treilhard, who was ousted on a legal technicality that had previously been ignored. LaRevellière and Merlin were then cajoled and intimidated into resigning when the Legislature placed itself *en permanence* and sent threatening deputations to them, hinting that they would be indicted for malfeasance if they failed to comply. Their reluctant resignations were wrested from them on 30 prairial VII (18 June 1799), which was hailed as another great *journée* in the Revolution. A parliamentary reshuffling rather than a real coup d'état, 30 prairial temporarily restored to the Legislature some of the influence and initiative that it had lost after Fructidor and Floréal.[40]

The replacements for the ousted Directors faithfully reflected the uncertain composition of the 30 prairial coalition. Barras remained on, adept and flexible enough to have escaped the purge, and liable to land on any possible side in the future. Unprincipled and self-interested, he nonetheless exhibited a levelheaded perspective that was attuned to political reality. The first and most important addition was Sieyès, whose well-known scorn for the deposed Directors

---

[39] *Ibid.*: reports for 13, 14, and 20 prairial, among others. One of the major signed pamphlets produced by this group was P. J. Briot, *Première réponse ... à l'acte d'accusation publiée par J. Ch. Bailleul contre la majorité du Corps législatif* (Impr. Vatar, 27 prairial VII), B.N. Lb42/2225.

[40] See Meynier, *Le 22 floréal*, pp. 202-30.

made him appear as a consensus candidate and likely strong man in a government that needed new leadership. That Sieyès was the most single-minded revisionist was not yet clear; that he was as decidedly anti-Jacobin as any of the deposed Directors was also partially veiled at first. Sieyès was seconded in everything by Roger Ducos, a *conventionnel* of the Plain whose chief asset was his reputation for integrity and the fact that for no good reason he had been floréalized in the Year VI. The new executive was rounded out with two men who were assumed to be staunch republicans and pro-Jacobins, and who had been floréalized as well: Gohier, Minister of Justice in the Year II, and the obscure but reliable General Moulin. The outstanding fact in the relationship of these five men seems to have been the tenacity with which Sieyès pressed his opinions and which obliged the others to appease him. It was not long before the balance was struck in Sieyès' favor—a balance that opened the way to Brumaire a mere four and a half months after the *journée* of 30 prairial, which was supposed to restore the republic to working order.[41]

[41] P. Bastid's *Sieyès et sa pensée* (Paris, 1939) is disappointing on this aspect of his career, but see pp. 223-25. G. Buffy's article on General Moulin (*R.F.*, L [1906]) is wholly unilluminating, but Gohier's memoirs are valuable: *Mémoires des contemporains: Mémoires de Louis-Jerome Gohier, président du Directoire au 18 brumaire* (2 vols.; Paris, 1824). There are no reliable secondary works on Barras.

CHAPTER XIII

The Last Stand: Jacobinism and Anti-Jacobinism in the War Crisis of 1799

THE FOUR and a half months between the *journée* of 30 prairial and the brumaire coup saw the last stand of Neo-Jacobinism. Because it coincided with a war crisis that was in certain ways reminiscent of the Year II, the final confrontation of Jacobins and anti-Jacobins took on a dramatic intensity. But the rush of events makes it difficult to assess the relative importance of special circumstances in this last and relatively minor crisis as against the on-going problem of whether or not a democratic movement could survive in France. In any case, the short-lived anti-Directorial coalition of 30 prairial soon dissolved into its constituent parts, leaving the Jacobins as a highly visible, vocal, and vulnerable minority. This development unfolded in three phases, which may be briefly described as a preliminary to pausing over the decisive issues.

Phase I. For about a month (messidor) the Jacobins appeared to be in the ascendant. A renewal of government personnel, the revival of certain newspapers, an outpouring of petitions, and the formation of new clubs constituted the classic pattern of resurgent Jacobinism in Directorial France. In Paris a new club united a number of Jacobin deputies with certain local democrats, much the way the old Paris Jacobin club had in the Year II. These deputies managed to enact three major pieces of legislation and seemed on the verge of achieving a fourth. (1) A call-up of all classes of conscripts —a kind of controlled mass levy—was easily passed on 10 messidor (28 June). (2) A forced loan to be levied on the rich was passed in principle on the same date, though the opposition managed to stall the implementing legislation until 19 thermidor (6 August). (3) A law of hostages was devised as a practical weapon against counterrevolutionary outbreaks (12 July). Finally, a bill of particulars against the ousted Directors as well as the alleged *dilapidateur,* ex-War Minister Scherer, was adopted by the Council of 500 on 24 messidor (12 July). After three readings, ten days apart, the council was then required to vote on it again, and if passed it would become an official indictment.[1]

Phase II. Starting as early as the official celebration of 14 July conservatives led by Sieyès began to warn against a return of terror, anarchy, and government by laws of exception. In newspapers, pamphlets, legislative speeches, as well as in the streets, the Manège Club in Paris came under assault. Meanwhile opposition grew to the indictment of the Directors. Preliminary to a decisive move against the club, Fouché was brought into the Police Ministry and investigations were launched both by the Legislature and the executive. On 26 thermidor (13 August) the club was preemptorily closed by Fouché at Sieyès' instigation and with the concurrence of all five Directors. Shortly thereafter the indictment of the deposed Directors was brought to a final vote and lost, 217/214 (18 August). The Neo-Jacobin ascendancy was over.[2]

Phase III. The tone of Jacobin opposition now reverted to the defensive hostility of pre-Prairial days. New acts of a alleged tyranny inspired by Sieyès, such as an attempt to suppress Jacobin newspapers on 17 fructidor (3 September), provoked counterattacks in the Legislature. The issue of freedom to dissent through clubs and newspapers became a rallying point for Jacobin opinion, as debate proceeded on proposed organic laws regulating both. But the situation remained fluid because of the outbreak of *chouannerie* and new military reversals. At the battle of Novi (15 August) General Joubert was killed and French forces compelled to retreat further out of Italy. Moreover an invasion of France itself was feared after a Russo-British expeditionary force landed successfully in the Netherlands on 27 August. "The extent of the danger to the fatherland" was once again extreme, as a young officer from Army of Italy headquarters wrote to his friend in Paris, Marc-Antoine Jullien, after Novi. "If the government does not determine to act energetically and with a kind of terror, this crisis may well mean the end of the republic."[3]

---

[1] See the standard work by Albert Meynier, Vol. III of his "Les Coups d'état du Directoire": *Le Dix-huit brumaire et la fin de la République* (Paris, 1928), Ch. I; Lefebvre, *Le Directoire*, pp. 174-76; Gohier, *Mémoires*, I, 61-68.

[2] The anti-Jacobin reaction is discussed in L. Madelin, *Fouché, 1759-1820* (2 vols.; Paris, 1913), I, 236-60, and Meynier, *Le Dix-huit brumaire*, Ch. III.

[3] G. Bourgin, ed., "Quelques lettres de Saint-Cyr Nugues à Jullien de Paris," *AHRF*, 1938 [No. 89], p. 458: letter dated 14 fructidor VII.

Such feelings focused on a symbolic issue: whether or not to declare *la patrie en danger*—a proclamation of martial law that could galvanize the government and the nation into effective resistance. Conservatives and pragmatists opposed this as either meaningless or dangerous. In a clandestine interview with the measure's legislative sponsor, General Jourdan, Barras decried this approach as "worn out . . . no longer productive of any results." The situation was not comparable to the Year II, he argued, since the present danger was not nearly as serious as the invasion of the first coalition. Moreover, the resources to oppose it were nonexistent then, whereas "we have today an organization, great civil and military organizations." The way to meet the crisis was simply to utilize existing resources and call on all citizens "in a regular way and without any shock." On 28 fructidor (14 September) the motion was brought to a vote in the Council of 500 and Barras' point of view prevailed. In a crucial division which is generally used to gauge the actual numerical strength of the Jacobins in the Council, the motion was defeated 245/171. Simultaneously the most prominent pro-Jacobin in the government, War Minister Bernadotte, was dismissed, possibly for fear that he would lead some kind of coup d'état.[4] Shortly thereafter Masséna's victory at the second battle of Zurich (27 September), and General Brune's successful repulsion of the Netherlands' invasion, seemed to confirm the wisdom of relying on normal methods. Having warded off the most immediate threats, the revisionists now set to work in earnest, fearful of next year's elections, and spurred on by the fortuitous return of General Bonaparte from Egypt.

‡ I ‡

To vanquish the allied coalition, Jacobins advocated the emergency legislation described above. Simultaneously they were preoccupied with the more complex problem of how to hold the forces of domestic anti-Jacobinism at bay and how to prevent the republic from lapsing into oligarchy. Distant military reversals seemed less palpable a threat than the decline of what they called freedom and public spirit. While much energy was expended on denouncing

[4] Barras, *Memoirs*, III, 569-72 (22 fructidor VII). Cf. René Valentin, *Le Maréchal Jourdan* (Paris, 1956), 185-93; Meynier, *Le Dix-huit brumaire*, pp. 61-73.

the foreign forces leagued against La Grande Nation, even more was directed against "tyranny" at home.

Jacobin publicists, petitioners, and orators would not let the pre-Prairial situation quietly recede into the realm of past history. Insistently they reminded whoever would listen how close to extinction the republic had come. Besides underscoring the alleged corruption, muzzling of generals, and betrayal of fellow patriots in places like Italy, they dwelled on the abridgment of rights and of sovereignty at home: on the floréal purge, the dismissal of patriots from office, and the police-state atmosphere created by the *mouchards* who hounded democrats, as one of them complained, "jusque dans la sanctuaire de sa pensée."[5]

> Public spirit extinguished, freedom of thought circumscribed, political clubs dissolved, citizens arrested arbitrarily . . . continuous demands for new taxes . . . blows planned and executed against the national representation; primary and electoral assemblies influenced, affronted, or dissolved by Directorial agents.[6]

Such was the Jacobins' indictment of the fallen Directors.

Would the *journée* of 30 prairial reverse this situation permanently? The most credulous knew by now that a dramatic *journée* was almost meaningless in itself. As a widely heralded petition from the "ouvriers" of the faubourg Antoine put it : "To escape from slavery does not suffice; it is necessary to assure the triumph of virtue over crime, of equality over oligarchy. A terrible experience has taught us that ephemeral victories are more harmful than defeats."[7] Each saving *journée*, like 13 vendémiaire or 18 fructidor, had

---

[5] D'Aubigny, *Le Pot aux roses decouvert*, esp. pp. 30-32; *Essai sur la nature et les divers agens de la conspiration presente ou lettres à un représentant du peuple* . . . (Impr. Vatar, an VII), B.N. Lb42/708, esp. pp. 143 and 178. (These essays were announced in the *J. hommes libres* No. 31, 1 thermidor VII and No. 47, 17 thermidor.) See also Guy Chaumont-Quitry, *Essai sur les causes qui, depuis le 18 fructidor, devaient consolider la République en France, et sur celles qui ont failli la faire perir* (Impr. Vatar-Jouannet, thermidor an VII), B.N. Lb42/2393.

[6] Rodolphe, *Acte d'accusation contre l'ex-Directoire exécutif et ses complices ou Tableau effrayant des causes secrètes qui ont amené la France au bord du précipice* (Chez Gauthier, an VII), pp. 7-8. B.N. Lb42/2237. Cf. a similar pamphlet by Rouy, B.N. Lb43/28.

[7] *Des Citoyens du Faubourg Antoine au Conseil des Cinq-Cents, séance du 17 messidor VII* (Impr. Nationale), Maclure Collection, University of Pennsylvania Library; *J. hommes libres* No. 23, 23 messidor VII.

ultimately been nullified by the policy of *bascule*—the "juggling of factions"; compensating measures against the Left after a blow against the royalists. *Bascule* had taken various forms. At worst it resulted in "judicial assassinations" like the Vendôme trial. Always it produced purges of *patriotes prononcés* who had been momentarily recalled to revitalize the government, and the suppression of clubs and newspapers that had been allowed to flourish briefly. The most recent type of *bascule* had of course been that act of "lèseconstitution," the law of 22 floréal VI.[8]

Now the Jacobins argued that the way to put an end to *bascule* was to indict and punish the so-called traitors: the deposed Directors (sometimes referred to as the "triumverate"), their principal ministers like Schérer, and agents like Trouvé, commissioner to the Cisalpine Republic. The "derogations and perfidies" of these men had been unmasked, according to the faubourg Antoine petition, yet they remained at liberty. Only a quick and severe punishment would assure permanent benfits from the *journée* of 30 prairial and truly restore confidence in the government. "Punish them, and you will have citizens to defend the fatherland," it concluded. Across the entire spectrum of Neo-Jacobinism, from petitioners in distant departments to orators at the Manège Club, this call was taken up. Whether in the incendiary language of Lebois' *Père Duchêne* that the guilty "must perish," or in the sober statement by Leclerc des Vosges that there would be no "tranquility or freedom" until they were punished, the issue was drawn.[9]

As the touchstone of Neo-Jacobinism after Prairial, the demand for punishment of the triumvirate became the issue on which the 30 prairial coalition split apart. There were a number of good rea-

[8] These phrases are taken from Publicola Chaussard, *Coup-d'Oeil sur l'intérieur de la République française, ou esquisse des principes d'une Révolution morale* (Impr. Moutardier, an VII), B.N. Lb42/2475, pp. 12-14; Chaumont-Quitry, *Essai sur les causes*, pp. 24 and 27; *Essai sur la nature et les divers agens*, pp. 120-24.

[9] Thus the *Essai sur la nature et les divers agens*, a 200-page statement of Jacobin grievances, concluded that to prevent the return of all the abuses described, another revolution was not needed. "Je ne vous connais qu'un seul moyen," it proclaimed, "c'est l'acte d'accusation" (p. 167). See also [Lebois], *Le Canon d'alarme tiré par le Père Duchêne sur les dangers qui menacent la patrie* (No. 6, 2 thermidor VII); Leclerc des Vosges, *Discours prononcé à l'inauguration de la Réunion des Amis de l'égalité et de la liberté* (Impr. Etienne Charles, 22 messidor VII), pp. 4-5.

sons why Directorials and revisionists resisted it. Many were themselves accomplices in such things as the floréal purge, while Barras in particular was likely to be called to account for these decisions if a precedent were set. The obscure conduct of Sieyès' prior diplomatic mission to Prussia put him too within the range of suspicion. Besides which, most of the Jacobins' accusations against the triumverate revolved around the latter's anti-Jacobinism, and the fact was that the conservative side of the 30 prairial coalition shared this point of view. It was extremely significant that LaRevellière stood his ground on this question in the successful defense that he published on 15 thermidor (2 August 1799). He had been accused of playing the politics of *bascule*, of consigning certain republicans to proscription by designating them as anarchists, and "provoking by such labels the exclusion of republicans from all public functions." To this he icily replied: "I maintain that it was with good reason that the Directory recognized the existence of an anarchist party."[10] By the time he wrote this, Sieyès was in open agreement and intended to act on that opinion.

The Jacobins' failure to secure the indictment and punishment of the triumverate was followed by the predicted consequences. True to previous patterns, *bascule* began in all the areas that traditionally served as indicators. A brief acquisition of initiative, freedom of expression, and a measure of public influence commensurate with the Jacobins' services to the republic quickly came to an end. The appointment of democrats to office, revival of their press, and formation of clubs were all reversed, signaling the reappearance of anti-Jacobinism, as if the *journée* of 30 prairial had never occurred. Since these three areas together formed the foundation of Neo-Jacobin activity, each warrants a last look.

‡ II ‡

Jacobin activists included numerous office-seekers, some motivated by ambition, others by sheer economic need. But in their quest for jobs the political side also counted for something, as the phenomenon of protest resignations indicates. A significant number of positions were subject to purges, and assignment to these posts entailed certain implied commitments. The Jacobins defined them-

[10] LaRevellière, *Mémoires*, III, 157-58.

selves as men whose dedication to the Revolution and experience in its ways had been proven decisively, and whose claim on these positions was well established. To purge such men was tantamount to betraying the republic, they felt.

The *journée* of 30 prairial seemed even more than 18 fructidor to restore these "proven patriots" to public positions, as petitions coming to the Legislature demanded. The appointment of Robert Lindet, former member of the Committee of Public Safety, as Finance Minister symbolized this. Previously Lindet's recognized talents had gone unused; instead he had been tried in absentia at Vendôme, and floréalized in the Year VI. To the war department came General Bernadotte, who was not long (as Barras put it) "in justifying the expectations that patriots felt the need of placing in him."[11] Bernadotte used the exigencies of the war crisis to fill his staff with Montagnards like Baudot, Choudieu, and Roux-Fazillac, and functionaries of the revolutionary government like D'Aubigny and Marchand, most of whom had been effectively barred from significant positions since Thermidor. Like Sotin's Police Ministry in the Year VI, Bernadotte's War Ministry became a bastion of Neo-Jacobinism whose "spirit" was celebrated in the Jacobin press.

The appointment of ex-conventionnel Quinette to the Interior Ministry, and the obscure Bourguignon to the Police Ministry was neutral in itself, but these men, too, extended patronage to former Jacobins. Tissot, Niquille, and others from Sotin's staff of the Year VI were brought back to the Police Ministry, while Quinette appointed men like the Montagnard Francastel to his staff. Quinette was also instrumental in having the departmental administration of the Seine completely renewed with a slate of veteran Jacobins including LaChevardière, Raisson, and Leblanc, who in turn purged at least half the hundred-odd employees under their jurisdiction and appointed men like Buonarroti's confidant Gabriel in their place. It was repeatedly claimed that Vatar's offices served as a clearing house for such patronage, which was probably true, and Vatar himself received the job of official printer to the Seine department.[12]

It suffices to suggest this pattern without describing it in detail

[11] Barras, *Memoirs*, III, 461-62.
[12] S. Lacroix, *Le Département de Paris et de la Seine pendant la Révolution* (Paris, 1904), 407-409 *et seq.* Cf. *Ami des Lois* for 8 and 19 messidor, 29 thermidor VII, cited in Aulard, *Paris*, v, 589, 627, 670.

since it was soon reversed. Barely installed, these officials one by one were removed or resigned. One of the first Jacobins to be eased out of a strategic position was General Marbot, commander of the 17th military division which was garrisoned around Paris, who was not the man to cooperate willingly in using force to close down a Jacobin club. A few days earlier Fouché was called to replace Bourguignon as Police Minister, and after a while people like Tissot felt compelled to resign. During the vote on the *patrie en danger* a resignation that Bernadotte never wrote was accepted, while three members of the Seine department were dismissed, with the others resigning in protest.[13] In these strokes the principal administrative rallying points of Neo-Jacobinism were eliminated. Shortly thereafter the Jacobin press, which as usual chronicled these comings and goings, featured a debate over whether protest resignations were a good tactic, or if it was not preferable to stay on until fired, using this dismissal as the grounds for a future indictment of the authorities![14] By the end of the Year VII the cycle was completed. Having been allowed momentarily to contribute to the commonweal, the Jacobins again found themselves outside the pale, sensible of their "absolute nullity," as Bonaparte had once put it. This sense was heightened by the depressingly familiar attempts to silence their newspapers and clubs.

As the ink dried on the resignations of 30 prairial, a proscribed

[13] To gauge the dismay over Bernadotte's dismissal see, e.g., "Marchand à ces concitoyens," *Ennemi des Tyrans* No. 50, 5th jour compl. an VII; "Les Républicains de Nancy au Corps Legislatif," *L'Abeille des gazettes* (Metz) No. 333, 10 vendémiaire VIII; Petition from the Metz Constitutional Circle, *Ibid.* No. 331, 6th jour compl. VII.

[14] Protest resignations were a familiar vehicle of opposition by now. Thus the *Démocrate* (No. 26, 11 fructidor VII) commented that Tissot had left the Police Ministry "voyant se manifester les symptomes de la réaction"; rumors that Sieyès had insisted he leave "est un titre de plus pour Tissot à l'estime et à l'attachement de tous les républicains-démocrates." About two weeks later Gabriel announced his resignation from the Seine department because of the dismissal of its administrators. He explained that it would be tacit consent to tyranny to retain his post under such circumstances, and that it was honorable to share the disgrace of those who had brought him to his post originally. (*Ennemi des Tyrans* No. 46, 1st jour compl. an VII.) But on the following day the same newspaper carried an "Avis important" urging republicans in the provinces not to resign, because of the imminent threat of royalism. And in its next number (No. 48) there was a column arguing that republicans in general should not resign from "amour propre," but should wait until they are arbitrarily dismissed.

press had returned to life. Quantitatively there is no doubt that royalists were the great beneficiaries. Badly decimated by the law of 19 fructidor Year V, which suppressed over forty royalist newspapers, royalist editors again took up their diatribes against the republic. Doubtless the Jacobins would have been as repressive as anyone against them, for anti-republicanism whether electoral or journalistic was outside the scope of legitimacy for them. But in their minority position they now had no choice but to advocate as free a press as possible, to denounce censorship, and to champion innocuous libel laws.[15] A free press became their watchword, not for philosophic reasons but for the pragmatic one that their existence as a public force depended heavily on the cohesiveness that an unfettered Jacobin press could provide.

The results were relatively meager, since the Directory's assaults against the fragile Jacobin newspapers of the Year VI had been effective. Few provincial newspapers recovered from their suppression, and it appears as if a number of erstwhile editors had been compelled to emigrate to Paris, notably Parent l'aîné (*Bulletin de la Nièvre*), Touquet (*Bulletin de l'Eure*), Pirolle (*Journal des Amis,* Metz), Ballois (*Observateur de la Dordogne*), and Latapy (*Courrier de la Gironde*).[16] None of these outspoken Jacobin organs seems to have revived after 30 prairial, nor did most of the shaky Parisian papers like the *Tribun du Peuple, Ami de la Patrie*, or *L'Indépendant*. Nonetheless 30 prairial was the occasion for several Jacobin newspapers to resume publication. The perennial and uninfluential René Lebois, for example, started a new version of his *Ami du Peuple* and also put out a *Père Duchêne* whose content, if not its language, was unworthy of the title.[17] More important was the re-

[15] See the pamphlets by deputies Blin, Dethier, Dessaix, and Guesdon, all published by Vatar or his cousin Vatar-Jouannet in the Year VII—conveniently listed in A. Monglond, *La France révolutionnaire et impériale*, IV, cols. 1179-82.

[16] Bégin's biographical dictionary of the Moselle department indicates that Pirolle migrated to Paris where he eventually became a horticulturalist; Parent l'aîné and Latapy both turn up in the deliberations of the Manège Club (see below), and Ballois is probably the same one who edited a Parisian newspaper at this time (see note 17 below).

[17] *Le Défenseur de la patrie, faisant suite à "L'Ami du Peuple"* (par R. F. Lebois), 7 messidor-6 fructidor VII: B.N. Lc2/829; *Le Père Duchêne* (Impr. de l'Ami du Peuple) par R. F. Lebois, messidor VII-brumaire VIII: B.N. Lc2/2674. Another short-lived democratic newspaper was founded somewhat later: *Le Défenseur des droits du peuple*, edited by L.J.P. Ballois and printed by E. Charles, 1-28 vendémiaire VIII: B.N. Lc2/2749.

appearance of the *Journal des hommes libres* and a revival of the *Défenseur de la Vérité*.

With placards announcing its imminent resurrection on 28 prairial (16 June 1799), Vatar's *Journal des hommes libres* reappeared on 1 messidor (19 June) as a forum for Jacobins across the country, and as an organ for the Jacobin deputation in the Legislature. Only the greatest tenacity could have kept Vatar from abandoning this hazardous enterprise in favor of the less trying trade of job-printing and bookselling, for the post office continued its harassment, making it difficult to get the paper out to his provincial subscribers.[18] Directorial as well as royalist newspapers waged a vindictive campaign against him, but more important, Sieyès soon embraced their point of view and proved as implacable in his pursuit of Vatar as the old triumverate. Several investigations and searches were carried out, and eventually Vatar was indicted by a grand jury upon recommendation from the Directory on the usual vague charges. His associates, Giraud, Eon, and Camus, were likewise hounded as they had been before Prairial; in what was clearly a politically motivated attack, Camus was savagely beaten on the street one night.[19]

Vatar could find an echo of support in at least one place, however, *Le Démocrate ou le défenseur des principes,* which started on 16 thermidor (3 August), and was a revival of Bescher and Lamberté's *Défenseur de la Vérité et des principes* of the Year VI. Like its predecessor, the *Démocrate* on the whole reflected the old Cordeliers attitudes towards popular democracy, which had opposed the centralization of revolutionary institutions in the Year II. At that time the *Démocrate* and the *Hommes libres* would likely have been on opposing sides in the controversy among democrats over the role of the Committee of Public Safety and the law of 14 frimaire.[20] But

---

[18] Placards on 28 prairial reported in Aulard, *Paris*, v, 572. On the post office see A.N. F⁷ 3449, correspondence for messidor VII; also the *Bulletin générale de Bordeaux* No. 106, 9 messidor VII in A.N. F⁷ 3677/10 (Gironde).

[19] See *Le Démocrate* Nos. 18 and 29, 3 and 14 fructidor VII; *J. hommes libres* No. 63, 3 fructidor; Aulard, *Paris*, v, 690-91; *Défenseur des droits du peuple* No. 6, 6 vendémiaire VIII. The attack on Camus is discussed in *Ennemi des Oppresseurs* Nos. 23 and 26, 4 and 7 vendémiaire VIII, as well as the *Ennemi des Tyrans* No. 54, vendémiaire VIII. Six men allegedly carried out the attack and were assumed to have mistaken Camus for Vatar himself in the dark, since they were of similar build. The victim, according to the police constable, was left in "la plus mauvaise situation."

[20] At various points Bescher, Bazin, Clement, Gabriel, Lambert, and Filhol

the overriding issues of that day were merely nuances that had lost their relevance in the more elemental struggles of the present moment. Now the two papers put up a united front (along with Ballois' *Défenseur des droits du peuple,* which began later), borrowing articles from each other, standing together against new reactions, pleading each other's cause when subjected to governmental harassment. Both were in fact suppressed together by the Directory in a decree of 17 fructidor (3 September) largely because of attacks they had printed against Sieyès.[21] Both soon reappeared under new titles whose similarity was surely by design: the *Ennemi des Oppresseurs* and the *Ennemi des Tyrans.* Vatar was more resourceful at this game of survival; whereas the *Ennemi des Tyrans* succumbed before Brumaire, he managed to carry on until after the coup.[22] Though the editors of each paper were forced to spend most of their time defending themselves and finding new presses, they effectively articulated the long-standing assumptions of the democratic movement.

THE *journée* of 30 prairial produced a sense of renewal which, along with the challenge of the war crisis, invited the formation of new clubs, as well as a revival of an independent press. This special confluence of circumstances proved sufficient to compensate for the previous frustrations of past efforts, and for the last time clubs again became the fulcrum of local and national politics. As always since the Year III the new Constitutional Circles took shape according to local situations.[23] But unlike the previous year they now

---

collaborated in its editing. On its "hébertism" see especially *Ennemi des Tyrans* No. 56, 10 vendémiaire VIII, discussed above in Ch. VI, n.2.

[21] Aulard, *Paris,* v, 714-15; *Le Démocrate* No. 16, 1 fructidor, explains that an article for which the *J. hommes libres* (No. 59) was censured came from their No. 13.

[22] The *Hommes libres* became the *Ennemi des Oppresseurs de tous les temps,* 18 fructidor VII-4 brumaire VIII, and was resurrected under other titles after that suppression. The *Démocrate* became the *Ami de la liberté* for three days, and then the *Ennemi des Tyrans,* 21 fructidor-18 vendémiaire VIII, after which it was definitively suppressed. On 27 vendémiaire the *Défenseur des droits du peuple* announced that it was taking over the subscription list of the *Ennemi des Tyrans.* But two days later Vatar's *Ennemi des Oppresseurs* reported the predictable news that the *Défenseur* (one of the few "écrivains indépendans") had in turn been suppressed (No. 48, 28 vendémiaire VIII).

[23] Amiens, Angers, Auxerre, Besançon, Bordeaux, Bruges, Chambéry, Clermont, Carrouge, Douai, Grenoble, Laon, LeMans, Lyon, Mâcon, Marseilles,

grew under the shadow of an imposing and controversial club in Paris on which national attention inevitably focused.

Founded on or around 18 messidor VII (6 July 1799)—and closed by the government on 26 thermidor (13 August)—the Society of the Friends of Liberty and Equality was almost certainly the creation of those Parisian democrats and Jacobin deputies whose collaboration before Prairial was described in the police surveillance reports. The club's inauguration reflected the moment's unusual circumstances, for it was granted permission to meet in the very precincts of the Legislature: in the recently vacated Salle du Manège, where once the Convention and later the Council of Elders had sat. After the initial elan of the prairial coalition dissipated, this permission was formally withdrawn by the Council of Elders (8 thermidor). The Manège Club (as it continued to be called) then repaired to the 10th arrondissement, whose municipal administration provided it with a public hall in the Rue du Bac. In the Year VI a much smaller and unheralded group of Jacobin deputies had been meeting in a club on the Rue de l'Université in the same vicinity. Scarcely noticeable among the country's other clubs, it apparently survived the floréal coup but had withered away in the repressive atmosphere of pre-Prairial days.[24] The new Manège Club was by comparison a colossus (to use the Directory's word), and one modeled after the original Paris Jacobin Club whose most prominent orators had been Montagnard deputies, and whose ranks were otherwise filled with

---

Metz, Moulins, Nancy, Nevers, Perpignan, Perigueux, Rennes, Valence, Toulouse, Thonon, Valenciennes, and Versailles were among the cities where clubs were formed in 1799.

[24] On the Rue de l'Université Club see below, Ch. VIII, n. 12. This club survived precariously into the Year VII. A printed letter dated 25 nivôse VII and signed with the name Merlino (deputy from the Nord) stated: "L'impossibilité de rassembler assez d'individu pour deliberer au cercle constitutionel de la rue de l'Université, dont vous êtes membre, m'oblige, étant chargé de sa depense, d'écrire à chacun d'eux pour l'informer de sa situation. Il est sur le point d'être dissout faute de fonds; vingt-quatre à vingt-cinq membres payant exactement une contribution de 3 à 5 francs par mois, suivant la saison, suffisent pour le soustraire à cette infamie. . . . Le nombre de réponses que je recevrai dirigera ma conduite ultérieure.

Salut et fraternité: (signed) Merlino

Under the circumstances, at that date, Merlino denied sending this, though he admitted that the signature was a good imitation of his! See A.N. F⁷ 6191, dossier 2482, plaq. 4.

Parisian revolutionaries from the middle class and petit bourgeoisie. The Manège Club attracted as many as 250 deputies at one time or another, while up to 3,000 citizens were reported to be nominally inscribed as members.[25] Most of its rotating officers were drawn from the deputies, while much of the committee work seems to have been carried out by local citizens. Typical of these meneurs were Gabriel (Buonarroti's Paris correspondent and employee of the regenerated Seine department), Boyer (a bureau chief in Bourguignon's Police Ministry), Marchand (a former employee of the Committee of Public Safety and now on Bernadotte's staff), and the ubiquitous Felix Lepelletier. Speeches printed under the club's auspices included those by veteran journalists Leclerc des Vosges and Caignard, and Oratoire elector Victor Bach.

Unlike the clubs of the Year VI, but like the old Paris Jacobin Club, the daily proceedings of the Manège were chronicled in the press, notably the cool *Moniteur*, the partisan *Hommes libres,* and later the equally partisan *Démocrate*. With this ample record it is possible to judge the nature of its proceedings: did it threaten the status quo or augur a revival of the "execrable regime of '93," as its enemies charged? Did it blatantly violate the constitutional articles on clubs? With the exception of an incident that was caused by a provocateur, the club committed itself to the constitutional framework. As its defenders later pointed out, nothing was ever said that was subject to prosecution under existing laws, like the law of 27 germinal IV under which Babuef had been convicted, or the kinds of laws under which Bach and Dubreuil had been unsuccessfully indicted before Prairial. Speakers were repeatedly interposing pledges of loyalty to the constitution and disavowing any call for a new Convention, revolutionary government, or terror. The Manège also abided by the constitution's rules to the same extent that most clubs did in the Year VI. It avoided any blatant violations but interpreted the fine points liberally. No permanent officers were designated, no categories of citizens barred from admission, no affiliation with other clubs attempted, no demonstrably collective acts undertaken. It did pass resolutions, set up study com-

[25] A. Aulard, "Les Derniers Jacobins," *R.F.,* xxvi (1894), 389. From articles in *J. Hommes libres* and the *Moniteur* Aulard established a roster of some 87 participants (pp. 391-92). Perusal of the *Démocrate*, which Auland did not know, brings to light a few others.

mittees, have speeches published under its auspices, and receive denunciations.[26]

Style was another matter. The rhetoric inspired by the war crisis and the vendetta against the deposed Directors was fiery and provocative. Speakers had the habit of stating relatively innocuous propositions extravagantly, and of invoking vague calls that could be interpreted in any which way, particularly the sentiment that in a republic "the people must save themselves." To the Jacobins it was obvious that one could espouse democratic ideas without reviving the regime of '93. Scarcely any notion advanced here (except for those pertaining to the temporary emergency on which the Legislature had already agreed) could not be found in the Year VI. The word "democracy" was invoked more often, but the attitudes behind it were familiar coin. Thermidor was reviled; democratic martyrs, including the Vendôme defendants, were celebrated; the right to censure and denounce public officials was affirmed; the meaning of sovereignty was expounded; the importance of public spirit, and its bulwarks—the press and the clubs—were emphasized.[27]

[26] This material is conveniently summarized in Aulard, "Les Derniers Jacobins," pp. 389-406, which is in turn the basis of Meynier's chapter in *Le Dix-huit brumaire*. Equally detailed coverage of the club in Metz was provided by the local newspaper *L'Abeille* (see my article, "The Revival of Jacobinism in Metz," *Journal of Modern History* [1966], pp. 34-35), while a much weaker club in Angers was publicized in the *Ami de la Liberté, Journal d'Angers* for thermidor and fructidor. See also *Manifeste des Jacobins au peuple français, en réponse aux calomnies . . .* (Impr. Phillipe), B.N. Lb42/2655, and other defenses whose titles are listed in M. Tourneux's *Bibliographie de l'histoire de Paris pendant la Révolution française*, Vol. ii, Nos. 9938, 9946, 9947, 9948, 9950.

[27] Compare this typical melange of concerns in a petition from the club in Perigueux: Continués donc, de resister aux scélerats qui voudraient vous effrayer ou vous desunir; protection constante aux républicains; prompte vengéance des crimes du triumvirat, des rapines de ses nombreuses suppots; activés par tous les moyens la fabrication des armes; ne tenez aucun compte des cris de l'avarice et de la corruption; que l'emprunt de cent millions s'effectue sans delai: les croiriez-vous les amis de la République ceux qui mettent ses besoins en balance avec leurs jouissances particulières[?] Non, ils sont faits pour l'esclavage, leur bassesse appelle la Royauté. Nous le savons les eternels calomniateurs des sociétés patriotiques, ne cessant de fouiller dans les crises de la Révolution, de vous en rappeler les malheurs pour émousser pour eteindre, s'il était possible, ce sainte enthousiasme qui les fait trembler. Les complices de Pitt ont bien pu fouler aux pieds la Constitution, ils ont bien pu la tremper dans le sang des boucheries de Vendôme et de Grenelle; mais les français dignes de ce nom ne cesseront de la porter dans leur coeur, et de la deffendre jusqu'à

Finally, though there was not much time to devote to this yet, the role of such a club in developing programs for progressive social legislation was asserted, notably in proposals by Victor Bach and Felix Lepelletier that drew together the issues discussed in a previous chapter.[28] At bottom, the Manège was a remarkably open forum for the exchange of sentiment and ideas among democrats. Demands that were supported nationally by what might be termed advanced or progressive opinion (as reflected in petitions) were translated into immediate pressure on the government.[29] However, the language and allusions of 1793 were used to pepper oratory that was addressed in substance to the world of 1799. The overexposure of publicity compounded this, making the Manège appear a more menacing organization than it really was.

For the prolific anti-Jacobin press (royalist and Directorial) the Manège Club was a target made to order. It proved a particular boon to the business of pamphleteering-for-profit, for it was the object of over fifty pamphlets and broadsides, most of them anti, a few pro, and a few simply timely but pointless. Their frenzied language and fantastic conceits were hawked through the streets by vendors who shouted their provocative titles: *Grande fureur de Moustache-sans-Peur; Chassez-moi les Jacobins, plus d'echafauds; A bas les Jacobins* [*pro!*]; *Mille bombes! voilà! voilà! les crimes*

---

dernier soupir. A.N. AF III 144B [Guerre: Objets divers]: Les Citoyens composans la société des amis de la liberté et de l'égalité de Perigueux (Dordogne) to the Council of 500 (late thermidor).

[28] *Premier discours du citoyen Bach à la réunion séant au Manège, sur les moyens de consolider la République* (Impr. Benoist, 30 messidor an VII); and Aulard, "Les Derniers Jacobins," pp. 404-405 on Lepelletier.

[29] Some of these petitions to the Legislature were even printed at its own expense during the ephemeral burst of solidarity following Prairial. See for example printed petitions in the Maclure Collection (University of Pennsylvania Library) from Nevers, Bordeaux, Grenoble, Rennes, the faubourg Antoine, the 10th arrondissement of Paris, and above all a petition from Mâcon, which among other things demanded: "Frappez le riche insensible et le froid egoiste, abordez sans crainte la grande question de l'impôt progressif. Les besoins de l'état et la justice sociale le demandent." (*Conseil des Anciens: Les citoyens de la commune de Mâcon . . . aux membres du Corps législatif . . . 4 messidor an 7* [Impr. Nationale].) In short, the point can amply be documented that Victor Bach's remarkable and well known pamphlet was by no means an isolated phenomenon. In his view the moment had come to draw together a number of long-standing issues in the hope of galvanizing support for the minority of activists who stood steadfast in the clubs. (See Bach, *Premier discours*, pp. 6 and 20.)

de Jacobins devoilés. . . . Dusting off accusations that were pre-posterous even in 1793, they depicted the Manège as a retreat of brigands, *égorgeurs*, and idolators of Robespierre. Some warned of their imminent domination, others merely reviled them.[30] The de-rogatory stereotypes also made fair game for a slightly higher level of political satire. One pamphlet entitled *Dites encore que les Jac-obins ne sont pas braves* hit the mark with a mock debate among Jacobins over whether they should form a legion to go to the front. A member objects that their place is here, so that denunciations can be processed. They decide to combine the two activities, depart for the front but leave behind a committee for denunciations.[31] Talk of proscription was especially common in these pamphlets—a some-what more ominous note than satire. Some accused the Jacobins of preparing proscription; others talked of the need for proscription *of* the Jacobins; while still others added to the overheated atmos-phere by publishing lists of patriotic Jacobins who were purport-edly being designated for such proscription after the club was closed.[32] Such manifestly exaggerated polemics created a smoke screen of images that obscured what the club was really doing—though that in itself would have been a legitimate matter of con-troversy for conservatives. The government's principal charge against the Manège was accordingly true: that the club was "stirring up hostility and reviving dangerous memories."[33]

[30] Tourneux's *Bibliographie de Paris*, II, 455-59 (Nos. 9920-72) lists most of these; Monglond, *La France révolutionnaire et impériale*, IV, cols. 807-12, adds a few additional titles.

[31] B.N. Lb42/2380 (n.l., n.d.). Cf. *Ami des Lois*, 22 thermidor VII (in Aulard, *Paris*, V, 672): "Tous les riches quittent Paris depuis la loi de 100 millions; les équipages ont disparu; on fuit les jurys [charged with allocating the forced loan] comme on fuyait les comités révolutionnaires. Les ouvriers sont sans ouvrage: il faut qu'ils aillent en demander aux clubs qui trouvent des remèdes à tout."

[32] See Tourneux, *Bibliographie de Paris*, II, Nos. 9932, 9956, 9959, and 9931, mostly pamphlets signed "Saunier," arguing (despite their misleading titles) that attacks on the Manège foretell the proscription of virtuous patriots, who are then named. Pamphlets like Nos. 9930 or 9961 were anti-Jacobin lists. Some weeks later there appeared a far more elaborate *Dictionnaire des Jacobins Vivans* (Hambourg, 1799). Its author had a good sense of the kinds of persons who were indeed "Jacobins vivans," though he erred in some individual cases, especially on former Montagnards who had retired completely from political life.

[33] *Conseil des Cinq-Cents: Message . . . du Directoire exécutif, 26 thermidor*

Thomas Lindet (writing from the Eure where he returned after being floréalized, and where he kept up-to-date by reading the *Hommes libres*) had predicted that "the patriots who devote themselves with a premature energy risk again becoming the victims of a new Machiavelism." "I feel sorry for the orators of the Manège who fashion a republicanism in the manner of 1793," he continued, since it was most unlikely that the "*moderateurs*" would be carried along without offering resistance.[34] In explaining his adherence to Sieyès' decree closing the Manège, director Gohier testified to a similar view. The Manège posed no real danger and was a source of potential good, in his estimation, but he felt that it was producing reaction in excess of such good. Though he objected to the inflammatory rhetoric that was sometimes heard there, he personally could tolerate it. He felt that its infractions of the constitution were easily corrected, and the real hotheads (*fous*) were few in number. In reality the club should have been causing concern only to the revolution's enemies, he concluded, but unfortunately it was frightening "weak-minded" citizens as well, instead of giving them confidence in the future.[35]

The closing of the Manège was a complex event that did not necessarily determine the fate of other clubs. For one thing, it was entangled in Sieyès' and Barras' maneuvers to block the indictment of the deposed Directors which the club stridently advocated. Another special circumstance was suggested by Vatar: that action against the Manège was demanded by the Parisian bankers whose loan on favorable terms the Directory was desperate to negotiate. That loan was concluded, he pointed out, on the same day that a report condemning the club was issued.[36] Both Barras and Gohier

---

an 7 (Impr. Nationale), p. 3. For the steps leading towards suppression see A.N. AF III 15: P. V. of the Directory for 13, 17, and 26 thermidor VII.

[34] Letter dated 8 thermidor VII, from Bernay (Eure) cited in A. Montier, *Robert Lindet, notice biographique* (Paris, 1899), pp. 367-68.

[35] Gohier, *Mémoires*, I, 91-92, 97, 104-107.

[36] *J. hommes libres* Nos. 46 and 48, 16 and 18 thermidor VII. This was but one of several attacks on the *gros capitalistes*, which culminated in an exposure of the relationship between the bankers and Bonaparte after Brumaire (*Journal des Républicains* No. 8, 29 brumaire VIII). The same charge was leveled by Gaultier-Biauzat in a letter to his daughter written on the very day of 18 brumaire: "Le parti financier de Paris, qui n'est pas étranger à tout ce qui s'est passé *depuis trois mois*, triomphe d'une manière éclatante, au point que dans l'acès de sa joie, il a donné plusieurs millions pour fournir aux dépenses actuelles." (Mege, *Biauzat*, p. 325; italics added.)

suggest yet another and less sinister consideration: that Sieyès' private animus against the club made it difficult for the executive to function harmoniously, since he would never let the matter rest. According to Gohier, the decision to close the Manège represented "the only way of calming our colleague's fright."[37]

In any case, Gohier and Moulin adhered to the decree on condition that it be accompanied by a special message to the Legislature urging passage of an organic law to regulate and guarantee the existence of political clubs, and thus to remove this issue from the arena of arbitrary decisions. It is possible to conclude that Gohier, and the kind of opinion he represented, was not being insincere. The closing of the Manège, while inevitably producing surges of anti-Jacobinism in the provinces,[38] did not interrupt the progress of most other clubs. And the Jacobins were likely to profit in the long run if that organic law was debated in an atmosphere unclouded by the kind of controversy that had raged around the Manège from its inception. Unforeseen at the time, no agreement was ever reached on this issue before Brumaire obviated the whole discussion. But a protracted debate on this organic law did ensue which, in its amplitude of detail and its range of revealed attitudes, was one of the era's most significant. In the Directory's twilight it illuminated the frustrated hopes and the equivocation that ushered in the Napoleonic dictatorship.

‡ III ‡

On the first of thermidor (19 July)—even before the Directory attacked the Manège—the Jacobin deputy Talot attempted to advance action on an organic law by a *motion d'ordre*, following which a special committee of five was established. Chairman Rollin (a

---

[37] Barras, *Memoirs*, III, 563, 566: Gohier, *Mémoires*, I, 110-11.

[38] See e.g., public prosecutor of the Doubs to the department's deputies, 29 thermidor VII: ". . . A peine avait-on scu que la Réunion de Paris avait été insultée que des jeunes gens de l'école centrale commencerent à ridiculiser celle d'icy [Besançon] qui avait tenu quelques séances." (A.N. F⁷ 7627, fol. 1362.) Des républicains de la Nièvre [residing in Paris] to Fouché, 3 fructidor: ". . . la nouvelle de la cloture du cercle de la rue du Bacq a fait pousser des cris de mort contre les républicains, surtout à Cosne." (F⁷ 7648, fol. 1789.) Les citoyens de Versailles to Directory, 28 thermidor (signators include Lepelletier and Germain), protesting the Directory's anti-Jacobinism which "va entrainer la République dans l'abime." (F⁷ 7656, fol. 1947.)

moderate professor of legislation) presented its draft proposal on the 16th (3 August), prefaced by a speech of his own. To reassure his colleagues he evoked a vision of prudent, patriotic, and useful clubs—clubs which would "take care to exclude all men of doubtful reputation"; where speeches would first be scrutinized by men of "known wisdom and intelligence"; where preference would be given to "respectable heads of families, peaceful men of commerce, heads of workshops, pure and honest artisans." However, the two Jacobins on the committee (Briot and Lamarque) evidently influenced the draft proposal more than the tenor of this speech would indicate. For it was actually a model of simplicity which thereby would have proven extremely favorable to the Jacobins. It had but four articles. I. Only French citizens could be members. (This was directed explicitly against foreign provocateurs; however, it might also have been interpreted to exclude such non-voting citizens as wished to participate, and this was later pointed out by other Jacobins.) II. Individuals who interfered with the right of clubs to meet were to be prosecuted as "disturbers of public order" under existing laws. III. Infractions of Articles 361-64 of the constitution were to be prosecuted through the existing channels of the *police correctionnelle*, and punished by maximum sentences of three months' imprisonment. IV. "All dispositions to the contrary are hereby repealed."[39]

As the organic law on clubs, this proposal would have effectively protected their right to exist and eliminated almost all cases where clubs were arbitrarily closed by the authorities. Conversely it said nothing to *further* restrict the clubs beyond the ambiguous wording of the constitution. It became increasingly evident as the debate proceeded that this ambiguity was to the Jacobins' advantage since it kept the situation open instead of spelling out cumbersome guidelines for the clubs' organization and behavior. The ambiguity that

[39] While the general outlines of this crucial debate may be followed in the *Moniteur*, it is essential to consult the printed speeches and draft proposals. They are available in the B.N., but I have drawn here on those in the Maclure Collection, University of Pennsylvania Library. Unless otherwise noted they were published by the Imprimerie Nationale by order of the Council of Five Hundred. See *Rapport fait par Rollin au nom d'une commission spéciale, sur le mode d'organisation des sociétés particulières s'occupant de questions politiques. Séance du 16 thermidor an 7*. The quotation is from pp. 16-17.

it did resolve served now to affirm the clubs' rights *against* arbitrary intervention by the authorities.

Before long a number of deputies labeled this committee report inadequate. While it protected the clubs, they pointed out, it did not protect the state from the clubs. By not anticipating and prohibiting the specific sources of past "disorders," it invited their repetition. In short the committee's draft did not implement the constitution's spirit by resolving its ambiguity and detailing the procedures that clubs must follow. Hence these deputies submitted their own proposals—all of which were longer, more detailed, and more restrictive.[40]

The Jacobins continued to press for decision on this issue, the closing of the Manège having underscored the need for a definitive guarantee of some sort. On 21 fructidor (7 September) Biggonet (who had escaped floréalizing in the Year VI from the Saône-et-Loire department) delivered a scathing attack on the government's anti-Jacobinism and the *malheurs* that continued to afflict the country—*malheurs* proving that 30 prairial had really changed nothing permanently. The term he used to encompass these issues was "réaction"; tyranny is reorganizing itself, he warned. To combat this Biggonet asserted that freedom to dissent had to be guaranteed—specifically freedom of the press and freedom of association, which always came under attack during periods of reaction. Every other daily session of the Legislature, he demanded, must be devoted to completing the organic laws on press and clubs. Hooted down by several deputies, he succeeded only in having his proposal sent to existing committees.

Five days later Bertrand tried another tactic that had evidently been planned by a group of Jacobin deputies. He moved to end debate on the issue of clubs and to bring to a vote a proposal previously submitted by Berlier. With Rollin's original draft obviously having

[40] Those submitting proposals included Luminais, Lafont, Renault, d'Outrepont, Declercq, Cholet, Ramel, Berlier, Guinard, D'André, Desnos, Mansord, Hello, Parent-Réal, Faulcon, Cabanis, and Scherlock. Those by Declercq, Berlier, D'André, and Mansord supported in one way or another the Jacobin position. Moreover, the speech that Declercq gave in introducing his proposal was an outspoken attack on the Directory's closing of the Manège, as well as being an eloquent defense of the principle of freedom for citizens in clubs to scrutinize and censure their officials. See *Opinion de H. Declercq (du Nord) . . . séance du 11 fructidor.*

no chance, they rallied to what must have appeared the least damaging of alternatives. A line was quickly drawn, as Jacobins like Clemenceau, Lesage-Senault, and Blin spoke in favor of Berlier's proposal, while the thermidorian Malès led a surprisingly vehement resistance, which foreshadowed the kind of debate that would greet Jourdan's motion on the *patrie en danger* the following day. All of the projects thus far still left the clubs in a position to become dangerous, Malès asserted. They "do not provide enough of a guarantee for the government," and may yet resemble those execrated popular societies of the Year II. In the end Bertrand's motion to stop debate and vote on Berlier's proposal was defeated. Speeches would henceforth be eliminated, but new proposals would still be accepted by the committee and decision would be postponed. Predictably, new draft proposals that were subsequently submitted were even more elaborate and repressive.[41]

OUT OF this welter of twenty-odd draft proposals, one can perceive certain points that would likely have drawn a majority consensus, and others whose resolution was in question. In other words one can see the problem posed before an ideologically divided legislature by the kinds of clubs that Neo-Jacobins insisted on protecting.

To begin with, any organic law that was passed, once Rollin's simple formula had been discarded, was likely to contain a number of explicit restrictions on clubs which the Jacobins would have had to accept.

1. Strict registration procedures would oblige a club to notify local authorities promptly and in writing of the time and place of meeting and of the membership roster.

2. These local authorities would have an unqualified right to enter and observe the meetings even though they were not members.

3. To be eligible for membership a man would have to be a Frenchman (that is, not a foreigner) and not otherwise excluded by certain categories spelled out in the constitution (bankruptcy, domestic service, etc.). In addition he must be domiciled in his canton for a year, could belong only to the club in his own canton, and could not belong to more than one club. In short, he would

---

[41] *Moniteur*, pp. 1434, 1436, 1454. See *Opinion de Berlier dans la discussion relative aux Sociétés s'occupant de questions politiques. Séance du 21 fructidor an 7.*

have to be a person of settled domicile who was known to his neighbors.

4. No one could come to a meeting armed.

5. Meetings would have to end by ten o'clock or some similar time.

6. The club's name could not be used by its members collectively outside its precincts. No petition could bear the name of a club under any circumstance.

7. A club would be prohibited from appointing deputations or committees to act outside its precincts, or to publish and distribute placards or pamphlets in its collective name.

Though the most determined opponents of the clubs would have opposed the following propositions, it seems likely, on the other hand, that any organic law passed by this Legislature would have granted certain prerogatives and extended certain guarantees to the clubs:

1. Clubs could screen their members individually, provided no categories of citizens (other than those earlier specified by law) were excluded. In effect Sotin's formula of the Year VI on judging an individual's "morality and civism" would have prevailed, and applicants could be voted on instead of being accepted indiscriminately.

2. Clubs could regulate their internal affairs, such as rules of procedure and monetary matters. However, their officers would have to be chosen on a rotating basis, possibly appointed newly at each meeting.

3. Law-abiding clubs would at last be free of arbitrary harassment by all manner of officials; the law would spell out the punishment of those who attempted to harass or prevent a club from meeting.

4. Conversely, infractions by the clubs would now be punished by due process. The law would designate which official would be involved (most likely the courts rather than the administrators) and what the punishments would be (most likely within reason rather than unusually severe).

Assuming that consensus would have prevailed on most of these points, the long-awaited organic law would have had to deal with a number of other proposals designed to restrict and limit the clubs. Against most of these potential roadblocks to effective civisme, Berlier's proposal would have defended the *de facto* condition of most Neo-Jacobin clubs.

A number of proposals sought to regulate further the size and in some cases the number of clubs. Several deputies urged that a two hundred-man limit should be set on the size of each club, since anything over that would be a disorderly assemblage. Berlier's draft had no such stipulations. Likewise his draft avoided entanglement in the constitution's highly ambiguous statement about public *vs* private meetings. Implicitly his position would have duplicated Sotin's rulings in the Year VI, which allowed the possibility for both kinds of meetings. Some conservatives, however, wished to strait jacket the clubs either in a requirement to maintain complete privacy, or a compulsion to hold only open meetings.

On the question of eligibility, the Jacobin position would have favored excluding various well-defined counterrevolutionary types as well as the intriguing "foreigners" whom all were anxious to keep out. But in a moving speech by the deputy Mansord, it was pointed out that allowing only "French citizens" into the clubs might be interpreted to exclude both the disfranchised "citoyen-ouvrier" who paid no tax and the youths who were called upon to fight but not to vote. The clubs must not accentuate the dichotomy of poor and rich, he argued. Berlier's proposal, though ambiguous on this point, was probably meant to be interpreted as Mansord wished. It did not use the limiting phrase "French citizen." Rather it excluded—besides foreigners—"all Frenchmen whose political rights have been lost or suspended by virtue of either the constitution or the laws of 3 brumaire Year IV and 9 frimaire Year VI," the latter aimed against ex-nobles. The likely interpretation of this text is that it refers specifically to Articles 12 and 13 of the constitution on the loss or suspension of citizenship, and not to Article 8 where the subject of registration and tax payment for voting is dealt with. The choice of the word "Frenchman" rather than "French citizen" seems to have been deliberate.[42]

---

[42] *Opinion de Mansord (du Mont Blanc)* . . . *séance du 26 fructidor an 7*, pp. 5, 9, 11 and *passim*. (To read this speech along with Declercq's is to feel the full emotional commitment of Jacobins to equality and civisme.) *Opinion de Berlier*, Art. I. Cf. *Opinion de D'André (du Bas Rhin)* . . . *séance du 22 fructidor*, Art I: "Ces sociétés ne sont composées que des Français qui exercent leurs droits politiques, et de ceux à qui il ne manque, pour les exercer, que l'âge, ou le paiement d'une contribution."

A third major dispute revolved around deliberation within the clubs. Guinard, for example, urged that "the members . . . may take no deliberations on any subject whatsoever," except those dealing with discipline and financing of the club itself. Cabanis (who was shortly found in the inner circle of revisionists) proposed: "They are prohibited from having recording secretaries, from naming committees, from hearing reports, from putting questions to a vote, from keeping registers of minutes." On the other hand, the moderate deputy Hello was willing to allow clubs to keep registers of minutes, to receive petitions and denunciations which could be edited by a committee and presented to the club, and to pass motions which, however, were not to be binding on the opposing minority. Likewise, D'André's relatively liberal draft specifically granted clubs the right to deliberate within their locale, though it added that "their voice may be manifested on the outside only individually." He argued that the club was a forum for expressing opinions and that since all citizens were not adept at public speaking they should be allowed to express opinions through votes. Nothing in Berlier's proposal would have prohibited deliberations, taking of votes, or keeping of records. It did, following the constitution's text, prohibit four kinds of collective acts which were external to the club's own deliberations: affiliation, collective correspondence, publication of addresses in the club's name, and sending out deputations. It also spelled out the interpretation of what collective petitions were, but in doing so it actually pointed to the obvious method of circumvention. The name of a club could never be used but "the simultaneous signatures of a number of citizens, even when they may all be members of the same club, does not at all constitute the collective aspect that is prohibited."[43]

Finally there was the issue of how to punish infractions. Consensus existed on the need to specify both the modes and the penalties, but there was considerable difference in substance about how to do this. The question of individual *vs.* collective responsibility for infractions was a particularly perplexing issue, and Berlier's draft attempted to put most of the weight on individuals, whereas other

[43] *Opinion de Guinard (de la Lys)* . . . *séance du 22 fructidor*, Art. XI; *Opinion de Cabanis* . . . (n.d.), Art IV; *Opinion de Hello (des Côtes du Nord)* . . . *séance du 26 fructidor*, Arts. IX and X; *Opinion de d'André*, Art. XIX, and pp. 12-13; *Opinion de Berlier*, Arts. XII, XV, XVI.

proposals made the case for collective responsibility. The latter usually entailed the closing of the club as one punishment. Cabanis' proposal was particularly severe in attempting to retain wide discretionary authority for local officials to close a club—a proposition which was anathema to the Jacobins. In Berlier's bill *only the refusal to allow public officials into the club was a cause for such action.* Another issue involved the severity of fines and prison sentences. Luminais and others wished to use the threat of prohibitive fines (2,000 francs) or long prison sentences as a deterent to infractions. Berlier, on the other hand, proposed fines of three *journées de travail* for certain offenses, and imprisonment from one to six months for the more serious infractions that involved the constitutional articles.

Presumably the Jacobin's commitment to Berlier's draft increased as the new proposals submitted grew increasingly repressive. The crypto-royalist deputy Felix Faulcon, for instance, would not only have limited the meeting time to eight o'clock—thus effectively barring working people—but he would have had all clubs closed during the months of ventôse and germinal, in other words before and during election time. Cabanis' proposal would have translated into law the repeated attempts—ranging for Mailhe's plan in the Year IV to Roederer's proposal in the Year VI—to reduce the clubs to mere discussion groups whose role was solely educative. And finally, there was General Scherlock, whose military mind cut through the self-deception, ambiguity, or sentimentality that prevented many conservatives from facing the logical consequences of their attitudes. No matter how stringently regulated, he warned, political clubs by their very essence were a threat to the "amis de l'ordre"—though, of course, they had once been indispensable to the nation. "Can one hope to succeed by means of an organic law to regenerate these clubs and guarantee them against all the abuses that are inseparable from their composition," he asked. In answering no, Scherlock suggested that this attempt to draft such a chimerical organic law be abandoned in favor of an unflinching application of the constitution. Its authors, he correctly pointed out, were more concerned with curbing the excesses of clubs than with guaranteeing their existence, and it must be applied in that spirit even if this involved certain drastic interpretations. Specifically, he called attention to a relationship between the press and the clubs that the

Jacobins had always prized. "The law is powerless . . . to prevent correspondence and affiliation among the clubs from the moment that they are in possession of publicity." This recognized, he invited the deputies to sacrifice the prerogative of publicity to the general interest, meaning, presumably, that newspapers should be barred from even mentioning a club's existence, let alone describing its activities.[44]

Undaunted by this thunder on the Right, Jacobins had no alternative but to continue pressing for an organic law that would stop short of such drastic prescriptions. This last hope was forcefully expressed and frequently reiterated even as Brumaire approached. "To democrats overwhelmed with disgust and bitterness," wrote one of the few remaining Jacobin organs in vendémiaire, "there remains only this single and legitimate hope of destroying, slowly but surely, the quaking foundations of despotism."[45] The prolonged struggle over the organic law on clubs thus illuminates the last agony of constitutional liberalism in France. Having long since recognized that the executive under Sieyès was their nemesis, democrats rested their fate on the will of the Legislature to uphold the freedom to dissent. The failure of that fragmented body to reach any decision on this issue serves as a perfect illustration of the division that made Brumaire possible.[46]

[44] *Projet de Résolution presenté par Felix Faulcon (de la Vienne)* [n.d., but after 26 fructidor], Arts. VI, X, and *passim*; *Opinion de Cabanis, passim*; *Opinion de Scherlock* [n.d., but after 26 fructidor], pp. 2-5, 9.

[45] *Défenseur des droits du peuple*, 25 vendémiaire VIII. See also petition from Nancy in *L'Abeille* (Metz) No. 333, 10 vendémiaire VIII, and a petition from Lyon with over 400 signatures complaining about the "marasme apathique; la fermeture d'une Réunion célebre [the Manège], foyer ardent de vertus, de talens, d'energie et d'esprit démocratique." The petition demanded that freedom of the press be assured, regardless of the "abus que le royalisme masqué ose en faire. Une prompte loi qui garantisse les sociétés politiques contre tous les coups du pouvoir. . . . Des loix philanthropiques qui viennent au secours du *peuple pauvre* . . . qui ne pouvant bientôt plus manger maudit la Révolution qui ne supplée point à ses privations." A.N. AF III 35 [Justice: questions de législation], dossier 128: Des républicains de Lyon au Corps législatif, 23 fructidor VII.

[46] Likewise the Legislature was unable to agree on a law designed to prevent the suppression of newspapers by the government, though both Jacobins and Directorials claimed to desire it. The law was supposed to guarantee freedom of the press, while setting out fixed procedures for punishing "abuses" and libel, much as the law on clubs was supposed to do. The inconclusive debates on this law are summarized from the *Moniteur* in G. LePoittevin, *La Liberté de la presse depuis la Révolution* (Paris, 1901), pp. 85-105.

‡ IV ‡

As a public force the Jacobins expired quite helplessly, but not without an acute consciousness of what they were fighting for. All things considered, it is understandable that they took their last stand on the issue of freedom to dissent—on the struggle for laws guaranteeing freedom of the press and freedom of association. For these were directly related to the larger question of whether opposition would be legitimized or excluded. Bonaparte's decisive "no" was already anticipated in the policies of the triumvirate and of Sieyès that the Jacobins fought so doggedly,[47] but with a crucial difference: as long as the Constitution of the Year III existed it remained an open question.

In its last manifestation before Brumaire permanently interred it, Jacobinism became so explicitly a defense of what Antonelle had called "representative democracy" that there is no mistaking it. Though the handwriting may have already been on the wall, they continued to maintain that a "democratic republic" could evolve out of the Constitution of the Year III. "Do you wish to know what these fearsome Jacobins want?" asked Marchand at the Manège Club. "They simply want the constitution, the democratic republic." It seemed so obvious. "We wish neither a triumvirate nor an oligarchy," a petition from Mâcon (Saône-et-Loire) declared; "we want representative democracy, we want a government where the people are everything, where its sovereignty is not a vain word." The resolution of social problems would in turn depend on the nature and vitality of that sovereignty.[48]

As a party organ in everything but name, the redoubtable *Journal des hommes libres* drove home the logic of the Jacobin position. Activist by definition, it ruled out apathy and acquiescence; pragmatic, it ruled out a public appeal to force. It remained to exhort the stalwart to carry on the struggle over implementation of that

[47] See "Réponse à Sieyès," reprinted from the *Démocrate* in *J. hommes libres* No. 59, 29 thermidor VII; *L'Ennemi des tyrans au dictateurs Sieyès et Barras* (Impr. rue du Fouare), B.N. Lb42/2461; Metge, *Panegyrique de Sieyès* (Impr. du *Démocrate*, 27 thermidor VII), B.N. Lb42/2161.

[48] Aulard, "Les Derniers Jacobins," p. 402 (9 thermidor); *Les citoyens de la commune de Mâcon . . . 4 messidor an 7*, p. 4; petition from the Constitutional Circle of Bruges (Lys), fructidor, in A.N. F7 7625, fol. 1336. See also the pamphlets by D'Aubigny, Chaumont-Quitry, and Chaussard, and the petitions from Perigueux and Lyon, cited above, notes 27 and 45.

remarkably pliable Constitution of the Year III on which the nation's "democratic existence" depended. This constitution had been abused repeatedly to deprive citizens of their rights and to circumscribe their activities almost totally. But according to the *Hommes libres* this could still be reversed by three related things: legislative supremacy; genuinely free primary assemblies; and the clubs—those "foyers of civisme"—which could guarantee this process.[49]

The rapid alternation of freedom (after 30 prairial) and renewed "tyranny" (under Sieyès) revealed the chasm that existed between this vision and reality. "Demoralization and every sort of crime" have been spread under the constitution's mantle, and this could not go unopposed.

> If they use the constitution as it is to maintain the democracy that the people desire, one should respect and assist those who govern. If ever, on the contrary, they abuse it in order to attack democracy, one must say to oneself that since democracy is the goal, and they are simply the means to a goal, it would be absurd on the part of the governed to sacrifice the one to the others. Democracy must be respected . . . instead of perjured and traitorous administrators, who work only for themselves against democracy and against us.[50]

This blunt statement aimed against Sieyès was later followed by an even more explicit justification of organized opposition. In an article entitled "Some definitions that are presently in order," Vatar recalled a distinction between faction and party that had been drawn in 1797 by ex-mayor Pache in his book attacking the Vendôme trial. The label of "faction" should be assigned to an ambitious group that would attack the principles of an established government (meaning its constitution)—a position that was illegitimate. But "party" should be defined as "discontented citizens who together attack the operations or the persons of those who govern." Not only was this deemed legitimate; under certain circumstances it was necessary.[51]

[49] *J. hommes libres* No. 5, 5 messidor, and No. 16, 16 messidor VII.

[50] *Ibid.* No. 49, 18 thermidor VII: "Developpment de quelques idées récemment offertes à Sieyès."

[51] *Ennemi des Oppresseurs* No. 30, 11 vendémiaire VIII: "Quelques definitions à l'ordre du moment."

Most Jacobins refused to confer any legitimacy on violent opposition. The most uncompromising and radical organ of Parisian democrats, the *Démocrate*, made it clear that they were an opposition disarmed and dependent on constitutional processes. "It is a far cry from the terrible truths that we proclaim . . . against all enemies (whatever mask they may cover themselves with), to the convulsive and disordered movement which would doom us all without profit to the cause of freedom." Wary of another massacre instigated by provocateurs, the *Démocrate* plumbed the limits of polemical confrontation, but drew the line against "thoughtless movements and illegal demonstrations." Instead, like Vatar, it simply offered an explicit defense of political opposition.[52]

Until 18 brumaire this could be argued. For all the repressive policies of the Directory, the Jacobin opposition was not subdued. True, the electoral campaign of 1798 had been a crucial turning point on the issue of legitimizing opposition, and in that sense the Directory prepared the way for Brumaire. But the final word must be in an opposite sense, for it is the difference between a tendency and its fulfillment, between probability and finality. Until that day on which it was unceremoniously scrapped, the constitution existed to remind the executive—as Declercq pointed out during the debate on the organic law—that they "were only directors and not dictators." This could scarcely be said after Brumaire.

‡ V ‡

The end of a lengthy study of the Directory era is not the place to assess the Napoleonic experience. But this much is certain: organized opposition was not tolerated. The Consulate's local administrators took it as their charge to prohibit the political clubs which were no longer guaranteed in its new constitution. Likewise the central government gradually muzzled the opposition press, limiting the number of newspapers that could appear as well as censoring those that survived. For their resistance on the *journée* of 18 brumaire, 62 deputies were promptly purged—an example not lost on the careerists who remained. To demoralize the cadres of Parisian "agitators," a random group of democrats, whose dossiers came readily to hand in the Police Ministry, was designated for arrest and then pardoned.

[52] *Le Démocrate* No. 21, 6 fructidor VII: "Avis important"; Nos. 27 and 29, 12 and 14 fructidor: "De l'Opposition."

Subsequently, however, over one hundred of these presumed oppositionists were sentenced by executive decree to deportation after the affair of the "infernal machine"—an attempt on Bonaparte's life in December 1800 that was actually perpetrated by royalists. Significantly, Vatar was among this group of former functionaries, journalists, and sectionnaires.[53]

This whole process of repression deserves careful scrutiny in its own right, as do the varieties of personal resistance and conspiratorial activity under Napoleon. But their details can scarcely alter the main conclusion. As a sustained political movement and as a practical political persuasion, Jacobinism was sentenced to wither away after Brumaire, if not in days then in weeks. Deprived of their structural base and channels of communication, the remaining cadres could not function in any effective way that was familiar to them. The incipient constitutional party of movement and reform that was the Jacobins' response to the thermidorian reaction now came to a dead end.

The Directorials had themselves thrown up obstacles to this opposition all along, but given their own commitments to republicanism they were unable to eliminate it. In that fact—in that ambiguity —lay the promise of the Directorial regime for men who shared the democratic persuasion. It is therefore possible to argue that instead of being an overdue or natural sequel to Thermidor, Brumaire was a marked change of direction. A counterrevolution of major proportions, Brumaire broke the fragile evolution of a certain kind of democracy, and closed off certain options, as Thermidor had not. The significance of that evolution is easily overlooked because fourteen years of Napoleonic rule produced an extreme discontinuity in political life. When democrats revived the revolutionary tradition and organized opposition to the constitutional monarchies of nineteenth-century France, it is safe to say that they were unaware of

[53] Among the most informative special studies are J. Destrem, *Les Déportations du Consulat et de l'Empire* (Paris, 1885); P. Gaffarel, "L'Opposition républicaine sous le Consulat," *R.F.*, XIV (1888), 530-50, 609-39; and R. C. Cobb, "Notes sur la répression contre le personnel sans-culotte de 1795 à 1801," *AHRF*, 1954 [No. 134], pp. 23-49. G. Lenôtre [Gosselin], *Les Derniers terroristes* (Paris, 1932) is his usual anti-revolutionary diatribe, but his liberal quotation from prefecture of police dossiers saves it from being useless. See also A.N. F⁷ 6276 (Attentat de 3 nivôse an IX).

their full heritage.[54] Babeuf was immortalized, Vatar forgotten. The Paris Jacobin Club thrust itself into memory, but the Constitutional Circles of the Year VI went unremarked. The elan and dramatic improvisations of the revolutionary government were justly celebrated; the mundane but crucial chapter that followed lay buried in the obscurity to which Bonaparte consigned it.

[54] Though this is not her particular concern, see E. Eisenstein, "The Evolution of the Jacobin Tradition in France: The Survival and Revival of the Ethos of 1793 under the Bourbon and Orléanist Regimes" (Ph.D. dissertation, Radcliffe College, 1952).

APPENDICES

Signatures on Petitions of the Constitutional Circle of the Faubourg Antoine

Aller
Alliot
Antoine

Bachelet
Bacon, père
Bal (or Bas)
Bamillie
Barbot
Barr
Beaufire
Berger
Bernard
Bertens
Beyne
Bion(?)
Blandeau
Blondon
Blussaud
Borie
Bouché
Bouet
Boullay
Bourloy
Boursol
Boutouny
Boyer
Brabant
Brement l'aîné
Brement jeune
Breton
Brisvin
Brochet
Bue

Camp
Captain
Caron
Caroy
Chappin

Chappuis
Chatelin fils
Chauvin
Chefdeville
Cochery
Corbel
Corillet
Cossard
Courton
Coutecher
Cresson
Crevel
Cuenier
Cuvillier

Debrie
Defouche
Delame
Delmont
Delande
Delaruelle
Delevigne
Delmos
Demery
Demons(y)
Dertiez
Dertus
Desouche
Despayal
Desterme
Desvignes
Diochet
Dion
Doirot
Dommeney
Dorienne
Dorlean
Dormoi
Douing
Dubée

Dubois
Dubourjale(?)
Dubusc
Ducatel
Ducatel cadet
Duclos
Duchesne
Dugreuse
Dulée
Dumont fils
Dumony
Dupuis
Duval

Expagnol

Fallain
Fainant(?)
Fergeret
Ferret
Fournerot
Fournier
Fournu

Gadton
Gareau
Gautier
Gillé
Goringlott(?)
Gregoire
Guet
Guidet
Guillaume

Hagnette
Hardivillé
Hardy
Hemmes
Henriet
Herré

Hesimetert(?)
Hesiné(?)
Hiver(t)
Horhof
Humbert
Humblet

Imbert

Joly
Janson

Kerchov

Lacroix
Laferein
Lafort
Lagoille
Lamotte
Landron
Lanoy
Lapeyrat
Laudet
Laurent
Lavalley
Leban
Leclerc
Lefrancais
Legendre
Leger
Lejeune
Lemoines
Letailleur
Letourné
Letourneur(?)
Linard
Loiseau
Louis
Louvain

Mablet	Nicole	Renaud	Songeray
Maquety(?)		Renault	Sully
Marcellin	Pairier	Retourné	
Marchais	Paschat(?)	Rocher	Tartavale
Martin	Pelis	Roophe	Thiboust
Martinaux	Pellegrin	Rossignol	Thiebaut
Massard	Pellgier	Rossignol frère	Thieblement
Mercier	Pepin	Rouisslot	Tinare
Merzet	Pinet	Roussel	Toussaint
Micouin	Placet	Royol	Tribous
Mithois			
Moly	Pornaz	Salbat	
Mopuiant	Potemont	Sard	Vacret
Moreau	Prevost	Saret	Vapaille
Moreau l'aîné		Seger fils	Vaquier
Moreaux	Rambour	Segretin	Vigner
Mougin	Remard	Solarin	Vingternier

SOURCE: see notes to Ch. VIII.

Signatures on Petitions of the Constitutional Circle of the 4th Arrondissement

Allard	Delechamps	Horut	Parent (fils)
Auffray (Auvray)	Drovalet		Pargme
Aurvot	Dumontier	Jacquinet	Perenaud
	Dumoy	Jouvre	Perers
Bazin	Duval		Peroud
Bertrand		Keller (Kelar)	Perouny
Blussaud	Fabre		Perrier
Bonifors	Filleau		Petyer
Boret	Filleau (2)	Lafontaine	Pouvert
Bot	Fortin	Langloy	
Boutaud	Frederick	Lassieur	Ravet
Bunelet	Funck	Le Brun	
Buquet		Leclerc	Sanylois(?)
Burguburu	Gautier	Lefebvre	Saviery
	Genet	Le Maitre	Secretain
Ceré	Girard	Lemort	
Chanu		Lenoir	Tabard
Chassein	Hailbron		Treham
Cousin	(Hartbron)	Monigom	
	Hamon		Vertun
Deladreux	Heuzé	Nicoud (Nicout)	Vigneury

SOURCE: A.N. F⁷ 7406, fol. 4264; A.N. F⁷ 3688/13.

Signatures on Petitions of the Constitutional Circle of the 7th Arrondissement

Aleff	Daverain	Jayer	Poitier
Altemaire	David	Jauseline	
Armand	Didot, A.		Roche
	Dimey	Lac	Rougierer
Bally	Dupléssis	Lamy	Royol
Baudequin	Duval	Lasquiene	Rozay
Bergeret		Laurent	
Bergeret (2)	Foures	Lebesque	Servant
Bernard		Le Blanc	Sonreset
Bistat	Garnier	Lesort	
Biston	Garriarp	Levarasseur	Teissedre
Boubled	Gobains		Thenault
Boucotte	Gothier	Mercier	Thiebaud
	Guerin	Mercier (2)	Toulorge
Caiveux	Guillemet	Micard	
Chapuis	Guilloumy	Miritoudine	Valée (Valet)
Chapuisat			Verner
Chevalier	Hainzelin	Neuiry(?)	Viget
Colignon	Haniques		
Coqué	Hardy	Payez	Wallier
	Herald	Peteil	
Darbyant	Houidaille	Poidevin	

Source: A.N. AF III 260/Seine; A.N. F⁷ 7353, fol. 9486.

Signatures on Petitions of the Constitutional Circle of the 10th Arrondissement (Rue du Bacq)

Accoyer	Bertier	Cadin	Copie
Alliman, fils	Besse	Caignart	Cretté
Andrieux	Biauzat	Caillot	
	Binow	Camus	Dauodre(?)
Bach	Blomart	Carré	David
Balardelle	Blondiot	Cassagne	Denron
Ballay	Blonsor	Castille	Depend
Bealle	Boillot	Cauvin	Dépid
Beauchamp	Bonjour	Chanin	Doite
Beidont	Bridont	Charpelier	Dorlé
Bellibart	Burgubun	Clesspur	Dubois, L.
Benoist		Coffin	Dubois

Duhamel	Jorden, J.	Marcellin	Rohaut
	Julien	Margery	Rolland, P.
Eon	Jullien, A.	Martin	Rondele
	Jullien, C. J.	Massieu	Rouillard
Favac		Muz	Rouillard, père
Faviot	Langlois		Rouillard, J. R.
Favre	Laugier	Olivier	Rouselant
Felix, S.	Lavalette		Roussel
Fleury	Laverriez	Paley	Rouval
Fleury, Jos.	Laveux	Parent	
Fontaine	Lavigny	Pargon	Scarif(?)
Forgery	Lebrun	Patin	Senéchal
Fouchet	Leclerc	Paulin	Sijas
	Lecourt	Peroimy	Suard, J.
Gautherot	Lefranc	Perrin	
Gillet	Leger	Perry	Tavernier
Girard, C.	Legras	Pierron	Thoury
Giraud	Lemonier	Pilon	Thurnot
Gogoreux	Leroy	Pons	Tobiéson
Gomegon	Lesnel	Porteroy	Touzet
Gremey	Lepinez	Poupré	Tréhan
Groslaire	Leymerey		
Gueouvas	Longpret	Quesnel	Vatar
Guis			Vinigigel(?)
	Magendie	Raisson	
Jacquemin	Maire	Ravesse	Zailler

SOURCE: A.N. C 431, fol. 167; A.N. F⁷ 7402/b, fol. 3906.

Signatures on Petitions of the Constitutional Circle of the 11th Arrondissement

Aimehume(?)	Burgebus	Crette	Garfaud
André		Cubières	Gaynailoy
Aubrey	Cahay		Geraud(?)
Avery	Caille	David	Godefroy
	Ceyrat	Desmaisons	Gonftel
Bach	Chapitel	Dobigny	Gousset
Beauchamp	Chartier	Dufayet	Grosselin
Bertier	Chavessey	Duval	Guilhemart
Borissel	Chevières		
Bormans	Comperot		Hache, G.
Boutat	Contamin	Etienne	Henri
Boutry	Coutarny		Heron
Brochet	Crappey	Fallot	Herrod

Husson	Lûnoy	Pelletier	Thumol
		Petit	Tinlot
Jaubert	Maillet	Piot	Tobiéson
Jolly	Martier		Tronc
Joyan	Martin	Raveau	
Juillot	Michalet	Revel	Vard
	Michelin	Rocher	Vary
Langlois	Mixelles	Rossignol	Veeten
Larchiel			Viée(?)
Launeet(?)		Simon	Velprony
Laymerie	Naulin		Velu
Le Bon		Thibautot	Vivin
Lejeune	Oliva	Thomas	

SOURCE: A.N. AF III 260/Seine; A.N. C 434.

APPENDIX II

Occupations and Political Background of some members of the Constitutional Circle of the Faubourg Antoine

*Berger (Section Indivisibilité). In the Year III "il fut expulsé à la presque unanimité de l'assemblée [sectionnaire], comme l'un des agents le plus prononcé du terrorisme." (Soboul, 558.)

*Boyer (Popincourt), porcelain worker; revolutionary committee. Jailed 2 floréal III, freed in vendémiaire IV; denounced as a Babeuvist. (Tonnesson, 361, 367.)

Brabant (Indivisibilité), box-maker [worker]; *armée révolutionnaire*; arrested thermidor III; on Babeuf's list. (Cobb, 207, 880, 883; F⁷ 4615, d. 3.)

*Brisvin (15/20), fabricant de crepin; civil commissioner; Extraordinary Commission of 15/20 in germinal III. "Designé comme agitateur en pluviôse an III, echappé mandat d'arrêt du 12 germinal III"; denounced as a Babeuvist. (Tonnesson, 221, 427.)

Chapuis (Montreuil), tailor; revolutionary committee; denounced as dangerous, nivôse III. (Markov, 458.)

*Chauvin (15/20), locksmith; stormed Tuilleries on 10 August 1792. (Rudé, *The Crowd in the French Revolution*, p. 108.)

*Cochery (15/20), harness-maker; author of the revolutionary 15/20 petition in germinal III; arrested in conspiration Lagrelet. (Tonnesson, 166, 180, 367-8; CSG fichier.)

*Chatelin (15/20), md. des sabots; denounced as an agitator in prairial III. (CSG, fichier.)

Demony (15/20), revolutionary committee; arrested prairial (?) III. (Markov, 516.)

Desouchet (15/20), "membre du bureau de l'assemblée illégale tenue les 1 et 2 prairial . . . motionner dangereux dans les assemblées générales et populaires." (Markov, 520.)

*Diochet (Montreuil), café-keeper; denounced prairial-thermidor III. (CSG fichier.)

Dion, locksmith; arrested floréal III. (CGS fichier.)

*Ducatel (15/20), gazier; denounced 20 thermidor II. (F⁷ 4683, d. 5.)

Duchèsne (Popincourt), café-keeper; justice of the peace, and president of sectional assembly; founded a popular society in his section after the closing of the Jacobin Club. Arrested in prairial III. (Soboul, 1082; Tonnesson, 432.)

*Fournerot (15/20), ribbon worker and carpentry worker; extraordinary commission 15/20 in germinal; disarmed; fled a *mandat d'arrêt*. (Tonnesson, 155, 180, 220-21, 359, 434-35.)

*Gille(t) (Montreuil), stonemason; leader of Société des Quinze-Vingts; revolutionary committee. (Soboul, 424; Markov, 512.)

*Hardevillé (15/20), arrested by CSG in pluviôse III for agitation in his section. (Tonnesson, 147; Markov, 458.)

*Henriet (Popincourt), revolutionary committee; arrested prairial III. (CSG fichier.)

Hiver(t) (Indivisibilité), bouillonnier (?); revolutionary committee. Denounced by the president of his sectional assembly; under suspicion for maintaining that the sections were sovereign above the Convention. (Soboul, 973-74.)

Humblet (15/20), shoemaker; revolutionary committee. A leader of the Société des Quinze-Vingts with Leban. Ordered arrested in germinal; arrested in messidor III (Tonnesson, 140, 147, 436.)

*Laudet (Montreuil), stonemason; cannonier section Montreuil; arrested with Potemont in germinal. (F⁷ 4768, d. 2.)

*Laurent (15/20), stonemason; revolutionary committee; joined *armée révolutionnaire*; extraordinary commission 15/20; arrested prairial III, rearmed vendémiaire IV. (Tonnesson, 208, 438; Cobb, 205, 543, 873.)

*Leban (15/20), cabinet-maker; leader of Société des Quinze-Vingts; arrested germinal III, freed fructidor III. On Babeuf's list. (F⁷ 4746, d. 2 and F⁷ 4770, d. 3.)

*Lejeune (15/20), harness-maker; civil commissioner.

*Letailleur (Montreuil), gazier; arrested prairial (?) III, freed thermidor III. (F⁷ 4774/21, d. 1 and F⁷ 4675, d. 4.)

*Loiseau, arrested prairial III, freed thermidor III. (CSG fichier.)

*Martin (Popincourt), sectionnaire. (Soboul, 576.)

*Mercier (Montreuil), civil commissioner. (Tonnesson, 290.)

Placet (15/20), *armée révolutionnaire*; arrested prairial. (Cobb, 172, 873, 879.)

*Potemont (Montreuil), locksmith; captain of a company of cannoniers in the *armée révolutionnaire*; arrested with Laudet in germinal III, freed thermidor III. With Placet he was on Babeuf's list for the insurrectionary provisional government. (Tonnesson, 443, 208; Cobb, 157, 159, 868, 872-73, 879, 885.)

Renault (15/20), accused of being a *septembriseur*. (Markov, 514.)

*Rossignol, famous sans-culotte general (formerly a watchmaker); "Babeuvist" acquitted at Vendôme.

Thiboust (Indivisibilité), paperhanger; revolutionary committee. "Resisté activement aux modérés en l'an III." Arrested variously in messidor II, brumaire III, nivôse III, and from floréal III to vendémiaire IV. (Tonnesson, 366, 446; Soboul, 974.)

*Toussaint, disarmed in floréal III; on Babeuf's list to command section 15/20. (CSG fichier.)

*Vacret (Montreuil), bonnetier; revolutionary committee; arrested ventôse III, released thermidor; denounced as Babeuvist; acquitted at Vendôme. (F⁷ 4774/37, l. 1.)

*Vaquier, wine-seller; arrested prairial III. (CSG fichier.)

*Vingternier, *armée révolutionnaire* officer; told his section that there was no other genuine assembly "que celle du peuple et des ouvriers." Arrested germinal III. (Soboul, 429-30.)

SOURCES:

CSG fichier: Comité de Sûreté Générale, alphabetical card file, A.N. In certain instances the dossiers themselves have been consulted, in which case they are listed.

Cobb: *Les Armées révolutionnaires.*

Markov: W. Markov and A. Soboul, eds., *Die Sans-culotten von Paris: Dokumente zur Geschichte der Volksbewegung.*

Soboul: *Les Sans-culottes Parisiens en l'an II.*

Tonnesson: *La Défaite des sans-culottes.*

References to those denounced as Babeuvists come from the documents collected in A.N. F⁷ 4276-78. Those names starred (*) signed at least two of the club's petitions.

Patronage in the Faubourg Antoine
under Sotin

"Liste des Citoyens préposés à l'administration Municipale du 8eme arrondisement, et à autres emploies."

Administration Municipale
Rollet, tappissier, rue fb. Antoine (15/20)
*Diochet, limonadier, id.
Damois (Montreuil)
*Toussaint, chez Damois
Armand père, peintre en porcelain
*Renaud, horloger (Popincourt)

Emplois militaires
*Moreau jeune, rue fb. Antoine (15/20): une place d'adjutant de section
*Placet, rue Reuilly (15/20) id.
*Henriet, rue fb. Antoine: Une place d'adj. de bataillon ou de brigade dans la garde nationale (Montreuil)
*Laudet, rue fb. Antoine, id. (Popincourt)
*Vingternier, ex-général de brigade, emploi dans son grade ou dans les bureaux de la guerre

Emplois Civiles, Police, Administration
Pellecat, rue fb. Ant (15/20) bon pour chef de bureau ou pour la comptabilité
*Hardivilliér, rue fb. Ant (Montreuil)
*Erray [Herré] rue fb. Ant (Popincourt)
Duquaine, bon pour expeditionnaire
*Vacret, bon pour officier de paix
*Martin, rue Marguerite, id.
*Humblet (Popincourt) bon pour commr de la ditte division
*Duchene, bon pour expeditionnaire
Lapeyre, id.
Duplessis, bon pour greffier dans les tribunaux

Bones & laternes, Inspections, Porteurs ou garçons de bureaux
*Caron, rue Margueritte, chez l'eppissier

*Hardivilliér, rue de Montreuil

*Erray, rue fb. Antoine

*Potemont, serrurier, rue fb. Ant, bon pour inspecteur des arsenaux

*Leclerc, rue de Bercy

*Moreau ainé, rue Traversière

*Chochery, rue fb. Antoine

*Brisvin, bon pour courrier de la malle, rue fb. Antoine

*Brement, inspecteur des bones et lanternes

A.N. F⁷ 6140, dossier 134, plaq. 2. Those starred (*) were members of the Constitutional Circle of the faubourg Antoine.

APPENDIX IV

The Career of René Vatar

THE ROLE of René Vatar and his *Journal des hommes libres* as a focal point for Jacobins during the Directory can scarcely be overstated. In the history of the Revolution, and in the annals of the press, Vatar merits a chapter of his own. To contemporaries he was by no means unknown, although he generally played his role behind the scenes. To posterity, however, he has become almost totally lost.

There is only one biographical sketch of Vatar to be found, and its origin is purely fortuitous. In the course of his researches on Charlotte Corday, the antiquarian historian Charles Vatel found that certain documents in the Corday affair had come into the possession of Vatar and his friend and collaborator, the conventionnel Charles Duval. Vatel's meticulous approach led him to write brief sketches of the two. (See *Charlotte de Corday et les Girondins,* 3 vols.; Paris, 1864-72, pp. 503-11.) In addition we have a statement made when, in the course of one polemic, Vatar stepped out from behind his usual impersonality to give a brief account of his own past (*J. hommes libres* No. 320, 15 germinal VI). Highlights included publishing a patriot newspaper in his native Rennes in 1789 and migrating to Paris after 1791, where he set up a new publishing and bookselling operation. The *Journal des hommes libres* was founded by Vatar and Duval after the August 1792 revolution.

The venerable lineage of the Vatar family in Breton publishing is traced briefly in Georges Lepreux, *Gallia Typographica ou Répertoire biographique et chronologique de tous les imprimeurs de France,* Vol. IV: *Province de Bretagne* (Paris, 1914), 121-22. An article by A. de la Borderie, while containing almost nothing about René, sets out in impressive detail the Vatar family publishing operations that continued into the nineteenth century ("Les Vatar, imprimeurs à Rennes et à Nantes," *Revue de Bretagne, de Vendée et d'Anjou,* X, Part 6 [1893], 405-21).

Vatar's role as printer of the Committee of Public Safety, and his difficulties after Robespierre's fall (political suspicion and uncollectable bills) unfold in A. N. AF II 33 (C.S.P.), plaqs. 270-72. He was, in fact, arrested briefly in the Year III (A.N. F⁷ 4774/40—Committee of General Security files). Upon exposure of the Babeuf plot, two arrest warrants were issued for him, as René Vatar and as the unnamed publisher of the *Journal des hommes libres*. However, his detention did not last very long. (See A.N. F⁷ 7148, fol. 4010; A.N. F⁷ 4276 [Affaire Babeuf].)

Police reports, including the daily bulletins of the Paris Central Police Bureau published by Aulard, repeatedly describe the association of Vatar with "anarchists," and also the use by such "anarchists" of his newspaper. Perhaps an even more significant indicator of his influence is in the records of the Ministry of Interior's censorship bureau, where it was common for conservative newspapers to be noted approvingly for their attacks on Vatar and Duval, and for other newspapers to be regarded as suspect for "echoing" the *Journal des hommes libres*. (See A.N. F⁷ 3448: Bureau général des analyses.) Though his newspaper was suppressed several times, Vatar's experience, his other publishing business, and a timely loan from friends kept his enterprise from collapsing. His protracted struggles with the censorship bureaucracy are recorded in A.N. F⁷ 3449-50 (Police—Presse).

Vatar's active role in the Jacobin resurgence of the Year VI is touched upon throughout this study. More than ever his newspaper was a forum for disseminating information; he himself was active in one of the Parisian clubs (the Constitutional Circle of the Rue du Bacq) and in the elections of that year. In the wake of the anti-Jacobin reaction that followed those elections his newspaper was again suppressed and he was placed under active surveillance. The resulting dossier is full of interesting political intelligence about Jacobin liaisons; in addition it sheds light on the half-world of fantasy in which the police observers lived. (See A.N. F⁷ 6194, dossier 2627, plaq. 5.) After the *journée* of 30 prairial VII, Vatar's offices again became a beehive of activity. The newspaper was revived and was as energetic as ever. Moreover Vatar became publisher to the newly installed and pro-Jacobin Paris departmental administration. All this ended with Brumaire, after which he was pressured into selling his newspaper. In the final anti-Jacobin repression that Bonaparte arranged after the famous assassination attempt, Vatar was prominent among those arrested. Despite some forceful intervention in his behalf, he was deported to Guiana. Eventually he died there, which explains the loss of his private papers and thus of a basic body of source material for the later history of Jacobinism (A.N. F[7] 6276: Attentat de 3 nivôse, an IX). Remarkably few traces of Vatar survive in subsequent memoirs, though there are a few lines of tribute in the *Notes historiques* of the conventionnel Baudot. For the "advocate-in-chief of the anarchists"—as his antagonist Poultier once labeled him—Napoleon's decree of exile was final.

NOTE ON SOURCES AND

BIBLIOGRAPHY

I. Manuscript Sources

The documentary basis for this study is dispersed primarily in a number of sub-series in the Archives Nationales. Their usefulness is not always apparent from the standard *instruments de travail,* which, as their titles warn, are regrettably summary.[1] Yet they offer clues enough to the surprisingly centralized structure of the Directory regime and to the resultant accumulation of information in Paris. The central government (meaning the Executive Directory and its ministries, as well as the Legislature) was deluged with a flow of correspondence from the provinces. Administrative councils of departments and towns, as well as the Directory's commissioners thereto, assumed it their duty to report all manifestations of dissidence in their areas. Moreover they were seconded by private citizens of various persuasions, and, of course, by the clubs who considered it a primary task to attack their enemies and defend their own conduct. Their letters, petitions, reports, denunciations, defenses, investigations, and pamphlets are liable to be found in anything from an unclassified bundle of papers on a particular department to the meticulously annotated file of *pièces annexes* in the Directory's records.

The bulk of such material touching on the democratic movement ended in the Police Ministry, Series F^7, particularly in a sub-series all-too-literally entitled *Affaires diverses* [F^7 7142-7674, an IV-VIII]. In over five hundred cartons for the Directory period, it rests along with documents on refractory priests, brigandage, malfeasance of local officials, and émigrés. A word about the series' arrangement is appropriate here, since its unwieldy size and diversity have undoubtedly deterred its exploitation. The series' structure is orderly if its subject matter is not. Much of the correspondence arriving at the ministry that was not passed along to a bureau or agent for specialized action was given a number and placed in a dossier. Other documents usually accumulated as the matter was followed up, and a dossier often ended by bulging with supplementary reports, supporting documents, and counter-claims. In addition, an entry (in-

---

[1] *Etat sommaire par séries des documents conservés aux Archives nationales* (1891) and *Etat sommaire des versements faits aux Archives nationales par les Ministères et les Administrations qui en dépendent (Séries F, BB Justice, et ADxix)* (4 vols., 1924-   ). Place of publication in all citations is Paris, unless otherwise noted.

cluding the date, place, name or title of correspondent, and some indication of the subject) would be made in a register with a number corresponding to each dossier. These registers [F⁷* 430-89] are therefore a ready-made inventory, and were systematically utilized to locate relevant dossiers. As a precaution, cartons for the Year VI were also consulted methodically to turn up material that had not been clearly indicated by the registers' entries.

A second major sub-series in the Police Ministry papers is called *Affaires Politiques: bureau particulier* [F⁷ 6139-6464]. Investigations of alleged subversion or suspicious *rassemblements* are concentrated here, especially where the ministry ordered close surveillance of individuals, cafés, or apartments by its agents. The bulk of this material is on Paris and was especially illuminating on dissident activity after the floréal purge, when police surveillance and censorship increased dramatically.

Wholly uncatalogued and unpredictable is a sub-series entitled *Statistique personnelle et morale, série départementale* [F⁷ 3647-3700]. Informative reports on clubs in Bordeaux and Marseilles turned up here, for example, as did the unprocessed rough notes of the *mouchards* who were set upon Paris. Provided that one carefully winnows out the obvious distortions from the revealing observations that were reported daily, these reports are far more valuable than the homogenized bulletins of the Paris Central Police Bureau that Aulard has edited. Also classified with Police Ministry papers are the voluminous files of the Convention's Committee of General Security [F⁷ 4577-4775/53]. This is indispensable for establishing the political background of members of the Parisian Constitutional Circles. An excellent card-index of names facilitates its use. Other Police Ministry papers that proved helpful included material on the ministry's own policies and personnel under Sotin [F⁷ 3006-07]; reports on Paris elections [F⁷ 3054]; press surveillance [F⁷ 3447-52]; and Babeuvism [F⁷ 4276-78].

Among the Executive Directory's papers, Series AF III, the minutes of its meetings have often been consulted and offer little that is not well known [AF III 1-16]. More useful were the reports and correspondence passed between the Directory and its ministers [e.g., AF III 35, 42, 45-47, 99-100, 144; AF III* 145-56], and certain documents included in the *pièces annexes* of its records for the Year VI [AF III 501-23]. The latter can be handily used, despite the mass of routine matter that swells its size, with the aid of detailed manuscript inventories. Most important among the Directory's papers was its *Série départementale* [AF III 211-267], with its abundance of petitions and detailed reports on local politics. Here, too, may be found the manuscript procès-verbaux of the Year VI electoral assemblies.

Perhaps the most precious of all sources for this study was in the *pièces annexes* of the Legislature's papers for the Year VI [C 426-37]: an untapped mass of petitions from the Constitutional Circles. Less concentrated in its yield, but occasionally rewarding, was a series in the Ministry of Interior's papers called *Esprit public et élections, série départementale* [F^{1c} III]. Like its counterpart in the F^7 series it is an uncatalogued miscellany of letters and petitions arranged alphabetically by department. Except for some documents on the Babeuf conspiracy [BB^3 21-22; W 564] the Ministry of Justice papers proved disappointing. Likewise the Archives Nationales' growing fund of private manuscript collections offered little except for some gleanings from the Barras and Lamarque papers [171 AP 1; 199 AP 2 and 4]. Relevant material classified under Press [F^{18} 14-23] proved sparse, and under Statistics offered valuable information only for the Seine department [F^{20} 381].

The Manuscript Division of the Bibliothèque Nationale holds a number of relevant items, including the Buonarroti and the Gautherot papers [Nos. 20803-04 and 21700], and the original procès-verbal and working papers of the Oratoire electoral assembly of the Year VI [No. 2718]. The latter can be supplemented with material on the Paris scene gleaned from the *Archives départementales de la Seine* [especially VD* 5414, 5416, 5463, and 2AZ 156]. Unfortunately the *Archives de la Préfecture de Police* (Paris) proved disappointing. A major source that Soboul and Rudé have used to great advantage is the procès-verbaux of the local police constables [Series Aa]. But during the Directory these officials were rarely called upon to make the political arrests or to carry out the kinds of surveillance and searches that had been common from 1792 to 1795.

Departmental and communal archives across France undoubtedly contain material that would enrich this study considerably, both in a general way and in the specific matter of identifying more precisely the Neo-Jacobin activists. But it would have taken an unfeasible amount of time to unearth it in any systematic way. Most of

421

these archives are inadequately catalogued, to put it mildly. (See *Etat des inventaires des Archives nationales, départementales, communales et hospitalières au 1ᵉʳ janvier 1937* [1938].) And a rubric like Series "1" (Police), in which local petitions would likely turn up, almost never appears in those inventories that have been published. On the other hand samplings made in the municipal archives of Bordeaux (Gironde) and Metz (Moselle) satisfied me that important information usually found its way to Paris in one manner or another.

II. PUBLISHED PRIMARY SOURCES

NEWSPAPERS

The Neo-Jacobin press is a neglected historical artifact of the first order. To those newspapers held by the Bibliothèque Nationale guidance is available in two places. Arranged alphabetically by title and covering both provincial and Parisian journals, there is A. Martin and G. Walter, *Catalogue de l'histoire de la Révolution française,* v (1943). More detailed and arranged chronologically is M. Tourneaux's *Bibliographie de l'histoire de Paris pendant la Révolution,* II (1894). The Archives Nationales, provincial libraries, and even American libraries contain newspapers that are missing in the B.N.'s collection.

Any scheme for classifying the newspapers used in this study is bound to be imperfect, but at least one dividing line commends itself: did the newspaper share or oppose the anti-Jacobinism that dominated both royalist and Directorial journalism. Two types of newspapers opposed it. Outspoken democratic organs, some of which cultivated an element of sans-culottisme; and moderate newspapers, addressed exclusively to a middle-class audience, which nonetheless defended the clubs and served as forums for certain democratic ideas. The most self-consciously democratic newspapers in Paris were the *Orateur plébéien* (Year IV); Labisol's *Père Duchêne* (Year V); the *Tribun du Peuple* (not to be confused with Babeuf's organ) and the *Défenseur de la Vérité* for the Year VI; and the *Démocrate* for the Year VII. The most interesting of the moderate pro-Jacobin journals—all of which solicited subsidies from the Directory, but largely refused to accept its "party line" on Jacobinism— were Coesnon-Pellerin's *Ami de la Patrie*; Colliot's *Journal des campagnes et des armées*; and Valcour's *L'Indépendant*. As the recognized *porte-parole* of Neo-Jacobins, the *Journal des hommes libres* drew upon and supported all of these journals, though its own persuasion reflected more of the first type. In a sense there is thus a formal criterion for establishing a list of pro-Jacobin newspapers: namely those with which Vatar fraternized in his columns. The same consideration applies to the provinces. Quite different in style and constituency, the self-consciously plebeian *Journal des Amis* (Metz) and the lofty *Observateur de l'Yonne* (Sens) both fought the Directory's line on Jacobinism and were embraced in Vatar's informal network of journalists. A number of newspapers like the *Bulletin de l'Eure* (Evreux) and the *Antiroyaliste* (Marseilles) approximated the position of the *Journal des hommes libres* on a local level.

Even leaving aside the royalists, anti-Jacobin journalism is easy enough to find. In Aulard's *Paris pendant . . . le Directoire*, for example, there are extensive excerpts from the quasi-official *Rédacteur* and from the *Ami des Lois*, which began a crusade against Vatar after Fructidor. The *Moniteur*, aside from being a journal of record, proved a surprisingly interesting source of conservative anti-Jacobinism, along with such papers as the *Clef du Cabinet*, the *Propagateur*, and the *Patriote française*. For the provinces I have sampled the *Courrier de l'Escaut* (Malines), the *Journal de la Côte-d'Or* (Dijon), the *Journal du département de Maine-et-Loire* (Angers), the *Journal du département de Seine-et-Oise* (Versailles), and the durable *Républicain du Nord* (Brussels)—all for the Year VI.

In the following list of what I call pro-Jacobin newspapers, information is supplied on the principal editor or publisher and on the extent of sometimes fragmentary holdings. An asterisk is used to note those located elsewhere than the Bibliothèque Nationale.

Paris

L'Ami de la Patrie, ou journal de la liberté française, ed. Coesnon-Pellerin; an IV-germinal VI; scattered nos. in B.N., others in A.N. ADxx/a 27.

L'Ami du Peuple ou le défenseur des patriotes persécutés, ed. Lebois; brumaire IV-vendémiaire VI; scattered nos.

Le Défenseur de la patrie, faisant suite à "l'Ami du peuple," ed. Lebois; messidor-fructidor VII.

Le Défenseur de la Vérité et des principes, ed. Bescher; pub. Lamberté; fructidor V-ventôse VI; scattered nos.

Le Défenseur des droits du peuple, ed Ballois; vendémiaire VIII.

Le Démocrate, journal politique et littéraire, ed. Méhée; fructidor V-vendémiaire VI (insignificant).

Le Démocrate ou le défenseur des principes, ed. Bescher, Bazin, Gabriel; pub. Lamberté; thermidor VII-vendémiaire VIII; name changed to *Ennemi des Tyrans* in fructidor VII; scattered nos.

Le Démocrate constitutionnel, ed. "Antoine"; pub. Vatar; fructidor V.

L'Indépendant, ed. Valcour; vendémiaire-fructidor VI.

*Journal des campagnes et des armées, pub. Colliot; an V-VI; scattered nos. in Newberry Library, Chicago, for an VI.

Journal des hommes libres de tous les pays, ou le Républicain, ed. Duval, Eon, Camus, Giraud, pub. Vatar; an IV-VIII. Major name changes were: *Le Républicain,* floréal-messidor VI; *Journal des Francs,* messidor-fructidor VI; *Correspondance des représentants du peuple Stevenotte, Desaix, Dethier et autres,* vendémiaire-frimaire VII; suppressed between frimaire-prairial VII; *Journal des hommes libres,* messidor-fructidor VII; *Ennemi des Oppresseurs de tous les temps,* fructidor VII-brumaire VIII.

Journal des Patriotes de '89, ed. Réal & Méhée; vendémiaire-thermidor IV; reluctantly and equivocally pro-Jacobin.

L'Orateur plébéien, ou le défenseur de la République, ed. Demaillot & Leuiliette; frimaire-germinal IV.

Le Père Duchêne, ed. Labisol; pub. Coesnon-Pellerin; an V; 44 nos.

Le Père Duchêne, ed. Lebois; messidor VII-brumaire VIII; 24 nos.

Le Révélateur, bulletin universel, ed. Errard; an V-VI; scattered nos.

Tableau politique, littéraire et moral de la France et de l'Europe, ed. Leclerc des Vosges, an VI.

Le Tribun du Peuple et l'ami des défenseurs de la patrie, ed. Prévost & Donnier; fructidor V-pluviôse VI; scattered nos.

The Provinces

L'Abeille des gazettes et journaux (Metz), pub. Verronnais; an V-VIII; Directorial in sympathy, but admirably tolerant of the Jacobins.

L'Ami de la liberté, Journal d'Angers, ed. Jahyer; an VII-VIII.

L'Ami des principes (Angers), ed. Jahyer; an V- prairial VI.

L'Antiroyaliste de Marseille, see *L'Observateur du Midi.*

Bulletin de l'Eure (Evreux), ed. Touquet; an V-germinal VI.

Bulletin de la Nièvre (Nevers), ed. Parent l'aîné; an VI; unavailable, but frequently cited by other Jacobin newspapers.

Chronique de la Sarthe (LeMans), ed. Bazin; an VI; used by means of the extensive citations in Reinhard's study.

Courrier de l'Armée d'Italie (Milan), ed. Jullien; an VI.

Courrier de la Gironde (Bordeaux), ed. Latapy; scattered nos. for an VI in Bibliothèque Municipale de Bordeaux.

L'Echo des Alpes (Chambéry), ed. Doppet; an VI; cautiously pro-Jacobin.

Journal de la Haute-Cour de Justice, ou l'écho des hommes libres, vrais et sensibles (Vendôme), ed. Hesiné; an V; Cornell University, Ithaca, New York.

Journal des Amis (Metz), ed. Pirolle & Trotebas; frimaire-germinal VI; scattered nos. in Bibliothèque Muncipale de Metz.

Journal des Hautes-Pyrénées (Tarbes), ed. Delaroy; scattered nos. for an V & VI in B.N. and in A.N. AF III 517, plaq. 3307.

Journal de Toulouse, ou l'observateur, ed. Dardenne; an V-VII.

Journal du département de l'Allier (Moulins); a few scattered nos. for an VI in A.N. C 530.

L'Observateur de la Dordogne (Perigueux), ed. Ballois; a few scattered nos. for an VI in A.N. C 531 and A.N. AF III 517, plaq. 3310.

L'Observateur démocrate ou le réveil des sans-culottes (Metz), ed. Trotebas; pluviôse-ventôse IV.

L'Observateur du département de l'Yonne (Sens), ed. Benoist-Lamothe; an IV-VIII; cautiously pro-Jacobin.

L'Observateur du Midi (Marseilles), ed. Peyre-Ferry & Reybaud; an IV-VI; later called *L'Antiroyaliste de Marseille.*

PAMPHLETS

Several types of pamphlets illuminate the nature and extent of the democratic movement. (1) Tracts written by individuals on questions of theory or policy. (2) Pamphlets emanating mainly from the Constitutional Circles in the form of political appeals, addresses, and polemics, all dating from Fructidor to the elections of the Year VI. (3) Pamphlets written in the wake of those elections, attacking or defending the conduct of local Neo-Jacobin cadres. (4) Polemics attacking the Directory between the floréal purge and Brumaire. A number of these items turn up only in police dossiers; guidance to those available in the Bibliothèque Nationale may be had in the standard reference works: Walter's *Catalogue*, Tourneux's *Bibliographie de Paris*, and Monglond's chronological-topical listings. In addition it proved useful to consult the Bibliothèque's *Catalogue de l'histoire de France* (12 vols.; 1855-95) directly.

Almost entirely omitted from the following list are the "official" pamphlets used in this study: proclamations, draft decrees, committee reports, and legislative speeches on such issues as franchise reform, the floréal purge, regulation of clubs, or freedom of the press. These are easily located in the B.N. or (for American researchers) in the University of Pennsylvania Library whose collection may be consulted systematically by means of the recent catalogue: Hardy, Jensen and Wolfe, eds., *The Maclure Collection of French Revolutionary Materials* (Philadelphia, 1966). In addition I have omitted listing large, repetitive groups of pamphlets attacking the Oratoire assembly and the Manège Club.

(1) Political Tracts

Antonelle, P.A. *Observations sur le Droit de Cité et sur quelques parties du travail de la commission des onze*. Chez Vatar, an III. B.N. *E/5718.

Chaumont-Quitry, Guy. *Essai sur les causes qui, depuis le 18 fructidor, devaient consolider la République en France.* . . . Impr. Vatar-Jouannet, an VII. B.N. Lb42/2393.

Chaussard, Publicola. *Coup-d'Oeil sur l'intérieure de la République française, ou esquisse des principes d'une Révolution morale*. Impr. Moutardier, an VII. B.N. Lb42/2475.

Didot, A. *Réflexions sur les ennemis de la République française*. Impr. de l'Institut National des Aveugles-travailleurs, an VI. A.N. F7 7408, fol. 4506.

Français (de Nantes). *Coup-d'Oeil rapide sur les Moeurs, les lois, les contributions, les secours publics, les sociétés politiques, les cultes, les théatres, les institutions publiques, dans leurs rapports avec le Gouvernement représentatif.* . . . Grenoble, an VI. Firestone Library, Princeton.

[Jullien, Marc-Antoine.] *Quelques Conseils aux Patriotes Cisalpins*. n.l., n.d. A.N. F7 3054.

Lefebvre, Edouard. *Considerations politiques et morales sur la France constituée en République.* Chez Bertrand, an VI. B.N. Lb42/1897 [anti-Jacobin].

Lenglet, E. G. *De la Propriété et de ses rapports avec les droits et avec la dette du Citoyen.* Impr. Moutardier, an VI. B.N. *E/1844.

Lepelletier, Felix. *Réflexions sur le moment présent, ou suite des celles déjà publiées . . . en floréal de l'an III.* Impr. Vatar, an IV. B.N. Lb42/ 1031.

Pache, J. N. *Sur les Factions et les Partis, les Conspirations et les conjurations; et sur celles à l'ordre du jour.* Impr. Vatar, an V. Weidner Library, Harvard.

Roederer, A. M. *Des Sociétés particulières, telles que clubs, réunions.* Impr. Demonville, an VII. B.N. Lb42/751 [anti-Jacobin].

[Satur, M. J.?] *Correspondance trouvée dans le porte-feuille d'un jeune patriote assassiné sur la route de Paris.* Impr. Leroux, an VI. B.N. Lb42/ 524.

Satur, M. J. *Les Préjugés constitutionnels de l'an VI, digression sérieuse et nécessaire sur la liberté politique.* Impr. Logerot, an VII. B.N. Lb42/1998.

Souhait, Julien. *Opinion . . . sur le droit de suffrage. . . .* Impr. Nationale, an III. B.N. Le38/1553.

(2) Pamphlets from the Constitutional Circles and Political Appeals

Adresse au Conseil des Anciens, sur les inscriptions réquises pour être admis à voter dans les assemblées primaires. Impr. Vatar, pluviôse an VI. B.N. Lb42/508.

Au Peuple. Chez P. Antoine, à Metz [an V]. A.N. AF III 250/ Moselle.

Au Peuple française. Impr. Leguay, an VI. A.N. F⁷ 3054.

Aux Habitans de Calvados [par le cercle constitutionnel]. Caen, an VI. A.N. F⁷ 7411, fol. 4759.

Aux Républicains de la Commune d'Evreux, par le Cercle constitutionnel séant aux ci-devant Ursulines. Impr. Touquet, an VI. A.N. F⁷ 7401, fol. 3769.

Avis au Républicains [par le Cercle constitutionnel de Moulins]. Impr. Burelle, an VI. A.N. F⁷ 7415, fol. 5161.

Avis de quelques individus du Cercle des Amis de la Patrie séant à la Montagne des ex-Récollets en cette commune à leurs con-citoyens. Maestricht, an VI. A.N. F⁷ 7414, fol. 5110.

Les Citoyens du Département de la Haute-Vienne soussignés, aux braves généraux, officiers et soldats composant les armées de la République française. n.l., n.d. A.N. AF III 267/Haute-Vienne.

Déclaration des Principes du Cercle constitutionnel établi à Vesoul. Impr. J. B. Poirson, frimaire VI. A.N. F⁷ 7404, fol. 4114.

Des Amis de la Constitution de l'an III à leurs concitoyens. Luxembourg, germinal VI. A.N. F⁷ 7417, fol. 5387.

Discours d'un grenadier près la représentation nationale, à ses camarades, prononcé au cercle constitutionnel. Paris, brumaire VI. B.N. Lb40/2362.

Discours lu le 20 nivôse an VI au Cercle Constitutionnel établi à Versailles. Impr. Jacob. A.N. F⁷ 7415, fol. 5227.

Discours prononcé le 2 brumaire de l'an VI . . . au Cercle constitutionnel de Vesoul, par le Citoyen Poirson fils, membre du dit cercle. Imprimé par ordre de l'administration centrale. A.N. F⁷ 7404, fol. 4114.

Discours prononcé par J. M. Lequinio le 2 pluviôse an VI à la cérémonie de l'anniversaire de la mort du Tyran, sur la place publique de Valenciennes, et imprimé par ordre du Cercle constitutionnel de cette commune. A.N. F⁷ 7386, fol. 2358.

Discours Prononcé par un membre du Cercle Constitutionnel de Toulouse le 22 frimaire an VI. A.N. F⁷ 7362, fol. 270.

L'Echo du Cercle Constitutionnel de Versailles Nos. 1 and 2. Impr. Locard fils, an VI. A.N. F⁷ 7415, fol. 5227.

Elections de l'An VI: Adresse des Citoyens français, membres du Cercle constitutionnel, séant rue de l'Université no. 932, 10ᵉᵐᵉ arrondissement. A.N. F⁷ 7415, fol. 5180.

Les Exaspérés (Air). Nevers, an VI. A.N. F⁷ 7411, fol. 4789.

Lamarque, F. *Lettre . . . à son collègue P. G. sur la clôture du cercle constitutionnel de Perigueux, et sur les destitutions qui l'ont accompagnée.* Impr. Baudouin, germinal VI. B.N. Lb42/1830.

Profession de foi politique des républicains de la commune de Lunéville, soussignées, réunis en cercle constitutionnel. Impr. Messuy, pluviôse VI. A.N. F⁷ 7399, fol. 3663.

Récit de ce qui s'est passé à la fête civique du Cercle constitutionnel de Versailles . . . le 21 Janvier (vs) ou 2 pluviôse an 6. Impr. Locard fils. B.N. Lb42/497.

Réflexions du Citoyen Coesnon-Pellerin, rédacteur de l'Ami de la Patrie, et électeur, sur la proclamation d'hier [Paris, an VI]. Melvin Collection, University of Kansas.

Règlement de police intérieur, adopté par la Réunion du 7eme arrondissement [de Paris]. Impr. de l'Institut National des Aveugles-travailleurs, an VI. B.N. Lb40/2364.

Règlement des Amis de la Constitution séant au faubourg Antoine. Impr. Lamberté, an VI. A.N. F^7 7292, fol. 2585.

Les Républicains membres du Cercle constitutionnel de Dôle, à leurs frères les habitans des autres communes du Jura. Impr. Briot [Besançon], an VI. A.N. F^7 7417, fol. 5361.

Résumé des travaux du cercle constitutionnel de la Rue du Bacq. Impr. de la Rue de l'Université [Vatar], an VI. B.N. Lb40/2363.

Réunion d'hommes libres, établie en Cercle à Toulouse, conformément à la loi [an VI]. A.N. F^7 7362, fol. 270.

Réunion Patriotique [*d'Orléans*]: *A la brave Armée d'Italie* [an VI]. A.N. F^7 7393, fol. 2996.

Thiébaut, A. *Le Tocsin de l'Opinion publique.* Impr. Guilhemat, an VI. B.N. Lb42/535.

Un Mot aux électeurs patriotes. Paris [an VI]. B.N. Lb42/1335.

(3) Post-Election Polemics, Year VI
(by departments)

Beauchamp et Chabot, *Sur la scission de l'Assemblée de l'ALLIER.* Impr. Ami des Lois, an VI. A.N. AF III 212/Allier [anti-Jacobin].

Faits relatifs à la scission des élections du département de l'ALLIER. Moulins, an VI. B.N. Lb42/ 547 [anti-Jacobin].

Rouchon, Boisset, Garilhe, *Sur les opérations de l'Assemblée électorale de l'ARDECHE.* n.l., an VI. B.N. Lb42/1870 [anti-Jacobin].

Réponse du Citoyen Gleizal, à une partie de l'écrit signé Rouchon, Garilhe. . . . Impr. Bailleul, an VI. B.N. Lb42/1871.

Courtois, E. B. *Précis de ce qui s'est passé dans le département de l'AUBE pendant la tenue de l'Assemblée électorale.* Impr. Bailleul, [an VI]. B.N. Lb42/551 [anti-Jacobin].

Sur les élections de la DORODGNE: organisation et plan . . . a dirigé les choix comme il a voulu. n.l., an VI. A.N. AF III 100 [anti-Jacobin].

Bulletin de l'Assemblée électorale du département des LANDES. Impr. Delaroy, germinal VI. A.N. AF III 239 Landes.

Batbedat, L. S. *Exposé de ce qui s'est passé dans le département des LANDES, relativement aux élections de l'an 6.* Impr. Lemaire. A.N. F⁷ 7421, fol. 5898.

Forest, Duguet et Meaudre. *Sur les élections du département de la LOIRE.* Impr. Baudouin, an VI. B.N. Lb42/572 [anti-Jacobin].

St. Didier. *Réponse au libelle diffamatoire des représentans Forest, Duguet et Meaudre. . . .* Impr. veuve Galetti, an VI. B.N. Lb42/573.

Doppet, A. *Essai sur les calomnies et les persecutions dont on peut être accablé en révolution. . . .* A Carouge, an VI. B.N. Ln27/6193.

Précis historique des causes et des effets de la scission dans le département de la NIEVRE. Impr. des républicains, an VI. A.N. F⁷ 7414, fol. 5054.

Aux Deux conseils . . . protestation des électeurs des cantons du PAS-DE-CALAIS. Impr. Ami des Lois, an VI. A.N. AF III 254/Pas-de-Calais [anti-Jacobin].

Gaultier-Biauzat, J. F. *Réfutation de toutes les imputations faites par le citoyen Desherbiers à l'Assemblée électorale du département de la SEINE.* n.l., an VI. B.N. Lb42/549.

Réfutation d'un libelle distribué au Corps législatif, ayant pour titre; procès-verbal de l'assemblée électorale scissionnaire du département de SEINE-ET-MARNE. Paris [an VI]. B.N. Lb42/553.

[Butaud]. *Sur les doubles élections de Poitiers (VIENNE).* Paris, Impr. Tutot, n.d. B.N. Lb42/554 [anti-Jacobin].

Dardillac, ex-administrateur [de la VIENNE]: Au Corps législatif, au Directoire exécutif, à tous les républicains. Poitiers, an VI. A.N. F⁷ 7414, fol. 5083.

(4) Anti-Directorial Polemics, Year VI-VII
(listed chronologically)

Gaultier-Biauzat, J. F. *Appel aux principes contre le système des scissions.* Impr. Guilhemat [an VI]. B.N. Lb42/1855.

Bach, Victor. *La Grande Conspiration anarchique de l'Oratoire, renvoyée à ses auteurs.* n.l., n.d. B.N. Lb42/550.

Lambert, J. (des Hautes-Alpes). *La Conspiration anarchique mise à la portée de tout le monde.* Paris, n.d. A.N. AF III 45, fol. 164.

Metge. *Des Représentans du peuple, au gouvernans, à nos très grands, très sublimes et très puissans membres du Directoire* (A l'insigne de la liberté violée) [an VI]. A.N. F⁷ 6175, dossier 2021 (pièce 616).

Projet d'Adresse: Des Citoyens du département de l'Ariège, au Corps législatif. n.l., n.d. A.N. F⁷ 7419.

Gilbert, L. *Des Invalides mutilés en combattant pour la République, au Corps législatif, sur les vexations et les injustices qu'on exerce envers eux et leurs camarades.* Paris, messidor VI. B.N. Lf221/13.

Crachet, R. *Appel aux principes, ou première lettre . . . aux républicains.* Impr. Rue de l'Université [Vatar], thermidor VI. B.N. Lb42/1952.

———. *Appel aux principes, ou deuxième lettre de Robert Crachet.* Impr. Rue de l'Université [Vatar], vendémiaire VII. B.N. Lb42/1997.

Antonelle, P. A. *Quelques observations qui peuvent servir d'appendice à la seconde lettre de Robert Crachet sur le 22 floréal.* n.l., n.d. B.N. Lb42/1894.

———. *La Constitution et les principes opposés aux floréalistes.* n.l., n.d. B.N. Lb42/1953.

Satur, M. J. *Le Cri de la Constitution contre l'immoralité des patriotes et la conspiration des flatteurs.* Impr. Baillis. B.N. Lb42/1896.

Dubreuil. *Hommage à la Vérité contre l'oppression, l'injustice, l'inhumanité, et les rapines du DIRECTOIRE et de ses représentants au Corps législatif.* [Paris, nivôse VII]. B.N. Lb42/582.

Analyse des proclamations . . . payés par la liste civile de dépradation. n.l., n.d. A.N. F⁷ 6175, dossier 2021, plaq. 10.

Briot, P. J. *Première réponse . . . à l'acte d'accusation publiée par J. Ch. Bailleul contre la majorité du Corps législatif.* Impr. Vatar, prairial VII. B.N. Lb42/2225.

Essai sur la nature et les divers agens de la conspiration présente ou lettres à un représentant du peuple. . . . Impr. Vatar, an VII. B.N. Lb42/708.

d'Aubigny, Villain. *Le Pot aux roses découvert et réponse au manifeste de Bailleul, deputé, propriétaire et seigneur suzerain des chateaux. . . .* Impr. Vatar, messidor VII. B.N. Lb42/729.

Rodolphe, *Acte d'accusation contre l'ex-Directoire exécutif et ses complices, ou Tableau effrayant des causes secrètes qui ont amené la France au bord du précipice.* Impr. Gauthier, an VII. B.N. Lb42/2237.

Les Citoyens de la commune de Maçon . . . aux membres du Corps législatif . . . 4 messidor an VII. Impr. Nationale. Maclure Collection.

Des Citoyens du faubourg Antoine au Conseil des Cinq-cents, séance du 17 messidor VII. Impr. Nationale. Maclure Collection.

Leclerc des Vosges. *Discours prononcé à l'inauguration de la Réunion des Amis de l'égalité et de la liberté.* Impr. E. Charles, messidor VII. B.N. Lb40/2196.

Premier discours du citoyen Bach à la Réunion séant au Manège, sur les moyens de consolider la République. Impr. Benoist, messidor VII. B.N. Lb40/2358.

Manifeste des Jacobins au peuple français, en réponse aux calomnies répandues contre eux par leurs ennemis. Impr. Phillipe [an VII]. B.N. Lb42/2655.

L'Ennemi des tyrans au dictateurs Sieyès et Barras. Impr. rue du Fouare [an VII]. B.N. Lb42/2461.

Metge. *Panégyrique de Sieyès.* Impr. du Démocrate, thermidor VII. B.N. Lb42/2449.

COLLECTIONS OF DOCUMENTS, CONTEMPORARY ACCOUNTS, AND MEMOIRS

A. Debidour's exhaustive *Recueil des actes du Directoire exécutif: procès-verbaux, arrêtés, instructions, lettres et actes divers* (4 vols.; 1910-17) stops abruptly at ventôse Year V. Like the *Archives parlementaires* (which does not extend to the Directory years), this publication was cut off by World War I, but unlike the former it was never resumed. Thus, the only significant collection of edited documents for this period is A. Aulard, ed., *Paris pendant la réaction thermidorienne et sous le Directoire* (5 vols.; 1898-1902)—consisting mainly of newspaper clippings and daily reports by the Paris Central Police Bureau. A gap in this collection for the crucial period of Fructidor was filled by C. Ballot, ed., *Le Coup d'état du 18 fructidor an V: rapports de police et documents divers* (1906). Both collections, however, barely scratch the surface of either police reports or available newspapers.

For parliamentary history the *Moniteur* and Buchez and Roux were consulted, but the most important material is in the speeches and committee reports published as pamphlets (see above). A contemporary survey of the intellectual and political scene in France is offered by A. M. Cécile, *Tableau historique, littéraire et politique de l'an VI de la République française* (Impr. Valade, 1798). The best diplomatic reports have been collected by P. Bailleu, *Preussen und Frankreich von 1795 bis 1807: Diplomatische Correspondenzen*, I (Leipzig, 1881), and by J. Godechot, "Le Directoire vu de Londres *AHRF*, 1949, pp. 311-36 and 1950, pp. 1-27. Standard documents like the various constitutions are most conveniently consulted in J. H. Stewart, ed., *A Documentary Survey of the French Revolution* (New York, 1951).

Babeuvism has generated several collections of documents. Babeuf's own writings are sampled extensively in M. Dommanget, ed., *Pages choisies de Babeuf* (1935) and C. Mazauric, ed., *Babeuf: textes choisis* (1965), while numerous documents are appended to Buonarroti's *Conspiration pour l'égalité dite de Babeuf* (2 vols.; 1954 edn.) and A. Saitta, *Filippo Buonarroti* (2 vols.; Rome, 1950). More important for my purpose were the documents seized and printed by the government to make its case against the conspirators (*Copie des Pièces saisies . . . dans le local que Babeuf occupait lors de son arrestation* [2 vols.; an V]); the trial transcript (*Débats du procès instruit par la Haute-Cour de Justice contre Drouet, Babeuf, et autres* [4 vols.; 1797]); and the prosecution's summary (*Discours des accusateurs-nationaux près la Haute-Cour de Justice, prononcé par le Citoyen Bailly* [Vendôme, an V]). As I have argued, this material (all available in Firestone Library, Princeton University) is a source not only for genuine Babeuvism but for Neo-Jacobinism as well. Private letters and other documents (many concerning Babeuf and his co-defendants) turn up occasionally in two other places: the *pièces-annexes* of older secondary works, and the "mélanges-documents-glanes" section of the *Annales historiques de la Révolution française*. Those that I have cited directly are mentioned in the footnotes.

The usual superabundance of memoirs is available, and a few are well worth attention, notably the tried, if not always true, productions of three directors: LaRevellière-Lépeaux (3 vols.; 1895); Barras (Eng. trans. by C. E. Roche, 4 vols.; 1895); and Gohier (2 vols.; 1824 under the title *Mémoires des contemporains*). Among the local chronicles only one was informative: *Souvenirs et Journal d'un bourgeois d'Evreux* (Evreux, 1850), B.N. Lk7/2707. Other useful items include the *Mémoires sur la Convention et le Directoire* (2 vols.; 1824) by the conservative A. C. Thibaudeau; the journal of the Irish revolutionary expatriate Wolfe Tone included in *Life of Theobold Wolfe Tone* (2 vols.; Washington, 1826); the partially factitious *Mémoires de R. Levasseur (de la Sarthe), ex-conventionnel* (4 vols.; 1831); and the ex-conventionnel M. A. Baudot's *Notes historiques sur la Convention Nationale, le Directoire, L'Empire et l'exil des votants,* ed. Veuve Quinet (1893). Finally, the specialist can savor with delighted skepticism two counter-revolutionary polemics: *Dix-huit fructidor, ses causes et ses effets* (2 vols.; Hambourg, 1799), and L. Calinau's malevolent *Dictionnaire des Jacobins Vivans* (Hambourg, 1799).

III. SECONDARY WORKS

GENERAL

Anti-republicans were the first serious historians of the Directory. Lavishing four pioneering volumes on a subject that he obviously detested, Ludovic Sciout portrayed the period as dominated by sterility, hypocrisy, and violence second only to the unspeakable Terror (*Le Directoire* [4 vols.; 1895-97]). In *Le 18 fructidor* (1893) and *La Terreur sous le directoire* (1887), Victor Pierre marshalled unpublished documents for the same argument. More significant monuments of French scholarship, like Albert Sorel's massive study of foreign relations or Marcel Marion's standard *Histoire financière de la France depuis 1715,* IV (1927), also served to tarnish the Directory's image, as did most local studies produced by clerics and antiquarians. Yet another assault on the men who governed France between 1796 and 1800 came from the genre of pro-Napoleonic literature, notably A. Vandal's *L'Avènement de Bonaparte* (2 vols.; 1902), which exalted its hero by deprecating his predecessors.

Inevitably this imbalance called forth a mildly "revisionist" treatment, heralded, for example, in Albert Goodwin's durable article of 1937: "The Executive Directory: a revaluation," *History,* XXII. Disguised polemics have been superseded by the valuable studies of scholars like Raymond Guyot, Jacques Godechot, and Marcel Reinhard, and the judicious surveys of Georges Lefebvre in *Le Directoire* (1946) and *La Révolution française* (1957). A consensus seems to remain, however, in which the "French Revolution" is seen as ending when the Directory was installed. Only in the area of counterrevolution and international relations—and specifically in R. R. Palmer's *Age of the Democratic Revolution*, II (1964) and J. Godechot's *La Grande Nation* (2 vols.; 1956)—are the lines of continuity taken very seriously.

Works which provide a thematic context for studying Directorial France include M. Deslandres, *Histoire constitutionnelle de la France* (1932); J. Godechot, *Les Institutions de la France sous la Révolution et l'Empire* (1951); P. Duclos, *L'Evolution des rapports politiques depuis 1750: liberté, intégration, unité* (1950); A. Soderhjelm, *Le Régime de la Presse pendant la Révolution française* (2 vols.; Helsingfors, 1901). The preceding "classic" phase of Jacobinism is examined in a multitude of works that were consulted but need not be cited here. Suffice to mention the complementary synthesis of C. Brinton's *The Jacobins* (1930) and L. deCardenal's *La Province pendant la Révolution: histoire des clubs Jacobins (1789-1795)* (1929), as well as the bibliographies therein. More recently, work or the Revolution "from below" provides an indispensable perspective on the limits of Jacobinism and Neo-Jacobinism, notably: A. Soboul, *Les Sans-culottes Parisiens en l'an II* (1958); K. Tonnesson, *La Défaite des Sans-culottes* (1959); and R. C. Cobb, *Les Armées révolutionnaires: instrument de la terreur dans les départements* (2 vols.; 1963). The latter is a particularly sensitive treatment of the tangential contacts between provincial Jacobinism and Parisian sans-culottism. Similarly, the impressive explosion of writing on Babeuvism is useful in assessing the nature of the Neo-Jacobinism that authentic Babeuvists so mightily disdained. (For a discussion of this literature see the notes to Chs. II and III.) Yet surprisingly little of this scholarship deals directly with the contrasting ideas and activities of the non-Babeuvist democrats. Exceptions are Professor Reinhard's discriminating Sorbonne lectures: *La France du Directoire: problèmes et résistance en 1796* (mimeographed, C.D.U., 1956); J. Suratteau, "Babouvisme, le péril rouge, et le Directoire," and A. Soboul, "Personnel sectionnaire et personnel babouviste," both in *Babeuf et les problèmes du Babouvisme,* ed. A. Soboul (1963).

The standard political history of the Directory is Albert Meynier's three-volume study *Les Coups d'état du Directoire* (1926-29)—

focusing on Fructidor, Floréal, Prairial VII, and Brumaire. Meynier examined in detail the political problems confronting the government and the misguided attempts to solve them. The Jacobin opposition, however, is treated here as the object of the Directory's politics, and its rather one-dimensional image is drawn on the basis of extremely meager material. Albert Mathiez began to construct his own interpretive history of the period (*Le Directoire: du 11 brumaire an IV au 18 fructidor V*, ed. J. Godechot [1934]). With his lively sense of politics and social issues he might well have done justice to the democratic resurgence of the Year VI. Unfortunately his death cut short his work at the coup d'état of fructidor. Previously he had attempted to deal indirectly with this subject in his dissertation *La Theophilanthropie et le culte décadaire, 1796–1801* (1904). Despite the fact that certain conservatives were instrumental in its founding, Mathiez treated theophilanthropy as an umbrella for democratic aspirations. On the whole, however, theophilanthropy was little more than window-dressing for the more pragmatic activities of democrats.

Other approaches since Mathiez include J. Godechot, *Les Commissaires aux armées sous le Directoire* (2 Vols.; 1937) on civil-military relations; J. Bourdon, "Le Mécontentement public et les craintes des dirigeants sous le Directoire," *AHRF*, 1946 [No. 103], on the conservatives' response to political instability; J. Dautry, "Les Démocrates Parisiens avant et après le coup d'état du 18 fructidor V," *AHRF*, 1950 [No. 118]—a tendentious appraisal of the movement's admittedly narrow base; J. Suratteau, "Les élections de l'an V au conseils du Directoire," *AHRF*, 1958 [No. 154], to be followed by publication of his *thèse secondaire* on the Year VI elections; and R. C. Cobb, "Notes sur la répression contre le personnel sansculotte de 1795 à 1801," *AHRF*, 1954 [No. 134]. This fascinating article discusses police methods in Paris, but significantly it jumps from the repressions that came in the wake of the Babeuf conspiracy in 1796 to the repressions under the Consulate. Hopefully the present study has suggested what went on between those two dates. Finally there are two vintage works on the last manifestations of Neo-Jacobinism: A. Aulard, "Les Derniers Jacobins," *R.F.*, xxvi (1894), and J. Destrem, *Les Déportations du Consulat et de l'Empire* (1885).

LOCAL STUDIES

There are literally hundreds of studies on individual towns, departments, or provinces—most by antiquarians, and few containing anything accurate on Neo-Jacobinism. In most of the older ones, the *faits divers* of local history are paraded, the authors' purpose being either to attack the Revolution in the person of the exagérés, exclusifs or anarchistes (as they are variously called), or to accumulate minutia. Following the references in G. Walter's *Répertoire de l'histoire de la Révolution française*, ii: *Lieux* (1951), it was my necessary task to go through these works, and gleanings from several are cited in the footnotes. The more useful and scholarly included B. Bois, *La Vie scolaire et les créations intellectuelles en Anjou pendant la Révolution* (1929); R. Doucet, *L'Esprit public dans le département de la Vienne pendant la Révolution* (1910); E. Labadie, *La Presse Bordelaise pendant la Révolution* (Bordeaux, 1910); H. Labroue, *L'Esprit public en Dordogne pendant la Révolution* (1911); R. Nicolas, *L'Esprit public et les élections dans le département de la Marne de 1790 à l'an VIII* (Chalons, 1909), and R. Paquet, *Bibliographie analytique de l'histoire de Metz pendant la Révolution* (2 vols.; 1926).

A handful of monographs deal with the Directory years. J. Brélot, *La Vie politique en Côte-d'Or sous le Directoire* (Dijon, 1932) and M. Reinhard, *Le Département de la Sarthe sous le Régime directorial* (St. Brieuc, 1935) are both concerned with areas where the Jacobins were strong, and both are eminently reliable. The same cannot be said for E. Delcambre, *Le Coup d'état jacobin du 18 fructidor an V et ses répercussions dans la Haute-Loire* (Rodez, 1942), which proved extremely disappointing despite its title. Recently two definitive studies have appeared that are models of meticulous scholarship: J. Suratteau, *Le Département du Mont-Terrible sous le régime du Directoire* (1965), and P. Clémendot, *Le Département de la Meurthe à l'époque du Directoire* (1966). Unfortunately neither department contained significant Jacobin cadres. Jean Beyssi has devoted a study entirely to the Neo-Jacobins of one area: "Le Parti Jacobin à Toulouse sous le Directoire," *AHRF* 1950 [No. 117], pp. 28-54 and [No. 118], pp. 108-33. See also the author's "The Revival of Jacobinism in Metz During the Directory," *Journal of Modern History*, xxxviii (1966).

BIOGRAPHICAL STUDIES

For the Directorial side of the spectrum we lack critical studies of Barras and Merlin de Douai, in addition to which the relevant section of P. Bastid's *Sieyès et sa pensée* (1939) are inadequate. The informative studies include R. Guyot, ed., *Documents biographiques sur J. F. Reubell* (1911); G. Robison, *Revellière-Lépeaux, Citizen Director* (New York, 1938); L. Madelin, *Fouché 1759–1820*, I (1901); M. Reinhard's outstanding *Le Grand Carnot*, II (1952).

As far as the democrats and pro-Jacobins are concerned, the results are meager. Most prominent revolutionaries of the Year II who managed to survive without repudiating their pasts either were forced into retirement or voluntarily abstained from politics. An example of the former is the conventionnel Châles, who having barely escaped with his life during the thermidorian reaction sought seclusion thereafter. Accordingly an excellent monograph, C. Pichois and J. Dautry, *Les Idées démocratiques du conventionnel Châles* (Aix, 1958), passes from a chapter on the reaction directly to a chapter on his hardships under the Empire. Even biographers of men who were active in Neo-Jacobinism tend to deal with the Directory years in cursory fashion. M. Dayot's sensitive study of the young Jacobin legislator Briot (*Un Révolutionnaire Franc-Comtois: Pierre-Joseph Briot* [1960]) is deficient on this score, as is Général Herlaut's otherwise discriminating portrait of Villain d'Aubigny: "La Vie politique de Villain d'Aubigny, adjoint de Bouchotte," *AHRF* 1934 [No. 61]. Particularly disappointing is the vague evaluation of a major Neo-Jacobin: E. Avenard and P. Guiral, "Essai d'explication du Marquis d'Antonelle," *Provence historique*, v (1955).

On the other hand an antiquarian biography of the jurist Gaultier-Biauzat yields precious information despite the author's unwillingness to recognize his hero's associations with the Left during the Directory: F. Mège, *Gaultier de Biauzat* (2 vols.; 1890). L. Bigard's *Le Comte Réal, ancien Jacobin* (Versailles, 1937), is enlightening about a lawyer who walked a tightrope between democrats and Directorials, while R. Montier's *Robert Lindet: notice biographique* (1899) treats a man whom the Left repeatedly tried to coopt into a leadership role. The exiled subject of L. Gershoy's *Bertrand Barère:*

A Reluctant Terrorist (Princeton, 1962) was less important to Neo-Jacobinism than his brother Jean-Pierre.

At least three biographical studies of democrats focus on the Directory years. G. Brégail, "Chantreau, journaliste et professeur sous le Directoire," *Annales révolutionnaires*, XIII (1921), 23-36, concerns an activist from the Gers department who was typical of the Neo-Jacobin intellectuals. R. Bois, "P. N. Hesiné, rédacteur du Journal de la Haute-Cour," *AHRF*, 1960, pp. 471-87, treats the most dedicated and appealing militant of his day during the difficult year of 1796. Utilizing his private notebooks to reconstruct the activities, ambitions, and thoughts of a young disciple of Robespierre's, V. M. Dalin gives us the most penetrating of biographical studies: "Marc-Antoine Jullien nach dem 9 thermidor," *Babeuf-Studien*, ed. W. Markov (Berlin, 1961). As indicated in Appendix IV, there is no biographical study of René Vatar, the "advocate-in-chief" of the Jacobins under the Directory.

INDEX*

* cc denotes constitutional circle.

441

Index

443

Index

Colliot, 213n, 221, 292
Committee of General Security, 217
Committee of Public Safety, 7f,
28, 36, 151n, 187, 189, 334, 337, 375,
378, 381, 413. *See also* Robespierre
communauté des biens, 34-35, 61n
conscription, 89, 194, 202, 369
conservatives, 4, 5, 17f, 89, 91, 100,
106, 107, 114, 150, 154, 155,
158, 159, 161, 162, 178f, 182,
188, 195, 204, 263f, 268, 271, 275f,
278, 280, 283, 301f, 303, 347f,
364f, 370, 371, 374, 388f, 393f. *See
also* Directorials
conspiracy, 21, 46f, 273f, 353, 358,
398
Constant, B., 66, 83, 94, 155f,
162, 178, 181, 198
Constant, P., 300
Constant (Sans-culotte), 213
Constitution of 1791, 5, 242, 263
Constitution of 1793, 25f, 46, 159,
170, 171, 185, 227, 241, 287, 314,
317, 319, 356, 362. *See also*
subsistence, right to
Constitution of the Year III, 20f,
25f, 31, 46, 84, 114, 123, 131f,
136, 170, 187, 197, 200, 204, 227,
256, 272, 342, 348f, 353, 356,
358, 365; Article 362, 17, 101ff,
104, 130, 211; and clubs, 15-18,
381, 387f, 395ff, 398f; and elections,
241f, 247f, 250, 263; Neo-Jacobins
and, 159-64, 185
Constitutional Circles, *see* clubs;
Rue du Bacq Club; Réunion
Politique du faubourg Antoine
CC of the Hôtel du Salm, 65f,
67, 83, 86. *See also* Salmistes;
B. Constant
CC of the Rue de l'Université,
161n, 212f, 380n
Convention, 7ff, 12, 15f, 19, 21, 165,
169f, 188, 189, 190, 207, 283,
291, 315, 381
Copie, 214
Cordebas, 44
Cordeliers Club, 151n, 378
Corrèze, 141f, 142, 163n, 254, 365;

election Yr. VI, 284, 300f.
See also Brive
corruption, 117, 364, 365, 372, 382n.
See also profiteering
Côte d'Or, 91, 286
Courrier de la Gironde, 87, 146,
281f, 285, 377
Courrier de l'armée d'Italie, 147
courts, clubs and, 133f
Cousin, 215
Crachet, R., 307n, 358f, 361
Cranfort, *ouvrier*, 37
Crassous, conventionnel, 15
Crespin, 59n, 317, 318
Creuzé-Latouche, deputy, 303
Crochon, 192f, 196, 197-201, 296f
Cusset (Allier), cc, 270

Dalin, V. M., 164
Damois, 318
D'André, deputy, 391n, 392
Danton, 8, 220
Dardillac, 303, 351
Darthé, 47, 52, 58, 60, 190
Dartigoyete, conventionnel, 284
D'Aubigny, V., 318, 325n, 332,
352, 366, 375
Dauchy, deputy, 178f&n
Daunou, deputy, 170, 290, 365
Dautry, J., 76
Daux, 317, 318, 325
Daviaud, 23, 43f
décadi, 121, 194, 195, 210, 224f
Declercq, deputy, 388n, 397
Défenseur de la Vérité, 61n, 72,
73, 78, 79, 146, 168, 176, 378
Défenseur des droits du peuple,
379&n
Delacroix, deputy, 301
Deladreux, 215
Delan, 284
Delattre, 89n, 285
Delavigne, 326
DeLormelle, 213
democracy (democrats), 6, 12&n,
14, 17f, 79, 109, 111, 115, 117,
136, 139, 149, 153, 158f, 163,
185f, 195f, 210, 241f, 253, 275f,
280ff, 311, 314; and Paris
elections, 316-25, 339-43, 352f,

444